International Human Resource Management

International Human Resource Management

From Cross-cultural Management to Managing a Diverse
Workforce

Edited by

Kate Hutchings and Helen De Cieri

Monash University, Australia

ASHGATE

Published by
Ashgate Publishing Limited
Gower House
Croft Road
Aldershot
Hampshire GU11 3HR
England

Ashgate Publishing Company
Suite 420
101 Cherry Street
Burlington, VT 05401-4405
USA

Ashgate website: http://www.ashgate.com

British Library Cataloguing in Publication Data
International human resource management : from
  cross-cultural management to managing a diverse workforce.
  – (The international library of essays on business and
  management)
  1. International business enterprises – Personnel management
  I. Hutchings, Kate II. De Cieri, Helen
  658.3

Library of Congress Cataloging-in-Publication Data
International human resource management: from cross–cultural management to
  managing a diverse workforce / edited by Kate Hutchings and Helen De Cieri
      p. cm. – (The international library of essays on business and management)
  Includes bibliographical references.
  ISBN-13: 978–0–7546–2654–1 (alk. paper)
   1. International business enterprises–Personnel management. 2. Personnel
  management. I. Hutchings, Kate. II. De Cieri, Helen.

  HF5549.5.E45157 2007
  658.3–dc22

                                                                                    2006048429

ISBN 978–0–7546–2654–1

Printed in Great Britain by TJ International Ltd, Padstow, Cornwall

Contents

PART II   COMPARATIVE HRM

PART III   INTERNATIONALISING HRM

Strategic Focus

Diversity Management

Acknowledgements

The editors and publishers wish to thank the following for permission to use copyright material.

Academy of Management and Copyright Clearance Center for the essays: Nancy J. Adler (1983), 'Cross-Cultural Management Research: The Ostrich and the Trend', *Academy of Management Review*, **8**, pp. 226–32. Copyright © 1983 Academy of Management Review; Parshotam Dass and Barbara Parker (1999), 'Strategies for Managing Human Resource Diversity: From Resistance to Learning', *Academy of Management Executive*, **13**, pp. 68–80; Anil K. Gupta and Vijay Govindarajan (2001), 'Converting Global Presence into Global Competitive Advantage', *Academy of Management Executive*, **15**, pp. 45–58.

American Psychological Association for the essay: Ron Garonzik, Joel Brockner and Phyllis A. Siegel (2000), ' Identifying International Assignees at Risk for Premature Departure: The Interactive Effect of Outcome Favourability and Procedural Fairness', *Journal of Applied Psychology*, **85**, pp. 13–20. Copyright © 2000 American Psychological Association.

Blackwell Publishing Limited for the essays: John T. Gullahorn and Jeanne E. Gullahorn (1963), 'An Extension of the U-Curve Hypothesis', *Journal of Social Issues*, **19**, pp. 33–47; Paul E. Spector, Caryl L. Cooper, Steven Poelmans, Tammy D. Allen, Michael O'Driscoll, Juan I. Sanchez, Oi Ling Siu, Phil Dewe, Peter Hart, Luo Lu, Lúcio Flávio Renault de Moraes, Gabrielle M. Ostrognay, Kate Sparks, Paul Wong and Shanfu Yu (2004), 'A Cross-National Comparative Study of Work-Family Stressors, Working Hours, and Well-Being: China and Latin America Versus the Anglo World', *Personnel Psychology*, **57**, pp. 119–42. Copyright © 2004 Personnel Psychology Inc; Olga Tregaskis, Noreen Heraty and Michael Morley (2001), 'HRD in Multinationals: the Global/Local Mix', *Human Resource Management Journal*, **11**, pp. 34–56; Nick Forster (2000), 'Expatriates and the Impact of Cross-Cultural Training', *Human Resource Management Journal*, **10**, pp. 63–78.

Paula Caligiuri for the essay: Paula M. Caligiuri (2000), 'Selecting Expatriates for Personality Characteristics: A Moderating Effect of Personality on the Relationship Between Host National Contact and Cross-Cultural Adjustment', *Management International Review*, **40**, pp. 61–80. Copyright © 2000 Paula Caligiuri.

Copyright Clearance Center for the essay: André Laurent (1983), 'The Cultural Diversity of Western Conceptions of Management', *International Studies of Management and Organization*, **13**, pp. 75–96.

Elsevier Limited for the essay: Gary C. McMahan, Myrtle P. Bell and Meghna Virick (1998), 'Strategic Human Resource Management: Employee Involvement, Diversity, and International Issues', *Human Resource Management Review*, **8**, pp. 193–214. Copyright ©

Introduction

The Field of IHRM and Its Importance

Since the late 1970s, academicians and practitioners of international management have paid increasing attention to the impact of globalization on the management of human resources across national boundaries. Just as international managers have turned their attention to issues such as expatriate management, managing in other cultures, working with transnational teams and managing diversity in multicultural domestic workforces, so too have academicians advanced understanding in these areas through the development of a distinct sub-field within the management discipline, namely international human resource management (IHRM). This field of research and practice draws upon human resource management (HRM) as a disciplinary base, and is embedded in the context of international business. As more markets internationalize, more nations become integrated with the global economy, and more businesses expand their operations across national borders, issues around the management of people become more critical to the international strategic planning and operations of firms. Many of these issues apply similarly to international non-profit organizations, such as relief and development organizations. The importance of IHRM as a field of academic endeavour has become more pronounced. This volume is the first publication to bring together a collection of key essays within the field of IHRM. We draw upon, and highlight, the major developments within IHRM, as well as emphasize recent advances within this important field.

In this volume we present the three major developments, or approaches, within the IHRM literature. De Cieri and Dowling (1999) identified these approaches as Cross-cultural Management, Comparative HRM and Strategic HRM, examining the latter more broadly by also making reference to more recent developments including global teams, global integration and diversity management. Importantly, the three broad approaches that have been identified in the academic literature correlate with developments in practice within internationalizing organizations. This clustering of the literature also has strong synergies with the well-cited works of Evans, Pucik and Barsoux (2002) and Evans and Genadry (1998), who suggest the need for human resource management and organizational behaviour generally to take a more international approach. They suggest the need for human resource managers and departments to be involved in international business from the beginnings of global operations in the form of mergers and acquisitions and establishment of subsidiary operations. Indeed, Evans *et al.* (2002) and Evans and Genadry (1998) suggest three modes of HRM, namely building HRM, realigning HRM and steering via HRM, which have similarities with the approaches outlined by De Cieri and Dowling (1999).

The genesis of research in IHRM was described by De Cieri and Dowling (1999) as cross-cultural management, which had a strong focus on expatriate management functions. Early work in this field emphasized a cross-cultural management approach and examined human behaviour within organizations from an international perspective. Focus was given to identifying the likely impact of cross-culturally similar and different human behaviour on the prescriptive elements of human resource management, such as recruitment and selection, training and development, performance management, and reward management. The second approach, which developed from the comparative industrial relations and human resource management literature, sought to describe, compare, and analyse human resource management systems across various countries (De Cieri and Dowling, 1999). This literature incorporated discussions about convergence and divergence in human resource management practices, corporate and social responsibility and analyses of the impact of political, legislative, cultural and developmental factors of specific subsidiary nations on the practice and policies of international organizations. A third, and erstwhile much less critiqued, approach focuses on aspects of human resource management in multinational firms in respect to implications of the process of internationalization for the activities and policies of human resource management (De Cieri and Dowling, 1999). This literature takes account of the relevance that IHRM may have for small and internationalizing firms that also face significant international management issues. It also incorporates the increasingly strategic focus of organizations that seek to outsource many of the prescriptive HRM functions to free IHRM managers to examine issues of greater strategic importance. This third approach, with its recognition of the dualities confronting human resource management as a discipline and human resource managers as practitioners, suggests that HRM departments will not only become involved in the international arena in respect to *ad hoc* management of expatriates and employees in other cultures. Rather, it is argued that human resource management departments will be increasingly involved in the whole process of internationalization from start-up of international operations and acquisitions and mergers, through detailing strategic levels of IHRM, managing the expatriation process and preparation of expatriates for managing in other cultures, steering the strategic expansion of international operations, managing diversity in multicultural domestic workforces, engineering of global teams, and engendering of global consciousness. Such an approach recognizes HRM's role in assisting the development of flexible, adaptive international organizations and highlights the role that human resource management can play when it broadens its function to that of *change agent* in transforming the global thinking of organizations (Evans *et al.*, 2002).

Given the increasing growth of interest and activity in IHRM, both by practitioners and academicians, it is essential to understand the problems, challenges, and future directions as perceived by those with intellectual and practical expertise in this field. In a comprehensive review and critique of IHRM, Schuler, Budhwar, and Florkowski (2002) highlighted the clear agenda of IHRM research as being one of studying human resources in context of industry and organizational strategy and other functional areas and operations within an international sphere. They also emphasized the importance of utilizing multiple levels of analysis, namely the external political, cultural, social and legal environment as well as considering the firm, the sub-unit, the group and the individual. In reviewing the existing state of IHRM literature in regard to the extent to which it incorporates the content, they conclude that, over three decades, this expansive and ever-expanding body of literature has covered substantive ground in exploring functional issues of human resources in an international context, through intercultural management and latter trends towards research on new forms of IHRM. Yet they also suggested that research published thus far has raised more questions that need to be examined in future research, given the increasing expectancy of competitive advantage being achieved by organizations that have strategic IHRM practices.

This volume addresses opportunities and challenges in the field of IHRM and highlights future directions for growth in the field by featuring practical and pedagogical developments of IHRM and encouraging practitioner and academician knowledge sharing by presenting critical and different IHRM perspectives. The volume is presented in order of the three major phases of developments in IHRM, namely Cross-cultural Management, Comparative HRM and Internationalizing HRM, with sub-headings provided where illustrative. In this introductory overview we provide a rationalization for the inclusion of each of the 28 essays in this volume and note the critical contribution that each essay has made to the development of the field of IHRM. We also make reference to other essays not included in this volume. In most cases the essays referred to are seminal works in the field of IHRM and have already been widely cited elsewhere but we make note of them to illustrate how the current selection of essays dovetail with, build upon, or critique, such earlier thinking.

Cross-cultural Management

Expatriate Management

Initial research into IHRM focused on the management of expatriates in subsidiary operations with writing in both academic circles and the popular press suggesting the need for expatriates to be cross-culturally sensitive, adaptive and responsive when managing across national borders. To achieve such adaptation was regarded as crucial to the avoidance of expatriate failure that had potentially damaging consequences for the individual expatriate, his/her spouse and family, and his/her organization. Expatriate failure was said to arise from culture shock experienced by expatriates as these individuals felt frustrated and alienated in foreign cultures (Oberg, 1960; Adler, 1975). Chapter 1 in this collection, by Gullahorn and Gullahorn (1963), made a valuable contribution in developing early research in the field of IHRM in pointing to reverse culture shock, a condition that could beset expatriates when returning to their home country. In revisiting the U curve of culture shock, and referring to a W curve that was representative of problems experienced in repatriation, the work of Gullahorn and Gullahorn set the stage for considerable subsequent research into the problems experienced on repatriation. While sociologists and anthropologists had previously devoted considerable discussion to the adjustment of individuals in foreign cultures, Chapter 2 by Black and Gregersen was the first research in IHRM to systematically characterize the adjustment or non-adjustment of expatriates when on international assignments. In so doing they referred to expatriates as either having their 'hearts at home' (with the consequence of being poorly culturally adjusted to the host country) or 'going native' (suggesting good cross-cultural adjustment but often an inability to translate the requirements of headquarters to the subsidiary operations). Black and Gregersen argued that the ideal international assignee was the individual they referred to as having 'dual allegiance', namely, someone who effectively balances his/her commitment to both headquarters and the host country subsidiary. Despite such early identification being made within the literature, subsequent research has continued to highlight the continuing problem of expatriates who grapple with the difficulties of achieving the dual allegiance which is integral to their effective adjustment and performance in international operations.

The majority of research within expatriate management has, however, focused on examining the prescriptive functions of human resource management as they relate to international assignees. While Welch (1994) provided a framework for understanding approaches to IHRM by examining interrelationships between IHRM activities and other organizational factors, such as industry, strategy, structure and internationalization stage, most researchers have explored individual functions. A founding researcher in IHRM, Tung (1981), led early research to explore the importance of selecting potential expatriates on the basis of personality characteristics to ensure a fit with the host country culture and identified the importance of also involving expatriates' spouse and children (if applicable) in the selection process. Caligiuri (2000), in Chapter 3, built on early work about selection for international assignments and theories of contact and social learning in arguing that interaction with the host country nationals assisted the cross-cultural adjustment of expatriates, but only in cases where the international assignees had the personality characteristics of openness and sociability. Arguing that an international assignment is not suitable for everyone within an organization, Caligiuri highlighted the essentiality of assessing personality characteristics early in the selection process. Chapter 4 by Harris picked up on the themes of selection when exploring why women are not selected for international assignments. Harris elaborated on groundbreaking but well-cited research by Adler (1984, 1987, 2002) into the myths surrounding, and barriers to, female international assignees, and some of the problems experienced by spouses and families on international assignments. Harris maintained that there is a continued need for expatriates and increasing reluctance of individuals to take international assignments, for reasons including dual career issues (see Harvey, 1996). However, she also suggested that despite these challenges in making international appointments, organizations' use of informal selection processes continues to result in an unintended gender bias in favour of males in recruiting for international postings.

Substantive research into training has indicated a direct relationship between expatriates' cross-cultural performance and their having been provided with cultural, political and economic knowledge of the host country, language skills, executive briefings about the subsidiary operations, and general local knowledge. Selmer (2001) has explored the relative merits of pre-departure verses post-arrival training, and has expanded the largely North American and West European focus within the IHRM literature to an examination of Hong Kong and China. Moreover, Richardson and McKenna (2000) have explored the phenomenon of self-selecting international sojourners as distinct from individuals transferred by their organisations and suggested that this has implications for the performance of such individuals on international postings. Yet, Forster's essay (Chapter 5), while concurring with previous research, also suggested the need for organizations to view international assignments as processes, rather than one-off events and to take a longitudinal approach to succession planning and career pathing for international assignees and potential international assignees within organizations. Importantly, Forster also highlighted new trends in expatriation, namely the employment of younger and early career employees as distinct from international assignments in earlier years which usually entailed posting of senior managers whom were completing their careers. While most research on performance appraisals in the IHRM field have focused on assessing expatriates' performance in international assignments, limited research has examined how performance appraisals are conducted cross-nationally. Chapter 6 by Milliman, Nason, Zhu and De Cieri, conducted as part of an international research consortium into best practices in

IHRM, explored approaches to performance appraisal across ten countries in Asia and North and Latin America, and found that the potential of appraisals are rarely realized in practice and that this was so across the range of countries examined.

Research into rewarding expatriates has focused largely on cost of living adjustments and hardship allowances, yet Milkovich and Bloom (Chapter 7), provided a model of strategic flexibility in compensation that allowed for a core package to be customized, to ensure that the total value of employment is structured so that employee contributions support organizational goals. Indeed, the approach advocated by Milkovich and Bloom allows employees the opportunity to select forms of returns that meet their individual goals; a flexibility that assists organizations to achieve competitive advantage and may contribute to their being viewed as employers of choice.

Early research in IHRM, such as that by Black, Mendenhall and Oddou (1991) examined approaches to international adjustment of expatriates and suggested that careful selection, followed by training and support, and well-developed compensation and appraisals systems (and subsequent follow-up repatriation programmes) should ensure expatriate effectiveness. However, the authors of Chapter 8, Garonzik, Brockner and Siegel focused on studying international assignees who were at risk of premature departure. They found that expatriates may consider departing prematurely from an assignment when they believed that their non-work, social outcomes were not favourable. Interestingly, their research also reported that the same expatriates were less inclined to depart international assignments in instances where they believed that procedural fairness was high. Importantly the authors suggested that many of the non-work issues may be beyond an employing organization's sphere of influence, although employers may exercise procedures that minimize costs of early return from international assignments. Much of the research within the expatriate management literature, with its focus on the need for careful selection, cross-cultural training, competitive reward packages, and effective appraisal, has been premised upon a belief that expatriate failure rates are high. It has been further assumed that these high failure rates prove very costly for organizations and hence there is need for all organizations that have, or are considering, international movement of employees, to utilize practices to minimize the effects of culture shock and non-adjustment of expatriates and/or their families that contribute to expatriate failure.

In Chapter 9, Harzing however, questioned whether expatriate failure rates were actually as high as had been previously documented by a range of well-regarded and well-published international researchers. Focusing on just one element of expatriate failure, premature re-entry, which she did acknowledge to be a limited categorization of failure, Harzing proffered that the perception of expatriate failure rates as being very high had been perpetuated by repetitive errors in quoting studies of expatriate failure from the early 1980s. In a landmark critique of many of the established names in the field of IHRM, she argued the need for much more empirical research into expatriate failure that draws upon broader samples of individuals and countries, and pays more attention to the reasons for failure – research which, at this time, has still not been systematically undertaken. Prior and subsequent research into expatriate failure rates, has, however, continued to argue that failure is likely to be considerably higher where there are substantive differences in the culture (and arguably also, the institutional framework) of the nation of headquarters' operation and the nation of subsidiary operation(s).

Managing Cross-culturally

As well as exploring the management of expatriates, the cross-cultural management literature has assessed how expatriates deal with local business partners and manage employees in subsidiary operations. In an examination of early research into the field, Adler (Chapter 10), found that, despite a trend towards greater internationalization of organizations throughout the 1970s, during that decade only one per cent of organizational behaviour essays published in top United States management journals explore interactions between employees of different (national) cultures. Indeed, she suggested that research and publishing activity did not keep pace with the internationalization of organizations and culture was a rarely examined issue within the literature until the start of the 1980s, which heralded the emergence of IHRM as an academic discipline. Despite two decades of subsequent research advocating the need for organizations to give increased attention to issues of human resource management in an international context, follow-up research conducted some two decades later by Wasti and Roberts (2004) found that only a low percentage of the human resource management essays which they examined concerned international issues. Further, they found that there was not a significant increase throughout the 1990s and they thus suggested the need for a more strategic approach and new theoretical developments within the HRM field of academic endeavour. While mainstream HRM research may have made insufficient reference to national culture, though, a significant body of literature has been devoted specifically to exploration of cultures and cultural adjustment and adaptation. In Chapter 11, Bird, Osland, Mendenhall and Schneider, amongst others, undertook a comprehensive exploration of acculturation and adaptation, which referred to the need to make sense of, and understand, other cultures and the importance of adapting managerial styles in order to ensure intercultural effectiveness and avoid interpersonal blunders when managing cross-culturally. Importantly, both of the chosen essays in this section on managing cross-culturally suggest the need for expatriates and organizations to avoid making cultural generalizations and to ensure that expatriates are responsive to local situations and changes when developing and implementing human resource management and management practices. The oft-cited Dutch researcher Hofstede (2002), has made an invaluable contribution to understanding of national cultures (as have Hampden-Turner and Trompenaars, 1997; Schwartz, 1994; Triandis, 1998; and the GLOBE study – see House, Hanges, Javidan, Dorfman and Gupta, 2004). Yet, Hofstede's research has also been widely critiqued (see, for instance, McSweeney, 2002; Williamson, 2002) for its assumed emphasis on universal cultural application within nations. Notably, these are issues which have been well-addressed within the IHRM literature.

While much of the research on managing cross-culturally has focused on sojourning between North America and Europe and Japan, a growing body of literature has explored management of employees and business relationships in other parts of Asia, Africa and Latin America. Hutchings (Chapter 12), explored cross-cultural management in China from the perspective of Australian expatriates, an erstwhile under-researched nation of international sojourners, with approximately one million Australian nationals currently living abroad. Hutchings suggested that, despite over twenty years of research recommending cross-cultural preparation of expatriates for international postings, the cohort of expatriates interviewed in her research claimed to be inadequately prepared for the demands of managing in China. Irrespective of the fact that many of the individuals who self-selected to work in China had prior language skills and cultural knowledge, they maintained that they were ill-prepared for the demands of cross-cultural management and considered themselves to be deficient in terms of their cultural adaptation. Her research does make an important contribution in suggesting that while organizations continue to invest little time or money in preparing employees for international assignments, they are recognizing the need to select individuals who already possess language and cross-cultural skills.

Comparative HRM

When managing cross-nationally, organizations and individual expatriates need to give consideration to various local factors including: culture and social practices; the political situation; legislation; economy; technology; and the labour market. Such recognition has led to the development of comparative human resource management literature that has specifically examined HRM practices (many of them in their infancy) that apply in individual nations, the extent to which the practices are determined by local factors, and the necessity for international organizations to develop policy and practice in subsidiary operations that accommodate pre-existing HRM practices. In an initial foray into comparative management within the European context in the early 1980s, in Chapter 13, Laurent found that the national origins of managers significantly affected their views of how effective managers should manage. He suggested that whether the manager should be viewed as a facilitator or expert differed markedly between the European countries he explored and could be attributed to pre-existing cultural attributes. There are other well-cited examinations of differing paradigms in human resource management (Brewster, 1999) and assessments of strategic integration and levels of decentralization (Brewster and Larsen, 1992). Begin (1992) undertook one of the first major systems analysis of comparative human resource management, in which he developed a framework for describing variations in HRM systems. Begin suggested a likely convergence of human resource management policies, practices and procedures internationally. While the latter theme of convergence/divergence has been widely explored within the international business literature, it was explored in detail in Chapter 14 by Sparrow, Schuler and Jackson, who addressed the question of whether global organizations utilize different human resource management practices throughout their international operations in order to achieve competitive advantage. While Sparrow *et al.* (Chapter 14) also concluded a trend towards convergence for competitive advantage, they cautioned that clear divergence remains and specific local aspects of culture, work structure, performance managing and resourcing need to be utilized when managing human resources across nations. It has also been suggested that such divergence can be expected to be more marked in cases where the nation of the subsidiary operation has dramatically different cultural and political practices than the nation in which the organization's headquarters is located.

Such divergence in human resource management practices internationally has been suggested by recent, and growing, research on particular nations and regions, including: Africa (Kamoche, 2004); China (Tung and Worm, 2001); Latin America (Osland, De Franco and Osland, 1999); the Middle East (Yavas, 1999); and Southeast Asia (Hutchings, 1996). Harvey (2002) presents a fascinating account of the development of human resource management in Africa, which he wrote with the use of the children's tale of *Alice in Wonderland* as a metaphor. Harvey quite rightly pointed to the difficulty of developing human resource management systems in Africa given its vast diversity on ethnic, political, economic and developmental lines. The same degrees of diversity are present throughout Asia, Latin America and the Middle East and present similar dilemmas for comparative human resource management. Yet, while research has illuminated our understanding of differences in human resource management practices between countries and regions, there is an ongoing need for research that undertakes a comparative examination of human resource practices, as noted by Bowen, Galang and Pillai (2002), who explored cross-cultural variance, based on findings of an international project examining best practice in IHRM. As an example of research that provides a comparative examination of human resource practices, Spector, Cooper, Poelmans, Allen, O'Driscoll, Sanchez, Siu, Dewe, Hart, Lu, de Moraes, Ostrognay, Sparks, Wong and Yu (Chapter 15), researched an increasingly important aspect of employment conditions at the individual level, namely work-life balance, working hours and well-being. Spector *et al.*'s research, (Chapter 15), was based on a study of China and Taiwan, Latin America and the Anglo countries, and examined the relationship between these three factors. Their research suggested that caution needs to be exercised when considering cultural differences and family structures in the work-family domain. Indeed, they concluded that, despite cultural differences, there is evidence to suggest that the relationship between work-family issues and outcomes such as job satisfaction and well-being cuts across countries.

Internationalizing HRM

As noted, in more recent years the IHRM literature has developed a focus on the need for organizations and researchers to think more strategically with recognition of the need for human resource departments and managers to move beyond just being involved in the international arena in respect to *ad hoc* management of expatriates and employees in other cultures. In their book, Evans *et al.* (2002) have suggested that human resource departments should be increasingly involved in the whole process of internationalization from start-up of international operations or acquisitions and mergers, through detailing strategic levels of international human resource management, managing the expatriation process and preparation of expatriates for managing in other cultures and steering the strategic expansion of international operations. Attention has also been given to the need for organizations to focus more on managing multicultural domestic workforces, creating global teams, managing diversity, engineering of global teams, and engendering of global consciousness. Such an approach recognizes the role of human resource managers and departments in assisting the development of flexible, adaptive international organizations and highlights the role that human resource management can play when it broadens its function to that of change agent in transforming the global thinking of organizations. The selected essays in this section explore and develop these themes.

Strategic Focus

In Chapter 16, Miller, Beechler, Bhatt and Nath discussed the relationship between human resource management functions and the need for human resources to be involved in global strategic planning. Importantly, they were amongst the first IHRM researchers to emphasize the requirement for human resource managers and departments to utilize their skills in recruiting and training to develop transnationally competent managers. At a time when the IHRM field was evolving, Miller *et al.* raised the important question for academic researchers and practitioners alike of whether IHRM was different from domestic human resource management. Throughout the 1980s and 1990s it was generally argued that yes, IHRM is different because of the added dimension of intercultural management in international operations but, from the late 1990s, researchers began to suggest that in fact domestic human resource management should also have an international orientation and borrow from the lessons of IHRM in managing domestic diversity. Schuler, Dowling and De Cieri (Chapter 17), presented the first integrated framework for strategic IHRM in which they linked strategy with human resource management in the international arena. Their essay drew upon an extensive body of literature from strategy and human resource management and IHRM, and suggested the need for multinational enterprises to also utilize a multidisciplinary set of tools from business as well as sociology and anthropology in managing human resource internationally. The authors developed a series of propositions and outlined a number of interrelationships and influences of exogenous and endogenous factors in IHRM. Moreover, they identified the need for organizations to balance their competitive demands of global versus local requirements with needs of coordination, control and autonomy. McWilliams, Van Fleet and Wright (2001) argued that there had been a void in knowledge and practice where global corporate strategy and human resource management intersect, and suggested how the strategic management of human resources could be used for global competitive advantage. Engle, Mendenhall, Powers and Stedham (Chapter 18), introduced a conceptual framework for bridging the gap between strategic needs of organizations and their human resource support practices. They presented a model, called the Global Competency Cube, with three balanced transnational competencies (cultural, functional and product) which can be utilized by organizations to balance these demands to ensure that micro and macro international human resource decisions can be made in a more timely and strategic manner. They suggested that the Global Cube could provide a template to assist the operating level 'entrepreneurs', senior management 'developers' and top level 'leaders' in developing and maintaining those new and radically different management roles required by the 'individualized' transnational organization, as earlier identified by Ghoshal and Bartlett (1997).

Diversity Management

While diversity management has been an issue highlighted in the general management literature for the past two decades and increasingly integrated into organizational human resource practices, it has only been in comparatively recent times that IHRM researchers have begun to recognize the synergies between cross-cultural management for international operations and diversity management in domestic operations. In Chapter 19, McMahan, Bell and Virick examined diversity and employee involvement with strategic IHRM and called for improved understanding and prediction of human contributions to the improvement of organizational systems. They suggested that strategic human resource management was at a crossroads and argued for three possible future scenarios for the field: stagnation and retrenchment; stability, slow growth and replication; and movement in new directions with a focus on improving understanding and predication of human contributions to the improvement of organizational systems. They argued for the third scenario with the use of some of the new arenas of enquiry (employee involvement, diversity and strategic international human resource management) which they addressed in their essay. While McMahan *et al.*'s essay addressed the need for appreciation of diversity in an international context, Dass and Parker (Chapter 20), concurred that there is no one best way to manage workforce diversity in organizations and developed a framework for linking managers' perspectives and priorities in respect to managing workforce diversity, organizational conditions and performance. In exploring internal and external pressures for and against diversity, Dass and Parker provided several scenarios for strategic responses to diversity management. While their essay did not specifically address diversity in the international context, it did provide valuable strategies for organizations to implement when dealing with diversity management both internationally and domestically. It also served as an important conduit to the growing numbers of researchers and organizational practitioners committed to understanding the linkages between domestic diversity management and international human resource management.

Global Teams

In Chapter 21, Snow, Snell, Davison and Hambrick undertook one of the first major explorations of international teamworking in demonstrating the key characteristics that differentiate transnational teams from other forms of work teams. Based on a two-year study conducted with thirteen organizations, Snow *et al.* argued that transnational teams are at the heart of the globalization process. The authors provided a practitioner-friendly step-by-step approach to assist managers and human resource departments to improve team performance and in so doing, argued that team effectiveness precedes company effectiveness. Further, they provided suggestions as to how human resource departments can ensure that existing multinational teams can be transformed into transnational teams. Welch, Worm and Fenwick examined in Chapter 22 new approaches to international management and suggested that virtual assignees, global teams and fly in/fly out postings are likely to replace many of the traditional expatriates posted for a fixed-term international assignment. Importantly, their research raised questions for researchers and practitioners of how to select, train, and support employees for such new forms of international assignments. Namely, they highlighted that transiting across a greater number of more frequent transitions (real or virtual) to differing cultural contexts suggests the need for employees to have a broader knowledge of a greater range of cultures as well as general global consciousness. This essay has important synergies with a recently published essay by Tharenou (2005) in which she addressed the increasingly international component of domestic jobs. Tharenou reported differences between the quantitative and qualitative data she collected, most notably that the factors quantitatively related to the amount of international work performed in the job differ from the main qualitative reasons employees give for why they would/wouldn't take up international work. She concluded, that as domestic jobs with international responsibilities are increasing in frequency, organizations need to provide environments to attract and assist employees who perform substantive amounts of international work in their jobs. This research accorded with the work of Welch *et al.* (Chapter 22) who argued that frequent transitions require as much cross-cultural knowledge, or perhaps even more, than for those people that are posted for one long-term, traditional, expatriate assignment.

Global Integration

Gupta and Govindarajan suggested in Chapter 23 how organizations may convert global presence into global competitive advantage. While most of their focus was on marketing, they provided some valuable issues for consideration by IHRM academicians and practitioners, such as the need to maximize knowledge transfer across global locations and achieve global integration of resources. In discussing global coordination they also provided valuable ideas for IHRM in terms of how to involve HRM in local-level decision making as well as in utilizing the skills of human resource departments in building global networks. In Chapter 24, Schuler and Jackson discussed the importance of involving human resource departments and managers in mergers and acquisitions in order to avoid some of the neglected human resources issues and activities that have been responsible for many mergers and acquisitions failures. They suggested ten key areas in which human resource departments can assist the achievement of well-integrated transitions, namely: developing key strategies; managing soft due diligence activity; providing input into change management processes; advising top management on merged companies' organizational structures; creating transition teams; overseeing communications; managing the learning process; re-casting the human resource department; identifying new roles for HRM leaders; and identifying and developing new competencies. Importantly they identify the necessity for human resource managers and associated professionals to work in partnership with line managers and employees and their representatives as mergers and acquisition activity proliferates in the future.

Chapter 25 by Tregaskis, Heraty and Morley, explored how multinational corporations differed from local companies in their human resource development practices and suggested that rather than there being a convergence to domestic practice, multinational corporations adapted their practices to accommodate national differences in a hybrid form of localization. They argued not for a complete integration of practice globally but rather suggested that the integrated management of local and international human capabilities offers multinational firms a means to address demands for local customer responsiveness, globally-operative cost efficiencies; and knowledge flows that lead to product and service innovation on an international scale. In respect to localization of human resource development practices, they suggested that country differences in career traditions and labour market skill needs are key drivers. Stahl, Miller and Tung (Chapter 26), examined international assignments and suggested that such sojourns are increasingly associated with boundaryless careers. The notion of a boundaryless career implies that employees are increasingly oriented towards personal and professional development and career advancement (which may or may not be linked to their current organization) and view the taking of an international assignment as part of their boundaryless career and as an important component to their career advancement. Despite the commonly held belief by respondents in this research project that there are deficiencies in corporate career management systems and that the international assignment probably will not assist their career advancement within their current organization, expatriates viewed their international assignment as a real opportunity for personal and professional development and long-term career advancement. Stahl *et al.*'s paper accorded with similar research which has also suggested the need to explore the contribution made by the 'perpetual' expatriate – the individual who moves from one international assignment to another, having allegiance neither to a particular organization nor to a particular nation, and the extent to which s/he is globally integrated and conscious. This research provides one example of the extent to which the IHRM field, in terms of both theory and practice, has transformed since the early research, such as that by Black and Gregersen (Chapter 2), which emphasized notions of allegiance to both host country and the organization.

As the world becomes increasingly internationally integrated another important emergent issue is that of creating and sustaining ethical capability in multinational corporations. While there have been a substantive number of essays written that have addressed corporate social responsibility (see, for instance, Etheredge, 1999; Wood, 1991), that by Buller and McEvoy, reproduced here as Chapter 27, examined how ethical capability could be achieved internationally through transformational leadership, organizational learning and human resource management. They suggested that while organizations need to become more sensitive to cross-cultural ethical differences and more sophisticated in applying the appropriate ethics in any given situation, the human resource department, which has traditionally been neglected in this area of management decision making, has an important role to play in facilitating processes of ongoing organizational change and improvement. Moving beyond the resource-based view of the firm, they suggested that ethical capability as an aspect of strategic international human resource management may become a future source of competitive advantage for internationalizing organizations.

The extent to which there are synergies between academicians' research and teaching in IHRM and organizational practice of IHRM and strategic or operative implementation of IHRM has been explored in research by Wasti and Robert (2004) and De Cieri, Fenwick and Hutchings (2005). Yet, in Chapter 28, De Cieri, Cox and Fenwick undertook a critical examination of philosophical approaches and processes in the teaching of strategic IHRM. They argued that internationalized management education suffers from elements of ethnocentrism and paternalism and that there is a need to move away from simply training or teaching about cross-cultural training as '(implied) inoculation' and consider other models. The authors suggested the need to 'move beyond the "safari mode" of taking the uninitiated out of the classroom on a "cook's tour" into strategic international human resource management territory' and in so doing, there might be a shift in emphasis from the expatriate to the host country national within IHRM research and practice. Importantly but also alarmingly they concluded that despite the supposed focus of international human resource management on appreciation of cultural diversity, when teaching human resource management and IHRM in Western nations, the teaching is often done from a Western model and when teaching offshore, teaching is still done from a Western model with token 'local' examples. So, rather than there being an emphasis on global integration, what has in fact occurred within teaching and education is a convergence towards Western methods and practice.

Conclusion

As an overall collection, the essays included in this volume provide an overview of the major developments in the field of international human resource management. We hope that, by exploring these developments, new directions for researchers and practitioners may be identified. As markets and economies become more globally integrated and more organizations expand their operations across national borders, issues around IHRM become critical to organizational sustainability and success. While there are many complexities and challenges for the research and practice of IHRM, there are many and varied opportunities for developing this field in the future. As Schuler *et al*. (2002, p. 463) noted, there are myriad opportunities for IHRM researchers to assist organizations to develop and sustain human resource-led strategies for success in their international operations and 'researchers and firms that chart these waters effectively will secure enviable market positions in the decades ahead'.

References

Adler, N. (1984), 'Women Do Not Want International Careers: and Other Myths About International Management', *Organizational Dynamics*, **13**, pp. 66–79.

Adler, N. (1987), 'Pacific Basin Managers: A Gaijin, Not a Woman', *Human Resource Management*, **26**(2), pp. 169–91.

Adler, N. (2002), 'Global Managers: No Longer Men Alone', *International Journal of Human Resource Management*, **13**(5), pp. 743–60.

Adler, P.S. (1975), 'The Transitional Experience: An Alternative View of Culture Shock', *Journal of Humanistic Psychology*, **15**(4), pp. 13–23.

Begin, J.P. (1992), 'Comparative Human Resource Management (HRM): A Systems Perspective', *International Journal of Human Resource Management*, **3**(3), pp. 379–408.

Black, J., Mendenhall, M. and Oddou, G. (1991), 'Toward a Comprehensive Model of International Adjustment: An Integration of Multiple Theoretical Perspectives', *Academy of Management Review*, **16**(2), pp. 291–317.

Bowen, D.E., Galang C. and Pillai R. (2002), 'The Role of Human Resource Management: An Exploratory Study of Cross-country Variance', *Asia Pacific Journal of Human Resources*, **40**(1), pp. 123–45.

Brewster, C. (1999), 'Strategic Human Resource Management: The Value of Different Paradigms', *Management International Review*, **39**(3), pp. 45–64.

Brewster, C. and Larsen, H.K. (1992), 'Human Resource Management in Europe: Evidence from Ten Countries', *International Journal of Human Resource Management*, **3**, pp. 409–33.

De Cieri, H. and Dowling, P.J. (1999), 'Strategic Human Resource Management in Multinational Enterprises', in P.M. Wright, L.D. Dyer, J.W. Boudreau and G.T. Milkovich (eds), *Research in Personnel and HRM, Supplement 4, Strategic Human Resources Management in the Twenty-first Century*, Stamford, CT: JAI Press, pp. 305–27.

De Cieri, H., Fenwick, M. and Hutchings, K. (2005), 'The Challenge of International Human Resource Management: Reconciling Strategic Academic Approaches with Practical Complexity', *International Journal of Human Resource Management*, **16**, pp. 584–98.

Etheredge, J.M. (1999), 'The Perceived Role of Ethics and Social Responsibility: An Alternative Scale Structure', *Journal of Business Ethics*, **18**, pp. 51–64.

Evans, P.A.L. and Genadry, N. (1998), 'A Duality Based Perspective for Strategic Human Resource Management', in P.M. Wright, L.D. Dyer, J.W. Boudreau and G.T. Milkovich (eds), *Research in Personnel and HRM, Supplement 4, Strategic Human Resources Management in the Twenty-first Century*, Stamford, CT: JAI Press, pp. 325–38.

Evans, P.A.L., Pucik, V. and Barsoux, J-L. (2002), *The Global Challenge: Frameworks for IHRM*, New York, NY: McGraw-Hill Irwin.

Ghoshal, S. and Bartlett, C.A. (1997), *The Individualized Corporation*, New York, NY: Harper Business Publishers.

Hampden-Turner, C. and Trompenaars, F. (1997), 'Response to Geert Hofstede', *International Journal of Intercultural Relations*, **21**(1), pp. 149–59.

Harvey, M.G. (1996), 'Addressing the Dual-career Expatriation Dilemma', *Human Resource Planning*, **19**, pp. 18–39.

Harvey, M.G. (2002), 'Human Resource Management in Africa: Alice's Adventures in Wonderland', *International Journal of Human Resource Management*, **13**(7), pp. 1119–45.

Hofstede, G. (2002), 'Dimensions Do Not Exist: A Reply to Brendan McSweeney', *Human Relations*, **55**(11), pp. 1355–61.

House, R.J., Hanges, P.J., Javidan, M., Dorfman, P.W. and Gupta, V. (2004), *Culture, Leadership, and Organizations: The GLOBE Study of 62 Societies*, Thousand Oaks, CA: Sage Publications.

Hutchings, K. (1996), 'Workplace Practices of Japanese and Australian Multinational Corporations Operating in Singapore, Malaysia and Indonesia', *Human Resource Management Journal*, **6**(2), pp. 58–71.

Kamoche, K. (ed.) (2004), *Managing Human Resources in Africa*, London: Routledge.

McSweeney, B. (2002), 'The Essentials of Scholarship: A Reply to Geert Hofstede', *Human Relations*, **55**(11), pp. 1363–72.

McWilliams, A., Van Fleet, D.D. and Wright, P.M. (2001), 'Strategic Management of Human Resources for Global Competitive Advantage', *Journal of Business Strategies*, **18**, pp. 1–24.

Oberg, K. (1960), 'Culture Shock: Adjustment to New Cultural Environments', *Practical Anthropology*, **7**, pp. 177–82.

Osland, J., De Franco, S. and Osland, A. (1999), 'Organizational Implications of Latin American Culture: Lessons for the Expatriate Manager', *Journal of Management Inquiry*, **8**(2), pp. 253–68.

Richardson, J. and McKenna, S. (2000), 'Metaphorical "Types" and Human Resource Management: Self-selecting Expatriates', *Industrial and Commercial Training*, **32**(6), pp. 209–19.

Schuler, R.S., Budhwar, P.S. and Florkowski, G.W. (2002), 'International Human Resource Management: Review and Critique', *International Journal of Management Reviews*, **4**(1), pp. 41–70.

Schwartz, S.H. (1994), 'Beyond Individualism/Collectivism: New Dimensions of Values', in U. Kim, H.C. Triandis, C. Kagitcibasi, S.C. Choi and G. Yoon (eds), *Individualism and Collectivism: Theory, Method and Applications*, Newbury Park, CA: Sage, pp. 85–110.

Selmer, J. (2001), 'The Preference for Predeparture or Postarrival Cross-cultural Training: An Exploratory Approach', *Journal of Managerial Psychology*, **16**(1), pp. 50–69.

Tharenou, P. (2005), 'International Work in Domestic Jobs: An Individual Explanation', *International Journal of Human Resource Management*, **16**(4), pp. 479–500.

Triandis, H.C. (1998), 'Vertical and Horizontal Individualism and Collectivism: Theory and Research Implications for International Comparative Management', *Advances in International Comparative Management*, **12**, pp. 7–35.

Tung, R. (1981), 'Selecting and Training of Personnel for Overseas Assignments', *Columbia Journal of World Business*, **16**, pp. 68–78.

Tung, R. and Worm, V. (2001), 'Network Capitalism: The Role of Human Resources in Penetrating the China Market', *International Journal of Human Resource Management*, **12**(4), pp. 517–34.

Wasti, S.A. and Robert, C.A. (2004), 'Out of Touch? An Evaluation of the Correspondence Between Academic and Practitioner Concerns in IHRM', in J. Cheng and M. Hitt (eds), *Advances in International Management*, Amsterdam: Elsevier, JAI Press, pp. 207–39.

Welch, D. (1994), 'International Human Resource Management Approaches and Activities: A Suggested Framework', *Journal of Management*, **31**(2), pp. 139–64.

Williamson, D. (2002), 'Forward from a Critique of Hofstede's Model of National Culture', *Human Relations*, **55**(11), pp. 1373–95.

Wood, D.J. (1991), 'Corporate Social Performance Revisited', *Academy of Management Review*, **15**(4), pp. 691–718.

Yavas, U. (1999), 'Training Needs in Saudi Arabia: A Survey of Managers', *Journal of Education for Business*, **75**(2), pp. 117–21.

Part I
Cross-cultural Management

Expatriate Management

[1]

An Extension of the U-Curve Hypothesis[1]

John T. Gullahorn and Jeanne E. Gullahorn

Introduction

An American student in a French provincial university tearfully presented this rather disorganized report of her adjustment difficulties:

> . . . it did hurt to feel so alone where not a soul seemed to care if you lived or died. That came as a shock to a young new college graduate . . . . The students in the university in my town were not friendly, but I know they were in other universities. Perhaps we at our university were exceptions, but all six of us were not entirely happy until we realized no one was going to care very much about us. As a result we stuck together and spoke English. . . .

Another American student who had recently returned to the United States described her readjustment problems as follows:

> I just can't seem to get adjusted back here. I just can't seem to settle down to work. I don't know what it is, but once you've lived abroad I guess you can't really come back . . . at least not if you're an artist. . . . Of course, I suppose eventually I'll be able to work this all out. . . . I'd like to keep on doing some creative work here, but it's very hard for artists to get by in America. I guess it's obvious that I won't be able to stay in Missouri; there is just no place out here for artists. I'll have to move to New York, and that's so expensive, and there are big disadvantages to living there, but really that's the only art center in the United States.

These cases illustrate some of the problems of alienation, anomie, and rejection frequently encountered in cross-cultural adjustment. Such reactions occur not only when a sojourner attempts to adjust to

[1] Paper presented in part at the symposium on "Human Factors in International Development Programs—Problems of Overseas Adjustment," at the meetings of the American Psychological Association (St. Louis, Missouri, September, 1962). We are grateful to the Program Evaluation Staff, International Educational Exchange Service, U.S. Department of State for sponsoring our interview and questionnaire study of 400 American students in France (1956) as well as our interview and questionnaire studies (1958 and 1960a) of 5,300 American Fulbright and Smith-Mundt grantees whose awards took them to all areas of the World. We also appreciate the funds for additional data analysis provided by the Office of International Programs, Michigan State University.

34   JOHN T. GULLAHORN AND JEANNE E. GULLAHORN

an alien social system; they also recur with varying intensities when the sojourners return to their home environments. In looking at the total exchange experience, therefore, we may speak of a W-curve rather than a U-shaped curve to characterize the temporal patterning in individual reactions to foreign settings and subsequently to their home cultures. Let us first look at adjustment in an alien social system.

Adjustment in an Alien Social System

During the last decade many researchers have recorded the adjustment process of foreign students in their host cultures (Lysgaard, 1953; DuBois, 1956; Gullahorn and Gullahorn, 1956; Smith, 1956; Coelho, 1958; Sewell and Davidsen, 1961). Initially the sojourners report feelings of elation and optimism associated with positive expectations regarding interaction with their hosts. As they actually become involved in role relationships and encounter frustrations in trying to achieve certain goals when the proper means are unclear or unacceptable, they become confused and depressed and express negative attitudes regarding the host culture. If they are able to resolve the difficulties encountered during this crucial phase of the acculturation process they then achieve a *modus vivendi* enabling them to work effectively and to interact positively with their hosts.

Essentially, the acculturation process may be interpreted as a cycle of adult socialization occuring under conditions where previous socialization offers varying degrees of facilitation and interference in the new learning context. As a consequence of previous socialization sojourners learn value orientations which provide a framework for evaluating behavior in role interactions. The result is that when two members of a particular social system are interacting each can anticipate the other's responses with sufficient accuracy so that his behavior is likely to elicit the results he desires (cf. Parsons' discussion of double contingency, 1951). This complementarity of role expectations generally becomes disturbed when an individual moves from one social system to another where differing value orientations and normative expectations are characteristic.

Actually, much the same patterning in the adjustment process seems to occur whenever one relocates geographically even within the United States if one encounters emotionally salient differences in social subsystems—for example, in moving from small town to metropolitan area, from Deep South to the North. Unless the new or old patterns of behavior or belief are of deep emotional significance, the depth or duration of the depression in the U-curve may be trivial, but it probably exists. For the recently retired individual moving to another sector of the country, the relocation process—physical and psychological—probably engenders the same intensity of response often found in cross-cultural contact situations. As with socialization, so with learning and creative endeavor in general: When one is seriously engaged in creative efforts or is deeply involved in a learning experience of emotional significance, the U-curve appears. That is, there is initial excitement or elation over new ideas or skills; feelings of depression and perhaps decrement in output as one encounters difficulties and complexities; and finally, a sense of satisfaction and perhaps even of personal growth if one emerges from the plateau and restructures the problem so he can work effectively.

The cross-cultural sojourner in the new environment generally behaves almost automatically in a manner compatible with his primary reference groups in his home culture. Thus at times he finds a lack of consensus between his own and his hosts' expectations regarding appropriate role behavior. For example, one woman professor of economics reported the following dilemma in adjusting to her host university:

> There is no established position for women professors in the . . . university where I taught. As a result my colleagues there did not know whether to treat me as a woman or as a professor. If I assumed all the privileges of a professor it was likely to be considered presumptuous behavior for a woman. But if I assumed the role of the woman I felt sure it would result in their refusal to accept my competence in my own profession.

Another American lecturer encountered an unexepected difference in role behavior in his host institution and found he had to change his usual practice of arriving early for class meetings:

> I started out early one day and my assistant, . . . grabbed me by the arm and said, "You mustn't go early." I didn't undestand this and told him that I often did because I liked to write things on the blackboard and liked to chat with students. He said, "But don't you see what happens?" I told him, no I couldn't see that anything was happening. He said, "Well, if you come early, not a student may come into the classroom after you have entered." It occurred to me that this was true. After I came in, not a single student did. They considered themselves late if they arrived after the professor, and so they would not enter, because to arrive late would be a mark of disrespect. Consequently, there the professor never went to class until fifteen minutes after the hour.

Aside from variations in classroom behavior in different university social systems there is considerable variance in the degree of social distance characteristic of faculty-student relations in different cultures. In commenting on his overseas experience, for example, one American professor noted,

> Another thing I did that proved extremely disturbing to the faculty was to invite the students to my home. . . . All in all, I think the faculty . . .

36   JOHN T. GULLAHORN AND JEANNE E. GULLAHORN

considered that the Americans have still remained rebels, and that the
revolution is aimed at the educational institutions. . . .

Conversely, foreign students at American institutions are at first confused and disturbed by what they perceive to be the lack of deference
their American peers exhibit toward their professors.

· Closely related to the issue of differing patterns of faculty-student
relations is the general area of cultural divergences in definitions
regarding the rights and obligations involved in friendship relationships (cf. Lewin, 1948). There is considerable variance across cultures
in the length of acquaintance preceding the establishment of first-
name relationships as well as in the introduction of a stranger into
one's home; furthermore, there are differences in the degree of in-
timacy of friendship implied by such behavior. Thus in a foreign
setting Americans behaving in terms of their norms of informality and
friendliness may find their hosts considering them forward and boorish.
The Americans, on the other hand, may perceive their hosts as cold
and distant. In the United States, foreign sojourners often initially
feel overwhelmed by the apparent openness and "friendliness" of their
hosts; however, when they find that an invitation to an American's
home does not necessarily indicate strong affective sentiments they
tend to characterize American friendship relationships as "superficial."

One area of cross-cultural contacts where lack of complementarity
in expectations may pose delicate personal problems involves dating
relationships. According to our student informants, in France it seems
to be an accepted norm that relationships between men and women
should be either completely platonic or completely sexual. The American dating practice of kissing and petting—but stopping at some
relatively undefined point—is considered dishonest and immoral. Thus,
a certain lack of international consensus might result if an American
girl indicates her willingness to have her French date kiss her good-
night.

Some of the situations encountered by foreign scholars in adjusting to their host cultures are amusing—at least they appear so in
retrospect. However, one should not underestimate the significance
of this period in the acculturation process in terms of the individual's
goals—and of those of agencies sponsoring international educational
exchange. We have already mentioned some of the cultural differences
creating varying degrees of confusion or frustration for grantees. Let
us mention a few more having even more direct bearing on the task-
fulfillment aspect of a grantee's sojourn. The first encounter with the
indexing system—if it is a system—of the Bibliotheque Nationale may
be traumatic to the goal-oriented humanities student who expects to
complete his dissertation research during his award year. And, after
this shock, encountering what such a student might perceive—probably

correctly—as the indifference of French professors toward American scholarly efforts is not likely to have a tranquilizing effect.

A vexation for researchers in the natural sciences who are accustomed to the plethora of readily available equipment in American laboratories involves the discovery of the paucity of such facilities abroad. Furthermore, discovering that their lab assistants are not exactly imbued with the Protestant ethic and cannot appreciate the necessity to "hurry" in building what the grantee considers standard equipment—all this puts a considerable strain on the goal-oriented researcher.

Or, we might take the situation of the idealistic teacher who ventures to a Far Eastern country expecting to make a contribution to the educational system only to find that he is expected to lecture from a set syllabus and that any deviation therefrom might jeopardize his students' chances of passing national examinations. Certainly a sojourner needs fortitude as well as ingenuity in discovering new means of achieving his objectives or formulating alternative goals which are realistic in terms of the situation confronting him.

Aside from cultural differences in role expectations a more covert source of potential misunderstanding among those involved in cross-cultural contact situations arises from the subtle expectations developed in the very process of learning a particular language. In the Japanese language, for example, the honorifics, syntax, and choice of lexical items are clustered for use depending upon the relative prestige of the interaction partners; consequently the language presents built-in status cues for its users. Such cues are absent in the relatively egalitarian structure of the English language, a factor contributing to what Bennett and associates (1958) characterize as "status-cue confusion" among Japanese sojourners in the United States. Thus the verbal cues occurring during a conversation with an American professor may lead a Japanese student to feel he is receiving what he perceives as peer treatment from someone he considers a superior status person. In the new cultural context, therefore, the Japanese sojourner can no longer depend largely upon language as an index of status but must learn to discriminate cues from other behaviors of his hosts.

Even in the area of non-verbal communication, opportunities for misinterpretation are legion. There are marked differences across cultures concerning such simple behavior as the spatial placement of partners in normal social interaction. Hall has noted (1959), for example, that a Latin American cannot talk comfortably with another person unless the interaction partners are close to the physical proximity that evokes either sexual or hostile feelings in the North American.

With so many potential sources of confusion and frustration for

38   JOHN T. GULLAHORN AND JEANNE E. GULLAHORN

the sojourner attempting to adjust to an alien social system it is not surprising that this phase of adjustment is sometimes termed "culture shock" to designate the psychological impact of the distortion or absence of familiar cues. Of course, individual personality differences account for some of the variance in the severity and duration of this anomic period. In addition, however, data from the SSRC studies of foreign students in the United States suggest that there are cultural patternings in the defense mechanisms exhibited at this time. For example, Indian and Pakistani students tend to display hypersensitive hostility in responding to the ego threat inherent in their perception of a derogatory American image of their homelands (Lambert & Bressler, 1956). Following Ichheiser's terminology, Coelho (1958) characterizes this reaction as the "mote-beam" mechanism of projection wherein the Indian student who is asked, for example, about the caste situation responds by attacking the American handling of Negroes. According to Bennett and associates (1958), Japanese students, on the other hand, respond to situations of threat to their national esteem by withdrawing—a reaction apparently consonant with their cultural norm of *enryo,* or reserve. Exploring further these cultural differences in preferred defense mechanisms would be a valuable research endeavor.

One method of such exploratory study is through computer simulation. At least one operating computer model of simple social behavior might be adapted to such research (Gullahorn and Gullahorn, 1962). The remaining requirements are to incorporate in the image lists of interaction partners data regarding values and defense mechanisms and to write routines which would express and execute the consequences of the hypotheses regarding the "sensitive area complex" and the "mote-beam" mechanism. The virtue of this approach is that computer simulation generates the dynamic consequences of a theory, showing the outcome of behavior specified by its principles. Furthermore, a practical benefit from this approach would ensue once the program was in operation, since modifications could be introduced to determine what inputs modify behavior. These could then be tested with actual subjects.

While speculating about research possibilities, let us mention a related topic. We have noted among American students in France and among foreign students we have studied in this country that two of the crucial determinants of the severity of culture shock involve the sojourner's flexibility of role behavior and his sensitivity in recognizing subtle sanctions and discriminating relevant cues for appropriate behavior. In terms of the familiar Riesman analogy, it appears that an other-directed radar system attuned to the feedback of the group in which one is interacting would have functional survival value when one shifts from one cultural system to another. It would be an interesting comparative study to see whether so-called market-oriented or other-directed individuals are able to adjust with less trauma to an alien cultural environment than are individuals with more traditionalistic or inner-directed orientations. In addition, of course, one would wish to know how the persons in the host culture respond to representatives of these value types. In effect, this would be a study of an individual's behavioral skill in a multiple-reference-group situation. Developing criteria and tests to operationalize the relevant concepts would in itself constitute a methodological contribution.

In addition, we may note that the problems encountered by the cross-cultural sojourner are those of marked cognitive reorientation, involving changes in feelings as well as overt behavior. For many years industry has been experimenting with such a retraining of relatively normal persons in stressful situations. Various labels are applied to this endeavor, such as sensitivity training or human relations in industry. It would appear to be worth experimenting with a similar approach and to set up a training program for sojourners to be conducted as a part of a research project such as that suggested here.

Post-Return Adjustment Problems

As a consequence of the resocialization experience in the alien environment, a sojourner tends to acquire expectation patterns compatible with his new social system. Indeed, if his interactions within the new society are particularly gratifying he may identify rather deeply with the new group. The result, of course, is that the sojourner typically finds himself out of phase with his home culture on his return. Our interview data concerning the experience of returned American grantees indicate that they undergo a reacculturation process in their home environments similar to that experienced abroad (Gullahorn and Gullahorn, 1958). Our data here are cross-sectional, based on interviews with different individuals at different periods after their return. Further research involving a longitudinal survey or a better-controlled panel study such as Coelho's (1958) would add valuable detail to our rather impressionistic data.

For most of the senior grantees—the professors and lecturers—the readjustment process was not particularly traumatic; the impact of their original socialization was sufficiently strong that relearning the patterns of their home social systems was not difficult. Nonetheless, they reported that their evaluations of certain situations and practices had changed sufficiently as a result of their participating in alien cultural systems that they felt annoyed and frustrated by American practices they had previously accepted. Many, for example, reported feelings of relative deprivation because in their home settings they

40   JOHN T. GULLAHORN AND JEANNE E. GULLAHORN

were not accorded the degree of respect they had come to feel was commensurate with their investments in their professorial statuses. Others expressed nostalgia for the greater time for reflection and prolonged consultation with colleagues they had enjoyed in their host universities. In particular, after experiencing the benefits of freedom from committee assignments in their host institutions, a number of professors expressed annoyance and regret at their home universities' committee obligations requiring them to concentrate precious time on group maintenance functions rather than on creative professional pursuits.

On the whole, however, faculty members who were fairly well established in their fields of work and in their university positions encountered relatively minor difficulties in readjusting to their home settings. Those who were able to become involved in creative work immediately on return reported less intense feelings of isolation and alienation.

For student grantees the situation generally was different. Those who had not previously experienced a major geographic move, or more precisely a "psychological relocation," seemed particularly likely to feel lost upon their return to the United States. For these individuals, it was a new experience to discover that in many subtle ways their patterns of expectations and, indeed, some of their values had changed as a result of their exposure and adjustment to a new social system. They had not before experienced such a shift in value identifications and the concomitant difficulties which ensue when one returns to his former environment only to find that he "can't go home again."

Particularly for those who had not yet "found themselves" in their own culture, the resolution of their identity conflict abroad often meant they had become zealously converted to new values, and they were reluctant to relinquish the security they had finally achieved. Students in the arts, such as the one quoted at the beginning of this paper, most frequently voiced feelings of alienation from American culture—and some reported finding a haven abroad where they felt their efforts, and they themselves, were considered legitimate and worthwhile. As one young painter expressed it,

> How can a man work effectively, achieve creative accomplishments, when his goals in life, his profession, and he himself are viewed and talked about as being not really masculine and not quite worthwhile?

Aside from the artists, members of other minority groups in their home culture also experienced serious feelings of relative deprivation after their sojourns in more gratifying social settings. One American Negro, for example, commented:

> Being a member of a minority group, the experience abroad was unique in every respect. At the same time, it made for very difficult readjust-

ment to many aspects of "the American Way of Life" upon return. This latter statement is not meant as a criticism of the experience—merely an observation made more revealing because of the experience. I doubt that a suggestion here would be of consequence.

The W-Curve

Our description of the W-curve of acculturation and reacculturation experiences involves a rather complex picture of variations in at least two variables which have long interested researchers in intergroup relations: interaction and sentiment. Important among the factors influencing the relationship between interaction and sentiment are the variables of proximity and similarity, characterized in the literature of Gestalt psychology as "unit-forming" factors in perception. Heider (1958) has noted that these factors may also be considered units for cognitive organization of social relationships; indeed, many reserchers have reported the importance of proximity in providing opportunity for people to interact (Festinger, *et al.*, 1950 and Gullahorn, 1952). In the case of the foreign scholar, of course, his travel award and presence in the alien society provide this opportunity. The outcome of the proximity insofar as continued interaction and positive sentiment are concerned depends largely on the factor of perceived similarity in what the interaction partners regard as salient areas of value orientation.

Data from the involvement phases of the W-curve support Heider's generalization that both proximity and interaction frequency increase the effect of perceived similarity on sentiments—expecially the effect of similarity or dissimilarity of attitudes and values. Given similar attitudes, proximity and frequent interaction tend to increase the degree of positive sentiment. With slight dissimilarity of attitudes a mutual assimilation seems to be produced, converting originally disparate values into common values, resulting in an increase in positive feelings. With strong dissimilarities, however, proximity and frequent interaction are likely to result in a greater clarification of the divergences and in a conflictful sequence of interaction—followed, perhaps, by mutual antipathy and dissociation.

The similarity of task-related values and goals seems particularly salient for the generation of positive sentiments. And it is precisely within this area of relationships that even across cultures the values characterizing university social systems are generally congruent—for example, dedication to one's profession and maintenance of certain standards in scholarship and research. Thus despite many differences in role expectations, sojourners participating in educational exchanges generally have at least some context of similarity in values and norms in which to operate. Their expected activities—teaching, conducting

42   JOHN T. GULLAHORN AND JEANNE E. GULLAHORN

research, studying, participating in professional discussions and professional meetings—generally require frequent interaction with their hosts; however, the interactions usually are of such a nature as to maintain emphasis on a common task, whether it be focusing on the substantive content of a course or seeking the discovery of new knowledge. Ideally, this situation of proximity and frequent interaction within a task-oriented context involving relative similarity in task-relevant values and norms should have salutary effects on the sentiment relationship of the interaction partners. Other aspects of the status positions of educational exchangees are also likely to provide structural support to the development of professional interaction having positive consequences (Gullahorn and Gullahorn, 1960b).

While they do not focus directly on adjustment processes, some of our questionnaire data are suggestive here (Gullahorn and Gullahorn, 1960a). On the basis of thirteen items concerning grantees' evaluations of the consequences of their award experiences we constructed a Satisfaction Index. This scale can be regarded as a rough subjective indication of how well a grantee resolved his adjustment difficulties. We found a significant positive relationship between the number of professional contacts a grantee reported having abroad and his own degree of satisfaction with his award experiences. Furthermore, there was a significant difference among the satisfied as contrasted to the dissatisfied grantees in the frequency of their contacts with professionals abroad. Our interview data indicate the reciprocal influence of the interaction-sentiment relationship. In most instances the generalized positive sentiment exhibited by grantees whose adjustment problems culminated highly satisfactorily was due to their initially sharing professional values and goals with their foreign colleagues so that their shared endeavors led to increased positive sentiment and more frequent interaction. In some cases, however, the interaction and sentiment variables were reversed. That is, the structured research positions the grantees occupied in their host institutions required a high frequency of interaction. To the extent that the interaction was constructive it led to an increased appreciation of the congruence between their own and their hosts' goals and thus increased positive sentiments.

The correlation between the number and the frequency of a sojourner's professional interactions with his hosts and his own relative satisfaction with his award experiences is interesting; however, possibly more important are questions regarding the quality of the interaction—the depth of the positive sentiments which apparently ensued. Unfortunately, most of our data concern only the feelings of the sojourners themselves; so we have only speculative evidence concerning their hosts. However, we may assume that in general relationships which are trivial or which are not rewarding will be terminated when it becomes convenient to do so, or when the cost of continuing them increases. Yet, grantees maintain their relationships after their return—and this implies cooperation of the host nationals in responding to their communications, or perhaps in doing the most to maintain them. In either event, we may consider continued contact one indicator of the significance of the relationships for the participants. Here it is of interest to note that significantly more of the satisfied grantees—as contrasted to the dissatisfied ones—have maintained contact with their host institutions abroad, have consulted on professional matters with colleagues and students from abroad and helped them apply for grants to come to the United States for educational purposes, have referred American colleagues going overseas to their foreign colleagues, and have arranged correspondence between American and foreign colleagues. All of these differences were significant at the .001 level and beyond.

From many viewpoints the opportunity for creative professional interaction has beneficial results. We found that in some cases a whole network of professional relationships across cultures resulted from a single scholar's award experiences. This facilitation of professional communication is of tremendous significance to the advancement of knowledge, especially in view of the time-lag in publication of research findings. There are other more far-reaching implications of this increased communication among scholars in different countries. Once established, relationships based on mutual professional respect and shared professional values and goals can lead to more sympathetic personal communication and understanding among colleagues in different countries. Hopefully, the constructive interaction leads the sojourners and their hosts to perceive each other as more similar in important areas and thus increases their tolerance and acceptance of differences in other areas.

So far we have presented some evidence supporting our extension of Heider's generalization concerning the impact of relative similarity in values and goals on the relationship between interaction frequency and positive sentiment. Let us turn now to the situation of strong dissimilarities in values where proximity and frequent interaction clarify the divergences. As an illustration we might cite the case of a Mormon girl who lived with a bourgeois French family. Because of her religious beliefs she refused to drink wine with her dinner. Her command of French was poor—which did not enhance communication between her and the family—and she was unable to make them understand that she was not rejecting French culture by her behavior. Trying to draw an analogy between her abstinence from alcoholic beverages and Catholic abstinence from meat on Friday was not effective inasmuch as food taboos are not strictly adhered to by many French Catholics. Thus this girl was unable to modify their beliefs about what is appropriate mealtime behavior (and eating practices are particularly important to the French). The end result was a breaking off of the relationship and a mutual antipathy.

As this case illustrates, a sojourner in the involvement phases of adjustment to a foreign culture or of readjustment at home frequently encounters situations of structural imbalance (Heider, 1958) or cognitive dissonance (Festinger, 1957). That is, he may find that people he had expected to like or to feel at home with actually hold strongly divergent values. Or, in response to the expectations of significant others in his environment and their manipulation of sanctions he may engage in role behavior that is at variance with his values. A relatively direct means of reducing the dissonance developed by such circumstances is by dissociation. Thus the sojourner may avoid engaging in role behavior which would be incongruent with his values by withdrawing completely from his status in the host society and going home; or the returnee may become an expatriate like some American artists who go back to Europe or like some former Fulbrighters who seek posts in government and university missions overseas.

However, the sojourner or ex-sojourner may decide that the rewards from his current status incumbency exceed his costs—or the costs of leaving the field exceed the anticipated rewards. In order to reduce his dissonance, while remaining in the cultural context, he might maximize the negative component in his ambivalent feelings toward others in his environment and withdraw as much as possible from interaction with them. To bolster this decision he may join a clique of fellow malcontents. We observed this reaction among some American students in France. In a study of colonial students in England, Carey (1956) also found that many of the students encountered frustration of their expectations of a close relationship with nationals of their "mother country," and responded to the perceived rejection by withdrawing into cliques of fellow colonials. Similarly, in American universities one often finds cliques of Europophiles—consisting of those possessing the distinction of having lived abroad and of never having returned home psychologically.

Rather than change positive sentiments concerning significant others, the sojourner or returnee may reduce the dissonance he encounters by modifying certain of his beliefs or expectations about appropriate role behavior—in short, by using those with whom he interacts as positive reference sources. Of course, the changes in sentiment or in belief structure are by no means mutually exclusive—indeed, individuals seem to vacillate between these two reactions. Nonetheless, the final resolution of the dissonance usually involves a relative dominance of one of these patterns. From several points of view the change in sentiment is less salutary. Obviously if a sojourner develops a strong antipathy toward his hosts, this will tend to produce a similar reaction on their part, and a vicious circle of antagonistic feelings may emerge—a result contrary to an explicit goal of cross-cultural exchange programs. Similarly, if a returnee cannot learn to interpret his new attitudes and goals in a manner which does not imply they are superior, then not only is he likely to be isolated, but his fellow countrymen may justify their rejection of him by claiming that he was brainwashed by his experience abroad. Such conflictful interactions may prevent the individual from ever coming to terms with his environment and of realizing either his original goals or realistic alternatives.

Related to our discussion of the impact of strong dissimilarities in values are some data from our questionnaire concerning the relationship between grantees' satisfaction with their award experiences and general cultural dissimilarities in social structure. The evidence is only speculative, however, since we do not have adequate means of ranking different cultures along dimensions of value similarities. Nonetheless, it is interesting to note that grantees sojourning in Europe tended to score higher on the Satisfaction Index than did those whose award periods were spent in the Near and Middle East or in Latin America, where presumably they encountered greater communication problems and value dissonance. For example, about two thirds of the grantees who had been to the Near and Middle East agreed with the questionnaire item, "My host country did not make maximum use of my experiences and abilities," while only slightly over one third of those sojourning in Europe or in Australia and New Zealand expressed such an evelution.

The findings regarding the relatively greater dissatisfaction with their award experiences among grantees to Near and Middle Eastern countries suggest an important area for research by social scientists. There is current interest in studies of the American university as a social system. Comparable research in academic institutions in other countries would be helpful so that one would have more definitive statements regarding the rights and obligations of a status incumbent in different university systems. For example, in a country characterized by particularistic relationships, such as India, an American professor may find he is expected to intercede for children of his friends to help them win fellowships in America—even though their fields of study have no relationship to his own. Individuals accustomed to the achievement orientation and universalism characteristic of the American pattern need to be apprised of such differences.

There is a related research question suggested by our findings on the relative satisfaction of grantees sojourning in different cultural areas. In the SSRC studies of foreign students in the United States, a finding of practical significance concerned varying degrees of culture shock exhibited by the nationality groups studied, suggesting

46   JOHN T. GULLAHORN AND JEANNE E. GULLAHORN

that different sojourn periods might have optimum benefits for diverse groups. Similarly, it appears that Americans require varying periods of time to adjust to different cultural areas. Thus the usual one-year grant may be unrealistic in certain countries in terms of the sojourner's and his hosts' achieving maximum professional as well as other benefits. Indeed, the one-year term seems questionable for most areas since even grantees reporting relatively mild acculturation difficulties felt that they were just becoming really effective as the year's end approached. The frustration of interrupting their work relationships and then having to renew others accounted in part for the reacculturation difficulties.

Probably few would argue with our belief that there are many important research problems concerning cross-cultural contact situations. We have tried to suggest that a number of them focus around patterns of adjustment both of the sojourner and of the returnee. Clearer evidence of the relationship of the W-curve to other psychological processes would enhance our understanding of international educational exchange and perhaps of theory in social psychology.

It would be helpful to have more specifications of cultural value dimensions as well as some means of calibrating them so that cross-cultural comparisons could be made realistically. Furthermore, we need to know more about the elements involved in the dissonance relationships encountered during the acculturation and reacculturation process. Under what conditions is the dissonance resolution likely to involve change in beliefs rather than in sentiments? In the intra-punitive withdrawal reaction noted among Japanese students, does their symbolic dissociation result in less cognitive reorganization and lessened probability of modification in beliefs? Does the motebeam mechanism of Indian student sojourners increase the probability of their hosts' dissociating themselves from further interaction? Do both interaction partners then tend to bolster their own prejudices? What is needed, of course, is what Brewster Smith and others have been suggesting for some years—more detailed careful study of the reciprocal process of interaction in cross-cultural contact situations. What happens to the sojourner and his host and the interactions between them? What happens to the returnee and his fellows at home and to subsequent interactions between them?

REFERENCES

BENNETT, J. W., PASSIN, H., & McKNIGHT, R. K. *In search of identity: the Japanese overseas scholar in America and Japan.* Minneapolis: University of Minnesota Press, 1958.

CAREY, A. T. *Colonial students: a study of the social adaptation of colonial students in London.* London: Secker and Warburg, 1956.

COELHO, G. V. *Changing images of America: a study of Indian students' perceptions.* Glencoe, Ill.: Free Press, 1958.

DuBois, C. *Foreign students and higher education in the United States.* Washington, D. C.: American Council on Education, 1956.

FESTINGER, L. *A theory of cognitive dissonance.* Stanford, Cal.: Stanford University Press, 1957.

FESTINGER, L., SCHACHTER, S., & BACK, K. W. *Social pressures in informal groups.* New York: Harper, 1950.

GULLAHORN, J. T. Distance and friendship as factors in the gross interaction matrix. *Sociometry,* 1952, **15**, 123-134.

GULLAHORN, J. T., & GULLAHORN, J. E. *American students in France.* Washington, D.C.: International Educational Exchange Service, U.S. Department of State, 1956 (mimeographed).

GULLAHORN, J. T., & GULLAHORN, J. E. *Professional and social consequences of Fulbright and Smith-Mundt awards.* Washington, D.C.: International Educational Exchange Service, U.S. Department of State, 1958 (mimeographed).

GULLAHORN, J. T., & GULLAHORN, J. E. *International educational exchange: an assessment of professional and social contributions by American Fulbright and Smith-Mundt grantees: 1947-1957.* Washington, D.C.: International Educational Exchange Service, U.S. Department of State, 1960a (mimeographed).

GULLAHORN, J. T., & GULLAHORN, J. E. The role of the academic man as a cross-cultural mediator. *American Sociological Review,* 1960b, **24**, 414-417.

GULLAHORN, J. T., & GULLAHORN, J. E. A computer model of elementary social behavior. In E. A. Feigenbaum and J. Feldman (Eds.) *Computers and thought.* New York: McGraw-Hill, scheduled for 1963. Also reprinted as SP-741, System Development Corporation, Santa Monica, California, March, 1962.

HALL, E. T. *The silent language.* New York: Doubleday, 1959.

HEIDER, F. *The psychology of interpersonal relations.* New York: Wiley, 1958.

LAMBERT, R. D., & BRESSLER, M. *Indian students on an American campus.* Minneapolis: University of Minnesota Press, 1956.

LEWIN, K. *Resolving social conflicts.* New York: Harper, 1948.

LYSGAARD, S. Adjustment in a foreign society: Norwegian Fulbright grantees visiting the United States. *International Social Science Bulletin,* 1955, VII, 45-51.

PARSONS, T., & SHILS, E. (Eds.) *Toward a general theory of action.* Cambridge, Mass.: Harvard University Press, 1951.

SEWELL, W., & DAVIDSEN, O. *Scandinavian students on an American campus.* Minneapolis: University of Minnesota Press, 1961.

SMITH, M. B. (Ed.) Attitudes and adjustment in cross-cultural contact: recent studies of foreign students. *Journal of Social Issues,* **12**, No. 1, 1956.

[2]

Serving Two Masters: Managing the Dual Allegiance of Expatriate Employees

J. Stewart Black • Hal B. Gregersen

A MANAGER WHO TAKES AN ASSIGNMENT IN A FOREIGN COUNTRY HAS THE IMMENSE TASK OF ADAPTING TO A NEW CULTURE AND NEW BUSINESS PRACTICES. The firm naturally wants to get the most out of this employee, both during the assignment and after repatriation. But the question of allegiance often gets in the way of the individual's and the firm's success. To whom is the expatriate most committed — the parent firm or the local unit? Black and Gregersen have studied and interviewed numerous expatriates. In this paper, they describe four allegiance patterns and the factors that affect them, and they suggest policies for promoting the most desired pattern: high dual allegiance. ☞

J. Stewart Black is assistant professor of business administration, and Hal B. Gregersen is visiting professor, the Amos Tuck School of Business Administration, Dartmouth College.

Each year hundreds of thousands of expatriate managers all over the world find themselves torn between their allegiance to the parent firm and their allegiance to the local foreign operation. To understand this tension, consider the following situation. A Dutch expatriate manager in a multinational consumer products firm is faced on the one hand with a parent firm that wants a set of products introduced in the host country (a large developing nation) as part of its global brand image strategy. On the other hand, the host country government wants high technology transferred into the country, not just consumer products placed on store shelves. Market research suggests that local consumers are interested in some of the core products but not others and in products not currently part of the firm's core set. The parent firm has a philosophy encouraging participative decision making, but host national employees expect managers to make decisions without burdening them.

Faced with serving two masters, many expatriate managers end up directing their allegiance too far in one direction or the other, creating serious costs and consequences for both themselves and their organizations. For example, if individuals are too committed to the local operation

relative to the parent firm, it is difficult for the home office to coordinate with them. A senior Honda executive commented to us that Honda had incurred "nontrivial" costs trying to coordinate its global strategy for the new Honda Accord because some expatriate managers were too focused on the local situation. Expatriates who are overly committed to the parent firm relative to the local operation often inappropriately implement policies or procedures from the home office. The medical equipment division of a large U.S. multinational firm recently tried to implement home office financial reporting and accounting procedures that simply did not apply to and would not work in its newly acquired French subsidiary.

Perhaps most important, the high competitive pressure, great geographical distances, and wide cultural diversity of global operations combined with ineffective management of expatriates can set off a vicious cycle that erodes or even destroys a firm's global competitive position:

1. Unbalanced allegiance can lead to a variety of failures during and after international assignments.

2. As managers hear about these failures, firms find it increasingly difficult to attract top international candidates.

3. Increasingly worse candidates are sent overseas, producing

even worse organizational results and more failed careers.
4. This further limits the pool of willing and qualified
candidates.
5. Over time the firm's overseas competitive position
erodes.
6. This cycle spirals downward until it becomes nearly
unstoppable.

Today's multinational firms need managers who are
highly committed to both the parent firm and the local
operation and who can integrate the demands and objectives of both organizations. As one senior executive put
it, the bottom line question is, "How can we get expatriate managers who are committed to the local overseas
operation during their international assignments, but
who remain loyal to the parent firm?" Unfortunately, our
research suggests that expatriate managers with high dual
allegiance are a rare commodity.[1]

This is not surprising in light of studies of dual commitment in domestic contexts, such as commitment to a
union and an organization (e.g., United Auto Workers
and General Motors) or commitment to a profession
and an organization (e.g., nursing and a specific hospital). These studies have found that certain factors have
different effects on the two targets of commitment and
that people hold different patterns of commitment.
Some individuals are unilaterally committed to one
organization over the other, some have low levels of commitment to both, and others have high levels of commitment to both.[2]

In this article we present a description of the patterns,
causes, and consequences of expatriate dual allegiance. In
brief, expatriate managers can be grouped into one of four
allegiance patterns. They can be overly committed to the
parent firm or the local operation, highly committed to
both organizations, or committed to neither. These four

basic patterns are presented in the Figure 1. matrix. Much
more important than the patterns of dual allegiance are
the factors that cause them and the related organizational
and individual consequences. We describe the causes and
consequences associated with each pattern and illustrate
them with actual cases generated through numerous interviews and surveys (most managers asked that their names
and firms be disguised). We also examine what firms are
doing now and what they can do in the future to more effectively manage their expatriate managers.

Free Agents

As an undergraduate, Paul Jackson majored in Asian
studies and studied for two years in Japan. At gradua-
tion, he had intermediate fluency in Chinese and near
fluency in Japanese. He immediately went on to receive a
master's degree from the American Graduate School of
International Management in Phoenix. He was hired by
a major east coast bank and two years later was sent on a
three-year assignment to Hong Kong. The expatriate
package Paul and his family received made life in Hong
Kong enjoyable. However, Paul felt little loyalty to the
parent firm back home or the Hong Kong operation.
First and foremost, Paul was committed to his career.
Because he was such a hard charger, the bank invested a
substantial amount of time and money into him for language and technical training. He worked hard but always
kept an ear out for better jobs and pay. Two years into
his Hong Kong assignment, he found a better position
in another firm and took it. Four years into that company and assignment, he took a job with a different U.S.
bank and its Taiwan operation. Four years later, he took
a job as vice-president and general manager for the Japan
subsidiary of a large west coast bank.

When we interviewed Paul about his work history, he
said, "I can't really relate to your question about which
organization I feel allegiance to. I do my job, and I do it
well. I play for whatever team needs me and wants me.
I'm like a free agent in baseball or a hired gun in the old
West. If the pay and job are good enough, I'm off. You
might say, 'have international expertise, will travel.' "

Interestingly, Paul was actually part of a network we
discovered of "hired-gun free agents" in the Pacific Rim.
The network consisted of a group of about ten American
managers hired as expatriates (not as local hires), who
were either bi- or trilingual, and who had spent over half
of their professional careers in Asia. This group of free
agents passed along information to each other about various firms that were looking for experienced expatriate
managers for their Asia operations.

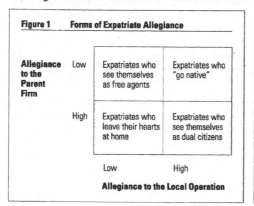

Figure 1   Forms of Expatriate Allegiance

Allegiance to the Parent Firm		Expatriates who see themselves as free agents	Expatriates who "go native"
	Low	Expatriates who see themselves as free agents	Expatriates who "go native"
	High	Expatriates who leave their hearts at home	Expatriates who see themselves as dual citizens
		Low	High
		Allegiance to the Local Operation	

Hired-Gun Free Agents

These expatriates have a low level of commitment to both their parent firms and their local operations. They are first and foremost committed to their own "gun-slinging" careers. When asked what long-term career implications this approach might have for them, these expatriates commonly indicated that it would be very difficult for them to ever "go back home" and move up the headquarter's hierarchy in any firm. However, most did not want to for several reasons. First, they felt the experience their children received from both an educational (schools are generally international, private, and paid for by the firm) and general life perspective was far superior to what they would receive back home. Second, the expatriates would be worse off financially if they went home and had to give up the extra benefits of their expatriate packages. Third, most were confident that they would not be given a job back home with the status, freedom, and importance of those jobs they held overseas. Consequently, most of these hired guns seemed happy with their lives and careers overseas.

Firms tend to view these expatriates with some ambivalence. On the one hand, even though these hired guns receive special benefit packages, they tend to be slightly less expensive than sending expatriates from the home country. Furthermore, these expatriates have already demonstrated their specialized skills, such as language, and their ability to succeed in international settings — qualities that are often lacking in a firm's internal managerial or executive ranks. This may be especially important to U.S. firms: on average 15 percent to 20 percent of their expatriate managers fail in their overseas assignments, at great cost to the firm, because they have serious problems adjusting to the foreign culture.

On the other hand, these free agent expatriates often leave the firm with little warning. Replacing them is usually costly and difficult and can have negative consequences for both the parent firm and the local operation. Sometimes these hired guns serve their own short-term career objectives at the expense of the firm's long-term interests. Also, as mentioned, few of these expatriates are willing to repatriate to the home office. This makes integrating their international experience or specific country or regional knowledge into the firm's global strategy formulation process next to impossible.

Plateaued-Career Free Agents

Our research uncovered another type of expatriate with low levels of commitment to both the parent firm and the local operation. This type of expatriate typically comes from the ranks of home country employees rather than of hired international experts. These expatriates are generally not committed to the parent firm before leaving for the overseas assignment in part because their careers have often plateaued. They take the international assignment because they don't see themselves going anywhere in the home operations, and they hope an international stint will change things. Or they are simply attracted by the sweet financial packages common to most overseas assignments. Unfortunately, many of the factors that led to low commitment before the international assignment result in low commitment to the local operation once the manager is overseas.

Several factors can contribute to development of this type of expatriate. First, if firms simply allow candidates for overseas assignments to self-select, they open the door for this type of expatriate. As one expatriate said, "I figured I was stalled in my job [back in North Carolina], so why not take a shot at an overseas assignment, especially given what I'd heard about the high standard of living even mid-level managers enjoyed overseas." Research has shown that certain personal characteristics correlate with successful adjustment to international assignments.[3] A self-selection process leaves personal characteristics of the expatriates to chance. Second, placing a low value on international operations can increase the probability that plateaued managers will apply for overseas assignments and decrease the probability that high-potential managers will volunteer for them. In such an environment, high-potential managers know that the place to get ahead is not overseas somewhere, out of sight and out of mind, but at home. Finally, lack of predeparture cross-cultural training can also reinforce low levels of commitment to the parent firm and the local operation. U.S. firms may be particularly vulnerable to this factor; roughly 70 percent of all U.S. expatriates receive no predeparture cross-cultural training.[4] Lack of firm-sponsored training can contribute to the view that "the company doesn't care about me, so why should I care about it?" Lack of training can also inhibit the expatriate from understanding the foreign culture and becoming committed to the local operation.

Unlike the hired guns, many of the plateaued-career free agents are not happy in their overseas assignments. Their low level of commitment often results in little effort to adjust to the local operation and culture. At worst, they fail the assignment. A failed overseas assignment not only inhibits the individual's career advancement, it can strike a severe blow to the individual's identity and self-confidence. Of course, there are also costs to the firm. Beyond the $100,000 to $250,000 it costs to bring the employee and family home and send out a replacement, the firm incurs the costs of damaged client and supplier relationships.[5] The lack of leadership during the replacement process can contribute to damaged internal and external relations. Failed assignments can also generate rumors back home that international posts are the "kiss of death" for a career, which in turn makes it more difficult to attract good candidates in the future.

Even if lack of commitment doesn't result in a failed assignment, it can still be costly to the person and the organization. Bob Brown was a typical plateaued manager for a major U.S. aircraft manufacturer who transferred to Taiwan three years before his interview with us. Bob was *not* very excited about living in Taiwan and neither was his family. His wife and daughter repeatedly asked to go back home. Bob pointed out that there was really no job for him to go back to. His daughter became so distraught

> ailed assignments can generate rumors back home that international posts are the "kiss of death" for a career.

that she began doing extremely poorly in school. This and other pressures put a severe strain on Bob's relationship with his wife. In an interview, Bob summed it up by stating that his home life was in shambles and that work was merely a paycheck, but a fat one (his compensation and benefit package was worth about $210,000 per year).

Perhaps the parent and local firm were getting their money's worth out of Bob, but it seems unlikely. Past studies have found that of those expatriates who complete their assignments, about one-third are considered ineffective.[6] Also, it is hard to imagine that a manager whose career has plateaued back home could be paid two to three times a normal compensation package and still provide a good return on that expense. If, as we suspect, such managers cannot, then this represents a serious economic loss to firms.

To summarize, low commitment to the parent firm and the local operation seems to be found in two general types of expatriate managers — hired-gun free agents and plateaued-career free agents. Although the causes and consequences of each type are different, both types represent potentially serious costs to the individual, parent firm, and local operation, since 41 percent of our sample fell into this group.

Going Native

The next allegiance pattern involves having high levels of commitment to the local operation but low levels of commitment to the parent firm. These expatriates usually form a strong identification with and attachment to the country's culture, language, values, and business practices. Consequently, these expatriates are often referred to as those who "go native."

Gary Ogden had been with a large computer company for fifteen years. He was the country manager for the firm's instrument division in France and had been in Paris for about four years, his third international assignment. Of his fifteen years with the parent firm, over half had been spent overseas, including six of the last eight years. Given that this was his third international stint, it hadn't taken long for Gary, his wife, and their three daughters (ages six, nine, and eleven) to settle in to life in France. His girls had enrolled in regular French schools when they moved to Paris and were now fluent for their ages. Gary's French was not perfect but he was comfortable in business situations. He had spent long hours trying to understand the local business situation, and he thought that corporate was constantly requesting and demanding things that either worked against objectives for the French unit or couldn't be done effectively or sometimes at all in France. Still, Gary loved it so much in France that he had already requested an extension, even though his contract only required him to stay another six months. When asked to describe his commitment to the parent firm and the local operation, he responded, "My first commitment is to the unit here. In fact, half the time I feel as if corporate is a competitor I must fight rather than a benevolent parent I can look to for support."

Our research suggests that individuals like Gary Ogden who have spent a number of years overseas, who adjust to the local culture, and who feel at odds with corporate headquarters are the most likely to go native. As managers spend more time away from the home office, their identities seem less and less tied to the parent firm. The firm becomes both literally and psychologically distant, as compared to the local operation. Additionally, the lack of formal communication with the home office through mechanisms such as sponsors (individuals assigned to keep in touch with specific expatriates) also serves to cause or reinforce this commitment pattern. Firms that are structured in international divisions and have cadres of "career internationalists" may be particularly vulnerable to this pattern.

What are the consequences of going native in terms of expatriate allegiance? Let's consider the individual's perspective. First, Gary felt that he had effectively managed the local situation. He pointed out that his knowledge of the language, culture, and union structure had enabled him to avoid an almost certain and probably very costly strike. Unfortunately, because the strike never happened, Gary felt that corporate did not recognize his achievement. Second, because Gary knew that his career depended to some extent on the evaluations made of him back at corporate, when he had to "fight" the parent firm, he had to do it subtly: "Sometimes I would simply ignore their directives if I didn't think they were appropriate or relevant to our operations. If it's really important, eventually someone from regional or corporate will hassle me, and I'll have to respond. If it isn't important or if they think I implemented what they wanted, they just leave me alone. As long as the general results are good, it doesn't seem as if there are big costs to this approach." Gary also indicated that on occasion he had to fight corporate more overtly. Although this may have cost him back at corporate, fighting these fights and especially winning them helped him gain the trust and loyalty of the local national employees. Their greater loyalty made it easier for him to be effective in the country. Interestingly, this effectiveness often later earned him points and slack back home.

Third, when Gary was repatriated after international assignments, he disliked the lack of responsibility compared to what he enjoyed overseas and the general lack of appreciation and utilization of his international knowledge. He nearly quit the firm both times he was repatriated. His low commitment to the parent firm heightened his dissatisfaction. Gary stated that both times it was receipt of another overseas assignment that kept him from leaving the firm.

From the parent firm's point of view, one of the common problems associated with expatriates who go native is the difficulty of getting corporate policies or programs implemented at the local level. Often the intense commitment to the local foreign operation leads these expatriates to implement what they think is relevant, in a way they deem appropriate, and then to ignore or fight the rest. This can be very costly, especially when the parent firm is trying to closely coordinate activities in a wide variety of countries for the good of global corporate objectives.

Also, to the extent that low commitment to the parent firm contributes to repatriation turnover, the parent firm loses the opportunity to incorporate the knowledge and experience of these expatriates into its global strategy or to incorporate some of these individuals into their succession plans. Interestingly, our research found that most expatriates, regardless of commitment pattern, do not feel that the international knowledge and experience they gained overseas is valued by their firms (91 percent of U.S. expatriates, 97 percent of Japanese expatriates, and 89 percent of Finnish expatriates). In general, firms do not seem to be utilizing these valuable resources.

Despite the negative aspects of expatriates who go native, many corporate executives recognize that these expatriates are not all bad. The high level of allegiance to the local operation generally leads these expatriates to identify with and understand the host national employees, customers, and suppliers. This understanding can translate into (1) new products and services or adapted products and services that are well targeted to the local market and (2) managerial approaches that are suited to the host national employees.

The importance of a managerial style modified to suit host national employees must not be overlooked, especially by U.S. firms. Although most U.S. firms assume that good managers in New York will do fine in Tokyo or Hong Kong and consequently select expatriates based primarily on domestic track records, evidence suggests that managerial characteristics that are related to performance in the United States are *not* related to performance in foreign countries.[7]

This potentially positive aspect of these expatriate managers may be particularly true in firms at a multidomestic stage of globalization.[8] In most multidomestic firms, each overseas unit competes in its national or regional market independent of the firm's other organizational units in other countries. The primary information flow is within the local operation, rather than between it and the parent firm. There is a premium on understanding the local market and the host national people and culture. Expatriates with relatively high allegiance to the local operation may be particularly beneficial in this situation.

In summary, managers who have spent a lot of time away from the parent firm, who can adjust to foreign cultures, and who lack formal communication ties to the parent firm are the most likely to go native; they constituted about 15 percent of our sample. There are pros and cons to this pattern for both the individual and the parent firm. Expatriates who go native often have valuable insights into the local operation, culture, and market; they can adapt procedures, products, or managerial approaches to fit the local situation. They may also be less likely to return prematurely and to invoke the serious costs associated with early returns. However, they also can frustrate global coordination efforts and may not be committed enough to the parent firm after repatriation to pass their knowledge on for country, regional, or global strategic planning.[9]

Hearts at Home

The third type of expatriate manager is highly committed to the parent firm but has little allegiance to the local foreign operation. We refer to these expatriates as those who "leave their hearts at home"; they constituted about 12 percent of our sample. These expatriate managers identify much more strongly with the parent firm than they do with the local operation and the local country's culture, language, and business practices.

Earl Markus was the managing director of the European headquarters of a large building supply firm's "do-it-yourself" retail division. This was Earl's first international assignment in his twenty-two years with the firm. He was married and had two children, both of whom were in college and therefore did not move with their parents to European headquarters in Belgium. Earl had worked his way up from a store manager to southwest regional manager and eventually to vice-president of finance over the previous twenty-two years.

The European operations were fairly new, and Earl saw his mission as expanding the number of retail outlets from the current nine in Belgium to fifty throughout western Europe. The president and CEO of the U.S. parent firm had assigned the COO, Frank Johnson, to work closely with Earl during his three-year assignment.

One year into the assignment, Earl was on schedule and had opened fifteen new outlets in three countries. But he was very frustrated. He said that he had seriously considered packing up and going home more than once during the year. He claimed Europeans were lazy and slow to respond to directives. When asked about his allegiance, he said that there was no contest. He was first and foremost committed to corporate, and when the next two years were up, he was headed back home. As an example of how things had gone, Earl described the implementation of the inventory system.

About eight months into the assignment, Frank Johnson suggested that Earl implement the new computerized inventory system that had just been phased into U.S. outlets. Frank was excited about the system's ability to reduce costs and shrinkage (i.e., theft), and he had high expectations of similar benefits for its use in Europe. For proper operation, the system required daily recording of sales and weekly random physical inventory of specific items. These reports needed to be transferred within forty-eight hours to the central office, which would generate total and store-by-store reports. The forms and procedure manuals were printed, and a two-day seminar was held for all European store managers and directors of operations and relevant staff members. Two months later, Earl inquired about how the system was operating. It wasn't. He said all he got from his managers were "lame excuses" about why the system wouldn't work, especially in Belgium.

This case illustrates some of the main causes and consequences of expatriates' allegiance being tilted strongly in favor of the parent firm. It is not surprising that our research found a significant correlation between long tenure in the parent firm and allegiance to it. These expatriates had invested time, sweat, and heartache with the parent firm, and they expected a "return" on this investment. Over time, the expatriates' identities had intertwined with the identities of the parent firm. A high level of allegiance to the parent firm was a natural consequence.

Our research found two other factors that, in combination, contributed to this allegiance pattern. The first factor was poor adjustment to the host country and culture, in part fostered by selection processes that primarily considered domestic track records. Because these expatriates could not relate to the host country's culture and people, they could not develop a strong sense of allegiance to the local operation. The second factor was having a sponsor in the home office who was formally assigned to the expatriate to maintain a formal tie. This tie focused attention and allegiance toward the parent firm and away from the local operation.

What personal and organizational consequences resulted from this allegiance pattern? Earl Markus was frustrated; he had considered leaving the overseas assignment several times. It was his fear of negative career consequences more than anything else that kept him from going. In addition to early return costs, which we discussed in the section on free agents, organizations can also incur the cost of having ineffectual managers. These managers often try to implement and enforce programs that are inappropriate for the local operation, or they implement them in ways that offend local employees, customers, or suppliers. Earl's inventory implementation effort antagonized employees and created an adversarial relationship that hampered other programs and changes he subsequently tried to initiate.

However, just as in the case of going native, not all the consequences of leaving one's heart at home are bad. Our research found that U.S. expatriates who had a high commitment to the parent firm during the international assignment were more likely to want to stay with the parent firm after their repatriation. Thus to the extent that these expatriates gain valuable experience, knowledge, and skills during their international assignments, their parent firms have greater opportunities to gain future returns from them. Unfortunately, the low commitment to the local operation reduces the knowledge these expatriates can gain. Nevertheless, expatriates who leave their hearts at home can provide another advantage. They often make it easier for the home office to coordinate activities between headquarters and the subsidiary. In Earl's case, it was very easy for the corporate purchasing agent to utilize the buying power of headquarters' centralized purchasing activities for the European operations. This coordination gave the European operations access to substantial price savings.

The ability to coordinate easily with the home office may be particularly beneficial for firms at the export stage of globalization. The primary objective of most firms at this stage is to sell in foreign markets products developed and manufactured in the home country. Information flows primarily from the parent firm to the local operation. The home office plays a key coordinating role, and good coordination with the subsidiaries is important. Expatriates with relatively high commitment to the parent firm are less likely to resist following the home office's coordination efforts than expatriates with low levels of commitment to the parent.

Dual Citizens

The final category consists of expatriate managers who are highly committed to both the parent *and* the local operation — dual citizens. We use the word "citizen" because it seems to reflect this group's behavior, attitudes, and emotions. These managers tend to see themselves as citizens of both the foreign country and their home country and as citizens of both the local operation and the parent corporation. They feel responsible for serving both organization's interests.

Joan Beckenridge was the director of a prominent U.S. consulting firm's Japan office. This was Joan's second international assignment in her thirteen years with the firm. Her first assignment was a one-year special project stint in Singapore seven years before. Joan was one of three candidates considered for the job in Japan and had been selected based not only on her past performance but also on assessments by outside consultants. Because the job required a high degree of interaction with host nationals in a novel culture, Joan was given five-months notice before departing for Japan. During this time she received about sixty hours of cross-cultural training. In addition, her spouse received about ten hours of survival briefing. Four months after arriving in Japan, Joan received another forty hours of cross-cultural training. She also took advantage of hundreds of hours of language training, paid for by the parent firm.

Perhaps most important, Joan had a clear set of objectives for her assignment. The Japan office had been established to serve the Japanese subsidiaries of the firm's U.S. clients. At this point, the office's growth was limited by the slowed pace of expansion of U.S. client firms to Japan. Joan was charged with developing Japanese clients. This would serve two objectives. First, it would increase the office's growth potential, and second, it would make it easier to secure Japanese firm's U.S. subsidiaries as clients. which would expand U.S. operations.

> # M
> ost U.S. firms do not provide any cross-cultural training for international assignments.

Despite these preparations, Joan found herself frustrated in one area. Headquarters and the local operation had differing expectations regarding business and entertainment expenses. Headquarters did not realize how much time and money it took to cultivate effective relationships in Japan. Joan's Japanese business associates were fond of pointing out that their country had the highest business entertainment expenses as a percent of sales in the world. Joan felt the tension between corporate "bean counters" who worried over entertainment expenses and local staff who floated contact opportunities that Joan couldn't develop. However, unlike many expatriates in similar situations, Joan had a mechanism for working out these differences. She had a high-level sponsor at corporate who was officially assigned to help her. Through this sponsor, Joan could educate corporate and bring corporate and local expectations in synch.

It was also clear from the beginning how this assignment fit Joan's overall career path and how her repatriation would be handled. Although she was not guaranteed a specific position upon repatriation, Joan knew what her general opportunities would be if she met her objectives in Japan.

Perhaps the most important factor in Joan's effectiveness was that she had a great degree of autonomy in deciding how to achieve the assignment's objectives. She had the flexibility to deal with the inevitable conflicts and ambiguities that cropped up in the job.

When asked about her allegiance, Joan said, "I feel a strong sense of allegiance to both companies [the local operation and the parent firm]. Although they sometimes have different objectives, I try to satisfy both whenever I can." When the two organizations conflicted, Joan would work to bring them together rather than simply following one or the other.

The personal and organizational consequences of Joan's dual citizenship orientation were primarily positive.

Joan indicated that it was sometimes frustrating to be torn between parent and local needs but that the clarity of her objectives, the latitude she had to pursue them, and the relative infrequency and small magnitude of the conflicts made the work rewarding and satisfying. Joan did well in her five years in Japan and received a substantial promotion upon repatriation to a position in which her knowledge was utilized in domestic and international expansion plans. For the organization, Joan's dual-citizen orientation helped her build solid relations with Japanese clients and government officials and helped the home office establish relationships with Japanese clients' U.S. subsidiaries. Joan believed her dual focus also gave her a greater ability to recruit high-quality Japanese employees, which was difficult for competitors.

Thirty-two percent of our sample of U.S. expatriate managers fit this allegiance pattern. Although it would be inaccurate to say that these expatriates never returned home early, never left the firm after repatriation, or never had adjustment or performance problems during international assignments, this group had a higher probability than the others of completing the foreign assignment, staying with the firm upon repatriation, and adjusting well to the overseas stay. These expatriate managers were much more interested than the others in understanding the needs, objectives, constraints, and opportunities of both the local operation and the parent firm. They talked of using this understanding to benefit both organizations. They could effectively implement corporate policies in the local operation and pass information from the local operation back to corporate in order to help shape strategy and policy development.

As indicated in Joan Beckenridge's case, *role conflict* played an important part in determining commitment. When the parent and local organizations had different expectations, demands, and objectives, the managers who had to negotiate these differences suffered from role conflict. The greater the role conflict, the less managers felt responsible for the outcomes and the less they felt committed to either organization. As one expatriate put it, "It's hard to feel responsible for what happens when you're being torn in opposite directions." In contrast, the greater the consistency between the two organizations, the more expatriate managers felt responsible for what happened and the more they felt committed to both organizations.

Role ambiguity produced a similar dynamic. Whereas role conflict follows from clear expectations that conflict, role ambiguity occurs when expectations from both organizations simply are not clear. Poor coordination between the parent firm and the local operation was a common source of role ambiguity. When we asked one

expatriate manager how much responsibility he felt for what happened on his job, he replied, "How can I feel responsible, when I don't even know what I'm supposed to do or what's expected of me?" In contrast, the clearer the role, the more expatriates felt responsible for what happened at work and committed to both organizations.

Another factor related to dual allegiance was *clarity of repatriation programs.* Over 60 percent of U.S. firms have no systematic or formal repatriation program.[10] Clear, systematic repatriation programs facilitate high levels of commitment to both organizations. Such programs seem to free expatriates from worrying about going home and allow them to focus on the job at hand. This facilitates allegiance to the local operation. Such programs also seem to communicate that the parent firm cares about their ex-

> # M
> any of the perks — company house, car, and driver — given to expatriate executives isolate them and inhibit their adjustment to the environment.

patriates and has thought about reintegration. This creates a greater sense of obligation to the parent firm.

The most powerful factor in creating dual allegiance was *role discretion.* Role discretion is the freedom to decide what needs to be done, how and when it should be done, and who should do it. The more discretion expatriate managers have, the more they feel responsible for what happens at work and committed to the local operation. Because they generally view the parent firm as responsible for the amount of freedom they enjoy, this translates into a greater sense of commitment to the parent firm as well. Part of the reason that discretion is the most powerful factor is that most expatriate managers experience some role conflict and ambiguity. Role discretion gives the manager the freedom to define expectations and resolve conflicting ones.

Although dual citizens are desirable for any firm at any globalization stage, they are most critical for firms at the coordinated multinational stage. Such firms need information to flow back and forth between the home office and foreign subsidiaries and from one foreign subsidiary to another. They need managers who identify with both the people back home and those in the local operation. They need managers who will stay in the assignment, who will try to meet the needs of both organizations, and who will stay with the firm after repatriation so that their international experience, knowledge, and skills can be utilized.

Policy Implications

Although most executives in multinational firms are aware of the issues concerning expatriate allegiance, few of the expatriates we interviewed said that their firms understood the causes and consequences of the different allegiance patterns or had systems for developing dual-citizen expatriates. However, many firms had found ways to counterbalance "lopsided" allegiance. Below we present what some of these firms are doing, and we propose steps for developing dual-citizen expatriates.

Strategy 1: Counterbalancing Going Native

Managers who have several years of international experience and who have successfully adjusted to foreign cultures in the past are most likely to go native. Although these managers tend to have a low commitment to the parent firm, they are also good candidates to send overseas because they lower the risks and associated costs of failed assignments and premature returns. What can firms do if their current policies tend to produce too many expatriate managers like Gary Ogden?

• **Limit Time away from Corporate.** Honda brings expatriates home to Japan for a few years before they go overseas again. This method reinforces the link between the manager and the parent firm. Honda believes that it is not logical to expect career internationalists who move from one foreign assignment to the next to be highly committed to the parent firm.

• **Send Managers with Strong Ties to Corporate.** Firms can send managers overseas who have longer tenure in the parent firm. The longer managers have been with the firm, the more they have invested in it, the more they identify with it, and the more they are committed to it. Also, long tenures build personal connections that keep individuals involved with corporate. However, this recommendation is problematic for firms such as General Electric (GE), General Motors (GM), and Ford, which increasingly use international assignments to develop younger, high-potential managers.

• **Establish Corporate Sponsor Programs.** GE uses sponsors to counterbalance the tendency to go native. The company assesses the expatriate's career objectives and chooses a senior manager, often in the function to which the expatriate is likely to return, who is willing to serve as sponsor. The sponsor maintains contact with the expatriate throughout the assignment, including face-to-face

meetings; evaluates the expatriate's performance during the assignment; helps clarify the expatriate's career objectives and capabilities before repatriation; and provides career advice and help finding a position back at headquarters. Some divisions even commit to hiring the expatriate manager back into a specific position before the foreign assignment begins.

Executives at several firms with sponsorship programs gave us additional advice. Overall, they recommended that sponsor assignment be systematized. First, the sponsor should be senior enough relative to the expatriate to be able to provide a broad view of the organization. Second, the sponsor should receive specific guidelines about the form, content, and frequency of contacts with the expatriate. Too often the sponsor is simply assigned, and that's it. If the sponsor takes the initiative and fulfills the responsibility, things go well. Otherwise, the sponsorship is in name only. Finally, the responsibility of planning for repatriation should not rest solely with the sponsor but should be incorporated into the firm's career systems.

• **Provide Predeparture and Postarrival Cross-Cultural Training.** Most U.S. firms do not provide any cross-cultural training for international assignments. While it may seem that predeparture training would increase a tendency to identify with the host culture and thus go native, our data indicate that such training creates a sense of obligation to the parent firm stemming from the firm's demonstrated concern for the expatriate.[11] Although we only examined the impact of predeparture training because fewer than 10 percent of the expatriates received postarrival training, we suspect that a similarly positive effect could be generated by providing training after arrival if the expatriate understands that the parent firm, and not the local operation, is paying for and sponsoring the training.

Strategy 2: Counterbalancing Hearts at Home

Although many U.S. executives seem unconcerned with the tendency of expatriates to leave their hearts at home, our research suggests that the consequences of this tendency are just as serious as those for going native. The lack of organizational practices in this area forces us to rely on our research for ways that firms might counterbalance the tendency of managers like Earl Markus to leave their hearts at home.

• **Send Younger Managers.** The managers most likely to be highly committed to the parent firm and much less committed to the local operation are those with long tenures at the parent firm and little international experience. Thus firms such as GE, GM, and Ford, which are increasingly sending younger managers overseas for career development, are perhaps unintentionally counterbalancing the hearts-at-home tendency.

• **Facilitate Cross-Cultural Adjustment.** Helping the expatriate manager adjust to the nonwork environment is another powerful counterbalancing force. Ironically, many of the perks — such as company housing, car, and driver — that are given to senior expatriate executives actually isolate them and inhibit their adjustment to the environment. Family members, especially the spouse, are often more directly exposed to the foreign environment because they do not have the insulation provided by the corporate structure. Therefore, a firm's efforts to facilitate the family's adjustment can have a positive effect on the manager's adjustment.[12]

• **Provide Cross-Cultural Training for the Family.** Ford is one of the few U.S. firms that tries to consistently provide training and preparation for the families and especially spouses of its expatriates. Although Ford executives did not intend this training to counteract the hearts-at-home tendency, our research suggests that this is a likely consequence.

• **Encourage Host National Sponsorship Programs.** Interacting with host nationals outside of work can help both families and managers adjust. Host nationals, who understand their own culture, are the best sources of instruction and especially feedback in getting along on a daily basis. However, such interaction is not always easy to develop. Firms can help by asking host national employees and their families to assist specific expatriates during the first few months. Care should be taken to match the sponsoring family's characteristics (e.g., number and ages of children) with those of the expatriate family. Several Japanese auto firms actually have hired Americans who speak Japanese to help their expatriate managers and families adjust to life in the United States.

The Amos Tuck School's joint M.B.A. program with the International University of Japan has a sponsorship program. A special employee in Japan is assigned to help U.S. professors with logistical problems, such as housing and travel, during their stay. Several Tuck professors who spent a term in Japan expressed pleasant surprise at the willingness of both the special employee and other employees to go beyond logistical assistance and to help them navigate the cultural and business terrain. This assistance gave them important insights into the culture and people and helped them adjust to the new environment.

Strategy 3: Creating Dual Citizens

Although these mechanisms are useful for counterbalancing negative tendencies, the most important steps firms can take are those that create high levels of dual allegiance.

Our research suggests that the primary target for fostering expatriates like Joan Beckenridge is the job.

• **Plan Overseas Jobs Strategically.** A firm that clearly defines the expatriate's job, reduces conflicts concerning job expectations, and gives the expatriate a fair amount of freedom in carrying out assigned tasks will foster a high level of dual allegiance. The idea is simple, but execution is complex.

One of the easiest but rarely utilized techniques for increasing role clarity is allowing the incumbent and the new manager an overlap period of several days or weeks. The more complex the job and the less experienced the new entrant, the longer the overlap. Several expatriates specifically mentioned this method as a relatively low-cost means of facilitating adjustment and effectiveness. Expatriates in Japan and Korea said that this overlap was necessary for properly introducing the replacement to employees, clients, and suppliers. Of course, sometimes there is no incumbent, and this option is not available.

Role clarification in and of itself does not necessarily reduce role conflict. In fact, clarification of job expectations can reveal previously hidden role conflicts, which most often stem from the differing expectations of the parent firm and the local operation. Thus firms must try to increase role clarity and decrease role conflict simultaneously. This requires understanding and integrating the perspectives of the parent firm and the local operation.

A firm's best intentions cannot entirely eliminate role ambiguity and conflict. This is probably why role discretion emerged as the single strongest factor in promoting high dual allegiance. Having a fair amount of freedom to decide what tasks to do, how and when to do them, and who should do them gives expatriates the flexibility to cope with ambiguity and conflict. However, too much discretion without clear objectives may make expatriates unintentionally work against the best interests of the parent firm, the local operation, or both. Firms need to consider all three job elements simultaneously.

We believe that role clarity, conflict, and discretion are best approached not as targets of manipulation but as outcomes of broader policy and strategic processes. If a firm wants to make significant, long-term, and effective changes in the expatriate manager's job, it should carefully assess the following issues:

1. Why is this expatriate being sent to this particular post? (Because there are no host nationals capable of filling the position? In order to provide developmental experience for the expatriate?)

2. How will job success be measured? What do you really want this particular person to do in this position?

3. Are the objectives of the parent firm and the local unit

consistent? Are they consistent between the local unit as a whole and the individual's department?

4. How much should the parent firm coordinate and control the local operation? How much freedom and autonomy should the local unit have? Is the expatriate's level of discretion consistent with these coordination needs?

Without an assessment of these strategic issues, firms may adjust expectations in ways that are dysfunctional for the firm's overall strategy. For instance, firms may provide overlap time that serves only to clarify the severe expectation conflicts between the two organizations. Or firms may give too much freedom to expatriate managers. Consequently, such ad hoc adjustments are likely to have short-term positive results at best and severe negative results at worst. In contrast, an analysis that begins with the broader context naturally leads to appropriate job adjustments and a higher probability of a high dual allegiance.

Some readers may feel that their firms have moved beyond the coordinated multinational stage. Global firms need managers who are capable not just of dual citizenship but of world citizenship. Many firms are moving in this direction, but our data suggest that most expatriate managers are still struggling to successfully reach dual allegiance. It seems to us that the first practical step toward developing global managers for global firms is to develop managers who see themselves as dual citizens. Dual-citizen expatriates are best developed through (1) careful selection processes; (2) cross-cultural training before and after arrival; (3) well-planned career systems that lead to clear, consistent job expectations and appropriate discretion levels; and (4) repatriation programs that effectively utilize expatriates' knowledge, skills, and experience. These steps will help expatriates more successfully serve two masters and help firms more effectively manage their expatriates. ◆

References

1. H.B. Gregersen and J.S. Black, "Antecedents to Dual Commitment during International Assignments," *Academy of Management Journal* 35 (1992): 65-90.
This article is based primarily on two international research projects. First, we did a questionnaire study of 321 U.S. expatriate executives and managers while they were on assignment in Europe (Belgium, England, the Netherlands, and Germany) and the Pacific Rim (Japan, Korea, Taiwan, and Hong Kong). These expatriates had worked on average more than fourteen years in their U.S. multinational firms representing a wide range of industries. We also completed in-depth interviews with more than 30 expatriates in both Pacific Rim and European countries. Second, we completed a study of expatriate commitment during repatriation for 174 Americans, 173 Japanese, and 104 Finns returning to their respective home countries after international assignments.

2. C.V. Fukami and E.W. Larson, "Commitment to the Company and Union: Parallel Models," *Journal of Applied Psychology* 69 (1984): 367-371;
M.E. Gordon and R.T. Ladd, "Dual Allegiance: Renewal, Reconsideration, and Recantation," *Personnel Psychology* 43 (1990): 37-69;
H.B. Gregersen, "Multiple Commitments at Work and Extrarole Behavior during Three Stages of Organizational Tenure," *Journal of Business Research* 25 (1992); and
N.B. Tuma and A.J. Grimes, "A Comparison of Models of Role Orientations of Professionals in a Research-Oriented University," *Administrative Science Quarterly* 26 (1981): 187-206.

3. J.S. Black, "Personal Dimensions and Work Role Transitions," *Management International Review* 30 (1990): 119-134; and
M.E. Mendenhall and G. Oddon, "The Dimensions of Expatriate Acculturation," *Academy of Management Review* 10 (1985): 39-47.

4. J.S. Black and M. Mendenhall, "Cross-Cultural Training Effectiveness: A Review and a Theoretical Framework for Future Research," *Academy of Management Review* 15 (1990): 113-136.

5. J.S. Black, "Work Role Transitions: A Study of U.S. Expatriate Managers in Japan," *Journal of International Business Studies* 19 (1988): 277-294;
J.S. Black and H.B. Gregersen, "Antecedents to Cross-Cultural Adjustment for Expatriates in Pacific Rim Assignments," *Human Relations* 44 (1990): 497-515;
L. Copeland and L. Griggs, *Going International* (New York: Random House, 1985); and
K.F. Misa and J.M. Fabricatore, "Return on Investment of Overseas Personnel," *Financial Executive* 47 (1979): 42-46.

6. See R.L. Tung, *The New Expatriates* (Lexington, Massachusetts: Lexington Books, 1988) for a review.

7. J.S. Black and L.W. Porter, "Managerial Behavior and Job Performance: A Successful Manager in Los Angeles May Not Be Successful in Hong Kong," *Journal of International Business Studies* 22 (1991): 99-114; and
E. Miller, "The International Selection Decision: A Study of Managerial Behavior in the Selection Decision Process," *Academy of Management Journal* 16 (1973): 234-252.

8. M. Porter, "Changing Patterns of International Competition," *California Management Review*, Winter 1986, pp. 9-40.

9. H.B. Gregersen, "Commitments to a Parent Company and a Local Work Unit during Repatriation," *Personnel Psychology* 45 (1992): 29-54.

10. M.G. Harvey, "Repatriation of Corporate Executives," *Journal of International Business Studies*, Spring 1989, pp. 131-144.

11. Research consistently shows that good predeparture training helps expatriate managers adjust to and perform well in their jobs overseas. See:
Black and Mendenhall (1990).

12. See also J.S. Black and G.K. Stephens, "The Influence of the Spouse on U.S. Expatriate Adjustment in Overseas Assignments," *Journal of Management* 15 (1989): 529-544.

[3]

Selecting Expatriates for Personality Characteristics: A Moderating Effect of Personality on the Relationship Between Host National Contact and Cross-cultural Adjustment

Paula M. Caligiuri

Abstract

- This study examines the process by which interactions with host nationals help facilitate expatriates' cross-cultural adjustment. The hypotheses are based on two related theories, (1) the contact hypothesis and (2) social learning theory.

- Personality characteristics (openness and sociability) are hypothesized to moderate the relationship between contact with host nationals and cross-cultural adjustment. The hypotheses are tested on a sample of expatriates from a US-based information technology company.

Key Results

- The findings suggest that greater contact with host nationals positively relates to cross-cultural adjustment when an individual possesses the personality trait of openness. The personality characteristic of sociability was also related to cross-cultural adjustment.

Author

Paula M. Caligiuri, Assistant Professor of Human Resource Management, School of Management and Labor Relations, Rutgers University, Piscataway, NJ, USA.

Manuscript received March 1998, revised July 1998, revised September 1998.

Paula M. Caligiuri

Introduction

International human resource experts agree it is imperative for multinational companies (MNCs) to attract, select, develop, and retain employees who can live and work effectively outside of their own national borders (Adler/Bartholomew 1992, Black/Gregersen/Mendenhall 1992, Mendenhall/Oddou 1985, Stroh/Caligiuri 1998,Tung 1988, Tung/Miller 1990). These employees, who are sent from a parent company to live and work in another country for a period ranging from two to several years, are colloquially referred to as "expatriates." The number of expatriates MNCs are sending on global assignments is increasing steadily (Laabs 1993, Stroh/Dennis/Cramer 1994). In the United States, for example, the number of American expatriate assignments has doubled from 1991 to 1993 and is predicted to double again before the year 2000 (Laabs 1993). The Conference Board (1992) survey of 130 multinational organizations found that half of these organizations had more than 50 high-level managers currently on global assignments, and 25% of the organizations had between 200 and 2,000 managers on global assignments. In a 1994 survey of 103 multinational organizations, the respondents stated that their number of global assignments had increased by 30% between 1993 and 1994, and 71% of this sample believed that this trajectory of growth would continue in the future (Windham International/National Foreign Trade Council, Inc. 1994).

Given the strategic importance MNCs place on global assignments (e.g., high-level negotiations, foreign subsidiary management, new market development), the harm an unsuccessful expatriate may cause in the host country can be detrimental to an MNCs' future global business (Gregersen/Black 1990, Zeira/Banai 1985). As Zeira and Banai (1985, p. 34) suggest, the real cost of an unsuccessful international executives extends beyond the monetary expenses of compensation: an unsuccessful expatriate, "almost invariably has a negative impact on future interactions between the MNCs and the host countries." For this reason, international HR practitioners and management researchers alike are particularly interested in understanding how to best predict individuals who can live and work successfully in cross-national settings.

Past research indicates considerable variation in the types of criteria used in evaluating how successful expatriate assignments have been. To date, the three most common criteria for evaluating expatriate success have been (1) cross-cultural adjustment, (2) completion of the global assignment, and (3) performance on the global assignment (Caligiuri 1997). McEvoy and Parker (1995) suggest that cross-cultural adjustment may be the antecedent of both performance and completion of the global assignment. Given that these are both important for MNCs, a better understanding of the factors which impact cross-cultural adjustment is necessary. To this end, many have been examining the topic of cross-cultural adjustment: That is, the extent to which expatriates feel comfortable and adapted to living and working in their host country. This study will examine how affiliating personality characteristics and host national contact relate to expatriate adjustment.

Cross-cultural Adjustment

Cross-cultural adjustment is the extent to which individuals are psychologically comfortable living outside of their home country (Black 1990, Black/Gregersen 1991). Cross-culturally adjusted expatriates "represent a more integrative approach to a new culture, (they) ... are open to the host culture, but integrate new behavior, norms and roles into the foundation provided by (their) home cultures" (Church 1982, p. 543). On the other hand, maladjusted expatriates are unable or unwilling to accept the host countries' behaviors, norms, and roles: They view the host cultures as inferior to their own. They tend to cling to their home cultures (e.g., other expatriates from their home country) whenever possible. Very simply, cross-cultural adjustment is "the individual's affective psychological response to the new environment" (Black 1990, p. 122). Therefore, cross-cultural adjustment is an internal, psychological, emotional state and should be measured from the perspective of the individual experiencing the foreign culture (Black 1990, Searle/Ward 1990).

To better understand how to maximize expatriates' cross-cultural adjustment, it is important to ascertain the factors which impact it. However, as Black, Mendenhall, and Oddou (1991, p. 293) note "(a)lthough international adjustment has received increased scholarly attention, the majority of the writing has been anecdotal in nature, and few scholars have rigorously investigated the phenomenon, empirically or theoretically." Many scholars have added to the list of factors which influence cross-cultural adjustment (e.g., Arthur/Bennett 1995, Baker/Ivancevich 1971, Black et al. 1991, Black/Stephens 1989, Harvey 1985, McEvoy/Parker 1995). The factors they identified were predeparture training, previous overseas experience, organizations' selection criteria, individual characteristics, country difficulty, and family adjustment. Although more rigorous empirical studies are now being conducted, the theoretical development for understanding *how* these factors impact cross-cultural adjustment has not advanced since the initial work of Black and his colleagues (Black et al. 1991, Black/Mendenhall 1990).

Host National Contact Affecting Cross-cultural Adjustment

Two theories have been proposed to date for understanding the process of cross-cultural adjustment (Black/Mendenhall 1990, Black et al. 1991). The first the-

Paula M. Caligiuri

ory uses social learning theory to explain why predeparture training is effective in improving cross-cultural adjustment (Black/Mendenhall 1990). The second theory uses the socialization and sensemaking literature (among others) to understand the process of cross-cultural adjustment (Black et al. 1991). These two theories have one key element in common: social interaction. Social interaction, in particular contact with host nationals, is the focus of the present study. The social aspect of the two existing theories will be described in greater detail below.

In 1990, Black and Mendenhall used social learning theory (Bandura 1977) to explain the theoretical underpinnings for how predeparture cross-cultural training could have a positive impact on the interactions expatriates would have with host nationals. In brief, Black and Mendenhall (1990, p. 120) suggest that "(c)ross cultural training enables the individual to learn both content and skills that will facilitate effective cross-cultural interaction by reducing misunderstandings and inappropriate behaviors." In the case of cross-cultural adjustment, according to social learning theory, the cross-cultural trainees would develop both the confidence in themselves to behave appropriately in the host country and the appropriate behaviors necessary for interacting successfully with host nationals, prior to going overseas (Black/Mendenhall 1990). Although predeparture cross-cultural skills training is important for cross-cultural adjustment, many organizations simply do not provide it for their expatriates (Black/Mendenhall 1990). Therefore, most of the expatriates' learning of culturally appropriate behaviors happens *in* the host country; The "trainers" will be the host nationals themselves; And the venue for training will be their daily interactions with their host national colleagues, neighbors, friends, etc. Although there is a shift in venue, from predeparture training to in-country learning, the social learning process described by Black and Mendenhall (1990) is essentially the same. The expatriates' cultural swimming lessons, however, just start in the host country's deep end.

One year later, Black et al. (1991) developed a more comprehensive model for understanding the cross-cultural adjustment process. This theoretical model integrated both the domestic and international relocation literatures (i.e., organizational socialization, career transitions and sensemaking, work role transitions). Their model had two chronological phases, anticipatory adjustment and in-country adjustment. The first phase focuses on what the expatriate expects based on predeparture cross-cultural training received, past experience, etc. The second phase focuses on the process of adjustment after he or she arrives in the host country. According to Black et al. (1991) the second phase is based on his or her individual characteristics, the job demands, the organizational culture and socialization, and the nonwork factors, such as country difficulty and family adjustment (see Black et al. 1991 for a detailed description of this theory).

A large part of the Black et al. model (in both phases) focuses on socialization (i.e., the ways in which individuals learn the culturally appropriate norms and behaviors). Testing a part of their model, this study will examine how socialization is affected by the individual characteristics of the expatriate. Then, in turn, how the socialization affects cross-cultural adjustment. This focus on individual characteristics and socialization is critical for two reasons: (1) expatriates often learn culturally appropriate norms and behaviors through host nationals, and (2) expatriates vary on the personality characteristics necessary for relating to others (affiliating personality characteristics; Mendenhall/Oddou 1985).

Affiliating Personality Characteristics Affecting Cross-cultural Adjustment

Many theorists have discussed the importance of individual characteristics in predicting an expatriate's cross-cultural adjustment. Mendenhall and Oddou (1985) proposed that there are three dimensions of individual characteristics that should be positively related to cross-cultural adjustment: (1) self-orientation, (2) perceptual-orientation, and (3) others-orientation. Relevant to this study, the latter dimension is the dimension of individual characteristics affecting "the expatriate's ability to interact effectively with host nationals" (Mendenhall/Oddou 1985, p. 41). Given the emphasis on social contact, these affiliating personality characteristics will be particularly important for expatriates' cross-cultural adjustment.

As Mendenhall and Oddou (1985) suggest, the "other-orientation" dimension encompasses two types of individual characteristics, or subfactors: The first is the individual's *ability to establish interpersonal relationships* with host nationals. Consistent with personality theory, this would be a persons' *sociability* (see McCrae/Costa 1987; Piedmont/McCrae/Costa 1991). Sociability includes the ability one has to be outgoing with others and the ability or desire one has to establish interpersonal relationships with others. The second is the individual's *willingness to communicate* with host nationals. Again, according to personality theory, this would be a person's *openness* (see McCrae/Costa 1987, Piedmont/ McCrae/Costa 1991). Openness is further defined as one's receptivity to learn and change in the new situation. In this context it is also one's belief that the host country has something to offer which will help one grow, develop, and learn. In particular, because of the focus on social interaction, this paper is interested in openness directed toward people, as compared to openness directed toward places or things (e.g., open to trying new food, open to new forms of art). These two personality characteristics, sociability and openness, (along with contact with host nationals) will be examined for their affect on cross-cultural adjustment.

Paula M. Caligiuri

Host National Contact and Personality:
The Contact Hypothesis

A theoretical perspective which elucidates the moderating effect of personality characteristics on the relationship between host national interaction and cross-cultural adjustment is the contact hypothesis or association hypothesis (Allport 1954, Amir 1969, Zajonc 1968). Originally posited to address race relations in the United States in the 1950's and 1960's, this theory suggests that the more inter-action (i.e., contact) a person has with people from a given cultural group, the more positive his or her attitudes will be toward the people from that cultural group (Allport 1954, Amir 1969, Zajonc 1968). Church (1982) suggested that the principles of the contact hypothesis can be applied to the interpersonal interac-tions between expatriates and host nationals. Having positive attitudes toward host nationals has been defined by Black (1988) as an important aspect of cross-cul-tural adjustment. This study attempts to explain how contact with host nationals will affect cross-cultural adjustment, in general. This is based on the assertion that the more expatriates interact with host nationals, the more likely they are to learn the culturally-appropriate norms and behaviors. As Black and Mendenhall (1990) proposed, learning these culturally appropriate norms and behaviors is positively related to higher cross-cultural adjustment.

Hypothesis 1:   Contact with host nationals will be positively related to cross-cul-tural adjustment.

Since the work of Allport (1954), Zajonc (1968), and Amir (1969), subsequent studies on the contact hypothesis have examined the impact of moderating vari-ables in the context of social interactions between minority and nonminority groups. These studies have examined a variety of moderating variables, such as percent of minorities living in a traditionally nonminority neighborhoods, the socioeconomic status of the minority group, relative to the majority group, and so forth (for a re-view, see Hewstone/Brown 1986). In the 1960's Amir (1969) noted that personal-ity characteristics would be a moderating variable in the contact hypothesis. That is, not all people will benefit equally from contact with host nationals (Amir 1969). In writing about personality characteristics as a moderating variable, Amir (1969, p. 335) stated "(t)here are always hindering factors which resist the influence of the contact or may even counteract it." That is, an expatriate who has much con-tact with host nationals, yet is not open to the interaction, will have lower cross-cultural adjustment, compared to a person with greater openness.

Despite the proposition of Amir (1969), personality as a moderator in the con-tact hypothesis has remained largely untested and the necessary personality char-acteristics have not yet been identified. This study will test the two personality characteristics, *openness* and *sociability,* as moderators of the contact hypothesis.

Again, these two personality characteristics were selected because they had been identified by Mendenhall and Oddou (1985) as relationship-building characteristics related to cross-cultural adjustment. In addition, numerous studies suggest that both openness and sociability are considered enduring, predisposed personality characteristics. As such, they are relatively fixed and will affect the way in which people behave in given situations, such as cross-national interactions (e.g., Buss 1989, Costa/McCrae 1992). Each characteristic will be discussed in greater detail below.

The Contact Hypothesis and Openness

As Mendenhall and Oddou (1985) and others (e.g., Abe/Wiseman 1983, Black 1990, Hammer/Gudykunst/Wiseman 1978) suggest, expatriates who possess the characteristic of *openness* tend to demonstrate greater cross-cultural adjustment. Contact theory may be one explanation for why this is true. By definition, individuals who are more open to people, should possess few (if any) negative predisposing attitudes that may impair their ability to develop relationships with host nationals. Openness should facilitate cross-cultural adjustment because individuals higher in this characteristic will have less rigid views of right and wrong, appropriate and inappropriate, etc. (Black 1990). Those who are more rigid "view their ideas, norms, and behavior patterns as correct and others as incorrect ... and will make little effort to understand host nationals or their culture or to modify their own behavior to make it more congruent with the cultural norms" and reduce their interactions with host nationals (Black 1990, p. 125). Expatriates who are unrestricted by their predisposing personality should be able to establish more interpersonal relationships with host nationals. Past research has inferred that establishing friendships with host nationals greatly improves expatriates' ability to learn culturally appropriate social skills and behaviors (Searle/Ward 1990), thus facilitating their cross-cultural adjustment. The host nationals with whom open individuals come in contact can be a source of information and feedback on how the expatriates should behave in the host country (Abe/Wiseman 1983, Black 1990, Brein/David 1971, Mendenhall/Oddou 1985, Searle/Ward 1990). This should result in a positive relationship with cross-cultural adjustment for these open individuals.

Hypothesis 2: Openness to people will moderate the relationship between contact with host nationals and cross-cultural adjustment.

The Contact Hypothesis and Sociability

Given the many uncertainties of living abroad, expatriates must have a social orientation and desire to communicate with others in order to learn about the host

Paula M. Caligiuri

country (Black 1990, Searle/Ward 1990). As Mendenhall and Oddou (1985) suggest, a personality characteristic positively affecting the expatriates' social interactions (i.e., *sociability*) may help facilitate interactions, acquaintanceships, and friendships with host nationals. With respect to contact theory, being sociable should improve the likelihood of making host national acquaintances or friends. Based on studies of immigrants, research suggests that those who establish close friendships in their host culture will have access to support networks and will experience less stress (Berry/Kim/Minde/Mok 1987).

Hypothesis 3: Sociability will moderate the relationship between contact with host nationals and cross-cultural adjustment.

Control Variables

Past studies examining the antecedents of expatriate adjustment have yielded six other possible predictor variables in addition to personality characteristics. Since the goal of this study is to understand the moderating affect of personality and contact on expatriate adjustment, the six *non-personality* antecedent variables will be used as control variables. Thus, this study will isolate the moderator variable beyond the influence of these other variables. The six control variables are briefly described below.

The first variable, *language skills,* are generally necessary for interpersonal communication and relationship building, and effective functioning at home and at work (e.g., Abe/Wiseman 1983, Benson 1978, Church 1982, Cui/van den Berg 1991, Mendenhall/Oddou 1985). The second variable, *past foreign experience* affects how confident an expatriate will feel in a new country and is positively related to success in a global assignment (Bochner/Hutnik/Furnham 1986, Bochner/McLeod/Lin 1971, Brein/David 1971). Given that it takes time for an individual to feel comfortable in a new culture (Oberg 1960, Church 1982), the *length of time in the global assignment,* the third variable, should also affect success on the global assignment. The fourth variable, *country distance,* is the extent to which the host country is culturally different from an expatriate's home culture (Mendenhall/Oddou 1985, Church 1982). The greater the cultural distance the more an expatriate will need to learn about the host culture. This cultural distance, therefore, will also affect expatriates' success (Searle/Ward 1990, Church 1982, Mendenhall/Oddou 1985, Torbiörn 1982). The fifth variable, *predeparture training,* helps expatriates learn the new behaviors of the host country that, in turn, should aid in their success (Black/Mendenhall 1990, Earley 1987). The sixth variable, *family adjustment,* affects whether an expatriate completes his or her assignment (Black/Gregersen 1991, Tung 1981), and how successfully the expatriate performs on that assignment (Black/Gregersen 1991, Black/Stephens 1989). Again, this study will examine the moderated relationship between contact and personality characteristics, as a predictor of expatriate adjustment, above and beyond these six control variables.

Method

Participants

Surveys were sent to *all* of the current American expatriate employees (in foreign countries) and inpatriate employees (in the United States) from a large multinational company based in the United States (total possible N = 280). One-hundred and forty-three surveys were returned, for a response rate of 51%. These expatriates were located in 25 different countries (Argentina, Australia, Belgium, Brazil, Canada, Chile, France, Germany, Guam, Hungary, Hong Kong, Italy, Japan, Korea, Malaysia, Mexico, New Zealand, Norway, Puerto Rico, Singapore, Spain, Sweden, Switzerland, Taiwan, United Kingdom). Seventeen of the participants were inpatriates (who are nationals of other countries) currently working in the United States. The average age of the participants was 40 years. Eighty-three percent were male and seventy-five percent were married. Eighty-one percent were American. Ninety-five participants brought their spouses with them on their overseas assignments and 83 participants reported having children (average number of children = 2). (Forty expatriates brought their children with them overseas.) Seventy percent of the participants had a bachelors degree or higher. The participants had been in their assignments an average of 1.8 years while they reported the expected length of their assignments to be an average of 3.2 years.

Measures

Independent Variables

Amount of Contact with Host Nationals

Expatriates were asked to divide 100 points among three categories, with respect to the amount of time they spend with the following people: (1) other expatriates from their home country, (2) other expatriates from countries other than their home country, and (3) host nationals (including friends, colleagues, etc.). The number of points allocated to number three was used as the measure of contact with host nationals.

Paula M. Caligiuri

Openness to People

This construct was measured by a seven-item scale adapted from Caligiuri's (1994, Caligiuri/Jacobs/Farr *forthcoming*) scale for openness. Each item was measured on a five-point scale ranging from 1 (strongly disagree) to 5 (strongly agree). The Openness to People Scale in this study had an alpha coefficient of .72. The items were totaled, whereas, a high score denoted greater openness. Sample items include: "I prefer parties where I know most of the people (reversed)" and "I dislike being with unpredictable people (reversed)" and "My friends' interests and hobbies are similar to mine."

Sociability

The Sociability subscale of the Hogan Personality Inventory (HPI, Hogan/Hogan 1992) was used to measure the construct sociability. This subscale has 24 true-false items. Sample items include "I am often the life of the party" and "Being a part of a large crowd is exciting." Note that, given the proprietary nature of the instrument, the participants completed the HPI, returned the HPI score sheet to the author, and the author sent the HPI score sheets to the test publisher for scoring. The scored data were returned to the author as *subscale* composite scores, rather than item-level scores. Since the author did not receive data back at the item level, the reliability estimate for the Sociability subscale could not be calculated directly from this data set. Rather, the reliability estimates presented below were those reported in the Hogan Personality Inventory Manual (Hogan/Hogan 1992). The scale has a reported reliability of 0.83.

Control Variables

Self-Report Language Skills

Language skills were measured by an item which asked "Describe your ability to speak the language of this host country." The participants rated their ability by rating their language skills on a five-point scale: 1 = I do not know the language of this host country; 2 = I am limited to very short and simple phrases; 3 = I know basic grammatical structure, and speak with a limited vocabulary; 4 = I understand conversation on simple topics; 5 = I am fluent in the language of this host country.

Foreign Experience

Foreign experience was measured by asking the expatriates to report how much time they had spent living in foreign countries (and in what countries). A total of number of months abroad minus the number of months in the foreign assignment was divided by the expatriates' age (in months) to create an index of foreign experience.

Predeparture Training

Training was measured by 2 items. The two items asked the expatriates to rate, on five-point scales (1 = poor, 5 = outstanding), their preparation for the foreign assignment, and the adequacy of the predeparture training this company provided for the assignment. The alpha coefficient of this two-item training measure was 0.64.

Family Adjustment

Expatriates rated how well their spouses and families have adjusted to the host country on 6 items. The items asked the expatriates to rate, on a five-point scale (1 = poor, 5 = outstanding), how well their spouses and children (1) speak the host country language, (2) interact with host nationals, and (3) have adjusted to living in the host country, in general. The alpha coefficient of the family adjustment measure was 0.83.

Length of Time in the Assignment

Expatriates reported how long they had been in their current foreign assignment (rounded to months).

Country Difficulty

Hofstede (1980) collected data on 40 countries (including the United States). The scores for each country on the four dimensions, uncertainty avoidance, individualism versus collectivism and masculinity versus femininity, were transformed to z-scores. For those expatriates who are American, the z-scores for the United States were subtracted from the z-scores for their respective host countries. The absolute values of the difference scores were used to create an additive composite score of country difficulty. (For non-American expatriates, the absolute values are taken relative to the scores from their respective countries.) Kogut and Singh (1988) implemented a similar method to quantify country difficulty from Hofstede's dimensions.

Dependent Variable

Cross-cultural Adjustment

Cross-cultural adjustment was measured by a 4-item scale adapted from Black's (1988) scale of general adjustment. The items ask the expatriates to rate, on a

Paula M. Caligiuri

five-point scale ranging from 1(poor) to 5 (outstanding), their degree of adjustment to living and working in their host national country. For example, items included "rate your adjustment to your current living conditions" and "rate your adjustment to living in this country, in general." The cross-cultural adjustment measure had an alpha coefficient of 0.86.

Design and Procedure

The surveys were sent to the expatriates via this company's country administrators. The country administrators had the current office addresses for the expatriates and sent them directly to the appropriate expatriate employees. Self-addressed, return envelopes were included with the surveys so that the completed surveys could be returned directly to the author. The individual characteristics were assessed at the front end of this larger survey, and the cross-cultural adjustment measure was placed at the end. This was done to lower the chance of self-generated validity (Feldman/Lynch 1988). The HPI also contains a Validity Scale to detect careless or random responses. None of the participants' results indicated that they were marking items randomly.

Results

Table 1 presents the descriptive statistics for the independent variables, control variables, and dependent variable in this study. As Table 1 suggests, all but one (training) of the multiple-item scales had acceptable alpha coefficients (above 0.70).

Next, the correlation matrix for all of the variables was calculated. These correlations are presented in Tables 2.

All of the control variables, except for country difficulty, were significantly related to cross-cultural adjustment. Country difficulty was removed from all subsequent analyses for two reasons. First, country difficulty demonstrated no linear relationship with cross-cultural adjustment. Second, Hofstede (1980) dimensions had data for only 40 countries. Not all of the countries in the current study were represented in Hofstede's study, therefore, including this dimension reduced the sample size and subsequently reduced the power of the analysis.

To test the first hypothesis, the correlation between host national contact and cross-cultural adjustment was examined in the correlation matrix. The correlation between these two variables is not significant ($r = -0.04$, *ns*). Thus, hypothesis one is rejected.

Expatriate Personality and Cross-cultural Adjustment

Table 1. Descriptive Statistics for the Variables Included in the Study

Variables[a]	N of Items	Alpha	Mean	Standard Deviation
Country Difficulty[b]	1		3.13	2.02
Length of Time on Assignment[b, c]	1		21.6	13.03
Ability to Speak the Host National Language [b]	1		4.06	1.24
Prior Foreign Experience[b, d]	1		0.08	0.17
Family Adjustment	8	0.83	3.42	1.02
Training Adequacy	2	0.64	3.95	1.69
Sociability[e]	24	0.83	14.41	4.39
Openness	7	0.72	19.38	4.26
Percent of Time Spent with Hosts[b]	1		51.46	28.16
Cross-Cultural Adjustment	4	0.86	3.94	0.70

[a] Sample size = 143
[b] No alpha is reported because it is a single item variable
[c] In months
[d] Ratio of total time spent in foreign countries, relative to age
[e] This information was reported in the HPI Manual

Table 2. Correlation Matrix of all Independent and Dependent Variables in this Study

	1	2	3	4	5	6	7
1 Country Difficulty							
2 Length of Stay	−0.08						
3 Ability to Speak	−0.36**	−0.09					
4 Foreign Experience	0.22*	−0.05	0.15				
5 Family Adjustment	−0.03	0.06	0.26**	0.12			
6 Training	0.04	−0.00	0.07	0.20*	0.20**		
7 Sociability	0.03	0.03	0.11	−0.01	0.30**	−0.02	
8 Openness	0.13	0.34**	−0.05	0.14	−0.06	−0.07	0.03
9 Contact	−0.13	0.12	0.34**	0.04	0.17*	−0.10	0.08
10 Cross-Cultural Adj.	−0.00	0.25**	0.15*	0.24**	0.37**	0.25**	0.30**

$* p < 0.05;\ ** p < 0.01$

To test the second and third hypotheses a hierarchical moderated regression analysis was conducted predicting cross-cultural adjustment. Predictors were entered in two blocks. The first block included the control independent variables: length of time in the assignment, training adequacy, language ability, family adjustment, and prior foreign experience. The second block included the independent variables and the moderator variables: sociability, openness, contact with host nationals, contact × sociability, contact × openness. Therefore, either hypothesis would be supported if both (1) the second block accounts for a significant portion of variance above and beyond the control variables in the first block and

Paula M. Caligiuri

Table 3. Hierarchical Regression Analysis Predicting Cross-cultural Adjustment

	Beta	t	
Block 1 – Control Variables			
Length of Stay	0.24	2.85**	
Ability to Speak	0.15	1.76, *ns*	
Foreign Experience	0.18	2.26*	
Family Adjustment	0.22	2.49**	
Training	0.17	2.06*	
R			0.51***
R^2			0.26***
Block 2 – Personality and Contact			
Sociability	0.46	2.95**	
Openness	−0.14	−1.08, *ns*	
Contact	−0.45	−2.88**	
R			0.06***
R^2			0.07***
Block 3 – Moderator Variables			
Contact × Sociability	−0.24	−1.58, *ns*	
Contact × Openness	0.41	2.20*	
R			0.04***
R^2			0.04***
Overall R	0.61***		
Overall R^2	0.37***		
Overall F	6.33***		

* $p < 0.05$; ** $p < 0.01$; *** $p < 0.001$

(2) the moderator variable is significant. Table 3 presents the results of the regression analysis.

The hierarchical regression analysis does demonstrate support for the second hypothesis. The contact × openness moderator variable is significant in the second block ($\beta = 0.41$, t = 2.20, $p < 0.05$). The third hypothesis was not supported in that the contact × sociability moderator variable was not significant in the second block. These results, taken together, suggest that greater contact with host nationals does not affect adjustment, unless expatriates possess the personality characteristic of openness.

Discussion

This study attempted to better understand how contact with host nationals will affect cross-cultural adjustment. Based on the contact hypothesis and social learning theory, this study suggests that the more expatriates interact with host nationals, the more likely they are to become cross-culturally adjusted – provided they possess the underlying "other oriented" (Mendenhall/Oddou 1985) personality characteristics of sociability and openness. The results of the hierarchical regression analysis partially support the hypothesis. The linear relationship between contact with host nationals and cross-cultural adjustment is moderated by the personality characteristic of openness. Sociability had a positive (non-moderated) relationship with cross-cultural adjustment.

This research supports Amir's (1969) assertion that not all people benefit equally from interactions with people from a different culture. In this case, these results suggest that those who have greater openness are less likely to have the personality characteristic that may impair their ability to develop relationships with host nationals. In the context of the social learning theory. expatriates who possess greater openness may have a greater interest in learning about new cultures from their host national friends and acquaintances. This is consistent with past research on cross-cultural interactions which suggested that having friendships with host nationals greatly improves expatriates' ability to learn culturally appropriate social skills and behaviors (Searle/Ward 1990). This cultural learning processed from the more frequent contact may have facilitated cross-cultural adjustment for this sample.

It was hypothesized that sociability would also moderate the relationship between host national interaction and cross-cultural adjustment. It was suggested through the contact hypothesis that if an expatriate is a sociable person, then not only host country nationals, but other expatriates, co-workers, neighbors, etc. will be attracted to him or her, possibly desiring to spend time interacting socially. Those expatriates who spend time interacting with other people in the host country (not just host nationals) may have greater opportunities to learn about aspects of daily living (e.g., where to shop, the best providers of medical care) and develop a support network of friends. This would be consistent with past research on immigrants suggesting that those who establish friendships in their "new" culture will have access to support networks and will experience less stress (Berry/Kim/ Minde/Mok 1987). Given that a positive association between sociability and cross-cultural adjustment was found, sociability may be a tool for making friends. It may be the case that the self-perception of having friends in a new country is related to expatriates' overall self-assessment of their adjustment to living in the host country.

The negative relationship in this study between amount of contact with host nationals and cross-cultural adjustment provides support for the assertion that mere contact with host nationals will not necessarily produce adjustment, and subsequent cross-cultural competence and sensitivity (Church 1982). This result suggests that not all contact is equally valuable. One interpretation is that contact with host nationals has a positive impact only when expatriates are open to the

Paula M. Caligiuri

relationship. And for those who are not open to people, greater contact may serve to reduce cross-cultural adjustment. Another interpretation of this negative linear relationship between contact and adjustment may be that expatriates prefer and receive more social support from other expatriates, rather than host nationals. Thus, in cases where other expatriates are not available to form social networks, the expatriates may then be forced to turn to host nationals. This interpretation would suggest that compatriot friends, as opposed to host nationals, positively affect adjustment. Additional research, comparing the influence of compatriot social interaction and host national social interaction on expatriates' cross-cultural adjustment is warranted.

Limitations

As with all studies, there are limitations to this study. The definition of contact was limited to a self-report variable of "percent of time spent with host nationals". Operationalized as such, the variable for "contact" did not delineate between social contacts (friends and acquaintances), work contacts (colleagues), and functional contacts (e.g., domestic help, store clerks). The nature of these relationships may be very different and may serve different roles in helping an expatriate learn cultural norms and behaviors which facilitate cross-cultural adjustment. Future research should explore the context of the interaction with host nationals.

Closely related, another limitation of the study was the lack of understanding of the underlying process for how cross-cultural adjustment is facilitated through host national interaction. This study makes the theoretical assertion that host national contact helps in the process of learning cultural norms, but only tests the amount of contact, rather than the process of contact. What happens during the host national interactions to facilitate learning? For example, are expatriates modeling behaviors of the host nationals? Or are they asking questions of clarification about what is correct and incorrect? This process of social learning should be examined for expatriates. As mentioned in the previous section, the source of the social interaction (and social learning) needs to be better understood in terms of its affect on cross-cultural adjustment. Is it the case that social interaction with host nationals produces similar cross-cultural adjustment as social interaction with other expatriates? Again, future research examining the effect of the source of interaction needs to be examined in future studies.

On the criterion-side of this study, the measure of cross-cultural adjustment was self-reported. Attention was paid to reduce potential biases that may result from a self-reported criterion. For example, the demographic and control variables were assessed at the front end of the survey, and the self-rated criterion measure was placed at the end of the survey. This placement was an effort to reduce self-generated validity (Feldman/Lynch 1988). In addition to self-ratings, future studies may include multiple raters (e.g., self, peers, supervisors, subordinates) and multiple raters with one rater-type (e.g., a host national and a compatriot peer). This is important because a compatriot peer might view socializing with other compatriots as a positive indicator of adjustment, whereas, the host national peer may view the expatriate's socializing as maladjustment to the host country. Two peers, in this case, would view the expatriate's adjustment in very different ways.

Self-reported adjustment as a criterion may pose additional problems when considering personality characteristics as predictors. Variables such as openness and sociability may have a positive response bias on the variable of cross-cultural adjustment. In other words, people who are open or sociable may be predisposed to respond more favorably to the cross-cultural adjustment scale, regardless of their true adjustment. If this response bias did exist, then the bias would provide an alternative explanation for the present study. However, that said, there are no studies which suggest that open or sociable people respond differently to dispositional questionnaires.

Future studies should move beyond the criterion of self-reported cross-cultural adjustment to examine the effect of host national contact on how well the expatriates perform their work assignments while they are abroad. There are very few sound empirical studies of expatriates where an assessment of job performance is used as the criterion. This represents a dearth of research in the field of expatriate management. We have not yet been able to conclude the relationship between cross-cultural adjustment and performance on the global assignment. Since we do not have statistics suggesting the proportion of people who would be considered "maladjusted" in the expatiate population and (presumably) since not all maladjusted expatriates necessarily leave their assignment, an examination of the expatriate performance criterion in the future would be valuable.

The sample was limited primarily to American expatriates. Given that the USA is a very individualistic society, personality may be especially important for Americans who are generally accustomed to doing things "their own way." People from more collectivist countries may have a tendency to learn culturally appropriate norms and behaviors more readily than Americans. Openness, therefore, should be tested across a comparative cross-cultural sample in future studies. In addition, when studying the relationships between host nationals and expatriates, one must consider the cross-cultural differences in the concept of "friend", "acquaintance" etc. (Church 1982).

Practical Implications

Given the extraordinary high financial, relational, and emotional costs for expatriates (Black/Gregersen/Mendenhall 1992), their families (Caligiuri/Hyland/Joshi/Bross 1998, Guzzo/Noonan/Elron 1994), and their organizations (Zeira/Banai 1985),

Paula M. Caligiuri

understanding who will benefit the most from being on a foreign assignment is important. In a practical sense, a question answered in this study was whether personality characteristics could be used to predict success in overseas assignments? Based on this study, the personality characteristics of openness and sociability are recommended for use in expatriate selection systems – especially in cases where the expatriates will be interacting more extensively with host nationals.

Selection systems for global assignments should include an assessment of personality very early in the selection process. As this research suggests, organizations should convey to its employees that a global assignment *is not right for everyone*. This should be conveyed early in the process. Organizations will get the best possible global assignees when they consider many possible candidates and engage the candidates' decision-making processes long before a position becomes available. This decision-making process, with a special assessment of their personality will help them decide whether the assignment is really right for them. That is, the selection decision needs to be mutual among the employee, his or her organization, and his or her family.

After selecting global assignees who will benefit most from the experience, multinational organizations should promote positive contacts between their host national employees and expatiate employees. In accordance with the theory (Amir 1969), this contact should be between perceived equals. Therefore, expatriates should not be led to believe that they are "the all-knowing headquarter's representative" in the subsidiary. The trend to send more middle-level global assignees would support this positive contact. A multinational organization should encourage its expatriates to learn from the host nationals – not placing them psychologically above the host nationals. This can be facilitated through performance assessment which encourages collaboration between the expatriates and their host national colleagues.

Thus, multinational organizations are encouraged to (1) assess their potential expatriates for these personality characteristics and, having selected carefully, (2) promote contact with host nationals once they are on the assignment. These practices combined could improve the MNCs' chances for having well-adjusted expatriates on these critical global assignments. In turn, the improved cross-cultural adjustment of expatriates should lead to better performance in the global arena – for both individuals and their organizations.

References

Abe, H./Wiseman, R. L., A Cross-cultural Confirmation of the Dimensions of Intercultural Effectiveness, *International Journal of Intercultural Relations*, 7, 1983, pp. 5–67.
Adler, N. J./Bartholomew, S., Managing Globally Competent People, *Academy of Management Executive*, 6, 1992, pp. 52–65.

Expatriate Personality and Cross-cultural Adjustment

Allport, G. W., *The Nature of Prejudice,* Cambridge, MA: Addison-Wesley 1954.

Amir, Y., Contact Hypothesis in Ethnic Relations, *Psychological Bulletin,* 71, 1969, pp. 319–342.

Arthur, W./Bennett, W., The International Assignee: The Relative Importance of Factors Perceived to Contribute to Success, *Personnel Psychology,* 48, 1995, pp. 99–114.

Baker, J. C./Ivancevich, J. M., The Assignment of American Executives Abroad: Systematic, Haphazard or Chaotic?, *California Management Review,* 13, 1971, pp. 39–44.

Bandura, A., *Social Learning* Theory, Englewood Cliffs, NJ: Prentice-Hall 1977.

Benson, P., Measuring Cross-Cultural Adjustment: The Problem of Criteria, *International Journal of Intercultural Relations,* 2, 1978, pp. 21–37.

Berry, J. W./ Kim, U./ Minde, T.,/Mok, D., Comparative Studies in Acculturative Stress, *International Migration Review,* 21, 1987, pp. 490–511.

Black, J. S., Work Role Transitions: A Study of American Expatriate Managers in Japan, *Journal of International Business Studies,* 78, 1988, pp. 277–294.

Black, J. S., The Relationship of Personal Characteristics with Adjustment of Japanese Expatriate Managers, *Management International Review,* 30, 1990, pp. 119–134.

Black, J. S./Gregersen, H. B., Antecedents to Cross-cultural Adjustment for Expatriates in Pacific Rim Assignments, *Human Relations,* 44, 1991, pp. 497–515.

Black, J. S./Gregersen, H. B., The Other Half of the Picture: Antecedents of Spouse Cross-cultural Adjustment, *Journal of International Business Studies,* 1991, pp. 461–477.

Black, J. S./Gregersen, H. B./Mendenhall, M. E., *Global Assignments: Successfully Expatriating and Repatriating International Managers,* San Francisco: Jossey-Bass 1992.

Black, J. S./Mendenhall, M. E./Oddou, G. R., Toward a Comprehensive Model of International Adjustment: An Integration of Multiple Theoretical Perspectives, *Academy of Management Review,* 16, 1991, pp. 291–317.

Black, J. S./Mendenhall, M. E., Cross-Cultural Training Effectiveness: A Review and Theoretical Framework, *Academy of Management Review,* 15, 1990, pp. 113–136.

Black, J. S./Stephens, G., Expatriate Adjustment and Intent to Stay in Pacific Rim Overseas Assignments, *Journal of Management,* 15, 1989, pp. 529–544.

Bochner, S./Hutnik, N./Furnham, A., The Friendship Patterns of Overseas Students and Host Students in an Oxford Student Resident Hall, *Journal of Social Psychology,* 125, 1986, pp. 689–694.

Bochner, S./McLeod, B. M./Lin, A., Friendship Patterns of Overseas Students: A Functional Model, *International Journal of Psychology,* 12, 1977, pp. 277–294.

Brein, M./David, K. H., Intercultural Communication and Adjustment of the Sojourner, *Psychological Bulletin,* 76, 1971, pp. 215–230.

Buss, A. H., Personality as Traits, *American Psychologist,* 44, 1989, 1378–1388.

Caligiuri, P. M., The International Orientation Scale, in Marcic, D./Puffer, S. (eds.), *International Management,* St. Paul, MN: West Publishing Company 1994, pp. 157–169.

Caligiuri, P. M., Assessing Expatriate Success: Beyond Just "Being There", in Aycan, Z. (ed.), *Expatriate Management: Theory and Practice,* Greenwich, CT: JAI Press, 1997, pp. 17–140.

Caligiuri, P. M./Hyland, M./ Joshi, A./Bross, A., A Theoretical Framework for Examining the Relationship Between Family Adjustment and Expatriate Adjustment to Working in the Host Country, *Journal of Applied Psychology,* 83, 1998, pp. 598–614.

Caligiuri, P. M./Jacobs, R. J./Farr, J. L., The Attitude and Behavioral Openness Scale: Scale Development and Construct Validation, *International Journal of Intercultural Relations,* forthcoming.

Church, A., Sojourner Adjustment, *Psychological Bulletin,* 9, 1982, pp. 540–572.

Costa, P. T./McCrae, R. R., Four Ways Five Factors Are Basic, *Personality and Individual Differences,* 13, 1992, 653–665.

Cui, G./van den Berg, S., Testing the Construct Validity of Intercultural Effectiveness, *International Journal of Intercultural Relations,* 15, 1991, pp. 227–241.

Earley, P. C., Intercultural Training for Managers: A Comparison of Documentary and Interpersonal Methods, *Academy of Management Review,* 39, 1987, pp. 685–698.

Feldman, J. M./Lynch, J. G., Self-Generated Validity and Other Effects of Measurement on Belief, Attitude, Intention, and Behavior, *Journal of Applied Psychology,* 73, 1988, pp. 421–435.

Gregersen, H. B./Black, J. S., A Multifaceted Approach to Expatriate Retention in International Assignments, *Group and Organizational Studies,* 15, 1990, pp. 461–485.

Paula M. Caligiuri

Guzzo, R. A., Noonan, K. A.,/Elron, E., Expatriate Managers and the Psychological Contract, *Journal of Applied Psychology*, 79, 1994, p. 617–626.

Hammer, M. R., Gudykunst, W. B./Wiseman, R. L., Dimensions of Intercultural Effectiveness: An Exploratory Study, *International Journal of Intercultural Relations*, 2, 1978, pp. 382–393.

Harvey, M. G., The Executive Family: An Overlooked Variable in International Assignments, *Columbia Journal of World Business*, 20, 1985, pp. 84–92.

Hewstone, M./Brown, R., *Contact and Conflict in Intergroup Encounters*, Oxford: Basil Blackwell 1986.

Hofstede, G., *Culture's Consequences*, Beverly Hills: Sage 1980.

Hogan, R./Hogan, J., *Hogan Personality Inventory Manual*, Tulsa, OK: Hogan Assessment Systems, Inc. 1992.

Kogut, B./Singh, H., The Effect of National Culture on the Choice of Entry Mode, *Journal of International Business Studies*, 1988, pp. 411–428.

Laabs, J., Rating the International Relocation Hot Spots, *Personnel Journal*, 72, 1993, p. 19.

McCrae, R. R./Costa, P. T., Validation of the Five-Factor Model of Personality Across Instruments and Observers, *Journal of Personality and Social Psychology*, 52, 1987, pp. 81–90.

McEvoy, G./Parker, B., Expatriate Adjustment: Causes and Consequences in Selmer, J. (ed.) *Expatriate Management*, 1995, pp. 97–114.

Mendenhall, M. /Oddou, G., The Dimensions of Expatriate Acculturation, *Academy of Management Review*, 10, 1985, pp. 39–47.

Oberg, K., Culture Shock: Adjustment to New Cultural Environment. *Practical Anthropologist*, 7, 1960, pp. 177–182.

Piedmont, R. L./McCrae, R. R./Costa, P. T., Adjective Check List Scales and the Five-Factor Model, *Journal of Personality and Social Psychology*, 60, 1991, pp. 630–637.

Searle, W./Ward, C., The Prediction of Psychological and Sociocultural Adjustment During Cross-cultural Transitions, *International Journal of Intercultural Relations*, 14, 1990, pp. 449–464.

Stroh, L. K./Caligiuri, P. M., Strategic Human Resources: A New Source for Competitive Advantage in the Global Arena, *International Journal of Human Resource Management*, 9, 1998, pp. 1–17.

Stroh, L. K./Dennis, L. E./Cramer, T. C., Predictors of Expatriate Adjustment, *International Journal of Organizational Analysis*, 2, 1994, pp. 176–192.

The Conference Board, *Recruiting and Selecting International Managers* (Report No. 998), New York: The Conference Board 1992.

Törbiorn, I., The Structure of Managerial Roles in Cross-cultural Settings, *International Studies of Management and Organizations*, 15, 1982, pp. 52–74.

Tung, R. L., *The New Expatriates,* Cambridge, MA: Ballinger 1988.

Tung, R. L., Selection and Training of Personnel for Overseas Assignments, *Columbia Journal of World Business*, 16, 1981, pp. 21–25.

Tung, R. L./Miller, E. L., Managing in the Twenty-First Century: The Need for Global Orientation, *Management International Review*, 30, 1990, pp. 5–18.

Windham International/National Foreign Trade Council, Inc., *Global Relocation Trends: 1994 Survey Report,* New York: Windham International 1994.

Zajonc, R. B., Attitudinal Effects of Mere Exposure, *Journal of Personality and Social Psychology Monograph Supplement*, 9, 1968, pp. 1–27.

Zeira, Y./Banai, M., Selection of Expatriate Managers in Multinational Corporations: The Host Environment Point of View, *International Studies of Management and Organization*, 15, 1985, pp. 33–51.

[4]

Think International Manager, Think Male: Why Are Women Not Selected for International Management Assignments?

Hilary Harris

Executive Summary

Studies of women in international management originating primarily from North America consistently highlight the lack of women in such positions. This trend continues despite the need for growing numbers of expatriates. Explanations for this phenomenon have centered on women's personal characteristics, home/family circumstances, organizational support, and host country nationals' attitudes. This study examines the status of women in international management from a United Kingdom (UK) perspective. A key finding arising from the study is the critical influence of selection systems for international assignments where the predominant use of closed, informal selection processes for international assignments was seen to create unintended gender bias in recruitment.

INTRODUCTION

n their search for competitive advantage in global markets, international organizations have traditionally experimented with varying forms of organizational structure and control to respond to the contextual exigencies facing them (Galbraith, 1987; Ghoshal, 1987; Porter, 1986; Prahalad & Doz, 1987; Schuler et al., 1993). Whilst these interventions may be beneficial for companies adopting either a purely ethnocentric or a completely devolved polycentric approach to internationalization, they have proved inadequate to deliver the corporate "glue" for those organizations striving to become truly global (Bartlett & Ghoshal, 1989; Kobrin, 1994). Bartlett and Ghoshal (1989, p. 212) explain the objectives of a "transnational" mindset:

Dr. Hilary Harris is Director of the Centre for Research into the Management of Expatriation (CReME). Dr. Harris has extensive experience as a HR practitioner with organizations in the security, engineering, and computing sectors.

Hilary Harris

> . . . the development of a transnational organization requires more than multidimensional capabilities and interdependent assets. It is crucial to change the mentality of members of the organization. Diverse roles and dispersed operations must be held together by a management mindset that understands the need for multiple strategic capabilities, views problems and opportunities from both a local and global perspective, and is willing to interact with others openly and flexibly. The task is not to build a sophisticated matrix structure, but to create a "matrix in the minds of managers."

Kobrin (1994) quotes Caproni et al. (1992, p. 1) in emphasizing a shift in the international management literature from the "fit" between strategy and structure to a "process" perspective that relies "on the assumption that the ways that organizations' members make sense of their organizations and the global environment, enhance or inhibit competitive advantage." He defines a geocentric mindset in terms of a global systems approach to decision making in which superiority is not equated with any nationality and ideas and resources, including human resources, but are valued according to their worth for the global entity, no matter where their source of origin might be.

By its very nature, the development of a global mindset can only be achieved through exposure to diversity. It is hardly likely that a homogenous group of managers will develop a global mindset unless the composition of the group is changed to reflect the diversity within the organization and potentially within its client base. In this respect, the fact that women (who represent half the population in most countries in the world) are barely represented at board level is problematic. In the UK for instance, women comprise only 2% of executive directors and 9.6% of non-executive directors in FTSE 100 companies.

In tandem with ensuring a diverse population amongst board members, many aspiring global organizations strive to develop a broad international cadre of managers amongst their most promising junior- and middle-management level employees who will feed into the most senior positions in the company. International management assignments constitute a vital component of the development of a geocentric mindset amongst this body of managers. Adler and Bartholomew (1992, p. 18) stress the importance of international assignments to developing a "global firm":

> Foreign assignments become a core component of the organizational and career development process. "Transpatriates" from all parts of the world are sent to all other parts of the world to develop their worldwide perspective and cross-cultural skills. Foreign assignments are used to enhance individual and organizational learning in all parts of the system.

In a recent survey by Organization Resources Counselors Inc. (ORC, 1997), 63% of responding organizations indicated that they were planning to increase the number of international assignments in Asia, with 54% also planning to increase international assignments in Europe. Over 60% of the assignments were single trips with planned repatriation. This confirms the importance of international experience as part of management development. As a result, one of the main international human resource challenges for multinational organizations is finding the right people with the requisite skills to send on global assignments (Stroh & Caligiuri, 1998).

Despite this increase in demand for international assignees, the numbers of women in such positions remains stubbornly low. Figures from the research currently being reported show a representation rate of 9% for women out of the total expatriate population studied (Harris, 1998). These figures are roughly in line with previous estimates of the number of women on international management assignments, with figures ranging from between 2 to 15% (Adler, 1984a; Brewster, 1991; Reynolds & Bennett, 1991; The Conference Board, 1992; Florkowski & Fogel, 1995; Tung, 1997). Given that women now constitute almost 50% of the UK workforce and form approximately 26% of junior- and middle-management positions (Labour Force Survey 1989, 1995), assumptions that diversity is being acknowledged and incorporated in the development of a geocentric mindset must be questioned.

The low incidence of women on international management assignments is even more puzzling when one looks at research into the criteria for effective international managers.

The low incidence of women on international management assignments is even more puzzling when one looks at research into the criteria for effective international managers. Here, the emphasis is on interpersonal, intuitive, and co-operative styles of management as the key skills for working internationally (Mendenhall & Oddou, 1985; Barham & Devine, 1991; Coulson-Thomas, 1992; Wills & Barham, 1994; Birchall et al., 1996). These same skills have been argued to be more suited to a woman's style of management (Marshall, 1984; Vinnicombe, 1987; Rosener, 1990; Sharma, 1990; Fondas, 1997). Why, therefore, do organizations continue to under-use such a valuable source of diversity and a potentially powerful aid towards developing a truly global mindset?

This article reports the result of a multi-stage study, examining reasons for the paucity of women in international management. The structure of the article consists of a review of the literature, a methodology section, and a results section detailing findings from both the preliminary research phase and the final case study phase.

Hilary Harris

REVIEW OF THE LITERATURE ON WOMEN IN INTERNATIONAL MANAGEMENT

Research into women in international management is fragmented. One of the earliest and most influential bodies of work was that of Adler (1984a, 1984b, 1984c, 1986, 1987). Working with a predominantly North American sample, she undertook a series of studies to investigate both the participation rates of women in international management and the reasons for the low rates revealed. In particular, she tested the veracity of three "beliefs" which had emerged from the academic literature and from managers themselves in attempting to explain the scarcity of females on international assignments. These beliefs or "myths" were:

- Women do not want to be international managers.
- Companies refuse to send women abroad.
- Foreigners' prejudice against women renders them ineffective, even when they are interested in international assignments and are successful in being sent.

Adler addressed the first myth in her research (Adler, 1984b) amongst 1,129 graduating MBA students in Canada, the United States, and Europe. Her findings showed that new women graduates expressed as much interest in international careers as their male colleagues. Women, however, saw organizational barriers facing females as greater potential constraints to achieving this goal than did the male sample. A more recent study amongst graduate and undergraduate business students in the U.S. as reported by Lowe et al. (1999), noted that gender was a significant predictor when specific referent countries were identified. Differences in cultural distance and human development explained substantial variance among males and females in their willingness to accept international assignments. Political risk was not deemed to be a significant factor. The authors acknowledge that their findings need further replication to ensure generalizability. However, they do raise issues for organizations, in terms of the amount of support needed to assist women to successfully undertake assignments in specific countries.

Myth 3 was also shown to be questionable by research carried out by Adler in 1987 amongst 52 North American female expatriates in Asia. Ninety-two percent of this sample self-reported their assignment as being successful, backed up by supporting organizational evidence. Adler concluded that this finding revealed that the female expatriates were seen as foreigners who happen to be women and were not therefore subject to the same cultural constraints as local women (Jelinik & Adler, 1988; Adler, 1993b; Westwood & Leung, 1994). Caligiuri and Cascio (1998) attribute such a phenomenon to the cognitive process of stereotyping subtypes (Brewer et al., 1981; Kunda & Thagard, 1996). They argue that according to this theory, Asian host nationals in Adler's study would have a sub-stereotype of "Western working women" and a very different sub-stereotype for "Asian working women." Reactions to the two groups can therefore be very different.

Organizational reluctance to send women overseas was confirmed by the research. In a survey of international personnel managers from 60 Canadian and American corporations, Adler (1984c) found that the majority perceived the following as barriers to women moving into international management assignments: foreigners' prejudice (72.7%) and dual career marriages (69.1%). In addition, more than half of the managers (53.8%) saw their own company's reluctance to select women as a major barrier. This reluctance was attributed to (a) traditional male chauvinism, (b) recognition of the higher risk involved in sending an unproven quantity, and (c) lack of suitably qualified or experienced women.

The issue of dual-career couples is becoming an increasing source of concern to organizations when sending individuals on international assignments (Brett et al., 1992; Reynolds & Bennett, 1991; McDonald, 1993; Swaak, 1995; Harvey, 1995, 1996a,b, 1997, 1998). It is estimated that 70% of expatriate managers are members of dual-career couples (Reynolds & Bennett, 1991; Karambayya & Reilly, 1992), creating immense problems for organizations in handling the position of both the trailing spouse and dependent children.

Reviewing the domestic literature on work/family interlinkages, Harvey (1997, p. 629) concludes that the consistent dimension in all theoretical approaches to analyzing dual-career couples' balancing work/family is the stress and tension that is generated in the couple relative to the demands associated with both spheres (p. 629). An extensive body of literature has examined the conflict, stress, and adjustment for dual-career couples in the case of domestic relocation (e.g., Bielby & Bielby, 1992; Brett et al., 1992; Higgins & Duxbury, 1992; Karambayya & Reilly, 1992; Williams & Alliger, 1994). The additional complexities and tensions involved in relocating to an international location are likely to increase stress and tension (Caligiuri et al., 1998). This can lead to poor job performance and ultimately, expatriate failure. Research into international assignments

Hilary Harris

failure reveals a key factor to be the inability to adjust on the part of both the expatriate and spouse (Tung, 1982; Mendenhall & Oddou, 1985; Black & Stephens, 1989; Black et al., 1991; Stone, 1991; ECA, 1994; Harvey, 1995, 1996a,b). Harvey (1997) therefore argues that existing theoretical approaches to willingness to relocate internationally, adjustment during international relocation and satisfaction with the international assignment need to be adapted in the case of the international relocation of a dual-career couple. Little has been done so far to rectify this situation from either an academic or an organizational perspective.

. . .it is argued that women will experience greater stress than men when faced with work-related pressures, including mobility requirements, due to the degree of incompatibility between role pressures from work and family domains . . .

Research into the problems facing dual-career expatriates indicates that this is equally problematic for men as for women. However, Adler (1984c) and Harris' (1999) research shows that potential dual-career couple restrictions are seen to be a key entry barrier for women wishing to gain international assignments. This may in part result from traditional sociocultural norms that identify the dominant gender-role profile of women as homemakers (Lewis & Cooper, 1988; Sandqvist, 1992). From this perspective, it is argued that women will experience greater stress than men when faced with work-related pressures, including mobility requirements, due to the degree of incompatibility between role pressures from work and family domains (Gupta & Jenkins, 1985; Sekaran, 1986; Rapoport & Rapoport 1971, 1976; Weirsma, 1994). In addition, it has been argued that male spouses face additional role transition obstacles in terms of adjusting to the role of secondary breadwinner (Paddock & Schwartz, 1986) or homemaker, if they cannot find work in the foreign location. Additional sociocultural barriers include the likelihood of the male spouse finding himself the lone man in a group of wives and the unavailability or inappropriateness of traditional volunteer activities that wives undertake in foreign locations, thus, limiting the extent of productive activities for males (Punnett et al., 1992).

Assumptions about the problems associated with sending a woman abroad if she is in a dual-career couple, have caused organizations to use this as a reason for not selecting potential female expatriates (Adler, 1984c). There is evidence, however, that male managers may be becoming less "psychologically immersed" in their work. They are, therefore, less prepared to make sacrifices which might harm their domestic lifestyles (Scase & Goffee, 1989; Forster 1992). As a result, organizations can no longer expect to supply their expanding global management requirements from male managers alone. The issues surrounding dual-career couples will remain a significant part of the decision as to whether or not to send an employee on an international assignment; however, organizations will need to look for solutions to the dual-career issue for both genders, not just for male employees.

An underlying theme arising from existing research into women in international management is that many of the reasons put forward for minimal participation rates are derived from assumptions about the likelihood of women experiencing problems whilst on assignments. An examination of the literature on expatriate failure however, provides no evidence with which to support these assumptions (Tung, 1981; Torbiorn, 1982; Copeland & Griggs, 1985; Mendenhall & Oddou, 1985; Stone, 1991; ECA, 1994). The most significant feature of the research into expatriate failure rates is that it is based on a male population. This research contains actual evidence of male expatriates facing cross-cultural adjustment problems and family problems. In contrast, research conducted on the outcome of women's global assignments indicates that female expatriates are successful in their assignments (Adler, 1987; Taylor & Napier, 1996; Caligiuri & Tung, 1998). The attribution of male expatriates' problems is, however, assumed to be a lack of adequate preparation on the part of the expatriate or lack of organizational support and is therefore seen to be open to remedy. This contrasts starkly with the situation for women where assumptions of potential problems, not linked to any concrete evidence of failure, are used on the part of home country managers as reasons for non-selection of female candidates.

ROLE OF HOME COUNTRY SELECTION PROCESSES IN DETERMINING WOMEN'S PARTICIPATION RATES

The previous section has revealed the prevailing arguments as it relates to minimal participation rates by women and have focused on individual perspectives. This was either from the point-of-view of the individual woman, in terms of constraints as a result of lack of experience/qualifications or domestic drawbacks; or from the point-of-view of the host country individuals who may be prejudiced against women managers. There is a lack of acknowledgment of the role of organizational processes in the home country as determinants of women's participation rates.

Organizational processes form part of Caligiuri and Cascio's (1998) four factor model for predicting the success of female global assignees. The four antecedents in the model are: personality traits,

Hilery Harris

organizational support, family support, and host nationals' attitudes towards female expatriates. Organization support is defined in the model in terms of cross-cultural and gender-specific training for women on assignments, and projecting female expatriate managers as being most suitable and highly qualified for the job to local nationals (Caligiuri et al., 1999, p. 167). The model does not, however, include the role of organizational selection systems for international assignments as a critical variable in organizational support.

It is not surprising that, given the paucity of research into women in international management, it is difficult to find any research into the role of organizational selection processes as a determinant of participation rates. However, an extensive body of literature from both North America and Europe highlights the pervasive influence of discrimination in selection processes. This work addresses the issue of "fit," both from a sociological and a social psychological perspective. From a sociological perspective, selection is seen as a *social* process, to be used by those in power within the organization as a means of determining the continuing form of the organization by recruiting and promoting only those individuals who most closely conform to organizational norms. Individuals would, therefore, be judged more on the basis of their *acceptability* than their *suitability* (Jewson & Mason, 1986).

Social psychological studies explore the role of individual values in perpetuating discrimination in selection through the use of schemas and stereotyping (e.g., Heilman, 1983; Futoran & Wyer, 1986). Such studies suggest that individual selectors will develop schemas of ideal "jobholders" and will use them as a yardstick against which all prospective candidates are measured during the process of selection. They also suggest that the less distinct the information concerning the vacancy, and/or the candidate, the more likely selectors are to use schemas and stereotypes.

Given the emphasis on "fit" as a key determinant of selection decisions in both the sociological and social psychological literature, the "gender-blindness" of research into expatriate management represents a significant gap for any study trying to assess the role of selection systems for international assignments on women's representation rates. Empirical survey results indicate that over 90% of expatriates are male. Previous research has argued that occupations where there is a predominance of one gender over the other can lead to gender-typed "job-holder" schema in the minds of selectors (Perry et al., 1994).

The gender of expatriates is, however, rarely acknowledged as a significant factor in the literature on expatriate selection. Descriptive and prescriptive studies of the features of expatriation therefore, tend to perpetuate the profile of an expatriate manager as being male and married with a trailing spouse. Discussions of appropriate selection, preparation, and repatriation systems subsequently tend to reflect both a lack of appreciation of gender-related needs and a reluctance to acknowledge the possibility of alternatives to the prevailing model.

The "gender-blindness" of the majority of research into expatriate management is reflected in feminist discussions concerning the patriarchal nature of organizations. They argue that the organizational population has traditionally been predominantly male and that therefore, the holders of organizational power, in terms of shaping structures and beliefs, have almost exclusively been male. The need to acknowledge this perspective is seen as critical since gender-role assumptions have been seen to be important components of decisions about "fit" (Webb, 1991; Alimo-Metcalfe, 1993, 1995; Rubin, 1997).

Descriptive and prescriptive studies of the features of expatriation therefore, tend to perpetuate the profile of an expatriate manager as being male and married with a trailing spouse.

The literature related to international management selection, however, does not address issues of gender discrimination or "fit" in any systematic or theoretical way. Nor does it explore the role of the type of selection system itself in constraining or enabling the use of individual values by selectors and how this might affect equal opportunities in the field of international assignments. This failure must increasingly be questioned, in light of extensive domestically-based research into the nature of gender-based discrimination in selection, and minimal evidence of business barriers to women undertaking international assignments.

STUDY METHODOLOGY

The main focus of the study was to examine the role of home country selection processes in influencing the number of women in international management positions. The absence of any empirical work in the UK on representation rates and barriers for women in international management called for a preliminary research phase. The purpose of this stage was to test the applicability of previous research findings into the numbers of women in management and potential barriers to participation. Following this initial phase, a second stage of research was carried out consisting of detailed case study explorations of the impact of selection systems for international management assignments on women's participation rates.

Hilary Harris

Preliminary Research Phase

In this first phase, a survey was sent to International Human Resource (IHR) Directors to obtain empirical data on the current usage of women in international management amongst UK-based international organizations and to ascertain IHR directors' perceptions as to the key barriers to women in obtaining international assignments. The survey was sent to international HR directors of 400 UK-based international organizations. The majority of organizations surveyed were from the private sector, with a sample of 286 companies. Private sector companies were identified by taking the *Times* Top 1,000 list of UK companies and cross-referencing them with Dunn and Bradstreet's volumes of "Who Owns Whom," in order to ascertain which out of the original 1,000 fitted the profile of UK-based organizations with a foreign subsidiary. In addition, professional firms and not-for-profit organizations were sampled given the high proportion of women in these sectors. Forty UK-based law firms with international offices were identified through professional directories, as were 30 UK-based finance houses. Forty-four UK-based organizations from the not-for-profit sector with overseas operations were also identified from published lists of not-for-profit bodies. The sample included all the major UK-based international aid agencies.

It was seen as essential to combine both public and private samples in the methodology in order to be able to gain a holistic picture of the situation for women expatriates in the UK context. It was also anticipated, particularly in the case study stage, that a comparison of the methods used in both sectors may provide some useful insights into reasons for the continuing scarcity of women in international positions. The difficult, and often hostile nature of the areas to which expatriates are sent by nongovernmental organizations (NGOs) precluded any argument that the situation would be easier for women to obtain international assignments in those organizations.

In-depth, qualitative interviews were then carried out with a small sample of female expatriates and IHR directors to confirm the importance of organizational processes in influencing opportunities for women in international management. Six female managers who had taken expatriate assignments in the recent past were interviewed. The women worked in the following sectors: telecommunications, gas exploration, transport, central government, and finance. They aged between 25–35 and all were single. The interviews with women expatriates were intended to obtain sensitizing information concerning individual experiences of expatriation, in order to assess the extent to which home country organizational influences affected the nature of the experience.

For the interviews with IHR directors, nine UK-based organizations (identified as organizations A-I), were picked to represent an established tradition of expatriation in many countries of the world, and to provide a broad, sectorial spread. The following sectors were represented: oil exploration (3), telecommunications (1), airlines (1), food and beverage (1), pharmaceuticals (1), production (1) and NGO (1). The interviews with IHR directors were intended to obtain a clearer understanding of expatriate selection based on actual organization practice. In this respect, the use of semi-structured interviews was seen to be an appropriate research tool, as it enabled the somewhat positivistic collection of standard company data on formal expatriate selection policy and practice, to be balanced by the individual views of managers on how the system worked in practice, which in most cases proved to be very different from an espoused norm.

A critical part of the research was seen to be the identification of personally held beliefs about the characteristics of effective international managers.

Main Research Stage

The main stage of the research consisted of a case study approach. This explored how the nature of selection systems for international management assignments might lead to a greater or lesser use of personal preferences by selectors, and the impact of this on the numbers of women entering international management assignments. A major consideration in the data collection phase was to ensure triangulation of methods. In this respect, it was decided to obtain information about international manager selection processes from two sources; the first through semi-structured interviews with HR personnel and key selectors within the individual organizations; the second via an examination of organizational literature in the form of policies and administration forms etc.

A critical part of the research was seen to be the identification of personally held beliefs about the characteristics of effective international managers. To try and ensure an unbiased summary of the characteristics of effective international managers (both from the researcher's part and that of the individual selectors), Repertory Grid technique was chosen as integral to the case study design. This consisted of asking individual selectors to compare and contrast nine international managers whom they knew personally, and then split them into the categories of highly effective, moderately effective, and not effective. As far as possible, women internation-

Hilary Harris

al managers were included in the sample. The results from the Repertory Grid interviews yielded a set of "constructs" or statements, concerning effective/non-effective international manager behavior which were further analyzed using the Grid Analysis Package (GAP) developed by Slater (1972). An explanation of how to interpret the results from this package is available from Smith (1986). In order to see if there was any inherent gender bias in the constructs used by the selectors, they were compared to the 92-item inventory designed by Schein (1973, 1975), known as Schein's Descriptive Index.

Survey Findings

A total of 90 usable questionnaires were returned, following reminder letters, before the cut-off date, giving a response rate of 22.5%. Of the responding organizations, approximately 85% were in the private sector, with the remainder in the not-for-profit sector. Industry sector breakdown of responses was as follows:

Metal and other manufacturing	40%
Energy an water	11%
Banking and finance	11%
Other services (including charities)	8%
Building	7%
Chemicals	5%
Retail and distribution	5%
Transport	4%
Health services	4%
Others	5%

Organization size reflected a wide range, with 32% of respondents with up to 500 employees; 18% with 500-1,000; 28% with 1,000-5,000, and 22% with over 5,000 employees.

Expatriate Population Demographics

The responding organizations employed a total of 3,619 expatriates, of which 3,290 (or 90.91%) were male, and 329 (or 9.09%) were female. The survey also split expatriate assignments into *management, technical, and others*. This allowed a further breakdown of the proportion of women in each of these categories. The majority of expatriates in this survey were categorized as technical (57%). Managerial expatriates accounted for 21%, whilst 22% fell into the "others" category. The survey figures indicated that women made up 9% of the total managerial expatriate population; 8% of the technical expatriate population, and 7% of the "others" category.

Despite women's low overall numbers, it was interesting to note that their numbers were relatively high in the less traditional, but high growth potential regions of the world for expatriation as follows:

Region	% Female Expatriates
Middle East	1%
Africa	8%
Western Europe	10%
Eastern Europe	16%
North America	9%
Central/S. America	20%
Asia	12%
Pacific Rim	5%

The survey responses indicated that women's participation in international management is likely to increase. One third of organizations indicated an increase in the numbers of female expatriates over the last five years, whilst nearly 50% believe that the number will increase over the next five years.

Status

In view of the perceived problems for women in taking their spouses or families with them on assignments, details were requested relating to the status of expatriates whilst on assignment. A rather surprising finding emerged from the data with respect to the fact that 50% of male expatriates were unaccompanied by their partner whilst on assignment. This may be a result of the high number of technical expatriates amongst the survey population. Thirty percent of male expatriates were accompanied, whilst 20% were designated as being single status. In contrast, figures for women show that only 6% of female expatriates were unaccompanied by their partner whilst on assignment; whilst a surprisingly high amount, 44%, were accompanied, and 50% were designated as being single status. This suggests that barriers to women with families or spouses may not be as rigid as generally assumed.

The survey was also interested in assessing whether the age at which employees were sent on expatriate assignments might be detrimental to women, based on research evidence at the domestic level into problems faced by women who were trying to follow chronological career timetables and have children. The survey findings showed that, for managerial assignments, the majority of organizations would arrange a first expatriate assignment between the ages of 31 and 40, whilst for technical assignments this was more evenly spread, with

Hilary Harris

33% sending staff on their first expatriate assignment between the age of 21 and 30, and 20% sending staff between 31 and 40. It is likely therefore, that women who wish to have families may face problems unless the organization can provide suitable support for childcare whilst on assignment.

Managers' Perceptions of Key Barriers to Women Obtaining International Management Positions

In order to address the reasons for the shortage of women in international management, the survey contained the question—"What are the key problems which restrict the number of females on expatriate assignments?" A breakdown of the replies are shown, in order of importance in Table 1.

. . . the locations of expatriate assignments appear to offer fewer possibilities for blanket refusal of women in expatriate positions.

It can be seen from this table that respondents identified lack of qualifications and experience as the key issues, with family obligations and dual-career obstacles also seen to be significant. In contrast to previous survey findings however, problems relating to host country employees and clients working with a woman were not seen as significant.

Summary

The analysis of the demographic data resulting from the survey corroborates existing research data (Adler, 1984a; ECA, 1994) with respect to current representation of women in expatriate management. It also presents some positive indicators for women to obtain greater representation in the future. Half of the organizations surveyed expected to increase the number of women in international management in the next five years. Likewise, the locations of expatriate assignments appear to offer fewer possibilities for blanket refusal of women in expatriate positions. Another positive sign is the extent of expatriation to first world countries where one would expect there

Table 1. Human Resource Managers' Perceptions of the Key Barriers to Women Obtaining Expatriate Assignments

Question	Managerial	Technical
Few women are qualified for assignments	39.0%	28.0%
Few women with enough experience	36.6%	26.8%
Family obligations	30.5%	20.7%
Dual career couple obstacles	25.6%	20.7%
Host country employees and clients will not work with a woman manager	15.9%	9.8%
Women are not interested in a foreign assignment	13.4%	8.5%
Physical safety and social concerns	3.7%	4.9%

to be very little possibility of women encountering prejudice. The figures relating to domestic status whilst on assignment show a surprisingly high number of women accompanied whilst on assignment, thus questioning the assumption that family ties will create insurmountable obstacles for women. On the negative side, the age range for expatriation is likely to cause problems for any woman who either has a family or wishes to start one, unless there is a high level of organizational support. It should also be remembered that the figures for representation are very low and whilst half of the organizations surveyed stated that they felt the numbers of women would increase, there was no estimation as to the amount of the increase.

Interview Results

The survey responses relating to perceptions of barriers for women expatriates were explored in more detail in semi-structured interviews with six women who had had expatriate experience. In addition, interviews were held with international HR directors from nine UK-based international organizations.

Qualifications and Experience

Linked in with the results concerning lack of experience and qualifications were more general findings from the interviews with international HR directors which pointed to the existence of strong functional ladders within organizations, where initial career choice could have extensive repercussions in terms of overall career development. Concerns could be seen for women in this respect given extensive research into occupational segregation at the domestic level (Doeringer & Piore, 1971; Reich et al., 1973; Barron & Norris, 1976; Joseph, 1983). The need for concern was also evident in responses from several of the women expatriates, who identified a significant lack of career planning on their part. There was also a perceived lack of strategic thinking about the likely nature of work involved in certain career options, which could lead to the women concerned being perceived as less interested in their particular role.

Personal Concerns

In relation to perceived barriers for women as a result of family/dual-career couple considerations, data from interviews with HR directors revealed a general assumption that taking on an international assignment would be more difficult for a woman with a spouse or dependents than for a man, although there was a recognition of the increasing problems faced by men in dual-career partnerships. However, there was no evidence to suggest that personal circumstances presented insurmountable barriers to women, and three of the organizations had provided flexible expatriation packages for women: for instance, one organization had amended the normal expatriate package to allow for a single mother's nanny to go as the "accompanying spouse."

The degree to which the organization is prepared to support and facilitate domestic issues whilst managers are on international assignments did appear to be a significant factor in determining whether a foreign assignment would be feasible for women expatriates. One of the women stressed that *perceptions* as to the willingness of the organization to be flexible with respect to expatriate arrangements were very important factors in determining the feasibility of undertaking an assignment. She commented that although the company might well be supportive to alternative arrangements for women going abroad, the standard package was geared to a male expatriate with a wife and children. She believed that, as a consequence, most women would not think to query whether arrangements could be made, but would just count themselves out as available.

Foreigners' Prejudice

With respect to problems of acceptance from host country nationals, there appeared to be a difference in viewpoint between organizational HR directors and the women expatriates. Several of the international HR directors felt that it would not be possible to send a female expatriate to the Muslim world, although they were not specific as to the region involved.

Evidence from one of the organizations and from several of the women expatriates, however, questioned the degree to which females face prejudice from foreigners. The international HR director from an NGO gave an example of a senior posting for a woman to work with Afghan refugees in Pakistan. The Afghan staff expressed that a woman could not come in and manage the program. The NGO, however, appointed a woman who managed perfectly well. She did come across tensions, but ultimately, but the local staff dealt with it by treating her as a notional man and as long as she obeyed tradition by keeping her head covered, etc., she was accepted and exploded the myth completely.

None of the women revealed any particular problems with prejudice from foreigners, stating that they had found their professional status to be an essential feature of acceptance with clients; however, acceptance from other expatriates was seen to be more problematic. The women in general considered that they would be accepted as expatriates in the majority of countries, with the exception of the Middle East. Two of the women had encountered more problems with acceptance from existing expatriates. This resistance to acceptance of women in international management positions did not merely arise from actual expatriates, but also from their spouses, who viewed unaccompanied women as a threat.

Women's Lack of Interest

In general, the interview transcripts from both the international HR directors and the individual women expatriates, did not reveal any significant acknowledgment of the fact that women were less interested in international assignments than men. However, the previous comments regarding lack of career planning on the part of individual women could be seen to be problematic. International manager selection is embedded within overall career processes within organizations, and is therefore strongly affected by assessments of commitment and potential which commence at the time an employee starts work and are continually build up throughout that person's organizational career.

The women in general considered that they would be accepted as expatriates in the majority of countries, with the exception of the Middle East.

The Role of International Management Selection Systems in Perpetuating Minimal Participation Rates for Women

Both survey responses and evidence from interviews with IHR directors, confirmed the embedded nature of selection for international manager assignments. Sixty-three percent of respondents to the survey saw management development as one of the main reasons for sending managerial staff on expatriate assignments. Fifty-seven percent of organizations also said that international assignments were important for progression to senior management. Managerial assignments were linked to overall career development in every organization with the exception of the NGO. The old image of the "career expatriate" who would spend the majority of his working life overseas, was seen by all respondents to be rapidly diminishing and only relevant for technical expatriate assignments. There was, however, a broader concept of a truly international manager who would be able to work wherever corporate headquarters or other strategically important centres were located.

The interview transcripts of eight out of nine IHR directors confirmed the embeddedness of selection for international management assignments within overall assessment of potential at the organization level. As a general rule, individuals needed to pass two hurdles to qualify for assignments. First, they needed to be judged as having "high potential," usually through the formal process of yearly

Hilary Harris

appraisals. This process identified them as potential international manager material.

The influence of informal processes was evident in many of the directors' responses concerning selection processes. These included the use of informal networks by either decision-makers or potential candidates in order to secure their desired outcomes. One IHR director commented that (line) managers generally had a too clear idea of the person they wanted. He felt that was the main weakness with a networking type of approach because if a manager knows of, for instance, two people who might do the job well, he or she won't stop to think "Now, is there anybody else?"

The literature notes that, in organizations in which the predominant profile of those in power is male, women may often by excluded from such networks (Marshall, 1984; Townley, 1989; Adler, 1993a; Rubin, 1997). Several of the IHR directors also echoed the importance of reputation in determining outcomes for international manager selection. For them, what was written in the performance appraisal was less important than general reputation.

The results of the interviews with IHR directors revealed the extent to which their organizations operated, i.e., if they had an open or closed selection system for international management assignments (Figure 1). An "open" system is one in which all vacancies are advertised and anyone with appropriate qualifications and experience can apply, and candidates are interviewed with greater or lesser degrees of formalized testing. Selection decisions are taken by consensus amongst selectors. In contrast, a "closed" system is one in which selectors at corporate headquarters nominate "suitable" candidates to line managers, who in turn have the option of accepting or rejecting them. In this situation, there may be only one manager involved in the selection process at the head office. The candidate is only informed after agreement about acceptability has been reached between head office personnel and the line manager. The interview

---

Figure 1. Plotting of Organisations onto the Open/Closed Continuum of International Management Selection Systems

Open   Closed
(_____)
C   B   A/D/E/F/G/H/I

A – I = Nine case study organisations

---

in this process consists of a negotiation about the terms and conditions of the assignment.

A further variation in selection systems was derived from both literature on discrimination in selection and expatriate management, and was confirmed during the interviews with IHR directors. There was a difference between a "formal" and an "informal" process. Within a "formal" system, selection criteria are made explicit, with objective debate amongst selectors as to which candidate more closely matches the criteria. An "informal" system consists of selecting using subjective and often unstated criteria for assessment with minimal systematic evaluation. Four possible variations of selection systems were therefore identified as being *open/formal, closed/formal, open/formal and closed/informal* (Table 2).

The implications of these variations in selection systems for international assignments in relation to women's participation are discussed. Following this typology, it was argued that an *open/formal* system would see greater clarity and consistency in international manager selection with a greater link to formal criteria. This system was seen to provide the greatest opportunities for women to be selected for international manager positions. A *closed/formal* system was seen to be similar to an *open/formal* system. However, the lack of personal contact with the candidate and the fact that the field of potential applicants is determined by the selector(s) with the attendant risk of omission of suitable candidates, may enable the use of individual preferences by selectors in terms of nominating individuals. An *open/informal* system would decrease clarity and consistency and linkage with formal criteria and was therefore seen to provide fewer opportunities

Table 2. Typology of International Manager Selection Systems

	Formal	Informal
Open	• Clearly defined criteria • Clearly defined measures • Training for selectors • Open advertising of vacancy (Internal/External) • Panel discussions	• Less defined criteria • Less defined measures • Limited training for selectors • No panel discussions • Open advertising of vacancy • Recommendations
Closed	• Clearly defined criteria • Clearly defined measures • Training for selectors • Panel discussions • Nominations only (networking/reputation)	• Selectors' individual preferences determine criteria and measures • No Panel discussions • Nominations only (networking/reputation)

Hilary Harris

for women to enter international management positions since selection decisions would be more subjective. A *closed/informal* system was seen to be the worst situation for equality of opportunity in this area, mixing as it does, the potential for subjectivity on the part of the selectors and lack of access on the part of potential candidates.

Case Study Findings

Organizations A, B, and C were picked for case study research as they represented the closed, middle, and open ends of the continuum. Organization A was in the petrochemicals sector, Organization B was in the airline industry, and Organization C was in the not-for-profit sector. A detailed analysis of the nature of selection systems for international assignments within the three organizations enabled them to be plotted on the typology of international management selection systems.

A closed/informal system was seen to be the worst situation for equality of opportunity in this area . . .

The analysis of features of the selection process at Organization A placed the organization at the *closed* end of the *open/closed* continuum. The selection process consisted of shortlisting by managers of existing employees, who remained unaware of this until asked whether or not they wished to accept the assignment. In addition, in order to be shortlisted, candidates for developmental international assignments must already have been identified as "high potential." The case study also revealed the extensive use of informal practices at both the stage of identification of high potential and the stage of selection for international assignments. Official organizational systems were seen to be subsumed by *informal* practices, including networking and informal debates about merit.

In contrast, Organization C was seen to have an *open* system of selection for international assignments. All international assignments were advertised internally *and* externally. In addition, the lack of integration of the overseas division with the UK-based head office career structure meant that assessment of suitability/acceptability is not embedded within concepts of effectiveness at home country organization level. It was acknowledged, however, that for internal candidates, details from annual performance appraisals are examined at the time of the shortlisting process. However, the ability to apply for international appointments is not subject to prior identification of high potential and the entire staff is free to apply if they feel they meet the *suitability* requirements.

The case study results from Organization C also revealed a high degree of conformity to official formal processes in most appointments. Shortcuts to the official process, were however, occasionally sanctioned in the case of emergency postings, due to the urgency of assignments. In general, there was strong adherence to panel interviews, with clear determination of person specifications and open debate about the type of behaviors and values required of candidates, coupled with the uniform use of a written test of the candidate's strategic planning abilities. It was seen therefore, that Organization C fell within the *open/formal* quadrant on the Typology of International Management Selection Systems.

Positioning Organization B on the Typology was far more complex. Organization B had initially been plotted between the *open* and *closed* ends of the continuum. Technically, selection for international assignments was *closed*, in that, all applicants have to be currently employed by the organization and in many cases, must already have been identified as being "high potential." However, the organization did not exhibit all the features of a truly *closed* system, as all international assignment vacancies are advertised internally and any employee with the relevant qualifications and experience can apply. The parallel process of contacting people who had attended the international development centers did exhibit features of a *closed* system again, but all applicants, whether contacted or not, still had to go through an open selection procedure. In terms of degree of *formality/informality*, there again appeared a fairly complicated picture. The case study revealed a well-established formal system administered by the HR function, but highlighted widespread variations in practice, and lack of adherence to HR rulings by line managers. This was apparent both within the process itself and the setting and measuring of criteria.

It was argued that Organization B therefore fell across the quadrants on the Typology. The description of the system was seen to fall almost equally between the *open* and *closed* quadrant, but in terms of degree of formality, it was argued that it fell more into the *informal* quadrant. This positioning was seen to indicate a very hybrid system in which there were real tensions between espoused formal policy and current organizational practice.

A composite picture of the positioning of the three organizations on the Typology of International Manager Selection Systems can be seen in Figure 2.

Repertory Grid Findings
The degree to which differences in selection processes resulted in the posited outcomes with respect to the use of selectors' individual preferences in selection decision making was explored via the Repertory

Hilary Harris

Figure 2. Positioning of Case Study Organizations on Typology of International Management Selection Systems

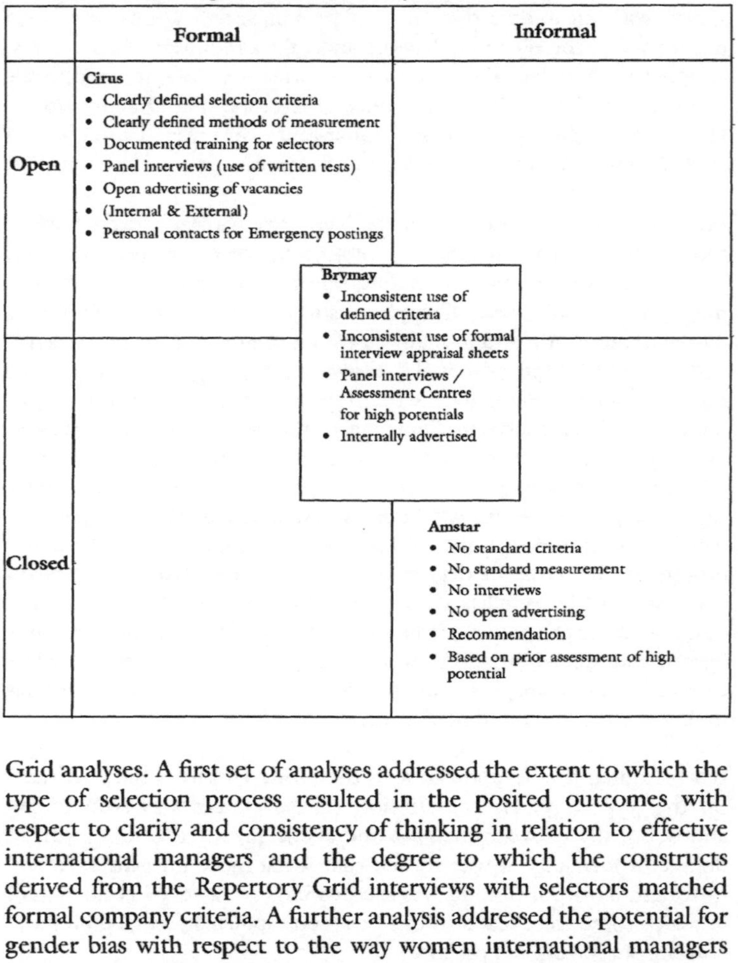

	Formal	Informal
Open	**Cirus** • Clearly defined selection criteria • Clearly defined methods of measurement • Documented training for selectors • Panel interviews (use of written tests) • Open advertising of vacancies • (Internal & External) • Personal contacts for Emergency postings	
	Brymay • Inconsistent use of defined criteria • Inconsistent use of formal interview appraisal sheets • Panel interviews / Assessment Centres for high potentials • Internally advertised	
Closed		**Amstar** • No standard criteria • No standard measurement • No interviews • No open advertising • Recommendation • Based on prior assessment of high potential

Grid analyses. A first set of analyses addressed the extent to which the type of selection process resulted in the posited outcomes with respect to clarity and consistency of thinking in relation to effective international managers and the degree to which the constructs derived from the Repertory Grid interviews with selectors matched formal company criteria. A further analysis addressed the potential for gender bias with respect to the way women international managers were viewed within the Repertory Grid responses and the degree to which the constructs used were masculine or feminine typed. For this last part, Schein's Descriptive Index (SDI) (1973, 1975) was used, as previously described in the Methodology section.

The results from the repertory grid interviews with selectors in each of the organizations supported the arguments posited for the outcomes of the various typologies. Under an *open/formal* system, there was evidence of more consistency and clarity in thinking in relation

Why Are Women Not Selected for International Management Assignments?

to the characteristics of effective international managers. In addition, in Organization C, the selectors had clear views of the women international managers included on the grids and were therefore less likely to be picking clones of male managers when selecting. None of the grids showed any negative thinking about the managers being female. The position of the managers on the grid was determined exclusively by their indicators of performance. In addition, the SDI analysis of the constructs elicited through the grid interviews showed a tendency towards a neutral/feminine gender-typing, thus, suggesting that equal opportunity considerations are used by selectors in the decision-making process.

In contrast, the *closed/informal* selection system in operation in Organization A did not force selectors to question their assumptions, thereby resulting in a marked lack of consistency and clarity in selecting criteria for effective international managers with little linkage with formal criteria. The majority of selectors were also not clear in their thinking about the female managers included in the cognitive maps. Although the female managers were positioned on the cognitive maps in relation to their performance ratings, in general, they were positioned closer to the center of the maps, which indicates that they were seen to be less distinctive than the male managers. In addition, the SDI analysis for the organization displayed a masculine-typed bias.

Under an open/formal system, there was evidence of more consistency and clarity in thinking in relation to the characteristics of effective international managers.

The picture at Organization B again provided tentative, but limited support for the posited relationship between *closed/formal* and *open/informal* systems and the number of women entering international management positions. In terms of consistency and clarity of thinking in relation to characteristics of successful international managers and link with formal criteria, the organization was positioned between the two extremes of A and C. The number of women selected for inclusion on the grids and their general lack of distinctiveness for the selectors reflected the situation in Organization A, where thinking about women managers was generally less clear than in Organization C. It was argued that this situation would give rise to cloning of existing male international managers. The SDI results for Organization B, however, show a more equal split between masculine and neutral typed constructs, which might again reflect it's positioning at the center of the Typology of International Management Selection Systems.

It is argued that the difference in the numbers of women in international management positions within the three case study organizations; A, B, and C (with Organization A having less than 5%

Hilary Harris

representation; Organization B a representation of 25%, and Organization C a representation of 45%), further support the arguments derived from the Typology of International Management Selection systems as presented in this article.

RECOMMENDATIONS

Findings from the research raise some fundamental issues for organizations and academics. Amongst the most critical are the following:

- Evidence that international assignment experience being a prerequisite for progression to senior management makes the minimal representation of women a fundamental equality issue for any organization operating in a global arena. Equally, from a business perspective, failure to utilize and develop a significant and growing proportion of their human resources in an increasingly knowledge-based global economy will result in organizations losing a vital component of competitive advantage.
- Evidence of widespread use of closed/informal systems for selection to international management assignments raises serious concerns with regard to ensuring objective and unbiased decision making in this process. Organizations need to:

  - Become more strategic in their planning for international assignments in order to prevent ad-hoc and informal placements that may replicate an existing expatriate profile and prevent the adoption of alternative approaches.
  - Adopt a sophisticated approach to the determination of criteria for effective international managers. Competencies should be developed and debated in as wide and diverse a forum as possible.
  - Monitor the selection processes for international management assignments to ensure that access is not unfairly restricted to specific sections of employees. This includes auditing career development systems leading up to international assignments for potential unintended bias.
  - Run selection skills training for all employees involved in the selection for international assignments. This training should include awareness raising of the advantages of using diverse groups of employees on international assignments and challenge existing stereotypes relating to women and other non-traditional groups.

- Provide full support for alternative arrangements for the domestic aspect of international assignments that might influence a woman's perceptions of accessibility.

CONCLUSION AND SUGGESTIONS FOR FUTURE RESEARCH

This article reports the results of a multi-stage study of women in international management in UK-based international organizations. The research confirmed the continuing minimal participation rates of women in international assignments. It reported, however, that prejudice of host country nationals was not seen to be a critical barrier to entry. The most critical barriers were assumptions about women's lack of qualifications and experience, and family obligations.

A key finding from the study was the identification of home country international management selection processes as a significant determinant of the numbers of women entering international management positions. This finding supports existing research into discrimination in selection in domestic environments. The typology of international management selection systems developed, as a result of the study, therefore represents a first step in developing a theoretical approach to this unexplored area of women in international management research.

It is acknowledged that it is not possible to generalize from an exploratory case study research methodology. However, the subtle nature of informal organizational processes calls for an in-depth qualitative research approach. Further research encompassing a wider range of organizations in both the private and public sectors would enable a more comprehensive understanding of the dynamics of the selection process for international assignments and the impact of this on the numbers of women being selected for such positions.●

REFERENCES

Adler, N. (1984a). Women in international management: Where ae they? California Management Review, 26(4), 78–89

Adler, N. (1984b). Women do not want international careers: And other myths about international management. Organizational Dynamics, 13(2), 66–79.

Adler, N. (1984c). Expecting international success: Female managers overseas. Columbia Journal of World Business, 19(3), 79–85.

Adler, N. (1986). Do MBAs want international careers? International Journal of Intercultural Relations, 10(3), 277–300.

Adler, N. (1987). Pacific basin managers: A Gaijin, not a woman. Human Resource Management, 26(2), 169–192.

Hilary Harris

Adler, N.J., & Bartholomew, S. (1992). Managing globally competent people. Academy of Management Executive, 6, 52–64.

Adler, N.J. (1993a). Women managers in a global economy. HR Magazine, 38, 52–55.

Adler, N.J. (1993b). Competitive frontiers: Women managers in the triad. International Studies of Management and Organization, 23, 3–23.

Alimo-Metcalfe, B. (1993). Women in management: Organizational socialization and assessment practices that prevent career advancement. International Journal of Selection and Assessment, 1(2), 68–83.

Alimo-Metcalfe, B. (1995). An investigation of female and male constructs of leadership and empowerment. Women in Management Review, 10(2), 3–8.

Barham, K., & Devine, M. (1991). The quest for the international manager: A survey of global human resource strategies. London, UK: Ashridge Management Guide/Economist Intelligence Unit.

Barron, K.D., & Norris, G.M. (1976). Sexual divisions and the dual labour market. In D. Barker & S. Allen (Eds.), Dependence and exploitation in work and marriage. London, UK: Longman.

Bartlett, C., & Ghoshal, S. (1989). Managing across borders. London, UK: Hutchinson Business Books.

Bielby, W., & Bielby, D. (1992). I will follow him: Family ties, gender-role beliefs, and resistance to relocate for a better job. American Journal of Sociology, 97(5), 1241–1267.

Birchall, D., Hee, T., & Gay, K. (1996, January). Competences for international managers. Singapore Institute of Management, 1–13.

Black, J., Mendenhall, M., & Oddou, G. (1991). Toward a comprehensive model of international adjustment: An integration of multiple theoretical perspectives. Academy of Management Review, 16(2), 291–317.

Black, J.S., & Stephens, G.K. (1989). The influence of the spouse on American expatriate adjustment in Pacific Rim overseas assignments. Journal of Management, 15, 529–544.

Brett, J.M., Stroh, L.K., & Reilly, A.H. (1992). What is it like being a dual-career manager in the 1990s? In S. Zedeck (Ed.), Work and family. San Francisco, CA: Jossey-Bass.

Brewer, M.B., Dull, V., & Lui, L. (1981). Perceptions of the elderly: Stereotypes as prototypes. Journal of Personality and Social Psychology, 41, 656–670.

Brewster, C. (1991). The management of expatriates. London, UK: Kogan Page.

Caligiuri, P.M., & Cascio, W.F. (1998). Can we send her there? Maximizing the success of western women on global assignments. Journal of World Business, 33(4), 394–416.

Caligiuri, P.M., Joshi, A., & Lazarova, M. (1999). Factors influencing the adjustment of women on global assignments. The International Journal of Human Resource Management, 10(2), 163–179.

Caligiuri, P.M., & Tung, R.L. (1998). Are masculine cultures female friendly? Male and female expatriates success in countries differing in work value orientations. In G. Hofstede (Chair), Masculinity/femininity as a cultural dimension. Paper presented at the International Congress of the International Association for Cross-Cultural Psychology. Bellingham, WA: The Silver Jubilee Congress.

Caproni, P.J., Lenway, S.A., & Murtha, T.P. (1992). Multinational minds sets: Sense making capabilities as strategic resources in multinational firms. Working Paper #679, Division of Research, School of Business Administration, The University of Michigan.

Copeland, L., & Griggs, L. (1985). Going international. New York: Random House.

Coulson-Thomas, C. (1992). Creating the global manager. Maidenhead, UK: McGraw-Hill.

Employment Conditions Abroad. (1994). Managing Mobility.

Doeringer, P.B., & Piore, M.J. (1971). Internal labor markets and manpower analysis. Lexington, MA: Heath.

Florkowski, G.W., & Fogel, D.S. (1995). Perceived host ethnocentrism as a determinant of expatriate adjustment and organizational commitment. Paper presented at the National Academy of Management Meeting, Vancouver, Canada.

Fondas, N. (1997). Feminization unveiled: Management qualities in contemporary writings. Academy of Management Review, 22(1), 257–282.

Forster, N. (1992, December). International managers and mobile families: The professional and personal dynamics of trans-national career pathing and job mobility in the 1990s. International Journal of Human Resource Management, 3(3).

Why Are Women Not Selected for International Management Assignments?

Futoran, G.C., & Wyer, R.S. (1986). The effects of traits and gender stereotypes on occupational suitability judgments and the recall of judgment-relevant information. Journal of Experimental Social Psychology, 22, 475–503.

Galbraith, J.R. (1987). Organization design. In J. Lorsch (Ed.), Handbook of organization behavior (pp. 343–357). Englewood Cliffs, NJ: Prentice-Hall.

Ghoshal, S. (1987). Global strategy: An organizing framework. Strategic Management Journal, 8, 425–440.

Gupta, N., & Jenkins, G. (1985). Dual-career couples: Stress, stressors, strains and strategies. In T. Beehr & R. Bhagat (Eds.), Human stress and cognition in organizations: An integrated perspective. New York: Wiley.

Harris, H. (1998). Women in international management: The times they are changing? International Review of Women and Leadership, 4(2), 6–14.

Harris, H. (1999). Women in international management. In C. Brewster & H. Harris (Eds.), International HRM: Contemporary issues in Europe. London, UK: Routledge.

Harvey, M. (1995). The impact of dual-career families on international relocations. Human Resources Management Review, 5(3), 223–244.

Harvey, M. (1996a). The selection of managers for foreign assignments: A planning perspective. Columbia Journal of World Business, 31(4), 102–118.

Harvey, M. (1996b). Addressing the dual-career expatriation dilemma in International relocation. Human Resource Planning, 19(4), 18–40.

Harvey, M. (1997). Dual-career expatriates: Expectations, adjustment and satisfaction with international relocation. Journal of International Business Studies, 28(3), 627–657.

Harvey, M. (1998). Dual-career couples during international relocation: The trailing spouse. International Journal of Human Resource Management, 9(2), 309–322.

Heilman, M. (1983). Sex bias in work settings: The lack of fit model. Research in organizational behavior, 5, 269–298.

Higgins, C., & Duxbury, L. (1992). Work-family conflict: A comparison of dual-career and traditional-career men. Journal of Organizational Behavior, 13, 339–356.

Jelinek, M., & Adler, N.J. (1988). Women, world class managers for global competition. Academy of Management Executive, 2, 11–19.

Jewson, N., & Mason, D. (1986). Modes of discrimination in the recruitment process: Formalization, fairness and efficiency. Sociology, 20(1), 43–63.

Joseph, G. (1983). Women at work: The British experience. London, UK: Philip Alan.

Karambayya, R., & Reilly, A. (1992). Dual-career couples: Attitudes and actions in restructuring work for family. Journal of Organizational Behavior, 13, 585–601.

Kobrin, S.J. (1994). Is there a relationship between a geocentric mind-set and multinational strategy? Journal of International Business Studies, Third Quarter, 493–511.

Kunda, Z., & Thagard, P.F. (1996). Forming impressions from stereotypes, traits and behaviors: A parallel-constraint-satisfaction theory. Psychological Review, 103, 284–308.

Labour Force Survey. (1989, 1995). London, UK: HMSO.

Lewis, S., & Cooper, G. (1988). Stress in dual earner families. In B. Gutek, A. Stromberg & L. Larwood (Eds.), Women and work: An annual review, vol. 3. Newbury Park, CA: Sage.

Lowe, K., Downes, M., & Kroek, K. (1999). The impact of gender and location on the willingness to accept overseas assignments. International Journal of Human Resource Management, 10(2), 223–234.

McDonald, G.M. (1993). ET go home?: The successful management of expatriate transfers. Journal of Managerial Psychology, 8(2), 18–29.

Marshall, J. (1984). Women managers: Travelers in a male world. London, UK: Wiley.

Mendenhall, M., & Oddou, G. (1985). The dimensions of expatriate acculturation: A review. Academy of Management Review, 10, 39–47.

Organization Resources Counselors Inc (ORC). (1997). Worldwide survey of international assignment policies and practices. European Edition.

Organization Resources Counselors Inc (ORC). (1998). 1998 North American survey of international assignment policies and practices.

Paddock, J.R., & Schwartz, K.M. (1986). Rituals for dual career couples. Psycotherapy, 23(3), 453–459.

Perry, E.L., Davis-Blake, A., & Kulik, C. (1994). Explaining gender-based selection decisions:

A synthesis of contextual and cognitive approaches. Academy of Management Review, 19(4), 786–820.

Porter, M.E. (1986). Changing patterns of international competition. California Management Review, 28(2), 9–40.

Prahalad, C.K., & Doz, Y. (1987). The multinational mission: Balancing local demands and global vision. New York, NY: Free Press.

Punnett, B.J., Crocker, O., & Stevens, M. (1992). The challenge for women expatriates and spouses: Some empirical evidence. International Journal of Human Resource Management, 13(3), 585–592.

Rapoport, R., & Rapoport, R.N. (1971). Dual career families. London, UK: Penguin Books.

Rapoport, R, & Rapoport, R.N. (1976). Dual career families re-examined. London, UK: Roberstson.

Reich, M., Gordon, D., & Edwards, R. (1973). A theory of labour market segmentation. American Economics Review, 63(2), 359–365.

Reynolds, C., & Bennett, R. (1991). The career couple challenge. Personnel Journal, March.

Rosener, J. (1990, Nov/Dec). Ways women lead. Harvard Business Review, 68(6), 119–125.

Rubin, J. (1997). Gender, equality and the culture of organizational assessment. Gender, Work and Organization, Special Issue.

Sandqvist, K. (1992). Sweden's sex-role scheme and commitment to gender equality. In S. Lewis, D. Izraeli, & H. Hootsman (Eds.), Dual earner families: International Perspectives. London, UK: Sage.

Scase, R., & Goffee, R. (1989). Women in management: Towards a research agenda. In Third Annual Meeting of British Academy of Management.

Schein, V.E. (1973). The relationship between sex role stereotypes and requisite management characteristics. Journal of Applied Psychology, 57, 95–100.

Schein, V.E. (1975). Relationships between sex role stereotypes and requisite management characteristics among female managers. Journal of Applied Psychology, 60(3), 340–344.

Sekaran, U. (1986). Dual-career families: Contemporary organizational and counseling issues. San Francisco, CA: Jossey-Bass.

Sharma, S. (1990). Psychology of women in management: A distinct feminine leadership. Equal Opportunities International, 9(2), 13–18.

Slater, P. (1972). Notes on Ingrid and grid analysis package. University of Manchester Regional Computing Centre, Manchester, UK.

Smith, J.M. (1986, Autumn). An introduction to repertory grids—Part Two: Interpretation of results. Graduate Management Research.

Stone, R. (1991). Expatriate selection and failure. Human Resource Planning, 41(1), 9–18.

Swaak, R. (1995, Jan–Feb). Today's expatriate family: Dual-career and other obstacles. Compensation and Benefits Review, 21–26.

Taylor, S., & Napier, N. (1996). Working in Japan: Lessons from women expatriates. Sloan Management Review, Spring, 76–84.

Torbiorn, I. (1982). Living abroad: Personal adjustment and personnel policy in the overseas setting. New York: Wiley.

Townley, B. (1989). Selection of appraisal: Reconstituting "social relations"? In J. Storey (Ed.), New perspectives on human resource management. London: Routledge.

Tung, R. (1981). Selection and training of personnel for overseas assignments. Columbia Journal, 23, 129–143.

Tung, R. (1982). Selection and training procedures of US, European and Japanese multinationals. Human Resource Management, 23, 129–143.

Tung, R.L. (1997). Canadian expatriates in Asia-Pacific: An analysis of their attitude toward and experience in international assignments. Paper presented at the meeting of the Society for Industrial and Organizational Psychology, St Louis, MO.

Webb, J. (1991). The gender relations of assessment. In J. Firth-Cozens & M. West (Eds.), Women at work: Psychological and organizational perspectives. Milton Keynes, UK: Open University Press.

Westwood, R.I., & Leung, S.M. (1994). The female expatriate manager experience: Coping with gender and culture. International Studies of Management and Organization, 24, 64–85.

Wiersma, U. (1994). A taxonomy of behavioral strategies for coping with work-home conflict. Human Relations, 47(2), 211–221.

Williams, K, & Alliger, G. (1994). Role stressors, mood spillover, and perceptions of work-family conflict in employed parents. Academy of Management Journal. 37(4), 837–868.

Wills, S., & Barham, K. (1994). Being an international manager. European Management Journal, 12(1), 49–58.

Vinnicombe, S. (1987). What exactly are the differences in male and female working styles? Women in Management Review, 3(1), 13–22.

[5]

Expatriates and the impact of cross-cultural training

Nick Forster, *University of Western Australia*

The development of effective international HR strategies is a major determinant of success in international business. The quality of management in companies is also extremely important in the international arena. Previous research on expatriate management indicates that any kind of under performance on international assignments can be extremely costly for employees in career terms. Potentially, they can be fatal to companies if they are entering a foreign market for the first time. It has also been suggested that companies with foreign operations need to employ sophisticated and rigorous pre-move policies in the areas of:

- selection procedures for international assignments – including, for example personality and psychometric testing
- language and cross-cultural training for both employees and their dependants

Research, over the last 20 years, has also indicated that many companies have failed to pay sufficient attention to both the screening, selection and training of potential expatriate staff and the non-technical skills that they should possess (*see* Harvey, 1998; Arthur and Bennet, 1995; Brislin and Yoshida, 1994; Business International Corporation, 1992; Barham and Devine, 1990; Black and Mendenhall, 1990; Tung, 1981, 1982, 1987, 1988a, 1988b; Schwind, 1985; Adler, 1981).

One of the main reasons put forward for a purported high failure rate among expatriate employees are the 'inadequate' selection criteria used by many multinational corporations (Dumaine, 1995; Black and Mendenhall, 1990; Adler, 1986). Consequently, many commentators have suggested a variety of criteria for improving selection. They imply that organisations who employ all, or most, of these will be more successful in selecting people with 'the right stuff' for international assignments than those that choose not to. These selection criteria include the employee's technical skills, empathy, managerial skills, sense of mission, political awareness, language skills, cultural sensitivity, ability to work with local nationals, good judgement, creativity, responsibility, alertness, initiative, self-confidence and willingness to change. (Baliga and Baker, 1985). Gertsen (1992), in a review of the literature on inter-cultural competence, found that researchers have put forward a whole range of different personality traits that the international employee 'should' possess in order to successfully complete a foreign assignment. These include empathy, openness, flexibility, tolerance, self-confidence, optimism, independence, good communication skills, initiative and intelligence. Many researchers, in the 1980s and 1990s, have also suggested that the family of the candidate should be considered and included in the selection process (*eg* Tung, 1982, 1987; Adler, 1986; Black and Mendenhall, 1989; Harvey, 1998; Forster, 2000).

Culture has a highly pervasive influence on the behaviour of individuals. A person's perceptions, attitudes, motivations, values, learning experiences and personality are all, to a very large extent, shaped by culture. The importance of culture lies in the fact that it provides the body of knowledge and techniques that enable us to act, both physically and socially, in the world and provides us with world views that enable us to make sense of ourselves and the people around us. We do not usually think consciously about our culture, unless we perceive it to be threatened by some external force or we are put in a situation where we are in a cultural minority. In other words our cultures operate largely at an unconscious level.

Culture includes many things, such as facial expressions, use of personal space, posture, gestures, personal appearance, etiquette, body contact and appropriate conduct in dealing with men and women. Understanding and respecting these differences are essential if we are to adapt to working and living in another culture. For example, the Chinese traditionally do not show emotion because the idea of 'saving face' is deeply rooted in their culture. For the Chinese, displaying emotion violates face-saving norms by disrupting harmony and causing conflict. In the West, a smile is usually a sign of happiness or friendly affirmation; in Japan, this can also be used to avoid answering a question or to mask an emotion. Sitting with crossed knees in the West is socially acceptable; in many Arabic cultures it is deeply offensive as it shows the sole of your foot. In Vietnam, men often express friendship by touching each other during conversations; in the UK, America or Australia this would be considered inappropriate. In many Muslim countries, touching the head is deeply offensive whereas touching the shoulders is seen as a sign of brotherhood. In Korea, young people are socially forbidden from touching the shoulders of their elders.

What we think and how we choose to act is a result of what we have been taught in our culture. Hence, a business executive who has been highly successful in one culture may find it difficult, if not impossible, to function in another culture, unless s/he is aware of the significance of cultural differences. Another important element of culture is that it takes years and years to learn and internalise. Yet, when it comes to international assignments, we expect expatriate staff to engage in business relationships with people from other cultures and learn their culturally prescribed ways of doing business in a matter of weeks, if not days. Goodman (1990: 41) has also pointed to another significant element of culture :

> In many respects, one can think of culture as being analogous to an iceberg. As with an iceberg, there is the part of the culture that is clearly in sight and there is a larger part of culture (the most dangerous) that is submerged, out of sight, below the waterline, waiting to destroy any business venture if people are unaware of its hidden dangers.

Cultural items 'above the waterline' include language, food, festivals, clothing and dress, architecture and art. Those 'below the waterline' are much more numerous and include business ethics, values, morality, facial and body language, male/female relationships, family fidelty, learning styles, work motivation and employee loyalty. Hence, anyone embarking on an international assignment has to be knowledgeable about the cultural aspects of the environment they are moving to.

This brief account indicates that the ability to adapt to new cultures is one of the most important elements of a successful international assignment. This is where cross-cultural training can play such an important role. The main purpose of these training programs is to introduce staff to the importance of culture and to sensitise them to cultural differences. They should also make them aware of the inevitable psychological stresses that occur when people adapt to living and working in new cultures. However, they can never be a 'cure-all'. As with all training programs, their success or otherwise rests on the willingness of the participants to learn new skills and aptitudes. In the next section, we look at the role of cross-cultural briefings during international assignments.

Nick Forster, University of Western Australia

The role of cross-cultural training in international assignments

Many researchers have stressed the importance of cultural empathy in training courses for expatriates (*eg* Tung, 1981; Brislin, 1981, Brislin *et al*, 1986; Bochner, 1982; Mendenhall and Oddou, 1986; Smith and Still, 1997; Forster, 2000). Training in cultural empathy can be broadly described as any procedure intended to increase an individual's ability to cope and work in a foreign environment. However, other studies have reported that many companies either do not provide formal cross-cultural training to their expatriates and spouses/families or only on a very selective basis (Baliga and Baker, 1985: Tung, 1988a; Black and Mendenhall, 1990; Scullion, 1994; Brewster and Pickard, 1994; Forster, 2000). The reasons given by organisations for this lack of cross-cultural training are: a lack of proven effectiveness (Baker and Ivancevich, 1971; Tung, 1981; Mendenhall and Oddou, 1985 and Schwind, 1986), time constraints reported by Tung (1982) and Gertsen (1990) and cost, reported by Gertsen (*ibid*).

Tung has classified cross-cultural training programs into six categories depending on, 'the rigour with which the programme seeks to impart knowledge and understanding of a foreign country' (1982: 65). These should include:

- factual information about geography, climate, housing and schools
- cultural orientation, providing information about the cultural institutions and value systems of the new country
- cultural assimilation training, consisting of brief episodes describing intercultural encounters
- language training
- sensitivity training to develop attitudinal flexibility
- field experience, where candidates can undergo some of the emotional stress of living and working with people from different cultures.

A survey in the early 1980s, of American MNCs, found that only 25 out of 80 companies had any formalised pre-departure training for overseas candidates (Tung, 1982). Tung also found that this training consisted mainly of environmental briefings, some cultural orientation and limited language training. In the same study, 20 out of 29 European companies reported using pre-departure training programs. These consisted largely of short environmental briefings, some cultural orientation, some language training and some field experience. In contrast, over half of the 35 Japanese companies used detailed pre-departure training programmes mainly covering environmental briefings and language training (Tung, *ibid*).

Another survey by Earley (*op cit*) showed that some participants received no training, some received documentary training, some received interpersonal training and others received a combination of documentary and interpersonal training. A more recent survey reported that formal cross-cultural training courses are used by about half of European companies (Brewster and Pickard, 1994). These companies arranged shadowing opportunities for employees prior to taking up a foreign assignment (where the employee takes responsibility for a country operation prior to moving across to that country). Further informal briefings, arranged either by the company or the expatriates themselves, take place in some organisations, and 'look-see' visits, similar to Tung's 'field experience', were quite common. Nearly all made arrangements for language training where necessary. Brewster and Pickard recommended that all cross-cultural training programmes should include:

- an awareness that there is a major influence on behaviour called 'culture'
- the knowledge necessary for survival or, preferably, success in other cultures
- an understanding of the emotional challenges which can arise and opportunities to acquire skills that can help with psychological adjustment overseas.

Brewster and Pickard (*op cit*) also looked at the effectiveness of pre-move training. They used a sample of expatriates and spouses who had received training at The Centre for International Briefings at Farnham Castle (CIB). The CIB runs residential briefing courses for UK employees who are planning to live and work overseas and for overseas staff coming to work in Europe. The authors found that although management in multinational companies might doubt the effectiveness of expatriate training, employees and partners believe it helps them to adjust to living and working in the host country. However, Brewster and Pickard add an important proviso to these findings. They discovered that both expatriates' and spouses' perceptions of the training programmes varied according to the size and cohesiveness of the expatriate community in the location of the foreign assignment.

The existence of an expatriate community can play a major role as a support mechanism. The larger the expatriate community the greater the support and the more likely that cross-cultural adjustment is facilitated (Marchant and Medway, 1987). As a result expatriates in these kinds of surroundings are likely to be more positive about this pre-departure training.

A review of 29 studies on cross-cultural training concluded that, 'the available empirical literature gives guarded support to the proposition that cross-cultural training has a positive impact on cross-cultural effectiveness' (Black and Mendenhall, 1989: 120). Another study found the relationship between cultural training and relocation outcomes to be 'generally non-significant' (Brislin and Yoshida: 119). They suggest that, 'cross-cultural training programmes should be viewed as one of several contributions designed to assist people who cross cultural boundaries and not a "cure-all" that guarantees cultural adjustment.' (*ibid*, 1994: 5).

There are six conclusions to be drawn from the literature on cross-cultural training. One, even though there are major disagreements about what the ideal expatriate 'is', most commentators on expatriate training recommend the same or similar types of training for staff. Two, the kinds of training policies recommended by these authors are always more rigorous and wide ranging than those employed by most international companies (Forster and Johnsen, 1996). Three, most are implicitly critical of either the lack of or the quality of training currently provided by many international companies. Four, most of the evidence seems to suggest that cross-cultural training positively effects cross-cultural adjustment, however varied this effect may be. Five, assessments of how effective cross-cultural training has been is based on either anecdotal evidence or on self-report questionnaires after the assignment, rather than looking at the effectiveness of training before and during the international assignment. That is, as a process. This study aims to redress this deficiency.

METHODOLOGY

The study employed a multivariate systemic theoretical model, a longitudinal research design and both quantitative and qualitative data gathering methods. The longitudinal design was employed primarily to look at processes over time rather than relying on the cross-sectional analyses characteristic of almost every other study in this area. Thirty-six UK-based companies were involved in the study. This was carried out between January 1995 and December 1996. The companies were selected from a mail shot of 200 leading UK-based organisations in autumn 1994. The selection of companies to involve in the study was based on a number of criteria. These included the range of their international operations (from multinationals to companies who were relative newcomers to the international scene), company sector, the number of expatriates who could be contacted during the research and the willingness of the companies to collaborate during the project, as this required sustained administrative assistance over a two-year period.

Nick Forster, University of Western Australia

Initially, 20 interviews were conducted with personnel/HR managers in a representative selection of the companies in order to obtain information on the management of international assignments from the companies' perspective and to elicit the views and opinions of HR and personnel managers dealing with expatriates. These also provided an opportunity to pilot the questionnaires in November 1994. The companies then provided the names and contact addresses of employees who had been notified of an international assignment. Separate questionnaires were sent to employees and, where appropriate, their partners. These were posted four to six weeks prior to the move. Two further questionnaires were posted four and eight months after the move. The questionnaire surveys were conducted between January 1995 and December 1996. A total of 1,630 questionnaires were returned over three time points. A breakdown of the questionnaire returns is presented below (Table 1).

Table 1 *Sample characteristics*

	Time 1	Time 2	Time 3*
Employees:	335	310	300
Men	243	236	228
Women	92	74	72
Partners:	245	230	210
Women	221	207	191
Men	24	23	21
Total(s)	580	540	510

* Time 1 questionnaires sent out 4-6 weeks prior to the move; Time 2 four months after the move and Time 3 four months later

The questionnaires employed a variety of measures. Some of these had been used in previous studies of domestic relocations and others were designed specifically for this study. Many were replicated at each time point in order to analyse changes (Forster, 1996 and 1992). The data from the surveys was analysed using a standard SPSSx statistical package.

To supplement the questionnaire surveys, a further 20 interviews were conducted with personnel and HR managers in 1995. Forty interviews were also conducted with expatriates, their partners and, in some cases, children in the spring and summer of 1996. Extracts from these interviews can be found in this article. In addition to this, extensive use was made of company policy documents and briefing papers. Forty employees and their dependants were interviewed (for about three hours using tape recorders) at their homes in the USA, France, Germany, Japan, China, Vietnam, Hong Kong and Singapore in 1996.

The sample characteristics data shows that, typically, British expatriates are in their mid to late thirties and married with children, although there are clear signs that the number of younger single expatriates is growing and there are more dual income couples going on international assignments. The data shows that they are successful professionals in middle and senior management positions who have enjoyed good upward mobility in career terms. On average, they have enjoyed three promotions during their careers and worked in a variety of industrial sectors (Table 2).

Expatriates and the impact of cross-cultural training

Table 2 *Industry sector (employees)*

Energy exploration/ distribution	=	16%	Motor manufacturing	=	15%
IT/electronics	=	15%	Chemicals	=	9%
Banking/finance	=	9%	Engineering	=	8%
Pharmaceuticals	=	7%	Retail	=	6%
Clothing/textiles	=	4%	Transport/distribution	=	3%
Construction	=	3%	Food/drink/tobacco	=	2%
General manufacturing	=	2%	Other	=	1%

Forty-three men and seven women experienced an international assignment prior to this survey. A high proportion of relocating partners were in paid employment prior to their international assignments. When compared with all other studies of expatriates over the last 10 years, there were a high number of women expatriate employees. This is a distinct change from the profiles of expatriate managers of a decade ago, but still untypical of the general world population of expatriate managers (Forster, 1999; Smith and Still, 1997).

The data also shows that the age of the expatriates in these companies has changed over the last 10 years. Traditionally, most commercial expatriates were senior managers who went abroad for long periods of time. The profile of this group ranges from ages 21 up to 53, with an average managerial age of 35. However, there are increasing numbers of young graduate staff embarking on international careers. International assignments were also becoming shorter, with postings of two to three years becoming the norm in many of these companies.

Training and support provided prior to the move

There was great variability in the level of support and training provided by the companies. Obviously, this provision is dependent on the nature of each international assignment and the knowledge and experience of the individual expatriate. In a few cases, neither language training nor cross-cultural briefings may be necessary or appropriate. Table 3 shows the types of training received by employees and their partners.

Table 3 *Training and support for staff and partners before and after move abroad*

	Staff	Partners
Cultural familiarisation training	77%	43%
Induction programmes	60%	32%
Language training	49%	7%
Mentor in the new job	48%	na
Job related training	40%	na

We also asked questions about the general preparation and support for the move. The HR and personnel managers we interviewed stressed methods such as statements of objectives, job descriptions, face to face briefings and written information. Employees also regarded these as being important but also stressed the importance of preliminary visits to the new country, the provision of a mentor in the new job, family support and cross-cultural training. Strangely, both employers and employees gave similar ratings to the importance of family support, although hardly any of these companies actually provided this on a regular basis.

Nick Forster, University of Western Australia

In the Time 1 survey, almost three-quarters of the employees in our sample wanted to see some changes to current pre-move training and support provisions. These included much clearer statements of how international assignments fitted into their overall career development and a greater involvement of their partners in the selection process. Less than one-quarter of the partners were involved in any part of the selection procedure. This is surprising for two reasons. First, because of the very high number of partners accompanying employees on international assignments. Secondly, because previous research has shown this to be a time and cost effective way of gaining the active support of the relocating partner for a geographical job move (Munton and Forster, 1993). The few companies that do include partners and families in this process do this essentially to assess 'suitability'. Very few indicated that that they would cancel an assignment if they thought the partner was unwilling to move or 'unsuitable' in some way. Where this does occur, the invariable response from the employer is to suggest an unaccompanied posting.

The importance of this support and preparation cannot be overstated. Unrealistic expectations about a move combined with inadequate information can create real problems. The interviews, with both employers and employees, show that this is seen to be a critical stage in the expatriation process. If people are well prepared and have realistic expectations, the chances of their succeeding will be greatly enhanced.

Cultural aclimatisation

In this section, we look at our respondents eight to 12 months after the start of their international assignments and the effects of pre-move training and briefings on their adaptation to living and working in the new country. A significant omission in the literature on expatriate management is the lack of attention devoted to the period immediately after the start of an international assignment. Almost all of the research has focused on the pre-arrival aspects of these moves rather than their post-arrival aspects. Clearly, this is an important phase in an international assignment. Employees have to get acquainted quickly with key players inside and outside the subsidiary operation. They have to settle down to work and start performing quickly. In many cases, they will have to get used to working in strange cultural environments. Outside work, they will have to find accommodation, settle into a new area, get their children established in new schools and do the rounds of welcoming lunches and dinner parties. Their partners, perhaps for the first time, will have to develop new social networks and learn to cope pro-actively with new cultures and lifestyles.

Pre-departure training and briefings

Our respondents had moved to all regions of the world but there was a noticeable concentration in East Asia. This is not surprising, given the rapid economic growth in this region between the early 1980s and the late 1990s. There were also significant numbers moving to European locations, reinforcing the notion that the 'Euro-manager' (Storey, 1992; Tailleu, 1992) is becoming a reality (Table 4).

Previous research in the UK has shown that the length of notice and the quality of the information given to people prior to a geographical move can effect their ability to cope with a relocation (Munton, Forster, Altman and Greenburg, 1993). In this research, the length of notice given to employees prior to their international assignment varied considerably, with less than one-third receiving more than three months advance notice. Thirty-nine per cent were given less than two months notice and a further thirty percent were given between two and three months notice.

Expatriates and the impact of cross-cultural training

Table 4 *Location of expatriates' international assignments*

	Region
East Asia (Japan, Hong Kong, Malaysia, Singapore, Vietnam China and Indonesia)	36%
Western Europe (EEC and non EEC)	21%
USA/Canada	16%
Middle East	10%
Eastern Europe/Russia	6%
India/Pakistan	4%
Australasia	3%
North Africa	2%
Thailand/Burma	1%

The expatriates were asked: 'Do you feel that you were given adequate time to prepare for your move?' The results indicate that while employees feel that they were, their partners wanted more time to prepare. They were also asked: 'Do you feel that you were provided with adequate information concerning the move? Once again, the results indicate that companies could give greater consideration to providing their employees' partners with more information about the impending assignment (Table 5). They were also asked to rate the accuracy of the information provided by their employer. Only 31 per cent of employees and 22 per cent of partners found the information 'very accurate'; 50 per cent of employees and 31 per cent of partners found it 'quite accurate' but 11 per cent of employees and 20 per cent of partners found the information 'quite inaccurate' and eight per cent of employees and 27 per cent of partners found the information given to them 'very inaccurate'.

Table 5 *Do you feel that you were given adequate time/information to prepare for move?*

	Adequate time		Adequate information	
	Employees	Partners	Employees	Partners
Very much so	63%	39%	63%	40%
To some extent	21%	28%	29%	43%
Hardly/ not at all	16%	33%	8%	17%

Collectively, this data shows that improvements can be made to the content, quality and timing of the information provided to some employees and their partners prior to their international assignments. At Time 3, the employees were asked to give retrospective assessments of the preparation and briefings that they had received prior to the move. Their answers are summarised in Table 6.

This table shows mixed opinions about the efficacy of the support and training received prior to and immediately after the start of an international assignment. While a majority of staff give positive ratings, between 20 – 40 per cent give negative ratings to specific aspects of these. This is a significant finding. At Time 2 we asked the employees to assess how important 'knowledge of local business practices' and 'knowledge of local customs and cultures' were in assisting their work performance. Eighty-six believed that 'knowledge of

Nick Forster, University of Western Australia

local business practices' was 'essential' or 'very important' and 83 per cent believed that 'knowledge of local customs and cultures was 'essential' or 'very important'. This contrasts with 'knowledge of local languages', where 44 per cent believed this to be 'essential' or 'very important' but 50 per cent saw this as 'unimportant' or 'not at all important'.

Table 6 *Ratings of the training and support provided by the companies at Time 3 (staff)*

		Rating (valid %)		
Job previews	**(% responding)**	**Essential**	**Useful**	**Little/no use**
(Verbal)	(97%)	11%	69%	20%
(Written)	(60%)	9%	68%	22%
Job related training	(40%)	21%	52%	26%
Language training	(29%)	8%	63%	31%
Cultural briefings	(77%)	18%	57%	25%
Induction programmes	(60%)	11%	49%	40%
Named mentor in new job	(48%)	22%	44%	33%

Given the time, effort and money spent on pre-move cross-cultural briefings (CCBs), these results indicate that a review of the management of the early stages of an international assignment is merited in some of the companies. Why were our employee respondents critical of this support and training? The interview data, gathered from expatriates working in China, Vietnam and Japan, provides some answers. For example, one interviewee (an investment analyst working in Guanxi Province, China) was scathing in his comments about the CCBs that he had received prior to starting his international assignment.

> I can honestly say that the briefings I had prior to coming here weren't that good. In purely information terms I suppose they were, but it would have been much more useful to have had briefings from experienced managers who have worked here recently and who were up to date with what's going on here.

One IT project manager in a Vietnamese electronics company said:

> The biggest criticism I would level at the pre-move briefings is that they were out of date... More recently there has been a upsurge in anti-western feeling with the public burning of western papers and videos and even raids on expatriate bars. I think the people doing the briefings were not really up to date with what is going on here.

The following quote from a senior investment bank manager in Japan was echoed by others working there:

> There are huge problems working in Japan unless you are really well prepared before you come out here. The first problem is the language... all the hidden and imperceptible body language... we really were very confused about what their management strategy was, for weeks. There is also the major cultural differences in that our individualistic, 'rational' approach to decision making does not fit with their more collectivist approach. Another obvious difference is that doing business in Japan is about building up trust and not being simply focused on getting the task achieved in the shortest possible time. I don't think two or three days at (name of training centre) helped enough to understand what I now think is the most subtle culture in the world – maybe four or five weeks might have!

These themes emerged again and again in the interviews, particularly among employees working in East Asian countries. Many felt that their pre-move briefings were too short and sometimes out of date. They also highlighted the difficulties of putting a few days training in the UK into practice in a foreign setting. In fact, at Time 3, more than 40 per cent of our staff respondents felt that they had insufficient knowledge of the country's culture, ethnic and religious divides and its economic and political background. The data also show that more than 40 per cent wanted more information about local business laws and customs and 32 per cent said that they would have benefited from more knowledge in dealing with host country nationals. This also applied to expatriates who had experienced international assignments in the past. One explanation for this lies in the false assumption of 'similarity of culture' in countries such as the USA and Australia. However on a more positive note, expatriates moving within Europe reported that they felt better prepared than those moving to the Middle East or to the Far East. This was particularly the case with the women employees in our sample (Forster, 1999).

The partners

At Time 3, the partners of relocated staff were asked to rate how useful, overall, they had found their CCBs (Table 7).

Table 7 *Ratings of the training and support provided by the company at Time 3 (partners)*

	Essential	Useful	Little/no use no use	Not provided or used
Language training	2%	5%	0%	93%
Cultural briefings	9%	21%	13%	57%
Induction programmes	2%	18%	12%	68%
Contacts with	4%	32%	8%	26%

Most of these women had received their briefings either in-house or at an expatriate briefing centre. The results show that while only seven per cent of partners received any language training, 57 per cent did receive some form of cross-cultural briefing. Of those who had received CCBs, just over two-thirds rated these as having been 'helpful'. However, if we compare their responses to the last three items with those of employees, their ratings are consistently lower. Those partners who were critical, to some extent, of the cross-cultural briefings and other support they had received from their husbands' companies were usually those moving to areas without well-established expatriate communities. This lends considerable support to Brewster's (1994) contention that expatriates moving to areas with large expatriate communities are much more likely to give positive rating to CCBs.

The main criticism leveled at these was that while they were usually good on basic facts and information, they were not particularly helpful in terms of preparing people for their psychological reactions to their moves. The following interview quote, from the partner (38 years old and in employment in the UK prior to her move) of an expatriate who had recently moved to Vietnam illustrates these points.

> In retrospect I was not really prepared for life (in Hanoi). I think the people at (name of briefing centre) glossed over some of the realities of life here but then I'm not sure what else they could have done. I suppose they did tell us that life is pretty primitive here and a lot of the basics we take for granted in the UK simply don't exist but what they really didn't get across was how isolated you

Nick Forster, University of Western Australia

can feel here. The expat community is small and it can all get a bit incestuous and it is very difficult to make friends with the local people because they are all paranoid about the police and the government is constantly shifting its attitudes towards foreigners working here.

These findings indicate that UK companies need to review the pre-move CCBs provided to the partners of relocating staff, particularly in terms of the psychological reactions that some can have in a new culture. Having said this, the results from the surveys show most staff adapt well to the demands of working in different business cultures around the world, although this can take over 12 months in some areas, particularly in areas with small expatriate communities. There is little doubt that pre-move training can help with adaptation, but this is mediated by other factors such as length of the time the company has been doing business in the particular location of the assignment. Some respondents in countries with superficially similar cultures (*eg* the USA) were as likely to report problems with adaptation as were staff moving to more 'novel' cultures. This is particularly the case when companies were moving into new markets for the first time. However, adaptability is statistically correlated to the length of the lead-in time that employees enjoyed prior to the move. The longer this preparatory time, the better the chances of adaptation. The accuracy of the briefings they had received about their job responsibilities were also extremely important as was the quality and relevance of the cultural briefings they received.

DISCUSSION

There is little doubt that pre-move cultural briefings benefit most staff and their dependants. However, the effectiveness of these are strongly influenced by other factors, for example by the length of notice prior to the move, the location of the international assignment and family relationships (Forster, 2000). A sizeable minority of staff were critical of the briefings they received either in-house, from consultants or at training centres. Their main criticisms concerned the lack of up to date knowledge concerning local business environments, the very short duration of most of these courses, the lack of advice on coping with family problems during international assignments and a lack of follow-up training after they had started international assignments. These criticisms were particularly common among expatriates who were acting as vanguards in new markets, particularly in East Asia and the former Soviet Union. This suggests that companies should either ensure that they are getting value for money from the providers of these services or seek alternative sources of information. Language training was not seen to be an important issue for almost all our respondents.

Companies, particularly those new to the international scene, need to be aware that there are a variety of cross-cultural training options now available (Figure 1). The choice of training is also dependent on what kind of 'international managers' companies are hoping to develop, the kinds of competencies they want to instill, the duration of the impending assignment and the time and resources available to the company. For example, an expatriate who is required to make fundamental changes to core business skills may require more time than an employee who simply needs to be aware of a few basic cultural differences. If the host culture is perceived to be very different to the UK, this will also require a longer period of cultural briefing. Women employees also expressed greater dissatisfaction with the quality of the pre-move training they received. Dissatisfaction with male oriented training programmes have also been expressed in more recent studies (Smith and Still, 1997). This indicates that a review of many training programmes is merited and the development of programmes specifically geared to the needs of women expatriates (Forster, 1999).

Expatriates and the impact of cross-cultural training

Figure 1 *Cross-cultural training methods*

Instructional strategies	Specific methods
Pre-move	
Simulations	Role playing and T-groups
	Case studies
	Instructional games
Behaviour modification	Drill and practice
	Modelling
PC based instruction	Cultural assimilator
Expositive instruction	Area briefings
	Briefings from expatriates
	Lectures and tutorials from people
	with recent expert knowledge
	Reading or PC-based assignments
	Audio/visual presentations
Field experience	Short (non-residential) assignments abroad
	Pre-move area visits
	Meetings with experienced international
	staff prior to start of new job
Post-move	
On the job training	Use of hand over period
	Use of coaching/mentors
	Monthly performance appraisals
	Use of additional instructional strategies
	Continuing cross-cultural training

Adapted from Baumgarten, 1995: 214-216

Baumgarten (1997) and others have also asked a simple but telling question: Why is it that companies all too often assume that cross-cultural training is something that takes place only prior to the move? International assignments are processes and not one-off events. Thus, it makes absolute sense to build on the learning curve initiated prior to the move and continue with both experimental and formal cross-cultural learning after moving abroad. The danger of one-off training events is that they all too often have a fast fading 'halo-effect'. This may mean the development of sequential training programmes that may start months or even years before the move and continue up to several months after the start of an international assignment. Another obvious and under-utilised resource are host-country nationals who could also be used through secondments to the companies' UK headquarters to provide pre-move briefings or provide training to new arrivals in the host country.

Although English is rapidly becoming the lingua franca of the international business community, it is always worth encouraging staff to learn a new language. Even if they would not be expected to conduct business in the local dialect, a visible effort to learn the courtesies of introductions and small talk can send out positive signals to host-country nationals. It is also a very useful method of getting under the 'surface' of the host-country's culture.

Employees want up to date and relevant information about the new country and practical hands-on help with the relocation. Most partners want more help in coping with the negative psychological reactions that they have. In short, they need more reassurance about the move. The staff in the host country want a new employee who is aware of local

Nick Forster, University of Western Australia

business practices and culturally sensitive. Hence, warning bells should be ringing for HR managers who are interviewing a potential expatriate who has little interest in discussing the implications of working in a foreign environment, either for themselves or their families.

Expatriates need to be able to combat culture shock and those with solid intercultural skills will invariably cope better than others. Even in cultures that appear superficially similar to the UK, there is still a place for intercultural briefings. For example, on a training course at Farnham Castle in 1996 for executives relocating to Denver in the USA, participants were provided with standard information about business laws and protocol, strategies to succeed in business in the USA and many other useful tips, such as coping with the weather.

Where they are provided, induction programs and the provision of mentors in the new job received mixed ratings from our respondents. This and other research has shown that effective induction programs and access to sympathetic and helpful mentors can greatly assist employees in their adaptation to new job roles (Selmer and de Leon, 1995). Wherever possible, companies should allow a long hand over period with the previous job-holder. This will improve employee performance appraisals that follow the move.

Many companies need to re-evaluate the training and briefing sessions for women employees. This means ensuring that pre-move cultural briefings are up to date, relevant and catered specifically for the needs of women expatriates. This should include appropriate protocol, customs and dress codes in highly patriarchal societies. Also there should be advice on coping with problems of isolation during the international assignment. Training companies could involve more women with previous experience of international assignments in their briefing sessions in the future (Forster, 1999).

Research on work stress over two decades has consistently demonstrated that feelings of control are an important safeguard against potentially stressful life events like international assignments. Research into domestic relocation has demonstrated four important principles. People who are able to plan effectively for their international assignments, who are kept informed about them, who have realistic expectations about these and maintain a strong sense of control over their moves are much more likely to be successful. So, companies should provide as much notice of the assignment as is possible. An absolute minimum of two months is recommended for married staff. If possible four or more months is recommended. Information about the move should be up to date and accurate.

Staff should be allowed as much time as possible prior to the move in order to familiarise themselves with this information and attend any training and briefing courses. This 'anticipatory socialisation' is seen to be a crucial factor in adjusting to new jobs in a domestic context (Nicholson and West, 1988). Companies should be open about exactly what the posting will involve, for both the employee and their partner or family. Support should be available from the moment of the job offer until the employee actually returns from the assignment. It should be made standard operating policy in all companies that the partners or spouses of relocating employees are always involved in discussions about the move. This will provide partners with real opportunities to talk through any worries and concerns they might have. This should not be regarded as undue interference if the reasons are explained and staff will accept this as normal procedure in time.

Most partners gave positive ratings to the relocation support and services provided by the companies, unless they are not enthusiastic about the move abroad. Our respondents' biggest criticisms were directed at issues such as disruption to children's education, lack of advice on new job opportunities and culture shock. UK companies should give serious consideration to employing suitably qualified clinical psychologists with expertise in this area.

In summary, the findings of this research confirm the view expressed by researchers over the last 20 years, that pre-move cultural briefings have a positive effect on adaptation to international assignments (Forster, 1996; Black and Mendenhall, *op cit*; Brewster and Pickard, *op cit*). However, this particular study has found that the efficacy of these is influenced by a number of other factors. This indicates that any analyses of expatriate managers must be systemic, encompassing the individual, his/her family, the employing organisation and the host country. It has also confirmed that international assignments are best viewed as processes, not one off events. This suggests that analyses into the efficacy of policies effecting the management of expatriates must be longitudinal (Forster, 2000, 1996) not cross-sectional.

CONCLUSION

In the future, the growth of global competition will necessitate the continuing development of training and briefings for employees. International assignments will probably involve more frequent cross-border job swops and short assignments (Price Waterhouse, 1998). Recent research has shown that the issues of dual-career couples, families and children's educational needs are already diminishing employees' desire to go on international assignments. More employees will find themselves working for short periods of time in different areas of a company' overseas operations, without the necessity of moving their families as well. There is certainly strong anecdotal evidence from airlines that this is happening, but this development is almost totally under-researched (Brewster, 1998).

There is no doubt that cross-border transfers will remain an important part of international HR strategies for the foreseeable future. However, rather than being the domain of senior managers, as they have been in the past, these will occur earlier in employees' careers, when the learning curve is likely to be greater and when they are usually unencumbered by family constraints. The new generation is much more amenable to learning about other cultures, many have travelled abroad and increasing numbers are embracing international careers. Most are tuned into the global learning possibilities of the Web and many are, technologically, highly literate. If organisations need to develop global mind-sets, then these are exactly the kind of people they will have to recruit in greater numbers.

In the future, the management of international assignments will need to evolve to cope with both the changing demographics of these 'third-wave' international workforces and the changing nature of the global economy. Only those organisations that are truly committed to learning quickly in this area of strategic HR management will succeed in the turbulent international business environment of the first decade of the 21st century (Turnbull, 1996).

REFERENCES

Abe, H. and Wiseman, R. 1983. 'A cross-cultural confirmation of the dimensions of intercultural effectiveness'. *International Journal of Intercultural Effectiveness*, Vol. 7, 53-68.

Adler, N. 1986. *International Dimensions of Organisational Behaviour*. Boston USA: Kent Publishing Company.

Arthur, W. and Bennett, W. 1995. 'The international assignee: the relative importance of factors perceived to contribute to success'. Personnel Psychology, Vol. 48, no. 1, 99-115.

Barham, K. and Devine, M. 1991. *The Quest for the International Manager: A Survey of Global Human Resource Strategies*. The Economist Intelligence Unit Report 2098, London: Ashridge.

Baker, J. and Ivancevich, J. 1971. 'The assignment of American executives abroad: systematic haphazard, or chaotic?' *California Management Review*, Vol. 13, no. 3, 421-443.

Nick Forster, University of Western Australia

Baliga, G. and Baker, J. 1985. 'Multinational corporate policies for expatriate managers: selection, training, and evaluation'. *SAM Advanced Management Journal*, Autumn, 43-58.

Baumgarten, K. 1995. 'The training and development of staff for international assignments' in Harzing and Ruysseveldt (*op cit*), 205-228.

Black, S. and Mendenhall, M. 1990. 'Cross-cultural training effectiveness: a review and theoretical framework for future research'. *Academy of Management Review*, Vol. 15, no. 1, 113.

Bochner, S. 1982. *Cultures in Contact: Studies in Cross-Cultural Interaction*, New York: Pergamon Press.

Brewster, C. 1999. '*International Commuting*'. Cranfield, UK: Cranfield School of Management.

Brewster, C., and Pickard, J. 1994. 'Evaluating expatriate training'. *International Studies of Management and Organization*, Vol. 24, no. 3, 18-35.

Brewster, C. 1991. *The Management of Expatriates*. London: Kogan Page.

Brewster, C. and Myers, A. 1989. *Managing the Global Manager: New Research Data*. Cranfield, UK: The Cranfield School of Management.

Brislin, R. and Yoshida, T. 1994. *Improving Intercultural Interactions: Modules for Cross Cultural Training Programs*. London: Sage Publications.

Brislin, R, Cushner, C, Cherrie, C. and Yong, M. 1986. *Intercultural Interactions: A Practical Guide*. Beverly-Hills: CA.

Brislin, R. 1981. *Cross Cultural Encounters*. New York: Pergamon Press.

Business International Corporation. 1992. *Managing People in Today's Global Economy*. New York: Business International Corporation.

Clark, C. 1993. 'Selection methods used by executive search consultancies in four European countries: a survey and critique'. *International Journal of Selection and Recruitment*, Vol. 7, no. 2, 53-71.

Darby, R. 1995. 'Developing the Euro-manager: managing in a multicultural environment.' *European Business Review*, Vol. 9, no. 1, 13-15.

Dumaine, G. 1995. 'Don't be an ugly American'. *Fortune*, Vol. 15, 33-35.

Earley, P. 1987. 'Intercultural training for managers: a comparison of documentary and interpersonal methods'. *Academy of Management Journal*, Vol. 30, no. 4, 19-35.

Forster, N. 2000. *Managing Staff on International Assignments: A Strategic Guide*. London: Pearson Educational/ Financial Times Publications.

Forster, N. 1999. 'Another glass ceiling? The experiences of women expatriates on international assignments'. *Gender, Work and Organisation*, Vol. 6, no. 2, 79-91.

Forster, N. and Johnsen, M. 1996. 'Expatriate management in UK companies new to the international scene'. *International Journal of Human Resource Management*, Vol. 7, no. 1.

Forster, N. 1996. *A Report on the Management of Expatriates in 36 UK Companies*. Cardiff, UK: Cardiff Business School.

Goodman, N. 1994. 'Cross-cultural training for the global executive' in *Improving Intercultural Interactions: Modules for Cross-Cultural Training Programs*. Brislin, R. and Yoshida, T. (eds). London: Sage Publications.

Gertsen, M. 1990. 'Intercultural competence and expatriates'. *International Journal of Human Resource Management*, Vol. 1, no. 3, 341-362.

Hamill, J. 1989. 'Expatriate policies in British multi-nationals'. *Journal of General Management*, Vol. 14, 18-33.

Harris, H. and Brewster, C. 1995. 'Preparation for expatriation: evidence about current needs'. Paper presented at the Second Conference on International Staffing and Expatriate Management. Braga: Portugal.

Harris, P. and Moran, R. 1991. *Managing Cultural Differences*. Houston: Gulf Publishing.

Harvey, M. 1998. 'Dual-career couples during international relocation: the trailing spouse'. *International Journal of Human Resource Management*, Vol. 9, no. 2, 309-331.

Harzing, A. and Van Ruysseveldt, J. 1995. *International Human Resource Management*. London: Sage.

Heller, J. 1980. 'Criteria for selecting an international manager'. *Personnel*, May-June, 4-9.

Johnson, C. and Blinkhorn, S. 1994. 'Desperate measures: job performance and personality test validates'. *The Psychologist*, April, 167-170.

Marchant, K. and Medway, F. 1987. 'Adjustment and achievement associated with mobility and achievement in military families'. *Psychology in the Schools*, Vol. 24, 289-294.

Mendenhall, M., and Oddou, G. 1986. 'Acculturation profiles of expatriate managers: implications for cross-cultural training programs'. *Columbia Journal of World Business*, Vol. 21, no. 4, 34-67.

Munton, A, Forster, N. Altman, Y. and Greenbury, L. 1993. *Job Relocation: Managing People on the Move*. London: Wiley.

Nicholson, N. and West, M. 1988. *Managerial Job Change: Men and Women in Transition*, Cambridge: Cambridge University press.

Price-Waterhouse Expatriate Compensation and Benefits Consultancy. 1993. *A Review of European Expatriate Policy and Practice*. London: Price-Waterhouse.

Schwind, H. 1985. 'The state of the art in cross-cultural management training' in *International Human Resource Development Annual (Volume 1)*, R. Doktor (ed).

Scullion, H. 1994. 'Creating international managers: recruitment and development issues' in *Human Resource Management in Europe: Perspectives for the 1990s*. London: Routledge.

Selmer, J. and de Leon C. 1995. 'Quality of overlaps: expatriate CEO succession procedures'. Paper presented at the Second Conference on International Staffing and Expatriate Management. Braga: Portugal, July 26-29th.

Smith, C and Still, L. 1997. 'Are women being prepared for international management?' *Industrial Employment Relations Review*, Vol. 3, no. 1, 21-35.

Smith, P. 1992. 'Organisational behaviour and national cultures'. *British Journal of Management*, Vol. 3, 39-51.

Sparrow, P. and Bognanno, M. 1993. 'Competency requirement forecasting: issues for international selection and assessment'. *International Journal of Selection and Assessment*, Vol. 1, no. 1, 50-58.

Storey, J. 1992. 'Making European managers: an overview'. *Human Resource Management Journal*, Vol. 3, no. 1, 1-11.

Tung, R. 1988a. *The New Expatriates: Managing Human Resources Abroad*, Cambridge Mass: Ballinger.

Tung, R. 1988b. 'Career issues in international assignments'. Academy of Management Executive, Vol. 11, 241-244.

Tung, R. 1987. 'Expatriate assignments: enhancing success and minimising failure'. Academy of Management Executive, Vol. 10, 117-126.

Tung, R. 1982. 'Selection and training procedures of US, European and Japanese multinationals'. *California Management Review*, Vol. 25, no. 1, 57-71.

Tung, R. 1981. 'Selection and training of personnel for overseas assignments'. Columbia Journal of World Business, Vol. 16, no. 1, 35-49.

Turnbull, N. 1996. *The Millenium Edge: Coping With Generation MM*. St. Leanards, NSW: Allen and Unwin.

[6]

An exploratory assessment of the purposes of performance appraisals in North and Central America and the Pacific Rim

John Milliman, Stephen Nason, Cherrie Zhu and Helen De Cieri

While performance appraisals are considered important management tools in many countries, their purposes and practices vary significantly between countries. Unfortunately, there is little empirical data on the specific practices of appraisals across countries. The focus of this study is to empirically examine the current purposes of performance appraisals in ten different countries and regions in Asia, North America, and Latin America. The purposes of appraisals studied here include documentation, development, administrative (pay and promotions), and subordinate expression. This paper also examines how the respondents believe the purposes of appraisals should ideally be practiced. Implications for research and practice are discussed.

Performance appraisals are viewed as a problematic, but important part of the performance management process in many countries. The performance appraisal concept is based on a similar fundamental premise in many countries, which is how to control individuals in organizations to achieve maximum performance (Nakane 1972; Ouchi 1982; Staw 1980). For example, even in countries as different as the US and Japan, this control process, as it relates to performance appraisals, involves the similar idea of developing social and performance norms, monitoring the actions of employees in relation to the norms, assigning responsibility for the actions, and then ultimately providing rewards or punishment based on performance towards those norms (Sullivan et al. 1986).

While performance evaluations are based on a similar fundamental notion in many countries, their specific purposes and practices vary significantly between different nations. However, much of the literature in many countries is based on conceptual articles or observation, rather than empirical data. Collecting empirical data is essential to ascertain how performance appraisal is actually practiced on a cross-national basis. Accordingly, one objective of this paper is to empirically determine the current purposes of performance appraisal in a variety of coun-

Correspondence to: John Milliman, College of Business, University of Colorado, Colorado Springs, 1420 Austin Bluffs Parkway, Colorado Springs, CO 80933-7150 USA; e-mail: jmillima@uccs.edu

106   *Asia Pacific Journal of Human Resources*   2002 | 40(1)

tries and regions including Australia, Canada, Indonesia, Japan, South Korea (hereafter stated simply as Korea), Latin America, Mexico, the People's Republic of China (PRC), Taiwan, and the US. Such data are needed if we are to begin to understand how and why appraisal practices vary across country boundaries.

It is important to recognize that at this point we are collecting country data without considering how various contextual factors influence the purpose of appraisals. In reality, a number of organizational contextual factors, such as organizational strategy and structure, industry, national and organizational culture and regulations, influence the purpose of appraisal. However, given the lack of empirical data on appraisals on a comparative management basis, we believe that collecting such data in a large number of countries is an important building block to understanding performance evaluation on a cross-national basis.

A second objective of this article involves determining what the purposes of performance evaluation should ideally be in these countries and comparing how the purposes 'should be' conducted versus the current practice of appraisal purposes. This analysis will provide insights into the future practice of appraisals and what change efforts need to be made from the existing practice of performance evaluations.

To accomplish these purposes, we first will review briefly the literature on the purposes of appraisals in the countries in our sample. Then, the mean scores of current practice, as well as how the respondents believe the appraisal should ideally be conducted, will be analyzed in these countries and regions. Finally, we will discuss the results and provide implications for future research and practice.

Literature review on appraisal purposes

Performance appraisals are viewed as a critical aspect of performance management practices and can influence the implementation of the business strategy of a firm (Schuler and Jackson 1987; Snell 1992) and organizational performance (Schuler, Fulkerson and Dowling 1991). In addition, performance appraisal is also seen as an important way to identify employee strengths and weaknesses, evaluate training needs, set plans for future development, and provide motivation by serving as a basis for determining rewards and career feedback (e.g., Cascio 1992; Cardy and Dobbins 1994). Furthermore, performance appraisals are seen as one important way by which multinational enterprises (MNEs) obtain the full abilities of their diverse workforce as well as control and co-ordinate their overseas operations (Schuler, Fulkerson and Dowling 1991).

While performance appraisals are viewed as important, they are also often seen as problematic. Many managers dislike giving appraisal reviews and employees often dislike receiving them. While some of this occurs because of problems in organizational performance appraisal systems (Gomez-Mejia, Balkin and Cardy 1995), it also occurs in part due to the inherent difficulties people have in giving and receiving feedback.

As the literature indicates, performance appraisal has a number of issues associated with it, but it can serve many important functions. However, despite its importance, the international management literature does not specify on an in-depth basis how performance appraisals vary across different nations (Milliman, Nason, Gallagher, Huo, Von Glinow and Lowe

1998). Establishing how and why performance appraisals vary across different nations is important for two major reasons. First, it is important for MNEs to understand how performance appraisals are practiced so that these organizations can adapt these management tools to meet the needs of the local context of their overseas business units. Second, learning about the diverse performance evaluation methods in different countries can provide insights into new and different ways of conducting appraisals and thereby provide a more comprehensive picture of best appraisal practices.

As previously noted, performance appraisal seeks to serve a number of specific objectives or purposes (e.g., employee development, career needs, linking performance to rewards, etc.). Thus, we believe that determining what the various purposes of appraisal are in different countries is an important step for the international human resource management (IHRM) literature. In this study, we use some of the most important purposes of performance appraisals, as they are conceptualized in the US, as a starting point to evaluate the intent of appraisals across different countries. These major appraisal purposes include documentation, development, administrative purposes involving pay and promotion, and subordinate expression (Milliman, Nathan and Mohrman 1991). Since the literature on performance appraisals is uneven on the various countries in our sample, we will focus our review on the following for which information is most available: Australia, Canada, Japan, Korea, PRC, Taiwan, Mexico, and the US. A concise summary of our literature findings regarding the purposes of performance appraisals is included in table 1.

Documentation

Performance appraisal is frequently viewed as having a documentation or legalistic perspective in the US (Laud 1984; Lawler, Mohrman and Resnick 1984) and Canada (Stone and Meltz 1992). This documentation perspective provides a

Table 1   **Summary of literature on current purpose of performance appraisal**

	Development	Documentation	Subordinate expression	Pay	Promotion
Australia	High	?	?	Low	High
Canada	High	High	High	Low	High
Japan	High	Low	High	Low	Moderate
Korea	High	?	Low	Low	High
Mexico	?	?	Low	Low	Low to moderate
PRC	High	?	Low	Low	Low to moderate
Taiwan	High	?	Low	Low	Low
USA	High	High	Moderate to high	Moderate to high	High

108   *Asia Pacific Journal of Human Resources*   2002 | 40(1)

retrospective look at the past performance time period (typically a year in the US) to determine positive and negative aspects of employees' work and whether they accomplished their goals (Gomez-Mejia, Balkin and Cardy 1995). In addition, organizations in the US keep detailed performance appraisal records as documentation and justification for administrative and termination decisions should they be challenged later in court (e.g., Milliman, Nathan and Mohrman 1991).

In contrast to the US and Canada, appraisals in Japan tend to have less emphasis on the evaluation of short-term goals and more focus on the future, such as long-term career and performance potential (Pucik 1984). Thus, we tend to expect that Japan would have less focus on documentation in appraisals than in the US and Canada.

Relatively little other explicit information was found on documentation in the other countries. This may be because the documentation perspective is largely assumed to occur as a fundamental aspect of appraisals (e.g., review of job-related work factors during the past performance time period) in many countries.

Development

Another fundamental objective of performance appraisal in the US (Gomez-Mejia, Balkin and Cardy 1995) is a developmental focus (e.g., training, planning, etc.) regarding how employees can improve their performance in the future. Similarly, studies have indicated that appraisals in Canada (Stone and Meltz 1992), Australia (Dowling and Fisher 1996; Shelton 1995), Korea (Steers, Shin and Unison 1989), Taiwan (McEvoy and Cascio 1990), and Japan (Hatvany and Pucik 1989; Pucik

1984) seek to determine future potential of employees and are used to determine job assignments and training opportunities. While development has not traditionally been viewed as playing a major role in appraisals in the PRC, there is some evidence that there is increasing use of this function in international joint ventures in the PRC (Shenkar and Nyaw 1995). All together we would expect that there would be a high emphasis on developmental activities in appraisals in Australia, Canada, Japan, Korea, Taiwan, and the US and a low to moderate emphasis in the PRC.

Administrative – pay

A third function of US performance appraisals is that they are often tied to administrative decisions, such as pay and promotion (Milliman, Nathan and Mohrman 1991; Thomas and Bretz 1994). This is based on the logic that connecting appraisal results to rewards can strengthen the motivational impact of performance evaluations on employees. We will first discuss the pay purpose.

Unions and collective bargaining agreements have a much stronger influence in both Canada (Stone and Meltz 1992) and Australia (Shelton 1995) than in the US. In general, unions tend to resist evaluations based on individual merit. Though there appears to be a trend toward greater discussion of performance-based rewards in appraisals in Australia (Shelton 1995), we would still expect that there would be only a low or moderate emphasis on pay in performance evaluations in these two countries due to the greater influence of unions.

Until quite recently the central purpose of performance appraisals in the PRC has been to access the 'political consciousness' of staff (Chen 1985; Liao 1991; Siu and Davies 1996; Su and Chu 1992). This emphasis is rapidly changing and using appraisals for promotions, demotions, and rewards is becoming more common (Chen 1985; Su and Chu 1992). Given that the PRC is currently in transition toward more western styles of management, we would expect only a moderate or low current use of appraisals for pay.

Taiwan places a high value on harmony, face, teamwork, and the importance of factors such as off-the-job behaviors and attitudes toward superiors (McEvoy and Cascio 1990). In Taiwan, this emphasis on face and harmony means it is particularly important that group or interpersonal harmony is not disturbed through the differentiation of employees in performance appraisals (Shaw, Tang, Fisher and Kirkbridge 1993) and in merit pay (Huo and Von Glinow 1993). For these reasons, it is less likely that firms with a Chinese culture will have extensive performance appraisals or use such systems for administrative purposes (Shaw, Tang, Fisher and Kirkbridge 1993), such as the determination of pay and hierarchical advancement. Similarly, Atchison (1990) observed that Taiwan is less likely than the US to tie pay to output.

Mexican law and custom emphasize the responsibility of the employer to treat employees as if they were an extended family. This, along with a collectivist culture with an emphasis on harmony, results in a situation where employees are quite sensitive to pay inequities (Schuler, Jackson, Jackofsky and Slocum 1996). Thus, we would expect relatively little enthusiasm for the use of performance appraisals for determining pay in Mexico.

Administrative – promotion

Performance appraisals are also often used to determine an employee's promotability in individualistic cultures, such as the US (cf. Milliman Nason, Gallagher, Huo, Von Glinow and Lowe 1998). As such, we would tend to expect there to be a relatively high emphasis on promotion (though reduced somewhat by their union influences) in Australia and Canada, which also have highly individualistic cultures.

Conversely, in collectivistic cultures, seniority is often seen as an important way to maintain harmony and preserve order within the group (Abdullah and Gallagher 1995; Milliman, Kim and Von Glinow 1993). The need to maintain harmony and cohesion are likely to be important reasons why Latin American (Quezada and Boyce 1988), Taiwanese (Shaw, Tang, Fisher and Kirkbridge 1993), and Japanese (Chang 1989a, 1989b; Elashmawi and Harris, 1993; Maher and Wong 1994) organizations are less likely to differentiate employees based on job performance and instead place a high emphasis on seniority. Thus, generally we would anticipate that appraisal would not be closely tied to promotion in the countries in our sample with collectivistic cultures which are more prominent in Asia and Latin America.

Our literature review does indicate, however, that some organizations in Japan (Pucik and Hatvany 1983) and Korea (Chang 1989b; Kim and Kim 1989; Steers, Shin, Unison and Nam 1990) and the PRC (Chen 1985; Su and Chu 1992) use appraisals to determine job assignments and ultimately promotion (Chang 1989b; Kim and Kim 1989; Steers, Shin, Unison and Nam 1990). Therefore, we would predict there to be a low to moderate emphasis on discussion of

110   *Asia Pacific Journal of Human Resources*   2002 | 40(1)

promotion potential in appraisals in these countries.

Subordinate expression

Another important objective of the appraisal review in Canada (Stone and Meltz 1992) and the US (Seddon 1987) is to provide a formal opportunity for subordinates to give feedback or express their views to their supervisors. US employees often feel they do not have much opportunity to discuss their career or personal needs and the appraisal review meeting does provide a once-a-year opportunity for the employees to discuss their views and feelings (Milliman, Nathan and Mohrman 1991).

In contrast, it has been proposed that high-power-distance cultures, such as those in much of Asia and Latin America, would not likely allow subordinates to express their views, since such expression would potentially threaten the status and power of the supervisor (Milliman et al. 1998). This assertion, supported by recent studies in Korea (Chung 1990), the PRC (Zhu and Dowling 1998), Taiwan (McEvoy and Cascio 1990), and Mexico (Schuler, Jackson, Jackofsky and Slocum 1996), indicates that employees place a low importance on expressing their views to superiors in appraisals.

It is important to note, however, that in high-power-distance Japan there is more emphasis on face-to-face communication (Hatvany and Pucik 1981b) whereby employees are expected to openly communicate with their direct superiors (Chang 1989a; Hodgetts and Luthans 1989) and are often actively involved in the appraisal via interviews and self-report instruments (Pucik 1984). Similarly, it was found that enabling employees to express their feelings in appraisal was linked

to effectiveness in international joint ventures in the PRC (Zhu and Dowling 1998). For these reasons, we would expect there to be low to moderate emphasis on employee self-expression in the performance appraisal process in Japan and the PRC.

Research methods

This study is part of a larger research effort to observe a number of HRM practices. For more extensive information on the research design and methodology of this project please see the article by Geringer, Frayne, and Milliman in this special issue entitled 'In search of "best practices" in international human resource management: Research design and methodology'. Eleven items focusing on performance appraisal are included in the survey. Respondents were asked the extent to which the items describe the current purposes of the company's appraisal system ('is now' *items*) and how appraisals should ideally be conducted ('should be' *items*). Thus, there were 22 total items on performance appraisal practices. The survey items were taken from Milliman, Nathan and Mohrman (1991) and were answered with a five-point Likert type scale with the anchors from 1 = not at all to 5 = to a very great extent.

At this point in our research, we will assess the various appraisal items on an individual basis. This is consistent with our intent to conduct an exploratory analysis of the data in order to establish a preliminary starting point for more rigorous research. However, based on the original intent of these items (Milliman, Nathan and Mohrman 1991), which is also supported by a preliminary factor analysis in four countries of these items by Milliman et al. (1995), these performance appraisal purpose items can be grouped in the following manner. Three items (#1 – pay, #4 – for salary administration, and #11 – to determine promotability) are related to administrative purposes of appraisals, such as pay and promotion. Four items are meant to reflect the documentation purpose (#2 – document the subordinate's performance, #5 – recognize the subordinate for things done well, #8 – evaluate the subordinate's goal achievement, and #9 – identify the subordinate's strengths and weaknesses). Two items were intended to focus on the future development of the employee (#3 – plan development activities of the subordinates and #6 – lay out specific ways in which the subordinate can improve performance). The two final items relate to subordinate expression in the appraisal review (#7 – discuss the subordinate views and #10 – allow the subordinate to express feelings).

The mean scores for the current practices ('is now') are included in table 2 and the desired practices ('should be') are shown in table 3. First, the 'is now' means is examined to understand the current practice and objectives of performance appraisals in each country. Second, the 'should be' means are examined to gain insight into future or best practices. In addition, the difference or change score from the 'is now' to the 'should be' means is examined. Comparing means across countries is problematic because the nature of how respondents interpret and respond to scales varies by country and culture (Cox, Lobel and McLeod 1991). For this reason, only general, rather than statistical, comparisons of the means across these countries are made. For the purpose of analysis, the following guidelines for a general interpretation of the data will be used. Mean scores below 3.0 will be considered low, 3.0 to 3.5 are moderate, 3.5

to 3.99 are moderately high, and 4.0 and above are high.

Results

The mean scores for the current practices ('is now') are included in table 2 and the desired practices ('should be') are shown in table 3. These mean scores for the performance appraisal items are grouped in the following purposes: documentation, development, administrative (pay and promotion), and subordinate expression.

Documentation/Retrospective

There are four items which are related to a documentation or retrospective evaluation of the employee's performance during the past-performance time period; #2 – document the subordinate's performance, #5 – recognize the subordinate, #8 – evaluate goal achievement, and #9 – identify strengths and weaknesses. Because there is a similar pattern of results among these four items, these items will be discussed jointly.

Most of the countries had moderate (e.g., between 3.0 and 3.5) 'is now' mean scores on all four documentation purpose items. The main exceptions to this were Mexico, which had means less than 3.0 on all four items, and Indonesia and the PRC, which had means lower than 3.0 on two of the four items. Thus, the current use of the documentation purpose in appraisals is categorized as being moderate in all of the countries except Indonesia, Mexico, and the PRC.

As noted earlier, little information was found in the literature regarding documentation in many of the countries in our sample. However, it does appear that Japan has slightly higher current mean (moderate score) than expected (low) and

Table 2 'Is now' mean scores – performance appraisal purposes

Items	Australia	Canada	Indonesia	Japan	Korea	Latin America	Mexico	PRC	Taiwan	USA
1. Determine pay	2.86	3.22	2.94	3.09	2.28	3.01	2.62	3.09	3.33	3.14
2. Document performance	3.78	3.33	3.05	3.05	3.11	3.46	2.82	2.71	3.53	3.56
3. Plan development activities	3.43	2.98	2.71	2.73	2.73	3.09	2.75	2.69	2.96	2.73
4. Salary administration	2.62	3.11	3.05	2.91	2.31	3.34	2.62	2.98	3.34	3.22
5. Recognize subordinate	3.46	3.27	3.00	3.18	3.13	3.30	2.82	3.21	3.42	3.31
6. Lay out ways to improve	3.48	3.23	2.74	2.85	2.50	3.43	2.74	2.90	3.14	3.07
7. Discuss subordinate views	3.50	3.19	2.71	2.55	2.49	3.14	2.80	2.69	3.08	2.91
8. Evaluate goals achievement	3.59	3.25	2.82	3.20	3.18	3.38	2.73	2.99	3.26	3.15
9. Identify strengths / weaknesses	3.55	3.27	2.86	3.11	2.62	3.56	2.87	3.09	3.18	3.35
10. Allow subordinate to express feelings	3.37	2.98	2.66	2.76	1.98	3.13	2.80	2.96	3.03	2.83
11. Determine promotability	3.13	2.92	2.91	3.07	3.34	3.30	2.79	2.90	3.29	2.69
Sample size	379–380	123–125	220–221	270–274	234–236	165–166	477–483	189–192	116–118	135–137

Table 3 'Should be' mean scores – performance appraisal purposes

Item	Australia	Canada	Indonesia	Japan	Korea	Latin America	Mexico	PRC	Taiwan	USA
1. Determine pay	3.40	3.64	3.90	3.90	3.18	3.82	4.44	4.01	4.15	3.78
2. Document performance	4.11	4.04	3.98	3.74	3.67	4.48	4.35	3.52	3.80	4.23
3. Plan development activities	4.38	4.27	4.05	3.70	3.83	4.61	4.48	3.66	4.15	4.23
4. Salary administration	2.92	3.32	3.66	3.26	2.90	4.07	4.31	3.83	4.06	3.45
5. Recognize subordinate	4.18	4.19	3.94	3.74	3.98	4.52	4.53	3.91	4.25	4.19
6. Lay out ways to improve	4.38	4.41	4.05	3.76	3.54	4.67	4.49	3.84	4.14	4.37
7. Discuss subordinate views	4.33	4.30	3.81	3.26	3.53	4.57	4.30	3.58	3.89	4.17
8. Evaluate goal achievement	4.36	4.32	3.84	3.96	3.78	4.69	4.47	3.80	4.06	4.36
9. Identify strengths / weaknesses	4.26	4.25	3.98	3.62	3.28	4.71	4.45	3.87	4.03	4.37
10. Allow subordinate to express feelings	4.22	4.18	3.79	3.40	2.55	4.47	4.37	3.71	3.90	4.02
11. Determine promotability	3.81	3.97	3.94	3.54	3.73	4.57	4.55	3.71	4.11	3.80
Sample size range	433–437	123–125	240–241	267–272	224–227	165–168	471–483	187–191	115–118	134–136

114   *Asia Pacific Journal of Human Resources*   2002 | 40(1)

Canada and the US have a slightly lower current mean score (moderate) than indicated in our literature review (high) on these documentation related purposes.

The 'should be' scores were higher than the 'is now' scores for all of the countries on all four documentation items. The 'should be' means were above 4.0 for Australia, Canada, Latin America, Mexico, Taiwan, and the US on virtually all four documentation purpose items. In contrast, the mean scores were mainly between 3.5 and 3.9 on these four items for Indonesia, Japan, Korea, and the PRC.

All together the data tend to indicate that organizations in the Latin and Anglo-based regions and Taiwan should consider a high priority on documentation, while the rest of the countries in Asia should consider only a moderately high emphasis on documentation in future appraisals.

Table 4 provides a concise summary of a general description of current practice of appraisal purposes ('is now') and how appraisal purposes 'should be' conducted in the future ('should be') for all five major types of purposes in the ten countries.

Table 4   **Descriptive summary of results**

Documentation

'is now': Moderate emphasis in all countries, except a low emphasis in Australia, Indonesia, and Mexico.

'should be': Increase in 'should be' scores in all countries with a high emphasis in the American continent, Australia, and Taiwan, but only a moderately high emphasis in the rest of the Asian countries.

Development

'is now': Only four countries tended to have a moderate emphasis (means at or above 3.0): Australia, Canada, Latin America, and Taiwan. The rest of the countries had scores close to or under 3.0, except for Korea which had the lowest means.

'should be': The results indicate that there 'should be' a high priority on development in the future in the American continent, Australia, and Taiwan. However, there should only be a moderately high emphasis in the remaining Asian countries.

Administrative purposes — pay and promotion

'is now': Low to moderate emphasis in most countries. There were low means in pay (< 3.0) in Australia, Korea, and Mexico and in promotion (< 3.0) in Canada, Indonesia, Mexico, the PRC, and the US.

'should be': The means increased in all countries, but still indicated only a moderate or moderately high emphasis 'should be' placed on these purposes in most countries. The exceptions to these are a high emphasis in the Latin bloc and Taiwan.

Subordinate expression

'is now': Overall, mainly low scores. Only Australia and Latin America had means above 3.0 on both items. Korea in particular had very low mean scores.

'should be': Means were much higher, particularly in the American continent and Australia where the means were above 4.0. However, the 'should be' scores indicated that only a moderate or moderately high emphasis 'should be' placed on subordinate expression in the rest of Asia.

Development

Two of the appraisal purpose items relate to development: #3 – plan development activities for the subordinates (e.g., training, new duties) and #6 – lay out specific ways in which the subordinate can improve performance. In relation to present practice, it appears that these two aspects of development are not highly utilized in most of the countries. Only Australia and Latin American had 'is now' means much above 3.0 on both items. Two countries, Canada and Taiwan, had scores close to 3.0, while the other six countries generally had scores less then 3.0. These scores show that most of these countries currently place a low to moderate emphasis on development, rather than a high emphasis as expected from the literature review.

There was a significant increase in the 'should be' means above the 'is now' scores for all of the countries on these two development-related items. The 'should be' mean scores (4.27 to 4.70) were the highest in the Latin and Anglo-based countries. With the exception of Indonesia and Taiwan, most of the Asian countries had means below 4.0. These results indicate that, in the future, organizations in Indonesia, Taiwan, and the Latin and Anglo-based regions should consider strongly emphasizing development in appraisals. Companies in the rest of Asia should place only a moderate or moderately high emphasis on development in performance evaluations.

Administrative purpose – pay

Two items focus specifically on pay: #1 – determine appropriate pay and #4 – for salary administration. Korea and Mexico were the only two countries with 'is now' mean scores substantially less than 3.0 on

these two pay purposes. Australia, Indonesia, Japan, and the PRC all have 'is now' mean scores generally at or lower then 3.0 on average on both pay items. The countries which emphasize pay more (e.g., 3.1 to 3.3), included Canada, Latin America, Taiwan, and the US. Overall, presently there is a low to moderate emphasis on discussing pay in appraisals in these ten countries. These data indicate that the US has a slightly lower emphasis on discussing pay in appraisals (moderate) than was anticipated from the literature (moderate to high). Otherwise the data is generally consistent with what was predicted from our literature review (low emphasis) for the emphasis of pay in appraisals.

The mean scores for the 'should be' pay items (2.90 to 4.44) were much higher than the 'is now' pay means (2.28 to 3.34) for each of the ten countries. Nonetheless, the pay 'should be' means tended to be a lower than the 'should be' means on the development and documentation purposes. For instance, 70% of the 'should be' pay means (14 out of 20) were still below 4.0 and two were below 3.0. The biggest changes from the 'is now' to the 'should be' means were in Mexico, the PRC, and Taiwan. The lowest difference in change scores from 'is now' to 'should be' were in the US and Canada. Overall, these 'should be' scores tend to indicate that pay 'should be' discussed to a high degree in Latin Bloc and Taiwan, but only to a moderate or moderately high extent in the rest of the countries.

Administrative purpose – promotion

One additional administrative-related purpose of appraisal, item (#11 – determine promotability) was also analyzed. In relation to current practice, one-half of the sample placed a low emphasis ('is now' means below 3.0) on determining promotability in appraisals: Canada, Indonesia, Mexico, the PRC, and the US. The other countries had moderate scores with the highest being in Korea (3.34), Latin America (3.30), and Taiwan (3.29).

Generally these data contradict our predictions from the literature review, which had predicted a higher emphasis on discussion of promotion in appraisals in the Anglo-based countries. These results are consistent with our predictions from the literature that promotions will be discussed to a low extent in appraisals in Indonesia, Mexico, and the PRC. However, the 'is now' means show that Japan, Korea, and Latin America had higher means (moderate) than what was expected based on previous studies.

The 'should be' items all had substantially higher scores than the 'is now' means for all of the countries (range of 3.54 to 4.57). The largest gap between 'is now' and 'should be' were in Mexico and Latin America (4.55 and 4.57). Taiwan was the only other country with a 'should be' mean above 4.0. These findings overall suggest that promotability 'should be' discussed only at a moderately high level in performance appraisals in most of these countries, with the exception of the Taiwan and Latin-based countries.

Subordinate expression

Two of the items relate to subordinate expression in performance appraisals: #7 – discuss the subordinate's views and #10 – allow the subordinate to express feelings. In terms of current practice, most of the countries do not emphasize this purpose very much as the 'is now' mean scores are largely below 3.0. Korea has by far the lowest scores on these items (1.98 and

2.49). Only Australia and Latin America has 'is now' mean scores above 3.0 on both of these items.

These results contradict our predictions from our literature search, which indicated that Canada, Japan, and the US would have moderate or high emphasis on subordinate expression in appraisals. Otherwise, these data are consistent with our prediction that countries with a collectivistic orientation will place a low emphasis on employee expression in appraisals.

The 'should be' items presented some interesting results by region. Countries in the Latin and Anglo-based blocs had the highest scores with means well above 4.0 on both subordinate expression items. In contrast, the scores of the countries in Asia were all below 4.0, with Korea again being, by far, the lowest. These findings suggest that allowing subordinates to express their views 'should be' an important purpose in Anglo- and Latin-based regions, but only to a moderately high level in Asia. An interesting question for future research will be to determine why the Latin-based and Asian countries believe such a different emphasis 'should be' placed on subordinate expression in appraisals given that both regions share a similar collectivistic and high power cultural orientation.

Discussion

Performance appraisal remains an enigma in management processes. On the one hand, it is viewed as an essential management tool that can enhance development, communication, and implementation of the company's strategy (Butler, Ferris and Napier 1991). On the other hand, critics contend that it can create more problems than it solves (e.g., Lawler 1994) and can lead to the demotivation of employees (Thomas and Bretz 1994). Clearly, performance evaluations have the potential to positively influence employee performance, but an important consideration with appraisals is whether they are practiced effectively and in alignment with their intended purposes.

The results in this study of appraisals in ten different countries largely support a mixed picture on whether performance evaluations accomplish their intended purposes. Referring back to table 2, it is interesting to note that only 6 of the 110 'is now' mean scores (11 appraisal items times 10 countries) are above 3.50 and of these the highest mean score was only 3.59. With the exception of Korea, a majority of the 'is now' means range from 2.70 to 3.39. Based on our mean score classification framework these results indicate that the various purposes of appraisal are currently practiced on only a low to moderate basis in virtually every country in our sample.

It is also important to observe that this 'is now' data to some degree contradicts our predictions from the literature review on two of the purposes in many of the countries. For example, the 'is now' documentation related means (moderate scores) were a bit lower than we expected in Canada and the US and somewhat higher (also a moderate score) than we had anticipated in Japan. In addition, we had predicted that the development-related items would be highly emphasized in many of the countries, but the data indicate that these purposes are emphasized to only a low extent in most of the countries.

The 'is now' mean scores were largely consistent with our predictions on the pay, promotion, and subordinate expression purposes for most of the countries. The biggest exception is the US. It is intriguing that even though the appraisal purposes studied here were derived mainly from the US literature, the US 'is now' means were lower (low to moderate) than what we had expected for the pay and promotion purposes.

Furthermore, it is interesting to note from tables 3 and 4 that the 'should be' means were higher than the 'is now' means on every purpose in every country. The 'should be' scores indicated that the five major purposes of appraisal ideally ought to be practiced on a moderately high to high basis on virtually every purpose in most of the countries. Taken together, these results indicate that the purposes of appraisal are not implemented or practiced nearly as much as is intended or desired in appraisals. As such, these data appear to reinforce the controversial nature of performance appraisal. It appears that the potential of appraisal is not fully realized in current practice, not only (as widely believed) in the US, but also in most other countries.

In stating this critical view of the current practice of performance evaluation, it is important to remember that the appraisal discussion typically lasts about one hour (and sometimes less) for the one time a year that it is conducted in the US. This raises the question of how realistic is it for five major purposes (and there are other purposes in addition to these studied here) to be accomplished in a one hour meeting. Perhaps part of the problem with performance evaluations are not just that their intended purposes are not wholly accomplished, but also that perhaps our expectations are too high of what realistically can be accomplished. In other words, if organizations really want to accomplish the various stated purposes of appraisal (e.g., documentation, development, subordinate expression, etc.) then organizations need to devote more time and effort to the performance appraisal process to effectively implement these objectives. Indeed, the fact that the 'should be' means are largely in the moderately high and high range indicates that the respondents do believe that these purposes or functions of appraisal ideally ought to be practiced. Thus, the intended purposes of performance evaluations are seen as useful, but clearly there are problems in the current practice and implementation of appraisals in many countries. Therefore, performance appraisals need to be substantially changed or improved to realize their full potential for impacting employee and organizational performance.

If the appraisal process is to be practiced differently, then an important question is what can be learned from this multi-country study? As stated before, it is difficult to draw any definite conclusions on best practices without assessing contextual factors such as culture, strategy, structure, etc. However, there are some interesting patterns that emerge by geographic regions in the 'should be' means that on a preliminary basis are suggestive of best practices. First, the countries in the American continent (Canada, Latin America, Mexico, and the US) along with Australia and Taiwan largely had 'should be' means above 4.0 on the development and documentation appraisal purpose items. These results were the highest of all of the appraisal purposes and indicate that performance appraisals 'should be' emphasized to a high degree in the future. In particular, two documentation items: #5 – recognize the subordinate and #8 – evaluate the subordinate goals achievement received, along with the two development items: #3 – plan development activities and #6 – lay out ways to improve performance overall, received the highest 'should be' mean scores in our study. The

scores on these items in the rest of the Asian countries were mainly in the moderately high category, suggesting these purpose items are important there as well.

A similar pattern (with the exception of Taiwan) occurred on the two subordinate-expression appraisal purpose items. The four countries in the American continent, along with Australia, all had 'should be' means above 4.0 on these two items, indicating that an important purpose of appraisal in these nations is to allow subordinates to express their thoughts and feelings. In contrast, the rest of the countries indicated that only a moderate to moderately high emphasis 'should be' placed on subordinate expression in appraisal review meetings. In fact, the 'should be' mean score in Korea was particularly low (2.55) on item #10 – allow the subordinates to express their feelings. It is possible that these scores reflect in part the high power distance orientation in many Asian countries which places a lesser value on subordinate input and participation into appraisals (Milliman et al. 1998).

In contrast to the appraisal purposes of documentation and development, there were more similar findings across all of the countries on the two administrative purposes of pay and promotion. In general, the 'should be' mean scores indicate there 'should be' only a moderate emphasis on the administrative purposes of pay and promotion in most of the countries. The exceptions to this are that a high emphasis 'should be' placed on these administrative purposes in Taiwan, Mexico, and Latin America. It is also interesting to note that the data generally suggest that there 'should be' higher emphasis on discussing promotions rather than pay in appraisals. Perhaps linking appraisal results to promotions is considered more consistent with the appraisal's other purposes (e.g., development, training, etc.) than pay. It is also possible that linking pay to appraisal is still too controversial or difficult to do in practice.

Altogether, the 'should be' data indicate that across all of the countries the development and documentation purposes are the most important. In terms of geographic patterns there appeared to be the some important similarities between the four countries in the American continent, Australia, and Taiwan and the other four Asian countries (Indonesia, Japan, Korea, and the PRC).

It is also interesting to note that by far the largest score changes were in Mexico. Mexico had low 'is now' mean scores (below 3.0) on every single purpose of appraisal. In contrast, the 'should be' means were the highest (4.30 to 4.55) overall of any of the ten countries. These generally large differences between the 'is now' and 'should be' means indicate that managers in Mexico particularly desire performance appraisals to be practiced much differently in the future.

While these findings provide a promising starting point for cross-national analysis of performance appraisal practices, there are a number of limitations which 'should be' considered. First, contextual variables were not considered and the analysis took place largely on individual items, although the items were grouped into four major types of appraisal purposes. Second, it 'should be' noted that there are some differences in the sample size and types of organizations sampled between the various countries, as well as when the data were collected. Finally, caution 'should be' used in viewing data since there are always issues in the translation and interpretation of surveys between countries

Future research on best practices in

performance appraisal should consider focusing on key organizational or societal contextual variables that are thought to influence performance appraisal. One particularly important area of study is culture where a number of propositions have been advanced (Milliman et al. 1998) on how culture is thought to influence appraisals. For instance, it has been predicted that countries with a low power distance culture will emphasize greater participation of the subordinate in appraisal meetings than high power distance countries. Another important area to study is the relationship between business strategy and performance appraisal. For instance, based on the strategic HRM literature (Schuler and Jackson 1987), we would expect that companies with a greater emphasis on quality and innovation would be more likely to emphasize the development purpose, while those with a cost efficiency focus would emphasize the documentation objective. Research in these areas along with other important contextual variables such as organizational size and structure, industry, unions, and government regulations should yield greater insights into a context-based perspective of best performance appraisal practices. Such studies should seek to include a number of countries based on their distribution (e.g., from low to high) along the predictor variable (e.g., culture). Obtaining larger samples should ensure that the full range of the predictor variable distribution is covered which will enhance the study's ability to contribute to the universal knowledge about performance appraisals.

It is clear that more rigorous empirical studies of appraisal and other IHRM practices are needed to better understand how and why this management practice differs across various countries and contexts. Research partnerships between

120   *Asia Pacific Journal of Human Resources*   2002 | 40(1)

academics from different countries as well as between academics and practitioners can be an important key to developing a greater understanding of such a fundamentally important and problematic management practice as performance appraisal.

John F. Milliman is an Associate Professor in the Department of Management at the University of Colorado at Colorado Springs. Dr Milliman obtained a BA in Business Economics at the University of California at Santa Barbara, an MS at UCLA, and a PhD at the University of Southern California. Dr Milliman worked in management in the health care industry for eight years and has taught at the University of Colorado for seven years. He has worked with organizations and published articles in the area of performance management, international human resource management, environmental management, and spirituality at work.

Stephen Nason is an Assistant Professor of Management at the Hong Kong University of Science and Technology, where he has taught since receiving his PhD in international management from the University of Southern California in 1994. His research interests focus on organizational learning, decision-making, and human resource management, all from an international perspective. Professor Nason has published papers in the Academy of *Management Journal, Journal of Management, Advances in International Comparative Management, Journal of Managerial Psychology,* and others. His latest book, co-authored with Arthur Yeung, David Ulrich, and Mary Anne Von Glinow, is titled *Organizational Learning Capability: Keys to Continuous Business Success in Today's Business Environment* has just been translated into Chinese.

Cherrie Zhu (BA, Nanjing Normal University; MBA, Monash; PhD, University of Tasmania) is a senior lecturer in the Department of Management at Monash University. She has published and presented papers internationally in the areas of human resource management and international management. Her PhD research was concerned with HRM systems and practices in China's industrial sector. In addition to teaching and conducting research, she offers consultation to businesses. She has been involved in the

development of management training programs, and has also helped to formulate HRM policies and regulations for Australian joint ventures in China.

Helen De Cieri (PhD) is an Associate Professor in the Department of Management, Monash University (Australia). Her academic experience includes appointments in Australia, China, Hong Kong, Malaysia, and the USA. Helen is the Editor of the *Asia Pacific Journal of Human Resources*. Her current research interests include strategic HRM in multinational enterprises, and HRM issues in international interorganizational networks.

References

Abdullah, A., and Gallagher, E. 1995. Managing with cultural differences. *Malaysian Mangement Review* 30, 1–8.

Atchison, T.J. 1990. Impression of compensation administration in the Pacific Rim. In *Research in personnel and human resources management,* eds G.R. Ferris and K.M. Rowland, Supplement 2, 187–99. Greenwich, CT: JAI Press.

Butler, J., G. Ferris and N. Napier. 1991. *Strategy and human resources management.* Cincinnati, OH: South-Western.

Cardy, R., and G. Dobbins. 1994. *Performance appraisal: Alternative perspectives.* Cincinnati, OH: South-Western.

Cascio, W. 1992. *Managing human resources,* 3rd edn. New York: McGraw-Hill.

Cascio, W., and E. Bailey. 1995. International human resource management: The state of research and practice. In *Global perspective of human resource management,* ed. O. Shenkar, 16–36. Englewood Cliffs, NJ: Prentice Hall.

Chang, S.K.C. 1985. American and Chinese managers in Taiwan: A comparison. *California Management Review* 27, 144–56.

Chang, C.S. 1989a. Comparative analysis of management systems: Japan, South Korea, Taiwan and the US. In *Management behind industrialization: Readings in Korean business,* eds D.K. Kim and L. Kim, 231–52. Seoul, Korea: Korea University.

Chang, C.S. 1989b. Human resource management in Korea. In *Korean managerial dynamics,* eds

K.H. Chung and H.C. Lee, 195–205. New York: Praeger.

Chen, S. 1985. *Comprehensive labor and personnel management in enterprises*. Shanghai: Shanghai Science and Technology Press.

Chung, B.J. 1990. Human resource management in Korea. Unpublished doctoral dissertation, University of Southern California.

Cox, T.Y., S.A. Lobel and P.L. McLeod. 1991. Effects of ethnic group cultural differences on Cooperative and competitive behavior on a group task. *Academy of Management Journal* 34, 827–47.

Dowling, P.J., and C. Fisher. 1996. The Australian HR professional: A 1995 profile. Work paper series, 96-04. University of Tasmania, School of Management.

Elashmawi, F., and P. Harris. 1993. *Multicultural mangement: New skills for global success*. Houston, TX: Gulf Publishing Company.

Gomez-Mejia, L., D. Balkin and R. Cardy. 1995. *Managing human resources*. Englewood Cliffs, NJ: Prentice Hall.

Hatvany, N., and V. Pucik. 1981a. Japanese management practice and productivity. *Organizational Dynamics* Spring, 5–21.

Hatvany, N., and V. Pucik. 1981b. An integrated management system: Lessons learned from the Japanese experience. *Academy of Management Review* 6, 469–80.

Hodgetts, R.M., and F. Luthans. 1989. Japanese HR management practices: Separating fact from fiction. *Personnel* April, 42–5.

Huo, Y.P., and M.A. Von Glinow. 1993. On transplanting human resource practices to China: A culture driven approach. Paper presented at ACME III/ICCM VI Joint International Conference, Los Angeles, CA.

Kim, D.K., and C.W. Kim. 1989. Korean value systems and managerial practices. In *Korean managerial dynamics*, eds K.H. Chung and H.C. Lee, 207–16. New York: Praeger.

Laud, R. 1984. Performance appraisal practices in the Fortune 1300. In *Strategic human resource management*, eds C. Fombrun, N. Tichy and M.A. DeVanna. New York: Wiley.

Lawler, E.E. 1994. Performance management: The next generation. *Compensation Benefits Review* May–June, 16–19.

Lawler, E.E., A.M. Mohrman and S.M. Resnick. 1984. Performance appraisal revisited. *Organizational Dynamics Summer*, 20–35.

Lee, H.C. 1989. Managerial characteristics of Korean firms. In *Korean managerial dynamics*, eds K.H. Chung and H.C. Lee, 147–62. New York: Praeger.

Lee, J.K., and R. Ellis. 1988. A framework of managerial promotion in a lifetime employment organizations: The D bank. *International Journal of Value Based Management* 1, 115–32.

Liao, C. W. 1991. *Human resource management*. Shanghai: Tungchi University Press (in Chinese).

Maher, T.E., and Y.Y. Wong. 1994. The impact of cultural differences on the growing tensions between Japan and the United States. *SAM Advanced Management Journal* 59, 40–6.

McEvoy, G.M., and W.R. Cascio. 1990. The US and Taiwan: Two different cultures look at performance appraisal. In *Research in personnel and human resources management*, eds G.R. Ferris and K.M. Rowland, Supplement 2, 201–19. Greenwich, CT: JAI Press.

Milliman, J.F., Y.M. Kim and M.A. Von Glinow. 1993. Hierarchical advancement in Korean chaebols: A model and research agenda. *Human Resource Management Review* 3, 293–320.

Milliman, J.F., S. Nason, E. Gallagher, P. Huo, M.A. Von Glinow and K. Lowe. 1998. The impact of national culture on human resource management practices: The case of performance appraisal. In *Advances in international comparative management*, eds J. Cheng and R.B. Peterson, 157–84. Greenwich, CT: JAI Press.

Milliman, J.F., S. Nason, K. Lowe, N. Kim and P. Huo. 1995. An empirical study of performance appraisal practices in Japan, Korea, Taiwan, and the United States. *Proceedings of the Academy of Management Conference*, 182–96, Vancouver, Canada.

Milliman, J.F., B. Nathan and A.M. Mohrman. 1991, August. Conflicting appraisal purposes of managers and subordinates and their effect on performance and satisfaction. Paper presented at the National Academy of Management Meeting, Miami, FL, August.

Nakane, C. 1972. *Japanese society*. Berkeley: University of California Press.

Nyaw, M.K. 1995. Human resource management in the People's Republic of China. In *Human resource management on the Pacific Rim: Institutions, practices, and attitudes*, eds L.F. Moore and P.D. Jennings. Berlin: Walter de Gruyter.

122   *Asia Pacific Journal of Human Resources*   2002 | 40(1)

Ouchi, W. 1981. *Theory Z.* New York: Addison-Wesley.

Pucik, V. 1984. White collar human resource management: A comparison of the US and Japanese automobile industries. *Columbia Journal of World Business* Fall, 19, 87–94.

Pucik, V., and N. Hatvany. 1983. Management practices in Japan and their impact on business strategy. *Advances in Strategic Management* 1, 103–31.

Quezada, F., and J.E. Boyce. 1998. Latin America. In *Comparitive management: A regional view*, ed. R. Nath, 245–70. Cambridge, MA: Ballinger Publishing Company.

Schuler, R., and S. Jackson. 1987. Linking competitive strategies with human resource management practices. *Academy of Management Executive* 1, 207–19.

Schuler, R., J.R. Fulkerson and P. Dowling. 1991. Strategic performance measurement and management in multinational corporations. *Human Resource Management* 30, 365–92.

Schuler, R., S. Jackson, E. Jackofsky and J. Slocum. 1996. Managing human resources in Mexico: A cultural understanding. *Business Horizons* May/June, 39, 1–7.

Seddon, J. 1987. Assumptions, culture, and performance appraisal. *Journal of Management Development* 6, 47–54.

Shaw, J.B., S.F.Y. Tang, C.D. Fisher and P.S. Kirkbridge. 1993. Organization and environmental factors related to human resource management practices in Hong Kong: A cross-cultural expanded replication. *International Journal of Human Resource Management* 5, 785–816.

Shelton, D. 1995. Human resource management in Australia. In *Human resource management on the Pacific Rim: Institutions, practices, and attitudes*, eds L.F. Moore and P.D. Jennings, 31–60. Berlin: Walter de Gruyter.

Shenkar, O., and M.K. Nyaw. 1995. Yin and yang: The interplay of human resources in Chinese-foreign ventures. In *Global perspectives of human resource management*, ed. O. Shenkar. Englewood Cliffs, NJ: Prentice Hall.

Snell, S.A. 1992. Control theory in strategic human resource management: The mediating effect of administrative information. *Academy of Management Journal* 35, 292–327.

Staw, B.M. 1980. Rationality and justification in organiztional life. In *Research in organizational life*, eds B. Staw and L.L. Cummings, vol. 2, pp. 45–80, of *Research in organizational behavior: A regional review*, eds B. Staw and L.L. Cummings. Greenwich, CT: JAI Press.

Steers, R.M., Y.K. Shin and G.R. Unison. 1989. *The chaebol.* New York: Harper and Row.

Steers, R.M., Y.K. Shin, G.R. Unison and S. Nam. 1990. Korean corporate culture: A comparative analysis. In *Research in personnel and human resources management*, eds B. Shaw, J. Beck, G. Ferris and K. Rowland, Supplement 2, 247–62. Greenwich, CT: JAI Press.

Stone, T.H., and N.M. Meltz. 1992. *Human resource management in Canada*, 3rd edn. New York: Harcourt Brace.

Siu, N.Y., and L. Davies. 1996. A study of managerial characteristics and practices in China, BRC Papers on China, Series No. CP 96010. Hong Kong: Hong Kong Baptist University.

Su, T.L., and C.F. Chu. 1992. *Fundamentals of personnel*. Beijing: Beijing Normal College Press.

Sullivan, J.J., T. Suzuki and Y. Kondo. 1986. Managerial perceptions of performance. *Journal of Cross-Cultural Psychology* 17, 379–98.

Thomas, S.L., and R.D. Bretz. 1994. Research and practice in performance appraisal: Evaluating employee performance in America's largest companies. *SAM Advanced Management Journal* Spring, 28–34.

Von Glinow, M.A., and B.J. Chung. 1989. Comparative human resource management practices in the US, Japan, Korea, and the People's Republic of China. In *Research in personnel and human resources management*, eds A. Nedd, G.R. Ferris and K.M. Rowland, Supplement 1, 153-71. Greenwich, CT: JAI Press.

Zhao, J.H. 1991. *Comparative management*. Jinan: Shan Dong University Press (in Chinese).

Zhao, L.K., and J.W. Pan. 1984. *Labor economics and labor management*. Beijing: Beijing Press (in Chinese).

Zhu, C.J., and P.J. Dowling. 1998. Performance appraisal in China. In *International management in China: Cross-cultural issues*, ed. J. Selmer, 115–36. London and New York: Routledge.

[7]

Rethinking International Compensation

George T. Milkovich
M.P. Catherwood Professor
Center for Advanced
Human Resource Studies
ILR School/Cornell University

Matt Bloom
Assistant Professor
College of Business Administration
University of Notre Dame

The logic of the global marketplace argues for strategic flexibility, rather than national culture, as the basis for managing compensation and reward systems internationally.

We are on the verge of a worldwide restructuring of compensation and reward systems. Even long-established, seemingly carved-in-granite cultural norms, such as lifetime employment in Japan and industrywide bargaining in Germany, are weakening in response to the pressures of a global economy. So also are our previously hard-and-fast assumptions about international compensation—the idea that pay systems should keep expatriates "ecoomically whole" and the notion that local compensation should be tailored to fit national cultures.

True, from a global perspective, there are still substantial differences in the ways people get paid. Consider, for example, that the pay packages offered by the same multinational operating in both Shanghai and Bratislava are very different. In Shanghai, the package may emphasize housing allowances and bonuses intended to retain scarce critical skills, while in Bratislava the package will place greater emphasis on productivity-based gainsharing and base pay.

Yet the logic of market-based economies suggests that these differences will narrow as players worldwide cope with similar pressures. All are affected by intense competition for customers and critical skills; all are influenced by global financial markets; and all seek to understand and leverage the enormous (and increasingly less restricted) flow of information and technology across national boundaries. All strive to harmonize their regional and global manufacturing and distribution systems. Exhibit 1 depicts some of the global forces at work.

While all companies playing in the international market face similar pressures, responses differ. In Europe, the French are changing their compensation systems only gradually. French voters continue to place a high value on their country's wide-ranging social safety net. Consequently, French managers are using share-the-work schemes to cope with the country's high unemployment. Other Europeans, notably the British, permit the parties to adopt more variable systems, including stock options and performance-based schemes. So even though the pressures created under market-based economies are similar, the players who determine how people get paid have considerable freedom when choosing how to respond.

Different responses to globalization highlight the fact that compensation and reward systems are part of the overall relationships between people and employers around the world. These relationships are entwined within social, political,

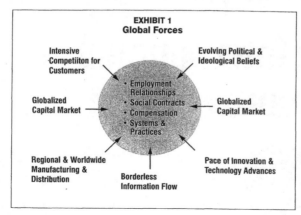

EXHIBIT 1
Global Forces

Intensive Competition for Customers

Evolving Political & Ideological Beliefs

Globalized Capital Market

Globalized Capital Market

• Employment Relationships
• Social Contracts
• Compensation
• Systems & Practices

Regional & Worldwide Manufacturing & Distribution

Borderless Information Flow

Pace of Innovation & Technology Advances

and economic contexts. We are witnessing different approaches to balancing these pressures within those relationships. The changes occurring bring to mind the old children's game of rock-scissors-paper: rock crushes scissors, scissors cuts paper, and paper covers rock. Rock, scissors, and paper interact with each other in the same way the pressures depicted in Exhibit 1 interact and, in turn, cause compensation and reward systems to adapt.

Creating Global Mind-sets

The pressures generated by globalization and market-based economies create unprecedented opportunities for multinational employers. Increasingly, company leaders are recognizing that global mind-sets are required to meet these challenges—and create opportunities.

A global mind-set means adopting values or attitudes to create a common mental programming.

A global mind-set means adopting values or attitudes to create a common mental programming for balancing corporate, business unit, and functional priorities on a worldwide scale. Such a mind-set has enormous intellectual and thus competitive advantages. According to Jack Welch, CEO at General Electric, "The aim in a global business is to get the best ideas from everyone, everywhere.... I think [employees] see that if you are going to grow in GE, you are not going to have

a domestic background all your life." This perspective goes beyond "think globally, act locally." It seems to imply the converse: "Think locally but act globally."

Compensation and reward systems can become crucial tools to support this global mind-set—or they can form major obstacles blocking the way. For organizations competing in worldwide markets, managing compensation and reward systems has always depended on understanding the economic, social, and political changes occurring in the countries in which they operate. What is emerging is that some companies are adopting global compensation and reward strategies that are aligned with and signal their global mind-sets. Rather than only reacting to and matching local conditions, companies with a global perspective shift to finding how they can best use compensation and rewards to compete on a worldwide basis.

Expatriate and National Systems Thinking

Ask compensation directors to describe how international compensation and rewards are managed in their firms, and they typically offer one of two responses. Some describe their recent efforts to modify the balance sheet approach for paying expatriates. Most of these efforts attempt to better align compensation costs with the purposes of different global assignments by distinguishing between developmental and longer-term technology transfers and leadership roles.

Other compensation directors think in terms of different national cultures. They point out the importance of localizing compensation decisions within broad corporate principles. Their purpose is to better align compensation decisions with differences in national cultures. Usually the broad corporate principles seem to be relevant only at 10,000 meters, as in "support the corporate values and global business strategy."

The reality is that local conditions dominate the compensation strategy. Justifications of this practice inevitably include statements like, "You must understand that the United States has a highly individualistic national culture. In other places in the world, particularly Asia, people are comfortable with more collective values. Security is more important than risk taking. You need to be sensitive to 'saving face,'" and so on. These executives seem to believe that something called "national culture" is a critical (perhaps the most critical) factor when managing international compensation.

Now ask those same executives the question posed above, but delete the word *international*, i.e., "Describe how your organization manages compensation." Executives now talk about initiatives to create a common culture of ownership and performance. They say they want to build flexible, agile cultures through practices such as broad banding, broad-based stock option eligibility, 360-degree assessment, and competency-based projects.

So, on the domestic front, they place emphasis on strategic choice and on crafting compensation strategies to help create an organization culture sensitive to markets and performance. Yet internationally, concern with aligning compensation with different national cultures dominates. Most managers subscribe to this approach as consistent with the belief that competitive advantage is achieved via transforming multinationals into local companies.

This view conforms to the often-heard conventional wisdom that the best, indeed, the *only* way to manage international compensation is to tailor it to local conditions and the national culture—to think globally but act locally. Too often the reality is a matter of *reacting*, not acting, locally.

Traditionally, "International" Means "National"

Generally, the traditional perspective is based on the premise that different national systems of compensation and reward are strategic. Discussions, for example, focus on contrasting the German, Japanese, and U.S. approaches. To a large measure, this view reflects the critical importance of government, laws, and regulations, especially tax policies, in determining pay practices. Consequently, understanding these regulations and perhaps undertaking initiatives to change them remain important responsibilities in international compensation.

But this national-system approach goes beyond focusing on regulatory differences among nations; it rests largely on three tenuous assumptions:

1. that national borders largely define the important attributes of people and must be considered when designing compensation and reward systems,

2. that differences between nations are greater

and more relevant to managing international compensation than differences within nations, and

3. that something called "national culture" exists and is a significant factor in global approaches to compensation and reward.

Nations and Regions versus Strategies and Markets

Does it still make sense to view international compensation in terms of national systems when there appears to be considerable variation in compensation and rewards *within* nations as well as between them?

Too often the reality is a matter of reacting—not acting—locally.

Recent studies in China, for example, report substantial differences in pay and reward systems associated with differences in the governance and ownership. In general, pay packages provided in state-owned enterprises emphasize services, benefit allowances (housing, food, healthcare, childcare, etc.), and relatively lower cash. Joint ventures and wholly foreign owned subsidiaries use widely divergent approaches, some emphasizing highly risky variable pay, others emphasizing careers, training opportunities, and moderate cash.

Studies of Japanese companies' HR strategies report differences in compensation approaches associated with organization profitability, size, degree of unionization, capital-labor ratio, and exposure to global competitive forces. For example, Japanese companies operating in protected domestic markets are more likely to use the more performance- and ability-based schemes. Among Korean chaebols, factors such as labor market conditions, customer and supplier relations, economic conditions, and technology account for differences in compensation strategies.

Studies of person-based rewards in samples from Hungarian and U.S. companies suggest that political, economic, and institutional forces, rather than national cultures, explain differences in Hungarian and U.S. reward practices. Recent surveys in the Central European countries of Slovenia and Slovakia also report differences among companies in their use of variable performance-based pay schemes, allowances and services, and even in the ratios of top managing directors' salaries to the average worker.

17

While the recent evidence does not suggest that national boundaries (national wage systems) should be ignored or overlooked, it does suggest that sufficient discretion for individual organizations exists within these national systems to allow organizations to customize compensation and reward systems. Hence, business strategy and markets are more appropriate than countries as the unit of analysis for globalizing compensation.

The Strategic (In)Significance of National Cultures

Are compensation and reward systems in a global context better understood by examining differences in *national* cultures—or by examining more *local* cultures, particularly those within organizations?

The assumption that compensation systems must fit national cultures is based on the belief that "most of a country's inhabitants share a national character...that...represents mental programming for processing ideas and information that these people have in common."[1] This belief, put forth by Geert Hofstede, leads to a search for distinct national characteristics whose influence is then assumed to be critical in managing international compensation systems.

Typical of this mode of thinking is the widely used list of cultural attributes proposed by Hofstede (power distance, individualism-collectivism, uncertainty avoidance, and masculinity/ femininity) or by H.K. Trompenaar (individualism versus collectivism, achievement versus ascription, universalism versus particularism, neutral versus affective, specific versus diffuse).

A "national culture" approach to pay engenders blatant stereotypes.

Following this view, some argue that compensation systems in countries where the culture emphasizes respect for status and hierarchy and thus produces higher power distance scores (Malaysia and Mexico) should exhibit more hierarchical pay structures, while those manifesting low power distance (Australia and the Netherlands) would choose more egalitarian systems. In nations identified as individualistic (U.S., U.K., Canada), compensation and rewards would support employability and individual and performance-based pay. Those in more collectivist nations (Singapore, Japan) would choose

more group-based approaches, and so on.

This national culture approach prescribes that compensation and reward policies must be aligned with and reinforce attributes of national culture. Proponents of this approach might argue, for example, that "Giving the kind of direct performance feedback required under most merit and bonus plans fails to account for saving face, which is so crucial in Asian cultures." Or they might say, "In Germany, MBO was favorably received, because Germans prefer decentralization and formal rules."

One might well react to such thinking by pointing out that it engenders blatant stereotyping. It parallels such biased notions as "all women desire time off because of their caring and nurturing values, while all men desire more time at work to pursue their more aggressive values."

It has long been recognized that compensation and reward systems, because of their social as well as economic significance, exemplify and reinforce cultural norms. However, this does not mean that social and cultural norms necessarily coincide with national boundaries. Indeed, 100 years ago, writers recognized that mining and textile companies developed their own unique social norms—and that the compensation systems of these companies reflected those norms.

The idea of a "national culture" requires a leap of logic in assuming that social norms and cultural values are solely national in character. Clearly, geopolitical boundaries alone do not determine cultural values and social norms. Nations comprise a variety of subgroups and subcultures, and anecdotal and empirical evidence suggest that local cultural values as well as values within organizations differ significantly.

Consider, for example, that the former Czechoslovakia included Czechs and Slovaks; now each of these two republics includes groups that exhibit Hungarian and Roman cultural characteristics. Historically, China has always been a composite of several groups; even today, Chinese make culturally laden distinctions between Shanghai, Beijing, and Hong Kong.

Listening to U.S. politicians during election time, one quickly realizes that the United States is made up of many different subcultures that do not conform to geographic boundaries. As pluralism and other influences of globalization increase around the world, some cultural researchers believe that the cultures of small subgroups will become much more important for shaping human behavior than norms at larger societal or national levels. Even when viewed at the national level, revisions may already have occurred. Recent studies suggest that work-related values are changing in China and the U.S. and that these changes are related to differences in reward allocation preferences.

Indeed, it seems increasingly inappropriate to begin analysis for compensation systems at the national level. We recently completed a study of values placed on individualism-collectivism and risk taking at four companies, two in the U.S. and two in Slovenia. The averages of these intra-country distributions were slightly different: Slovenian employees tended to be more individualistic and more inclined to take risks than U.S. employees. Yet Hofstede's work suggests that Yugoslavs, of which Slovenia is a former republic, should be risk averse and collectivistic. The striking feature, however, was that the variances of the distributions were virtually the same. Thus, one can find risk averse collectivists and risk-taking individualists in the U.S., Slovenia, and most likely in many other nations as well.

Our research suggests that paying attention to average levels across national cultures may be misleading. It fails to account for the significant variation within countries that creates sufficient overlap with the distributions in other countries. Closer analysis reveals that political, economic, institutional, and other forces (rather than national culture) explain a significant amount of variation in the expressed desires of employees from different countries. For example, U.S. workers may desire two weeks of vacation, not because of culture, but because that is the norm in the U.S. In Germany, the norm is one month or more. Transfer a U.S. worker to Germany, and the employee will likely want the month; two weeks will no longer be sufficient.

Does It Pay to Be Different?

Are compensation and reward systems in a global context better understood by examining competitive strategies of specific enterprises, or by focusing on differences in national culture and institutions (e.g., public policy)?

Obviously, national public policy, which reflects social contracts among unions, employers, financial institutions and people, is an important influence on compensation and reward systems. For example, differences in the use of stock options in Germany and Japan compared with the United States and United Kingdom are directly related to national tax and regulation policies. Differences in marginal tax rates are directly associated with the use of vari-

able pay schemes. In Korea or Japan, for example, employees prefer increases in bonuses and allowances (not based on performance) rather than base pay increments. Social security and national health insurance rates paid by employers are calculated on base pay, not bonuses or allowances. In the U.S., many benefit forms are not subject to income tax and are therefore a relatively tax effective way to increase the value of employment for people.

Strategic flexibility means customizing multiple compensation and reward systems.

The degree of discretion available to managers when they respond to governmental initiatives is often not a simple matter of compliance. Except in rare cases, firms usually have alternatives in terms of the strength and pervasiveness of their response to governmental actions.

For example, structuring compensation practices around U.S. tax laws has led to some very creative and innovative new compensation schemes (e.g., deferred compensation plans, ESOPs, phantom stock options). These are used by some firms, but certainly not all. Thus, even the "how" of complying with public policies is a strategic choice.

In the same way, firms operating within so-called national cultures exhibit a variety of responses. Each organization's human resource policies and practices create a distinctive and unique culture that influences people's attitudes and work behaviors. Those people who do not fit the organization culture because they possess different values will either not join or will soon leave the organization.

Signaling Organization Cultures, Not National Cultures

Compensation and reward systems can become an important signal of an organization's culture and values. As such, the systems help create cultures or mind-sets that are different and distinct from the cultures and values of competing firms. Hewlett-Packard and Microsoft both compete vigorously for software engineers, yet each company exhibits a different corporate culture, signaled by and reinforced in their respective compensation systems. The same logic applies to

19

EXHIBIT 2
Rethinking International Compensation
Traditional to Strategic Flexibility

TRADITIONAL	STRATEGIC FLEXIBILITY
Ensure Expatriates' Balance Sheet	⟶ Create Global Mind-set; Achieve Strategic Priorities
Focus on Differences Among Nations	⟶ Leverage Differences Within Nations
Act Like National Culture	⟶ Grow Corproate Culture
Focus Total Compensation Package	⟶ Manage Total Value of Employment and Relational Forms
Manage Multiple Compensation Systems	⟶ Manage Multiple Deals

Toyota and Toshiba—different cultures and different compensation and reward systems.

Given sufficient variation in values among the people in the labor pools of a nation, firms can structure compensation policies that are consistent with the firm's culture and simultaneously attract individuals from the applicant pool who have similar values. When considered from a strategic perspective, organizations can customize compensation systems to help create a culture and attract a workforce that possesses the values, knowledge, skills, and abilities that support the organization's strategic goals and objectives.

Strategic Flexibility: Managing Multiple Deals

Strategic flexibility in global compensation and reward systems starts with understanding how the company plans to win. What is its strategic intent? What is its global mind-set?

The strategic flexibility model offers managers the opportunity to tailor the total compensation system.

As depicted in Exhibit 2, strategic flexibility is based on the premise that understanding and managing total compensation in a global business shifts thinking away from using a balance sheet to keep expatriates economically whole or relying on stereotypical notions of differences among nations. The focus, rather, is on under-

standing and leveraging differences within and between nations.

To be sure, national laws, particularly tax and welfare regulations, are important forces. Yet logic argues that understanding differences and variability within as well as between nations reinforces strategic concerns. In the U.S., no manager presumes all the people are equal to the U.S. average; differences matter. It's the same around the world. In addition, the focus on differences helps managers think in terms of shaping a common mind-set and creating and energizing a workforce with shared values and the capabilities necessary to achieve success.

·If the global business strategy involves paying less attention to boundaries, sharing ideas and intelligence, harmonizing manufacturing and the distribution process to take advantage of economies of scale, and presenting one face to the customer, then a global compensation system should be crafted to signal this—and reward behaviors to achieve it.

At the same time, we need to recognize that creative tension occurs when a global business strives to achieve a common mind-set and common strategic objectives while simultaneously operating in numerous, complex, rapidly changing markets and locations.

Strategic flexibility means that companies achieve advantage by customizing multiple compensation and reward systems. This is already the state of practice in companies operating in multiple markets or employing contingent and core workforces. The art is to avoid the chaos created when multiple systems go off in multiple directions. This results in numerous compensation systems, one for each country in which the company operates. To overcome the chaos, the company must ensure that the multiple deals signal the organization's global mind-set and support its strategic priorities.

The strategic flexibility model presumes that all these complexities cannot be predetermined and indeed are constantly changing. So an adaptive, more flexible approach is required—one that creates a total value of employment consistent with local conditions, while at the same time forging the common mind-set required by business priorities. It supports business priorities not through a set of chameleon-like systems tailored to varying conditions, but from systems that focus attention on what matters to business success and influences employees' actions consistent with an organization's priorities.

Creating and managing multiple deals to support a global business is consistent with the current practice of broadening the definition of total compensation to include the total value of employment. As shown in Exhibit 3, total compensation includes cash, benefits, and long-term incentives as well as employment security conditions, flexible work schedules, learning opportunities, and so on. There is a growing realization that focusing only on the financial forms of total compensation creates transactional relationships that can be easily copied or purchased by competitors. Financial returns alone cannot extract the unique, value-adding ideas and behaviors possessed by employees. Financial returns alone are ineffective in creating the common mind-set that creates peoples' willingness to share the insights and tacit knowledge required to achieve and sustain advantage.

Relational Returns

Broader thinking that includes both financial and relational returns is required. Relational returns may bind individuals more strongly to the orga-

nization because they can answer those special individual needs that cannot be met as effectively with economic returns (e.g., providing for childcare via the noneconomic return of flexible work schedules, versus the financial return of salary to pay for childcare; the flexible schedule puts a parent, not a caregiver, at home). The total value of employment, comprising both relational and financial returns, creates broad, flexible exchanges or deals with employees. Multiple deals encompass a broad range of exchanges and can help create commitment to common values, goals, and the pursuit of mutually beneficial long-term objectives.

Thus, an adaptive, more flexible approach is required. It must permit multiple employment relationships that allow organizations to recognize local conditions when necessary, while at the same time creating the common mind-set among employees required to direct their efforts toward strategic priorities. This approach recognizes that variations in beliefs, opinions, and values within countries provide opportunities for organizations to attract people who thrive in the organization's unique culture, rather than trying to make the organization conform to national cultures.

Flexibility, choice, and managing risk form the essence of this thinking. It begins by viewing the employment relationship as an exchange. Under this view, both the employer and employee make contributions and extract returns from the rela-

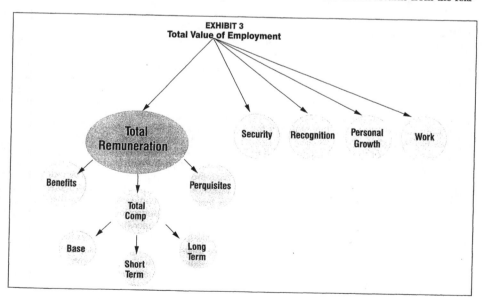

EXHIBIT 3
Total Value of Employment

Total Remuneration — Security — Recognition — Personal Growth — Work

Benefits — Perquisites

Total Comp

Base — Short Term — Long Term

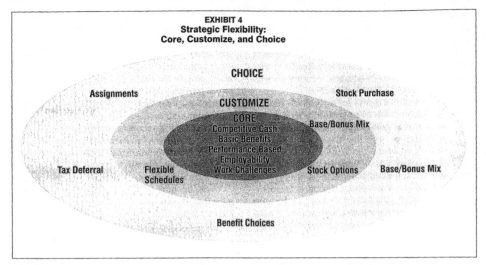

EXHIBIT 4
Strategic Flexibility:
Core, Customize, and Choice

CHOICE

Assignments   Stock Purchase

CUSTOMIZE

CORE
Competitive Cash   Base/Bonus Mix
Basic Benefits
Performance Based
Employability
Tax Deferral   Flexible   Work Challenges   Stock Options   Base/Bonus Mix
Schedules

Benefit Choices

tionship. A critical principle is that the returns offered by the employer are the primary determinants of the contributions provided by employees. That is, what employees are willing to give to the organization is determined in large part by what the employer is willing to give to the employee. There is no chicken-and-egg search here; the employer's choices come first and determine the employees' response. However, once this relationship is underway, it becomes dynamic and recurring.

Total Compensation

The objective, then, is to structure the total value of employment so that employee contributions support organizational goals.

The model in Exhibit 4 groups different forms of total compensation into three sets: core, crafted, and choice. It includes any return an organization can offer that employees see as a reward or a return for the contributions they make on the organization's behalf.

The *core* section of the model includes compensation and reward forms that signal the corporate global mind-set (e.g., creating a performance/customer service culture or a culture of ownership, ensuring a basic level of services and benefits). Specific practices may vary according to market and local conditions but must be consistent with the core policies.

The *crafted* set of compensation elements in Exhibit 4 assumes that business unit or regional leaders have discretion to choose among a menu of total compensation forms that may be impor-

tant to gain and sustain advantage in the markets in which they operate. For example, some form of housing assistance (loans, allowances, dormitories) may make sense in Shanghai, whereas in London or Tokyo, transportation assistance may make more sense. A single company with operating units in San Jose and Kuala Lumpur may find that specific elements (e.g., risk sharing, bonuses, language training, and flexible schedules) may be more important in California than in Kuala Lumpur.

The critical focus of the crafted alternatives is to offer operating units the ability to further customize their total compensation package to achieve their business objectives. This crafted portion is created within the framework of core returns so that it supports and reinforces corporate priorities and culture as well. Thus, managers of R&D units can craft returns to support their goals and satisfy the preferences of scientists, while the sales units can craft a different set of returns consistent with sales goals and preferences of sales personnel.

Finally, the alternatives in the *choice* set offer flexibility for employees to select among various forms of total compensation. Analogous to flexible benefits, the choice set shifts the focus of customizing compensation from managers to employees. Examples here might include opportunities to take educational leaves to become eligible for regional or global assignments, 401(k)-like wealth creating arrangements, or differing employment security arrangements (e.g., contract terms for managers and professionals).

The choice set recognizes the difficulties in identifying national cultures by taking the notion of customizing to the individual level. Within a total cost framework, employees would be given the opportunity to select from a set of returns those that are of most value to their particular situations.

So the strategic flexibility model offers managers the opportunity to tailor the total compensation system to fit the context in which they compete within a framework of corporate principles. Additionally, the approach offers some opportunity for employees to select forms of returns that meet their individual needs as well.

Many companies are already using some of this strategic flexibility model. In global organizations, the business units or regions often have discretion to customize their compensation system within corporate guidelines. For some companies, the strategic flexibility model simply draws existing practices under one umbrella. For example, it treats expatriates as simply another group, much like sales disciplines.

At the same time, however, other companies operate with their international compensation and reward systems pointed in many different directions. Global mind-sets may not be obvious and the global strategic priorities may not be supported. For these firms, directing compensation and reward systems strategically provides an opportunity to gain a competitive advantage.

Endnotes

1 Hofstede, Geert. "Motivation, Leadership and Organizations: Do American Theories Apply Abroad?" *Organizational Dynamics*, Summer 1980, pp. 42-55.

George T. Milkovitch is the M.P. Catherwood Professor and Research Director at the Center for Advanced Human Resources Studies, ILR School, Cornell University. He recently chaired the National Academy of Sciences Committee on Pay for Performance and the Congressionally appointed Committee on Strengthening the Relationship Between Pay and Performance. He is the co-author of Compensation, *the most widely used text in the field.*

Matt Bloom is an assistant professor in the College of Business Administration at the University of Notre Dame. His current research and teaching focus on managing total compensation, understanding high-performance employment relationships, and strategic international human resource management. Bloom received his Ph.D. from Cornell University.

● ●

[8]

Identifying International Assignees At Risk for Premature Departure: The Interactive Effect of Outcome Favorability and Procedural Fairness

Ron Garonzik
Hay/McBer Corporation

Joel Brockner
Columbia University

Phyllis A. Siegel
Rutgers, The State University of New Jersey

Two studies examined factors that predict expatriate managers' tendencies to think seriously about departing prematurely from their international assignments. Previous research (conducted outside of the expatriate context) has shown that individuals' willingness to stay with or leave their positions is an interactive function of outcome favorability and procedural fairness. A conceptually analogous interaction effect was found in the present studies. Whereas expatriates more seriously thought of departing prematurely when they perceived the non-work-related outcomes of their overseas assignments to be less favorable, this tendency was much less pronounced when procedural fairness was relatively high. Theoretical and practical implications are discussed, as are limitations of the studies and suggestions for future research.

The consequences of managers' international assignments are of great significance, both to the organization and to the managers themselves. From the organization's perspective, whether international assignees successfully complete their tour of duty is a matter of considerable importance (Bird & Dunbar, 1991; Black, Gregersen, & Mendenhall, 1992; Naumann, 1992). Moreover, international assignments may have significant effects on managers' professional and personal lives. For example, international assignments may affect managers' longer-term career prospects, either inside their employing organization (Adler, 1996; Grant, 1997) or outside of it.

Given the many significant consequences of expatriation, it is both practically and theoretically important to understand the factors that make expatriation more or less successful (Black, Mendenhall, & Oddou, 1991). Although the success or failure of expatriation has been conceptualized in a variety of ways, one frequent operational definition is the extent to which managers

Ron Garonzik, Hay/McBer Corporation, Boston, Massachusetts; Joel Brockner, Graduate School of Business, Columbia University; Phyllis A. Siegel, Faculty of Management, Rutgers, The State University of New Jersey.

Ron Garonzik and Joel Brockner contributed equally to this research; their order of authorship is random.

We thank Allan Bird, Ya-Ru Chen, Chris Earley, Mark Mendenhall, and Batia Wiesenfeld for their constructive comments on an earlier version of the article. We also are extremely grateful to the late David McClelland, who not only offered helpful comments on an earlier version of the article but who also served more generally as a source of guidance and inspiration for many years.

Correspondence concerning this article should be addressed to Joel Brockner, 715 Uris Hall, Columbia University, New York, New York 10027. Electronic mail may be sent to jb54@columbia.edu.

prematurely depart from their international assignments. Studies have shown that the costs of premature departure may be considerable to the organization, the expatriates, or both. For example, it has been reported that the average annual cost to send an employee overseas for a year or two is in the range of $250,000–300,000 (Milkovich & Newman, 1996). Thus, for organizations that have a sizable number of expatriates, the total cost of premature repatriation may be enormous. Costs to the expatriates may include threatened career advancement, reduced managerial self-confidence, and lowered prestige in the eyes of their peers.

The purpose of the present research is to identify factors that lead expatriate managers to think seriously about departing prematurely from their international assignments. Theory and research have suggested that turnover typically is preceded by several related withdrawal cognitions, such as serious thoughts of leaving and the intention to turnover (Mobley, 1982; Naumann, 1992; Shaffer & Harrison, 1998). Moreover, previous research has found moderate-to-strong relationships between behavioral intentions and actual behavior, both generally in social psychology (Ajzen & Fishbein, 1980) and specifically in the context of organizational turnover (Mobley, 1982; Naumann, 1992). For example, Steel and Ovalle (1984) reported a weighted average correlation of .50 between intention to turnover and actual turnover in their meta-analytic review. Thus, expatriates who are thinking seriously about departing prematurely may be described as being at risk to leave. Given the magnitude of the potential costs associated with premature expatriate departure, it is important to identify those who are at risk.

The potential conceptual advances offered by the present research are threefold. First, we seek to extend the literature on premature expatriate departure by providing a theory-driven analysis of some of its antecedents. More specifically, the present studies are grounded in a considerable body of theory and research in organizational justice (e.g., Greenberg, 1990). Second, the theoretical underpinning of the present studies offers an extension to existing models of expatriate adjustment and turnover (e.g., Black et al., 1991; Naumann, 1992), which suggests that expatriates' thoughts of premature departure may be influenced by a variety of factors. The existing models, however, have not considered how the various factors combine with each other to influence expatriates' thoughts of premature departure. The organizational-justice framework guiding the present studies suggests that several antecedents of expatriates' withdrawal cognitions interact to predict the extent to which they are seriously thinking of departing prematurely.

A third goal of the present studies is to extend the generality of organizational-justice theory. Although justice factors have been shown to influence a variety of important work attitudes and behaviors (e.g., Folger, 1993; Greenberg, 1996), few studies have examined the role of fairness perceptions as predictors of expatriates' reactions.

Theoretical Grounding

Organizational psychologists have shown that employees' work attitudes and behaviors are jointly determined by outcomes (i.e., what happens) and procedures (i.e., how things happen). Outcome factors have been considered by social exchange theorists (e.g., Blau, 1964). According to this viewpoint, employees give back to the organization (e.g., show signs of commitment) in proportion to the perceived favorability of the outcomes received from the organization. Relevant outcomes may be economic (e.g., favorable levels of compensation) or psychological (e.g., individuals' perceptions that they are valued and respected by their employers).

The role of procedural fairness has been discussed extensively by organizational justice theorists (e.g., Folger & Greenberg, 1985; Greenberg, 1987; Lind & Tyler, 1988). According to these viewpoints, employees will be more organizationally committed (e.g., they will be less likely to think of leaving) to the extent that organizational authorities use fair procedures in planning and implementing decisions. Individuals' perceptions of procedural fairness, moreover, are based on two categories of factors: (a) the structural aspects of decision processes, such as whether people are allowed to provide input into decisions (Thibaut & Walker, 1975), and (b) the interpersonal behavior of those responsible for implementing decisions (also known as interactional justice; Bies, 1987), such as whether they treated the affected parties with dignity and respect.

The present research examines whether expatriates' thoughts of premature departure are affected by both the outcomes associated with their overseas assignment as well as the procedural fairness exhibited by organizational authorities. Interestingly, many recent studies (conducted outside of the expatriation context) have shown that outcome favorability and procedural fairness combine interactively to influence employees' attitudes and behaviors. It is therefore plausible that expatriates' thoughts of premature departure also will be an interactive function of outcome favorability and procedural fairness. Brockner and Wiesenfeld (1996) reviewed 45 independent samples that showed that individuals' perceptions of outcome favorability had much less of an impact on a variety of dependent variables (including withdrawal cognitions)

when they perceived the procedures enacted by organizational authorities to be relatively fair.

A number of explanations have been advanced to account for the interactive relationship between outcome favorability and procedural fairness. It is beyond the scope of the present research to describe and compare the various explanations (but see Brockner & Wiesenfeld, 1996, for a review). Moreover, the present studies were not designed to be a critical test of competing explanations. Rather, our primary purpose was to evaluate whether expatriates' thoughts of premature departure varied as a function of the interaction between outcome favorability and procedural fairness. Specifically, whereas expatriates were expected to be more seriously thinking of departing prematurely when the outcomes associated with their overseas assignment were relatively unfavorable, this tendency was expected to be less pronounced when procedural fairness was relatively high.

Outcome Favorability in the Present Research

Although many outcomes of significance to expatriates reside in the workplace (e.g., compensation, feeling valued), the outcomes selected for investigation in the present studies referred to the nonwork aspects of expatriates' assignments. Nonwork factors, such as living conditions, health care, and the perceived adjustment of participants' spouse or significant other, were chosen for several reasons. First, previous research has shown that the perceived favorability of these nonwork outcomes is meaningful to expatriates; for example, it predicts the extent to which expatriates consider departing prematurely from their overseas assignments (Black et al., 1992; Shaffer & Harrison, 1998). Second, previous research examining the interactive relationship between outcome favorability and procedural fairness outside of the expatriate context invariably has examined work-related outcomes (e.g., Greenberg, 1994). By focusing on nonwork factors in the present studies, we evaluated whether the outcomes associated with a broader array of factors (than those residing in the workplace) interact with procedural fairness to influence employees' work attitudes and behaviors.

Procedural Fairness in the Present Research

Procedural fairness in the present research referred to expatriates' perceptions of the methods generally used by the parent organization to plan and implement decisions. Participants rated the fairness of the organization's usual procedures in making decisions, which may include, but need not be limited to, their expatriate experience (e.g., compensation, work assignments, etc.). Previous research has shown that perceptions of procedural fairness are related to various indexes of organizational commitment, including the desire to remain with (rather than depart from) the organization (Brockner & Wiesenfeld, 1996). Moreover, the procedural fairness of an organization relates to several components of Naumann's (1992) model of expatriate turnover, such as corporate culture (i.e., the perceived fairness of how things are done around here).

In sum, we conducted two studies that examined the extent to which expatriates were thinking seriously about departing prematurely from their international assignments as a function of their perceptions of (a) the favorability of the nonwork outcomes of their assignments and (b) the procedural fairness of the organization's decision-making processes. Whereas expatriates were expected to be more seriously thinking of departing prematurely when outcomes were perceived to be less favorable, this tendency should have been less pronounced when procedures were seen as relatively fair.

Study 1

Method

Participants. Participants were 58 international assignees employed by a United States-based service company with significant international markets. The survey was mailed to all expatriates in the company; the response rate was 75%. Participants were located in 20 countries drawn from five continents. The average age of participants in the sample was 37 years, and 95% of them were men. In addition, all of the participants in the main analyses were accompanied by a spouse or significant other on their assignment. The group was evenly divided between technical specialists and first-level managers versus second-level or higher managers (senior managers, managing directors, and vice presidents). Their average tenure with the company was 8.7 years. Participants had been in their assignments for an average length of 1.6 years at the time that the study was conducted. The typical length of an expatriate assignment in the organization was approximately 3 years.

Procedure. Participants were asked to complete a survey in the context of the organization's routine efforts at assessing and improving the quality of its human resource practices. Prior to receiving the survey, all participants received an in-house notice from the Vice President of International Personnel that informed them of the study's significance and implored them to take part. Ron Garzonik then mailed the survey to all participants. In the cover letter accompanying the survey, Garzonik introduced himself and described the basic purpose of the survey ("to gauge the experiences and reactions of international personnel to their assignments"). The cover letter also assured respondents that (a) their participation was voluntary, (b) their responses would be confidential, and (c) only aggregate data would be presented to the sponsoring organization.

Survey instrument. All of the measures were included in the survey, which consisted of more than 100 items and which entailed a comprehensive assessment of expatriates' perceptions of the assignment and the parent organization. The independent and dependent variables of the present study were embedded in the survey (Hay/McBer Co., 1996).

Dependent variable. Six items were developed to measure the extent to which participants were thinking seriously about departing prematurely from their expatriate assignment. A 6-point rating scale was used for each item, with endpoints labeled *strongly disagree* (1) and *strongly agree* (6). Items were coded such that higher scores reflected fewer thoughts of premature departure (or more of an expressed likelihood of remaining with the assignment). Sample items were, "I wouldn't seriously consider leaving my current job assignment prematurely," and "I often discuss with my spouse (or significant other) the possibility of returning to the U.S. prematurely" (reverse scored). Coefficient alpha was .76. Participants' responses to the six items were averaged into an index.

Independent variables: Outcome favorability. Seven items measured participants' perceptions of the favorability of the outcomes associated with their expatriate assignment. Six-point rating scales were used. Six of the seven items required participants to indicate how much they had adjusted to various aspects of their nonwork lives. Endpoints ranged from *very unadjusted* (1) to *very adjusted* (7). Aspects covered included (a) living conditions in general, (b) housing conditions, and (c) health care management. An additional item measuring an important nonwork outcome was, "How well has your spouse (or significant other) adjusted to living overseas?" Presumably, participants viewed their outcomes more favorably to the extent that they perceived adjustment to be higher. Re-

sponses to the measures of outcome favorability were internally consistent (coefficient alpha = .85) and averaged into an index.

Procedural fairness. Whereas questions pertaining to outcome favorability referred specifically to the expatriate assignment, the measures of procedural fairness were intended to be more general, reflecting participants' judgments of the organizational climate of their work units based on typical day to day experiences (Hay/McBer Co., 1997; McClelland & Burnham, 1995). Thus, evaluations of procedural fairness could be based on events associated with their expatriate assignment or organizational experiences encountered outside of the expatriate setting. Five items tapping various aspects of procedural fairness were included in the climate survey. Some of the items referred to the structural aspects of the organization's procedures (Leventhal, Karuza, & Fry, 1980; Thibaut & Walker, 1975), such as whether people were allowed to have input into the organization's decision-making policies ("Problems are solved and decisions are made at the lowest appropriate level in the business"). Other items focused on the interpersonal behavior of the parties responsible for planning and implementing decisions ("Employees are treated with respect and dignity in this company"). Six-point rating scales were used with endpoints consisting of diametrically opposed statements. All items were coded such that higher scores reflected stronger perceptions of procedural fairness. Coefficient alpha was .61. Participants' responses to the five measures of procedural justice were averaged into an index.

Control variables. Four factors that have been theoretically or empirically linked to expatriates' thoughts of premature departure were included in the survey (e.g., Black et al., 1992; Gregersen & Black, 1992). The control variables consisted of (a) whether participants have had any prior international work experience (measured by either a "yes" or a "no" answer); (b) perceptions of predeparture training, which was assessed with four items (e.g., "I am satisfied with the quality of the predeparture preparation I underwent"; coefficient alpha = .77), (c) perceived support from the home office during their overseas assignment, which was based on six items (e.g., "Overall, I am satisfied with the level of support I have received from the home organization to help me solve work-related problems"; coefficient alpha = .77), and (d) beliefs about being successfully repatriated on completion of their overseas assignment, which were based on five items (e.g., "I am confident that I will be repatriated in a manner that will take advantage of my international experience"; coefficient alpha = .85). Responses to the measures of predeparture training, perceived support from the home office, and beliefs concerning repatriation could range from *thoroughly disagree* (1) to *thoroughly agree* (6).

Results and Discussion

Summary statistics for and correlations between all of the continuous variables are reported in Table 1. Four factors were significantly related to expatriates' thoughts of premature departure (perceived support from the home office, beliefs about being successfully repatriated, outcome favorability, and procedural fairness), all in the expected direction.

The primary hypothesis was tested with a hierarchical multiple regression. In the first step, we simultaneously entered the four control variables. As reported in Table 2, Step 1, the only one to attain significance was the measure of perceived support from the home office ($p < .01$). In the second step, we simultaneously added the main effects of outcome favorability and procedural fairness to the terms entered in Step 1. As can be seen in Table 2, Step 2, only the main effect of outcome favorability was significant ($p < .001$), such that expatriates were more apt to think seriously about departing prematurely when their nonwork outcomes were more unfavorable.

Finally, and of greatest importance, the interaction between outcome favorability and procedural fairness was added in the

Table 1

Summary Statistics and Correlations for Continuous Variables (Study 1)

Variable	M	SD	1	2	3	4	5	6
1. Home office support	2.83	0.93	(.77)					
2. Successful repatriation	2.79	1.19	.58**	(.85)				
3. Predeparture training	2.37	1.10	.52**	.28*	(.77)			
4. Outcome favorability	4.50	0.88	.35**	.15	.18	(.85)		
5. Procedural fairness	3.67	0.92	.45**	.34**	.27*	.25*	(.61)	
6. Thoughts of premature departure	4.38	1.06	.51**	.28*	.11	.49**	.32**	(.76)

Note. Higher scores reflect greater levels of all variables except thoughts of premature departure, in which case higher scores reflect fewer thoughts of premature departure. All scores could range from 1–6. Coefficient alphas are in parentheses. One of the control variables (whether participants had overseas experience) was a categorical variable. We conducted a series of t tests to evaluate whether this factor was related to any of the variables included in Table 1. The only significant effect emerged on the measure of predeparture training, $t(56) = 2.49$, $p < .025$, such that perceptions of predeparture training were more favorable among participants who did not have (rather than did have) previous overseas experience ($Ms = 2.61$ and 1.94, respectively).
* $p < .05$.   ** $p < .01$.

third step; it was found to be significant ($p < .01$). The fact that the sign of the beta weight was negative suggests that the interaction took the predicted form (i.e., that outcome favorability and thoughts of premature departure were more strongly related when procedural fairness was relatively low). To illustrate further the nature of the interaction effect, we classified participants as relatively high or low in their perceptions of procedural fairness on the basis of a median split. We then computed the correlation between outcome favorability and thoughts of premature departure for each of these two groups. As expected, expatriates' perceptions of outcome favorability were more closely related to their thoughts of premature departure among those who perceived relatively low levels of procedural fairness, $r(22) = .66$, $p < .01$, rather than high levels of procedural fairness, $r(32) = .32$, $p > .05$.

Although the measure of outcome favorability referred to tangible factors of known significance to expatriates (e.g., living conditions), the rating scales asked participants to indicate how adjusted they felt toward these factors rather than their perceptions of favorability per se. An alternative measure of outcome favor-

ability consisted of an item which assessed the construct more directly (and more generally) than the measure reported above. Specifically, participants indicated on a 6-point rating scale their level of agreement with the following statement: "All in all, the benefits of my current assignment outweigh its costs." As might be expected, participants' evaluations on this alternative measure of outcome favorability item were significantly related to their evaluations on the previously reported measure of outcome favorability, $r(56) = .52$, $p < .001$.

We also conducted a hierarchical multiple regression in which the alternative measure of outcome favorability was substituted for the one used previously. Of greatest concern was whether the interaction between procedural fairness and the alternative measure of outcome favorability would be significant. In fact, it was, $F(1, 50) = 5.88$, $p < .025$, and took the same form as the one reported above. That is, outcome favorability was more strongly related to expatriates' thoughts of premature departure when procedural fairness was relatively low rather than high. These findings provide converging evidence in support of the primary hypothesis. Furthermore, in conjunction with the significant correlation between the two measures of outcome favorability, the regression results provide evidence supporting the construct validity of the original measure of outcome favorability.

Study 2

Although the results of Study 1 supported the primary hypothesis, several methodological weaknesses should be noted. First, the sample size was fairly small ($N = 58$). Second, the internal consistency of the measure of procedural fairness was modest (.61). Given these shortcomings, it seemed worthwhile to attempt to replicate the findings; hence, a second study was conducted.

Method

Participants. Participants were 70 international assignees employed by a European-based consumer products company with significant international markets. The survey was mailed to all expatriates in the company; the response rate was 35%. Participants were located in more than 40 countries spanning five continents.

Table 2

Hierarchical Multiple Regression Results (Study 1)

	Thoughts of premature departure		
Independent variable	β	R^2	Change in R^2
Step 1		.26**	.26**
Home office support	.68**		
Successful repatriation	−.05		
Previous overseas experience			
Yes	2.08		
No	.00		
Predeparture training	−.10		
Step 2		.43***	.17***
Procedural fairness	.21		
Outcome favorability	.40***		
Step 3		.50***	.07**
Procedural Fairness × Outcome Favorability	−.06**		

** $p < .01$.   *** $p < .001$.

The average age of the participants in the sample was 40 years, and 95% of them were men. All of the participants in the main analyses were accompanied by a spouse or significant other. The group was largely composed of middle- to senior-level managers (e.g., directors, vice presidents, and regional general managers). Their average tenure with the company was 12 years. At the time the survey was administered, participants had been on assignment for an average of 1.6 years. The usual length of an international assignment in the organization was approximately 5 years.

Procedure. The procedure was highly similar to the one used in Study 1. Participants completed the survey in the context of the organization's efforts to assess its human resource practices. The survey was highly similar to the one used in Study 1. Because two of the control variables in Study 1—previous overseas experience and predeparture training—were unrelated to the dependent variable in both correlational analyses (see Table 1) and multiple regression (see Table 2, Step 1), they were deleted from Study 2.

Results

Summary statistics for and correlations between all of the variables are reported in Table 3. As can be seen, all of the measures had acceptable internal reliabilities (including procedural fairness). Moreover, each of the independent variables and control variables was significantly related to participants' thoughts of premature departure and in the expected direction.

As in Study 1, a hierarchical multiple regression was conducted. In the first step, we entered the two control variables. As can be seen in Table 4, Step 1, only perceived support from the home office was significant ($p < .01$). In the second step, we added the independent variables of outcome favorability and procedural fairness. Although neither effect was significant, outcome favorability was marginally related to thoughts of premature departure ($p < .08$).

Finally, we added the interaction between outcome favorability and procedural fairness on the third step. As can be seen in Table 4, Step 3, the interaction was significant ($p < .025$), and the sign of the beta was negative, as predicted. Subgroup analyses (analogous to those conducted in Study 1) further illustrated the nature of the interaction effect. Among those who perceived relatively low levels of procedural fairness, higher outcome favorability was associated with fewer thoughts of premature departure, $r(36) = .50$, $p < .01$. In contrast, among those who perceived relatively high levels of procedural fairness, the relationship between outcome favorability and thoughts of premature departure was not significant, $r(24) = .23$, $p > .15$.

General Discussion

Taken together, the results of both studies show that (nonwork) outcome favorability and procedural fairness combine interactively to predict expatriates' thoughts of premature departure. Although it may come as little surprise that participants thought more seriously about departing prematurely when their nonwork outcomes were relatively unfavorable, it is intriguing that the relationship between outcome favorability and thoughts of premature departure was significantly less pronounced when the organization's procedures were judged to be more fair. Both studies included control variables that have been linked to expatriates' thoughts of premature departure (e.g., perceived home office support). Thus, the interaction between procedural fairness and outcome favorability accounted for a significant portion of the variance beyond that attributable to the control variables. Furthermore, the fact that similar results emerged across two samples drawn from different countries and industries bodes well for the generalizability of the findings.

Theoretical Implications

Expatriation. The extent to which expatriates successfully complete their overseas assignments is a matter of considerable significance to organizations and individuals alike. Extant models designed to predict premature expatriate departure, however, have not considered possible complexities in how the antecedent factors combine with each other, such as interaction effects between the antecedents. Drawing on recent research and theory in the organizational-justice literature (Brockner & Wiesenfeld, 1996), the present studies hypothesized and found that important nonwork outcomes combine interactively with procedural fairness to predict the extent to which expatriates were seriously considering departing prematurely from their overseas assignments.

Organizational justice. Although the interaction between outcome favorability and procedural fairness has been found on numerous occasions (Brockner & Wiesenfeld, 1996), the present studies enhance the generalizability of previous findings in two important respects. First, none of the preceding studies examined the interaction effect in the context of expatriates' reactions to their overseas assignments. Instead, many of the previous studies looked at the interaction between the outcomes and procedures associated with a significant organizational change, such as layoffs (Brockner et al., 1994), a pay freeze (Schaubroeck, May, &

Table 3

Summary Statistics and Correlations (Study 2)

Variable	M	SD	1	2	3	4	5
1. Home office support	3.41	0.95	(.77)				
2. Successful repatriation	2.62	0.88	.51**	(.77)			
3. Outcome favorability	5.53	0.80	.28*	.19	(.81)		
4. Procedural fairness	3.84	0.78	.44**	.32**	.15	(.70)	
5. Thoughts of premature departure	4.35	0.92	.34**	.30**	.37**	.32**	(.74)

Note. Higher scores reflect greater levels of all variables except thoughts of premature departure, in which case higher scores reflect fewer thoughts of premature departure. All scores could range from 1–6. Coefficient alphas are in parentheses.
* $p < .05$. ** $p < .01$.

Table 4
Hierarchical Multiple Regression Results (Study 2)

	Thoughts of premature departure		
Independent variable	β	R^2	Change in R^2
Step 1		.22***	.22***
Home office support	.33**		
Successful repatriation	.20		
Step 2			
Procedural fairness	.11	.26***	.04
Outcome favorability	.20		
Step 3			
Procedural Fairness × Outcome Favorability	−.21*	.32***	.06*

$^* p < .025.$ $^{**} p < .01.$ $^{***} p < .001.$

Brown, 1994), and the introduction of a smoking ban (Greenberg, 1994).

Second, the outcomes examined in previous tests of the focal interaction effect in organizational settings always were work related. In contrast, the present studies dealt with perceptions of nonwork outcomes, such as expatriates' beliefs about the adjustment of their spouse/significant other, housing conditions, and health care management. Perceptions of nonwork outcomes may have been particularly meaningful to the current participants, given that all of them were accompanied by a spouse or significant other.

In fact, in both studies there also were a small number of expatriates who had not been accompanied by a spouse/significant other ($N = 17$ and 20 in Study 1 and Study 2, respectively). To evaluate whether nonwork outcomes interact with procedural fairness when those not accompanied by a spouse/significant other were included in the analyses, we computed a measure of nonwork outcome favorability that applied to all expatriates, regardless of whether they had been accompanied by a spouse/significant other. This was achieved by deleting the item tapping the perceived adjustment of the spouse/significant other; all other items tapping outcome favorability applied to all expatriates. We then repeated the hierarchical regression analyses conducted in Studies 1 and 2. Of greatest importance, the interaction between outcome favorability and procedural fairness took the same form (but was weaker) in both studies ($p < .03$ in Study 1, and $p < .11$ in Study 2).

One possible explanation of why the interaction effect became weaker is that the nonwork outcomes chosen for investigation (e.g., living conditions, health care management) were less important to expatriates who had not been accompanied by a spouse/ significant other relative to those who had been accompanied. To evaluate this possibility, we computed the correlation between outcome favorability and thoughts of premature departure separately for expatriates who had been accompanied by their spouse/ significant other versus those who had not. The correlation was significant among those who had been accompanied in both studies; $r = .45$ and .35 in Study 1 and Study 2, respectively, $p < .01$. In contrast, the correlations were not significant among those who had not been accompanied by a spouse/significant other in both studies; $r = .15$ and .22, respectively. Similar findings also were reported by Shaffer and Harrison (1998).

Limitations and Suggestions for Future Research

The present studies have a number of methodological and conceptual limitations. In discussing these limitations, we simultaneously are suggesting avenues for future research.

Correlational design. Given the methods used in the present research, the causal impact of the interaction between outcome favorability and procedural fairness on expatriates' thoughts of premature departure has not been definitively established. On the basis of previous studies examining the interactive effect of outcome favorability and procedural fairness, however, there is reason to believe that the interaction between these two independent variables was causally related to the dependent variable in the present studies. Many of the previous demonstrations of the interaction between outcome favorability and procedural fairness were obtained when one or both of the independent variables were experimentally manipulated (e.g., Folger & Martin, 1986; Folger, Rosenfield, & Robinson, 1983; Greenberg, 1987, 1994). The fact that the interaction has been found repeatedly in well-controlled studies suggests that the present findings have internal validity. However, the interactive effect of outcome favorability and procedural fairness on expatriates still needs to be explored in future research with methods that allow for stronger forms of causal inference.

Common methods. Another possible limitation of the present studies is that the results may have been an artifact of common methods. Although this alternative explanation cannot be eliminated entirely, the fact that the primary findings were interaction effects makes the common-methods explanation less compelling. Participants in both studies completed measures of procedural fairness, outcome favorability, and thoughts of premature departure in the same survey at the same point in time. Whereas the common-methods account may explain why the three measures generally were correlated with each other, it is less able to explain why the relationships between variables were more pronounced under some conditions than others. For example, the relationship between outcome favorability and thoughts of premature departure was stronger when procedural fairness was relatively low rather than high.

Dependent variable. A basic premise of the present studies is that premature departure is one operational definition of the success or failure of an expatriate assignment. Participants' actual level of premature departure was not measured in the present studies. Rather, we assessed the extent to which they thought seriously about leaving. Several turnover models (Mobley, 1982; Naumann, 1992) suggest that individuals who quit usually think seriously about doing so prior to their departure. Thus, it is useful to identify the factors that affect expatriates' thoughts of premature departure (Shaffer & Harrison, 1998; Steel & Ovalle, 1984). However, it is important for future researchers to evaluate whether the interaction between outcome favorability and procedural fairness similarly predicts actual premature departure.

Accounting for the interaction effect. Numerous theories have been offered that can account for the interaction between outcome favorability and procedural fairness; see Brockner and Wiesenfeld (1996) for a review. One theory that is quite compatible with the present findings is the updated version of referent cognitions theory (Folger, 1993). According to this viewpoint, people are particularly resentful toward a party whom they associate with unfavorable outcomes when they view the party as responsible for, or intentionally causing, the unfavorable outcomes. When the party is seen as less responsible for, or less intentionally causing, unfavorable outcomes, resentment toward the party will be muted. The present findings suggest that expatriates who viewed procedures to be more fair may have perceived the organization as less responsible for unfavorable nonwork outcomes relative to those who perceived procedures to be less fair. For example, those who perceived procedures to be more unfair may have blamed the organization more for not arranging better living conditions for them, thereby eliciting more serious thoughts of premature departure.

Although the present findings are consistent with referent cognitions theory, they also are at least somewhat compatible with other explanations of the interaction effect (Lind & Tyler, 1988; Thibaut & Walker, 1975). The present studies did not evaluate the relative merits of the various explanations of the interactive relationship between outcome favorability and procedural fairness, nor were they intended to. Thus, future research is needed to ascertain more definitively why expatriates' thoughts of premature departure were more strongly related to outcome favorability when procedural fairness was low rather than high.

Practical Implications

Many of the factors examined in previous research on premature expatriate departure are proximal to the expatriation process, for example, whether the right people are selected or whether the organization provides adequate levels of predeparture and on-assignment training and support for managers and accompanying family members (Black et al., 1991; Naumann, 1992). The present findings suggest that organizational authorities also need to attend to the fairness of their ongoing procedures, which are more distal to the expatriation process but nevertheless may influence expatriates' reactions to their overseas assignments. In fact, proximal factors such as the favorability of living conditions interact with distal factors such as procedural fairness to predict expatriates' thoughts of premature departure.

The present studies also have important implications for organizations seeking to minimize the extent to which expatriates are thinking seriously about departing prematurely. On the one hand, it could be argued that organizations can reduce the odds of premature departure by trying to ensure that the expatriates receive favorable nonwork outcomes. On the other hand, organizations may encounter at least two problems in their attempts to provide favorable outcomes outside of the workplace. First, many of the relevant outcomes (e.g., adjustment of family members) may not be under the organization's direct control. Second, it may not be economically feasible to provide expatriates with favorable outcomes. In fact, many globally oriented organizations are under increasing cost pressures to minimize the perquisites often associated with international transfers (Brewster, 1997). The nature of the interaction effect suggests that nonwork outcome favorability may be less consequential as long as the organization's procedures are seen as fair. Although it may be challenging for managers to ensure that the institution's procedures are fair, the economic or material costs associated with ensuring procedural fairness are likely to be far less than those needed to produce favorable nonwork outcomes (Folger & Pugh, 1999). In short, the present findings may help organizations find cost effective ways to minimize the extent to which their international assignees seriously contemplate departing prematurely.

References

Adler, N. (1996). *International dimensions of organizational behavior* (3rd ed.). Boston: PWS-Kent Publishing Co.

Ajzen, I., & Fishbein, M. (1980). *Understanding attitudes and predicting social behavior.* Englewood Cliffs, NJ: Prentice-Hall.

Bies, R. J. (1987). The predicament of injustice: The management of moral outrage. In L. L. Cummings & B. M. Staw (Eds.), *Research in organizational behavior* (Vol. 9, pp. 289–319). Greenwich, CT: JAI Press.

Bird, A., & Dunbar, R. (1991, Spring). Getting the job done over there: Improving expatriate effectiveness. *National Productivity Review,* 145–156.

Black, J. S., Gregersen, H. B., & Mendenhall, M. E. (1992). *Global assignments.* San Francisco: Jossey-Bass.

Black, J. S., Mendenhall, M., & Oddou, G. (1991). Toward a comprehensive model of international adjustment: An integration of multiple theoretical perspectives. *Academy of Management Review, 16,* 291–317.

Blau, P. (1964). *Exchange and power in social life.* New York: Wiley.

Brewster, C. (1997). International human resource management: Beyond expatriation. *Human Resource Management Journal, 7,* 31–40.

Brockner, J., Konovsky, M., Cooper-Schneider, R., Folger, R., Martin, C. L., & Bies, R. J. (1994). The interactive effects of procedural justice and outcome negativity on the victims and survivors of job loss. *Academy of Management Journal, 37,* 397–409.

Brockner, J., & Wiesenfeld, B. M. (1996). An integrative framework for explaining reactions to decisions: The interactive effects of outcomes and procedures. *Psychological Bulletin, 120,* 189–208.

Folger, R. (1993). Reactions to mistreatment at work. In J. K. Murnighan (Ed.), *Social psychology in organizations: Advances in theory and research* (pp. 161–183). Englewood Cliffs, NJ: Prentice-Hall.

Folger, R., & Greenberg, J. (1985). Procedural justice: An interpretive analysis of personnel systems. In K. Rowland & G. Ferris (Eds.), *Research in personnel and human resource management* (Vol. 3, pp. 141–183). Greenwich, CT: JAI Press.

Folger, R., & Martin, C. L. (1986). Relative deprivation and referent cognitions: Distributive and procedural justice effects. *Journal of Experimental Social Psychology, 22,* 531–546.

Folger, R., & Pugh, S. D. (1999). *The Churchill paradox in managing hard times: Kicking employees when they're down and out.* Manuscript submitted for publication.

Folger, R., Rosenfield, D., & Robinson, T. (1983). Relative deprivation and procedural justification. *Journal of Personality and Social Psychology, 45,* 268–273.

Grant, L. (1997, April). That overseas job could derail your career. *Fortune, 135,* 166.

Greenberg, J. (1987). Reactions to procedural justice in payment allocations: Do the ends justify the means? *Journal of Applied Psychology, 72,* 55–61.

Greenberg, J. (1990). Organizational justice: Yesterday, today, and tomorrow. *Journal of Management, 16,* 399–432.

Greenberg, J. (1994). Using socially fair treatment to promote acceptance of a work site smoking ban. *Journal of Applied Psychology, 79,* 288–297.

Greenberg, J. (1996). *The quest for justice on the job: Essays and experiments.* Thousand Oaks, CA: Sage.

Gregersen, H., & Black, J. S. (1992). Antecedents of commitment to a parent company and a foreign operation. *Academy of Management Journal, 35,* 65–90.

Hay/McBer Co. (1996). *The international assignment inventory.* Boston: Hay/McBer Publications.

Hay/McBer Co. (1997). *Organizational climate survey II*. Boston: Hay/McBer Publications.

Leventhal, G., Karuza, J., & Fry, W. R. (1980). Beyond fairness: A theory of allocation preferences. In G. Mikula (Ed.), *Justice and social interaction* (pp. 167–218). New York: Springer-Verlag.

Lind, E. A., & Tyler, T. R. (1988). *The social psychology of procedural justice*. New York: Plenum.

McClelland, D. C., & Burnham, D. H. (1995). Power is the great motivator. *Harvard Business Review, 95,* 126–139.

Milkovich, G. T., & Newman, J. M. (1996). *Compensation* (5th ed.). Chicago: Richard D. Irwin.

Mobley, W. H. (1982). *Employee turnover: Causes, consequences, and control*. Reading, MA: Addison-Wesley.

Naumann, E. (1992). A conceptual model of expatriate turnover. *Journal of International Business Studies, 3,* 499–531.

Schaubroeck, J., May, D. R., & Brown, F. W. (1994). Procedural justice explanations and employee reactions to economic hardship: A field experiment. *Journal of Applied Psychology, 79,* 455–460.

Shaffer, M. A., & Harrison, D. A. (1998). Expatriates' psychological withdrawal from international assignments: Work, nonwork, and family influences. *Personnel Psychology, 51,* 87–118.

Steel, R. P., & Ovalle, N. K. (1984). A review and meta-analysis of research on the relationship between behavioral intentions and employee turnover. *Journal of Applied Psychology, 69,* 673–686.

Thibaut, J., & Walker, L. (1975). *Procedural justice: A psychological analysis*. Hillsdale, NJ: Erlbaum.

Received July 22, 1998
Revision received February 15, 1999
Accepted February 17, 1999 ∎

[9]

The persistent myth of high expatriate failure rates

Anne-Wil K. Harzing

Abstract

This paper provides a critical analysis of research and notably quotations in the field of expatriate failure rates. Over the last three decades it has become almost 'traditional' to open an article on expatriate management by stating that expatriate failure rates are (very) high. Virtually every publication on the topic defines and measures expatriate failure as the percentage of expatriates returning home before their assignment contract expires. Of course, premature re-entry might be a very inadequate way to measure expatriate failure. One can easily argue that those expatriates who stay on their assignment but who fail to perform adequately are (potentially) more damaging to the company than the ones who return prematurely. Furthermore, successful completion of a foreign assignment does not mean that the possibility of expatriate failure has been avoided. Sometimes, returning home poses even larger problems than the foreign assignment itself. The repatriate must face re-establishing himself within the home organization and readjusting to the home culture. Failure to do so, for whatever reason, can also be regarded as expatriate failure. These reservations being made, in this paper it is argued that there is almost no empirical foundation for the existence of high failure rates when measured as premature re-entry. The persistent myth of high expatriate failure rates seems to have been created by massive (mis)quotations of three articles. Only one of these articles contained solid empirical evidence on expatriate failure rates and in fact showed them to be rather low.

Keywords

Internationalization, expatriate failure, expatriate adjustment, international human resource management, international mobility, research methodology

Anne-Wil Harzing

Introduction

The growing internationalization of the world's markets is drawing more and more players into the international business arena. One of the results is that not only large multinational corporations, but also smaller and recently internationalized companies are encountering the problems associated with sending their employees, so-called expatriates, abroad. They may believe that their bigger brothers and sisters can provide answers to their practical problems, but in fact large multinationals are themselves coping with trends such as a changing work ethos and dual career couples, all of which has made their employees less willing to accept an assignment abroad (Shell, 1993). When the pool of candidates gets smaller, it becomes increasingly important that the expatriates who *are* sent abroad are successful in their assignments: on the one hand, because a low failure rate reduces the number of candidates needed and, on the other hand, because a high failure rate is likely to discourage potential candidates, shrinking the pool even further.

Over the last three decades it has become almost 'traditional' to open an article on expatriate management by stating that expatriate failure rates are (very) high. Virtually every publication on the topic defines and measures expatriate failure as the percentage of expatriates returning home before their assignment contract expires. Of course, premature re-entry might be a very inadequate way to measure expatriate failure. One can easily argue that those expatriates who stay on their assignment but who fail to perform adequately are (potentially) more damaging to the company than the ones who return prematurely. Furthermore, successful completion of a foreign assignment does not mean that the possibility of expatriate failure has been avoided. Sometimes, returning home poses even larger problems than the foreign assignment itself (Harvey, 1982; Forster, 1994). The repatriate must face re-establishing himself within the home organization and readjusting to the home culture. Failure to do so, for whatever reason, can also be regarded as expatriate failure.

These reservations being made, in this article I will argue that there is almost no empirical foundation for the existence of high failure rates when measured as premature re-entry. Unfortunately, there has been no reliable large-scale empirical work on this subject for more than fifteen years. As argued at the end of this article, however, some small-scale studies suggest that we might be equally justified in claiming that expatriate failure rates are generally rather low, at least in Europe. Before launching into this discussion, however, I will first

The persistent myth of high expatriate failure rates

describe a chain of references in the field of expatriate failure rates – measured as the percentage of expatriates who return home before their assignment contract expires – that grew stranger and stranger as I traced back the various links.[1]

A promising start

I would like to start my story by reviewing some of the recent contributions in this field, gradually working backwards through various references and taking a few detours when necessary. In their book *International Business Studies*, Buckley and Brooke (1992) claim that '*Empirical* studies over a *considerable period* suggest that expatriate failure is a significant and persistent problem with rates ranging between 25 and 40 per cent in the developed countries and as high as 70 per cent in the case of developing countries (Desatnick & Bennett, 1978; Holmes & Piker, 1980; Mendenhall & Oddou, 1985)' (Buckley and Brooke, 1992: 528, emphasis added). Let us take a look at the references Buckley and Brooke quote, starting with Desatnick and Bennett. (See Figure 1 for a summary of the publications and the pattern of references in this field.) At first sight there seems to be nothing wrong with this reference. Desatnick and Bennett do indeed say that '30–50 per cent of U.S. expatriates do not complete their assignments in developed countries; and the proportion rises to 70 per cent in developing countries' (Desatnick and Bennett, 1978: 173). In my opinion, however, there are two problems with this reference. First, Desatnick and Bennett refer to US expatriates only, and as we will see later there is quite a big difference between US expatriate failure rates on the one hand and Japanese and West European expatriate failure rates on the other. Second, and perhaps more seriously, we cannot verify the source of these figures. Desatnick and Bennett do not mention any research project conducted by themselves, nor do they refer to any other study. In fact, throughout the entire book, no single reference can be found, not even a bibliography at the end, so this source can hardly be counted as empirical evidence. Holmes and Piker (1980) describe a number of techniques 'which have been found to reduce the failure rates of expatriates to adjust and to succeed overseas from around 40 to 25 per cent' (Holmes and Piker, 1980: 31). But, once again, there is no indication of where these figures might originate from. As Buckley and Brooke are the only ones to refer to this article (see Figure 1), I will not probe into this study further, but once again empirical evidence does not seem to have been delivered. Mendenhall and Oddou's (1985) article, which, as we will see later, is

459

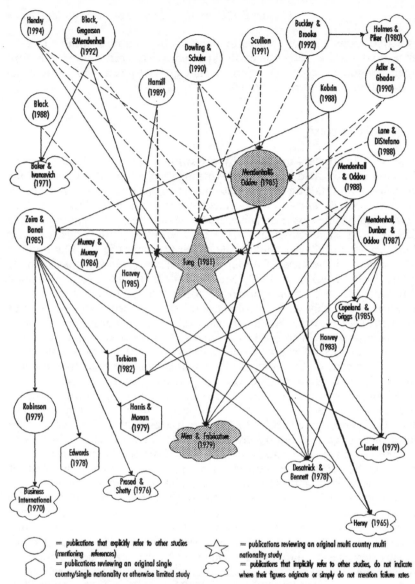

The figure shows the various publications in more or less chronological order, with the most recent publications at the top.
The size of the symbols is adjusted to the names within and does not have any special significance, except in the case of Tung (1981), Mendenhall & Oddou (1985) and Misa & Fabricatore (1979) where size indicates importance.

Figure 1 *Publications and pattern of references in the field of expatriate failure rates*

The persistent myth of high expatriate failure rates

one of the most crucial articles on expatriate failure rates (see also Figure 1), simply asserts that 'It has been estimated that the expatriate failure rate from 1965 to the present has fluctuated between 25 percent and 40 percent (Henry, 1965; Misa & Fabricatore, 1979; Tung, 1981)' (Mendenhall and Oddou, 1985: 39). I will discuss the sources Mendenhall and Oddou refer to later in this article. For now I would like to continue with a number of more recent contributions. The somewhat older study by Tung, however, will be discussed next, as this seems to be the most crucial study in this field; no less than twelve other publications refer to it (see Figure 1).

Tung's research on expatriate management

Tung (1981, 1982, 1984, 1987, 1988)[2] is one of the very few researchers up till now who has conducted empirical research on expatriate management. In a sample of eighty American, twenty-nine West European and thirty-five Japanese multinational firms with subsidiaries in Western Europe, Canada, Middle/Near East, Eastern Europe, Latin/South America, Far East, Africa and the United States, she has conducted survey research on the following subjects:

- staffing policy. To what extent and at which levels are the subsidiaries of the multinational company (MNC) in question staffed by parent country nationals, host country nationals and third country nationals;
- selection criteria for overseas assignments;
- procedures used to determine the suitability of a prospective expatriate for a foreign position;
- the type and extent of predeparture training; and
- the success rate and the reasons for success.

The last subject is, of course, highly relevant for this article. Respondents were asked to indicate the percentage of expatriates who had to be recalled before the end of their assignment. Table 1 summarizes the results.

Generally speaking, the recall rate of American multinationals is considerably higher than that of their European and Japanese counterparts. While 76 per cent of the US multinationals in Tung's study have recall rates above 10 per cent, this goes for only 3 per cent and 14 per cent of the European and Japanese multinationals respectively. The group of Japanese multinationals included the highest percentage of companies with recall rates below 5 per cent. Still, we can conclude from this study that there are in fact very few companies with recall

461

Anne-Wil Harzing

Table 1 *Recall rates in American, European and Japanese companies*

Recall rate %	% of companies
US multinationals	
20–40	7
10–20	69
< 10	24
European multinationals	
11–15	3
6–10	38
< 5	59
Japanese multinationals	
11–19	14
6–10	10
< 5	76

rates above 20 per cent. Only 7 per cent of the US multinationals fall in this category, and there are no European or Japanese firms in this group at all.

Referring to others: how (not) to do this?

Before continuing with our chronological search backwards, I would like to take a look at the most recent contribution to mention expatriate failure rates, a book entitled *Human Resource Strategies for International Growth* by Chris Hendry (1994). Hendry correctly refers to Mendenhall and Oddou (1985) when he states that they 'estimate the expatriate failure rate to have varied between 25 and 40 per cent in the period 1965–1985', to Desatnick and Bennett who 'put it up to 70 per cent in developing countries' and to Tung when he quotes the percentage of US, West European and Japanese MNCs that have expatriate failure rates above 10 per cent (Hendry, 1994: 91). He also mentions two recent British surveys by Scullion and Brewster, which will be discussed in the final section of this article. Apart from the fact that he gives credence to two studies whose empirical content is not beyond doubt, there seems to be nothing wrong with his references.

This is not true for Scullion (1991), the next author in our chronological search backwards. According to him 'An earlier study of American multinationals showed that between 25 and 40 per cent of

The persistent myth of high expatriate failure rates

all international assignments ended in failure' (Scullion, 1991: 32). To substantiate this statement, he refers to Tung (1982). As we have seen above, in Tung's study only 7 per cent of the American MNCs had expatriate failure rates between 20 (not 25) and 40 per cent, which is very hard to reconcile with Scullion's statement. Two pages later Scullion attributes the statement 'Research suggests that the estimated expatriate failure rate in American multinationals has fluctuated between 25 and 40 per cent over the last 20 years' to Mendenhall and Oddou (1985). However, by converting Mendenhall and Oddou's 'from 1965 to the present' (Mendenhall and Oddou, 1985: 39) to 'the last 20 years' in an article published in 1991, Scullion effectively excludes two of the three references which Mendenhall and Oddou's article was based on (Henry, 1965; Misa and Fabricatore, 1979) and only just includes the third: Tung, 1981.

Scullion is not the only one to make this kind of mistake, however. Dowling and Schuler (1990: 59) claim that 'Mendenhall and Oddou report that the estimated expatriate failure rate from 1965 to the present has fluctuated between 25 and 40%'. They do, but by citing this in a book published in 1990 the suggestion is raised that the present is 1990, especially because the year of publication of Mendenhall and Oddou's article (1985) can be found only in a note fifteen pages later at the end of the chapter. Apart from this, Dowling and Schuler correctly refer to Desatnick and Bennett (for the 70 per cent expatriate failure in developing countries) and Tung.

Alternative ways to substantiate claims of high failure rates

Adler and Ghadar (1990) refer to the 25–40 per cent range of Mendenhall and Oddou (1985) to substantiate their statement that American expatriates have high failure rates. Mendenhall and Oddou, however, did not reserve this percentage for American expatriates alone. For expatriate failure figures on West European and Japanese expatriates, Adler and Ghadar refer to Tung (1982). Of course Tung does mention these failure rates (see above), but in the same article (in fact in the very sentence before the section dealing with West European and Japanese expatriate failure rates) she also mentions that only 7 per cent of American MNCs had expatriate failure rates between 20 and 40 per cent.

Hamill (1989) states that 'There is an extremely high failure rate amongst expatriate employees, at least in U.S. multinationals, with between 25 and 40 per cent of all foreign assignments ending in failure' (Hamill, 1989: 18). To substantiate this claim he refers to Tung

Anne-Wil Harzing

(1981, 1982) and a newcomer in the field: Harvey (1985). We have already seen that Tung's research can in no way be interpreted as claiming 25–40 per cent expatriate failure rates (even for American MNCs). Harvey (1985) states that 'depending on the source, 25% to 40% of all expatriates from the United States fail', claiming the source of these figures to be: Tung (1981, 1984)!

Black (1988) presents us with yet another, slightly different version. He also refers to Tung, but puts the expatriate failure rate at 20–40 per cent. This is indeed one of Tung's categories, but – as we have seen above – only 7 per cent of the American companies fall in this category. Black's second reference, substantiating his statement that 'between 20 to 40% of the expatriate managers do not successfully make the transition and return early' (Black, 1988: 277), is even stranger. He refers to Baker and Ivancevich (1971), who have indeed written an historic article on the inadequate way in which American firms handle(d) foreign assignments. There is one thing they do not do, however: mention figures on expatriate failure rates, making this indeed one of the strangest references of all.

New leads and loose ends

Kobrin (1988) takes a fresh approach to the field by providing two new leads: Harvey (1983), who notes that 'depending on the source, from 33 to 80 percent of expatriated families return to the United States before their contract expires', and Zeira and Banai (1985), who are said to 'summarize eight studies of failure rates of expatriates abroad that range from 30–70 per cent' (Kobrin, 1988: 66). But before tracking down these new leads, I would like to tie up three loose ends, shown in Figure 1 as having a limited number of links with other articles.

Lane and DiStefano (1988), for instance, simply refer to Mendenhall and Oddou (1985) when they state that 'Estimates of expatriate failure run between 25 and 40%'. Murray and Murray (1986) refer to Tung (1984) in citing differences in expatriate failure rates between American and Japanese companies. However, the way in which they present Tung's data, although in principle correct, might easily lead to a gross overstatement of American expatriate failure rates. According to Murray and Murray, more than three-quarters of American multinationals have expatriate failure rates between 10 and 40 per cent. If we look back at Tung's original figures, we do indeed see that 76 per cent of American multinationals had expatriate failure rates between 10 and 40 per cent. Crucial, however, is that the vast majority of

464

The persistent myth of high expatriate failure rates

these firms had expatriate failure rates *below* 20 per cent. We are equally justified in saying that 93 per cent of the total American sample had expatriate failure rates below 20 per cent, which puts the American expatriate failure rate in a much more favourable light. Finally, Copeland and Griggs (1985) write that 'Data suggest that somewhere between 20 and 50 percent of international relocations end with premature return. In developing countries the expatriate failure rate has been as high as 70 percent' (Copeland and Griggs, 1985: xix). Unfortunately, they do not tell us precisely which data suggest these expatriate failure rates. We can assume that the 70 per cent can be traced back to Desatnick and Bennett, because they are the only writers who mention it. Perhaps the 20–50 per cent is jut a misreading of Desatnick and Bennett's 30–50 per cent? But even Copeland and Griggs have their followers, as we will see later.

Two new leads!

I promised to come back to Harvey and Zeira and Banai. We already encountered the first above in a publication (1985) in which he incorrectly attributes the 25–40 per cent expatriate failure rates to Tung. Two years earlier (Harvey, 1983), he had held another view, already using the words 'depending on the source' but claiming that '33 to 80 percent of expatriated families return to the United States before their contract expires' (Harvey, 1983: 72). This time his source was Lanier (1979), who says '*Current studies* put actual failures – i.e. returns – at about one-third of all personnel; *some companies* have had 79% returns' (Lanier, 1979: 160, emphasis added). Quoting this as a 33–80 per cent expatriate failure rate can be considered a rather liberal presentation of these data, which in and of themselves already did not contain any verifiable empirical information.

Zeira and Banai (1985) reviewed no less than nine (and not eight as Kobrin claimed) studies on expatriate failure rates. Two of them, however, only say that expatriates are less successful than in their home country and do not mention expatriate failure rates at all. Two of the remaining seven studies have already been dealt with above, namely Desatnick and Bennett and Lanier, and have been criticized for not substantiating their claims. A study by Business International (1970) – Zeira and Banai refer to the citation of this study in a book by Robinson (1979) – states that 'it has been estimated that the rate of turnover of expatriate executives of U.S. firms may be as high as 30%' (Business International Research Report, 1970:1). No indication is given in this report as to where these estimates originate from. (In

Anne-Wil Harzing

view of the year of publication of the report, it could well be Henry's article, which is discussed below.) Besides in my opinion an *estimate* of the turnover of *American* expatriates *in the 1960s* can hardly be considered a valid source of *present* general expatriate failure figures. A second study mentioned by Zeira and Banai, Edwards (1978), quotes Gary Lloyd, director of the Business Council for International Understanding: 'Lloyd tells of one firm with a hospital management contract which experienced a failure rate of 120% that by last January had jumped to 142%' (Edwards, 1978: 42). How can we explain an expatriate failure rate above 100 per cent? It turns out that in this article expatriate failure rates are annualized. Edwards comes up with a second example where more than half of the expatriate construction team in Saudi Arabia had returned within two months, resulting in an annualized expatriate failure rate of 368 per cent! Of course, we cannot compare these figures with studies that measure expatriate failure rates as the percentage of expatriates returning before their contract expires. Quite apart from this, however, these examples are too idiosyncratic to base general statements on about expatriate failure rates. Indeed, the same goes for Harris and Moran (1979), who discuss two multinational corporations working in Iran in the late 1970s that reported premature return rates of 50 and 85 per cent respectively of the Americans they had sent to Iran. In later editions of the same book Harris and Moran no longer refer to these studies. The fourth reference mentioned by Zeira and Banai, Prasad and Shetty (1976: 113), claims very high expatriate failure rates (approximately 80 per cent) for American executives in Japan in the early 1960s, without however mentioning the source of these claims. Finally, Torbiörn (1982: 44) states that 25 per cent of the expatriates in the (Swedish) companies he studied returned home before the end of their contracts. Interestingly, Zeira and Banai ascribe to Torbiörn the statement that 257 – perhaps a misreading of 25 per cent? – of the 639 expatriates returned prematurely.

Diving back into the 1960s

To summarize: so far we have not found any solid empirical foundation for the claim that expatriate failure rates lie in the region of 25–40 per cent or even higher, except for the modest support provided by Torbiörn's study, which puts the failure rate of *Swedish* expatriates at 25 per cent. The only study that provided solid empirical and verifiable results was Tung's, which suggests that 93 per cent of American multinationals have expatriate failure rates *below* 20 per cent, with

The persistent myth of high expatriate failure rates

expatriate failure rates in West European and Japanese firms being even lower. But I haven't yet traced back all the sources of the article by Mendenhall and Oddou (1985), cited by so many other researchers. There are two references I have not dealt with yet: Misa and Fabricatore (1979) and Henry (1965). I will start with the latter.

As far as I have been able to trace, Henry's (1965) article on 'What Business can Learn from Peace Corps Selection and Training' is the first piece to mention expatriate failure rates. It is an important one, as the two most crucial articles in this field (Tung, 1981; Mendenhall and Oddou, 1985) both refer to it. It is the reason that quite a number of articles (most of them with Mendenhall and Oddou's article as an intermediate) claim that expatriate failure rates have fluctuated between 25 and 40 per cent *since 1965*, the year Henry's article was published. Henry states 'It has been estimated that about 30 percent of the people sent overseas by American companies are mistakes, and have been – *or should have been* – sent home' (Henry, 1965: 17, emphasis added). In a footnote Henry admits that 'I have no precise, comprehensive statistical basis for this 30 percent figure, but from the more or less informal data I have been able to obtain it seems to be a conservative estimate.' More or less informal data can hardly be considered solid proof for an expatriate failure rate of 30 per cent in 1965. For our purpose, however, there is one additional and rather serious problem associated with using this estimate as a source when discussing expatriate failure rates. The 30 per cent given by Henry includes not only employees who have been sent or who have returned home (the way expatriate failure is measured in all other publications) but also employees who *should have been* sent home (but were not). So the 'actual' expatriate failure rate as it is measured in all other articles (premature re-entry) might lie anywhere between 0 and 30 per cent in Henry's article.

Misa and Fabricatore, two employees of an American firm of management consultants, published a short article on 'Return on Investment of Overseas Personnel' in *Financial Executive*. In this article they say that 'A recent review of the overseas operations of 245 multinational corporations concludes that "the adjustment problems of Americans abroad are severe"' (Misa and Fabricatore, 1979: 42) Unfortunately, the authors do not provide any clues as to which review they are citing (it could even be the one by Tung, the results of which were presented in 1978). However, a second quotation from this article is far more important: 'Even when things were going right for expatriate managers overseas in the glorious days prior to the devaluation of the dollar and closing of some of the beneficial tax advantages, the premature return rate on foreign assignments ranged

467

Anne-Wil Harzing

from 25 to 40 percent.' The glorious days Misa and Fabricatore are referring to are probably the days before the collapse of the Bretton Woods system in 1971. This collapse led to a downwards fluctuating dollar, which did not stabilize until 1978/1979 (Samuelson and Nordhaus, 1985: 885). The period Misa and Fabricatore are referring to with respect to their expatriate failure rates is therefore most likely the 1960s. Could this then be the source of all of these references on expatriate failure rates, both for US companies and in general, right through to 1994? Two management consultants claiming, out of the blue, that in the glorious past (the 1960s) American expatriate failure rates were 25–40 per cent? It seems unbelievable, and yet this is the earliest publication that comes up with these percentages and the only one that does not refer to others to substantiate them.

Evidence that this figure is generally and unquestioningly accepted can be found in the large number of references to it via Mendenhall and Oddou's (1985) article. This general acceptance is nicely illustrated by Borg (1988), who mentions, without references, in a commercial edition of his dissertation that 'The general opinion among American writers is that the failure rate, i.e. premature return of expatriates, fluctuates between 25 and 40%' (Borg, 1988: 31).

Mendenhall and Oddou revisited

Amusingly, while almost every author who has contributed to the literature on expatriate management since 1986 has referred to 'Mendenhall and Oddou's' 25–40 per cent expatriate failure rate, Mendenhall and Oddou themselves came up with different figures in later publications. An article which they wrote in 1987 with Dunbar puts the failure rate of American expatriates at 20–50 per cent. The reference to Henry has been omitted, but Misa and Fabricatore and Tung were retained, the latter inappropriately. Other references were added. The first was their own article from 1985, which simply duplicates the references to Misa and Fabricatore and Tung and adds an indirect reference to Henry. I have already criticized three other references – Copeland and Griggs (1985), Desatnick and Bennett (1978) and Lanier (1979) – for mentioning completely unsubstantiated figures. The reference to Torbiörn can be considered useful, as he indeed mentions an expatriate failure rate of 25 per cent. But the reference to Zeira and Banai only duplicates another three references and on top of that adds some very doubtful and country-specific studies that for the most part do not even mention expatriate failure rates in the 20–50 per cent range.

The persistent myth of high expatriate failure rates

So we see that Mendenhall and Oddou themselves gave up the idea of 25–40 per cent expatriate failure rates, while still claiming that these rates were very high. Or at least they did so until their next article, in 1988: 'The Overseas Assignment: A Practical Look'. In this article they claim that 'It has been estimated that approximately 20 percent of personnel sent abroad return prematurely from an overseas assignment' (Mendenhall and Oddou, 1988: 78). In a footnote they refer to Tung, which can still be considered inappropriate. Even stranger in this case, however, is their reference to Misa and Fabricatore, Copeland and Griggs and Torbiörn, who put expatriate failure rates at 25–40 per cent, 20–50 per cent and 25 per cent respectively, all of these above and mostly way off the approximate 20 per cent Mendenhall and Oddou now embrace. It looks as if they have changed their ideas without, however, changing their references. Finally, in a book written in collaboration with Black and Gregersen in 1992, Mendenhall retained this 20 per cent expatriate failure rate, still referring to Tung and Misa and Fabricatore. The authors do, however, come up with one new reference, namely Baker and Ivancevich (1971), which is probably a remnant of one of the first author's previous publications (Black, 1988). I already noted above that Baker and Ivancevich do not mention expatriate failure rates at all in this publication.

Brewster's explanations

There is one publication in this field, Brewster (1991), which I did not include in Figure 1 because it refers to more than half of the other publications mentioned in the figure; including it would make the figure too complicated and difficult to read. As has become 'traditional' in this field, Brewster's book contains some incorrect references (e.g. citing Tung, 1981, as mentioning 20–50 per cent expatriate failure rates) and a very large number of duplicate references (e.g. Robinson and Business International; Murray and Murray – who are also misquoted – and Tung; Kobrin and Lanier; Mendenhall and Oddou, and Henry, Misa and Fabricatore and Tung, etc.) Brewster is the *first one*, however, to note that 'in most cases it is unclear where the figures originate' (Brewster, 1991: 85) and states that 'in general more solidly research-based studies show that the situation might not be quite that bad' (ibid.). Brewster cites a number of recent research-based estimates on expatriate failure rates (Hamill, 1989; Tung, 1982; Brewster, 1988, see my conclusions for a description of the first and last of these studies) that suggest that expatriate failure rates may be much lower

Anne-Wil Harzing

than previous estimates have indicated. He offers a number of explanations for this difference:

- First, expatriate failure rates may have declined over time. We would expect MNCs to learn from their mistakes and to pay more attention to careful selection and training, which might reduce expatriate failure rates. However, since Tung – who conducted the only solid empirical study in this field – already found very low expatriate failure rates for European and Japanese multinationals in the late 1970s, this explanation can hardly be sufficient.
- Second, different industries and different nationalities may have different expatriate failure rates. Many of the studies referred to in this article deal with American companies (although this is not always stated explicitly). From Tung's research we have learned that expatriate failure rates of American companies are probably higher than those of European and Japanese companies. Recent studies that focus on European companies should therefore find lower expatriate failure rates than older studies involving American companies. However, Tung's research also suggests that even American companies have much lower expatriate failure rates than claimed by other publications. Unfortunately, I cannot assess the influence of industry, because the vast majority of earlier studies do not in any way indicate the origin of the figures, let alone state in which industry these figures were found.
- This leaves us with a third, and possibly far more important explanation: methodological differences. The vast majority of publications discussed above do not present any original data at all. The authors simply refer to other publications which, in a large number of cases, also do not mention research results, referring in turn to yet other publications. Except for the studies by Tung and Torbiörn and a few very idiosyncratic studies (Harris and Moran, 1979; Edwards, 1978), those studies that do provide us with 'original' figures either state these figures *without any* foundation or say something like 'current studies suggest' or 'it is estimated'. These figures might just as well be based on very rough estimates or on only one respondent. Furthermore, I consider it very likely that estimates such as 'about one-third', 'about a quarter' and 'between one-fifth and half of the group' have been converted into 33 per cent, 25 per cent and 20–50 per cent respectively, giving these figures a precision not present in the original estimate. (An actual illustration of this process is given in the publication by Harvey, who refers to Lanier's 'about one third' as 33 per cent.) All in all, I can heartily agree with Brewster's suggestion that 'It may be that failure rates have never been as high as the earlier estimates' (Brewster, 1988: 87).

The persistent myth of high expatriate failure rates

Conclusions

In view of the *very, very* limited number of solid empirical studies in this field, my suggestion would be to refrain from any exact figures on expatriate failure rates – measured as premature re-entry – in American and Japanese MNCs until at least one solid large-scale empirical study has been conducted on this subject. The only thing we can say with respect to Tung's study is that failure rates among American expatriates are generally higher than failure rates among West European and Japanese expatriates. But then, this study dates back to the late 1970s and I would expect some changes to have occurred in the last fifteen years.

Although not overwhelming, there is some empirical evidence with regard to expatriate failure rates in West European and notably British firms. Tung's assertion that the majority (59 per cent) of West European firms had expatriate failure rates below 5 per cent is supported by three recent studies. Brewster's (1988) study of twenty-five West European (British, Dutch, German, Swedish and French) firms showed that eighteen of them (72 per cent) had expatriate failure rates below 5 per cent, nine even below 1 per cent. Of the remaining seven, only one had more than a 7 per cent failure rate. Hamill (1989) reports that all seven (British) firms in his survey had expatriate failure rates below 5 per cent. Scullion's (1991) survey of forty-five companies (forty British, five Irish) found that only 10 per cent of these firms had expatriate failure rates above 5 per cent. So we can state with some confidence that West European and notably British expatriate failure rates lie somewhere around 5 per cent on average, which is actually very reasonable. Although I do not have any material on failure in domestic assignments to serve as the basis of comparison, I can hardly imagine that domestic failure rates are much lower than 5 per cent. So may we please see an end to the claim of high expatriate failure rates except when backed by solid empirical evidence?

This article revealed that there is very little empirical proof for the persistent claim of high expatriate failure rates when measured as premature returns. The discussion above, however, does not imply that expatriate failure is not a subject worthy of further attention. I must emphasize the importance of research on expatriate failure and international mobility in a broader sense. With regard to expatriate failure, such research would involve using a much broader definition of failure, including underperformance and repatriate failure as defined in the introduction. It would also mean paying more attention to the *reasons* for failure, which then draws in variables such as selection and recruitment procedures, cross-cultural training, cultural nov-

Anne-Wil Harzing

elty and family situation (a.o. dual-career couples). In my opinion, the model presented by Forster in this journal (Forster, 1992) would be a very good starting point for this kind of research.

University of Limburg
Maastricht
The Netherlands

Notes

1 Please note that my criticism below concerns only the way in which the various authors handle data and references with regard to expatriate failure rates. It does not extend to their research efforts as such, which are – in some cases – extremely valuable.
2 All these publications refer to the same study, the results of which with regard to expatriate failure rates are summarized in Table 1.

References

Adler, N.J. and Ghadar, F. (1990) 'Strategic Human Resource Management: A Global Perspective'. In Pieper, R. (ed.) *Human Resource Management: An International Comparison*. Berlin: de Gruyter, pp. 235–60.

Baker, J.C. and Ivancevich, J.M. (1971) 'The Assignment of American Executives Abroad: Systematic, Haphazard, or Chaotic', *California Management Review*, XIII: 39–44.

Black, J.S. (1988) 'Work Role Transitions: A Study of American Expatriate Managers in Japan', *Journal of International Business Studies*, 19: 277–94.

Black, J.S., Gregersen, H.B. and Mendenhall, M.E. (1992) *Global Assignments*. San Francisco: Jossey-Bass.

Borg, M. (1988) *International Transfers of Managers in Multinational Corporations*. Uppsala: Acta Universitatis Upsaliensis.

Brewster, C. (1991) *The Management of Expatriates*. London: Kogan Page.

Buckley, P.J. and Brooke, M.Z. (1992) 'International Human Resource Management'. In *International Business Studies*. Oxford: Blackwell, pp. 523–39.

Business International (1970) *Compensating International Executives*. New York: Business International.

Copeland, L. and Griggs, L. (1985) *Going International*. New York: Random House.

Desatnick, R.A. and Bennett, M.L. (1978) *Human Resource Management in the Multinational Company*, New York: Nichols.

Dowling, P.J. and Schuler, R.S. (1990) *International Dimensions of Human Resource Management*. Boston, MA: PWS-Kent.

Edwards, L. (1978) 'Present Shock and How to Avoid it Abroad', *Across the Board*, 15: 36–43.

Forster, N. (1992) 'International Managers and Mobile Families: The Professional and Personal Dynamics of Trans-national Career Pathing and Job Mobility in the 1990s', *The International Journal of Human Resource Management*, 3: 605–23.

The persistent myth of high expatriate failure rates

Forster, N. (1994) 'The Forgotten Employees? The Experiences of Expatriate Staff Returning to the UK', *The International Journal of Human Resource Management*, 5: 405–25.

Hamill, J. (1989) 'Expatriate Policies in British Multinationals', *Journal of General Management*, 14: 18–33.

Harris, P.R. and Moran, R.T. (1979) *Managing Cultural Differences*. Houston, TX: Gulf Publishing.

Harris, P.R. and Moran, R.T. (1991) *Managing Cultural Differences*. Houston, TX: Gulf Publishing.

Harvey, M.G. (1982) 'The Other Side of Foreign Assignments: Dealing with the Repatriation Dilemma', *Columbia Journal of World Business*, 18: 53–9.

Harvey, M.G. (1983) 'The Multinational Corporations Expatriate Problem: An Application of Murphy's Law', *Business Horizons*, 26: 71–8.

Harvey, M.G. (1985) 'The Executive Family: An Overlooked Variable in International Assignments', *Columbia Journal of World Business*, 20: 84–93.

Harzing, A.W.K. and Van Ruysseveldt, R. (eds) (1995) *International Human Resource Management, an Integrated Approach*, London/Heerlen: Sage Publications/Dutch Open University.

Hays, R.D. (1974) 'Expatriate Selection: Insuring Success and Avoiding Failure', *Journal of International Business Studies*, 5: 25–37.

Hendry, C. (1994) *Human Resource Strategies for International Growth*, London: Routledge.

Henry, E.R. (1965) 'What Business can Learn from Peace Corps Selection and Training', *Personnel*, 42: 17–25.

Holmes, W. and Piker, F.K. (1980) 'Expatriate Failure: Prevention Rather than Cure', *Personnel Management*, 12: 30–3.

Kobrin, S.J. (1988) 'Expatriate Reduction and Strategic Control in American Multinational Corporations', *Human Resource Management*, 27: 63–75.

Lane, H. and DiStefano, J. (1988) *International Management Behavior*, Nelson, Canada: Scarborough.

Lanier, A.R. (1979) 'Selecting and preparing personnel for overseas transfers', *Personnel Journal*, 58: 160–3.

Mendenhall, M. and Oddou, G. (1985) 'The Dimensions of Expatriate Acculturation: A Review', *Academy of Management Review*, 10: 39–47.

Mendenhall, M. and Oddou, G. (1988) 'The Overseas Assignment: A Practical Look', *Business Horizons*, 78–84.

Mendenhall, M.E., Dunbar, E. and Oddou, G.R. (1987) 'Expatriate Selection, Training and Career-Pathing: A Review and Critique', *Human Resource Management*, 26: 331–45.

Misa, K.F. and Fabricatore, J.M. (1979) 'Return on Investment of Overseas Personnel', *Financial Executive*, 47: 42–46.

Murray, F. and Murray, A. (1986) 'Global Managers for Global Businesses', *Sloan Management Review*, 27: 75–80.

Prasad, S.B. and Shetty, K.Y. (1976) *An Introduction to Multinational Management*, Englewood Cliffs, NJ: Prentice-Hall.

Robinson, R.D. (1979) *International Business Management. A Guide to Decision Making*, Hinsdale, IL: The Dryden Press.

Samuelson, P.A. and Nordhaus, W.D. (1985) *Economics*, 12th edition. New York: McGraw-Hill.

Scullion, H. (1991) 'Why Companies Prefer to Use Expatriates', *Personnel Management*, 23: 32–5.

Anne-Wil Harzing

Shell (1993) *The Shell Review*, July, London.

Stone, R.J. (1991) 'Expatriate Selection and Failure', *Human Resource Planning*, 14: 9–18.

Torbiörn, I. (1982) *Living Abroad: Personal Adjustment and Personnel Policy in the Overseas Setting*, New York: Wiley.

Tung, R.L. (1981) 'Selection and Training of Personnel for Overseas Assignments', *Columbia Journal of World Business*, 15: 68–78.

Tung, R.L. (1982) 'Selection and Training Procedures of U.S., European, and Japanese Multinationals', *California Management Review*, 25: 57–71.

Tung, R.L. (1984) 'Human Resource Planning in Japanese Multinationals: A Model for U.S. Firms', *Journal of International Business Studies*, 15: 139–49.

Tung, R.L. (1987) 'Expatriate Assignments: Enhancing Success and Minimizing Failure', *Academy of Management Executive*, 1: 117–25.

Tung, R.L. (1988) *The New Expatriates: Managing Human Resources Abroad*, Cambridge, MA: Ballinger.

Zeira, Y. and Banai, M. (1985) 'Selection of Expatriate Managers in MNCs: The Host-Environment Point of View', *International Studies of Management & Organisation*, XV: 33–51.

Managing Cross-culturally

[10]

Cross-Cultural Management Research: The Ostrich and the Trend[1]

NANCY J. ADLER
McGill University

The trends in cross-cultural management papers published in 24 journals during the last decade, 1971 to 1980, are examined. Less than 5 percent of organizational behavior articles published in top American management journals focused on cross-cultural issues. The majority of the cross-cultural articles were single culture studies; less than 1 percent investigated the interaction between employees of different cultures. No increase was seen in the number of international organizational behavior articles over the decade.

The corporate world is becoming more and more interrelated—more and more international. Improvements in transportation and communication and lower production costs abroad have made global markets more accessible. Even United States-based firms, with their immediate access to extensive domestic markets, have steadily increased the proportion of their foreign to total operations. As shown in Table 1, major economic indicators of internationalization (including foreign direct investment, international sales, and profits earned overseas) have been steadily increasing. Increased multinational operations mean increased multiculturalism within the organization, increased interaction between employees and managers of different cultures. Increased multiculturalism calls for new strategies for organizations.

The United States historically has been in the forefront in the development of management theory, research, and practice. Given the current internationalization of business, the United States could be expected to lead the development of a cross-cultural perspective to management. What have researchers publishing in American management journals written to help managers understand the behavior of people in multinational and transnational organizations? Although there has been a proliferation of books in the field (Bass & Burger, 1979; Harris & Moran, 1979; Heenan & Perlmutter, 1979; Hofstede, 1980),

the survey presented here questions the extent to which management journals have provided theories, models, and research focusing on managers working in multinational and multicultural environments. Have authors chosen to submit and journal editors to publish cosmopolitan papers or papers that reflect a strictly parochial point of view?

Method

Cross-cultural management is the study of the behavior of people in organizations located in cultures and nations around the world. It focuses on the description of organizational behavior within countries and cultures, on the comparison of organizational behavior across countries and cultures, and, perhaps most importantly, on the interaction of peoples from different countries working within the same organization or within the same work environment. The present survey sought to identify the trends in the publication of cross-cultural management articles in major American management journals over the last decade, 1971-1980.

Based on reviews of the literature in the field (Barrett & Bass, 1976; Hofstede, 1980; Kraut, 1975; Roberts, 1970), *it was hypothesized that (1) the published articles in cross-cultural management would be few relative to the amount of international business activity, and (2) there had been an increasing awareness of the importance of international and cross-cultural issues as reflected in increased publication of cross-cultural management articles during the*

[1]The author would like to thank Arshad Ahmad, research assistant, for his many hours analyzing the publishing trends.

Table 1

Economic Indicators of Internationalization in the United States[a]

Year	A	B	C	D	E
1966	51,792	5,259	3,467	1,791	1,163
1967	56,560	5,605	3,847	1,757	1,354
1968	61,907	6,592	4,152	2,440	1,431
1969	68,093	7,649	4,819	2,830	1,533
1970	75,480	8,169	4,992	3,176	1,758
1971	82,760	9,159	5,983	3,176	1,927
1972	89,878	10,949	6,416	4,532	2,115
1973	101,313	16,542	8,384	8,158	2,513
1974	110,078	19,156	11,379	7,777	3,070
1975	124,050	16,595	8,547	8,048	3,543
1976	136,809	18,999	11,303	7,696	3,530
1977	149,848	20,081	12,795	7,286	3,793
1978	167,804	25,165	13,696	11,469	4,775
1979	192,648	37,815	19,400	18,414	5,042

[a]A is foreign direct investment position (in millions) of U.S. corporations; B is income; C is interest, dividends, and earnings of unincorporated affiliates; D is reinvested earnings of incorporated affiliates; E is fees and royalties. Source: U.S. Department of Commerce (1980).

decade 1971-1980.

As listed below, 24 journals were selected that either (1) are recognized to be the better journals in the field of management and organizational behavior and/or (2) tend to carry more international management articles. These selection criteria were designed to identify the maximum number of international organizational behavior articles published during the past decade.

  ** *Academy of Mangement Journal*
  ** *Academy of Management Proceedings*
  ** *Academy of Management Review*
  ** *Administrative Science Quarterly*
  ** *California Management Review*
  ** *Columbia Journal of World Business*
  * *Conference Board Record*
  * *Dun's Review*
  ** *Group and Organization Studies*
  ** *Harvard Business Review*
     International Journal of Intercultural Relations
     Journal of Applied Behavioral Science
     Journal of Applied Psychology
  ** *Journal of International Business Studies*
  * *Journal of Management Studies*
     Journal of Social Psychology
  * *Management International Review*
  * *Management Japan*
  * *Management Science*
  ** *MSU Business Topics*
  ** *Organizational Dynamics*
  ** *SAM Advanced Management Journal*
  ** *Sloan Management Review*
     The Bridge

Of these 24, 19 are management (* and **), 3 are applied psychology, and 2 are international journals. Of the 19 management journals, 13 are published in the United States and are considered top academic journals in management. These formed a separate subgroup for purposes of analysis and are double-starred (**).

As shown in Table 2, articles were classified as to their management focus: general management, organizational behavior, or general interest. They were classified further in two ways according to their cross-cultural focus: as either international or domestic (i.e., as including a country other than the United States or not) and as either cultural or not cultural (i.e., as including culture as a variable or not). Organizational behavior articles that were both international and cultural were defined as cross-cultural management articles. This category, which was the primary focus of the survey, was further categorized as follows into (1) unicultural, (2) comparative, or (3) intercultural articles:

1. Unicultural articles are those organizational behavior articles that focus on the management of organizations in any country other than the United States, such as an article on motivating workers in Israel.
2. Comparative articles are those organizational behavior articles that focus on a comparison between (among) the organizations in any two or more countries or cultures, such as a comparison between leadership styles in Brazil and Japan.
3. Intercultural articles are those organizational behavior articles that focus on the interaction between (among) organization members from two or more countries or cultures, such as a description of the process of negotiation between the Chinese and the French.

Culture has been defined in many ways (Kroeber & Kluckhohn, 1952) and in management studies often has been equated with nation-state. For this survey, it was not found necessary to categorize articles ac-

Table 2
Categorization of Articles in Cross-Cultural Management Literature Review, 1971-1980

| | International | | Domestic | | |
	Geographic Number (%)	Cultural Number (%)	Not Cultural Number (%)	Cultural Number (%)	Total Number (%)
Organizational behavior articles					
$n = 24$	54 (.48)	400 (3.6)	2,225 (19.8)	159 (1.4)	2,838 (25.3)
$n = 13$	39 (.85)	193 (4.2)	1,239 (27.0)	83 (1.8)	1,554 (33.9)
Management articles, not organizational behavior					
$n = 24$	658 (5.9)	29 (.26)	2,659 (23.7)	42 (.37)	3,388 (30.2)
$n = 13$	474 (10.3)	18 (.39)	1,431 (31.2)	18 (.39)	1,941 (42.3)
General articles, not management					
$n = 24$	644 (5.7)	55 (.49)	4.036 (35.9)	258 (2.3)	4,993 (44.5)
$n = 13$	241 (5.3)	2 (.04)	819 (17.9)	26 (.57)	1,088 (23.7)
Total articles					
$n = 24$	1,356 (12.1) + 1,840 (16.4)	484 (4.3)	8,920 (79.5) + 9,379 (83.6)	459 (4.1)	11,219 (100.0)
$n = 13$	754 (16.4) + 967 (21.1)	214 (4.6)	3,489 (76.1) + 3,616 (78.9)	127 (2.8)	4,583 (100.0)

cording to a particular definition of culture. Articles were categorized as cross-cultural if the researcher used any implicit or explicit definition of culture, including nation-state. It also should be noted that including the concept of culture did not mean that the researcher had claimed that culture was a significant variable. It simply meant that culture, as a variable or a construct, was not ignored. Furthermore, other salient dimensions of international organizations—such as geographical dispersion—were recognized but not combined with the cross-cultural category.

Results

As shown in Table 3, the results of the literature survey showed that 4.2 percent of the articles published in top American management journals were in the cross-cultural management category. Even fewer, 3.6 percent, of the articles published in all 24 surveyed journals were in the cross-cultural management category.

The majority of the articles published in the surveyed journals were domestic; in the top 13 American management journals, 19.6 percent were international. Of these international articles, the majority, 76.3 percent, were geographically international but did not refer to the concept of culture.

About a third (33.4 percent) of the articles published in the 13 top American management journals focused on organizational behavior issues. Of these organizational behavior articles, more than three-

quarters, (84.9 percent), were domestic; 15.1 percent were international.

The remaining category of interest to this study was domestic articles that included cultural issues: 5.5 percent of the articles fell into this category. An example of an article in this category would be the decision making practices of Hispanics living in Los Angeles.

Table 3 presents the breakdown of cross-cultural management articles into unicultural, comparative, and intercultural articles. Of the total articles, 4.2 percent were cross-cultural management articles. Of these, 1.9 percent were unicultural, 1.4 precent were comparative, and .9 percent were intercultural. Within the cross-cultural management category, nearly half of the articles were unicultural (47.2 percent); about a third were comparative (34.2 percent); and about a sixth (18.6 percent) were intercultural. Table 4 and Figure 1 show that there was not a rising trend across the decade. The proportion of cross-cultural management articles did not increase substantially from 1971 to 1980. Furthermore, the relative proportions of unicultural, comparative, and intercultural articles did not follow a stable trend.

As summarized in Table 5, these aggregate trends appeared to hold for the individual journals. Of the 13 top American management journals, the range in cross-cultural management articles was from 9.7 percent (*Journal of International Business Studies*), 7.8 percent (*Administrative Science Quarterly*), and 7.3 percent (*Columbia Journal of World Business*) to .8

Table 3
Publishing Trends
in Cross-Cultural Management

	All Surveyed Journals	Management Journals	Top Academic Management Journals
Number of journals	24	19	13
Number of articles	11,219	8,795	4,583
	%	%	%
Of the total articles			
Domestic	83.6	81.8	80.4
International	16.4	18.2	19.6
Of the total articles			
General	44.5	37.9	31.3
Organizational behavior	25.3	24.3	33.4
Management	30.2	37.8	35.3
Of the total international articles			
Cross-cultural	26.3	21.9	23.7
Geographic	73.7	78.1	76.3
Of the total organizational behavior articles			
Domestic	84.0	82.3	84.9
Cultural	5.6	4.9	5.5
Not cultural	78.4	77.4	79.4
International	16.0	17.7	15.1
Cultural	14.1	15.2	12.6
Unicultural	6.8	7.9	5.9
Comparative	4.2	4.5	4.3
Intercultural	3.1	2.9	2.4
Geographic	1.9	2.5	2.5
Of the total cross-cultural articles			
Unicultural	1.7	1.9	1.9
Comparative	1.1	1.1	1.4
Intercultural	.8	.6	.9

Table 4
Trends in the Publication of Cross-Cultural Management Articles in 24 Journals, 1971-1980

Year	Total Articles	Interna-tional Articles %	Organiza-tional Behavior %	Cross-Cultural Management %	Of the Total International Articles				Of the Total Organizational Behavior Articles			
					Cross-Cultural %	Uni-cultural %	Compar-ative %	Inter-cultural %	Cross-Cultural %	Uni-cultural %	Compar-ative %	Inter-cultural %
1971	973	17.2	28.2	5.4	31.4	19.2	8.1	4.1	19.1	11.7	4.9	2.5
1972	1229	17.7	23.4	4.8	27.1	15.3	6.8	5.0	20.4	11.5	5.1	3.8
1973	1154	16.9	25.5	2.9	17.1	8.3	4.7	4.1	11.3	5.5	3.1	2.7
1974	990	14.8	26.3	2.6	17.6	5.4	6.8	5.4	9.8	3.0	3.8	3.0
1975	1140	15.8	23.8	2.3	14.6	4.4	5.1	5.1	9.7	2.9	3.4	3.4
1976	1200	14.4	25.3	2.7	18.8	10.4	5.6	2.8	10.7	5.9	3.2	1.6
1977	1197	15.2	26.1	3.9	25.7	13.2	6.6	5.9	14.9	7.7	3.8	3.4
1978	1227	15.1	27.5	4.1	27.1	11.9	10.6	4.6	14.8	6.5	5.8	2.5
1979	1170	11.3	23.5	3.4	30.0	11.5	8.8	9.7	14.5	5.5	4.3	4.7
1980	939	14.8	24.2	3.9	26.4	12.2	8.1	6.1	16.0	7.4	4.9	3.7
Total	11,219	16.4	25.2	3.6	26.3	10.8	7.1	5.3	14.1	6.8	4.2	3.1

percent (*Organizational Dynamics*) and 1.8 percent (*Harvard Business Review*). The journals that publish more international articles—*Journal of International Business Studies* (97.3 percent international) and the *Columbia Journal of World Business* (91.6 percent international)—seem to publish relatively fewer organizational behavior articles (15.6 percent and 11.2

percent, respectively). On the other hand, those journals that have published the greatest number of organizational behavior articles—*Organizational Dynamics* (83.3 percent), *Group and Organization Studies* (56.4 percent), and *Administrative Science Quarterly* (44.9 percent)—have not published as many international articles (1.7 percent, 4.9 percent,

Figure 1
Cross-Cultural Management Articles
as a Proportion of the Total Articles

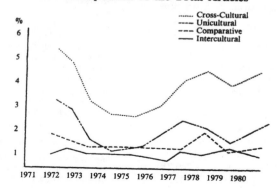

Table 5
Organizational Behavior, International, and Cross-Cultural
Management Articles Published in 24 Journals, 1971-1980

Journal	Total Articles	Organizational Behavior %	Inter-national %	Cross-Cultural %	Unicultural %	Compar-ative %	Intercultural %
Management Journals	8,795	23.3	18.1	3.6	1.9	1.1	.6
*Academy of Management Journal***	412	37.9	5.0	4.3	1.9	2.4	0.0
*Academy of Management Proceedings***	825	29.9	9.4	4.6	1.6	1.9	1.1
*Academy of Management Review***	218	39.4	3.2	3.2	1.8	0.0	1.4
*Administrative Science Quarterly***	347	44.9	8.1	7.8	4.3	2.6	.9
*California Management Review***	398	32.2	15.0	3.5	2.0	.5	1.0
*Columbia Journal of World Business***	508	11.2	91.6	7.3	4.1	2.4	.8
Conference Board Record	1,227	8.1	16.7	1.0	.4	.1	.5
Dun's Review	1,018	9.9	12.5	.3	.1	.1	.1
*Group and Organization Studies***	101	56.4	4.9	4.9	.1	0.0	3.9
*Harvard Business Review***	703	21.8	11.6	1.8	.9	.6	.3
*Journal of International Business Studies***	154	15.6	97.3	9.7	3.9	3.2	2.6
Journal of Management Studies	192	62.5	16.2	14.1	8.9	4.2	1.0
Management International Review	342	45.3	51.2	15.5	8.5	3.5	3.5
Management Japan	112	18.8	73.3	18.8	15.2	3.6	0.0
Management Science	1,321	1.4	.6	.2	0.0	.1	0.0
*MSU Business Topics***	293	30.0	12.9	3.7	2.0	1.0	.7
*Organizational Dynamics***	114	83.3	1.7	.8	0.0	.8	0.0
*SAM Advanced Management Journal***	328	69.5	4.5	1.5	.3	.9	.3
*Sloan Management Review***	182	32.9	8.1	1.0	.5	.5	0.0
13 Double Starred Management Journals	4,583	33.5	8.1	4.3	1.9	1.4	.8
Psychology Journals	2,245	9.8	5.8	2.7	.9	.8	.4
Journal of Applied Behavioral Science	310	46.5	4.2	2.9	2.3	.3	.3
Journal of Applied Psychology	1,143	47.6	2.7	2.8	.9	1.2	.7
Journal of Social Psychology	792	4.4	1 .5	.7	.3	.3	0.0
Cross-Cultural Journals	179	29.1	64.2	22.9	5.0	5.6	12.3
The Bridge	103	26.2	65.0	23.3	4.8	7.8	1 .7
International Journal of Intercultural Relations	76	32.9	63.1	22.4	5.3	2.6	14.5
All Journals	11,219	25.2	16.4	3.6	1.7	1.1	.8

230

and 8.1 percent, respectively). Although there are numerous international management articles in the various functional areas (i.e., finance, marketing), there have been few international articles in organizational behavior.

Discussion

This survey clearly demonstrates that corporate activity has internationalized faster than has the publishing of articles in American management journals. The majority of the total articles and of the organization behavior articles published in American management journals focus on the domestic U.S. environment; they do not refer to culture in any way. Within the category of international organizational behavior articles that do refer to culture, the majority are studies of a single foreign country or studies comparing two countries' organizational practices. The minority are articles that refer to the interaction between people from different cultures within a single organizational setting. Over the decade 1971-1980 there appeared to be no trend either toward increasing the overall proportion of cross-cultural management articles or toward increasing the relative proportion of unicultural, comparative or intercultural articles.

If, at a minimum, organizational behavior research is to remain relevant to managers and not become an ivory tower aside, it must begin to include in its leading journals a substantially greater proportion of articles that go beyond the purely domestic perspective. It also must begin to address international problems and issues. An international perspective is particularly important for the field of organizational behavior. Recent studies (Brossard & Maurice, 1976; Child, 1981; Hofstede, 1980; Laurent, 1979) have concluded that there are major impacts of culture on the ways individuals and groups work within systems. The impact on the behavior of people within work systems appears to be greater than the cultural impact on the systems themselves.

It is suggested that journal editors, scholars, management professors, and working managers need to address the growing internationalism of the work environment more directly. All four groups need to question whether paradigms developed in and for the domestic U.S. environment are applicable outside of the United States. It is recommended that:

Journal editors and reviewers be aware of the importance of cross-cultural and international management to their readership and seek to lead the profession in this new area.

Scholars question the applicability of their research (a) beyond the U.S. management community—that is, that they question the universality of their research—and (b) beyond the shrinking segment of the U.S. management community that works strictly within a domestic, unicultural milieu.

Management professors question the relevance of material that is based strictly on a domestic, unicultural U.S. population; that they question the types of environments that their students are most likely to be facing during their professional careers and design courses accordingly (AACSB, 1978-1979).

Managers question the relevance of management articles that do not address international issues; furthermore, that they question the universal applicability of research results and consultant programs that do not consider the cultural dimension.

Beyond awareness of the international dimension, there are many dilemmas impeding cross-cultural management research. The first is funding. International studies are more expensive than domestic studies. The second is methodological complexity. Issues involving access to representative samples, translation, equivalence of concepts, instrumentation, administration, analysis, and interpretation are difficult, time consuming, and expensive. Frequently they are impossible to solve with the rigor usually required of within-culture studies (Bennett, 1977; Brislin, Lonner, & Thorndike, 1973; Hofstede, 1980; Kraut, 1975; Sekaran, 1981; Triandis, 1972). Compared with the study of organizational behavior in domestic settings, cross-cultural management research is in its infancy. Perhaps reviewers and journals editors will need to keep this fact more closely in mind when evaluating international organizational behavior studies submitted for publication.

The field of cross-cultural management does not exist with a set of ready answers. Management, as a professional and an academic discipline, must address itself more directly to a new set of issues. Kuhn (1962) suggested that it is very difficult for the scientific community to give up a cherished paradigm. Growing internationalism demands that a narrow domestic paradigm be replaced with one that can encompass the diversity of a global perspective.

References

AACSB. *Policies, procedures and standards.* St. Louis: American Assembly of Collegiate Schools of Business, 1978-1979.

Barrett, G. V., & Bass, B. M. Cross-cultural issues in industrial and organizational psychology. In M. D. Dunnette (Ed.), *Handbook of industrial and organizational psychology.* New York: Rand McNally, 1976, 1639-1686.

Bass, B. M., & Burger, P. C. *Assessment of managers: An international comparison.* New York: The Free Press, 1979.

Bennett, M. Testing management theories cross-culturally. *Journal of Applied Psychology,* 1977, 62 (5), 578-581.

Brislin, R. W., Lonner, W. J., & Thorndike, R. M. *Cross-cultural research methods.* New York: John Wiley & Sons, 1973.

Brossard, M. & Maurice, M. Is there a universal model of organization structure? *International Studies of Management and Organization.* 1976, 6 (3), 11-45.

Child, J. Culture, contingency and capitalism in the cross-national study of organizations. In L. L. Cummings & B. M. Staw (Eds.), *Research in organizational behavior* (Vol. 3). Greenwich, Conn.: JAI Press, 1981, 303-356.

Harris, P. R., & Moran, R. T. *Managing cultural differences.* Houston, Texas: Gulf Publishing, 1979.

Heenan, D. A., & Perlmutter, H. V. *Multinational organization development.* Reading, Mass.: Addison-Wesley, 1979.

Hofstede, G. *Culture's consequences: International differences in work related values.* Beverly Hills, Cal.: Sage Publications, 1980.

Kraut, A. I. Some recent advances in cross-national management research. *Academy of Management Journal.* 1975, 18, 538-547.

Kroeber, A. L., & Kluckhohn, C. *Culture: A critical review of concepts and definitions.* Papers of the Peabody Museum of American Archaeology and Ethnology (Vol. 47, No. 1). Cambridge, Mass.: Harvard University, 1952.

Kuhn, T. S. *The structure of scientific revolution.* 2nd ed. Chicago, Ill.: University of Chicago Press, 1962.

Laurent, A. Cultural dimensions of managerial ideologies: National versus multinational cultures. Paper presented at the 5th Annual Meeting of the European International Business Association, London Business School, England, 1979.

Roberts, K. On looking at an elephant: An evaluation of cross-cultural research related to organizations. *Psychological Bulletin,* 1970, 4 (5), 327-350.

Sekaran, U. Methodological and theoretical issues and advancements in cross-cultural research. Paper presented at the McGill International Symposium on Cross-Cultural Management, Montréal Canada, 1981.

Triandis, H. C., Vassiliou, V., Vassiliou, G., Tanaka, Y., & Shanmugan, A. V. *The analysis of subjective culture.* New York: Wiley-Interscience, 1972.

U.S. Department of Commerce. *Survey of current business.* 1980, 60 (8), 24-25.

Nancy J. Adler is Assistant Professor of Organizational Behavior and Cross-Cultural Management in the Faculty of Management, McGill University, Montreal, Canada.

[11]

Adapting and Adjusting to Other Cultures
What We Know but Don't Always Tell

ALLAN BIRD
California Polytechnic State University

JOYCE S. OSLAND
University of Portland

MARK MENDENHALL
University of Tennessee, Chattanooga

SUSAN C. SCHNEIDER
HEC University of Geneva

A scrutiny of international management textbooks yields some common themes. Inevitably they present the reader with a set of dimensions on which cultures can be differentiated, the most popular of these being Hofstede's (1980) work-related values dimensions. They also provide some analysis of culture and of the challenges of working across cultures. For the most part, however, the treatment is simple, even superficial, bearing little resemblance to the complexity that most managers confront when they get overseas. What these books all seem to be short on is concrete advice that carries the marks of experience, won with risk and trial and error rather than academic research. What specifically should someone do when entering an intercultural context? What strategies can one confidently adopt? How can managers unfamiliar with a given culture make sense of what is going on around them?

We pulled together a group of people who not only have researched and taught about managing across cultures for the past 10 to 15 years but who also have extensive experience living and working abroad. We had a conversation about what we ourselves do when crossing cultures and the advice we give to others, about the challenges of teaching culture, and about what currently intrigues us. The outcome was a dialogue about what we know but don't always tell.

The four people we brought together, two men and two women, have collectively worked in Asia, Latin America, North America, Africa, and Europe. Our work experiences range from the Peace Corps to employment in host national organizations to consulting with North American, European, and Japanese multinational companies on a range of international human resource issues. We share a common passion for the value and rewards of international experience and passionately disagree about the best way to go international.

THE DIALOGUE

We began with a simple question that every manager who has ever prepared for entering a new culture raises shortly after immersing themselves in it: "Why don't people act the way I was told they would act?" Managers asking this question are not so naive that they expect everyone to fit a particular stereotype. Nevertheless, they inevitably confront a situation in which cultural behaviors are not simply different but paradoxical. The behaviors appear to violate the very norms one was told to expect.

Osland: The longer I live in a country, the more uncomfortable I become making generalizations about the culture because 10 examples immediately come to mind where the generalization does not hold true. To further muddy the waters, we usually characterize cultures on binary dimensions, like Hofstede's values, that are used as shorthand stereotypes. But people with experience in the culture can usually come up with examples of both individualism and collectivism or both high- and low-uncertainty avoidance within those cultures and in their business practices. So, what interests me is, "How are cultures paradoxical?" That is the question that Allan and I have been grappling with over the past few years.

Mendenhall: If we teach people that everybody is different in all the cultures, they have nothing they can refer to. The idea of stereotypes is critical, in that you have to have a very educated understanding of what the basic values and accepted norms are for a population. That way you have in your mind a reference point from which you can begin to make sense of behavior. At the same time, you must also have the understanding that no one you meet will fit that "reference point stereotype" perfectly. They're all individuals. The problem is that it's a paradox. You need a stereotype, an informed set of reference points against which you can begin to make sense out of host nationals' behavior. But then you have to remember that no one fits that

stereotype perfectly. You're constantly having to adjust your perceptions and your attributions about everything on an individual level but with that stereotype in place.

Schneider: Being at INSEAD the last 10 years has been an interesting experience. INSEAD is multicultural: There is no one nationality. Neither the French nor British, for example, represent more than 20% of the M.B.A. program or the faculty. Supposedly there's no dominant culture except, of course, that it is very Anglo-Saxon being a business school. Many people consider INSEAD to be an American spaceship that landed in the middle of Fontainbleau. Interestingly enough, what happens is that after a while, every stereotype you ever had about any nationality gets reinforced. And that's interesting because it reminds me of Hofstede's (1980) and Laurent's (1983) work. They found that even within multinationals, such as IBM, despite a strong corporate culture and pressures to converge, there remains a large variation due to nationality. It seems that these forces for convergence create a backlash—a greater reassertion of cultural identity. All those stereotypes become more obvious because it is only by comparison that you can see them. When you're only looking within a country, however, you only see the variation. But when you compare, let's say, a group of German managers with a group of French, you see the difference—and that is when your stereotypes get reinforced. Stereotypes are only meaningful by comparison.

People have to make sense of their environment. They have categories or stereotypes, which are formed on information they have gathered, on impressions they have experienced over time. So, when I meet somebody and they say to me, "Oh, you're from New York! I know somebody from New York," I say, "Great, there are 8 million people in New York!" But what they've done is they've called up the file cabinet in their head and found the file which is that stereotype of New Yorkers. Whatever the accumulation of their information is, that's what is applied. The research that has been done that relates indirectly to those people basically says it's not the stereotype that is good or bad; it's that stereotypes get used in certain ways that become dysfunctional.

Osland: And whether you hang onto the stereotype in light of contrary new information.

Schneider: Well, whether you can adapt the stereotype. The whole point of new information is that you're developing that file, enriching that file.

Bird: This gets back to the initial question. We have students come through, or we work with companies, and we teach them, not "Mexicans are lazy" (an inaccurate stereotype), but Mexicans have a large power distance and Americans have a small power distance. All we've done is change the stereotyping that we've taught them to do. How do you teach this in a way that, instead of reinforcing existing stereotypes or giving new ones to replace old ones, weakens the inclination to use stereotypes in a rigid way?

Mendenhall: It's a very difficult thing to pull off. I've done seminars with senior executives in Japan, trying to help them understand the Japanese business culture. What we've found is that, left to their own devices, managers very quickly start to develop stereotypes in order to make sense out of what they're seeing. And what they're developing is often way off base in terms of the reality of where the Japanese are operating from. So they have dangerous stereotypes. If they've been there about 6 months or longer, they are very unwilling to break those notions. It is hard to get them to disassemble their frameworks, listen to some new input, and reassemble the stereotype. The ones who had not been over there very long were much more open.

In seminars we consistently say, "Now, this is based upon our reading, our research, our experience. We are not telling you that we know everything about Japan. We're giving you enough to get started so that now you can be a self-learner and add to or subtract from what we've said."

Some expatriates in Japan say that understanding Japan is like peeling an onion. It goes, "They're just like us; they're not like us; they're just like us; they're not like us." But you become wiser as you go through that process. Many expatriates never peel the onion. They create their own small, very inaccurate stereotypes and operate that way for 2 or 3 years.

Schneider: What do you mean "inaccurate stereotype?" What does that mean actually?

Mendenhall: I mean a stereotype that doesn't access the reality of the culture. Not that you can ever develop one that accesses the reality completely.

Schneider: Could you give me an example of an inaccurate stereotype?

Bird: How about, "Japanese are polite"? I hear that repeatedly from people who just arrive in Japan or who have never been in Japan before, who clearly have never been pushed off a train in rush-hour Tokyo.

Schneider: Do you think that's impolite? I'm from New York. That's normal.

Mendenhall: But it's inaccurate, so that then as people move through experiences in Japan, it becomes a negative colorization of everything they perceive. "Japanese aren't polite; I thought they were," and then those people make lots of internal attributions about Japanese that are negative.

Schneider: I think that's what the role of dimensions such as Hofstede's are for. Hofstede didn't invent collectivism, certainly not with the few items he uses. The collectivism dimension has been around for so long and keeps coming back. There seems to be some convergent validity. This dimension helps in understanding certain kinds of behaviors and can serve as a label. Other dimensions serve the same purpose. Therefore, I think it's important to have a set of dimensions when you're going into a situation so that one is able to assess it.

Osland: I agree that it's best to start with cultural dimensions; they're certainly useful. Give people the dimensions first so they have something to guide them in the very beginning. Otherwise, people who are more likely to be seeking black-and-white answers at this time may respond, "Well, if there are so many exceptions to cultural stereotypes, why bother with these dimensions at all?" But once people understand the dimensions and are beginning to see the paradoxes themselves, it makes sense to introduce the idea of cultural paradoxes.

We'd be remiss if we didn't. For example, Americans are characterized as a low power distance culture, and yet we have some of the most autocratic CEOs in the world. People should be prepared to encounter that. In certain situations, you would be committing a major faux pas if you operated only with the stereotypical cultural dimensions as a guide.

Schneider: People's reactions, though, are often, "So why bother learning this stuff when we can't get a straight answer?" On the other hand, to say "it's a dimension on which a given culture has distributed a wide variety of responses" begins to unravel some of those paradoxes. Paradoxes such as, "Yes, of course, a French person would bend the truth and testify that a friend was not speeding in a car accident because that's what you do." But on the other hand, one would never go to a restaurant and say the food was good if it wasn't. That would be a sacrilege because cuisine is an art form. Even if it was your mother's or your best friend's cooking, you would say, "No, I'm sorry, the food's lousy." But you'd protect your friend vis-à-vis the police or vis-à-vis the system.

Mendenhall: I don't know anything about France, but my guess is that there is some kind of value around which "one needs to be honest about food" that flows from something deeper. If you can look at the interdisciplinary research from sociologists, historians, and anthropologists, you can start to uncover what a culture's core values are and start to see what norms flow from them.

I was on the plane coming here, talking with two professors from Germany. We got into a discussion about gun control. This was a rather strange thing to them, this obsession Americans have to own guns. I was able to help them to understand why Americans might feel so strongly on this issue by connecting "gun control" to the values of individualism and independence. In some ways, owning a gun is one of the last vestiges of being able to "feel" independent. Many of our behaviors and things that we focus on, both at a mundane level and at other levels, flow from deep-seated constructs or values, things, or ideas that a lot of people in a culture hold dear.

Bird: Adapting, then, is not just the identification of some construct or some deep-seated value but the ability to create a logic around why something should be valued and how that value should be applied. There are two tasks. One is understanding the logic, and the other is situating the value. Once the logic behind a value is laid bare and the value is clearly situated, it all makes sense.

I like to tease people who tell me about the Japanese having a high uncertainty avoidance and Americans having a low uncertainty avoidance by talking about what lawyers in each country do. In Japan, they write ambiguous clauses, which doesn't seem like a very effective way to reduce un-

certainty. Of course, in America, every "i" has to be dotted, every "t" crossed, and every contingency planned for in the contract, which doesn't seem like a tolerance for risk at all. The logic is far more interesting and helpful than the dimension alone. In Japan, you don't need a written contract because the uncertainty is resolved through a host of other mechanisms. Once you understand that, for the Japanese, resolving the uncertainty through those other mechanisms is more important than what is in a contract, then people have a way of making sense. Or, when you understand that Americans don't like to take needless risks and a contract can remove needless risk, then you are giving people a context that simple dimensions don't encompass.

However, this approach is a more difficult, tortuous process than saying, "Here are some dimensions; be careful." Like the warning on cigarette packs, it's there to indemnify, not to inform or to help. I warn people not to generalize, but it's clear that they do.

Mendenhall: When I first started out in the field, I was really trying to push predeparture cross-cultural training. Now I think it is much less important. It's important to do some predeparture training as inoculation. But what we found in our work with American executives in Japan is that they did not have the experience base to be able to listen to what we said in America and project that onto experiences they'd never yet had. So now, I really advocate "in-country training" about 3 months after arrival.

Schneider: You also gave them the language to talk about these experiences.

Mendenhall: I do not know how you can provide that to people who have never had the experience. I don't know how you can give an in-country sort of experience to people who have never had to wrestle with these things.

Schneider: I sometimes get executives with a lot of experience who say, "It's just people, not culture." But then I also get people who sit there when I'm presenting Hofstede's dimensions—and I'm thinking everybody in the world has heard of Hofstede, and I am embarrassed to put it up at this point—and these people say, "Oh, that explains it." All of these lightbulbs go off in their heads because you're giving them something, however rudimentary it is, that helps them make sense of the experience they had. They've just never had words to put around the experiences.

And that's the dilemma. The danger of getting stuck in these dimensions and yet needing some sort of term, or word, or some way of categorizing what these differences are without the dimensions taking on a life of their own and becoming handcuffs.

Osland: What we're talking about is an evolutionary process. Before people go overseas, they don't need these concepts that Mark thinks are just-in-time learning. They need to know enough to not be rude. But once there, they need concepts to help them make sense of what they observe and feel. Also, I think it's more the long-term expatriates who love paradoxes because they've cracked the easy code and now they can perceive and get excited about the more difficult puzzles, which are the paradoxes.

Schneider: For 10 years I've been living in France and quite regularly something happens and I think, "Wow, I never thought of that!" I explain it as levels of codes or paradoxes. Initially, you start out with very gross kinds of categories. The evolutionary process you describe is what I call refining your categories. Little by little you begin to see, "Oh, that's why they're doing that." Things that you've read all of a sudden hit you and make sense. Even with me, who supposedly knows this field with all its vocabulary and frameworks, I am still in this kind of shock mode—"Oh, my God"—or discovery mode—"Wow, can you believe this?"—and it happens almost on a daily basis. I don't know if it ever stops.

Mendenhall: And that's what I meant by self-learning. It never stops. But the problem is some expatriates very quickly develop a rudimentary software system—the "inaccurate stereotypes." They go just far enough to be able to get through each day, and they stop and never change. "The French are this way, the Japanese are that way, and that's the way it is." They never have those subsequent "Ah-ha!" experiences because they freeze themselves, unlike the self-learners such as you and other expatriates who continually peel away more layers of the onion. At this point we're talking more about personal motivation.

Schneider: But even with strong personal motivation, and even with being able to understand these

things cognitively or being able to figure them out afterwards, it is a difficult process. I had an experience today where I saw somebody I knew. I immediately went into French mode—"Hello," with two kisses—and they recoiled. I thought "Oh, my God, my own behaviors have become so automatic." Even with people who are very good friends, when they only gave me one kiss, I felt rejected because it's supposed to be two, or four if they are really close to you. I realized that I have become programmed in ways that I wasn't even aware of.

Bird: You're talking about unconsciously taking on the norms of another culture, but let's consider an opposing view. Do you think people who journey abroad reach a point where they're comfortable asserting their own culture and not adopting local cultural norms? I think about my having lived in Japan for 8 years and more recently traveling back and forth on a regular basis. I'm now comfortable adapting to the Japanese in some modes, but in other situations in Japan, I'm perfectly willing to impose my American values and my sense of who I am. We tell people to adapt, but I don't always do that. Why is it that I'm willing to do that in some situations and not others? What is it about those situations that makes me feel comfortable to behave differently?

Osland: I've thought about that too because in every country I've lived in, there's been a point where I've made a conscious decision to act in a way that is truer to who I really am. For example, in Colombia I reached the point where I decided, "Well, I'm not going to drink coffee anymore." I've always hated coffee, and I only started drinking it there because they bring it around four times a day and it's somewhat rude to say no. Granted, by this time I had also learned that it was polite to turn it down if you could claim a liver problem. You reach a point where you say, "I'm an American, for God's sake!" Or, "This is more of who I really am—take it or leave it."

Reaching this point relates to the balance between perceived eccentricity and perceived competence. If you are perceived as competent, you are allowed to be more eccentric and deviate from normal behavior. "Joe is a little weird, but that's okay because, boy, does he do a great job!" Minorities, like women, people of color, expatriates, etc., are by definition more eccentric than the norm of the majority group. They often feel compelled to de-emphasize their eccentricity in order to fit in. I think effective expatriates intuitively realize when they are perceived as competent enough to allow themselves to express more of their eccentricity. By effective expatriates, I mean people who try to integrate, who learn the language and work at learning the culture, who do whatever it takes to be successful at work, and who try very hard not to offend. One day they look around and see that this effort has paid off—they have good relationships with the locals, and they've done well on the job. They think to themselves, "I've mastered this—I am perceived as competent, and now I'm going back to be more who I really am."

Schneider: That's not obvious to me. I was just thinking about how you subtly get shaped by a new culture, even a corporate culture, to start doing things that you never would have done had you been somewhere else. How did I end up writing cases? I never intended to write cases. Well, I'm at INSEAD so I'm writing cases. You get shaped to do things that you would never plan to do and at some point you say, "Well, now that I'm sort of arrived at full professor, or I've got tenure, I can now step back and really be me." Well, what does that mean?

Osland: I agree that you pick up a lot of another culture in this process, organizational or national, so it's not as if you totally revert to the person you were in the beginning. After a point, however, rather than continuing to struggle to fit in, you demand that they adjust to you a little.

Mendenhall: Most host nationals expect some differences from you if you are from a foreign country. They don't expect you to become French or Japanese. In fact, they would probably consider it to be impossible. With time, as you understand not just that you shouldn't take your shoes off but maybe why you shouldn't, you start to understand which situations are less critical in terms of culture as it relates to overseas effectiveness. Host nationals expect some eccentricity; so it's okay to be American or whatever you are to some degree. You might feel a little more free to act American in certain situations, but in Japan there would be some situations where you would never do that.

Bird: For example, you'd never wear your shoes on *tatami* (straw mats) in a Japanese house.

Mendenhall: Or if a Japanese employee comes to you and starts to talk about his family, you would not just say, "Oh, that's very nice" and blow it off and then get back to the task. You would know that this is a very important situation and that you have to listen to this person. But there might be other situations at work where it's not as critical to obey Japanese norms, where you say no because now you know that you don't have to conform every time.

Schneider: But what if you just assume that, "Well, I'm an American. They know I'm an American, so why play games and pretend to be anything else?" I think this attitude is a kiss of death because it's arrogant.

Mendenhall: Asserting yourself in this way—being more American—only works if you have a lot of cross-cultural experience. Teaching this would be very dangerous. I wouldn't teach this notion about "sometimes it's okay to be an American and sometimes it's not" to undergraduates.

Schneider: But we have to discuss and teach it. This whole issue of when we adapt and when we don't is critical. I understand that there are these cultural differences, and I understand that at work I might see a behavior that I can accurately interpret. So, do I adapt or do I say, "No, we're not going to do it that way"? You have to confront that dilemma! That's what managers are demanding to know. When should managers adapt and when should they say, "Look, this is the corporate way, and this is what we're going to do. And if you don't like it, we'll hire some French person who does."

Mendenhall: But there are no simple answers to those questions. When we get executives in seminars, they'll raise their hand and say, "I have this situation. . . ." And our response is, "There's no 100% way to know exactly what you should do, but here are some principles. It's most likely that 'x' is happening. Therefore, here is a logic for thinking about 'x.'"

The freedom to be yourself a little bit more only comes after you have paid a self-learning price over a period of time. That's what I meant before when I said I would never teach "just be yourself whenever you feel like it" because the only person who can make that decision is the individual.

Schneider: But I think you are yourself, whether you're trying to be or not. I think it's very hard to be otherwise. It's a constant process of being very much aware of what being yourself means and how it is perceived by others. It's a constant process of back and forth, adapting and not adapting. It's impossible for me to walk into a situation and pretend to be French, no matter how much I want to.

Osland: Maybe it's a matter of how we frame the examples. What were you thinking of, Allan, when you brought this up?

Bird: Here's an example of the types of situations I mean. I was out to dinner with some Japanese. In the past I would have eaten whatever the Japanese ate. When I first went to Japan, I did that because that's adapting, that's fitting in. Right now I'm at the comfort stage where I say, "I don't like that." And I feel I can do that without insulting them or creating problems.

Schneider: But I don't think you have to go through a stage where you have to eat things you don't like just so that you won't insult them.

Osland: Oh, I always did!

Mendenhall: But Allan knows how to do that. In Japan there's a certain way you can get out of eating unpleasant things. But if you're a neophyte and you just say, "I don't want to eat that," then you are in trouble. At this point Allan knows when to decline and how to decline in a way that's not offensive.

Schneider: Why does it have to get to that point to be able to decline? Do you mean somebody who's a neophyte can't learn how to decline in a socially acceptable way?

Mendenhall: Not at first. Not until they learn how to do it. Not until they've earned the right to decline.

Osland: You can teach some things upfront, but I think it's an important, essential step in acculturation to work very hard at fitting in and meeting host country expectations. When you're living overseas, there are tremendous identity issues with all this flexing and taking on aspects of other cultures and questioning one's own cultural values. Maybe another way to explain what Allan described is that sometimes we go too far and then decide to retrench and be ourselves more. I don't think it's an issue of being Ugly Americans. When expatriates talk about being themselves a little more, they are usually talking about not going along with peripheral values and customs rather than fighting cultural imperatives (key norms in a culture that everyone must observe).

(At this point Schneider left the conversation to go to a meeting.)

Osland: Let's switch gears here to discuss something Allan and I have been talking about called "value trumping." It goes back to what you mentioned, Mark, where if people learn the key cultural values, then it helps them figure out in what circumstance or what context those values would be most important. In your gun control example, individualism and independence apparently trump other U.S. values like the sanctity of human life and the right to live in peace. The idea of trumping helps us understand how something that looks paradoxical on the surface has an underlying logic to it that makes sense.

Mendenhall: When we are teaching executives in Japan, they say things like, "We have never seen Japanese get angry, really angry at each other and just say what's on their mind. Do they ever really do that?" We say, "Well, they get angry and they are direct. But they usually do it in situations and contexts where foreigners are not present." There are times when Japanese are quite blunt with each other, where they chew each other out, or at least are very open and direct. But it is always in situations and in places where there are no outsiders. That is one of those paradoxes for foreigners. How do Japanese get anything done if they never seem to say what is on their mind?

If you make the assumption that there is always a logical reason behind any behavior—that there is a logic to what appears to be dysfunctional behavior in another culture—you learn more. If you believe that it is all completely irrational and that these people are weird, then you start to make negative attributions about the people and the culture, and you think and say things like, "These people are stupid. They are backwards."

This brings us back to the problem with generalized cross-cultural, predeparture training programs. I used to think it was enough to teach general principles to adjustment. But in order to truly adjust, you need in-country training and culture-specific training. There are general principles of adjustment, and they have to be taught. But in each culture you are going to have to work through those principles in very, very different ways and learn very, very different things.

Osland: I can certainly relate to your frustration with predeparture training. But a general exposure that helps participants realize that there are many things to take into consideration overseas and that there is more to be learned is still valuable and better than nothing. Given the general lack of expatriate training provided by companies, such courses may be all some expats ever receive.

Mendenhall: It seems to me there are levels to it. At some point, to really truly assist people, the cultural specificity issues have to be addressed. If we just want to expose people to the first layer, we can stay at a general level. That is perfectly fine as long as we let them know that adjustment for them in Great Britain is going to be different than in Japan, even though the basic principles of adjustment probably remain the same.

Osland: Tell me what you think about this idea as a way to teach cultural paradoxes or culturally specific behaviors. Have you ever run into the notion of "language acquisition made practical?" It's a form of learning a language where you work with a teacher, an expert in the foreign language, who also speaks your own language. You decide what you want to learn each day—for example, you may decide you want to learn how to get a haircut in French. Your teacher gives you the rudiments of how to ask the right questions, such as, "How do I ask for a haircut?" "How do I say 'just take a little off the top'?" And then you take those questions to five "informants," native speakers who are willing to spend 10 minutes a day answering your questions. You tape all of this and tell your teacher the next day what you learned. I've always thought this was a wonderful way to learn languages. What about taking this method and using it for cross-cultural adaptation?

Bird: That'd be like a modified, personalized cultural assimilator. With cultural assimilators you are given a critical incident and then asked, "Now what would be the appropriate response?" In Joyce's example, what you do is have a critical incident that you might take and show to five people in the office. For example, say it's a motivational problem—someone isn't doing his job the way it should be done. You would take that problem to five different people in the office and say, "If this happened to you, how would you solve this problem?"

Mendenhall: Or even, "How would you process what's going on?" Just getting at what's going on might take you beyond the issue of solving it.

Bird: Maybe you would even start that way, "Tell me how you would work through this problem?" "What would you look at?" "What concerns would you have?" Or you may even start with, "Here's a story. Tell me what you think is going on here."

Mendenhall: Let me change the subject. I am very interested in the idea that many people have the need to become a chameleon overseas. It is not so much that you become a chameleon but that you remain yourself, that you express parts of yourself that the cultural norms of your home country perhaps do not allow to surface. This other culture you go into may allow those things, those aspects of yourself, to surface and play out. That is maybe what people should be looking for. If you go to Japan or any culture, there are probably parts of that culture that you can plug into.

Osland: Or that resonate with you. I've seen people go to another culture and experience a different side of themselves. Buttoned-down people say, "I was never like this at home, but I love this gesturing with my hands and dancing every weekend."

Mendenhall: We were doing a training session with spouses and managers, and this woman came up to us during the break. She was clinically depressed. She was from an Italian background in America, very outgoing, could always make friends wherever she went, and had lived overseas before. She said that she could not break through to the Japanese. Her words of frustration were, "I think that if you cut these people open there would be nuts and bolts inside." My colleague said, "Well, let's look at it this way. There's got to be something in this culture, some part of it, that you can plug into, or admire, or respect." I could see in her eyes she really wasn't buying it. My colleague spoke about something that he liked, and I spoke about some things that I really liked about Japanese culture. Our message was, "Find it, whatever you can plug into, because otherwise you are just going to be miserable."

Bird: E. M. Forester had that great two-word piece of advice on crossing culture: "Just connect." Adaptation is ultimately about making connections: with a culture, with a group of people, with an individual.

I don't think I have ever given that advice to people before. A critical part of adaptation is about being flexible, it's about being open—those things may all be important—but another critical part of adaptation is simply finding something in the new culture that you feel comfortable with and good about.

I was thinking about what Susan said earlier about the files people call up when they meet new people. Maybe that is a clue to something that is universal. We look for a connection when we meet somebody. At this conference you meet somebody new who happens to be from Texas Tech and immediately you start to think, "Who do I know at Texas Tech?" And when you can think of someone and mention their name, you're establishing a connection, then you're more comfortable. It's the connection. That's what is critical.

The art of really adapting and being effective in the new culture is looking to make those connections, finding the place where those connections can be made, and building from there.

Mendenhall: And this notion of hidden or suppressed aspects of yourself coming out might be surprise connections. Connections that are made so naturally that they surprise you. Then there are other connections you might have to work at more.

Osland: I can remember an office party when I was a new Peace Corps volunteer in Colombia. My colleagues were playing a game where we each took a turn standing up in the middle of the circle and doing whatever the group ordered. They made me dance the *cumbia*, which I'd barely seen and had certainly never done before. I was embarrassed and self-conscious with all of them watching, but I knew I had to be a good sport and do it. Now I'm more willing to make a fool of myself; I take the microphone and sing (badly) at seminars in Latin America. Left to my own devices in my own culture, would I do that? Probably not, but I enjoy doing it now, and it does help you connect with people.

Bird: So, on the one hand, we can suggest finding something and connecting with it. On the other hand, to be effective managers and to work effectively in that other culture, we need to identify what are the critical connections that have to be made. Whether you like it or not, you are going to have to connect at this point, or you will not be effective in this culture.

Osland: I had to get up and do that dance. I had no choice if I was to be accepted.

Bird: Many expatriates reach a particular point and then they decide to freeze themselves; they never get any further. The connections they have made stop at that point, and they cannot be more effective without changing. They may be effective at a particular level, and that may be sufficient or adequate, but eventually, they reach a situation or a position where it's no longer functional.

Osland: It's a lot like language acquisition. You reach a plateau where you can get along; some people stay there and never improve further. You can survive at that level—do the shopping, take care of household affairs. But then if you force yourself to go beyond that level of fluency, it's amazing the words that you begin to perceive. Maybe you've lived in a country for years, and all of a sudden you learn a new word and begin to hear it everywhere, several times every day. And you think, "Gosh, people have been using this word all along and I've been missing it?" The same phenomena happens with cultural factors—you don't see what you're missing unless you force yourself to a higher level of acculturation.

Mendenhall: I've always felt there was a commonality between language acquisition and cultural adaptation. In Japan for the first 4 months, I wasn't understanding anything. It was frustrating. And then it seemed, all of a sudden, there was some Berlin Wall that fell, and I felt like I could converse and that I was understanding all of it. It was great. But later, I ran into a higher level of complexity, and it was frustrating. I couldn't break through it and I thought, "I can't even speak this language," and then there was another bursting through. It's like those layers of the onion. "Oh, I understand," and then you don't understand. But you are always moving to higher levels of complexity. But you can choose to stop at any of those levels. You can choose to say, "I will go this far and no more."

Bird: And why does somebody stop while somebody else goes on? One thing that comes to mind is Susan talking about how every day she sees new things. I think that is the hook, the adventure of being an expatriate. There are constantly new things to figure out, and that is so exciting. I have a friend who had moved to Japan when his father was an expatriate and he had grown up there for 6 or 7 years. After he got his degree he moved back to Japan. We were working together, and one day I said, "John, why do you enjoy living in Japan?" He looked at me and said, "Because I get up each morning knowing that there is likely to be something that will happen to me that I cannot possibly anticipate. Every day is an adventure in this country. I know if I go back to the States that it won't be an adventure."

Osland: Because we assume we understand it.

Bird: Right, we assume we understand it at home, but we know we can't assume it in another culture. I'm not sure that I love being in Japan to the extent that he does, but I know that when I am living and working outside the United States, every day is an adventure. Even my attitude changes. I become more adventurous and more curious than I am when I am living at home.

Mendenhall: I think this is where the idea of self-efficacy comes into play. The reason people stop at different levels relates to their self-efficacy in dealing with differing levels of adventure. There is a risk and a scariness to adventure, but it is fun if you feel like you can handle the risk. As I look at expatriates or look at myself in different areas of life, there is a point beyond which it stops being an adventure and becomes more of a nightmare. Low self-efficacy at this point may keep them from learning more about the culture.

Bird: You can get in situations where it's no longer thrilling. It's terrifying.

Mendenhall: Or potentially dangerous. You walk into the wrong part of town and maybe you're accosted or threatened. You get away okay, but now this place is not just adventurous; there is also some real danger here. Or there are career threats. It could be that your career in this company is riding on this assignment. Coming into work every day ceases to be an adventure; it's torture. It might be different for an expatriate who says to himself, "Well, if this doesn't work out, I can get something else. No problem," versus "I have got to be successful here in order to climb the next rung."

Osland: Maybe it is also that some people approach it from a very expedient point of view—just learn enough to get by. This might be called a more extrinsic approach, whereas other people are much more into the intrinsic, adventurous aspects of the experience.

Bird: People's willingness to adapt is driven to a certain extent by how they see the international assignment. Whether it is an assignment for growth and development or whether it is just one more stop along the way. Their perspective on the reason for the assignment influences other factors, such as whether they learn the language. If you are adapting just to be expedient, then you don't want to go too far in learning the language. That can happen even with career expatriates because they know, "I'm going to be here 4 years, and then I'm going to Australia, and from Australia, it's off to Saudi Arabia, so I don't want to get too settled here. I don't want to learn too much about this place." Then they get to Saudi Arabia and go through the same cycle. They don't feel it's worth getting that deep into the culture.

Osland: Yet some expatriates advise others to "treat it like you're going to be here for the rest of your life. Get involved as quickly as you can and learn as much as you can." That's one of the things they have learned from experience, probably to reduce marginality.

Mendenhall: I have been thinking about an experience we had with an Australian guy. We were working with bright, top managers in a multinational company, and we did a little bit of a language component. It wasn't to learn the language fluently; it was to foster a willingness to communicate. If you have at least conversational-level language ability, your sense of confidence to embark and engage increases. So we began to prove that to these managers. We told them, "There are three different alphabets in Japan, and we're going to teach you how to learn this stuff really quickly." We were using visual mnemonic devices and were getting them to repeat how to pronounce the characters. You could tell some of them were willing to do it, and others were thinking, "I feel like I'm in kindergarten again, and I'm a Harvard M.B.A. What's going on?" This one Australian fellow was like that. You could tell he was not buying into this portion of the seminar at all. Then this woman, bless her heart, raises her hand and says, "Oh, before you get started, I just want to share something with all of you. I went and tried this and I was amazed. I went on the subway, and I could—I don't know exactly what I'm reading, because I didn't get a dictionary yet—but I could read everything. I could sound out the *katakana* and everything!" She was sharing something that she had actually accomplished. I glanced over at the Aussie, and his mouth was wide open. He couldn't believe such a thing could be done. He thought we were just up there blowing smoke trying to make money.

There are so many instances with expatriates where to some degree it's whether they believe they can adjust or not. I don't know if it goes to issues of faith. But he did not believe it could be done and was shocked to learn that it could be.

Bird: This takes us back to the issue of identity. Your sense of who you are is tied to how confident you are about some things and also about what you are willing to do and what you're not willing to do. Joyce, you got up and danced. I suspect there are other people who would not have been willing to do that. The question is, why wouldn't they do that? Especially if you were to sit down in advance and say to that person, "There is a possibility you may be called on to dance, and this is really critical to your being an effective manager." There would be some who, even knowing it was critical, would not get up and dance. Self-efficacy plays a part, but it is also an issue of who you are and how you see yourself and how you want others to see you.

Mendenhall: I teach people that if you are going to be living overseas, you have to think about who you are. There are going to be a lot of behaviors that you are going to have to adjust to or take on. You have to conform, at least initially, until you create trust. But I also tell them there may be some behaviors where they have to draw the line, regardless of how strong the custom is, due to their personal beliefs. Before you go overseas or very soon afterwards, you have to determine in your own mind what the boundaries are. There are ways to learn how to "nonconform," without alienating the host nationals. I think to delineate an identity boundary, you've got to know ethically, from a business sense and from a social sense, what those lines are. Dancing could be a moral concern for some, but for most people it's more a matter of, "Am I willing to risk embarrassment?" which is common overseas.

Osland: I think you have to have a strong identity. If I were selecting expatriates, I would look for those with a fairly strong sense of self, who knew what pieces of themselves they could jettison and not jettison. Where does this willingness to make a fool of yourself in the service of being an effective expatri-

ate come from? There is a lot of self-sacrifice involved with being an expatriate. Why are some people willing to make sacrifices and others are not?

Bird: That's a good question. I can remember the first time I traveled overseas, and I knew I was going to be there for some time. I had studied the language but not enough to really be able to communicate. I don't know whether somebody told me this or whether I just reached this conclusion on my own, but I decided that for the first 6 months I was not going to be concerned about making mistakes. I wasn't going to intentionally commit them. I was certainly going to work as hard as I possibly could to avoid them and to fit in. But I wasn't going to let mistakes get me down. I just had to accept the fact that I was human. I was going to make mistakes, and because I was in a completely different culture, there were going to be a lot of mistakes I would get to make. But at the end of 6 months, I felt I ought to have learned the basics of living in that country and getting around. After 6 months, it was okay for me to not only be embarrassed but also irritated with myself for making those mistakes. At that point, I should have learned how to speak and act.

There is value in going through that process. Consequently, I entered a lot of situations during that first 6 months where I felt comfortable not knowing what the rules were. I felt comfortable making mistakes because I had given myself permission to make them.

Mendenhall: You're on to something very, very important, and that's a personal strategy when going overseas. My wife had never lived overseas, and we had an opportunity to go to Switzerland for 4 months. Before we left, I shared with her some things about culture shock. Also, I began to learn German because I had decided that we were not going over there and have to grunt and point because that affects your self-image. By the time we got off the plane, I was able to get around language-wise. My wife started to attend some language classes when she got there. I kept telling her, "Just talk." My strategy for learning the language was simple. "I don't care if it's *die, der,* or *das* plus the noun. I'm going to just put one of those in. I'm never going to be fluent in this language. I'm probably never going to study it again, so I don't care." But she wanted to speak the language perfectly. She thought I was amazing. I knew I wasn't speaking it that well, but she just couldn't believe that I could go from zero to a point where I could kind of chat with people. It wasn't until right before we went home that she realized that by waiting until she spoke German perfectly, she learned nothing.

It is not just like that in language, it's like that in everything else. This is one of the problems with expatriates. They are usually bright—even brilliant—people, and they are used to being very, very successful. To be put in a situation where schoolchildren know more than they do about most things, where schoolchildren may occasionally laugh at something they do or say, can create an identity crisis. Unless you have a very strong sense of self and create a strategy for yourself, it's going to be pretty rocky for a while.

Osland: That's part of the transformation process. If you use the metaphor of a heroic adventure (referring to Joseph Campbell's myth of the hero's adventure), then you would be willing to humble yourself, give up who you were at home, and be willing to become someone different (Osland, 1995).

Mendenhall: And I think a fair amount of expatriates are not willing to do that because nobody has told them what we have just talked about, and they haven't figured it out on their own. They have to develop an internal strategy.

Bird: Without a strategy you end up simply defending yourself, and you become concerned with how other people see you. We're back to the issue of identity; it includes your own self-concept but also the identity that you are trying to project to others. Mark's right when he says executives, particularly very effective executives, have a very hard time doing that.

Osland: Maybe Bennis and Nanus's (1985) research on high-level leaders who don't talk about setbacks as failures but as mistakes that they learn from is relevant here. It's all just grist for the mill; they learn from it and move on.

Mendenhall: In doing all these things that we think makes for cultural adjustment, I've found that host nationals care not so much about how skillful you are but your sincerity in wanting to understand their culture. That is almost more important than the skills. They sense the degree to which you are really working hard, the degree to which you want to know, and the degree to which you want to make

those connections. The process of trying to learn generates something intangible that actually creates your ability to be productive. Host nationals see you are sincere. In their experience, many expatriates have never really done this, and all of a sudden you become unique in their eyes.

Bird: Most host nationals have worked with enough expatriates that they think they can distinguish between those who are sincere and those who aren't. When they put you in the sincere category, you get different treatment.

Mendenhall: They protect you. They direct you a little bit more. But you have to really want to make the connections and want to understand.

IN CONCLUSION

This dialogue was an exercise in making tacit knowledge explicit (Nonaka & Takeuchi, 1995). The act of groping for words and trying to make ourselves understood compels us to crystallize in our own mind ideas and lessons that may be half-formed or taken for granted. As our dialogue wound to a conclusion, we discovered those things we want to share with others about the art of teaching and crossing culture. Below is a summary of the most relevant points.

Tips About Teaching Culture

- The cultural dimensions we refer to are the binary characteristics used to teach cross-cultural management.[1] They are also useful points of reference that help people chart a course of analysis when exploring and trying to understand another culture. These dimensions are more useful and accurate in explaining between-culture differences because when we compare cultures, these stereotypes are often reinforced.
- When we focus on a single culture, we perceive the variance, paradoxes, and exceptions to stereotypical cultural dimensions. Thus, cultural dimensions are necessary but not sufficient tools for making sense of complex behavior within another culture. There is a danger of using these dimensions in a stereotypical manner that prevents us from seeing and understanding behavior that does not fit the stereotype. On the positive side, the dimensions provide a language for assessing culture as well as beginning hypotheses that help expatriates simplify the confusing new environment in which they find themselves.
- Prolonged exposure to a culture reveals its paradoxical nature. We should not be surprised to find both

ends of the continuum of cultural dimensions or values (e.g., collectivism and individualism) within the same culture, depending on the context in question. It is the context that determines what cultural values trump other values.

- Adaptation goes beyond identifying cultural values to encompass both an understanding of the logic of a culture and being able to situate specific cultural values within that logic.
- At least three factors seem to determine a person's willingness to make the sacrifices necessary to adapt in another culture and continue onto higher levels of acculturation:
  - 1. High self-efficacy, which allows a person to see the expatriate experience as an adventure rather than a nightmare.
  - 2. Perceiving the purpose of the overseas assignment as a growth and development opportunity versus just another rung on the ladder.
  - 3. A focus on the intrinsic rewards of living overseas, which motivates them to continue learning, versus an expedient focus in which expatriates just learn enough to get by.
- Predeparture training is helpful in providing people with cultural dimensions they can use to decode the other culture and with information about general adjustment and country conditions. Basic principles of adjustment, however, must be specifically applied to individual cultures. The overall effectiveness of predeparture training is hindered because people are not living the experience; they lack a frame of reference to make the material relevant. In-country training about 3 months into the experience is a better vehicle than predeparture training for providing culture-specific information that responds to the complexity and paradoxes expatriates are actually confronting and for helping people through more specific adjustment difficulties.

Tips for Adjusting and Adapting

- Make connections: Find something in the culture to connect with, be it people, activities, and/or ideas. Don't be surprised to discover new sides of yourself that are more readily expressed in a foreign culture than at home. Identify the connections that have to be made for you to be accepted and effective.
- We signal host nationals of our strong desire to adapt and be accepted by our willingness to make sacrifices (looking foolish, eating strange foods, giving up our own norms to conform to theirs). When expatriates conform to the other culture's norms, host nationals find it easier to trust them. This is an essential step in the adaptation process.

- Another signal to host nationals is being sincere about wanting to learn and adapt to the other culture and in your dealings with host nationals. They sense this sincerity and treat expatriates more favorably as a result.
- If expatriates have worked hard at integrating themselves, learned the language and the culture, and been effective at work, they may reach a point where they decide to be themselves more and not adapt to all of the other culture's customs. They have built up enough idiosyncrasy credits to allow them to politely pass on peripheral cultural values. There may even be a need to assert key aspects of their self-identity after having previously sacrificed some of their identity to gain acceptance in the other culture. However, if they are not perceived as competent in the other culture (have not earned their spurs, so to speak), expatriates are not allowed to be as eccentric; their failure to adapt is usually attributed to or perceived as arrogance.
- Expatriates need a strong sense of identity. To be accepted, expatriates take on values of the other culture and may give up some of their own peripheral values. A cross-cultural experience almost always involves self-reflection and questioning one's own cultural values. It's necessary to accept looking stupid and foolish without losing one's self-respect and not be overly concerned if host nationals perceive the expatriate less favorably than people do at home.
- The more connections people make and the harder they try to adapt to the other culture, the more likely that they will find themselves transformed by living overseas. Therein lies the value of a cross-cultural assignment; it is a tremendous opportunity for learning, growth, and development.
- Many expatriates limit their growth overseas; they should avoid stopping at threshold or survival levels of cultural understanding (and language fluency). Learning a culture is described as peeling away the layers of an onion; there is usually much more to be discovered before one truly understands the logic of another culture and how to behave in a variety of contexts.
- Another danger to avoid is forming and adhering to inaccurate stereotypes. Instead, we should make tentative hypotheses about the other culture that can be modified or jettisoned as we gather more information and experience. Moving beyond cultural stereotypes and continually refining one's categories and knowledge of the other culture characterize self-learners.
- Be open and flexible and approach the new culture with humility and a sense of humor.
- Develop a personal acculturation strategy. How will you make connections, become fluent in the language, find friends, locate a cultural mentor, and so on?

- Give yourself permission to make mistakes, with both cultural norms and the language, in the beginning of the assignment and simply try to learn from them.
- Approach an overseas assignment as an ongoing learning opportunity. Many longtime expatriates enjoy the novelty and adventure of confronting new experiences abroad. Because we do not assume we understand what is happening around us, we open ourselves up more to learning overseas than we do in our home culture.

NOTE

1. The dimensions most commonly taught were developed by Parsons and Shils (1951), Kluckhohn and Strodtbeck (1961), Hofstede (1980), Hall and Hall (1990), Trompenaars and Hampden-Turner (1993), and Trompenaars (1994).

REFERENCES

Bennis, W., & Nanus, B. (1985). *Leaders*. New York: Harper & Row.

Hall, E. T., & Hall, M. R. (1990). *Understanding cultural differences*. Yarmouth, ME: Intercultural Press.

Hampden-Turner, C., & Trompenaars, A. (1993). *The seven cultures of capitalism*. London: Doubleday Currency.

Hofstede, G. (1980). *Culture's consequences: International differences in work-related values*. Beverly Hills, CA: Sage.

Kluckhohn, F., & Strodtbeck, F. L. (1961). *Variations in value orientations*. Evanston, IL: Row, Peterson.

Laurent, A. (1983). The cultural diversity of Western conceptions of management. *International Studies of Management & Organization, 13*(1-2), 75-96.

Nonaka, I., & Takeuchi, H. (1995). *The knowledge-creating company*. New York: Oxford University Press.

Osland, J. S. (1995). *The adventure of working abroad: Hero tales from the global frontier*. San Francisco: Jossey-Bass.

Parsons, T., & Shils, E. (1951). *Toward a general theory of action*. Cambridge, MA: Harvard University Press.

Trompenaars, F. (1994). *Riding the waves of culture*. New York: Irwin.

[12]

Cross-Cultural Preparation of Australian Expatriates in Organisations in China: The Need for Greater Attention to Training

KATE HUTCHINGS   k.hutchings@qut.edu.au
School of Management, Queensland University of Technology, GPO Box 2434, Brisbane Q 4001, Australia

Abstract. The historically unprecedented pace of internationalising organisations in the last twenty years has made the need for cross-cultural awareness, sensitivity and adaptability of expatriates in the daily operations of international businesses in host nation subsidiaries much more salient. One of the key aspects identified in literature as contributing towards achieving intercultural effectiveness of expatriates is cross-cultural training. The research presented in this paper examines the training provided to Australian expatriates in China, a nation that has loomed large in the current and future trading and expansion plans of many Australian corporations since it opened its doors to international commerce in the late 1970s. While academic literature has given increasing attention to recognising the skills necessary to achieve intercultural effectiveness in China, organisations are continuing to give scant time and resources to developing their expatriates' China awareness. Based on information gathered through semi-structured interviews conducted with Australian expatriates in Shanghai, this research indicates that while Australian organisations are recognising the need to employ expatriates that have prior China knowledge, organisational preparation remains negligible.

Keywords: China, Australia, expatriates, cross-cultural training

The removal of national protectionist trade policies, de-regulation of international fiscal and monetary markets, and rapid advances in communications and distribution channels, has contributed to the increasing numbers of organisations that have decided to expand their operations across international borders in the last two decades. The international movement of labour that has been concomitant to such expansion of international business has meant that issues associated with the management of human resources across international borders have become of increasing importance to international Human Resource Management (HRM) managers and academics. As such, much has been written about the saliency for individuals and organisations to be cross-culturally sensitive, adaptive and responsive when managing internationally if non-adjustment and expatriate failure is to be avoided.

Expatriate failure, presently estimated to cost organisations in the range of US$250000–US$1000000 (Varner and Palmer, 2002:9), was initially defined by organisations and IHRM literature as being the measurable financial costs of early return of expatriates and disruption to international operations or as expatriates who are not retained by their organisation following completion of an international assignment (Garonzik, Brockner and Siegel, 2000; Milkovich and Newman, 1996). The definition was later expanded to include the less measurable financial costs of expatriates who may complete international assignments but who contribute to loss of business confidence and damaged relations to the host country market through committal of cultural *faux pas* (Harzing, 2002; Selmer, 2002).

Since the 1970s a plethora of literature in the field of IHRM has highlighted the vital importance of organisations providing comprehensive, strategic, country-specific programs of preparation for expatriates managing abroad if the costs of expatriate failure for organisations and expatriates are to be minimised and cross-cultural capability achieved (Caligiuri, 2000; Forster, 2000; Osman-Gani, 2000; Sargent and Matthews, 1998). At the core of this argument was the belief that better selection techniques (Black, Gregorsen and Mendenhall, 1992; Harvey and Novicevic, 2001; Richardson, 2000; Tung, 1982), cross-cultural training (Black, Mendenhall and Oddou, 1991; Desphande and Viswesvaran, 1992; Selmer, 2001; Tung, 1988; Zakaria, 2000), and in-post support (De Cieri, Dowling and Taylor, 1991; Harris, 1989; Hippler, 2000; Kraimer, Wayne and Jaworski, 2001), can play a major role in contributing to expatriates' intercultural effectiveness. Despite a recent survey suggesting that expatriates want their employers to provide cross-cultural assistance to them and their families (Britt, 2002), research conducted over two decades has consistently shown that expatriate cross-cultural preparation is either neglected outright or handled poorly by international organisations (Osman-Gani, 1999).

This paper examines the training provided to Australian expatriates in China (the broader research project also included examination of selection techniques and in-situ support—for discussion of these issues, see Hutchings, 2002). Advocating the broadest definition of expatriate failure as being the lack of intercultural effectiveness that highlights the most potentially damaging effects for expatiates, organisations, and subsidiary operations (Harzing, 2002), I assess the extent to which this cohort of expatriates are trained to maximise their intercultural effectiveness in China. Interview data from expatriates elucidates the training that these expatriates received from their organisations, the problems that they have experienced while in China, and their perceptions of whether training would have helped maximise their intercultural effectiveness. China is currently recording amongst the highest rate of expatriate assignments (GMAC, 2002) and is of particular strategic importance to many Western organisations that are expanding their Asian operations. The world's largest recipient of international foreign direct investment, worth US $312 billion utilised capital in 340,000 foreign investments (Tung and Worm, 2001:519), and recently admitted into the World Trade Organisation (WTO), China is currently Australia's third largest trade partner in two-way trade (Austrade, 2002; DFAT, 2002).

Yet, despite the obvious worth of this nation to Australian organisations, Australian managers have been ranked poorly in their cross-cultural skills (Commonwealth of Australia, 1995; IRIC, 1995) and young Australians still favour Britain as their first choice for international work experience (Harvey, 2001). Moreover, little attention has been given in the literature to analysing the cross-cultural training provided to Australian expatriates. To this end, this research serves a valuable purpose in (a) broadening the existing literature base focusing largely on North American, European and Japanese studies, that makes scant reference to Australian organisations, and (b) informing Australian business about Australian expatriates' perceptions of the value of training for intercultural effectiveness in China.

1. Expatriate training

Literature has consistently highlighted the problems inherent for individual expatriates and their families, organisations, and subsidiary employees and business partners where expatriates lack cross-cultural skills (Forster, 2000; Osman-Gani, 2000; Sargent and Matthews, 1998; Zakaria, 2000). It is suggested that acculturation and adaptation (Bird et al., 1999; Ward and Rana-Deuba, 1999), the need to make sense of, and understand, other cultures (Osland and Bird, 2000; Osland, DeFranco and Osland, 1999), and to adapt managerial styles (Hammer et al., 1998; Osland, Snyder and Hunter, 1998) is essential to ensuring intercultural effectiveness, and avoiding interpersonal blunders (Zakaria, 2000:493). The need to develop cross-cultural skills in expatriates is even greater where the gap between cultures is very wide (Forster, 2000), or as Kaye and Taylor (1997) note of China, where culture shock is marked.

The literature suggests that key to achievement of acculturation and intercultural effectiveness of expatriates is the provision of pre-departure and/or post-arrival training, especially cross-cultural training (CCT). Fundamental to the rationale for providing CCT is the belief that management skills are not necessarily generalisable as "good management is not good worldwide" and that existing management skills of expatriate managers need to be integrated with cross-cultural skills (Osman-Gani, Tan and Toh, 1998; Osman-Gani, 1999) in order to attain intercultural ineffectiveness.

Most of the literature advocating CCT provides a variation on the categories Tung (1982) identified as being essential in imparting knowledge and understanding of a foreign nation. These categories (Tung, 1982:65) include: factual information; cultural orientation; cultural assimilation training; language training; sensitivity training; and field experience. Zakaria (2000) notes that other aspects of training that have been referred to in the last twenty years include: areas studies and intercultural effectiveness skills. For discussion of an intercultural training effectiveness model, see Bhagat and Prien (1996), for discussion of the relative benefits of pre-departure or post-arrival training, see Selmer (2001).

1.1. Asia, China and expatriates

Incidence of expatriate failure rates have been cited as being ranging from 4–15% (Tung, 1981), 16–40% (Black, Mendenhall and Oddou, 1991), 25–40% (Ralston et al., 1995), 20–50% (Morley, Burke and Finn, 1999) and as high as 70% (Hendry, 1994; Shay and Bruce, 1997). However, Harzing (1995, 2002) suggests that the IHRM literature has maintained a persistent myth of high expatriate failure rates and claims that the most reliable empirical studies are those done by Tung (1981) and Forster (1997) who suggest that failure is in the range of 4–15% and 0–18% respectively (Harzing, 2002). Even so, it should be noted that these two studies examined Japanese, US, European (Tung, 1981) and UK expatriates (Forster, 1997) and overall failure rates may actually be much higher as intercultural ineffectiveness results from marked distance between cultures (Hofstede, 1980; Trompenaars and Hampden-Turner, 1997) such as that between China and Australia. Despite this, few researchers have examined the training and intercultural effectiveness of expatriates working in Asia, generally (Osman-Gani, 1999) and China specifically. Huo, Huang and Napier

(2002) actually suggest that IHRM research is overwhelmingly parochial in its focus on Western expatriates and nations.

The literature on business management practices in Asia suggests that Western expatriate managers assigned to Asia need to make considerable sociocultural adjustments to their roles at work (Child, 1994; Goodall and Warner, 1997; Selmer, 2002). However, few researchers have specifically studied expatriates in China. Bjorkman and Schaap (1994) discuss some problems encountered by expatriates in Chinese-Western joint ventures and suggest practical ways to handle these issues. In more recent work on expatriate adjustment, Selmer, Torbiorn and Leon (1998) excluded 18 Australian expatriate managers from a sample of 154 expatriates leaving a group comprising exclusively Western European and North American managers. While Selmer (1999, 2001, 2002) has contributed significantly to the literature on expatriates in China and Hong Kong, there is still very limited research available on Australian expatriates in Asia and China. Welch (1994) studied the expatriate management practices of four Australian companies and found low rates of failure, while Enderwick and Hodgson's (1993) study of New Zealand companies found there to be little or no failure rate amongst their expatriate employees. However, neither of these studies specifically examined expatriates in China (for a discussion of Australian expatriates' responses to specific Chinese cultural characteristics (Hutchings and Murray, 2002).

2. Methods

The information on which this study is based was obtained through semi-structured interviews conducted with expatriate Australian managers in China in 1999. Organisations were interviewed only in Shanghai because this is the location in which the vast majority of Australian organisations have their operations (Bevan, 2000). Qualitative interviews were conducted with the aim of hearing in detail and complexity how expatriates describe and contextualise the training provided to them, the cultural difficulties they have encountered, and their perceptions of whether training could have contributed to intercultural effectiveness.

2.1. Procedure

From databases of Australian organisations operating in China maintained by the China Secretariat in Australia and the Australian Business Association and Austrade in China, 24 organisations were selected for study. Of the 24 organisations that met the criteria, 22 organisations agreed to participate in the research. The high response rate was attributed to two factors. First, a belief that the need for training of expatriates is increasingly considered to be of vital importance to organisations with an international profile. Second, because of the fact that the author had insider status with a number of the expatriate managers as a result of other research conducted in China (for a discussion of participant observation and the advantages of insider status in doing research (Siu, 1996). The elimination of random sampling in favour of snowballing/convenience sampling through use of personal contacts (*with the organisations providing listing of Australian organisations*) does suggest the potential for bias on the part of the interviewer and the organisations providing contacts. However, it is a strategy that was also used by an international team of researchers currently reporting best practice in IHRM (Von Glinow, Drost and Teagarden, 2002:150). This approach was adopted given the difficulties associated with gaining an adequate sample when utilising random sampling in Asia.

Interviewer and interviewee bias was minimised by the use of a neutral setting, by establishing trust and rapport by referral via Australian business associations, and the use of funnelling and presentation of questions in unbiased form. To ensure that all interviewees were interviewed in the same manner clarifying questions were avoided (for further information on interviewee and interviewer bias (Sekaran, 2000). While it could be argued that the sample are specific in that they share similar characteristics, other research (such as Forster, 2000) suggests that there is a trend towards expatriates being younger, single and having limited international experience, and the predominance of large companies in the sample reflects the make-up of Australian organisations in China at this time as determined in Australian trade records (see, for instance, DFAT, 2002).

A semi-structured interview was designed to be of one-hour duration. In practice, interviews were between forty minutes and two hours in duration. The interview notes were transcribed and, where necessary, returned to the interviewees for clarification. If interviewees disagreed with how their comments were transcribed, they were requested to make the necessary corrections and return the interview notes to the researchers. None of the interviewees elected to make changes to notes of their personal interview. At the interviewees' request, interviews were not audio-recorded. At all stages throughout the process interviewees were assured that all information provided was given on a purely voluntary basis. Moreover, they were reminded that their names, the names of their organisations, and names of their employees who facilitated interview scheduling would be kept strictly confidential.

2.2. Sample

The sample of organisations and expatriates was drawn from a multi-industry background of organisations with the proviso being that senior management of the organisations must be Australian. The ethnic background of the participants is Australian of Anglo-Saxon (20) or European (2). Of the respondents, 17 are male and 5 are female. Six of the interviewees have had prior international experience and 9 have some formal education in Chinese culture. Seven of the interviewees speak Mandarin fluently, and 3 claim to have a basic or working knowledge of Mandarin. The average age of the respondents is in their 30s and 5 interviewees self-selected to move to China rather than being posted to China by an organisation. For biodata on the expatriates interviewed (Table 1).

2.3. Measurement

The interviews with expatriates asked them about whether generalist training was provided pre-departure or post-arrival, cultural training, language training, practical training (including short visits prior to posting), executive briefing, and notice of posting. The questions were developed on the basis of the areas identified by Tung (1982) (and highlighted in subsequent literature) as needing to be provided by organisations sending managers on expatriate

Table 1.   Bio data of expatriates interviewed.

Interviewee code	Self selected China	Company type	Years in China	Previous international experience	Mandarin fluency	Education in Chinese culture	Age	Highest study
1 Bac-X-EM	No	MNC	11	2	Fluent	Yes	40s	Degree
2 Re-X-AM	Yes	MNC	1	1	Fluent	Yes	25	Degree
3 Print-X-AM	Yes	MNC	3		Fluent	Yes	25	Degree
4 Elec-X-EF	No	MNC	3	2	Nil	No	28	Trade
5 Prop-X-AM	Yes	MNC	2		Fluent	Yes	29	Degree
6 Hosp-X-AM	No	MNC	11		Fluent	No	42	High School
7 Hosp-X-AM	No	MNC	5		Nil	No	28	High School
8 Food-X-AM	No	Private	5		Nil	No	44	High School
9 Educ-X-AF	No	Private	3		Nil	No	42	High School
10 Educ-X-AF	No	Private	6		Nil	Yes	40s	Degree
11 Rec-X-AM	Yes	MNC	1		Basic	Yes	30s	Degree
12 Rec-X-AM	No	MNC	2		Basic	Yes	20s	Degree
12 Cat-X-AM	No	MNC	3	3	Basic	No	30s	High School
14 Law-X-AF	No	MNC	1		Nil	Yes	20s	Degree
15 Law-X-AF	No	MNC	1		Nil	No	20s	Degree
16Trans-X-AM	No	MNC	3		Nil	No	20s	Trade
17 Bac-X-AM	No	MNC	2	3	Fluent	No	30s	Degree
18 Bac-X-AM	No	MNC	7		Fluent	Yes	30s	Degree
19 Bac-X-AM	No	MNC	1		Nil	No	30s	Degree
20 Bac-X-AM	No	MNC	1	7	Nil	No	30s	Degree
21Man-X-AM	No	MNC	2		Nil	No	40s	Degree
22 Food-X-AM	Yes	MNC	2		Nil	No	30s	High School

a. Respondent codes: *Industry type*: Bac: building and construction, Re: real estate, Print: printing, Elec: electronic and components, Law: legal, Trans: transportation, man: manufacturing, Prop: property, Hosp: hospitality, Food: food and beverage, Educ: education and training, Cat: clothing and textiles.
Company type: Private: small, privately-owned, Owner: respondent owns and manages a private company, MNC: publicly listed multinational corporation.
Ethnicity: A: Australian (as defined as Caucasian or Anglo Saxon), C: Chinese, E: European.
Gender: M: Male, F: Female.

postings. The discussion of pre-departure and post-arrival generalist training refer to Tung's category of training, and my category of cultural training collapses three of Tung's categories associated with culture. I also refer to Tung's categories of language training and practical training (and consider the provision of short visits within the latter). The category of executive briefing refers to Tung's country knowledge and also incorporates provision of information about the subsidiary operations. I also include notice of posting, in agreement with Forster's (2000) recognition of the need for adequate notice to ensure time for delivery of CCT. In their responses, interviewees were requested to refer to China-specific examples, where possible.

2.4. *Analysis*

Differing conceptions of the interviewees are contextualised, re-contextualised and grouped, where possible. The transcribed interviews were manually coded and analysed by qualitative inquiry by the researcher. The results are presented in a detailing of numbers of interviewees that had received training. The results are also described in more detail with reference to individuals' comments where informative and illustrative.

It was intended to group responses of interviewees on the basis of their companies' size, type and ownership, and on the basis of ethnicity and gender of the respondents. However, the relative homogeneity of the sample in terms of the expatriates themselves and the form of company in which they are employed made this problematic. Hence, grouping has been done on the basis of company size, but not type. Arguably grouping has also been done in terms of whether the ownership of the company is private or publicly-listed. However, it should be noted that this also relates to size in that the privately-owned companies are all small in size relative to the employment size of the MNCs in this cohort. The arguments made about size can equally be applied to private ownership, although it would not be possible from this small sample size to confer that ownership is as important a factor as size in determining disposition towards offering training. To group on the grounds of gender would be dubious given that there are only 5 females represented (less than a quarter of the cohort of interviewees). However, although there are only 2 respondents of Chinese ethnicity in the cohort, some attempt has been made to group their responses as they do have the benefit of being able to understand, and make the connections between, Australia's and China's culture.

It is acknowledged that the process of coding and analysing the interview data, like the data collection itself, is something of a selective process in terms of a determination of what to add in and what to leave out. Coding provides an efficient method for data-labelling and retrieval, yet it is acknowledged that qualitative data analysis has a potentially ad hoc character (Miles and Huberman, 1994), the process is eclectic and there is no right way (Tesch, 1990, cited in Creswell, 1994). Nevertheless, some consideration does needs to be given to issues of validity and reliability associated with the data analysis.

Taking a reduction and interpretation approach based on coding, I began with a first-level coding start-list that divided the collected data into clusters of topics representing each question. Memos were also compiled for detailing more reflective comments of interviewees. My first-level coding elucidated distinct differences between small and large companies and between lengths of time expatriates had spent in China. To facilitate reliability of my findings I then had a colleague check the groups and do a second-level coding to ascertain whether the findings could be construed as atypical. The colleague also suggested coding characteristics of the expatriates, such as gender and ethnicity. To minimise bias, interviewees' reference to dramatic incidences were removed from the usable data and checks for representativeness were undertaken (as detailed above in relation to procedure and sample).

Internal validity was assisted by: having a colleague check decisions made throughout the analysis process; by having the interviewees check my interpretation of the data; the interviewees being involved throughout various stages of the research; and researcher/interviewer bias minimised. External validity was assisted by the use of a colleague serving as external advisor throughout the research process and the context from which the data was gathered being made clear. The interview questions are detailed in the research findings (and are adapted from previous researchers' categories), and therefore, the study could be replicated. Issues of representativeness of the particular sample are discussed above. It is acknowledged that another researcher may not arrive at the same findings using either this sample set or another set in other organizations/locations, as interviews were undertaken only at one point in time. However, the researcher has recently replicated the study, with similar findings. This is not, however, to suggest that all the findings could be generalised.

3. Results

One of the key findings of this study is that despite a significant body of literature suggesting the need for organisations to adequately prepare their prospective expatriate managers for the cross-cultural demands of managing internationally, still very little attention is given to training. This suggests that organisations are still not prepared to invest resources (both monetary and time) in preparing their expatriates, but at least acknowledge the demands of operating in a foreign environment are quite different from that of the home environment.

3.1. Training

Despite convincing argument in the literature highlighting the importance of training to cultural adjustment, and hence success for the expatriate and the organisation, the organisations in this study are providing very little training. For a summary of the issues that expatriates identified as being necessary components of pre-departure and post-arrival preparation and training to assist their work and non-work adjustment to China (Table 2).

3.2. Training and problems

Of the twenty-two interviewees, only 6 claimed to have received formal training prior to arriving, or during their assignment, in China. It should be noted, however, that as 5 of the interviewees had self-selected to work in China and had not been actually posted to China by an organisation, one would not expect them to have had any formal training. Of these 5, all work in MNCs yet none have received any in-post training. All 6 interviewees that had received pre-departure training from their organisations prior to posting to China work in MNCs. All of these 6 interviewees also claimed that their organisations would be amenable to providing follow-up in-post training should it be warranted and should the individual expatriate ask for assistance. None said that such in-post training had automatically been offered to them by their organisation. The majority of the interviewees argued that some training is essential to maximise the expatriate experience. One manager did, however, suggest that

> I have done some consulting on other Chinese societies—Hong Kong, Taiwan, Malaysia and Singapore. So, I did not need so much training. I had only a week's notice of this

CROSS-CULTURAL PREPARATION OF AUSTRALIAN EXPATRIATES 383

Table 2. Factors associated with training that Australian expatriates in China identify as contributing to cross-cultural adaption.

Pre-departure and post-arrival training and information

Other than cultural information about the host nation

Weather—be aware of the cold climate and dress accordingly

Economic—appreciate the differences in socio-economic and educational standards throughout the nation

Communications—appreciate the differences in telecommunications and other infrastructure across the nation

History—Show reverence for China's history and cultural development—indeed, there is much to be appreciated in it

Politics—do not discuss politics and certainly do not criticise political leaders or senior administrators or military officials

Language

English is taught in schools but thus far, few people even in the cities in China, have English fluency

Mandarin but local dialect also useful for those working outside the eastern seaboard

Non-verbal knowledge is crucial e.g. do not point, give way to locals in entering doorways, avoid direct eye contact, sit upright and recognise signs of disinterest or anger

Executive briefing

In order to operate effectively in China, a thorough briefing about the subsidiary operations must be provided—this should include information about the nature of company's operations, host nation organisational strategies, interaction with host country institutions, the networks with whom the company is already enmeshed

Notice of posting

A couple of months at least is required to ensure time for a comprehensive cross-cultural preparation, relocation orientation and development of basic conversational language skills

Relocation assistance

Medical facilities are not what they are in Australia—ensure that the company offers airlift to Hong Kong for major illness. Be prepared for minor illness from contaminated water and/or pollution—know where to find assistance

Western doctors and dentists are very costly—in some cases be prepared to try local medicine

Shopping is not the same as in Australia but is a fascinating experience—receive advice on how to bargain and negotiate and enjoy!

Seek advice about the best ways to make contact with home and use of postal and telecommunications services

Information about educational facilities for spouse and children should be provided—China does have some top universities but quality throughout the nation is very mixed

Preparation, training and support for cultural sensitivity and acceptance of difference

Understand cultural values such as guanxi, mianzi and renqing—exercise them at work and socially

Appreciate the importance of feng shui, the value of the group and consensus, the value of family, respect for authority, modesty, ancestor worship, avoidance of confrontation,—show respect!

Contacts are essential to doing business and moving towards insider status and business dress should be conservative

Greetings are quite formal and seniority must be recognised—also important in seating arrangements. Business cards are essential and gift giving is an art form that must be learnt

Despite being a bureaucratic society, foreigners need to be flexible and accept that sometimes rules are bent

Negotiations should be win win and require much patience on the part of the Westerner. Principles are usually discussed first details follow later (and sometimes not at all)

Bargaining only means that discussions are open—not necessarily that any decision will be made. Discussions are not usually sequential and confrontation should be avoided

---

(Continued on next page.)

Table 2. (*Continued*).

Pre-departure and post-arrival training and information

Contracts establish relationships—they are not viewed as necessarily committing anyone to anything—the word of a Chinese person is seen as more valuable than a document.

The food will be quite different from Western Chinese but it is important to be polite. Table etiquette is quite different from Australia e.g. communal bowls, and banquets have their own set of protocols

Queues are not usual (do not be offended at being pushed!) but automated ticketing systems for transport are common

Many parts of China do not have adequate infrastructure e.g. public amenities, power, hot water, telephone and email access—do not judge, but improvise!

When shopping, just as in business, negotiating is the norm

Expect quite dramatic lifestyle differences—e.g. in respect to outdoors and sport

a. The headings for this table have been compiled from the literature about what should be included in expatriate pre-departure and post-arrival training programs. The specifics about Chinese culture have been compiled from responses of expatriates about issues that they believe it is necessary to have some knowledge to assist intercultural effectiveness as expatriate managers. These issues relate to expatriates' effectiveness on business and social levels. It should also be noted that literature suggests that the greatest effectiveness will be achieved when these practices are also adopted for expatriates' spouses and families, where applicable.

posting—but I did move back and forth between home and China for a few months. (4Elec-X-EF)

Significantly, the vast majority (18) claimed to have encountered problems on a business and/or social level, many of whom argued that could have been at least partially avoided had they received some, or more, training than they did. Most of these problems are consistent with transition stresses and adjustment stresses and are exhibited at a work and non-work level. Responses to this question included comments such as

Numerous examples—where to find things, how to shop, different food styles. Social needs have to be met before you can get on with doing business. (6Hosp-X-AM)

There are vast differences in practices and logistics. It's hard to define. How can you educate about this? Previous managers left China suddenly so there was no changeover period. (17Bac-X-AM)

Though a number of interviewees argued that training can never fully prepare you for a new culture until you experience it, most did suggest that some training would have given them some preparation for what to expect. The major problems faced included social issues of knowing where to find food and services they were accustomed to at home, and business issues relating to differing cultural practices. The majority of interviewees expressed feelings of alienation and frustration consistent with cultural shock, at least in the initial stages of working and/or living and studying in China. Two of the major business issues mentioned were loss of face and dealing with customers. As one respondent argued

definitely the most difficult thing to deal with is loss of face. Even if people are not performing, it is difficult to reprimand them. (7Hosp-X-AM)

CROSS-CULTURAL PREPARATION OF AUSTRALIAN EXPATRIATES 385

3.3. Cultural training

None of the expatriates interviewed had received any specific training about aspects of Chinese culture. While most interviewees believed that their initial adjustment to China and intercultural effectiveness on both work and non-work levels would have been increased by having received some pre-departure cultural awareness, a few interviewees believed that no training could prepare one for the experience of dealing with a new cultural environment. As one commented,

> There was not really any (*training*), but I do not think it matters. You need to experience it for yourself. I am glad I did not have training—it made much more sense to me when I lived it. (4Elec-X-EF)

The majority of respondents said there was a very real need to have some knowledge of China's culture prior to arrival because of the advantages they perceived that it could provide in terms of immediate awareness of different business practices. Awareness of these differences, it was argued, could decrease the likelihood of committing serious cultural *faux pas* due to simple ignorance of what was considered acceptable and unacceptable behaviour in certain situations. Whilst it has been noted that a significant number of the interviewees already had some formal education in Chinese culture and were likely to have been chosen on this basis, there still seems to be a need for organisations to provide some additional training that is company-specific. One interviewee noted,

> not as such did I receive training in culture. There is a mentor provided. When I looked for help, I was told, 'Do what you can'. I was not aware of time constraints. One needs to be very self-sufficient here. Informally, you have to seek your own support, and this can pose difficulties. (2Re-X-AM)

3.4. Language training

Language training was somewhat better accommodated by organisations with 10 of the interviewees claiming that their organisation provided them with some language classes or would do if there were the requirement. Of those, 6 said there was also the facility for some training in multicultural communication as part of the language course. Of the 10 that were offered language training by their organisation, 3 said that they had not actually acquired basic communication skills. All of these interviewees argued that the language training they were offered pre-departure was only of a couple of days duration. While these 3 said that their organisations would fund the cost of language training while in-post, all argued that they simply did not have them time to participate in language classes. Of the remaining 7 interviewees that said they had language skills, 3 claimed their skills were basic while 4 said they were fluent in Mandarin.

One of the interviewees that said his language skills were basic had self-selected to work in China and had arrived with these basic skills but he also said that his company was currently covering the costs of his undertaking further language study. Those that were fluent said that much of their skills had come from in-post language training (in all cases, company funded) and practicing speaking with locals. Of the remaining 4 of the 5 interviewees that had self-selected to work in China, 1 said that he had nil proficiency in Mandarin but his company would provide financial assistance with language study if he requested it. The other 3 of the self-selected interviewees claimed to have Mandarin fluency. These individuals had all done some formal study of Chinese culture and had moved to China to further their language skills prior to seeking work.

Despite the various proficiencies in language, all interviewees argued that pre-departure language training is not really sufficient and only provides the most rudimentary skills. One expatriate did suggest, however, that language skills were not as important as the ability of an individual to adapt and take a "big picture" view. As she said,

> I did three weeks [language skills] on my own when I first arrived in China but have had no time to follow up since. However, I do not see this as a problem. People with language training but no company knowledge ... do not work. You want to convey company knowledge to locals—systems need to be implemented. We are meant to train as international managers, not as China experts. (4Elec-X-EF)

An additional problem with the development of language skills is that there is an onus placed on the expatriates themselves to follow-up their language skills either through practice or study. Issues of intercultural communication are rarely addressed within the language classes offered, although several interviewees said the language classes they had attended included reference to the importance of acquiring flexibility and resilience.

3.5.   Practical training

Practical training (or logistical assistance with relocation) that is given most attention by organisations. All but one of the expatriates that had been posted to China by an organisation had received some assistance with relocation. Those that had not received relocation assistance because they were already situated in the Asian region or China itself all said that generous financial assistance would be available from their organisations. Relocation generally covered financial assistance with the move for the expatriate (and family, if required). In most cases, additional allowances were also provided to trailing spouses. One expatriate argued that the assistance she had received was very comprehensive. As she said,

> It was perfectly organised from hotel accommodation to an orientation program to medical assistance and regular trips home. I am also able to meet with someone from the company and discuss problems when at home. (4Elec-X-EF)

In some cases organisations also provide assistance in helping expatriates to settle in to their new environment by providing information about shopping, medical facilities, schools, social activities and clubs. One interviewee is actually employed by her organisation to serve just that purpose and acts as an on-going liaison consultant to expatriates.

None of the expatriates interviewed in this research project had been sent on a short visit to China prior to commencing their posting, although a number of them had been to China previously whether on short-term work visits with other organisations or as language students. Almost all interviewees argued, however, that it was most desirable for an organisation to send expatriates on such a visit to ensure that they would have some prior practical knowledge of the country in which they would live and work. Clearly, having such experience would assist expatriates in their awareness of the country in which they will be living and hence make it easier for them to cope in terms of non-work socialisation. This is an aspect which is often more difficult to adjust to than the work environment and the area which actually may be such a negative experience that it results in expatriate failure at a work level. One expatriate said,

> no, I was not sent on a short visit, but I would have liked it. I only received two weeks notice of this posting—more preparation and initial exposure would have given me a better understanding of China's culture and what I would be experiencing and would have assisted my transition greatly and (I believe) made me more effective as a manager in China. (15Law-X-AF)

Importantly, it was argued, expatriate failure could be somewhat minimised by allowing expatriates to have some exposure to China prior to being posted. Several expatriates argued that it was difficult to have an understanding of China just from theory alone and that being able to spend even just a short term in the country would allow people to know what they were "getting themselves into".

3.6. Executive briefing

Less than half (10) of the expatriates in this cohort had received an executive briefing on their organisation's operations in China, and only 6 of these had received comprehensive information about China's history, economy, and political situation. Of the 12 other expatriates, 2 had received information about China's political and economic history but scant details on the subsidiary operations. Of the 10 that did receive a briefing on the subsidiary operations, most argued that the briefing had been fairly comprehensive and covered the economic environment in China, the organisation's specific long-term strategies in China, and the role that the given expatiate was to play in this process. As one expatriate said,

> My briefing was fairly comprehensive. It was one month's familiarisation in Sydney about organisational changes in China. (14Law-X-AF)

However, other expatriates claimed that while they had received an overall strategic outline, there probably was more need to have a sense of how the subsidiary operation actually worked on a daily basis. One expatriate (12Rec-X-AM) said that he has been briefed by the local manager and that this was probably more beneficial than having received the information from headquarters in Australia.

3.7. *Notice of posting*

The majority of interviewees argued that they had received what they considered to be inadequate notice of their posting to China and hence there was little time for their organisation to fully train and prepare them for the demands of the new environment. Two of the expatriates had received three months notice, 1 had received six weeks notice, and 11 had received one month's notice. The remaining 3 expatriates that had been posted to China received between two and three weeks notice of their posting. In these 3 cases, the individuals were aware that their organisations had been "looking for someone" for the China post, so the notice provided to these individuals refers to the time at which these expatriates were specifically chosen by their organisation. The majority of expatriates complained that they had not had enough time to organise themselves for the move or prepare themselves emotionally, much less to have received adequate training. One expatriate summarised the experience of many others in stating that,

> I was just asked if I was willing to live in China for 2 years and then sent on a 1 day language course. I arrived in China two weeks later. (21Man-X-AM)

Most believed that they had in effect received no training, and certainly not training which would prepare them culturally for the demands of the new environment. As one expatriate lamented,

> The only training I can really say I received was about company specific briefs in relation to China and the product's market. Training is certainly a very neglected part of this company's preparation for foreign postings. (18Bac-X-AM)

4. Discussion

While the organisations in this cohort still give very little attention to training, they are clearly making a much greater effort to choose expatriates who have language and cross-cultural knowledge skills, and have, in many cases, completed other foreign postings. This suggests that organisations are still not prepared to invest resources in preparing their expatriates, but at least they are acknowledging that the demands of operating in China are quite different from Australia. Hence, they are recognising that there is a necessity to choose people who already possess some of the skills to make them more successful than managers who do not have these skills. A not insignificant percentage of the expatriates in this study have had prior international work experience and several of these have worked in Hong Kong and/or Taiwan (that have close cultural proximity to China). This decision making is consistent with the literature that argues that in addition to technical competence, expatriates should be chosen who exhibit personality traits which make them more suitable for expatriate posting, such as knowledge of the country in which they will live (Tung, 1981, 1990).

Certainly, that many of the expatriates interviewed in this cohort have had prior experience and some formal education in the cultural and social practices of China is likely to suggest that they will exhibit greater tolerance to the values of this society, and that they are likely to have "faster acculturation" (Zakaria, 2000).

4.1. Training

4.1.1. Cultural training. The perceptions of this cohort of expatriates confirms 20 years of research that suggests that pre-departure and post-arrival cultural preparation has a positive effect on adaptation to international assignments and that the best CCT is that which works in concert with other strategies for effective international assignments such as correct selection techniques and provision of in-post support (Forster, 2000). The view expressed by these expatriates suggests support for the realisation that international assignments are an on-going process of adaptation, not something that occurs just prior to an international move (Baumgarten, 1995).

4.1.2. Language training. Though some authors argue that CCT is more important than language skills (Zakaria, 2000), and English is accepted as the predominant international business language, most authors suggest that language skills (including non-verbal) are more important than ever in reducing uncertainty in the new environment (Frazee, 1999; Osman-Gani, 2000), ability to process information (Ashamalla and Crocitto, 2002) and send out positive signals of interest and willingness to the host nation employees and business partners (Forster, 2000).

4.1.3. Relocation assistance, executive briefing, and notice of posting. While the expatriates received very good assistance with relocation and were well briefed on the requirements of the organisation for the subsidiary operations, much less attention was given to providing a briefing on the host nation's political, economic, historical and geographic positioning—identified in the literature as being of considerable importance to effective adaptation (Osman-Gani, 2000; Tung, 1982). It is also lamentable that organisations are giving very limited notice of posting to their expatriates, particularly given the importance of adequate notice in respect to having time to organise one's life, prepare emotionally and participate in training programs prior to departure for the international assignment. Nicholson and West (1988) note such "anticipatory socialisation" is a crucial factor in adjusting to new jobs in a domestic context. It is surely even more important in an international setting.

Much of the onus is placed on individual expatriates to seek out support, assistance and information for themselves as organisations are not providing long handover periods that may ensure effective induction programs as Forster (2000) suggests. Such a transition seems even more important in a nation that is culturally very distant from Australia and one in which expatriates believe that it would have been beneficial for them to have received some CCT. Moreover, expatriates suggested that they would have liked more support to provide guidance about dealing with specific practicalities of doing business in China with respect to such issues as *guanxi* and *mianzi* (Buttery and Wong, 1999; Guthrie, 1998; Luo, 2000).

4.2. Company size, company ownership and an expatriate's time in China

The findings from this cohort of individuals suggest that there are two factors at play when considering issues around training. The first is the size of the organisation (and ownership) in question and the second is the length of time and experience that the individual expatriate has had in China. The first factor of size is relevant in that expatriates in large organisations have overwhelmingly provided more training. Arguably grouping has also been done in terms of whether the ownership of the company is private or public. However, it should be noted that this also relates to size in that the privately-owned companies are all small in size. The arguments made about size can equally be applied to private ownership, although it would not be possible from this small sample size to confer that ownership is as important a factor as size in determining disposition of the organisation towards preparation of expatriates.

In respect to the second aspect, there is a distinct difference noted in the observations of those expatriates who have been in China for more than/less than three years. The expatriates who have been in China for three or more years (the majority of whom also speak Mandarin), do suggest that language skills and increasing length of time in China increases adjustment and that understanding cultural practices decreases the likelihood of committing the *faux pas* that may lead to early return from the assignment. Those who have been in China longer than 5 years no longer regard themselves as expatriates but suggest that they are now making a conscious choice to live in China. The expatriates who have been in China for a shorter time period highlight the importance of working to build relationships with local Chinese business partners if they are to improve their sensitivity to the Chinese culture and assist their own adaptation. Further, smaller companies are very well represented amongst those individuals who have only been in China for short times and expatriates employed in large companies tend to have greater international experience and/or knowledge of China's culture. It can be argued that there appears to be a correlation between length of experience/company size and consequent response to the necessity of developing cultural understanding.

4.3. Gender and ethnicity

While it was originally intended to examine issues of gender and ethnicity in their impact on expatriates' perceptions of organisational training, the sample size does not allow for an exploration of gender. While there are not divergent views amongst the Chinese and non-Chinese expatriates in the cohort in respect to their belief in the value of training, there are obvious differences in the degree of adaptation in that those who have a Chinese background already have cultural knowledge and language skills. There was not a marked difference in the comments of those who have a Chinese background and those who have prior experience working in Chinese-based societies accompanied by language skills and formal study of Chinese culture. While those who have a Chinese background do have some advantage in being able to move into business networks, those who have language skills and prior experience suggest that they need much less organisational support than those who do not possess these skills/experience. The individuals who have invested time in learning Mandarin argue for consequent dividends in their business activities. However, some of the non-Mandarin speaking expatriates do cite the benefits of utilising local Chinese as intermediaries (sometimes their marriage/defacto partner) in business negotiations.

5. Conclusions

5.1. Implications for practice

The literature referred to in this paper suggests that expatriate training is rarely provided and, where it is, tends to be very much ad hoc in nature, and that expatriate training or preparation needs to be improved in a number of important aspects. The research on which this paper is based firmly supports the literature and it is suggested that there is a patent need for Australian expatriates working in China to be fully briefed prior to being sent on overseas postings. Such preparation would be more effective if it included goal-setting, performance expectations, and awareness of socio-cultural limitations of operating from a business and social perspective in China. Moreover, while the findings of this research would suggest that for the expatriates in this cohort, their organisations are not adverse to providing some assistance in the form of language training and cross-cultural communication, often the onus is on the expatriate him/herself to seek out training and then request the organisation to provide some financial assistance. As all the expatriates interviewed are in favour of organisations expanding the extent of training they provide, this research affirms the need for organisations to pay greater attention to the need to develop strategic expatriation processes that value the importance of comprehensive pre-departure and in-situ training for expatriates and their families.

Arguably greater attention to training for expatriates posted to China is warranted, specifically in relation to increasing expatriates' awareness of: the importance of relationship building; the value of family, hierarchy and authority; the giving and preserving of face; trust; reciprocity and payback; and negotiating and bargaining. The time and costs invested in providing expatriates and their families with such cultural awareness briefings that would reduce their difficulties in adjusting in both business and social fora would certainly contribute to minimising the risk of early returns of expatriates and the potentially more damaging cultural offence and alienation of local employees and business partners. An understanding of these uniquely Chinese cultural characteristics would be of assistance to an expatriate operating in any of the Chinese-based societies throughout Asia. However, being able to operate effectively and efficiently in China also requires an understanding of other factors. As a society transiting from Communism to capitalism, China provides a fascinating interplay of remnants of a Communist polit-bureau and military with an overarching capitalist economic system determined by market forces—a situation that creates interesting contradictory elements of great efficiency with elements of great inefficiency. Expatriates need to be prepared by their organisations to be familiar with: the great disparities in skill and education levels of the workforce; the variable availability of telecommunications (such as the internet); the rapidly expanding, but still limited infrastructure, and the paradoxical inflexibility and flexibility (dependent on insider status) of the Communist bureaucracy.

5.2. Contributions to theory

This research supports findings in existing literature in that expatriates in this cohort argue for the need to receive training that would reduce any perceived lack of cross-cultural skills and help them to achieve intercultural competence (Forster, 2000; Osman-Gani, 2000; Zakaria, 2000) particularly given the greater cultural distance between China and Australia (Hofstede and Bond, 1988; Trompenaars and Hampden-Turner, 1997) than many of the nations that have been previously examined in the literature. The expatriates also concurred with arguments made in the literature for the need for language training, cultural orientation, provision of factual information (Tung, 1982; see also Zakaria, 2000) if acculturation and adaptation (Bird et al., 1999; Osland, De Franco and Osland, 1999) is to be achieved. Expatriates were also in agreement with the literature that emphasises the importance of providing longer handover periods from one manager to the next (Forster, 2000).

While supporting existent literature and research, this research does make some valuable contributions to the literature. Despite the breadth, and often, depth, of research into the need for better expatriate preparation, the focus has overwhelmingly been on North American, European and Japanese cases (Black, Mendenhall and Oddou, 1991; Forster, 2000; Tung, 1981, 1982) and the research that has examined expatriates in China and Hong Kong (Bjorkman and Schaap, 1994; Selmer, 1999; Selmer, 2001, 2002) has rarely included Australian expatriates or organisations. So, first this research examining training of Australian expatriates in China broadens the base of nations covered in the literature.

Second, and related to the first issue, is that this research contributes to the existing body of literature in highlighting that the actual process of selection for Australian expatriates does appear to differ from other nations, which has implications for the amount of training that needs to be/is provided. There are three respects in which the selection of Australian expatriates in China differs. First, the majority of Australian companies in China are small to medium enterprises (SMEs) whereas the majority of North American and European companies are multinational corporations (MNCs). Australia's history as being a relatively new nation and one that does not have a history of being a seafaring and maritime society means that its experience of internationalisation is relatively new compared to other Western nations. This is important because it means that Australians potentially face a steeper learning curve than expatriates from elsewhere because there is not a large accumulated knowledge of cross-cultural understanding and preparation within their organisations. This would suggest that their need for training may be greater than for other Western nationalities whose organizations have been internationalised for generations.

A second aspect of this lack of long-term internationalisation is that Australian companies do not as yet have a large pool of individuals from whom to choose for sending on international postings and given the increasingly younger ages of those taking international assignments, the China posting may be an Australian expatriate's first overseas sojourn. This suggests that there will be limited career planning of these individuals. Third, Australia's experience in selection for international postings is markedly different from the traditional expatriate experience in that increasing numbers of Australians working in China have self-selected. The cohort of individuals in this study are in contrast to the traditional expatriate (identified in the literature as being middle-aged, married and towards the end of their working life) in that they are generally young and single (this has synergies with findings in recent research such as Forster's (2000) study) and many have voluntarily moved to China in search of work rather than being posted by their organisation. These individuals are thus, very unlikely to benefit from succession planning, which also has implications for lack of cross-fertilisation of China-knowledge within organisations.

Third, this paper suggests differences in orientation towards training between small (usually privately-owned) and large companies in that large companies overwhelmingly offer more training per se, and in more forms. Fourth, this paper highlights that expatriates who speak Mandarin and/or have lived in China for more than three years cite lesser problems of adjustment (consistent with the previously cited literature on what is required to achieve intercultural competence) and there is a correlation with these individuals generally being employed in large organisations (which the literature suggests are more likely to provide training).

The findings of this research, with its focus on a younger expatriate cohort that is increasingly self-selecting to work in China, suggests that the nature and style of expatriation (at least for some Australian expatriates and organisations) is changing. While strictly speaking these findings relate only to this specific cohort and it is difficult to generalise to other expatriates and organisations, the findings do suggest that organisations are increasingly valuing prior international work experience (particularly in nations that have similar cultures), formal cultural studies and language skills, and individuals who freely elect to work in another nation rather than relying upon posting individuals who may not have the requisite personal orientation for working cross-culturally. The findings are consistent with a large body of literature that maintains that organisations offer very little CCT. However, the findings do also auger well for proposing that organisations will increasingly utilise individuals with a predisposition to working cross-culturally and whom already possess some cross-cultural skills that will assist them to achieve intercultural competence and avoid expatriate failure.

5.3. Issues for future research

This research is limited by being based on a small sample and the future research based on a larger sample is warranted. For comparative purposes, a larger sample could also include a wider range of nationalities of expatriates. Moreover, while most Australian organisations are located in Shanghai it is acknowledged that there is likelihood of responses to *guanxi* differing from the Eastern seaboard to more remote parts of China given the influence of clans and family networks in the rural areas. Hence, research that examined differences based on geographical areas would also be warranted. Further research could broaden this initial study to include a quantitative survey of expatriates as well as triangulation of results through a quantitative survey of the expatriates' local employees. This research has provided a macro view of Australian organisations operating across a range of industries. However, literature and practice would also be better informed by future research considering whether the need for organisational training is affected by variables such as company market positioning, geographic location of the organisations in China, and industry-specific regulations.

References

Ashamalla, M.H. and M. Crocitto. (1997). "Easing Entry and Beyond: Preparing Expatriates and Patriates for Foreign Assignment Success." *International Journal of Commerce and Management* 7(2), 106–114.

Austrade (Australian Trade Commission). (2002). *China Profile*. Canberra, Australian Trade Commission, Commonwealth Government of Australia, http:www.Austrade.gov.au, accessed 23/09/02.

Baumgarten, K. (1995). "The Training and Development of Staff for International Assignments." In A. Harzing and J. Van Ruysseveldt (eds.), *International Human Resource Management*. London: Sage.

Bevan, S. (ed.). (2000). *Jobson's Year Book of Public Companies 1997–1998*. Sydney: Dunn and Bradstreet Publishers.

Bhagat, R.S. and O.K. Prien. (1996). "Cross-Cultural Training in Organizational Contexts." In D. Landis and R.W. Brislin (eds.), *Handbook of Intercultural Training*, 2nd edition. Thousand Oaks: Sage.

Bird, A., J.S. Osland, M. Mendenhall, and S.C. Schneider. (1999). "Adapting and Adjusting to Other Cultures. What We Know But Don't Always Tell." *Journal of Management Inquiry* 8(2), 152–165.

Bjorkman, I. and A. Schaap. (1994). "Outsiders in the Middle Kingdom: Expatriate Managers in Chinese-Western Joint Ventures." *European Management Journal* 12(2), 147–154.

Black, J., H. Gregorsen, and M. Mendenhall. (1992). *Global Assignments*. San Francisco: Jossey-Bass.

Black, J.S. et al. (1999). *Globalizing People Through International Assignments*. Massachusetts: Addison-Wesley.

Black, J., M. Mendenhall, and G. Oddou. (1991). "Toward a Comprehensive Model of International Adjustment: An Integration of Multiple Theoretical Perspectives." *Academy of Management Review* 16(2), 291–317.

Britt, A. (2002). "Expatriates Want More Support from Home." *HR Magazine* 47(7), 21–22.

Buttery, E.A. and Y.H. Wang. (1999). "The Development of a Guanxi Framework." *Marketing Intelligence and Planning* 17(3), 147–154.

Caligiuri, P. (2000). "Selecting Expatriates for Personality Characteristics: A Moderating Effect of Personality on the Relationship Between Host National Contact and Cross-Cultural Adjustment." *Management International Review* 40(1), 61–80.

Child, J. (1994). *Chinese Management During the Age of Reform*. Cambridge: Cambridge University Press.

Commonwealth Government of Australia. (1995). Industry Taskforce on Leadership and Management Skills (Karpin Report). *Enterprising Nation: Renewing Australia's Managers to Meet the Challenges of the Asia-Pacific Century*. Canberra: AGPS.

Creswell, J.W. (1994). *Research Design*. Thousand Oaks: Sage.

De Cieri, H., P. Dowling, and K. Taylor. (1991). "The Psychological Impact of Expatriate Relocation on Partners." *The International Journal of HRM* 2(3), 377–414.

Desphande, S. and C. Viswesvaran. (1992). "Is Cross-Cultural Training of Expatriate Managers Effective?" *International Journal of Intercultural Relations* 16, 295–310.

DFAT (Department of Foreign Affairs and Trade). (2002). *Australia Economic and Trade Statistics. Market Information and Analysis Section. June*. Canberra, Department of Foreign Affairs and Trade, Commonwealth Government of Australia, http:www.dfat.gov.au, accessed 23/09/02.

Enderwick, P. and D. Hodgson. (1993). "Expatriate Management Practices of New Zealand Business." *The International Journal of HRM* 4(2), 407–423.

Forster, N. (1997). "The Persistent Myth of High Expatriate Failure Rates: A Reappraisal." *The International Journal of Human Resource Management* 8(4), 414–437.

Forster, N. (2000). "Expatriates and the Impact of Cross-Cultural Training." *Human Resource Management Journal* 10(3), 63–78.

Forster, N. and M. Johnsen. (1996). "Expatriate Management in UK Companies New to the International Scene." *International Journal of HRM* 7(1), 165–178.

Frazee, V. (1999). "Send Your Expats Prepared for Success." *Workforce* 4(2), 6–8.

Garonzik, R., J. Brockner, and P.A. Siegel. (2000). "Identifying International Assignees at Risk for Premature Departure: The Interactive Effect of Outcome Favourability and Procedural Fairness." *Journal of Applied Psychology* 85(1), 13–20.

GMAC. (2002). *Global Relocation Trends 2001 Survey Report*. New Jersey: GMAC Global Relocation Services.

Goodall, K. and M. Warner. (1997). "Human Resources in Sino-Foreign Joint Ventures: Selected Case Studies in Shanghai, Compared with Beijing." *The International Journal of Human Resource Management* 8(5), 569–594.

Guthrie, D. (1998). "The Declining Significance of Guanxi in China's Economic Transition." *The China Quarterly* 3, 254–282.

Hammer, M.R., R.L. Wiseman, J.L. Rasmussen, and J.C. Bruschke. (1998). "A Test of Anxiety/Uncertainty Management Theory: The Intercultural Adaptation Context." *Communication Quarterly* 46(3), 309–326.

CROSS-CULTURAL PREPARATION OF AUSTRALIAN EXPATRIATES 395

Harris, P. (1989). "Moving Managers Internationally: The Care and Feeding of Expatriates." *Human Resource Planning* March, 49–54.

Harvey, C. (2001). "Britannia Rules OK for Young and Restless." *The Australian* 17 July, 4.

Harvey, M. and M.N. Novicevic. (2001). "Selecting Expatriates for Increasingly Complex Global Assignments." *Career Development International* 6(2/3), 69–86.

Harzing, A.-W. (1995). "The Persistent Myth of High Expatriate Failure Rates." *The International Journal of Human Resource Management* 6(2), 457–474.

Harzing, A.-W. (2002). "Are Our Referencing Errors Undermining Our Scholarship and Credibility? The Case of Expatriate Failure Rates." *Journal of Organizational Behavior* 23(1), 127–148.

Hendry, C.A. (1994). *Human Resource Strategies for International Growth*. London: Routledge.

Hippler, T. (2000). "On-Site Adjustment Support for German Expatriates in the Republic of Ireland: An Exploratory Study." *IBAR* 21(2), 15–38.

Hofstede, G. (1980). *Culture's Consequences: International Differences in Work-Related Values*. Beverly Hills: Sage.

Huo, H.P., J.H. Huang, and N.K. Napier. (2002). "Divergence or Convergence: A Cross-National Comparison of Personnel Selection Practices." *Asia Pacific Journal of Human Resources* 40(1), 38–54.

Hutchings, K. (2002). "Cross-Cultural Adjustment of Expatriates in Organisations in China: Selection and In-Post Support." *Cross Cultural Management* 9(3), 15–40.

Hutchings, K. and G. Murray. (2002). "Australian Expatriates' Experiences in Working Behind the Bamboo Curtain: An Examination of Guanxi in Post-Communist China." *Asian Business and Management* 1, 1–21.

Institute for Research into International Competitiveness (IRIC). (1995). *Customer's Views of Australian Management: Asian-Pacific Viewpoints*. Perth: Curtin University.

Kaye, M. and G.K. Taylor. (1997). "Expatriate Culture Shock in China." *Journal of Managerial Psychology* 12(8), 496–514.

Kraimer, M.L., S.J. Wayne, and R.A. Jaworski. (2001). "Sources of Support and Expatriate Performance: The Role of Expatriate Adjustment." *Personnel Psychology* 54(1), 71–100.

Luo, Y. (2000). *Guanxi and Business*. Singapore: World Scientific.

Miles, M.B. and A.M. Huberman. (1994). *Qualitative Data Analysis*. Thousand Oaks: Sage.

Milkovich, G.T. and J.T. Newman. (1996). *Compensation*, 5th edition. Chicago: Richard Irwin.

Morley, M., C. Burke, and G. Finn. (1999). "Irish Expatriates in Moscow: Exploratory Evidence on Aspects of Adjustment." In C. Brewster and H. Harris (eds.), *International HRM: Contemporary Issues in Europe*. London: Routledge.

Nicholson, N. and M. West. (1988). *Managerial Job Change: Men and Women in Transition*. Cambridge: Cambridge University Press.

Osland, J. and A. Bird. (2000). "Beyond Sophisticated Stereotyping: Cultural Sense Making in Context." *Academy of Management Executive* 14(1), 65–79.

Osland, J., S. DeFranco, and A. Osland. (1999). "Organisational Implications of Latin American Culture." *Journal of Management Inquiry* 8(2), 19–234.

Osland, J., M. Snyder, and L. Hunter. (1998). "A Comparative Study of Managerial Styles Among Female Executives in Nicaragua and Costa Rica." *International Studies of Management and Organisations* 28(2), 54–73.

Osman-Gani, A. (2000). "Developing Expatriates for the Asia-Pacific Region: A Comparative Analysis of Multinational Enterprise Managers from Five Countries Across Three Continents." *Human Resource Development Quarterly* 11(3), 213–235.

Osman-Gani, A.M. (1999). "Expatriate Development for the Asia-Pacific Region: A Comparative Study of Expatriates from Five Countries Across Three Continents." In *Proceedings of the Academy of Human Resource Development Conference*, K. P.

Osman-Gani, A.M., W.L. Tan, and T.S. Toh. (1998). "Training Managers for Overseas Business Operations in the Asia-Pacific Region: A Study of Singapore-Based Companies." *International Journal of Training and Development* 2(2), 119–127.

Ralston, D., R.H. Terpstra, M.K. Cunniff, and D.J. Gustafson. (1995). "Do Expatriates Change Their Behaviour to Fit a Foreign Culture." *Management International Review* 35(1), 109–122.

Richardson, J. (2000). "Metaphorical 'Types' and Human Resource Management: Self-Selecting Expatriates." *Industrial and Commercial Training* 32(6), 209–218.

Sargent, J. and L. Matthews. (1998). "Expatriate Reduction and Mariachi Circles." *International Studies of Management and Organisations* 28(2), 74–96.

Sekaran, U. (2000). *Research Methods for Business*. 3rd edition. New York: John Wiley.

Selmer, J. (1999). "Western Business Expatriates' Coping Strategies in Hong Kong vs. the Chinese Mainland." *Asia Pacific Journal of Human Resources* 37(2), 92–107.

Selmer, J. (2001). "The Preference for Predeparture or Postarrival Cross-Cultural Training: An Exploratory Approach." *Journal of Managerial Psychology* 16(1), 50–55.

Selmer, J. (2002). "Practice Makes Perfect? International Experience and Expatriate Adjustment." *Management International Review* 42(1), 71–88.

Selmer, J., I. Torbiorn, and C.T. de Leon. (1998). "Sequential Cross-Cultural Training for Expatriate Business Managers: Pre-Departure and Post-Arrival." *International Journal of Human Resource Management* 9(5), 832–840.

Shay, J. and T. Bruce. (1997). "Expatriate Managers." *Cornell Hotel and Restaurant Quarterly* 38(1), 30–35.

Siu, Y.-M.N. (1996). "Getting in, Getting on, Getting out: The Role of Participant Observation Research in a Professional Organisation." BRC Working Paper Series Number 960202, Hong Kong: Hong Kong Baptist University.

Trompenaars, F. and C. Hampden-Turner. (1997). *Riding the Waves of Culture. Understanding Cultural Diversity in Business*. 2nd edition. London: Nicholas Brealey.

Tung, R. (1981). "Selection and Training of Personnel for Overseas Assignments." *Colombia Journal of World Business* 16, 68–78.

Tung, R. (1982). "Selection and Training Procedures of US, European and Japanese Multinationals." *California Management Review* 25(1), 57–71.

Tung, R. (1988). *The New Expatriates: Managing Human Resources Abroad*. Cambridge: Ballinger.

Tung, R. (1990). "IHRM Policies and Practices: A Comparative Analysis." *Research in Personnel and Human Resource Management* Supplement 2, 171–186.

Tung, R. and V. Worm. (2001). Network Capitalism: The Role of Human Resources in Penetrating the China Market." *International Journal of Human Resource Management* 12(4), 517–534.

Varner, I.T. and T.M. Palmer. (2002). "Successful Expatriation and Organizational Strategies." *Review of Business* 23(2), 8–11.

Von Glinow, M.A., E.A. Drost, and M.B. Teagarden. (2002). "Converging on IHRM Best Practices: Lessons Learned from a Globally Distributed Consortium on Theory and Practice." *Asia Pacific Journal of Human Resources* 40(1), 146–166.

Ward, C. and A. Rana-Deuba. (1999). "Acculturation and Adaptation Revisited." *Journal of Cross-Cultural Psychology* 30(4), 422–442.

Welch, D. (1994). "Determinants of International Human Resource Management Approaches and Activities." *Journal of Management Studies* 31(2), 139–164.

Zakaria, N. (2000). "The Effects of Cross-Cultural Training on the Acculturation Process of the Global Workforce." *International Journal of Manpower* 21(6), 492–502.

Kate Hutchings (Ph.D., University of Queensland) is Senior Lecturer in International HRM in the School of Management, Queensland University of Technology, Australia. Her principal research interests focus on Australian expatriates in China and Southeast Asia, and the impact of culture on HRM decisions in subsidiary operations. She held a prior appointment at the University of Queensland, has taught short courses in Malaysia and China, and has held visiting positions in the United States and Denmark. She is currently undertaking research on network building in Australian organisations in China, and knowledge sharing in China.

Part II
Comparative HRM

[13]

THE CULTURAL DIVERSITY OF WESTERN CONCEPTIONS OF MANAGEMENT

André Laurent (France)

Background

In the last few years, I have been looking at the process of managing as an implementation process by which managers translate into behavior some of their basic, implicit beliefs about effective action in organizations. This interest emerged while I was attempting to introduce managers to alternative models of managing and organizing. I realized that any attempt to communicate alternative ideas about the process of management was headed for failure if it could not in some way first address the implicit management gospel that managers carried in their heads. This became a growing conviction a few years ago when I was, for instance, trying to communicate to groups of French managers the potential interest of matrix organization design (Laurent, 1981). The idea of reporting to two bosses was so alien to these managers that mere consideration of such organizing principles was an impossible, useless exercise. What was needed first was a thorough examination and probing

Dr. Laurent is Professor of Organizational Behavior at INSEAD, Fontainebleau, France. He was formerly (1967-1970) Study Director at the Survey Research Center, Institute for Social Research, University of Michigan, Ann Arbor, Mich., USA, and before that (1963-1967) served as an industrial psychologist in Guinea, West Africa.

of the holy principle of the single chain of command and the
managers' recognition that this was a strong element of their
own belief system rather than a constant element in nature.

Every manager has his own management theory, his own set
of representations and preferences that in some way guide his
potential behavior in organizations; and it is critical for managers, management researchers, and educators to identify and
understand these implicit theories of management better. This
conviction that every manager has his own management gospel
provided the initial ground for the research reported here, research that was not originally designed to be comparative.

In order to elicit managers' implicit theories of management,
I had developed a questionnaire proposing 56 different statements about the management of organizations. A five-point
opinion scale was attached to each statement to record the respondent's degree of agreement or disagreement with those
statements. Owing to the bilingual setting in which the survey
was to be administered, the questionnaire was developed in
both English and French simultaneously rather than formally
translated from one language into the other. A great deal of
care was taken to avoid words, expressions, or sentence constructions that could not communicate fairly equivalent meaning in both languages.

The questionnaire was initially administered to a group of
60 upper-middle-level managers from various companies attending an executive development program at INSEAD, a European management institute located in France. This first group
was composed of 40 French managers and 20 managers from
several other European countries.

The original idea was simply to use the recorded opinions
of the managers as an input in the pedagogical process. The
objective was to explore and discuss the participants' implicit
theories of management.

Since I was aware of the work conducted by my colleague
Geert Hofstede, who was, at the time, analyzing his bank of
comparative survey data from the Hermes multinational corporation (Hofstede, 1980a), I decided to compare the results

Diversity in Concepts of Management   **77**

of the group of 40 French managers with those of the 20 non-
French managers. The differences in opinion between these
two <u>ad hoc</u> cultural groups appeared to be so great on so many
items of the questionnaire that they could not be ignored.

These results led to the main working hypothesis of this subsequent research study, namely, that <u>the national origin of</u>
<u>European managers significantly affects their views of what</u>
<u>proper management should be.</u> National culture seems to act
as a strong determinant of managerial ideology. The objective
of the research thus became to assess and identify some of the
national differences in concepts of management.

Research Methodology

The 56-item Management Questionnaire was systematically
administered to groups of upper-middle-level managers attending the various INSEAD executive development programs
between 1977 and 1979. The managers came from a large number of different enterprises and from a variety of Western
countries. So as not to influence the responses, the data were
always collected before beginning a program. Most of the
questionnaires were administered in their English version to
respondents of all nationalities, all of whom were fluent in
English. For a few French-speaking programs, the French
version was used.

The first part of this report summarizes the results obtained with 817 respondents from 10 Western countries (9
European countries and the United States). National sample
size varies from a low of 32 for Italy to a high of 219 for
France. Within each national sample there is some variance
in terms of function, educational background, age, types of
companies, etc. The only common characteristic of the respondents is their participation in management-education programs attracting upper-middle-level managers from a large
number of business firms. The data-collection strategy was
designed to randomize, as much as possible, all variables except nationality. Attempts at controlling other sources of vari-

ance in the data are presented in the second part of this report.

Statistical analysis of the data was performed by computing "ecological" correlations among country mean scores across the 56 items. This approach of ecological factor analysis, which has been used and advocated by Hofstede (1980a. Chap. 2), considers the group — national culture, in the present case — as the unit of analysis. Thus, correlations are run among country scores, not individual scores, in an attempt to identify groups of questions in which the distribution of scores for the various countries shows similar patterns from low to high agreement across the clustered questions. These groups of questions or indices suggest factors or dimensions that may meaningfully differentiate national cultures in terms of their managerial ideologies.

Four indices or dimensions emerged from the statistical analysis. Three of them cluster three questions each; one of them clusters four questions. The four dimensions have been labeled: organizations as political systems (Table 1), organizations as authority systems (Table 2), organizations as role-formalization systems (Table 3), and organizations as hierarchical-relationship systems (Table 4). Ecological correlations among country mean scores computed across the 56 items and leading toward the selection of these four dimensions are presented in Table 5.

The four dimensions or indices do not pretend to be exhaustive. They have been selected strictly on the basis of the high level of statistical association among countries, the number of items they cluster, and the conceptual meaning of the clustered items.

The indices represent attempts to capture a structure of collective managerial ideologies that meaningfully differentiates national cultures. They do not account for individual ways of thinking within a given culture. Indeed, whereas correlations among country scores are very high across the clustered items within a given index, correlations among individual scores for a given country within the same index have proved to be remarkably low. (1) Once again, the purpose here is not

Diversity in Concepts of Management   79

to analyze the structure of individual opinions, but to compare countries.

Although statistical analysis was performed initially on country mean scores from five-point opinion scales, the results are presented here in terms of percent average agreement scores ("strongly agree" and "tend to agree" responses) and percent average disagreement scores ("strongly disagree" and "tend to disagree" responses) for ease of reading and interpretation. Each table thus presents the percentage of managers agreeing or disagreeing with each statement and their percent average score across the clustered questions (last row of the table) for each country. This last measure indicates the country score or position on the index. In each table, countries are ordered from left to right according to their increasing degree of identification with the measured dimension.

<u>Results</u>

<u>Organizations as Political Systems</u> (Table 1)

The dimension "organizations as political systems" clusters three items dealing, respectively, with the political role played by managers in society (item No. 40), their perception of power motivation within the organization (item No. 49), and an assessment of the degree to which organizational structures are clearly defined in the minds of the individuals involved (item No. 33). In countries such as France and Italy, where managers report a stronger perception of their political role in society, they also emphasize the importance of power motivation within the organization and report a fairly hazy notion of organizational structure. Danish and British managers, on the other hand, express a significantly lower political orientation, both within and outside the organization, and a clearer notion of organizational structure.

These results may provide some insight into the extent to which managers from different countries tend to interpret their organizational experience in power terms. Clearly, the

80

772 MANAGERS FROM NINE COUNTRIES *	DENMARK	GREAT BRITAIN	NETHERLANDS	GERMANY	SWEDEN	U S A	SWITZERLAND	FRANCE	ITALY
SAMPLE SIZE	54	190	42	72	50	50	63	219	32
% AGREEMENT WITH : 40. THROUGH THEIR PROFESSIONAL ACTIVITY, MANAGERS PLAY AN IMPORTANT POLITICAL ROLE IN SOCIETY.	32	40	45	47	54	52	65	76	74
% AGREEMENT WITH : 49. MOST MANAGERS SEEM TO BE MORE MOTIVATED BY OBTAINING POWER THAN BY ACHIEVING OBJECTIVES.	25	32	26	29	42	36	51	56	63
% DISAGREEMENT WITH : 33. MOST MANAGERS HAVE A CLEAR NOTION OF WHAT WE CALL AN ORGANIZATIONAL STRUCTURE.	22	23	36	31	30	42	38	53	61
% AVERAGE AGREEMENT / DISAGREEMENT	26	32	36	36	42	43	51	62	66

TABLE I - ORGANIZATIONS AS POLITICAL SYSTEMS

* Belgium has been excluded from this table because of its indecision rate, more than 20% for 2 items (40 & 33)

Diversity in Concepts of Management 81

political orientation of Italian (index score 66) and French managers (index score 62) appears much stronger than the political orientation of Danish (index score 26) and British managers (index score 32). Furthermore, these findings indicate an interesting association at the country level between a lower inclination toward political behavior and a greater perceived clarity of structure (in Denmark and Great Britain) versus a greater inclination toward political behavior and a greater perceived haziness of structure (in Italy and France).

I should like to suggest at this point that it may not be by accident that the contrasting results demonstrated by the British and the French managers seem to parallel to a considerable extent the contrasting perspectives on organizations taken a decade ago by mainstream schools of organizational sociology on each side of the Channel. While the British Aston School researchers were conducting their rational analyses of structural characteristics of organizations, French sociologists were describing organizations as sets of games and power strategies played by actors seeking to maintain some uncertainty around their function so as to play even more power games. Organizations were certainly perceived and defined far more as political systems by the latter than by the former. Thus, cultural differentiation may affect not only managers' implicit concepts of organizations but also researchers' explicit theories. Organization and management theory may be as much culturally bounded as the actual processes of organizing and managing (Brossard and Maurice, 1974; Derossi, 1978; Hofstede, 1980b, 1981).

In summary, this index suggests some important effects on organizational behavior of cultural differences in the political outlook of managers in neighboring Western countries.

Organizations as Authority Systems (Table 2)

"Organizations as authority systems" groups three questions dealing with a conception of hierarchical structure as being designed to specify authority relationships (item No. 14),

82

817 MANAGERS FROM TEN COUNTRIES	U S A	SWITZERLAND	GERMANY	DENMARK	SWEDEN	GREAT BRITAIN	NETHERLANDS	BELGIUM	ITALY	FRANCE
SAMPLE SIZE	50	63	72	54	50	190	42	45	32	219
% AGREEMENT WITH : 14. THE MAIN REASON FOR HAVING A HIERARCHICAL STRUCTURE IS SO THAT EVERYONE KNOWS WHO HAS AUTHORITY OVER WHOM.	18	25	24	35	26	38	38	36	50	45
% AGREEMENT WITH : 52. TODAY THERE SEEMS TO BE AN AUTHORITY CRISIS IN ORGANIZATIONS.	22	29	26	40	46	43	38	64	69	64
% AGREEMENT WITH : 43. THE MANAGER OF TOMORROW WILL BE, IN THE MAIN, A NEGOTIATOR.	50	41	52	63	66	61	71	84	66	86
% AVERAGE AGREEMENT	30	32	34	46	46	48	49	61	61	65

TABLE II - ORGANIZATIONS AS AUTHORITY SYSTEMS

Diversity in Concepts of Management 83

a perception of authority crisis in organizations (item No. 52), and an image of the manager as a negotiator (item No. 43). It differentiates three country clusters of managers' perception of organizations as authority systems. Latin countries such as Belgium, Italy, and France, at the upper end of the continuum (index score 61 to 65), present a sharp contrast to countries such as the United States, Switzerland, and Germany at the lower end (index score 30 to 34), and the remaining four countries fall in the middle (index score 46 to 49).

The belief that "The main reason for having a hierarchical structure is so that everyone knows who has authority over whom" is associated across countries with the perception that "Today there seems to be an authority crisis in organizations" and the expectation that "The manager of tomorrow will be, in the main, a negotiator." However, national culture strongly affects the popularity of such conceptions. For instance, organizations are seen significantly more frequently as authority systems by French managers (65 percent average agreement rate across items) than by American managers (30 percent average agreement rate).

French, Italian, and Belgian managers report a more personal and social concept of authority that regulates relationships among individuals in organizations. American, Swiss, and German managers seem to report a more rational and instrumental view of authority that regulates interaction among tasks or functions. For the former, authority appears to be more a property of the individual; for the latter, it appears to be more an attribute of the role or function.

This index reveals important national variations in managers' views of authority in organizations that are likely to influence their behavior.

Organizations as Role-Formalization Systems (Table 3)

The three items clustered in "organizations as role-formalization systems" all focus on the relative importance of defining and specifying the functions and roles of organizational

84

817 MANAGERS FROM TEN COUNTRIES	SWEDEN	U S A	NETHERLANDS	DENMARK	GREAT BRITAIN	FRANCE	BELGIUM	ITALY	GERMANY	SWITZERLAND
SAMPLE SIZE	50	50	42	54	190	219	45	32	72	63
% AGREEMENT WITH : 1. WHEN THE RESPECTIVE ROLES OF THE MEMBERS OF A DEPARTMENT BECOME COMPLEX, DETAILED JOB DESCRIPTIONS ARE A USEFUL WAY OF CLARIFYING.	56	76	71	87	86	87	89	90	89	91
% AGREEMENT WITH : 13. THE MORE COMPLEX A DEPARTMENT'S ACTIVITIES, THE MORE IMPORTANT IT IS FOR EACH INDIVIDUAL'S FUNCTIONS TO BE WELL-DEFINED.	66	69	79	85	85	83	84	94	93	94
% DISAGREEMENT WITH : 38. MOST MANAGERS WOULD ACHIEVE BETTER RESULTS IF THEIR ROLES WERE LESS PRECISELY DEFINED.	50	54	52	67	68	72	71	69	73	71
% AVERAGE AGREEMENT / DISAGREEMENT	57	66	67	80	80	81	81	84	85	85

TABLE III – ORGANIZATIONS AS ROLE FORMALIZATION SYSTEMS

Diversity in Concepts of Management 85

members. They stress the values of clarity and efficiency that can be obtained by implementing such organizational devices as detailed job descriptions, well-defined functions, and precisely defined roles. Here the results seem essentially to indicate a relatively lower insistence on the need for role formalization in Sweden, the United States, and the Netherlands (index score 57 to 67) than in the remaining seven countries (index score 80 to 85).

Hence, there may be national variations in the degree of formalization, often considered an important structural characteristic of organizations, that is judged desirable.

Organizations as Hierarchical-Relationship Systems (Table 4)

The last index, "organizations as hierarchical-relationship systems," which groups four questions, shows sharp differences in management attitudes toward organizational relationships as one moves from Northern Europe and the United States on the lower end of the continuum to the Latin countries of Europe on the higher end.

Across countries, the dream of eliminating conflict from organizations is associated with the belief that a manager should definitely know more than his subordinates and that organizations should not be upset by such practices as bypassing or having to report to two bosses.

As suggested elsewhere (Laurent, 1981), an index such as this one can provide some assessment of the feasibility of new organizational arrangements — such as the matrix structure — that deviate from more classic hierarchical forms. Indeed, in matrix-type organizations, as opposed to more classic hierarchies, potential conflicts of interest about resources tend to surface more, bosses can no longer pretend to have answers to most of their subordinates' questions, bypassing of authority lines becomes more of a way of life, and, obviously, some managers have to report to two or more bosses.

Thus, the contrasting results obtained from Swedish managers (index score 25) and Italian managers (index score 66)

817 MANAGERS FROM TEN COUNTRIES	SWEDEN	U S A	NETHERLANDS	GREAT BRITAIN	DENMARK	SWITZERLAND	GERMANY	BELGIUM	FRANCE	ITALY
SAMPLE SIZE	50	50	42	190	54	63	72	45	219	32
% AGREEMENT WITH : 19. MOST ORGANIZATIONS WOULD BE BETTER OFF IF CONFLICT COULD BE ELIMINATED FOREVER.	4	6	17	13	19	18	16	27	24	41
% AGREEMENT WITH : 24. IT IS IMPORTANT FOR A MANAGER TO HAVE AT HAND PRECISE ANSWERS TO MOST OF THE QUESTIONS THAT HIS SUBORDINATES MAY RAISE ABOUT THEIR WORK.	10	18	17	27	23	38	46	44	53	66
% DISAGREEMENT WITH : 2. IN ORDER TO HAVE EFFICIENT WORK RELATIONSHIPS, IT IS OFTEN NECESSARY TO BYPASS THE HIERARCHICAL LINE.	22	32	39	31	37	41	46	42	42	75
% AGREEMENT WITH : 8. AN ORGANIZATIONAL STRUCTURE IN WHICH CERTAIN SUBORDINATES HAVE TWO DIRECT BOSSES SHOULD BE AVOIDED AT ALL COSTS.	64	54	60	74	69	76	79	84	83	81
% AVERAGE AGREEMENT / DISAGREEMENT	25	28	33	36	37	43	47	50	50	66

TABLE IV - ORGANIZATIONS AS HIERARCHICAL RELATIONSHIP SYSTEMS

Diversity in Concepts of Management 87

Table 5

Ecological Correlations*

Index I (politics)			Index II (authority)		
Items	49	33	Items	52	43
40	0.73	−0.85	14	0.86	0.69
49		−0.89	52		0.88

Index III (formalization)			Index IV (hierarchy)			
Items	13	38	Items	24	2	8
1	0.95	−0.91	19	0.88	−0.90	0.82
13		−0.83	24		−0.87	0.80
			2			−0.64

*Pearson r among country mean scores. Coun-
try mean scores per item were computed for each
of the ten national samples on the basis of the managers' responses to the five-point opinion scale attached to every questionnaire item.

suggest that matrix-type organizational arrangements might
have better prospects in Sweden than in Italy. National variations in conceiving organizations as hierarchical relationship
systems may affect the structuring of organizations in different
countries and have implications for the transfer of organizational forms across cultures.

Limitations of the Findings

The four dimensions reported above that seem to differentiate national cultures in terms of their managerial ideologies
represent one attempt at mapping some of the cultural differences in concepts of management and organization within the
Western world. Looking at organizations as symbolic systems

of social representation, this research elicits findings that emphasize the need to recognize and identify cultural specificity
as a critical element in the texture of organizations. Furthermore, the reported cultural diversity poses significant challenges for both management theory and practice and seriously
questions claims of universality in both.

These findings have important limitations, however.

First, they reflect the limitations of the questionnaire itself.
Another researcher with different interests would have devised
different questions and would have obtained other dimensions
of differentiation among cultures.

Second, these findings probably reflect the French cultural
identity of the author through the questions he thought of and
included in the list in the first place. Indeed, it may not be ac-
cidental that whereas the positions of other countries tend to
vary from index to index, the position of the Latin countries,
including France, is on the high-score side on all four indices.
Thus, the research findings indicate that French managers,
more than managers from non-Latin countries, tend to view
organizations as political, authority, role-formalization, and
hierarchical-relationship systems.

From this perspective, the findings provide clearer indications about Latin countries such as France than about others
in the sample. They reveal the widest gap in conceptions of
management between the Latin cluster (France, Belgium, Italy)
and the Nordic cluster of America and Europe (United States
and Sweden). Would a British questionnaire designer have elicited dimensions illustrating the same gap? Even though Hofstede's work (1980a) partly eliminates such questions by inter-
correlating the results of various independent comparative
studies, and in spite of attempts by multicultural teams of researchers to design research tools jointly, the methodological
challenge persists.

A third limitation of the findings stems from the limited
number of countries represented in the sample. Similar data
subsequently collected from Japan and Indonesia do indicate
the Western bias of some of the dimensions. For instance,

Diversity in Concepts of Management   89

Japanese managers obtain both high and low scores on questionnaire items regrouped in the same Western index, thus
challenging the validity of the ecological factor. The validity
of the four dimensions is therefore restricted to the ten Western countries represented in the initial sample.

Finally, one may seriously wonder whether the ad hoc sampling method of surveying relatively small groups of managers
attending executive development programs at INSEAD is valid
for making inferences about national cultures. Since legitimate
questions could be raised concerning the representativeness
of the population surveyed in the initial study, several subsequent studies were conducted to assess the validity of the preliminary results.

Replications of the Study

A partial replication of the original survey was initially obtained by administering the same Management Questionnaire
to a much younger population of British and French MBA students at INSEAD. The results, reported elsewhere (Laurent,
1981), confirmed, on a preliminary index, the differences observed between British and French experienced managers.

Another partial replication was performed with a group of
55 French MBA students from ISA, a French business school.
Their index scores are reported in Table 6, along with the index scores of the experienced French managers from the initial survey. The scores of these French MBA students run
parallel to the scores of the experienced French managers,
with a tendency toward perceiving organizations even more as
role-formalization and hierarchical-relationship systems than
the managers.

Fuller replication was then obtained in two, large, U.S.-
based, multinational companies. Since the initial results had
been obtained from ad hoc samples of managers in executive
programs, the question arose of whether similar differences
in management and organizational concepts would persist within the potentially homogenizing, corporate culture of a single

90   André Laurent (France)

Table 6

Index Scores of French MBA Students and French Experienced Managers

Subjects	Index I (politics)	Index II (authority)	Index III (formalization)	Index IV (hierarchy)
55 French MBA students (ISA)	61	64	90	66
219 French experienced managers (INSEAD)	62	65	81	50

multinational company, or whether the multinational culture would be sufficiently strong and pervasive to swamp national differences.

National versus Multinational Cultures

The MNC-A Study

In order to test the above hypothesis, carefully matched national samples of managers were selected from a large, U.S.-based, multinational, chemical firm (MNC-A) with subsidiaries in France, Germany, and Great Britain. Every attempt was made through sampling to control for all conceivable sources of variance other than nationality. A description of sample characteristics is presented in Table 7.

Index scores are reported for the three national groups in Table 8, along with the index scores obtained by the ad hoc INSEAD national samples from the original study. Although a few variations — perhaps due to corporate culture — did appear, the results clearly indicated the consistent and pervasive

Diversity in Concepts of Management 91

Table 7

MNC-A Study — Survey Sample Characteristics

Characteristics	France	Germany	Great Britain
Sample size	48	39	56
Percentage of response rate	80	91	97
Average age	42	43	40
Average number of years of work experience	17	18	18
Average number of years of service with company	15	15	14
Average number of years lived abroad	2.5	1	1.5
Percentage of respondents working in primarily line position	70	65	59
Percentage of respondents working in primarily staff position	30	35	41
Percentage of respondents with higher education at university level	91	81	85
Percentage of respondents with major professional experience in technical fields (production, engineering, maintenance, etc.)	60	58	59
Percentage of respondents with major professional experience in marketing	18	25	23
Percentage of respondents with major professional experience in administration	22	17	18

effects of national cultures for the three countries involved. The average distance among the three countries' scores across the four indices remained essentially the same (INSEAD sample = 13.3; MNC-A sample = 13.0), as did the average range

Table 8

Index Scores of MNC-A and INSEAD Managers

	Index I (politics)				Index II (authority)		
	Great Britain	Germany	France		Germany	Great Britain	France
MNC-A managers	24	33	45	MNC-A managers	38	42	53
INSEAD managers	32	36	62	INSEAD managers	34	48	65

	Index III (formalization)				Index IV (hierarchy)		
	Great Britain	France	Germany		Great Britain	Germany	France
MNC-A managers	71	88	88	MNC-A managers	29	45	54
INSEAD managers	80	81	85	INSEAD managers	36	47	50

93

Table 9

Index Scores of MNC-B and INSEAD Managers for Opposite Clusters of Countries

Index I (politics)

	Denmark + Great Britain + Netherlands + Germany	France + Italy
MNC-B managers	33	56
INSEAD managers	33	64

Index II (authority)

	USA + Switzerland + Germany	Belgium + Italy + France
MNC-B managers	30	69
INSEAD managers	32	62

Index II (formalization)

	Sweden + USA + Netherlands + Germany + Switzerland	Denmark + Great Britain + France + Belgium + Italy
MNC-B managers	57	78
INSEAD managers	63	82

Index IV (hierarchy)

	Sweden + USA + Netherlands	Belgium + France + Italy
MNC-B managers	32	53
INSEAD managers	29	55

of the country scores across the four indices (INSEAD sample = 20; MNC-A sample = 19.5).

Actually, when the results were analyzed not only across
the 13 questions that constitute the 4 indices but across the
totality of the 56 questions initially asked in the survey, it was
found that:

— the range of MNC-A country averages (variance of the
country means) was 28 percent greater than the range of
INSEAD country averages;

— the MNC-A country averages were more widely spread
than the INSEAD country averages on 41 of the 56 questions
answered (73 percent).

A homogenizing effect of a large multinational corporation
toward standardization of managerial concepts across national cultures was certainly not found in these data. If anything, the opposite hypothesis could be advanced.

The MNC-B study

Finally, another replication of these findings was obtained
within another large American multinational company in the
office-equipment industry (MNC-B). This time a different
research strategy was used. A small ad hoc group of 30 large
account managers from the 10 Western countries represented
in the INSEAD study was surveyed with a condensed questionnaire containing only the 13 questions that constitute the 4 indices. "National" sample sizes were a low 2 for the United
States, Sweden, Denmark, Belgium, and Italy; a medium 3 for
Germany and the Netherlands; 4 for France and Switzerland;
and a high 6 for Great Britain. Minute sample sizes were,
however, compensated for by a very high degree of occupational homogeneity among respondents and a very strong company culture.

Results from opposite clusters of countries on each of the
four indices are presented for this group of respondents in
Table 9. They demonstrate once again an intriguing overall
stability of the national patterns of managerial ideologies,

Diversity in Concepts of Management 95

given the very tight conditions of the research design. The average distance among clustered countries' scores across the four indices again remained the same (INSEAD sample = 26.5; MNC-B sample = 26.0). There was no indication of any reduction in cultural differences in management concepts within MNC-B.

Conclusions

The findings summarized here provide an illustration of nationally bounded collective mental maps about organizations that seem to resist convergence effects from increased professionalization of management and intensity of international business. Neighboring Western nations seem to be forming fairly differentiated images of organizations and their management. This attempt to use a comparative phenomenological approach to the study of organizations seems to elicit findings that cast serious doubt on the universality of management and organizational knowledge and praxis.

It may very well be that the management process in these ten Western countries is as much culture bound as their cooking, and that international management has to avoid the trap of international cuisine. National cultures may still offer some genuine recipes.

Note

1) A. Laurent (1980) "Dimensions Culturelles des Conceptions de Management. Une Analyse Comparative Internationale." Working Paper 80-02. Fontainebleau: European Institute for Business Administration (INSEAD), February 1980.

References

Brossard, M., and Maurice, M. (1974) "Existe-t-il un modèle universel des structures d'organisation?" Sociologie du Travail, No. 4, pp. 402–426. (English translation: "Is

96   André Laurent (France)

There a Universal Model of Organization Structure?" International Studies of Management & Organization, 1976,
VI(3), pp. 11–45.)

Derossi, F. (1978) "The Crisis in Managerial Roles in Italy."
International Studies of Management & Organization,
VIII(3), 64–99.

Hofstede, G. (1980a) Culture's Consequences: International
Differences in Work-related Values. Beverly Hills, Calif.:
Sage Publications.

Hofstede, G. (1980b) "Motivation, Leadership and Organization: Do American Theories Apply Abroad?" Organizational Dynamics, Summer, pp. 42–63.

Hofstede, G. (1981) "Culture and Organizations." International
Studies of Management & Organization, X(4), 15–41.

Laurent, A. (1981) "Matrix Organizations and Latin Cultures.
A Note on the Use of Comparative Research Data in Man-
agement Education." International Studies of Management
& Organization, X(4), 101–114.

[14]

Convergence or divergence: human resource practices and policies for competitive advantage worldwide

Paul Sparrow, Randall S. Schuler and Susan E. Jackson

Abstract

The world is becoming far more competitive and volatile than ever before, causing firms to seek to gain competitive advantage whenever and wherever possible. As traditional sources and means such as capital, technology or location become less significant as a basis for competitive advantage, firms are turning to more innovative sources. One of these is the management of human resources. While traditionally regarded as a personnel department function, it is now being widely shared among managers and non-managers, personnel directors and line managers. As the management of human resources is seen increasingly in terms of competitive advantage, the question that arises is: What must we do to gain this advantage? Many of the most successful firms now have to operate globally, and this gives rise to a second question: Do firms in different parts of the globe practice human resource management (HRM) for competitive advantage differently? Because of their importance, these two questions form the primary focus of this investigation. Data from a worldwide respondent survey of chief executive officers and human resource managers from twelve countries are cluster analysed to identify country groupings across a range of human resource policies and practices that could be used for competitive advantage. Differences and similarities on fifteen dimensions of these policies and practices are statistically determined and the results interpreted in the light of relevant literature. This investigation concludes that there is indeed a convergence in the use of HRM for competitive advantage. However, in pursuing this convergence there are some clear divergences, nuances and specific themes in the areas of HRM that will take the fore and in the way in which specific aspects such as culture, work structuring, performance management and resourcing will be utilized. These patterns of HRM bear understanding and consideration in managing human resources in different parts of the world.

Paul Sparrow, Randall S. Schuler and Susan E. Jackson

Introduction

As firms pursue, aggressively, their short-term and long-term goals, they are realizing that their success depends upon a successful global presence (Ghoshal and Bartlett, 1989). In turn, their success as global players is being seen as increasingly dependent upon international human resource management: In a comparative context, human resource management (HRM) is best considered as the range of policies which have strategic significance for the organization (Brewster and Tyson, 1991) and which are typically used to facilitate integration, employee commitment, flexibility and the quality of work life as well as meeting broader business goals such as changing organizational values, structure, productivity and delivery mechanisms. Therefore, in order to explain the various 'brands' of HRM on a worldwide basis in sufficient detail, any analysis must include 'subjects which have traditionally been the concern of personnel management and industrial relations . . . as well as . . . more innovative and strategic approaches to people management' (Brewster and Tyson, 1991: 1). Differences between countries in the historical role and function of the personnel management function make it necessary to take a more strategic perspective of the underlying people issues.

This increasing reliance upon successful HRM as a key to gaining competitive advantage in the global arena is mirroring the same phenomenon that effective firms witnessed during the 1980s on the domestic scene. As technology and capital became commodities in domestic markets, the only thing left really to distinguish firms, and thereby allow them to gain competitive advantage, were skills in managing their human resources (Reich, 1990). While attention has been devoted to international comparisons of production systems and management strategies for many years, the comparison of people management systems has until recently been overlooked (Brewster, Hegewisch and Lockhart, 1991; Pieper, 1990).

Successful global human resource management

If long-run as well as short-run corporate goals are dependent upon successful global HRM, an interesting question is: What is successful global management of human resources? At the risk of oversimplifying, we argue that it is best defined as the possession of the skills and knowledge of formulating and implementing policies and practices that effectively integrate and cohere globally dispersed employees, while at the same time recognizing and appreciating local differences that impact on the effective utilization of human resources.

268

HRM practices and policies for competitive advantage worldwide

This definition of the successful global management of human resources can be decomposed into two distinct components of international HRM. The first component represents the body of knowledge and action that multinational firms use in allocating, dispersing, developing and motivating their global work-force. The major HRM concerns tend to focus on expatriate assignment, payment schemes and repatriation (Black, Gregersen and Mendenhall, 1992; Dowling and Schuler, 1990). Concerns for third country and local nationals are reflected in issues relating to the management of global operations, such as who is going to run the various geographically dispersed operations. Thus relatively few individuals tend to be encompassed by this component of international HRM.

The second component represents the body of knowledge and action concerned with actually staffing and running the local operations. The topics and issues enacted at this level are essentially focused around an understanding of local differences relevant to attracting, utilizing and motivating individuals (Adler, 1991; Poole, 1986; Punnett and Ricks, 1992).

As Ronen (1986) suggested, for global firms to be successful in managing their worldwide work-forces, they need to have an understanding and sensitivity to several local environments. They must utilize local information and adapt it to a broader set of human resource policies that reflect the firm itself. Of the two components of successful global HRM, this appears to be the lesser developed. Consequently, the focus of this article is on providing a greater understanding of selected aspects of HRM on a worldwide, comparative basis. We should note, however, that many successful organizations have prospered without following a global route.

Human resource practices and concepts for gaining competitive advantage

Porter (1980) suggested the concept of gaining competitive advantage to firms wishing to engage in strategic activities that would be difficult for competitors to copy or imitate quickly. Schuler and MacMillan (1984) applied this concept to HRM. They, and others since (for example, Reich, 1990), have suggested that firms can use HRM to gain competitive advantage because it is difficult for competitors to duplicate. That is, while technology and capital can be acquired by almost anyone at any time, for a price, it is rather difficult to acquire a ready pool of highly qualified and highly motivated employees. It is increasingly difficult to plan strategy in an era of discontinuous change. A number of writers have focused on the importance of underlying competencies –

Paul Sparrow, Randall S. Schuler and Susan E. Jackson

technical, marketing or strategic capabilities – reflected in unique sets of corporate skill and HRM activities (Grant, 1991; Hamel and Prahalad, 1991).

At the global level, firms can seize competitive advantage through the selection and use of human resource policies and practices. The most important questions to ask then are: What human resource policies and practices can firms consider using in their worldwide operations that might assist them in gaining competitive advantage? Are they likely to be the same across countries? Is there some uniformity that firms can pursue in their efforts to manage their worldwide workforces successfully?

Given the analysis by Moss-Kanter (1991) and Porter (1990), it seems reasonable to proceed on the basis that any understanding of comparative HRM would aid firms in seeking to develop and implement human resource policies and practices worldwide to gain competitive advantage.

Key policies and practices in gaining competitive advantage

While there are several specific ways that firms can gain competitive advantage with HRM policies and practices, it is most useful to gather data on generalizable policies and practices that are consistently seen as central to the management of human resources. In order to provide a basis for international comparison, we elected to focus on five major groupings of HRM policies and practices identified in the literature (see Poole, 1990; Schuler, 1992; Walker, 1992). Broadly, these include: culture; organizational structure; performance management; resourcing; and communications and corporate responsibility.

Culture   The present study addresses two aspects of culture. The first is the problem of creating a culture of empowerment, of including all employees in the decision making and responsibility of the organization. This aspect of HRM represents a significant trend in a number of US and UK organizations (Lawler, 1991; Wickens, 1987). How important is it worldwide? The second aspect is the promotion of diversity management and the development of a culture of equality. These two practices are tied together by a policy of inclusion, of bringing everyone into the operation and treating them equally with respect. Equality based on diversity covers the recruitment, placement and advancement of all groups (regardless of race, age, sex or religion) in the organization. More specific and detailed concepts of equality are not examined by the research.

270

HRM practices and policies for competitive advantage worldwide

Organization structure Associated with the issue of culture is that of organization structure. Organization structure refers to the relationship among units and individuals in the organization. It can be described as ranging from a hierarchical, mechanistic relationship to a flatter, horizontal and organic relationship (Burns and Stalker, 1961). Obviously, these represent rather contrasting approaches to structuring organizations. Although their impact on individuals has been explored, more investigation specifically related to comparative HRM appears warranted. Are all countries pursuing strategies of reducing the number of vertical layers (delayering) with the same vigour?

Performance management Another important group of HRM policies and practices reflects those associated with performance management. This process links goal setting and rewards, coaching for performance, aspects of career development and performance evaluation and appraisal into an integrated process. As firms seek to 'manage the most out of employees' they are turning their attention to issues associated with employee performance. Because of the nature of international competition, the specific concerns in performance management are with measuring and motivating customer service, quality, innovation and risk-taking behaviour (Peters, 1992).

Resourcing As important as motivating employees once they are employed are issues associated with obtaining the most appropriate individuals (external resourcing); training and developing them with regard to technology and business process change; and managing the size of the work-force through reductions, downsizing and skills reprofiling. Beer *et al.* (1984) describe these issues as part of a human resource flow policy. Seen in aggregate, we also regard them as part of a total resourcing dimension to HRM, as discussed by a number of writers (Boam and Sparrow, 1992; Mitrani, Dalziel and Fitt, 1992; Torrington *et al.*, 1991).

Communication and corporate responsibility The fifth and final group of HRM policies and practices to which we give consideration are those by which firms may seek to describe their philosophy of communication and corporate responsibility. These two aspects of HRM capture the flow and sharing of information, internal and external to the organization (Daft, 1992). Both can be vital as firms seek to empower and include employees in the organization; and as they seek to recognize and incorporate aspects of the external environment such as the general quality of the labour force, legal regulations or concerns about environmental quality and social responsibility.

Paul Sparrow, Randall S. Schuler and Susan E. Jackson

In summary, while these five groupings of HRM policies and practices may not capture all the human resource policies and practices relevant to global firms seeking to gain competitive advantage, they represent some of the major contemporary policies and practices being considered by academics and organizations, and are, therefore, worthy of international comparison.

The current literature suggests that these five aspects of HRM policies and practices may have varying levels of effectiveness throughout the world (Moss-Kanter, 1991; Porter, 1990). Indeed, Whitley (1992a) notes that, as organizations move towards greater integration, there is increasing recognition of national differences in higher level business systems. Despite increasing internationalization within many industries, national institutions remain quite distinct. The role of the state and financial sectors, national systems of education and training, and diverse national cultures, employment expectations and labour relations all create 'national business recipes', each effective in their particular context but not necessarily effective elsewhere. These different national business recipes carry with them a 'dominant logic of action' that guides management practice. This logic of action is reflected in specific management structures, styles and decision-making processes, growth and diversification strategies, inter-company market relationships and market development (Hofstede, 1993). There is also greater recognition of the effects of both sector (Räsäsen and Whipp, 1992) and regional networks (Sabel *et al.*, 1987) in patterning HRM activities.

The institutional argument against unconstrained globalization and business integration runs broadly as follows. There are a number of different and equally successful ways of organizing economic activities (and management) in a market economy (Whitley, 1992a). These different patterns of economic organization tend to be a product of the particular institutional environments within the various nation states. The development and success of specific managerial structures and practices (such as HRM) can be explained only by giving due cognizance to the various institutional contexts worldwide. Not all management methods are transferable. The effectiveness therefore of any worldwide conceptualization of HRM will very likely be constrained by the different institutional contexts for national practice.

Hypotheses and expectations

Based on the world of Moss-Kanter (1991) and Hofstede (1993), two hypotheses are developed in direct relationship to the concept of convergence or divergence of human resource policies and practices. Moss-Kanter (1991) found in her worldwide survey of management

HRM practices and policies for competitive advantage worldwide

practices and expectations that the results could be clustered, not necessarily according to geography but according to culture. Thus she coined the phrase 'cultural allies' to signify results from several countries being identical (e.g. US, UK and Australia) and 'cultural islands' to signify results from individual countries being unique (e.g. Korea; Japan). Using her results and rationale leads to these testable hypotheses:

> *Hypothesis 1*: With regard to using human resource policies and practices for competitive advantage, there will be cultural islands and cultural allies. The cultural islands will be Korea and Japan and the cultural allies will be Europe, North America, UK and Australia; and Latin America.

Our second hypothesis is more tentative, more exploratory than the first. Thus, while we can propose cultural allies and islands to exist, given the existing literature we are unable to make specific predictions about how human resource policies and practices will differ across nations. While it might be argued that they will reflect national cultures (it might also be argued that they will reflect differences in local law, custom and union–management history), we have no guidance suggesting specific relationships between aspects of culture and specific human resource policies and practices. This research is intended to provide such information. Thus, at this time, what we are able to offer is a second and somewhat exploratory hypothesis:

> *Hypothesis 2:* There will be differences in which human resource policies and practices are seen as important for gaining competitive advantage across nations.

Methodology

Questionnaire

To explore these hypotheses, we conducted secondary analyses on data obtained as part of a larger international survey conducted in 1991. This was a worldwide study of human resource policies and practices conducted by IBM and Towers Perrin. The survey data which form the basis of the analysis in this paper have been published elsewhere (Towers Perrin, 1992). In developing the survey questionnaire, some of the authors of this paper were invited to incorporate policies and practices and then write survey items that represented the academic and practitioner research and literature through 1990. These items were reviewed for representation and agreement by a series of other academics and practitioners identified by the IBM Corporation.

Paul Sparrow, Randall S. Schuler and Susan E. Jackson

A major topic addressed in one section of the questionnaire was 'human resource concepts and practices for gaining competitive advantage'. In this section, respondents were asked to indicate the degree of importance they attached to each item in their firm's attempt to gain competitive advantage through human resource policies and practices. They indicated this for the current year (1991) and for the year of 2000. For the purposes of this study, we have analysed the data for the year 2000. This allows us to consider the extent to which future plans and expectations within the firms surveyed are likely to converge.

The specific firms included were those identified jointly by IBM and Towers Perrin as being the most effective firms in highly competitive environments in each of several countries. Details of the sample are provided by Towers Perrin (1992). In summary, the following information is of relevance in order to draw attention to the nature of the sample and the limits to which the data may be generalized. Effective firms in highly competitive environments were identified for each country surveyed. Given the global nature of firms discussed in the introduction, major employers in one country were, in some cases, subsidiaries or divisions of firms headquartered in other countries. In all cases, Towers Perrin (1992) surveyed two executives from each firm. Invitation letters and questionnaires were mailed to respondents in spring 1991. The respondents included the chief operating officers and the senior human resource officers (2961 respondents or 81 per cent of the sample). Of these respondents 22 per cent were from firms that employed over 10,000 employees, 46 per cent were from firms employing 1,000 to 10,000 employees and 32 per cent were from firms employing fewer than 1,000 employees. The other 19 per cent of the sample comprised leading academics, consultants and individuals from the business media. The total sample of respondents was located in twelve countries throughout the world (the figures in brackets denote the sample size for each country): Argentina (42), Brazil (159), Mexico (67), France (81), Germany (295), Italy (212), the United Kingdom (261), Canada (120), the United States (1,174), Australia (94), Japan (387) and Korea (69). The strategy of gathering data from major employing organizations led to a natural bias in the sample towards those countries with significant numbers of large organizations (e.g. the United States, Japan, Germany and the United Kingdom). To overcome the potential bias this might introduce into the analysis, the statistical tests (as discussed later) used to establish significant differences between national samples are those that control for sample size. The analysis that follows then is primarily based upon responses from respondents in effective firms in highly competitive

HRM practices and policies for competitive advantage worldwide

environments in twelve countries worldwide responding to surveys that were translated into the language of the representative country.

When survey responses are used for comparative analysis, there are a number of issues that have to be acknowledged. Different political, economic, social and cultural considerations lead to a reinterpretation of management agendas at a local level. For example, in carrying out the pilot studies for their surveys on European HRM, Brewster, Hegewisch and Lockhart (1991) noted that identical questions about specific HRM tools or issues were interpreted differently by respondents within their national cultural and legal context. For example, the issue of flexible working in Britain and Germany has been linked to demographic change and the need to reintegrate women into the labour market, whereas in France flexible working is seen as a response to general changes in lifestyle and has little to do with female labour force participation. Another problem is that the actual level of rating is difficult to interpret. For example, a low rating to a particular item might reflect the fact that the firm does not think the issue critical because they do not have the competence or desire to pursue the issue, or it might reflect the fact that the firm is very good already in the area under question and so no longer thinks the issue critical (although it will still form part of their activity). Survey findings reflect a pot pourri of past cultural constraints and future expectations based on new practices. Surveys are also cross-sectional and examine perceptions (current or future) at only one point in time. The analysis in this paper is based on expectations and plans for the year 2000, and therefore should not be coloured by short-term factors (such as economic problems) that might influence respondents. This is not to say that short-term factors should be dismissed, but, when considering global patterns of similarity and difference in HRM, the longer-term objectives, directions and pathways provide a more consistent picture. Nevertheless, ratings reflect current mindsets only and these may change over the next ten years as organizations implement the findings of the survey. The data are then not a guarantee of eventual action. Great care is needed in interpreting comparative survey results and where possible we support the survey findings by reference to other published work.

Having noted the methodological constraints of empirical survey work, we would point to the general dearth of large-scale empirical data and the opportunities afforded by an analysis of the Towers Perrin worldwide data. The addition of new empirical data we believe outweighs possible limitations. The statistical analysis in this paper therefore uses the Towers Perrin (1992) survey data to shed light on hypotheses described above:

Paul Sparrow, Randall S. Schuler and Susan E. Jackson

- is there any underlying pattern (i.e. statistical clusters of countries) in the national data on HRM policies and concepts?
- what is the nature of differences between countries or groups of countries across a range of HRM variables?

Statistical analysis

We analysed the responses to thirty-eight questions asked about various HRM practices and concepts. In the first analysis we used the cluster analysis package on S.P.S.S. to ascertain whether there was any pattern in the anticipated HRM policies and concepts across the twelve countries included in the sample. The basic procedure of all agglomerative techniques (such as cluster analysis) is similar. They compute a similarity or distance matrix between a series of variables. Differences between methods arise because of different ways of defining similarity or distance between two groups of dependent variables. The dependent variables for this analysis are the percentage of respondents stating each of the thirty-eight items (human resource concepts or practices) are of critical importance or importance in order to achieve competitive advantage. The successively combined independent variables are the twelve countries. The analysis uses the cosine measure of similarity and fuses countries according to the least 'distance' from their furthest neighbour.

Each fusion decreases by one the number of country groupings or clusters and occurs at a point where increasingly dissimilar countries are being combined (i.e., more and more 'mathematical force' is required to fuse them). Ultimately the data are reduced to a single cluster containing all the original countries. Consequently, great importance is attached to the decision rule that provides the criterion to stop 'forcing' combinations. While such rules are to some extent arbitrary, they are acceptable given that the purpose of cluster analysis is only to classify and interpret differences between countries rather than attributing any further quantitative qualities. The accepted practice is to limit the degree of fusion by calculating coefficients of similarity and stopping the fusion at the point which would require the greatest amount of change (or mathematical force) in this coefficient of similarity once the fusion has begun.

Once the underlying clusters (or grouping of countries) were identified, the differences between the importance these clusters of countries attribute to various HRM policies and practices were analysed. In order to facilitate this analysis of difference, the thirty-eight survey questions were reclassified (on a conceptual basis) into fifteen underlying dimensions. These dimensions identify elements of culture change,

HRM practices and policies for competitive advantage worldwide

structuring the organization, performance management, resourcing, and communication and corporate responsibility. They, therefore, broadly correspond with current conceptualizations of strategic human resource management as discussed in the Introduction (see, for example, Schuler, 1992; Walker, 1992). Questions relating to each of the dimensions examined are listed in Table 1. It is important to note here that we have grouped survey items on a logical basis rather than an empirical basis.

An alternative approach would be to factor analyse the thirty-eight questionnaire items and to create composite scores on the resultant factors. We feel that such an analysis should not be conducted at this stage of investigation, particularly as we do not yet know (but shall test for) significant sub-groupings within the HRM data across countries. The approach we have adopted of creating dimensions based on conceptual similarity, is of more value in linking our comparative analysis back to the academic literature on HRM practices. We shall discuss the possibility of creating categories of HRM practices based on factor analysis later in the paper.

The analyses of statistical differences between the resultant clusters across the fifteen dimensions of HRM were conducted by selecting one (the more representative) country from each cluster. For each of these countries, scores for the fifteen variables were created by averaging the percentage of people who rated the topic as important or very important for achieving competitive advantage across the relevant questions (shown in Table 1). The primary data summary published by Towers Perrin (1992) reported the percentage responses to questions as well as the sample size. A statistical technique had to be chosen that allows for meaningful secondary analysis and comparison. Because country samples have widely varying numbers of respondents it would not be valid to test for simple differences in percentages without controlling for variation in sample size. The most appropriate statistical measure therefore is the Standard Error of Difference between Proportions. This can be used to test whether the percentage difference between any two samples (countries) represents a significant difference or is just due to sampling variation. It is calculated using the formula:

$$\text{Standard error of difference between proportions} = \sqrt{\frac{p_1 q_1}{n_1} + \frac{p_2 q_2}{n_2}}$$

where: p = sample proportion in favour
q = sample proportion against
n = sample size

Paul Sparrow, Randall S. Schuler and Susan E. Jackson

Table 1 *The fifteen HRM dependent variables and the questionnaire items combined to create them*

CULTURE CHANGE VARIABLES:

---

(1) Promoting an empowerment culture
Facilitate full employee involvement
Require employees to self-monitor and improve
Promote employee empowerment through ownership
(2) Promoting diversity and an equality culture
Promote corporate culture emphasizing equality
Manage diversity through tailored programmes

ORGANIZATION STRUCTURE AND CONTROL VARIABLES:
(1) Emphasis on flexible organization/work practices
Require employee flexibility (i.e. jobs and location)
Flexible cross-functional teams/work groups
Flexible work arrangements
Utilize non-permanent work-force
(2) Emphasis on centralization and vertical hierarchy
Maintain specialized and directed work-force
(3) Emphasis on utilizing IT to structure the organization
Promote advanced technology for communications
Provide more access to information systems
(4) Emphasis on horizontal management
Increase spans of control and eliminate layers
Establish multiple and parallel career paths

PERFORMANCE/PROCESS MANAGEMENT VARIABLES:
(1) Emphasis on measuring and promoting customer service
Reward employees for customer service/quality
Peer subordinate customer ratings
(2) Emphasis on rewarding innovation/creativity
Reward employees for innovation and creativity
Opportunity includes autonomy, creative skills
Reward employees for enhancing skills/knowledge
(3) Link between pay and individual performance
Reward employees for business/productivity gains
Focus on merit philosophy, individual performance
(4) Shared benefits, risks and pay for team performance
Implement pay systems promoting sharing
Flexible benefits
Share benefit risks and costs with employees

HRM practices and policies for competitive advantage worldwide

RESOURCING VARIABLES:
(1) Emphasis on external resourcing
Emphasize quality university hiring programmes
Recruit and hire from non-traditional labour pools
(2) Emphasis on internal resourcing – training & careers
Identify high potential employees early
Emphasize management development/skills training
Require continuous training/retraining
Provide basic education and skills training
(3) Emphasis on internal resourcing – managing outflows
Provide flexible retirement opportunities
Develop innovative and flexible outplacement

COMMUNICATION/CORPORATE RESPONSIBILITY VARIABLES:
(1) Emphasis on communication
Communicate business directions, problems and plans
(2) Emphasis on corporate responsibility
Active corporate involvement in public education
Ensure employees pursue good health aggressively
Offer personal/family assistance
Encourage/reward external volunteer activities
Provide full employment (life-time security)

Given the large number of two-country comparisons that need to be made on any one variable, a more conservative significance level of $p < .01$ is adopted. In order to be significant at the $p < .01$ level, the observed percentage difference has to be 2.58 times greater than the standard error of the difference (3.29 times greater for significance at $p < .001$).

Results

Hypothesis 1

The dendogram in Figure 1 shows the result of the successive fusions of countries, starting from the most similar. There are five resultant clusters of countries. The first cluster initially comprises the Anglo-Saxon business culture countries of the United Kingdom, Australia, Canada and the United States. These countries (the most similar) are subsequently joined by Germany and finally by Italy. The second cluster (a cultural island) consists solely of France. The third cluster is

Paul Sparrow, Randall S. Schuler and Susan E. Jackson

another cultural island consisting of Korea. The fourth cluster reveals another set of cultural allies comprising the South American or Latin countries of Brazil, Mexico and Argentina, while the fifth cluster represents another cultural island consisting of Japan alone. These results, which are largely consistent with those we hypothesized, are discussed and interpreted later in this article primarily in relation to two other studies that have considered international patterns in business practice: the work of Hofstede (1980, 1993) on culture and the work of Moss-Kanter (1991) on attitudes towards change.

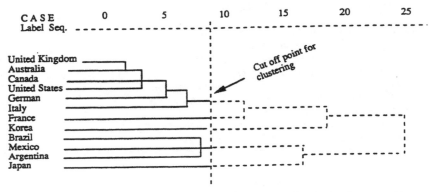

Figure 1 *Rescaled dendogram showing the average for the twelve countries*

Three of the clusters contained only a single country. In order to complete the analysis of HRM differences between the other two clusters, the United States was chosen to represent the Anglo-American cluster (as the largest sample contained within the cluster) and Brazil was chosen to represent the Latin American cluster on the same basis. The results are summarized in Table 2 below. Scores which are significantly 'higher' or 'lower' (using the Standard Error of Difference in Proportions) than those of other countries on each variable are highlighted in the shaded boxes. In some cases, three grades of significant difference existed, i.e. higher, medium and lower.

Exploratory differences on Hypothesis 2

In this section we outline those comparisons that resulted in significant differences regarding HRM practice to be used to gain competitive advantage. Interpretation and discussion of these differences are left until later in the paper. On the *cultural items* Japan scores signifi-

HRM practices and policies for competitive advantage worldwide

cantly lower on 'promoting an empowerment culture' compared to the Anglo-American representative United States (z = –6.40, p<.001) and the Latin American representative Brazil (z = –6.30, p<.001), while the United States scores significantly higher on 'promoting diversity and an equality culture' compared to France (z = 2.98, p<.01) and Japan (z = 3.62, p<.001).

On the *structuring items* the United States scores significantly higher on 'emphasis on flexible work practices' compared to France (z = 3.56, p<.001) and Brazil (z = 2.97, p<.01). Nearly all the comparisons on the 'emphasis on centralization and vertical hierarchy' variable are significant. France and Korea score higher than Japan (z = 3.82, p<.001 and z = 3.25, p<.01), and Japan scores higher than the United States and Brazil (z = 9.87, p < .001 and z = 6.01, p<.001). Variations in the 'emphasis on utilizing IT to structure the organization' are less marked, but Japan scores significantly lower than Korea (z = –2.85, p<.01) and Brazil (z = 3.59, p<.001) and the United States scores lower than Brazil (z = –3.04, p<.01). No significant differences were found between the clusters on the 'emphasis on horizontal management' variable.

Less variation was found between the clusters on the *performance management items*. There were no significant differences on the 'emphasis on rewarding innovation/creativity' and 'link between pay and individual performance' variables. The extent to which emphasis was put on 'customer service' and its measurement varied significantly. France placed significantly higher emphasis on customer service than the United States (z = 3.23, p<.01), while the United States placed more emphasis on customer service than Korea (z = 2.59, p<.01) and Japan (z = 6.06, p<.001). The emphasis placed on 'shared benefits, risks and pay for team performance' also varied significantly. The United States placed greater emphasis on this than Brazil (z = 2.60, p<.01), France (z = 3.79, p<.001), Korea (z = 3.57, p<.001) and Japan (z = 10.84, p<.001). The Japanese score was also significantly lower than that for Brazil (z = –4.34, p<.001).

The *resourcing items* yielded virtually no significant differences. Korea placed a higher 'emphasis on training and career management' than Japan (z = 3.32, p<.001), while Brazil placed greater 'emphasis on managing outflows' of staff than the United States (z = 3.14, p<.01) and Japan (z = 3.54, p.<001).

Finally, there were no significant differences between the cluster country representatives in their emphasis on *communication and corporate responsibility*.

Paul Sparrow, Randall S. Schuler and Susan E. Jackson

Table 2 *Summary of differences in HRM between the five clusters of countries*

Survey items	US Anglo American cluster	France	Japan	Korea	Brazil South American cluster
	Differences between the five clusters of countries on the Culture Change Variables				
Promoting empowerment culture	71.0% HIGHER	64.0%	52.7% LOWER	64.3%	78.7% HIGHER
Promoting diversity and equality culture	53.0% HIGHER	36.5% LOWER	42.5% LOWER	49.5%	47.5%
	Differences between the five clusters of countries on the Structuring Variables				
Emphasis on flexible work practices	59.8% HIGHER	39.8% LOWER	54.5%	53.3%	47.3% LOWER
Emphasis on centralization and vertical hierarchy	6.0% LOWER	53.0% HIGHER	30.0% MEDIUM	51.0% HIGHER	10.0% LOWER
Emphasis on utilizing IT to structure the organization	50.0%	54.5%	46.0% LOWER	64.0% HIGHER	62.5% HIGHER
Emphasis on horizontal management	62.0%	55.5%	61.0%	58.5%	68.5%
	Differences between the five clusters of countries on the Performance Management Variables				
Emphasis on measuring and promoting customer service	67.5% MEDIUM	82.0% HIGHER	50.0% LOWER	51.5% LOWER	66.5%
Emphasis on rewarding innovation/creativity	70.3%	62.7%	66.3%	67.3%	74.0%
Link between pay and individual performance	67.5%	64.5%	72.0%	70.0%	60.5%

HRM practices and policies for competitive advantage worldwide

Survey items	US Anglo American cluster	France	Japan	Korea	Brazil South American cluster
Shared benefits, risks and pay for team performance	71.3% HIGHER	49.7%	40.1% LOWER	49.3%	60.7% MEDIUM
Differences between the five clusters of countries on the Resourcing Variables					
Emphasis on external resourcing	57.5%	50.0%	56.5%	42.0%	52.0%
Emphasis on training and careers	71.0%	60.7%	64.0% LOWER	81.5% HIGHER	73.3%
Emphasis on managing outflows	29.5% LOWER	40.5%	26.5% LOWER	34.0%	42.5% HIGHER
Differences between the five clusters of countries on the Communication and Corporate Responsibility Variables					
Emphasis on communication	85.0%	86.0%	83.0%	72.0%	81.0%
Emphasis on corporate responsibility	39.0%	28.6%	32.4%	37.4%	41.6%

Discussion and summary

There are several ways in which we could discuss the results of this analysis of possible differences among firms from different nations as they seek to gain competitive advantage through their HRM practices. We could look at differences between countries across each of the fifteen dimensions of HRM that have been examined, or focus on overall country strategies (as reflected by the different priorities given to each area of HRM), or consider the relationship between cultural stereotypes of nations and the results obtained in this study. Each of these approaches provides complementary insights, therefore we discuss the findings from all three angles.

Paul Sparrow, Randall S. Schuler and Susan E. Jackson

Relationship to cultural stereotypes

It is useful to compare and contrast the results regarding our hypothesis (particularly the national clusters of countries) with other identified clusters of countries associated with cultural stereotypes (Adler, 1991; Hofstede, 1980, 1993; Phatak, 1992; Johnson and Golembiewski, 1992; and Laurent, 1991) or with studies on the management of change (Moss-Kanter, 1991). The Anglo-American cluster identified in this study contains very similar members to those identified in Moss-Kanter's (1991) study of 12,000 survey respondents worldwide. The United States, Australia, the United Kingdom and Canada were also grouped into a common cluster by Moss-Kanter (1991). There is an Anglo-American or Anglo-Saxon business culture that unites these countries. It is stereotyped in terms of openness and equality. This is reflected in the results on both the culture change items (particularly the 'promoting diversity and equality' variable) on which the Anglo-American cluster scores significantly higher than, for example, France and Japan. Firms in the Anglo-American cluster see this cultural openness as one of their most important ways of gaining competitive advantage, reflecting the academic literature that describes future problems of demography in terms of the need to cope with diversity (Johnston and Packer, 1987). This cultural stereotype of openness and equality is also reflected in the results on the structuring items, where the Anglo-American cluster places a significantly higher emphasis on the criticality of flexible work practices and the lowest emphasis on the need for centralization and vertical hierarchy. It is interesting to note that in Moss-Kanter's (1991) study, Germany formed part of a North European cluster of countries and Italy formed part of a Latin cluster of countries. In contrast, our study suggests that, where people management issues are concerned, the relative emphasis these countries expect to give in the year 2000 to the fifteen dimensions of HRM places them in the Anglo-American camp.

Our study indicated that Japan stands alone with a unique cluster of HRM emphases. This was also the case in Moss-Kanter's (1991) study, which is why she called Japan a cultural island. It is interesting to note that, although Japan faces even more severe demographic problems than the Anglo-American countries, it does not place as high an emphasis on the cultural variables of empowerment, diversity and equality, but places greater emphasis on centralization and vertical hierarchy. Japan gave lowest importance for gaining competitive advantage to promoting empowerment, diversity and equality, reflecting the cultural importance given in Japan to respect for authority and its more homogeneous ethnic culture.

HRM practices and policies for competitive advantage worldwide

In Moss-Kanter's (1991) study France formed part of a North European cluster of countries. The only difference noted in this study is that Germany does not share the same pattern of HRM emphases as France. The results obtained for the French cluster also strongly reflect Hofstede's (1980) findings on culture. In Hofstede's analysis French managers have a higher power distance score (68) in comparison for example with British managers (35). There are greater differences in formal power across management hierarchies in France and managers are more tolerant of such inequalities of power. French managers also have a higher uncertainty avoidance score (86) in comparison to British managers (35) and might be expected to seek to eliminate uncertainty and ambiguity in their tasks. The way in which the manager–subordinate relationship enables them to do this nevertheless remains a delicate point in France (Poirson, 1993). The fear of face to face conflict, the way in which authority is conceived, and the mode of selection of senior managers all act as powerful cultural forces that make it difficult for French organizations readily to adopt Anglo-American management concepts (such as performance management). Rojot (1990) paints French corporate culture as one that creates situations in which subordinate managers seek more responsibility, but in fact remain passive, fear to commit themselves to specific objectives and mostly look for protection from above. Senior managers rule autocratically and see the organization as an élite school in which they are the most intelligent and subordinates therefore cannot conceivably have valid ideas. French managers are therefore more possessive of their individual autonomy. Their reaction is: 'I know my job, if I am controlled, this means they have no confidence in me' (Poirson, 1993). Even where Anglo-American concepts of HRM are adopted, they become 'the stake of a different game' (Rojot, 1990: 98).

Both our study and that of Moss-Kanter (1991) revealed Korea as another cultural island. The Korean results in our study reflect Korea's higher emphasis on protectionism, strong sense of corporate paternalism, preference for centralization and greater optimism for the future, as noted by Moss-Kanter (1991). The utilization of information technology to help do so appears consistent with the image of Korea as a nation that is respectful of authority and very hierarchically organized.

Recently, attention has been directed to the unique features of Latin America in terms of HRM (Baker, Smith and Weiner, 1993; Baker *et al.*, 1992; Nash, 1993). Moss-Kanter (1991) identified a Latin cluster of countries consisting of South American nations, Italy and Spain. Similarly, we found that the South American countries of

285

Paul Sparrow, Randall S. Schuler and Susan E. Jackson

Mexico, Argentina and Brazil were clustered together. The one difference was that Italy seems to adopt an Anglo-American perspective on future HRM practices for competitive advantage. Recent analyses of HRM in Italy and the European Latin countries (Camuffo and Costa, 1992; Filella, 1991) support this finding. The Latin cluster has many features similar to the Anglo-American cluster, such as promotion of an empowerment culture, high decentralization, high emphasis on using IT to support structuring in organizations and a high desire to seek a sharing of benefits and risks in reward systems which may reflect the high levels of privatization occurring in those countries. The Latin cluster differs from the Anglo-American cluster in that it places more value on the need to manage outflows from organizations and less emphasis on the need for flexible work practices.

National HRM strategies

In this section we discuss the survey findings in relation to national patterns of HRM and draw upon other research to provide the necessary context to interpret the survey findings. Naturally, this section focuses on differences between countries. These differences should not be overstated, however, for balanced against these are the underlying convergences that are reducing many of these differences. These convergences will be discussed in the following section.

> European-style class consciousness, a serious socialist movement . . . penetration of Marxist ideology in 'old Europe' . . . have variously served to structure both the perception and reality of superior–subordinate and management–worker relations in industry.
>
> (Lawrence, 1992: 12)

Lawrence (1992) argues that HRM is essentially an Anglo-Saxon construct that has been 'grafted on', but has not 'taken root', in Continental Europe. Classic HRM functions such as recruitment, socialization, training and development are determined by different conceptions of management in Europe, and underpinned by a related set of values. Historically, HRM has not had the same élan and in part has been socially and culturally bypassed. When compared with American (or indeed British) concepts of HRM, a European model needs to take account of a number of factors. The distinctions drawn between concepts of HRM prevalent in continental Europe as opposed to the Anglo-American model (Brewster and Hegewisch, 1993; Pieper, 1990) include more restricted employer autonomy, difficult hiring and firing decisions, lower geographic and professional employee mobility and a stronger link between type of education and career progression. There is an increased role of 'social partners' in

HRM practices and policies for competitive advantage worldwide

the employment relationship, a stronger role of trade unions' influence in the setting of HRM policy, collective bargaining at the state and regional level and direct co-determination at the firm level. Finally, there are higher levels of government intervention or support in many areas of HRM, a state role in education through public school and university systems, formal certification systems influencing personnel selection and careers and more comprehensive welfare policies.

It is therefore all the more interesting that Germany and Italy, as two continental European countries, actually fell within the Anglo-American cluster. However, a preliminary analysis of this cluster suggests that, while the constituent members are all more like each other than they are like the other countries (France, Korea, Japan and so forth), there are still likely to be some significant differences in HRM practices within the cluster. Germany and Italy 'joined' the Anglo-American cluster only towards the end of the mathematical forcing process (see Figure 1), and could be considered as worth separate investigation. A useful area for further investigation would be national pathways and statistical differences within the regional clusters.

The characteristics of French HRM (recently discussed by several authors such as Barsoux and Lawrence, 1990; Besse, 1992; Poirson, 1993; Rojot, 1990) as revealed by our analysis support many of the cultural distinctions drawn above. For example, the strong French educational élite, distinct cadres of management and an extremely rigid hierarchical approach to both performance and career management is reflected in the significantly lower rating given to a culture based on diversity and equality as well as a significantly higher emphasis given to centralization and vertical hierarchy. However, the context within which HRM in France is practised has changed considerably over the last ten years (Poirson, 1993; Rojot, 1990). Increased and globalized competition, the growth of multinational organizations, the shortening of product life-cycles and the growing importance of product quality have all provided a new justification of managerial authority in France, and a new language among the employers' associations and bodies has legitimized a number of management and HRM practices, including performance management (Rojot, 1990). A 1987 survey by Hay France of 220 French organizations employing more than 65,000 managers found that 91 per cent had a policy of fixing individual objectives for managers, 81 per cent evaluated performance in relation to these objectives and 87 per cent had an annual performance appraisal review meeting. This renewed fervour for and emphasis on objectives-based performance management is reflected in the French sample high rating for the need to emphasize the promotion and measurement of customer service.

Paul Sparrow, Randall S. Schuler and Susan E. Jackson

Many of our findings reflect the existing competence and perceived priorities in the Japanese HRM system (see Aoki, 1988; Dore, 1986; Koike, 1987) and reveal the unique approach to HRM created by its internal labour market. Japanese HRM has been characterized by hierarchical pyramid-type organizations with bureaucratic control. The Japanese respondents rated an emphasis on centralization and vertical hierarchy as significantly more critical than the Anglo-American cluster (30 per cent compared to 6 per cent). However, the Korean and French samples placed an even greater emphasis on these issues. Performance in Japan is evaluated in the long term and there is a model of life-time employment. Skills are firm-specific and there is a reliance on in-house specific on-the-job training. Not surprisingly, our Japanese sample rated the need to manage outflows from the organization significantly lower than Brazil or France and placed a lower emphasis on training and development (linked to careers as opposed to jobs) given the existing high levels of informal on-the-job training.

Communication in Japan is more informal and relies on managerial networks. Promotion systems (particularly to senior management level) are more geared to an educational élite (Koike, 1987; Whitley, 1992b), female participation rates are low and there is a marked labour market segmentation between core (65 to 90 per cent) employees and lower status, higher mobility, temporary workers. This is reflected in the survey finding that the Japanese sample provided a significantly lower rating to the criticality of promoting a culture that promotes diversity and equality (42 per cent compared to 53 per cent in the Anglo-American cluster).

Japanese wage differentials are based on hierarchy and have remained fairly stable, despite the pressures for change discussed later. Bonuses in Japan are not regarded as a reward or dividend of profit, as in the Anglo-Saxon countries, but are taken more for granted and assumed to be part of regular earnings. Despite the fact they account for around 33 per cent of nominal salaries (Aoki, 1988), they do not decrease even in difficult times (Sano, 1993). Jobs are also highly segmented. The survey data reflected this paradox with the Japanese sample giving a significantly lower rating to pay systems that share risks and benefits or reward team performance (40 per cent compared to 71 per cent in the Anglo-American cluster).

More recently a number of reviews have pointed to growing pressure for change in the Japanese model of HRM (see, for example, Sano, 1993; Sasajima, 1993; Takahaski, 1990). Japanese organizations are facing a crisis and their traditional patterns of HRM are under structural pressure to change. Increasing difficulties are being faced in maintaining employment security and automatic pay increase systems.

HRM practices and policies for competitive advantage worldwide

Demographic pressures have resulted in an ageing work-force with an increasingly long length of service (Sano, 1993), creating fears about skills shortages and upward pressure on labour costs. Education levels have increased markedly, as have female participation and part-time work (these pressures are also apparent in the US and Europe). It is interesting to note that the Japanese sample provided the lowest rating to the importance of promoting an empowerment culture. This could be interpreted in two contrasting ways: a reflection of the fact that the Japanese HRM system already achieves this, and so it is a lower priority for the future, or a recognition by Japanese managers that external pressures may interfere with their ability to maintain this type of culture.

Some authors have argued that in Japan new technology is being used increasingly to deskill jobs and combine business processes because productivity of more senior and skilled employees is falling. However, our survey data do not appear to reflect this concern. The Japanese sample viewed the use of IT to structure the organization as significantly less important compared to, for example, the Korean and Brazilian samples.

Wilkinson (1988) has noted that some features of the Korean labour system resemble those of the Japanese, such as the segmentation of the labour market (our data supported this with both countries rating the need to promote an empowerment culture or culture based on diversity and equality as low) and overall philosophy behind their reward systems (similarly supported by our analysis showing no significant differences between Korean and Japan on any of the four dimensions used to examine performance management). However, a number of writers have noted a number of striking differences between Japanese and Korean labour systems (Biggart, 1989; Chung and Lee, 1988; Deyo, 1989; Michell, 1988; Park, 1992; Sharma, 1991; Shin and Chin, 1989; Whitley, 1992b; Yoo and Lee, 1987). In contrast to Japan, labour turnover in the manufacturing sector in Korea is high (Amsden, 1989) and managerial mobility is high (Biggart, 1989). This is perhaps reflected in our finding that Japan places a low emphasis on the importance of managing outflows from the organization (27 per cent) in comparison to Korea (34 per cent), although the difference is not significant. Similarly, Michell (1988) reported lower employer commitment to employee welfare in Korea than Japan, mainly because its labour-intensive industries (such as textiles) are following cost leadership strategies. Even in capital-intensive industries, lifelong employment is not seen as an ideal. Our analysis revealed that the Korean sample placed a significantly higher emphasis on work structuring through the use of IT and on centralization

International Human Resource Management

Paul Sparrow, Randall S. Schuler and Susan E. Jackson

and the vertical hierarchy. These are two dimensions of structure that are often associated with newly industrializing countries and their attempts to drive cost savings and improvements to the business process and productivity.

Attention has also been drawn to the greater scope for manager and owner discretion in Korea, more authoritarian and directive supervisory style focused on task performance as opposed to the facilitation of group performance (Park, 1992; Whitley, 1992b), limited scope for supervisors to organize groups' work and lower levels of autonomy for workers in comparison to Japan (Deyo, 1989). We found only a marginally lower emphasis on the importance of horizontal management in Korea than in Japan and a more marked (but still insignificant) difference in the importance given to communication (72 per cent in Korea, the lowest of all five clusters, compared to 83 per cent in Japan). Perhaps reflecting a national desire to reduce this differential, recent moves towards democratization and the atypical Korean trends towards greater unionization (Park, 1992), the Korean sample placed higher importance on promoting an empowerment culture than did Japan (which, as discussed previously, may feel it has already achieved much in this area).

Recruitment decisions, while based on a university élite as in Japan, also differ in Korea. Shin and Chin (1989) argue that Korean selection and promotion decisions are more influenced by personal and regional networks and relationships than in Japan. Therefore, despite the acute labour shortages experienced in Korea since 1986 (Park, 1992) the lower level of formality in selection is reflected in our results, which show that in Korea only 42 per cent of the sample felt that an emphasis on external resourcing was critical, compared to 57 per cent of the Japanese sample, although again the difference was not significant. Amsden (1989) has also drawn attention to the high wages and fringe benefits (such as company housing, bonus payments and schooling for children) that characterize the Korean reward system. This is essentially a paternalistic system (without the Japanese guarantee of lifelong employment) in which loyalty is less directly incorporated into rewards systems than in Japan. However, as already noted, there were no significant differences between Japan and Korea on the four dimensions of performance management, although the Korean sample placed a lower emphasis on reward systems that share both benefits and risk or pay for team performance, but a higher emphasis on linking pay and individual performance, which seems to reflect the description of reward systems given by Amsden (1989).

HRM practices and policies for competitive advantage worldwide

Predictions about HRM practices for competitive advantage

The comparison of differences thus far have been made using the data for the year 2000. These data were used for two primary reasons. First, using HRM to gain a competitive advantage takes time; thus historical data would not be as much use as data which reflect expectations and plans for the year 2000. Second, data for the year 2000 would enable us to assess the extent to which there is a convergence or divergence occurring worldwide in the practice of HRM.

In making predictions about HRM practices and policies for competitive advantage, it is necessary to establish the baseline from which we started. In this study, the baseline is 1991. If we look at these results in conjunction with the results for the year 2000 we have a better basis not only for prediction but also for comparison across the clusters. Table 3 shows the differences in the importance ratings from respondents for the fifteen dimensions of HRM.

One clear pattern revealed by Table 3 is that the respondents in all the clusters rated all HRM items higher in the year 2000 than they did in the year 1991. This appears to be consistent with the academic and professional literature that suggests that management of people is becoming a more significant force in organizations, particularly now that capital, technology and the like are readily available to everyone. It also reflects the points we made in the section on national strategies which showed that in France and Japan there are increasing pressures to adapt their highly nationalistic models of HRM. Another observation and prediction is that, while people management is becoming important in all the countries surveyed, the countries will continue to exhibit differences, both in degree and in kind. For example, when it comes to promoting an empowerment culture, the Japanese are increasing as are the French, but the Anglo-American cluster is increasing much more (40–71 per cent vs. 40–53 per cent).

When examining Table 3 it is important to keep these percentage differences in mind. They often provide explanatory evidence as to why the differences are indeed different. For the item 'emphasis on communication' both Japan and Korea have small differences compared to the Anglo-American cluster. However, an examination of the original percentage shows that both Japan and Korea had originally rated this item substantially higher than the Anglo-American cluster. Is this suggesting that the Anglo-American cluster is 'playing catch-up'? Are we to assume that an understanding of future events is to be found in the Asian nations? Probably not. These differences more likely still reflect cultural and economic differences. Note that, while Japan and Korea are geographical neighbours to the United States,

Paul Sparrow, Randall S. Schuler and Susan E. Jackson

Table 3 *Differences in HRM between the five clusters: change from 1991–2000*

Survey items	US Anglo American cluster	France	Japan	Korea	Brazil South American cluster
Differences between the five clusters of countries on the Culture Change Variables					
Promoting empowerment culture	40–71 +31%	38–64 +26%	40–53 +13%	34–64 +30%	41–79 +38%
Promoting diversity and equality culture	31–53 +22%	20–37 +17%	28–43 +15%	18–50 +32%	23–40 +17%
Differences between the five clusters of countries on the Structuring Variables					
Emphasis on flexible work practices	26–60 +34%	24–40 +16%	32–55 +23%	15–54 +39%	17–47 +30%
Emphasis on centralization and vertical hierarchy	0–6 6%	15–53 +38%	13–30 +17%	25–51 +26%	11–10 −1%
Emphasis on utilizing IT to structure the organization	16–50 +34%	19–55 +36%	21–46 +25%	23–64 +41%	21–63 +42%
Emphasis on horizontal management	36–62 +26%	30–56 +26%	37–61 +24%	30–59 +29%	37–69 +32%
Differences between the five clusters of countries on the Performance Management Variables					
Emphasis on measuring and promoting customer service	40–68 +28%	47–82 +35%	31–50 +19%	34–52 +18%	36–67 +31%
Emphasis on rewarding innovation/creativity	35–70 +35%	32–63 +31%	41–66 +25%	40–67 +27%	40–74 +34%
Link between pay and individual performance	52–68 +16%	42–65 +23%	44–72 +28%	45–70 +25%	48–61 +13%

292

HRM practices and policies for competitive advantage worldwide

Survey items	US Anglo American cluster	France	Japan	Korea	·Brazil South American cluster
Shared benefits, risks and pay for team performance	40–71 +31%	23–50 +27%	18–40 +22%	23–49 +26%	24–61 +37%
	Differences between the five clusters of countries on the Resourcing Variables				
Emphasis on external resourcing	24–58 +34%	37–50 +13%	41–57 +16%	40–42 +2%	23–52 +29%
Emphasis on training and careers	38–71 +33%	43–61 +18%	52–64 +12%	60–82 +22%	59–73 +14%
Emphasis on managing outflows	13–30 +17%	13–41 +28%	7–27 +20%	7–34 +27%	14–43 +29%
	Differences between the five clusters of countries on the Communication and Corporate Responsibility Variables				
Emphasis on communication	57–85 +28%	57–86 +29%	74–83 +9%	62–72 +10%	48–81 +33%
Emphasis on corporate responsibility	18–39 +21%	14–29 +15%	16–32 +16%	18–38 +20%	27–42 +15%

overall their results are rather different. In fact, Australia is regarded by some as being in the Asia Pacific region, yet it falls into the Anglo-American cluster in the original analysis.

These observations about Table 3 being so noted, what other predictions about convergence can we offer concerning HRM practices and policies for competitive advantage?

1. The *culture change* dimensions: Firms in all clusters are seeing that it is likely to be useful to empower their employees more than today, and to promote a more diverse and egalitarian culture. As the world's work-force becomes more educated it is demanding more involvement and participation in work-place decisions and events. Tasks and knowledge, as well as employee

needs and abilities, appear to be driving this trend in huma resource practices. A related prediction here is that there will b continued examination of the role of the manager, with contir ued pressure for change in that role.

2. The *structuring* dimensions: Following from the first prediction i the second: as the task and knowledge determine the involve ment of employees and the role of the manager, they also impac on the structure of the operation. In particular, they make it nec essary for work practices to be more flexible to change as the skills and abilities needed to do them change. This removes the sole responsibility for decision making from the hierarchy to those in the know and those generally nearest the action.

3. The *performance management* dimensions: There is likely to be enhanced emphasis on obtaining performance and making performance a centre of attention. In particular, performance related to serving the customer would appear to be of most importance. This will be closely followed by an emphasis on the performance related to innovation, new products and services (of course, designed with the customer in mind). To reinforce these emphases, remuneration schemes at both the individual and team level are likely to be implemented in significant numbers during this decade. There will be a greater sharing of risks and rewards. With the emphasis on promoting a culture of equality, this might also mean that greater sharing will occur at all levels of management and non-management employees.

4. The *resourcing* dimensions: Flexibility will be desired and sought regarding all areas of the business. Just as there is likely to be more flexibility with regard to job assignments and decisions, there is likely to be more flexibility regarding staffing decisions, both at the entry and exit stages. That is, firms might be likely to seek greater use of part-time or temporary workers to fill positions, and not bring them into full-time employee status. Perhaps for the full-time employees, firms will dedicate more resources to training and retraining. This will make the current work-force (the one that is more empowered and is making more decisions) more important to the organization. Nevertheless, even this work-force may need to be replaced. Knowledge is doubling every seven years. To capture this, firms may need to be constantly incorporating new members and new ideas. This will demand constant change and adaptation by all. For some this may mean a need to exit from the organization. Consequently, firms will be equally concerned about managing the egress of employees. They will want to ensure that this is

HRM practices and policies for competitive advantage worldwide

predictable and that employees with key skills, today and in the future, do not suddenly leave the firm.

5. The *communication and corporate responsibility* dimensions: While organizations are likely to get more involved in community activities, particularly training and education, they are likely still to want employees to focus on the firm. Consequently, they will devote more resources to communicating and sharing the goals and objectives of the organization with all employees. This will facilitate the empowerment of employees and help ensure that the decisions made by employees are as consistent with the needs of the business as those made by top management.

Conclusions

The function of managing people in organizations is perceived as important today for firms to gain competitive advantage. This level of importance, however, pales in comparison to the importance it is expected to have in the year 2000. While this is likely due to greater access organizations have to capital and technology, it is also likely due to a growing recognition that people do make a difference. Thus, this relatively under-utilized resource called 'people' is likely to receive greater attention from organizations throughout this decade, at least for firms seeking to be effective in highly competitive environments.

While 'to receive greater attention' is likely to vary across firms, it is not expected to vary widely concerning several key themes or foci. These include the following: a greater emphasis on empowerment, equality, diversity management, flexibility in job design and assessment, flatter organizational structures, customer-based measures of performance and related remuneration schemes, flexibility in staffing decisions, training decisions and exiting decisions, and greater communication of the objectives and goals of the firm to all employees.

Although the country clusters reported in this study did illustrate differences to these key themes, they also reflected similarity. The differences are probably better described as being more 'in degree' than 'in kind'. Thus, while it might be tempting to conclude that there is clearly a convergence rather than divergence in the practices and policies used by organizations to manage their human resources, this might be overstating the reality (as well as the complexity) of managing human resources effectively. Employees do reflect the larger society and culture from which they come to the organization. From this they bring education and skill, attitude towards work and organization and general expectations about their role and responsibility in the

Paul Sparrow, Randall S. Schuler and Susan E. Jackson

organization. The impact and relevance of these should not be under-stated. Thus, while it may be tempting to conclude by using the term 'convergence', it may be more an attempt to simplify reality prematurely. Our research findings revealed a number of disjunctures with the academic literature, particularly with regard to the use of new technology in Japan to deskill jobs, differences between Japanese and Korean reward systems, and the level of similarity between German and Italian patterns of HRM and Anglo-American patterns. Such disjunctures should be noted as areas for further research.

This state of affairs, however, offers opportunity more than it does frustration. It offers competitive advantage to those firms willing to survey systematically their employees and adopt and adapt human resource practices appropriate for the situation. Yet, this situation is likely to reflect the nation in which the operation is located. But, at the end of the day, these reflections may be more at the margin than at the core. Observe the operations of Nissan and Honda in England in comparison to their operations in Japan (Wickens, 1987). Thus organizations seeking to have a truly global operation are likely to pursue the above stated key themes in the work-place with human resource practices that have some cross-cultural variation, but that can all be fitted under a common policy umbrella.

Paul Sparrow
Manchester Business School
UK
Randall S. Schuler
Susan E. Jackson
New York University
USA

Acknowledgements

The authors wish to thank the IBM Corporation and Towers Perrin for conducting the worldwide study and their report entitled *Priorities for Gaining Competitive Advantage*.

References

Adler, N.J. (1991) *International Dimensions of Organisational Behaviour*. Boston, MA: PWS-Kent.
Amsden, A.H. (1989) *Asia's Next Giant*. Oxford: Oxford University Press.
Aoki, M. (1988) *Information, Incentives and Bargaining in the Japanese Economy*. Cambridge: Cambridge University Press.

296

HRM practices and policies for competitive advantage worldwide

Baker. S., Smith, G., Weiner, E. and Jacobson, K. (1992) 'Latin America: The Big Move to Free Markets', *Business Week*, 15 June: 50–62.

Baker. S., Smith G. and Weiner, E. (1993) 'The Mexican Worker', *Business Week*, 19 April: 84–92.

Barsoux, J.L. and Lawrence, P. (1990) *Management in France.* London: Cassell Education.

Bartlett, C.A. and Ghoshal, S. (1992) 'What is a Global Manager?', *Harvard Business Review*, 70 (5): 124–32.

Beer, M., Spector, B., Lawrence, P.R., Mills, D.Q. and Walton, R.E. (1984) *Managing Human Assets.* New York: The Free Press.

Besse, D. (1992) 'Finding a New Raison d'Etre: Personnel Management in France', *Personnel Management*, 24 (8): 40–3.

Biggart, N.W. (1989) 'Institutionalised Patrimonialism in Korean Business', Program in East Asian culture and development research, *Working Paper No. 23, Institute of Governmental Affairs.* University of California: Davies.

Black, J.S., Gregersen, H.B. and Mendenhall, P. (1992) *Global Assignments.* San Francisco: Jossey-Bass.

Boam, R. and Sparrow, P.R. (eds) (1992) *Designing and Achieving Competency.* London: McGraw-Hill.

Brewster, C. and Hegewisch, A. (1993) 'Personnel Management in Europe: A Continent of Diversity', *Personnel Management*, 25 (1): 36–40.

Brewster, C. and Tyson, S. (eds) (1991) *International Comparisons in Human Resource Management.* London: Pitman.

Brewster, C., Hegewisch, A. and Lockhart, J.T. (1991) 'Researching Human Resource Management: Methodology of the Price Waterhouse Cranfield Project on European Trends', *Personnel Review*, 20 (6): 36–40.

Burns, T. and Stalker, G.R. (1961) *The Management of Innovation.* London: Tavistock.

Camuffo, A. and Costa, G. (1992) 'Strategic Human Resource Management – Italian Style', *Sloan Management Review*, 34 (2): 59–67.

Chung, K.H. and Lee, H.C. (eds) (1988) *Korean Managerial Dynamics.* London: Praeger.

Daft, R.L. (1992) *Organization Theory and Design.* St Paul, Minneapolis: West Publishing.

Deyo, F.C. (1989) *Beneath the Miracle: Labour Subordination in the New Asian Industrialism.* Berkeley, CA: University of California Press.

Dore, R.P. (1986) *Flexible Rigidities.* Stanford, CA: Stanford University Press.

Dowling, P.J. and Schuler, R.S. (1990) *International Dimensions of Human Resource Management.* Boston: PWS-Kent.

Filella, J. (1991) 'Is There a Latin Model in the Management of Human Resources?', *Personnel Review*, 20 (6): 14–23.

Ghoshal, S. and Bartlett, C.A. (1989) 'The Multinational Corporation as an Interorganisational Network', *Academy of Management Review*, 15 (4): 603–25.

Grant, R.M. (1991) 'The Resource-Based Theory of Competitive Advantage: Implications for Strategy Formulation', *California Management Review*, 33 (3): 114–35.

Hamel, G. and Prahalad, C.K. (1991) 'Corporate Imagination and Expeditionary Marketing', *Harvard Business Review*, 69 (4): 81–92.

Hofstede, G. (1980) *Culture's Consequences: International Differences in Work-Related Values.* London: Sage.

Hofstede, G. (1993) 'Cultural Constraints in Management Theories'. *Academy of Management Executive*, 7 (1): 81–93.

Paul Sparrow, Randall S. Schuler and Susan E. Jackson

Johnson, K.R. and Golembiewski, R.T. (1992) 'National Culture in Organization Development: A Conceptual and Empirical Analysis', *International Journal of Human Resource Management*, 3, 1: 71–84.

Johnston, W.B. and Packer, A.E. (1987) *Workforce 2000: Work and Workers for the 21st Century*. Washington, DC: US Government Printing Office.

Koike, K. (1987) 'Human Resource Development and Labour Management Relations'. In Yamamura, K. and Yashuba, Y. (eds) *The Political Economy of Japan. 2. The Domestic Transformation*. Stanford, CA: Stanford University Press

Laurent, A. (1991) 'Managing Across Cultures and National Borders'. In S.G. Makridakis (ed.) *Single Market Europe: Opportunities and Challenges for Business*. London: Jossey Bass.

Lawler, E.E. (1991) 'The New Plant Approach: A Second Generation Approach', *Organizational Dynamics*, Summer: 5–15.

Lawrence, P. (1992) 'Management Development in Germany'. In Tyson, S., Lawrence, P., Poirson, P., Manzolini, L. and Vincente, C.S. (eds) *Human Resource Management in Europe: Strategic Issues and Cases*. London: Kogan Page.

Michell, T. (1988) *From a Developing to a Newly Industrialised Country: The Republic of Korea, 1961–82*. Geneva: International Labour Organisation.

Mitrani, A., Dalziel, M. and Fitt, D. (eds) (1992) *Competency-Based Human Resource Management*. London: Kogan Page.

Moss-Kanter, R. (1991) 'Transcending Business Boundaries: 12,000 World Managers View Change', *Harvard Business Review*, 69 (3): 151–64.

Nash, N. (1993) 'A New Rush into Latin America', *The New York Times*, 11 April, Sec. 3: 1–6.

Park, D.J. (1992) 'Industrial Relations in Korea', *International Journal of Human Resource Management*, 3 (1): 105–24.

Peters, T. (1992) *Liberation Management: Necessary Disorganisation for the Nanosecond Nineties*. London: Macmillan.

Phatak, A.V. (1992) *International Dimensions of Management.*. Boston, MA: PWS-Kent.

Pieper, R. (ed.) (1990) *Human Resource Management: An International Comparison*. Berlin: de Gruyter.

Poirson, P. (1993) 'The Characteristics and Dynamics of Human Resource Management in France'. In Tyson, S., Lawrence, P., Poirson, P., Manzolini, L. and Vincente, C.S. (eds) *Human Resource Management in Europe: Strategic Issues and Cases*. London: Kogan Page.

Poole, M.J.F. (1986) *Industrial Relations: Origins and Patterns of National Diversity*. London: Routledge.

Poole, M.J.F. (1990) Editorial: 'Human Resource Management in an International Perspective', *International Journal of Human Resource Management*, 1: 1–16.

Porter, M.E. (1980) *Competitive Strategy: Techniques for Analysing Industries and Competitors*. New York: Free Press.

Porter, M.E. (1990) *Competitive Advantage of Nations*. New York: The Free Press.

Punnett, B.J. and Ricks, D.A. (1992) *International Business*. Boston: PSW-Kent.

Räsäsen, K. and Whipp, R. (1992) 'National Business Recipes: A Sector Perspective'. In Whitley, R. (ed.) *European Business Systems: Firms and Markets in National Contexts*. London: Sage.

Reich, R.B. (1990) 'Who is Us?', *Harvard Business Review*, 68 (1): 53–64.

HRM practices and policies for competitive advantage worldwide

Rojot, J. (1990) 'Human Resource Management in France'. In Pieper, R. (ed.) *Human Resource Management: An International Comparison.* Berlin: de Gruyter.

Ronen, S. (1986) *Comparative and Multinational Management.* New York: Wiley.

Sabel, C., Herrigel, G., Deeg, R. and Kazis, R. (1987). 'Regional Prosperities Compared: Massachusetts and Basen-Württemberg in the 1980s', *Discussion Paper of the Research Unit Labour Market and Employment.* Wissenschaftszentrum: Berlin.

Sano, Y. (1993) 'Changes and Continued Stability in Japanese HRM Systems: Choice in the Share Economy', *International Journal of Human Resource Management*, 4 (1): 11–28.

Sasajima, Y. (1993) 'Changes in Labour Supply and their Impacts on Human Resource Management: The Case of Japan', *International Journal of Human Resource Management*, 4 (1): 29–44.

Schuler, R.S. (1992) 'Strategic Human Resource Management: Linking the People with the Strategic Needs of the Business', *Organizational Dynamics*, 21 (1): 18–31.

Schuler, R.S. and MacMillan, I. (1984) 'Creating Competitive Advantage Through Human Resource Management Practices', *Human Resource Management*, 23: 241–55.

Sharma, B. (1991) 'Industrialisation and Strategy Shifts in Industrial Relations: A Comparative Study of South Korea and Singapore'. In Brewster, C. and Tyson, S. (eds) *International Comparisons in Human Resource Management.* London: Pitman.

Shin, E.H. and Chin, S.W. (1989) 'Social Affinity among Top Managerial Executives of Large Corporations in Korea', *Sociological Forum*, 4: 3–26.

Takahashi, Y. (1990) 'Human Resource Management in Japan'. In Pieper, R. (ed.) *Human Resource Management: An International Comparison.* Berlin: de Gruyter.

Torrington, D., Hall, L., Haylor, I. and Myers, J. (1991) *Employee Resourcing*, Wimbledon:. Institute of Personnel Management.

Towers Perrin (1992) *Priorities for Gaining Competitive Advantage: A Worldwide Human Resource Study.* London: Towers Perrin.

Walker, J. (1992) *Human Resource Strategy.* New York: McGraw-Hill.

Whitley, R. (ed.) (1992a) *European Business Systems: Firms and Markets in their National Contexts.* London: Sage.

Whitley, R. (ed.) (1992b) *Business Systems in East Asia: Firms, Markets and Societies.* London: Sage.

Wickens, D. (1987) *The Road to Nissan.* London: Macmillan.

Wilkinson, B. (1988) 'A Comparative Analysis'. In *Technological Change, Work Organisation and Pay: Lessons from Asia.* Geneva: International Labour Organization.

Yoo, S. and Lee, S.M. (1987) 'Management Style and Practice of Korean Chaebols', *California Management Review*, 29 (4): 95–110.

[15]

A CROSS-NATIONAL COMPARATIVE STUDY OF WORK–FAMILY STRESSORS, WORKING HOURS, AND WELL-BEING: CHINA AND LATIN AMERICA VERSUS THE ANGLO WORLD

PAUL E. SPECTOR
Department of Psychology
University of South Florida

CARY L. COOPER
Department of Management
University of Manchester Institute of Science and Technology, U.K.

STEVEN POELMANS
IESE Business School
University of Navarra, Spain

TAMMY D. ALLEN
Department of Psychology
University of South Florida

MICHAEL O'DRISCOLL
Department of Psychology
University of Waikato, New Zealand

JUAN I. SANCHEZ
Department of Management
Florida International University

OI LING SIU
Department of Politics and Sociology
Lingnan University, Hong Kong

PHIL DEWE
Department of Organizational Psychology
Birkbeck College, U.K.

PETER HART
Insight SRC Pty. Ltd., Australia

LUO LU
Department of Psychology
Fu-Jen University, Taiwan

The authors thank Alfonso Bolio (IPADE, Universidad Panamericana, Mexico), Pablo Ferreiro De Babot (Universidad de Piura, Peru), Raul Lagomarsino (IEEM, Universidad de Montevideo, Uruguay), Antonio Rodriguez Lopez (IDE, Ecuador), Alejandro Sioli (IAE, Universidad Austral, Argentina), and Carlos Portales (Escuela de Administracion y Economia, Universidad Catolica, Chile) for their help in the data collection in Latin America.

Correspondence and requests for reprints should be addressed to Paul E. Spector, Department of Psychology, University of South Florida, Tampa, FL 33620; spector@chuma.cas.usf.edu

120   PERSONNEL PSYCHOLOGY

LÚCIO FLÁVIO RENAULT DE MORAES
Department of Administrative Sciences
Federal University of Minas Gerais, Brazil

GABRIELLE M. OSTROGNAY
International Survey Research, Australia

KATE SPARKS
Department of Management
University of Manchester Institute of Science and Technology, U.K.

PAUL WONG
Department of Psychology
Trinity Western University, Canada

SHANFA YU
Department of Occupational Health
Henan Institute of Occupational Medicine, PR China

A comparative study of work–family stressors, work hours, and well-being was described contrasting 3 culturally distinct regions: Anglo (Australia, Canada, England, New Zealand, and U.S.), China (Hong Kong, People's Republic of China, and Taiwan) and Latin America (Argentina, Brazil, Colombia, Ecuador, Mexico, Peru, and Uruguay). Samples of managers were surveyed in each country, and country data were combined for the 3 regions. Support was found for the hypothesis that Anglos would demonstrate a stronger positive relation between work hours and work–family stressors than Chinese and Latins. In all 3 samples, work–family stressors related to increased job satisfaction and reduced well-being. Latins were found to work the most hours, have the most children, and report the highest job satisfaction. China was the only region in which being married and having more children related positively to all measures of well-being.

The past decade has steadily seen increasing interest in the impact that work–family issues have on employees, family members, and organizations. This rising interest in the nexus between work and family is not surprising because new technologies are placing increasing demands on many employees. For instance, employers have now the ability to reach employees 24 hours per day, 7 days per week. This "24/7" access may distract employees' attention from family matters, and it can be expected that the more time a person spends on the job, the more conflict there is likely to be between work and family (Bruck, Allen, & Spector, 2002). It goes without saying that work–family issues are at least as important to organizational functioning as family functioning (Barnett, 1998). Much of the research on these issues has been from the occupational stress perspective, focusing on how an unbalanced work–family relationship can function as a stressor that affects strains and well-being both at work and at home. This literature has clearly shown a connection between work–family stressors and employee strain (e.g., Allen, Herst, Bruck, &

Sutton, 2000). However, most work–family research has been conducted in predominantly Anglo countries (e.g., Canada, U.K., and the U.S.) and other western countries that share similar cultural backgrounds and family structures. Work done elsewhere has been conducted mainly in Asia (see for example Aryee, Fields, & Luk, 1999), and little of it is comparative, limiting the extent that we can draw conclusions about generalizability of western findings.

The only published comparative work–family study of which we are aware is based on research reported by Yang, Chen, Choi, and Zhou (2000). They presented a theoretical analysis suggesting that Americans and Chinese will view work and family differently, due in large part to differences in their individualism–collectivism (I-C) values. We extended their thinking to predict that reactions to work hours will differ between western individualist nations such as the U.S. and not only collectivist China but collectivist Latin America as well. We followed their lead and adopted I-C as the core element of our theoretical framework because the only comparative study of work–family found support for it, and because I-C is a construct well researched in cross-cultural and cross-national studies.

Work–Family Issues From a Stress Perspective

A variety of work–family constructs has been studied in the context of occupational stress. By far the most popular has been work–family conflict (WFC), which is defined as a form of interrole conflict in which demands between family and work are incompatible (Greenhaus & Beutell, 1985). Based on role theory (Kahn, Wolfe, Quinn, Snoek, & Rosenthal, 1964; Katz & Kahn, 1978), the notion of WFC as a job stressor parallels the idea of within-role conflict as a stressor. Frone (2003) discussed a broader concept of work–family balance that includes both the negative side of conflict and the positive side of work–family facilitation in which one role enhances the other. In both cases he distinguishes work to family from family to work, that is, the extent that work conflicts with family versus family conflicts with work. Reviews of the WFC literature have clearly linked these constructs to strains. For example, Allen et al. (2000) conducted a meta-analysis linking WFC to a variety of attitudinal (e.g., job dissatisfaction), psychological (e.g., depression), and physical (e.g., somatic symptoms) strains. Kossek and Ozeki (1998) found in their meta-analysis that job satisfaction was associated with WFC (mean $r = -.27$).

Other family-related measures have been linked to strains. For example, Vinokur, Pierce, and Buck (1999) found that a measure of family stress (conflict among family members) and family distress (strength of negative emotional reactions to family members) related to depressive symptoms in U.S. Air Force women. Similarly, work interference with family was shown to relate to depression and somatic health symptoms (Major, Klein, & Ehrhart, 2002). All of these work–family conflict and stressor variables may be the result of family responsibilities that make both emotional and physical demands.

Family Responsibilities

Family responsibilities involve having to care for other family members, most commonly children and, increasingly, older family members. The level of family responsibilities can be considered a source of work–family stress, and it can be operationalized rather objectively as the number of children or others for whom the respondent has care responsibility. The life stages of children can be used to get a more precise indicator of demands (Rothausen, 1999).

Family responsibilities have been tied to perceptions of work–family conflict and other work–family stressors, as well as to strains. For example, Grandey and Cropanzano (1999) found that having children at home related to several work–family stress-related variables, including family distress, family role stress, and family/work conflict. Other researchers have linked family responsibilities to blood pressure levels (Brisson, et al., 1999; Lundberg & Frankenhaeuser, 1999). However, not all studies have shown such connections. For example, Major et al. (2002) failed to find a connection between parental demands and strains (depression and somatic health complaints). However, as a whole, these studies establish a connection between work–family stressors and at least some strains.

Working Hours

One of the major causes of work–family stressors has to do with insufficient time for both (Greenhaus & Beutell, 1985). Although relations are relatively small, some studies have shown that work–family conflict is related to number of working hours (e.g., Bruck et al., 2002; Eagle, Miles, & Icenogle, 1997; Major et al., 2002; Wallace, 1999; Yang et al., 2000). However, the relation of work hours with strains has been inconsistent (Barnett, Gareis, & Brennan, 1999). Although Frone, Yardley, and Markel (1997) found a significant correlation between work hours and WFC, they failed to find a significant correlation of work hours with family distress. In a meta-analysis Sparks, Cooper, Fried, and Shirom (1997) reported small mean correlations of weekly work hours with physiological health ($r = .06$) and psychological health ($r = .15$). In a recent study, Major et al. (2002) found only a .10 correlation of work hours with depression and no relation with somatic health symptoms. These weak effects on employee strains suggest that the mechanism through which work hours generate work–family stressors is still largely unknown. Barnett et al. (1999) cleverly argue that an important element that has been neglected has to do with fit; specifically whether or not the individual wants to work the hours he or she works. Indeed, any sample contains both people who are working the hours they want and people who are working more hours than they want. The fact that number of work hours fails to capture the employee's motivation to do so may explain the weak correlations with strains.

Work–Family Issues From a Cultural Perspective

Most studies on work–family issues have been conducted in predominantly Anglo countries (Canada, U.K., and the U.S.) and other western countries that share a number of important characteristics that distinguish them from many other regions of the world. For example, these countries tend to be economically developed and people live in nuclear families, often remote from more distant relatives, such as parents and siblings. In other areas, such as China and Latin America, people are more likely to live in close proximity to extended family, possibly due to a combination of their lower level of economic development and their higher level of familism (which can be seen as a facet of collectivism). The Anglo countries also share an important cultural characteristic of individualism as opposed to collectivism. In individualist countries, the primary concern of people may lie with their own goals and preferences, and those of their immediate nuclear families (Triandis, 1995). Markus and Kitayama (1998) termed this the independent self, whereas Kagitcibasi (1994) explains how individualists focus on personal autonomy. In collectivist countries, such as in Asia and Latin America (Hofstede, 1984), people view themselves as part of a larger social network that can include extended families and workgroups. Markus and Kitayama (1998) explain that collectivists express the interdependent self, and Kagitcibasi (1994) argues that in such cultures people are encouraged to explore belongingness needs. Falicov (2001) contrasts individualist Anglo Americans with collectivist Latinos, noting that for the latter, family connectedness and cohesiveness can take priority over the self.

There have been a few work–family studies outside of individualist countries, mostly in Asia. We were able to locate nine in Asian countries (Hong Kong, Japan, and Singapore), but only one was a comparison with the U.S., and the range of variables studied has been limited. Furthermore, these studies merely applied western ideas about WFC and similar constructs to Asia. Aryee et al. (1999) surveyed 320 working individuals in Hong Kong. Contrary to results in the U.S., they found a nonsignificant correlation of −.02 between WFC and job satisfaction. Likewise, Aryee, Luk, Leung, and Lo (1999) found a nonsignificant correlation between WFC and job satisfaction, and Aryee and Luk (1996) found nonsignificant correlations between WFC and career satisfaction for husbands and wives, both studies conducted in Hong Kong. On the other hand, Chiu (1998) found a significant −.24 correlation of WFC and job satisfaction in Hong Kong, and Aryee (1992) found significant correlations between WFC and job satisfaction for at least some subgroups in a Singapore sample. Chan, Lai, Ko, and Boey (2000) collected data on 2,589 professionals in Singapore, finding that WFC was related to job dissatisfaction and strain when controlling for a number of work-related, personality and demographic variables.

Aryee (1993) studied employed couples in Singapore, finding WFC to be associated with burnout. Matsui, Ohsawa, and Onglatco (1995) surveyed a sample of working women in Japan, including measures of parental demands (number of children), family/work conflict (FWC), and strain. They found that demands related to FWC ($r = .28$) but not to strain ($r = -.03$). However, FWC and strain were correlated at .47.

Yang et al. (2000) argued that I-C is an important variable in the work–family domain. Individualists emphasize personal accomplishment and achievement through work. There is a tendency for individuals to perceive time at work as time spent fulfilling personal ambition rather than tending to their family. Consistent with this view, Brett and Stroh (2003) found in a sample of managers working extremely long hours that a large part of their motivation involved achieving intrinsic rewards from the work. Thus, the individualist will tend to view the needs of the self and the family as distinct, and will experience conflict when there are demands made by both. In other words, the work and family domains are seen as exerting competing demands where addressing one will likely be at the expense of the other. As a result, when work time demands are high, individualists are bound to experience higher levels of work–family stressors and consequent strain than are collectivists.

In collectivist societies, according to Yang et al. (2000), people's focus is on the family's welfare. Work is seen not as a means of enhancing the self, but as a means of supporting the family. For example, Chinese traditionally view work as more important than leisure, and as contributing to family welfare instead of competing with it (Redding, 1993). Bu and McKeen (2000) found that Chinese business students were more committed to work than were Canadians and expected to work more hours. In addition, there may be less tendency for Chinese and other collectivists to consider home and work as independent domains, which may reflect more of a western point of view that is not universally held (Ishii-Kuntz, 1994).

The Yang et al. (2000) paper was concerned specifically with China in relation to the U.S. However, their theoretical arguments were based on I-C, which should generalize to other countries and regions that share cultural values with the U.S. (individualism) or China (collectivism). As Hofstede (1984) discusses, the most individualist countries in the world are Anglo countries, such as Australia, Canada, England, New Zealand, and U.S. The most collectivistic include China and Latin America, especially Colombia and Peru. Of course there are differences other than I-C among these countries/regions.

All this evidence leads to our expectation that, in comparing people from individualist versus collectivist countries, I-C at the country level will moderate the relation between working hours and work–family stress. Individualists will have a greater tendency to see work time as taking time from family, and so they will experience greater work–family stress in response to working long hours than will collectivists. This leads to our main hypothesis:

Hypothesis 1: Region of the world will moderate the relation between work–family stress and work hours; work hours will be positively related to work–family stress, with a stronger relation in individualist Anglo countries than in collectivist China or Latin America.

Current Study

There were two major purposes to this study. The first was to test our hypothesis that the relation between work hours and work–family stress would differ in collectivist and individualist countries. We chose three categories/regions of the world to compare: Anglo, China, and Latin America, because the latter two are considered the most collectivist regions of the world, whereas Anglo countries are the most individualistic (Hofstede, 1984). We did not assess I-C, but rather draw inferences about region differences based on prior research concerning average I-C levels in various countries. Although countries may vary in mean levels, it should be kept in mind that individuals within countries vary in I-C, and so not all individuals within a country will be individualists or collectivists. We report elsewhere (Spector et al., 2001b) results with Hofstede's VSM94 (Hofstede, 1994) I-C measure that managers show country differences as expected between four of our Anglo samples and our Chinese samples, that is, the Anglo samples were high (I) and the Chinese samples low (C) on the I-C scale. Although there were individual differences found within the 23 countries/regions compared, 11% of the variance was accounted for by country/region. We kept the occupation constant by limiting our participants to managers in order to control, at least to some extent, the nature of work. Clearly, there can be cultural and country differences in managers' jobs, but limiting the sample to managers should produce more homogeneity than studying a variety of different jobs. Another reason for studying managers is that this is a fairly demanding job with the likelihood of considerable variance in hours worked per week, as reflected in the range we observed in working hours.

A second purpose was to explore regional differences in other variables that have been important in the work–family domain, both in terms of mean level and intercorrelations. We included gender, number of children, marital status, intention of quitting, job satisfaction, mental well-being, and physical well-being. There is a great deal of research showing that greater work–family stress is associated with lesser job satisfaction and well-being. Thus, in Anglo samples, we would expect that work–family stress should be negatively associated with measures of job satisfaction, mental well-being, and physical well-being. There is no theoretical reason to expect different results outside of this region, and in fact, Chan et al. (2000) found similar results in Singapore with WFC as are typically found in the U.S. However, there has been very little comparative research upon which to base hypotheses, so this aspect of the present study was exploratory.

Method

Overview of the Study

The data reported here were from the Collaborative International Study of Managerial Stress (CISMS) founded in 1996 as a joint effort among a group of international researchers. Subsets of the CISMS data have been published elsewhere (Spector et al., 2001a; Spector et al., 2001b; Spector et al., 2002). Data were collected between 1997 and 2000. The current study includes data on additional Latin countries not previously published and incorporates data not previously reported.

Participants

Data were collected from 2,487 participants (all managers) across 15 samples that were placed into three groups according to region. Five samples were from English-speaking, Anglo countries: Australia, Canada, England, New Zealand, and U.S. Three were Chinese samples from Hong Kong, People's Republic of China (PRC), and Taiwan. Seven were from Latin American countries: Argentina, Brazil, Colombia, Ecuador, Mexico, Peru, and Uruguay. Our strategy was to classify the countries into regions based on country-level I-C scores in order to test our moderator hypothesis. We decided to break the collectivist countries into two regions because there are considerable cultural differences between China and Latin America. As noted below, analyses were conducted to control within-region differences, showing that results were not affected much by analyzing by region rather than country. To the extent possible samples were chosen to represent a wide range of organizations and industries.

The Anglo group was 66% male, with a mean age of 44.6 ($SD =$ 8.9), and mean job tenure of 11.2 years ($SD = 9$ years). The majority (84%) were married, 31% had children, and 56% had a partner working. The Chinese group was 60% male, with a mean age of 37.3 ($SD = 9.5$), and mean job tenure of 10.8 years ($SD = 9.3$ years). Most (72%) were married, 59% had children, and 61% had a partner who was working. The Latin group was 77% male, with a mean age of 37.8 ($SD = 9.2$), and mean job tenure of 10 years ($SD = 9.9$ years). Three-fourths (75%) were married, 92% had children, and 47% had a partner who worked. For the Anglo and Latin samples, a small percentage (11% and 8%, respectively) were first/low level managers compared to 40% for the Chinese. Managers indicated their functional area in five categories. About one-fifth of participants were in production (18% to 22% across the three samples), about one-sixth were in finance (13% to 19%), and about a tenth were in personnel (10% to 13%). The Anglo sample had 13%, whereas the Chinese and Latin samples had 22% and 32%, respectively in marketing. The remaining participants indicated other for their functional area.

Measures

A questionnaire was administered that contained the Occupational Stress Indicator-2 (OSI2; Williams & Cooper, 1996), and some additional scales that are not of interest here. Four subscales of the OSI2 were used in the present analyses: work–family pressure, job satisfaction, mental well-being, and psychological well-being. The OSI2, and its longer version the OSI is an instrument that was carefully developed to measure sources of stress (pressure), strains, and other variables relevant to the occupational stress process. Evidence for validity for these scales in the U.K. can be found in a number of sources (e.g., Cooper & Williams, 1991; Robertson, Cooper, & Williams, 1990). The *work–family pressure scale* consisted of 9 of the 60 pressure items asking the participant to rate on a 6-point scale the extent that each item is a source of pressure for them. Response choices range from 1 = *very definitely is not a source* to 6 = *very definitely is a source*. Items concern sources of pressure or stress that involve work and home, which is somewhat different from WFC, which assesses the extent that an individual perceives conflict but not the extent that it is perceived as stressful. Sample items include "taking my work home," "not being able to 'switch off' at home," "demands my work makes on relationships with spouse/children," and "pursuing a career at the expense of home life." High scores represent high levels of work–family pressure. The internal consistencies of this scale across the three regions ranged from .79 to .85. We conducted an exploratory factor analysis (common factor model with maximum zero-order correlation among items as the communality estimate) on these 9 items for the entire sample. The scree plot suggested a clear single factor with the first eigenvalue being 3.50 and accounting for 77% of total variance and all others being well below 1.0 (the second was .57). Factor loadings ranged from .51 to .72 on a single factor.

Three scales from the OSI2 assessed job satisfaction, mental well-being, and physical well-being. For consistency, all three were scored such that low scores indicate strain. The *job satisfaction scale* consisted of 12 items that ask for ratings of satisfaction on 6-point scales rating from to 1 = *very much dissatisfaction* to 6 = *very much satisfaction*. A sample item is "The kind of work or tasks that you are required to perform." Coefficient alphas ranged from .91 to .93 across our samples. The *mental well-being scale* contained 12 items concerned with psychological strain, focusing mainly on symptoms of anxiety and depression, such as feeling melancholy, miserable, panicky, upset, and worried. Each item had six response choices, but they varied across items. For example, the item "concerning work and life in general, would you describe yourself as someone who is bothered by their troubles or a 'worrier'?" had choices ranging from definitely yes to definitely no. The coefficient alphas ranged from .77 to .86 across our three samples. The *physical well-being scale* consisted of 6 items concerning physical symptoms, such as "feeling unaccountably tired or exhausted," "shortness of breath," and "muscles trembling." Response choices range from 1 = *never* to 6 = *very frequently*. Coefficient alphas ranged from .79 to .86 across our three samples.

In addition, a single question asked about intentions of quitting the job, "How often have you seriously considered quitting your job" with six response choices from 1 = *never* to 6 = *extremely often* (Spector, Dwyer, & Jex, 1988). Single questions asked gender (coded 1 = *male*, 2 = *female*), age, tenure on the job, number of children living in the home, management level, and marital status, which was coded 1 = *married* or 2 = *not married*.

Respondents were also asked how many hours they worked in a typical week. We excluded 35 cases that reported working 15 or fewer hours per week, with 28 of these reporting 8 to 10 hours. We assumed that these either represented errors (reporting daily rather than weekly hours) or part-time casual employment that did not consume a significant amount of time each week. An additional 4 outliers were deleted who reported 90 or more hours—one of which was an impossible 575.

Procedure

The organizers of the CISMS project (Cooper & Spector) designed the original questionnaire and recruited partners from a variety of countries, some of whom recruited additional partners. In countries where English was not the native language, the questionnaire was translated and independently back translated to assure equivalence of meaning. The original plan was to sample managers broadly from companies to provide as representative a sample as possible. In two of our samples (England and PRC) data were collected from one or two organizations. In the other samples, data were collected in a wide range using a variety of methods. For example in Canada, Hong Kong, and New Zealand, members of professional management organizations were contacted and asked to participate. In others (all Latin samples except Brazil), participants were practicing managers taking college courses who were recruited in classes. For some (Hong Kong and the U.S.), multiple methods were used, including recruiting participants taking classes. All analyses except for scale equivalence were done using SAS 8.02.

Scale Equivalence

It is generally recommended that measures used cross-nationally, particularly when translation is involved, be tested for equivalence. Following procedures recommended by Riordan and Vandenberg (1994) and Schaffer and Riordan (2003), we compared the variance/covariances among items within each scale across the three samples. We chose to use the most stringent approach of comparing the interitem variance/covariance matrices for equivalence, which is recommended as the first step in equivalence analysis (Riordan & Vandenberg, 1994; Schaffer & Riordan, 2003). It should be noted that results are not always consistent with other tests, such as comparisons of number of factors and equality of factor loadings (Raju, Laffitte, & Byrne, 2002). The analyses were conducted with LISREL 8.0, which allows for a comparison of variance/covariance matrices among groups. For each of our four multi-item scales, we compared the three samples simultaneously. As can be seen in Table 1, chi square statistics were significant in each case, but such statistics are widely known to be overly sensitive, particularly with large samples as we have here (Ryan, Chan, Ployhart, & Slade, 1999). However, an inspection of the various fit statistics shows that they are

TABLE 1

Summary of Fit Statistics For Scale Equivalence Tests Using LISREL

Scale	Chi square/df	RMSEA	GFI	NFI	CFI	IFI
Job satisfaction	520.4/156	.031	.97	.97	.98	.98
Mental well-being	1,041.7/156	.047	.89	.86	.89	.89
Physical well-being	319.9/42	.051	.94	.93	.94	.94
Work–family pressure	836.3/90	.058	.89	.88	.90	.90

Notes: RMSEA = Root mean square error of approximation; GFI = Goodness of fit test, NFI = Normed fit index, CFI = Comparative fit index; IFI = Incremental fit index. All chi square tests are statistically significant.

within or close to generally accepted values for good fit. For example, in all four cases the RMSEA was within the range considered indicative of good fit (less than .08). The remaining fit statistics ranged from .86 to .98, with the best fit found for job satisfaction. Given these results, we were satisfied that our measures showed sufficient evidence for equivalence to justify further analyses.

Results

Means, standard deviations, ranges, and internal consistencies (for multiple item measures) are shown in Table 2 for the continuous variables. As can be seen, the internal consistencies (coefficient alpha) for all measures were above .75, suggesting that these scales maintained internal consistency across translation and culture. Table 3 contains results of a one-way ANOVA for each of the six continuous variables, including the effect size (R^2). In each case, region was the independent variable and in each case it was statistically significant. Duncan post hoc tests were run to compare all three means. The table contains means for each variable with superscripts that indicate whether they were different among the three regions. Different superscripts within rows indicate significant differences between means. For example, the Anglo mean for turnover intent (superscript a) was significantly higher than the means for China and Latin America, which were not significantly different from one another (both superscript b). The last two columns show the effect sizes (R^2) for comparisons of Anglo versus China and Anglo versus Latin separately. This was done by including individual contrasts in the analysis and dividing the sums of squares for each by the total sums of squares.

Table 2 shows that the Latins work the most hours and the Chinese the fewest. However, work–family pressure does not follow the same pattern, as the Chinese reported the highest level and the Anglos the lowest. Anglos reported the highest intentions of quitting the job and the best mental well-being. Chinese reported the lowest job satisfaction and physical well-being. It should be kept in mind that the magnitude of

TABLE 2

Descriptive Statistics

Variable	n	M	SD	Range	Possible range	Coefficient alpha
Anglo						
Work hours	1,152	49.3	8.2	30–80	30–80	na
Children	1,130	.58	1.0	0–5	0–	na
work–family	1,108	25.7	8.5	9–50	9–54	.85
Intent to quit	1,142	2.7	1.33	1–6	1–6	na
Job satisfaction	1,137	47.5	10.5	14–72	12–72	.91
Mental well-being	1,143	49.2	9.9	20–72	12–72	.86
Physical well-being	1,141	25.6	6.4	6–36	6–36	.86
China						
Work hours	768	47.5	8.5	30–82	30–80	na
Children	768	.97	.97	0–5	0–	na
work–family	738	33.6	7.5	9–54	9–54	.84
Intent to quit	766	2.5	1.2	1–6	1–6	na
Job satisfaction	765	45.3	10.0	13–71	12–72	.92
Mental well-being	768	47.6	8.7	21–72	12–72	.80
Physical well-being	768	27.2	5.4	7–36	6–36	.79
Latin						
Work hours	574	50.4	8.2	30–80	30–80	na
Children	553	2.2	1.3	0–5	0–	na
work–family	528	32.2	8.6	9–51	9–54	.79
Intent to quit	572	2.5	1.2	1–6	1–6	na
Job satisfaction	574	49.6	11.2	14–72	12–72	.93
Mental well-being	572	46.1	9.4	17–72	12–72	.77
Physical well-being	572	26.4	6.0	6–36	6–36	.79

TABLE 3

Comparisons of Means

Variable	Error DF	F	R^2	Anglo mean	China mean	Latin mean	Anglo vs. China R^2	Anglo vs. Latin R^2
Work hours	2,491	20.22	.016	49.3[b]	47.5[c]	50.4[a]	.002	.0002
Children	2,342	430.04	.269	.58[a]	.97[b]	2.2[c]	.018	.262
Work–family	2,371	236.78	.166	25.7[c]	33.6[a]	32.2[b]	.141	.084
Intent to quit	2,477	6.65	.005	2.7[a]	2.5[b]	2.5[b]	.004	.003
Job satisfaction	2,473	27.97	.022	47.5[b]	45.3[c]	49.6[a]	.009	.005
Mental well-being	2,480	20.73	.016	49.2[a]	47.6[b]	46.1[c]	.004	.018
Physical well-being	2,478	24.3	.019	25.6[b]	24.2[c]	26.4[a]	.011	.001

Notes: Error DF = Degrees of freedom for error term; All F values are significant at $p < .01$; Different superscript letters within each row comparison indicate significant mean differences using a Duncan test.

effects for all but work–family pressure was rather small, with R^2 being .02 or less. The work–family pressure effect size was relatively large with an R^2 of .166.

TABLE 4

Summary of Moderated Regressions of Work–Family Pressure on Work Hours, Region, and Their Product Both With and Without Gender, Marital Status, Children, and Job Level as Control Variables

Predictor	Anglo vs. others		Anglo vs. China		Anglo vs. Latin America	
	Unstandardized coefficient	t-value	Unstandardized coefficient	t-value	Unstandardized coefficient	t-value
Gender	.80	2.14*	.68	1.68	.72	1.5
Married	-.10	-.21	.48	.90	-1.29	-2.09*
Children	.06	.40	.38	1.91	.31	1.57
Job level	.27	1.50	.09	.44	.18	.73
Work hours	-.01	-.62	.01	.45	-.05	-1.42
(No controls)	(-.02)		(.01)		(-.05)	
Region	-14.96	-9.01*	-13.91	-7.47*	-15.50	-7.37*
(No controls)	(-14.88)		(-13.88)		(-15.65)	
Hours*Region	.16	4.67*	.13	3.39*	.19	4.43*
(No controls)	(.15)		(.12)		(.18)	
Constant	32.00		30.74		34.22	
Overall F	74.36		65.65		37.90	
Degrees of freedom	7, 2382		7, 1853		7, 1626	
R^2	.18		.20		.14	

Notes: Gender 1 = *male*, 2 = *female*, Married 1 = *married*, 2 = *not married*; Children = number of children living at home, Job level ranged from 1 = *top level* to 4 = *first level*. Coefficients in parentheses were from an analysis without the four control variables entered.

Our main hypothesis, that region would moderate the relation between working hours and work–family pressure, was tested with a series of moderated regressions (see Table 4). In the first analysis, we coded region as 1 for Anglo and 0 for China or Latin America. In the first analysis, we coded region as $1 = Anglo$ to $0 = China$ or *Latin America*. We entered four variables as controls: Gender, marital status (married vs. unmarried), number of children in the home, and management level. The main variables of interest were work hours, region, and the product of the two, with work–family pressure as the criterion. Table 4 shows the results. The overall regression was significant (F (7, 2382) = 74.36, $p <$ .0001, R^2 = .18), and the product term was significant. The slope of the line relating work hours to work–family pressure was .15 for the Anglo sample and –.01 for the other two combined, thus supporting our hypothesis that there would be a larger positive relation for the Anglo sample than for the others. We conducted two additional analyses to compare the Anglo sample with the Chinese and Latin American separately. As can be seen in Table 4, results for each were quite similar to the combined Chinese and Latin regions. In both cases there was the expected positive relation for Anglos (.14), and little or even slightly negative relations for the other samples (.01 and –.05 for China and Latin, respectively). The table also shows the regression coefficients for work hours, region, and their product without the controls entered (values in parentheses). As can be seen, results were only slightly different, and in no case did it affect significance. A final analysis was conducted adding whether or not the spouse worked as an additional control for only those participants who were married. As with the other four control variables, results were practically identical.

Table 5 contains the zero-order correlations among the variables of the study for each region separately. It should be noted that we also computed pooled within-class correlations for each region to control for the subsample (individual country) differences. Although there were some minor differences in correlations, almost all differences were quite small (+/–.04) and the pattern of results was similar across regions. This evidence suggests that the results were not affected by differences that existed among the countries within each region. We report the uncorrected correlations here.

The correlation pattern across regions between work hours and work/family stress was consistent with the moderated regression results. There was a small but statistically significant correlation for the Anglo group (.17) but not for the other two. Furthermore, a z-test for independent correlations indicated that the Anglo correlation was significantly larger than the correlations for the other two regions. Likewise, the work hours–job satisfaction correlation was significant for the Anglos ($r = .15$)

134   PERSONNEL PSYCHOLOGY

TABLE 5

Correlations Among Study Variables For Anglo, China, and Latin Regions

Variable	1	2	3	4	5	6	7	8
Anglo								
1. Work hours								
2. Gender	−.18*							
3. Marital status	−.07*	.19*ab						
4. Children	−.08*b	−.11*b	−.15*ab					
5. Work–family	.17*ab	−.03a	−.08*a	.10*ab				
6. Intent to quit	−.01b	.07*	.04a	.04a	.13*			
7. Job satisfaction	.15*a	−.04	−.03a	−.10*ab	−.06*	−.54*		
8. Mental well-being	.08*a	−.06	−.03a	−.07ab	−.35*a	.33*	.35*	
9. Physical well-being	.01	−.01ab	.01ab	−.12*ab	−.22*a	.22*	.27*	.56*ab
China								
1. Work hours								
2. Gender	−.06							
3. Marital status	.05	.09*c						
4. Children	−.02c	−.17*	−.61*c					
5. Work–family	.03	.09*	.13*c	−.09*c				
6. Intent to quit	.09*c	.12*	.35*c	−.28*c	.20*			
7. Job satisfaction	−.02c	−.03	−.21*c	.17*	−.10*	−.42*c		
8. Mental well-being	−.08*c	−.10*	−.18*c	.12*	−.24*	−.30*	.35*	
9. Physical well-being	−.09*c	−.12*	−.19*	.18*	−.14*c	−.20*	.20*	.46*
Latin America								
1. Work hours								
2. Gender	−.09*							
3. Marital status	−.04	.32*						
4. Children	.11*	−.26*	−.56*					
5. Work–family	−.01	.04	−.03	−.01				
6. Intent to quit	−.13*	.05	.04	−.09*	.11*			
7. Job satisfaction	.10*	−.00	−.01	.09*	−.16*	−.51*		
8. Mental well-being	.04	−.04	−.05	.04	−.34*	−.24*	.31*	
9. Physical well-being	.05	−.14*	−.13*	.17*	−.29*	−.22*	.23*	.38*

Notes: Anglo $n = 1090–1145$; China $n = 733–768$; Latin $n = 514–574$. Gender 1 $= M$, 2 $= F$; Marital status 1 $=$ *married*, 2 $=$ *not married*.

[a] Corresponding correlation significantly different between Anglo and China samples
[b] Corresponding correlation significantly different between Anglo and Latin samples
[c] Corresponding correlation significantly different between China and Latin samples
*$p < .05$ for significance of correlation

but not the Chinese ($r = -.02$), and these correlations were significantly different from one another.

For all three regions, work–family stress was related to all three strains, suggesting that this phenomenon may be universal, at least among these three regions. However, child responsibilities and marital status showed stronger relations with job satisfaction and well-being in China than among Anglos and Latins, with better well-being associated with being married and having more children. Among Anglos there was a small but significant relation ($r = -.10$) between child responsibilities and job satisfaction and physical well-being, but in the opposite (negative) direction.

There were few relations with gender in these data. The only significant gender correlation in the Anglo group was for marital status (women more likely to be unmarried) and intent to quit (women higher intent), but the latter correlation was smaller than .1. The Chinese sample had similar findings to the Anglos, with the addition that women reported fewer family responsibilities, more work–family pressure, and poorer mental and physical well-being. For the Latins, women were less likely to be married, had fewer family responsibilities, and reported poorer physical well-being.

To test for the moderator effect of gender, we computed correlations for each region for men and women separately. There were only 4 significant differences out of 108, which is about the number expected by chance if these were independent tests. For the Anglos, males had a stronger correlation between child responsibilities and physical well-being and a smaller correlation between intent to quit and physical well-being. For the Chinese, males had a smaller correlation between work hours and marital status and between intent to quit and job satisfaction.

Discussion

Work–family issues are vital to the well-being of employees, their families, and their organizations. Despite the large amount of research in this area in recent years, very few studies have explored cultural and international differences, and most studies that have been conducted outside of the U.S. and culturally similar countries have not been comparative. Our study compared results in three of the largest (by population) regions in the world: Anglo, China, and Latin America. We showed that some results generalize nicely, but others produced differences.

We focused on the number of hours worked, which can seriously impact work–family issues in today's global workplace where managers are often asked to be available on a "24/7" basis. Our major hypothesis, based on the theorizing of Yang et al. (2000), was that there would be a stronger relation between number of hours worked and work–family pressure in individualist regions (Anglos) than among collectivists (Chinese and Latins). Moderated regression results supported this hypothesis. Our theory presumes that Anglos view working extra hours as taking away from their families, which may provoke feelings of guilt and greater levels of work–family pressure. This may not be the case in China and Latin America, where employees and their families may view working long hours differently.

Although the theoretical explanation for these results concerns values, there are alternative explanations, which seem quite plausible. The economies in the Anglo countries tend to be stronger than those in China and Latin America, resulting in a higher average household income. Thus, working longer hours in the Anglo world may appear to be less necessary for family survival. It makes sense that where making a living is more difficult, people would be more accepting of working long hours. Similarly, higher unemployment rates than those in Anglo countries may force managers in less developed areas to protect their jobs by working longer hours. Such extended hours would be tolerated by the family as a necessary evil, or even celebrated as a further guarantee of job security in an uncertain job market where having a management job is certainly an unusual privilege. Furthermore, there may be greater extended family support in collectivist countries on matters such as babysitting children, thereby making it easier for families to manage with one or even both parents working long hours (Ishii-Kuntz, 1994). There is also the possibility that cultural norms in some nations may discourage managers from spending time taking care of children, which may be seen as better fit for unemployed spouses or hired helpers. The presence of such cultural norms might provide legitimate excuses that would free managers from feelings of guilt for spending too much time away from family. All of these explanations need empirical testing, but seem like plausible, alternative explanations to I-C.

Another area where there were region differences concerned the relation of marital status and family responsibilities with strain. Among Anglos there were no significant relations of strain with marital status, and having children was associated with better job satisfaction and lower physical strain. For Latins, being married was associated with lower strain across all three variables, but having children was associated with higher strain. For Chinese, the pattern was similar to the Latins, although only half the correlations were significant, one for marital status and two for having children. For Latins and to some extent Chinese, perhaps having a spouse can facilitate balancing of both work and family (Frone, 2003).

There were also areas in which results were consistent across regions. First, there were few gender differences across the correlation tables, and gender did not function as a moderator of relations between the other variables in the study for any region. Perhaps the most notable difference is that women in China (but not the Anglo or Latin regions) reported more work–family distress and lower mental and physical well-being. Second, work–family pressure was related to job satisfaction and well-being universally, with the strongest correlation for mental well-being. In fact, the correlation for mental well-being was more than twice as large as for job satisfaction for all three samples, and the correlation with physical well-being was larger than job satisfaction as well. This suggests that more attention should be paid to these well-being variables in the work–family arena, rather than just focusing on job satisfaction.

Interpretation of results should consider alternative causal connections among these variables. For example, job satisfaction is often considered an outcome of work–family stressors, but it is possible that job satisfaction may act as a cause rather than effect. For instance, those who are satisfied with their jobs might tend to put more time and energy into work, to the detriment of family. Interestingly, for the Anglos and Latins, but not the Chinese, work hours related positively to job satisfaction, although none of the correlations was sizeable in magnitude. It should also be kept in mind that the notion of family and work can vary across countries.

Methodological considerations should be kept in mind in the interpretation of these results. First, the cross-sectional, single-source design makes it impossible to draw causal conclusions. Thus, we can say something about relations among variables, but not whether or not work–family stressors are the cause, consequence, or concomitant of job satisfaction and well-being. It is certainly possible that shared biases among some of these measures could partly account for observed relations among at least some variables. For example, the well-being measures contain items concerning affective responses to the job that might have been affected by affective traits, such as negative affectivity (Watson, Pennebaker, & Folger, 1987). This seems unlikely to have affected the factual items, such as gender, number of children, or working hours, which are not vulnerable to subjective interpretation. In any event, it is important to establish the existence of relations among variables as a first stage in research. It goes without saying, however, that future research should use a variety of methodologies to address possible causal connections with work–family issues, including additional sources of data such as coworkers, significant others, and supervisors.

A second issue concerns the interpretation of results across countries. Although we were able to successfully back translate our scales, and we have been able to demonstrate elsewhere with the OSI2 that job satisfaction and well-being subscales maintained internal consistency (Spector et al., 2001) and factor structure (Spector et al., 2002) across a variety of countries/languages, one cannot be absolutely certain about similar scale calibration across countries. This is particularly problematic with the multi-item scales where means are compared. A response of 6 to a particular item for a Canadian using the English version may not be exactly the same as for a Colombian using the Spanish version. Subtle connotation differences in words, or the scale value of an item, can differ between countries and languages. However, it is less likely that this would distort correlations among variables, especially with those that are more factual, such as hours worked per week or marital status.

Another calibration issue concerns the possibility of country-specific response styles that may have affected mean comparisons across samples, and also could have produced distortions in relations. Triandis (1994) and Van de Vijver and Leung (1997) discussed how response styles can be in part culturally determined. Asians, for example, have a tendency to avoid strong positive responses (Iawata, et al., 1998).

Finally, it should be noted that this study was based on instruments and theories developed in the Anglo world and transported to China and Latin America. It is certainly possible that had the constructs and scales been developed in China and/or Latin America, the nature of this work and the findings might have been different.

Despite its limitations, this study was able to show that some relations of work–family variables with job satisfaction and well-being generalize across three regions of the world, whereas others do not. However, our study was of managers, who are certainly above average in education and income in all these countries. It is important to see the extent that our regional differences might be the same or different with other employed groups from these regions.

One practical implication of our findings is that the policies that have been found to be effective in reducing work–family pressure in western society may not be as effective in other regions of the world. For example, research concerning family-supportive benefits has shown that flexible work options are among the most highly related to reduced WFC and job strain (Allen, 2001; Thomas & Ganster, 1995). Flexible work options may be less effective in regions where long hours are not strongly related to work and family pressures. In addition, the provision of dependent care supports has been another focus of benefits in western organizations endeavoring to provide a family-friendly workplace. Dependent care supports provided by the organization may be less necessary or helpful in other countries where extended kinship systems provide dependent care support.

Perhaps the most important implication of our study for future cross-national work–family and other research is that one cannot assume that western findings will or will not generalize to culturally dissimilar countries/regions. In the work–family area, there are important cultural differences that can affect relations among variables. Our findings that work hours may appear to affect work–family stress differently across regions need to be replicated with other measures and methods. For example, will results with WFC be the same as work–family stress? What about family interference with work as well as work interference with family? Additional sources of data should also be used, such as having partners/spouses indicate their level of work–family stress and conflict. More explicit measures of how spouses and families perceive working hours could more directly address our main hypothesis that individualist and collectivist people may view them differently. As well, it might be useful for future research to explore individualism–collectivism as a moderator at the individual employee level of the relation between working hours and WFC. Finally, it would be useful to look within countries to see if variation within family structure can affect relations of working hours to work–family stress, such as proximity of extended family members. For example, would having grandparents or relatives living nearby reduce the effects of working hours on work–family stress? Such extended family structures would be expected to be more common in collectivist countries, so there is a possible confound between family structure and culture values.

Our findings regarding work hours strongly suggest that caution must be exercised when considering cultural differences and family structures in the work–family domain. For instance, our data are interesting in that they run counter to stereotypical thinking about collectivist cultures, which are often depicted as too focused on family and ingroups and, thus, unwilling to work long hours. It appears that a collectivist orientation may indeed act as a buffer of WFC effects. For this reasons, solutions to the work–family dilemma, such as a mandatory 35 or 36 hour work week in Western Europe may fail to reduce work–family stressors when implemented in other parts of the world such as Asia or Latin America. Differences may also exist within country/region as there can be a variety of family arrangements among people. Perhaps most importantly, our results provide initial evidence suggesting that the relationship between work–family issues and outcomes such as job satisfaction and well-being cuts across nations and continents.

REFERENCES

Allen TD. (2001). Family-supportive work environments: The role of organizational perceptions. *Journal of Vocational Behavior, 58*, 414–435.

Allen TD, Herst DEL, Bruck CS, Sutton M. (2000). Consequences associated with work-to-family conflict: A review and agenda for future research. *Journal of Occupational Health Psychology, 5*, 278–308.

Aryee S. (1992). Antecedents and outcomes of work–family conflict among married professional women: Evidence from Singapore. *Human Relations, 45*, 813–837.

Aryee S. (1993). Dual-earner couples in Singapore: An examination of work and nonwork sources of their experienced burnout. *Human Relations, 46*, 1441–1468.

Aryee S, Fields D, Luk V. (1999). A cross-cultural test of a model of the work–family interface. *Journal of Management, 25*, 491–511.

Aryee S, Luk V. (1996). Work and nonwork influences on the career satisfaction of dual-earner couples. *Journal of Vocational Behavior, 49*, 38–52.

Aryee S, Luk V, Leung A, Lo S. (1999). Role stressors, interrole conflict, and well-being: The moderating influence of spousal support and coping behaviors among employed parents in Hong Kong. *Journal of Vocational Behavior, 54*, 259–278.

Barnett RC. (1998). Toward a review and reconceptualization of the work/family literature. *Genetic, Social and General Psychology Monographs, 124*, 125–182.

Barnett RC, Gareis KC, Brennan RT. (1999). Fit as a mediator of the relationship between work hours and burnout. *Journal of Occupational Health Psychology, 4*, 307–317.

Brett JM, Stroh LK. (2003). Working 61 plus hours a week: Why do managers do it? *Journal of Applied Psychology, 88*, 67–78.

Brisson C, Laflamme N, Moisan J, Milot A, Masse B, Vezina M. (1999). Effect of family responsibilities and job strain on ambulatory blood pressure among white-collar women. *Psychosomatic Medicine, 61*, 205–213.

Bruck CS, Allen TD, Spector PE. (2002). The relation between work–family conflict and job satisfaction: A finer-grained analysis. *Journal of Vocational Behavior, 60*, 336–353.

Bu N, McKeen CA. (2000). Work and family expectations of the future managers and professionals of Canada and China. *Journal of Managerial Psychology, 15*, 771–794.

Chan KB, Lai G, Ko YC, Boey KW. (2000). Work stress among six professional groups: The Singapore experience. *Social Science and Medicine, 50*, 1415–1432.

Chiu RK. (1998). Relationships among role conflicts, role satisfactions, and life satisfaction: Evidence from Hong Kong. *Social Behavior and Personality, 26*, 409–414.

Cooper CL, Williams J. (1991). A validation study of the OSI on a blue-collar sample. *Stress Medicine, 7*, 109–112.

Eagle BW, Miles EW, Icenogle ML. (1997). Interrole conflicts and the permeability of work and family domains: Are there gender differences? *Journal of Vocational Behavior, 50*, 168–184.

Falicov CJ. (2001). The cultural meanings of money: The case of Latinos and Anglo-Americans. *American Behavioral Scientist, 45*, 313–328.

Frone MR. (2003). Work–family balance. In Quick JC, Tetrick LE (Eds.) *Handbook of occupational health psychology* (pp. 143–162). Washington, DC: APA.

Frone MR, Yardley JK, Markel KS. (1997). Developing and testing an integrative model of the work–family interface. *Journal of Vocational Behavior, 50*, 145–167.

Grandey AA, Cropanzano R. (1999). The conservation of resources model applied to work–family conflict and strain. *Journal of Vocational Behavior, 54*, 350–370.

Greenhaus JH, Beutell NJ. (1985). Sources of conflict between work and family roles. *Academy of Management Review, 10*, 76–88.

Hofstede G. (1984). The cultural relativity of the quality of life concept. *Academy of Management Review, 9*, 389–398.

Hofstede G. (1994). *Values Survey Module 1994 manual.* University of Limburg, Mastricht, The Netherlands.

Iwata N, Umesue M, Egashira K, Hiro H, Mizoue T, Mishima N, et al. (1998). Con positive affect items be used to assess depressive disorder in the Japanese population? *Psychological Medicine, 28*, 153–158.

Ishii-Kuntz M. (1994). Work and family life: Findings from international research and suggestions for future study. *Journal of Family Issues, 15*, 490–506.

Kagitcibasi C. (1994). A critical appraisal of individualism and collectivism. In Kim U, Triandis HC, Kagitcibasi C, Choi S, Yoon G (Eds.). *Individualism and collectivism: Theory, method, and applications* (pp. 52–65). Thousand Oaks, CA: Sage.

Kahn RL, Wolfe DM, Quinn RP, Snoek JD, Rosenthal RA. (1964). *Organizational stress: Studies in role conflict and ambiguity.* New York: Wiley.

Katz D, Kahn RL. (1978). *The social psychology of organizations* (2nd ed). New York: Wiley.

Kossek EE, Ozeki C. (1998). Work–family conflict, policies, and the job–life satisfaction relationship: A review and directions for organizational behavior–human resources research. *Journal of Applied Psychology, 83*, 139–149.

Lundberg U, Frankenhaeuser M. (1999). Stress and workload of men and women in high-ranking positions. *Journal of Occupational Health Psychology, 4*, 142–151.

Major VS, Klein KJ, Ehrhart MG. (2002). Work time, work interference with family, and psychological distress. *Journal of Applied Psychology, 87*, 427–436.

Markus HR, Kitayama S. (1998). The cultural psychology of personality. *Journal of Cross-Cultural Psychology, 29*, 63–87.

Matsui T, Ohsawa T, Onglatco ML. (1995). Work–family conflict and the stress-buffering effects of husband support and coping behavior among Japanese married working women. *Journal of Vocational Behavior, 47*, 178–192.

Raju NS, Laffitte LJ, Byrne BM. (2002). Measurement equivalence: A comparison of methods based on confirmatory factor analysis and item response theory. *Journal of Applied Psychology, 87*, 517–529.

Redding SG. (1993). *The spirit of Chinese capitalism.* New York: De Gruyter.

Riordan CM, Vandenberg RJ. (1994). A central question in cross-cultural research: Do employees of different cultures interpret work-related measures in an equivalent manner? *Journal of Management, 20*, 643–671.

Robertson IT, Cooper CL, Williams J. (1990). The validity of the occupational stress indicator. *Work and Stress, 4*, 29–39.

Rothausen TJ. (1999). "Family" in organizational research: A review and comparison of definitions and measures. *Journal of Organizational Behavior, 20*, 817–836.

Ryan AM, Chan D, Ployhart RE, Slade LA. (1999). Employee attitude surveys in a multi-national organization: Considering language and culture in assessing measurement equivalence. PERSONNEL PSYCHOLOGY, *52*, 37–58.

Schaffer BS, Riordan CM. (2003). A review of cross-cultural methodologies for organizational research: A best-practices approach. *Organizational Research Methods, 6*, 169–215.

Sparks K, Cooper C, Fried Y, Shirom A. (1997). The effects of hours of work on health: A meta-analytic review. *Journal of Occupational and Organizational Psychology, 70*, 391–408.

Spector PE, Cooper CL, Sanchez JI, O'Driscoll M, Sparks K, Bernin P, et al. (2001a). Do national levels of individualism and internal locus of control relate to well-being: An ecological level international study, *Journal of Organizational Behavior, 22*, 815–832.

Spector PE, Cooper CL, Sparks K, Bernin P, Büssing A, Dewe P, et al. (2001b). An international study of the psychometric properties of the Hofstede Values Survey Module 1994: A comparison of individual and country/province level results. *Applied Psychology: An International Review, 50*, 269–281.

Spector PE, Cooper CL, Sanchez JI, O'Driscoll M, Sparks K, Bernin P, et al. (2002). A 24 nation/territory study of work locus of control in relation to well-being at work: How generalizable are western findings? *Academy of Management Journal, 45*, 453–466.

Spector PE, Dwyer DJ, Jex SM. (1988). The relationship of job stressors to affective, health, and performance outcomes: A comparison of multiple data sources. *Journal of Applied Psychology, 73*, 11–19.

Thomas L, Ganster DC. (1995). Impact of family-supportive work variables on work–family conflict and strain: A control perspective. *Journal of Applied Psychology, 80*, 6–15.

Triandis HC. (1994). *Culture and social behavior,* New York: McGraw-Hill.

Triandis HC. (1995). *Individualism and collectivism.* Boulder: Westview.

142   PERSONNEL PSYCHOLOGY

Van de Vijver F, Leung K. (1997). *Methods and data analysis for cross-cultural research.* Thousand Oaks, CA: Sage.

Vinokur AD, Pierce PF, Buck CL. (1999). Work–family conflicts of women in the Air Force: Their influence on mental health and functioning. *Journal of Organizational Behavior, 20,* 865–878.

Wallace JE. (1999). Work-to-nonwork conflict among married male and female lawyers. *Journal of Organizational Behavior, 20,* 797–816.

Watson D, Pennebaker JW, Folger R. (1987). Beyond negative affectivity: Measuring stress and satisfaction in the workplace. In Ivancevich JM, Ganster DC (Eds.), *Job stress: From theory to suggestion* (pp. 141–157). New York: Haworth Press.

Williams S, Cooper CL. (1996). *Occupational Stress Indicator Version 2.0.* Windsor, UK: NFER-Nelson.

Yang N, Chen CC, Choi J, Zou Y. (2000). Sources of work–family conflict: A Sino–U.S. comparison of the effects of work and family demands. *Academy of Management Journal, 41,* 113–123.

Part III
Internationalising HRM

Strategic Focus

[16]

The Relationship Between the Global Strategic Planning Process and the Human Resource Management Function

Edwin L. Miller, Schon Beechler, Bhal Bhatt and Raghu Nath

This article discusses the relationship between the Human Resource Management function (HRM) and the global strategic planning processes of five leading U.S. multinational corporations. Data were collected by means of interviewing HRM and strategic planning executives, as well as corporate or strategic business unit senior-level line executive personnel. An HRM presence occurred most frequently in discussion pertaining to the implementation of the global strategy, and management succession and management development activities were the most frequently mentioned areas of involvement. Edwin L. Miller and Schon Beechler are with the Graduate School of Business Administration, University of Michigan. Bhal Bhatt is with the University of Toledo, and Raghu Nath is with the University of Pittsburgh.

The rapid increase in U.S. multinational corporations' (MNCs) foreign direct investment has generated a series of intersections between MNCs' human resource management systems and their global strategic planning processes. As the MNCs strive to administer their overseas operations, the control mechanisms developed by the corporate headquarters to regulate the activities of their overseas subsidiaries impact the structure, the human resource management system and the enterprise's internal environment. Structural changes within the parent company or its overseas subsidiaries frequently lead to greater decentralization and increased emphasis on management development. Simultaneously, Human Resource Management (HRM) is placed under increased pressure to solve problems associated with promotion and management succession, measurement of performance, and issues pertaining to the distribution of power between corporate headquarters and overseas subsidiaries.

Because of the increasing importance of human resource issues in the management process of multinational corporations, a longterm research project has been undertaken to examine the nature of the linkages between HRM and the global strategic planning processes of multinational corporations. The first phase of the project has been completed, and this article presents the results of that part of the study. The purpose of this article is to describe the nature of Human Resource Management's participation in the formulation and implementation of global strategic plans of leading American multinational corporations. It also provides information about the role of HR professionals in the planning process.

A review of the strategic planning literature indicates that MNCs have adopted a strategic planning perspective as a means for helping them make rational decisions in the face of rapidly changing and complex environments. As the management teams of these corporations begin to develop and implement their firms' global strategic plans, do they concern themselves with human resource issues? Lorange reports that they do, and these issues appear in the context of discussion concerned with such topics as acquisitions or divestitures of overseas production facilities, entering or withdrawing from markets, proposed redesign of corporate structures to accommodate different cultures or nations, the means for controlling relationships between overseas subsidiaries and the parent, and the procedure for effectively managing the fundamental elements of the human resource system, (Lorange and Vancil, 1977).

Bartlett's work on the evolving nature of multinational corporations supports Lorange's conclusion, (Bartlett, 1983). He stresses the importance of human resource issues associated with the structural problems generated by multiple and often conflicting pressures emanating from most host country and global competitors. Bartlett writes:

> "Human resource issues become critical to the formulation and implementation of the MNC's strategic plan. It is management that must develop the perspective, viable organization structures and systems through which they can interact as well as develop an appropriate decision making apparatus," (Bartlett, 1983).

When does HRM fit into these strategic concerns of the MNCs? Is the function an active, contributing partner in the global strategic planning activities of MNCs? Or, is it viewed as contributing little of value to the strategic planning process? The strategic planning literature indicates that at least at the corporate level, human resource concerns are a collective top management responsibility rather than that of the HRM function, (Hofer and Schendel, 1981). If this is so, just what is the nature of HRM's involvement? These are important questions because they deal with the future direction and contribution of HRM.

In the HRM literature, it has become fashionable to cast the human resource system into a strategic context. To add legitimacy to their conceptual frameworks, authors and scholars have provided examples of: (1) companies that have successfully linked their human resource management systems to strategic planning, (2) top human resource management executives who have been instrumental in tying the HRM function and its activities to their respective corporations' strategic plan, and (3) procedures for moving a human resource management function into the strategic arena, (Tichy, Fombrun and Devanna, 1984).

K.R. Andrews was one of the earliest advocates for linking business strategy with human resource management, (Andrews, 1957). Although he used different terms, the essence of his argument stressed the value to be achieved by integrating these organizational activities. After almost two decades, HRM scholars and authors have begun to express themselves about the relevance of linking HR activities to the strategic planning process. A plethora of articles and books have appeared, and they have concentrated on strategic human resource management. For example, authors have written about the relationship between staffing and product life cycles, (Leontiades, 1982; Miller, 1984) performance appraisal and business strategy, (Latham, 1984; Tung, 1984) management succession and stockholder wealth (Reinganum, 1973) and compensation structures and business strategy, (Salter, 1973).

The HRM literature offers a picture of an important and relevant role for the function as well as providing concrete examples of what can be. However, Dyer has written that the interrelationship between HRM and strategic planning represents an uncharted area, (Dyer, 1984). Notwithstanding Dyer's comments, a consensus is emerging among leading HRM scholars and professionals that the function is expanding far beyond the traditionally accepted activities of staffing, training and development, rewards and appraisal.

A distinguishing characteristic of the developing HRM model is its strategic orientation. The HR professional and executive is a central element in the emerging model, and it is noted that the HRM professional is confronted by a twofold challenge: (1) to develop viable processes whereby HRM contributions can and do occur in the strategic planning process, and (2) to adopt and promote strategic thinking within the human resource function itself.

What are the variables that differentiate strategic human resource management from previous definitions of the function? We believe that it is helpful to use Miles and Snow's strategic human resource management dimensions (Miles and Snow, 1984), and the following attributes appear to capture the spirit of the developing model:

1. Top managers of the human resource function should possess at least a conceptual familiarity with all services needed to acquire, allocate and develop managers and employees.

2. The function should have a comprehensive understanding of the language and practices of strategic planning. Appropriate human resource representatives must continually participate in the planning process to assess the probable demand for their unit's services.

3. The human resource function should pursue appropriate strategies of its own to match the organization's business strategy.

4. The function must act as a professional consultant to the line. In addition to their expertise in strictly human resource matters, the human resource specialist should be knowledgeable about organization structure, management processes including communication and control, and organization change and development.

Given these benchmarks, how does one classify the nature of the decisions made by HRM as it goes about discharging its responsibilities? Anthony's classification of management decision making is a useful tool for classifying the nature of HRM participation in the strategic planning process, (Anthony, 1964). According to his classification scheme, there are three levels of decision making: strategic, managerial, and operational. Anthony defined the levels in the following way: (1) Strategic level decisions are concerned with policy formulation and setting of overall goals, (2) Managerial level decisions are more pragmatic in orientation, and these decisions are associated with the development of programs to guarantee the availability of resources to carry out the strategic plan, and (3) Operational level decisions are concerned with the execution of day-to-day activities, and these decisions are the consequence of programs and issues developed at the managerial level.

Applying Anthony's framework to HRM's responsibility for staff, Table 1 provides an example of the three levels of decision making.

TABLE 1
Human Resource Management Involvement
in the Organizational Employee Staffing Process

Strategic Level	Strategic Planning Relationship to Human Resource Management System
	"What kinds of people will be needed to lead the organization in the years to come?"
Managerial Level	Development of Activities to Satisfy Forecasted Organizational Human Resource Requirements
	"What programs and activities must be developed to satisfy forecasted human resource requirements?"
Operational Level	Implementation and Monitoring of Specific Human Resources Programs and Activities
	"What are the specific plans for this year's college recruiting? What colleges will be visited? How many college recruits must be interviewed? And, what will be the college recruiting budget?"

Conceptual Framework

Although there are many variables that could be considered as important determinants of HRM's contribution to the planning process, it is our opinion that three variables are central to a meaningful understanding. Based upon the strategic planning and the HRM research and literature, the following variables comprise the framework that was used in the study: Organizational Level of Strategy, Human Resource Management Functions, and Global Strategic Planning Process.

ORGANIZATIONAL LEVEL OF STRATEGY

The nature of a corporation's business strategy can be viewed in several different ways. In this study, however, strategy was limited to two organizational levels: corporate and strategic business unit. At the corporate level, strategy is concerned primarily with such issues as long-run organizational survival, domain differentiation, resource allocation and goal formulation. Strategy associated with the strategic business unit is concerned with competition in a particular industry or product market segment. Attention is centered on competencies and competitive advantage and major functional area policy decisions.

HUMAN RESOURCE MANAGEMENT FUNCTIONS

This variable is divided into the HRM activities of staffing, training and development, rewards and appraisal. In this context the Human Resource system is defined by the breadth and quality of services needed to acquire, allocate, develop and evaluate managerial personnel.

GLOBAL STRATEGIC PLANNING PROCESS

This variable can be divided into four categories: strategy preplanning, strategy formulation, strategy implementation and strategy control and evaluation. For purposes of this research project, only strategy formulation and strategy implementation were used in the analysis. Much of the previous work on strategy has been limited to these two categories, and in the pilot phase of this study, it was found that respondents were familiar and comfortable discussing the formulation and implementation phases of strategy. The respondents found it difficult to describe the involvement in strategy preplanning and evaluation activities because they generally don't view the strategy cycle as being divided into four distinct categories.

The framework for classifying HRM involvement in the global strategic planning process is presented in Figure 1. As one can observe in this framework, HR involvement in the strategic planning process can be divided into four different categories. First, HRM can be involved in the formulation of corporate level global strategic planning. Second, it can participate in the formulation of the SBU's global strategic plan. Third, HRM can be involved in the implementation of the MNC's corporate level global strategic plan. And fourth, HRM can participate in the implementation of the SBU's global strategy.

FIGURE 1

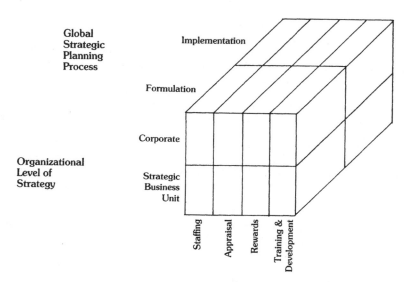

THE RELATIONSHIP BETWEEN THE GLOBAL STRATEGIC PROCESS AND THE HUMAN
RESOURCE MANAGEMENT FUNCTION **13**

METHODOLOGY

Since very little has been published about HRM linkages with MNC's global strategic planning processes, it was decided to gather data by means of the structured interview technique. The rationale for that decision flowed from the commonly acknowledged fact that structured interviews allow an investigator the freedom and flexibility to explore a wide range of topics as well as the opportunity to collect qualitative data on attitudes, values and opinions. At this stage of the research project, qualitative information was critical for successive phases of the investigation. It was imperative to obtain the subjects' cooperation, and from past experience it was known that more relevant information could be obtained by means of the interview method than by use of the questionnaires. Experience indicated that executives and staff specialists would be much more willing to spend time talking about their participation in the planning process than they would by filling out a survey instrument.

The managers and executives who participated in the study occupied positions in one of the following areas: the strategic planning function, the human resource management system, or as corporate or SBU senior-level line executive. Regardless of their official titles, each participant was involved in the overseas activities of his or her organization. As such, they were able to provide several different and relevant perspectives about the global strategic planning process and HRM involvement in it.

Five U.S. multinational corporations comprised the sample, and they represented several different types of manufacturing industries. The following criteria were used as the basis for choosing the MNC's: (1) The enterprise must have a significant overseas presence i.e., (the firm must have manufacturing, marketing or administrative facilities in at least six different countries), (2) The firm must have been engaged in international business for at least 20 years.

Net annual sales for the corporations ranged from approximately three billion to over twenty billion dollars, and foreign sales represented at least 20% of total sales for each corporation. These were large U.S. firms and their foreign sales represented a significant portion of these firms' total annual sales.

Twenty-two interviews were conducted during the data collection phase of the study. Twelve of the participants were involved in the global strategic planning process at the corporate level. The 10 remaining participants were involved in the global strategic planning process of those SBU's engaged in the production and sale of goods overseas. Consequently, interview data have been obtained on five MNC's global strategic planning processes at corporate and SBU levels.

Among the 12 participants at the corporate level, five were senior HR executives in their respective corporations, four were top-level line executives, and three were responsible for development of their corporations' global strategic plan. At the SBU level, the 10 participants were divided in the following manner: five were in charge of the SBUs' HR systems, four were general managers of the SBUs, and one was responsible for the development of business planning.

DISCUSSION

What was the nature of HRM involvement in the global strategic planning process? In each of the MNCs it was found that HRM was participating in the global planning process. However, the degree of participation did vary across the corporations, which was not surprising. What was interesting was where and how the HR system linked with the MNC's global strategic planning processes and the role the top HR executive played in bringing about those linkages. In this section, we will discuss some of the more interesting findings.

The Nature of Human Resource Management Involvement in the Global Strategic Planning Process at the Corporate Level

Incorporation of a HRM perspective at the corporate level was informal and limited. In two of the MNCs, the senior line executives and strategic planners reported that it wasn't clear how HRM could contribute to the MNC's global strategy. In the words of one of these executives:

"Human resource issues are considered when they are pertinent to the topic at hand, but we would never think of asking the HR people to participate in those strategic discussions. Although those guys are nice people, they are soft and they have little to contribute to the broader strategic issues of the corporation."

When there was HRM involvement in the strategic planning process, the CEO played an instrumental role in that relationship. Three of the top HR executives attributed their effectiveness to their personal relationship with the CEO. As one HR executive said:

"I see or talk to the CEO on a daily basis, and we talk about personnel related matters. However, you must understand that he trusts me or else I wouldn't be in this job. We go back a long way together."

Involvement of HRM was fragile and subject to change given the nature of the personalities involved, and the function's effectiveness was influenced by the executive's ability to develop and maintain personal relationships with the CEO. The presence and participation of HRM at the corporate level required constant revalidation because each time there was a change of CEO or the senior HR executive, a period of testing and critical review occurred. The HR executive had to win acceptance on the basis of value added to strategy matters or else win acceptance on the basis of personal qualifications. However, it was not an either-or situation.

HRM involvement in the formulation and implementation of the MNCs' global strategic planning process varied across organizations and the HR system's four basic activities of staffing, training and development, appraisal of performance, and compensation. It was the area of staffing which represented the major arena in which HR made its presence felt. Management development was another area in which there was a reasonably strong degree of HRM participation in the strategic planning process. Apparently discussions about executive compensation and performance appraisal were considered by these five MNCs to be the responsibility of top management itself, and there was little reason to include an HRM contribution.

Among several of the MNCs, HRM contributions to staffing had moved to the strategic decision-making level, and considerable time and effort were devoted to the process of choosing the very best executives for overseas positions. Many times these assignments were designed to meet three objectives: (1) to assign the very best person to the vacant post, (2) to gather evidence about the expatriate's capabilities to manage in a foreign environment, and (3) to provide the executive with an overseas experience prior to advancing to still higher and more responsible positions within the management hierarchy of the parent organization. The HRM executive was expected to help develop the criteria that an executive must possess in order to successfully perform on the overseas assignment. In two of the MNCs, the senior HR executives indicated that they participated in discussions about the selection of executives to head major geographic regions overseas. In both companies, the HR executive helped develop the slate of candidates and the HR executives offered their opinions about each candidate's qualifications to the CEO and other members of the management committee.

In several of the MNCs, the HRM function was responsible for administering the management succession and career development plans for high potential managerial personnel. These executives and managers were holding key positions within the management hierarchies of their respective firms, and they were judged to possess the potential to rise to senior management positions within the near future. The HR executives who participated in those discussions, reported their opinions were sought out with respect to the following subjects: (1) The managerial qualities required to successfully manage the MNC in the future, (2) The types of domestic as well as foreign assignments that would help the executives build the competencies that would be necessary to lead the corporation in the future, and (3) Which individuals should be considered for overseas assignments as part of their career progression. A particularly helpful insight into HR involvement was provided by the following comments of a senior HR executive:

> "I was requested to generate a slate of candidates for the position of president of the Southern Asia region. In my opinion, that geographic region no longer warranted a 'star' just because we had little market share and there were no plans to try and expand it. The job required nothing more than a figurehead, and all we needed to do was to show the flag. An executive close to retirement seemed to be the ideal type of person to assign to the job. I used the BCG framework as the basis for my argument to the management committee because I knew they were familiar with that terminology and approach. Much to my surprise they went along with my argument."

Given the nature of HR involvement in the global strategic planning process at the corporate level, it is somewhat artificial to try to force the function's involvement into formulation or implementation of strategy. It was more meaningful to state there was an HR presence at the corporate level, and the content of the HR decisions was, in Anthony's framework, essentially strategic and managerial in substance. Table 2 summarizes the nature of HRM involvement in the global strategic planning process at the corporate level.

The Nature of HR Involvement at the Strategic Business Unit Level

At the SBU level, HRM participation in the global strategy was well established, valued, and expected by management and planners alike. They reported that an HR perspective added value to the strategic planning process, and there was high regard for the professional competence of the HRM staff and, in particular, the senior HR manager. In general, the HR professionals were considered to be sensitive to the environmental pressures on the SBU, they understood the dynamics of the business and they brought a long-term orientation to the strategic problems facing the business. In the words of one senior SBU HR manager:

> "Management and the business planners trust me, and they look for ways to take advantage of my expertise. On technical matters, management will routinely ask me if I see any HR issues. Let me give you an

TABLE 2

HRM Involvement in Global Strategic Planning Process at the Corporate Level

DECISION	FORMULATION HUMAN RESOURCE MANAGEMENT ACTIVITIES				IMPLEMENTATION HUMAN RESOURCE MANAGEMENT ACTIVITIES			
	STAFFING	DEVELOPMENT	APPRAISAL	REWARDS	STAFFING	DEVELOPMENT	APPRAISAL	REWARDS
STRATEGIC	Participation in the development of qualifications necessary for success in an overseas position.				Administration of management succession program.	Integration of management development and management succession programs.		
MANAGERIAL	Participation in the development of management succession program.	Participation in the development of management development program.			Administration of management development program.	Determination of other type of development assignments for executives and high potential managerial personnel.		
OPERATIONAL					Development of slate of candidates for overseas. Participation in the selection and assignment of executives to overseas assignments.			

THE RELATIONSHIP BETWEEN THE GLOBAL STRATEGIC PROCESS AND THE HUMAN RESOURCE MANAGEMENT FUNCTION **17** example, as part of our global strategy we began thinking about going into Mexico and opening up a manufacturing facility. As part of the feasibility study, I was asked to provide an HR input. I raised questions and provided information about the reactions of our union if we outsourced part of production, I provided information about the skill level of the potential workforce, its commitment to work and its stance relative to outside management."

Among this sample of companies, HRM was deeply involved in the strategic planning process, and its participation crossed all four HRM functional activities. Perhaps one of the most dramatic statements pertaining to HRM involvement in the planning process was made by one of the HR managers in the following way:

"I have an excellent staff, and it handles the day-to-day HR routine much better than I can. As for me, I'm concerned about the 21st century for this company."

Management succession and career development again represent two of the main ways in which HRM was involved in the formulation of the SBU's global strategic planning process. In two of the SBUs, the HR executives reported that a key element for tying HRM to the SBU strategic plan occurred by means of the management succession plan, and it was important for the function to play an important role in that relationship. As an example of that, HR executives indicated that they were participants in discussions about the SBU's strategy for a particular market or product and the human resource requirements needed to implement that strategy. Several of the HR officials reported they devoted a large amount of their time to locating managerial and technical professional personnel who could fill vacancies that opened up as a result of the strategic discussions about the future of the SBU's international involvement.

Relatively speaking, HRM was much more involved in the implementation rather than the formulation of the SBU's global strategic plan. One HR executive made a statement that seemed to be a common thread through many of the discussions, "I'm a doer. Give me a direction, and I'm off and running." Examples of such behavior were most evident in the area of staffing. HRM was responsible for the development and administration of programs associated with internal movement and development of managerial and professional technical personnel. In contrast, the performance appraisal and reward programs required HRM to do nothing more than administer them, and it was limited to monitoring the decisions of overseas management to determine if they were in compliance with the corporation's guidelines and stated policies and procedures. In several of the firms, the reward system had been designed by an outside consulting group, and the HRM function did little more than oversee a compensation program that had been developed by a group external to the MNC.

Classifying HRM decisions according the Anthony's classification scheme, the majority of its decision making occurred at the operational level. The HR function was responsible for preparing managerial, professional and technical personnel for impending overseas assignments. For instance, arrangements were made for language training, presentation of indoctrination programs for the soon-to-be expatriates, preparations for moving household goods overseas, making travel arrangements prior to departure from the U.S. and responding as best it could to the personal requirements of the person about to be sent abroad. While the expatriate was away from the United States, the function was in touch with the overseas employee, and it responded to personal requests ranging from seeking college application forms for college-age dependent children, to gathering information about legal issues that sometimes arise between the expatriate and the state and federal government, and finally, locating hard-to-find food and personal products. Prior to repatriation, the function prepared the expatriate and family members for their return to the U.S. This included: (1) locating an assignment within the SBU that would be similar in authority and responsibility to the expatriate's present position, and (2) helping with preparations to move the family back to the U.S. Table 3 summarizes HRM involvement in the global strategic planning process at the strategic business unit level.

TABLE 3
HRM Involvement in Global Strategic Planning Process at the Strategic Business Unit Level

DECISION

FORMULATION
HUMAN RESOURCE MANAGEMENT ACTIVITIES

	STAFFING	DEVELOPMENT	APPRAISAL	REWARDS
Strategic	Participation in discussion of qualification necessary for success in an overseas position.			
Managerial				
Operational				

DECISION

IMPLEMENTATION
HUMAN RESOURCE MANAGEMENT ACTIVITIES

	STAFFING	DEVELOPMENT	APPRAISAL	REWARDS
Strategic				
Managerial	Adminstration of management succession program.	Administration of management development program.	Administration of performance program.	Administration of reward program.
Operational	Identification of potential candidates for overseas assignments Preparation of personnel for overseas assignment and repatriation to the U. S.	Individual specific development assignments	Monitor performance appraisals	Monitor individual compensation decisions

THE RELATIONSHIP BETWEEN THE GLOBAL STRATEGIC PROCESS AND THE HUMAN RESOURCE MANAGEMENT FUNCTION 19

CONCLUSION

This article has reported the results of the first phase of a long-term research project designed to examine the interrelationship between HRM and the global strategic planning processes of large multinational firms. It is our opinion that this study has helped to bridge part of the knowledge gap that has existed with respect to the linkages between HRM and the planning processes of MNCs. When considering the findings of this study, one of the most striking results is the potentially influential role that senior HR executives can play in the strategic planning process. That is, among those firms in which there was a high level of HRM involvement in the planning process, the HRM executives were viewed as the functional leaders, and they were judged by senior management as having something of value to contribute to the strategic planning discussions. The professional competence and personal characteristics of the senior HR executive were critical determinants for MNC management willingness to include HRM contributions to the planning process. This finding held true at the corporate as well as the strategic business unit levels.

Professional competence was a necessary but not sufficient condition for inclusion in strategy decisions. In those companies where there were effective HRM inputs, the senior HR executive was described in the following terms: professionally competent, value added, personal confidante, trustworthy and insightful. However, there was not a direct correlation between the power and prestige of the senior HR executives and the involvement of the function, and in some cases the HR executive was involved in the strategic planning process while similar status was not enjoyed by the HRM function.

It is our conclusion that if the senior HR executive and ultimately the function is to be included in the global strategic planning process, several conditions must be met. First, the senior HR executive, as the key legitimate function leader, must be included in the strategic planning process, and legitimacy is the result of professional competence. Although there may be times when HRM contributions to the planning process will be limited, there will be other times when the function's contributions will be critical and participation active. Without inclusion, HRM contributions to the strategic planning process will be minimal and of little consequence.

Second, the senior HR executive must be competent and sensitive to the problems, needs and circumstances confronting the organization. Members of management and strategic planners alike must recognize the value added by the contributions made by the function and its senior executive. As a corollary, HRM must conscientiously strive to understand the language and practice of strategic planning, the nature of the business and a demonstrated sensitivity to the demands and circumstances impacting the manger and his or her job. It is our opinion that such an awareness is just beginning to occur, and the results of this study support such a conclusion.

As firms become more deeply involved in international business, there will be more opportunities for strategic HRM to become active and full participants in the global strategic planning process. The function must seek ways to exploit these opportunities to contribute to the planning process, and the HR professionals must prepare themselves professionally to contribute. The perspective and competence of the HR professionals will be critical for their inclusion in the strategic planning process, and the senior HR executive must provide an important example to management and to lower level HR professionals of how the interface can occur. In this regard the HR executive must be an excellent teacher, and teaching must occur by deeds not words alone. It is our opinion that more HR professionals are becoming aware of the need to prepare themselves and to develop a perspective that will be helpful for building viable and important relationships between HRM and the global strategic planning processes of MNCs.

Third, integrity and the quality of the interpersonal skills possessed by the senior HR executive are critical contextual determinants of his or her participation in the planning process. Several of the HR executives reported that being viewed as trustworthy and the confidante of the CEO were two of the most important elements contributing to the degree of influence they exerted on the MNC's global strategic planning process. However, they were quick to add that without demonstrated professional competence, being trustworthy or a good sounding board to the CEO or other members of management meant very little in terms of the likelihood of being included in the strategic planning process.

If human resource management is to begin moving out of a role of just responding to the global strategic plan, if it is to participate in the strategic arena of the multinational corporation, senior HR executives must begin to recognize and understand at least conceptually the nature of the services needed to acquire, allocate, develop, reward and evaluate managerial personnel. The HR executive must understand how the HRM function relates to other functional activities of the enterprise as well as its contribution and importance for managerial and organizational effectiveness. Finally, the executive must be sensitive to his or her personal image including integrity and interpersonal and communication skills.

It is our conclusion that if senior corporate level HR executives wish to improve upon the degree of participation in the global strategic planning process there are steps that can be taken. Several of these are as follows:

1. Design a Human Resource Management system that meets the needs of management. In part, be concerned with providing the types of services and support that enable management to do its job more efficiently and effectively. Furthermore, strive to guarantee that management consider human resource issues as they plan and implement the global strategic plan.

2. Develop a personal strategy for building a meaningful relationship with his or her CEO. It is our opinion that the strategy must be proactive in its orientation and perspective, and the executive must be committed to it.

3. Assess one's listening and communication skills. These skills are important components for building and maintaining a strong, personal relationship with the CEO. Carl Rogers' work on effective communication and the means for developing nondirective counselling skills should be helpful in this regard, (Rogers and Farson, 1976).

4. Carve out an active, helping and consulting role with top management. The HR executive should be viewed as an individual of high integrity, one who will be available to listen and talk, and one who provides nonjudgemental but sound advice.

5. Interpret the organizational political signs accurately. Although the HR professional may be politically literate, it should not be construed to mean the successful HR executive is a master politician who relies solely upon political influence to achieve an HR presence in the global strategic planning process.

At the SBU level, HR managers can increase their involvement in the global strategic planning process too. Our recommendations are similar to those that we offer to corporate level HR executives interested in improving relationships with their respective CEOs. For example, SBU level HR managers can develop supportive communication skills, acquire an understanding of the organizational, political and cultural environment, demonstrate professional competence, establish links between HRM and SBU global strategic planning processes. These skills and activities are essentially short-term in their perspective. However, there are activities that will have long-term consequences that should be undertaken too. One such activity is the need to develop strong and meaningful relationships with SBU line management. These managers are the future leaders of their respective MNC's and it is important for the HR manager to establish the relevance of the function's contribution in the eyes of these managerial personnel. The findings of this study indicate that several of the corporate level HR executives indicated their influence could be traced to the strong and trusting relationships they had developed with current top level management while they both served at the SBU level.

Given the findings and our interpretation of them, the second phase of the research project will be developed, with several different dimensions to be explored. For example, one aspect of the new project will be the revalidation of the current findings in a wider sample of MNCs. More firms will be involved in the study, and there will be in-depth investigations occurring in several of those firms. Another dimension of the research project will be to study firms that have successfully integrated HRM into the global strategic planning process in contrast to those companies that have not been as successful in the integration process.

The senior HR executive was a central person in the process of linking HRM and the global strategic planning process of MNCs. As a third facet of the new research project, we are especially interest in studying the senior HR executive role and its occupant closely. Is there something that can be learned from an in-depth study of HR executives who have been successful in bringing about an effective, formal HRM presence in the global strategic planning process? We believe there is.

It is our opinion that we have much to learn about HRM participation in the management process of firms' international business activities. Just what is the scope of HRM involvement in the strategic planning process as well as its responsibilities for maintaining the HR system overseas? Is international HRM different from domestic HRM? This type of research should be of interest and value to the practitioner as well as the academic researcher concerned with the evolving nature of the field.

We would like to express our appreciation for the helpful comments provided by Professors V.K. Narayanan, The University of Kansas; Richard Peterson, the University of Washington; Rosalie Tung, The Wharton School; as well as Noel Tichy and David Ulrich at the University of Michigan.

REFERENCES

Andrews, Kenneth R., "Is Management Training Effective?", *Harvard Business Review*, March - April 1957, Vol. 35.

Anthony, Robert, *Planning and Control Systems: A Framework for Analysis*, Division of Research, Graduate School of Business Administration, Harvard University, 1964.

Bartlett, Christopher, "How Multinational Organizations Evolve," *Journal of Business Strategy*, Summer, 1983 pp. 10-32.

Dyer, Lee, "Studying Human Resource Strategy: An Approach and an Agenda," *Industrial Relations*, Spring, 1985, pp. 156-169.

Hofer, Charles and Dan Schendel, *Strategy Formulation: Analytical Concepts*, (St. Paul, MN, West Publishing Co., 1986.).

Gary Latham, "The Appraisal System as a Strategic Control" in Fombrun et. al. *Strategic Human Resource Management*, (New York: John Wiley & Sons, 1984).

Leontiades, Milton, "Choosing the Right Manager to Fit the Strategy," *Journal of Business Strategy*, Fall, 1982, Vol. 3, pp. 58-69.

Lorange, Peter and R. Vancil, *Strategic Planning Systems*, (Englewood Cliffs, N.J., Prentice Hall Book Co., 1977).

Miles, Raymond E. and Charles C. Snow, "Designing Strategic Human Resource Systems," *Orangizational Dynamics*, Summer 1984, pp. 36-52.

Miller, Edwin L., "Strategic Staffing," in Fombrun, Charles, Tichy, Noel and Mary Anne Devanna (editors), *Strategic Human Resource Management*, (New York, John Wiley & Sons, 1984).

Reinganum, Marc R., "The Effect of Executive Succession on Stockholder Wealth," *Administrative Science Quarterly*, 30, 1985, pp. 46-60.

Rogers, Carl and R. Farson, *Active Listening*, (Chicago: Industrial Relations Center. 1976.).

Salter, Malcom S., "Tailor Incentive Compensation Strategy," *Harvard Business Review*, March-April, 1973, pp. 94-102.

Tichy, Noel, Fombrun, Charles and Mary Anne Devanna, "The Organizational Context of Strategic Human Resource Management," in Fomburn, Charles, Tichy, Noel and Mary Anne Devanna (eds.) *Strategic Human Resource Management*, (New York, John Wiley & Sons, Inc., 1984).

Tung, Rosalie, "Strategic Management of Human Resources in the Multinational Enterprise," *Human Resource Management*, Summer, 1984, pp. 129-144.

[17]

An Integrative Framework of Strategic International Human Resource Management

Randall S. Schuler
New York University

Peter J. Dowling
Monash University

Helen De Cieri
Monash University

The globalization of business is making it more important than ever to understand how multinational enterprises (MNEs) can operate more effectively. A major component of this understanding appears to be the field of human resource management, and in particular, the field of international human resource management (Brewster, 1991; Hendry, 1992; Desatnick & Bennett, 1978; Dowling, 1986; Dowling & Schuler, 1990; Evans, 1986; Laurent, 1986; Tung, 1984). The trend over the past few years has been to identify the linkage of human resource management with strategy and offer an understanding of how single country or domestic human resource management can facilitate organizational understanding and effectiveness (Wright and McMahan, 1992). In this article we attempt to extend this line of work into the international arena. We do this by offering a framework of strategic international human resource management (SIHRM). Anchoring SIHRM in the strategic components of MNEs, namely their interunit linkages and internal operations, strategic aspects of international human resource management are described. Using several theoretical bases, numerous propositions are offered. These propositions reflect the single and multiple influence of the strategic components of MNEs and several exogenous and endogenous factors on SIHRM. The intention is to offer a framework that can serve both academics and practitioners in furthering our understanding of strategic international human resource management.

The world has become more competitive, dynamic, uncertain and volatile than ever (Kanter, 1991; Kobrin, 1992). To be successful, many firms have to compete on the global playing field because the costs associated with the development and marketing of new products are too great to be amortized only over one market, even a large one such as the United States or Europe (Bartlett & Ghoshal, 1991). Yet there are some products and services that demand accommodation to location customs, tastes, habits and regulations. Thus for many multinational enterprises (MNEs), the likelihood of operating in diverse environments has never been greater. While these scenarios suggest paths that multinational enterprises have indeed taken to being internationally competitive, they are being superseded by the need to manage globally, as if the world were one vast market, *and* simultaneously to manage locally, as if the world were a vast number of separate and loosely connected markets (Bartlett & Ghoshal, 1991). The trend is creating a great deal of challenge and opportunity in understanding and conceptualizing exactly how multinational enterprises can compete effectively.

Thus there is a significant desire to seek models, frameworks and perhaps solutions in the management of MNEs, particularly with respect to human resource management. While the temptation exists to extrapolate from existing and less global management practice, the requirements of managing global businesses are different and require unique solutions (Bartlett & Ghoshal, 1991; 1992; Adler & Bartholomew, 1992; Casson, 1982; Hennart, 1982; Kogut, 1989; Toyne, 1989; Teece, 1983; Williamson, 1985; Buckley & Casson, 1976; Black, Gregersen & Mendenhall, 1992). Differences also exist at theoretical and conceptual levels: MNEs do appear to have characteristics that are unique or substantially different from domestic organizations (Sundaram and Black, 1992). This is reflected in Sundaram and Black's (1992) definition of an MNE as:

> any enterprise that carries out transactions in or between two sovereign entities, operating under a system of decisions making that permits influence over resources and capabilities, where the transactions are subject to influence by factors exogenous to the home country environment of the enterprise (p.733).

Thus the competitive arena for MNEs is that of the world. However, the competition can be carried out in different forms, with different strategic and organizational responses and organizations often have latitude in selecting the form to use in the competition. According to Bartlett and Ghoshal (1991):

> Even within particular industries, worldwide companies have developed very different strategic and organizational responses to changes in their environment (p.37).

Bartlett and Ghoshal (1991) then go on and describe the arena in which these different strategic and organizational responses are played out. Their basic premise is that MNEs are represented by units spread throughout the world that need to be coordinated or integrated in some form and to some degree.

The differentiation and integration of units (Lawrence & Lorsch, 1967) needs to be done with some attention paid to being globally competitive, efficient, responsive and flexible to local needs and conditions and being able to transfer their learning across units. In essence, MNEs are firms that need to be global and local (multidomestic) at the same time. There are, however, varying levels of globalness and localness that MNEs need to achieve. And there are varying ways to attain similar levels of globalness and localness (Bartlett, 1992).

With the concern for being global and the concern about the transfer of learning and being multidomestic and, therefore, sensitive to local conditions simultaneously, several strategic concerns relevant to international human resource management arise. For example, can and how do MNEs link their globally dispersed units through human resource policies and practices? Can and how do MNEs facilitate a multidomestic response that is simultaneously consistent with the need for global coordination and the transfer of learning and innovation across units through human resource policies and practices?

Thus for strategic international human resource management these characterizations of some possible issues facing multinational enterprises imply several things (Kochan, Batt, & Dyer, 1992). They imply that MNE generally confront several strategic international human resource management decisions. Yet they may also confront several other strategic international human resource decisions that vary depending upon specific characteristics of the MNE. And they also imply the *importance* of strategic international human resource management (SIHRM) for MNEs. As such, the aims of this article are:

- To offer a definition of the field of strategic international human resource management (SIHRM) and to present an integrative framework for this new field of practice and research which identifies key factors and characteristics and their inter-relationships.
- To present testable propositions suggested by the framework.
- To suggest some implications of this framework for academics and practitioners working in the field of SIHRM.

Definition of SIHRM

As the area of human resource management has expanded and become more linked with the strategic needs of the business, it has taken on the characterization of *strategic* human resource management (Schuler, 1992; Lengnick-Hall & Lengnick-Hall, 1988; Wright & McMahan, 1992). We are witnessing a similar phenomenon in the area of international human resource management as well, viz., the linkage of international human resource management with the strategic needs of the business (Galbraith & Kazanjian, 1986; Bartlett & Ghoshal, 1991); and thus the development of strategic international human resource management (Bartlett & Ghoshal, 1992; Adler & Bartholomew, 1992; Black et al., 1992). This linkage is having a substantial impact on identifying and defining what is to be included in strategic international human resource management. Developed more in the discussion of our integrative framework are these three major components of SIHRM: *issues*; *functions*; and *policies and practices*. All three are included here because they are influenced by an MNE's strategic activities and because they in turn influence the concerns and goals of an MNE.

Reasons for the development of strategic international human resource management include the recognition: a) that human resource management at any level is important to strategy implementation (Hamel & Prahalad, 1986; Hambrick & Snow, 1989); b) that major strategic components of multinational enterprises have a major influence on international management issues; functions; and policies and practices (Edstrom & Galbraith, 1977); c) that many of these characteristics of SIHRM can influence the attainment of the concerns and goals of MNEs (Kobrin, 1992); and d) that there are a wide variety of factors that make the relationship between MNEs and SIHRM complex, thereby making the study of SIHRM challenging as well as important (Bartlett & Ghoshal, 1991; Evans, 1992).

Consistent with Schuler (1992) and Wright and McMahan (1992) who define *strategic* human resource management, and thus distinguish it from human resource management, we define strategic international human resource management as:

> human resource management issues, functions, and policies and practices that result from the strategic activities of multinational enterprises and that impact the international concerns and goals of those enterprises.

While this definition is certainly consistent with the definition of human resource management presented within a single country or domestic context (e.g., Schuler & Huber, 1993; Boam & Sparrow, 1992), it greatly expands the coverage of what is to be included in a discussion of strategic international human resource management. It also facilitates the inclusion of a significant number of factors discussed in the international literature, both in the areas of international management and business and international human resource management (Punnett & Ricks, 1992; Dowling & Schuler, 1990; Phatak, 1992). These factors and the definition of SIHRM are melded together and described next in the section presenting the Integrative Framework of SIHRM.

Overview of The Integrative Framework of SIHRM

To address the issues associated with strategic international human resource management, it is most useful to consider utilizing a framework that enables us to integrate the aspects most relevant to our understanding SIHRM. The proposed framework is illustrated in Figure 1. The inspiration for a framework to encompass our thoughts on SIHRM and then to offer some testable propositions was provided by several recent and notable works in the field including Gregersen and Black (1992); Naumann (1992); Begin (1992); Adler and Ghader (1990); and Sundaram and Black (1992). These sources also stimulated the specification of propositions that might be testable and thereby

AN INTEGRATIVE FRAMEWORK 423

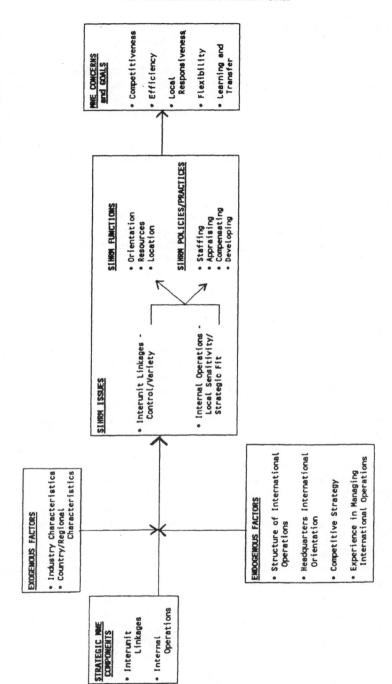

Figure 1. Integrative Framework of Strategic International Human Resource Management in MNE.

offer revisions to what is suggested here. These and a great many other sources provide the support and guidance via discussions of theory in the human resource management, organizational behavior, sociology, psychology, economics and organizational theory literatures. Because this article is meant to focus more on developing a conceptual framework than offering a theoretical perspective (cf. Wright & McMahan, 1992), the utilization of theory is intended to offer suggestions and guidance to others who might wish to develop the theoretical base further (Dubin, 1976).

All the aspects of our integrative framework are described in this section. The following sections then describe their relationships and offer propositions applicable to SIHRM.

Strategic MNE Components

There are two major strategic components of MNEs that give rise to and influence strategic international human resource management. These are the interunit linkages and internal operations (Hennart, 1982; Phatak, 1992).

Interunit Linkages. Multinational enterprises are concerned with operating effectively in several different countries. Consequently, MNEs are continually discussing how to manage their various operating units. In particular, they are interested in how these units are to be differentiated and then how they are to be integrated, controlled and coordinated (Punnett & Ricks, 1992; Ghoshal, 1987; Galbraith, 1992). Differentiation and integration questions are important because they influence the effectiveness of the firm (Lawrence & Lorsch, 1967). In addition to this importance, is the challenge that tends to be associated with selecting from among the several choices and alternatives that exist in differentiating and integrating an MNE (Phatak, 1992; Vernon & Wells, 1991; Prahalad & Doz, 1987). Because of this importance and the challenge associated with them, general questions about differentiating and integrating the units of the firm are regarded as strategic ones (Hambrick & Snow, 1989). Thus, for international human resource management they are also strategic. In fact, for SIHRM, the issues associated with differentiating and integrating the units of an MNE represent a major influence on SIHRM issues, functions and policies and practices (Schuler, Fulkerson, & Dowling, 1991; Fulkerson & Schuler, 1992). Depicted in Figure 1, issues and questions associated with differentiation and integration are covered by the term "Interunit Linkages" under the general heading "SIHRM Issues."

Internal Operations. MNEs are also concerned about strategic issues other than those dealing with the linkage of the units. They are concerned about the internal operations of those units. In addition to working together, each unit has to work within the confines of its local environment, its laws, politics, culture, economy and society. Each unit also has to be operated as effectively as possible relative to the competitive strategy of the MNE and the unit itself. Thus for MNEs, these concerns regarding the internal operations of units are also strategic (Prahalad & Doz, 1987). They can influence the level of effectiveness of the MNE in significant ways. And for our integrative framework, they also influence SIHRM in significant ways. Consequently, the internal operations are also included in Figure 1 under the heading "SIHRM Issues." More precisely, how these internal operations and the interunit linkages of MNEs are expected to influence SIHRM will be suggested after the remaining discussion of the integrative framework of SIHRM.

SIHRM Issues

SIHRM issues address an MNE's interunit and within unit and needs and challenges. Although the MNE is separated across several nations it is a single enterprise. It needs to consider how to balance the needs for differentiation and integration (Lawrence & Lorsch, 1967; Galbraith, 1987). As an MNE it needs to be aware of how much automony it can and needs to grant to local units. It needs to decide how much to control and how to coordinate those units. As an MNE, it needs to decide how much control it will exert over the internal operations of the local unit, particularly how much sensitivity to the local environment is needed. Because these issues of differentiation and integration are often facilitated by human resource management activities, they represent a critical component in our framework.

SIHRM Functions

SIHRM functions represent three areas: the MNE's human resource orientation; the time, energy and financial resources devoted to operating the human resource organization in the MNE; and the location of those resources and the human resource organization. In managing its human resources, the MNE elects to manage in one of several ways. As discussed later, this can range from allowing the units to manage independently to deciding that the units will be managed the same as they are at the center (i.e., the headquarters) of the MNE.

MNEs can devote considerable time, energy and financial resources towards managing their human resources. The center can staff a rather extensive Human Resource department that is exclusively devoted to SIHRM decisions, such as deciding how to select and repatriate expatriates and how to compensate these employees. It can also hire a staff of individuals devoted to management training and development, largely to develop a global management cadre. Of course, many of these activities could be rather minimal if the number of expatriates is small and the units are given a great deal of automony (these alternatives are sometimes discussed under the labels of centralization and decentralization). Thus, the location of these activities can vary, from the center all the way out to the local units. Thus, the resources devoted to and the location of SIHRM operations can be expected to vary considerably across MNEs.

SIHRM Policies and Practices

SIHRM policies and practices represent the last component of SIHRM. This involves the development of general guidelines on how individuals will be managed and the development of specific practices. For example, an MNE might have an HR policy that indicates that performance will be rewarded. Given that this is a rather general statement, each MNE unit could be free to develop specific practices that are simultaneously consistent with local conditions and the general policy. For example, under the above policy, one local unit might develop an individual incentive plan for the general manager tied to the sales of the local operation while another unit might develop a group incentive plan for the entire top management team tied to the sales of the local operation (Fulkerson & Schuler, 1992).

SIHRM policies and practices that are most relevant to the strategic needs of MNEs include those related to staffing, appraising, compensating, and training and developing (Dowling & Schuler, 1990). Only general statements, however, are made about them in the presentation of the propositions here. While potentially significant, the reference of labor-management, employee rights and safety and health practices are not treated in this article.

Exogenous and Endogenous Factors

While these three components of SIHRM are critical to our framework, they are only part of the whole. As suggested, these components, while representing an important part of the framework of SIHRM, are also influenced by factors inside and outside the MNE. As shown in Figure 1, these factors are identified as exogenous (outside the MNE) and endogenous (within the MNE).

The exogenous factors include industry characteristics and country/regional characteristics. Industry characteristics include: a) type of business and technology available; b) nature of the competitors; and c) extent of change. The country/regional characteristics include: a) political conditions; b) economic conditions; c) legal requirements; and d) socio-cultural conditions.

The endogenous factors include: a) structure of international operations; b) the MNE's headquarters international orientation; c) competitive strategy being used; and d) the MNE's experience in managing international operations. The nature of the impact of these exogenous and endogenous factors will be predicted in specific propositions after the discussion of the framework.

Support for inclusion of these factors is offered by Kobrin (1991; 1992); Evans (1992); Porter (1980; 1986; 1990); Bartlett and Ghoshal (1987; 1988; 1991; 1992); Punnett and Ricks (1992); and Phatak (1992); and Miller, Beechler, Bhatt, and Nath (1986). Essentially all these factors impinge upon the MNE's management of its human resources and its effort to be locally responsive and adaptable and globally coordinated and controlled (Edstrom & Galbraith, 1977; Egelhoff, 1988; Galbraith & Kazanjian, 1986). Other factors that could be included in a more extended version of this framework include industry maturity, history, national industrial policy and extent of unionization (Kochan et al., 1992).

As will be developed in this article, the factors are proposed to influence SIHRM in rather specific ways. And while the theoretical base in the SIHRM literature is still evolving, we will attempt to draw upon a variety of theoretical viewpoints to support our propositions (cf. Gregersen & Black, 1992). This utilizes and extends the suggestions of Wright and McMahan (1992) in describing several theoretical bases for strategic human resource management (Kobrin, 1992).

The framework in Figure 1 obviously oversimplifies the reality of the MNE and the factors that influence SIHRM in MNEs, e.g., the type of business and the structure of international operations may be related. It might be reasonably argued that in fact, the type of business could be an antecedent of the structure of international operations (Phatak, 1992; Heenan & Perlmutter, 1979). However, because the exact nature of the possible relationships among these factors can be debated, we offer them here as independent factors subject to empirical investigation (Kobrin, 1992).

Concerns and Goals

The last portion of our integrative framework of SIHRM is "MNE Concerns and Goals." The five concerns and goals shown in Figure 1 are: a) global competitiveness; b) efficiency; c) local responsiveness (sensitivity); d) flexibility; and e) organizational learning (and transfer of information) (Bartlett & Ghoshal, 1991). As Bartlett and Ghoshal (1991) suggest, while these concerns and goals are important to MNEs, their degree of importance and the nature of how the importance is constructed may vary with the specific MNE. Being globally competitive for an MNE that is really in a global industry has implications for competitive behavior that are different from an MNE that is in a multidomestic industry (Porter, 1986, 1990). Nevertheless, for survival, all MNEs need to be concerned with global competitiveness.

They also need to be concerned with being efficient, with having and utilizing the most appropriate methods and processes to make and deliver their products and services worldwide. Also, because of the intense global competitiveness, MNEs are seeking to identify the methods and processes that are most appropriate. They are realizing that every possible source of competitive advantage must be identified and utilized. And as they are searching, particularly firms pursuing total quality management, they are realizing that a systematic approach to developing human resource policies and practices may, in fact, give competitive advantage (Galbraith, 1992). Furthermore, these MNEs are also realizing that SIHRM policies and practices may indeed travel well, i.e., they may actually transfer across cultures more easily than once assumed (Wickens, 1987). Of course, this application of human resource practices across environments is typically done with recognition for local conditions. Local conditions such as laws and culture make it imperative for MNEs to be aware of the need to adapt their human resource practices. Thus, an MNE's SIHRM policies and practices need to be locally responsive and globally competitive at the same time (Bartlett & Ghoshal, 1991).

MNEs also need to be concerned with being flexible to changing conditions, whether from local conditions or from technology, strategy, or nature of the competition. These and other factors may require new human resource policies and practices in the MNE center and the MNE local units.

Lastly, a major goal of MNEs is facilitating learning and the transfer of this learning across units. As MNEs face more competition, their degrees of freedom, their slack, tends to be constrained. Consequently, they must encourage new learning, and ultimately the development of new products and services. In addition to encouraging new learning, MNEs must encourage and facilitate the transfer and sharing of this new knowledge. It is in this way that the synergies of being one company can be seized (Prahalad & Doz, 1987; Bartlett & Ghoshal, 1991).

These five concerns and goals of MNEs are not necessarily the only ones on which MNEs focus, but they appear to be some of the most important. They are also ones that can be influenced by SIHRM (Evans, 1992; Walker, 1992; Dowling & Schuler, 1990). Thus, they are an integral component of our integrative framework shown in Figure 1.

Development of the Integrative Framework

With this integrative framework as our brief guide for what is included in SIHRM, we will now expand on the descriptions of each part. In so doing, propositions will be offered that represent our understanding of the field. They certainly are not intended to represent all the propositions that one could generate, but we would hope that they represent many of critical ones.

The presentation of these propositions reflects the integrative framework in Figure 1. Because a central premise of the framework is that the SIHRM *issues* are the major drivers in SIHRM, i.e., they really are the focal point and help determine the characteristics of the SIHRM *functions* and SIHRM *policies and practices*, they are used as major organizers of the discussion. The interunit linkages and internal operations however, serve as the first two primary headings. Within these discussions, SIHRM issues and relevant HR policies and practices are identified, based upon the literature (cf. Sundaram & Black, 1992). Exogenous and endogenous factors that appear to have a rather direct and immediate impact upon these interunit linkages and internal operations are also presented here. After the discussion of them under the first two primary headings, further discussion of the possible impact of the exogenous and endogenous factors is presented. Throughout, propositions most relevant to the immediate discussions are offered.

Interunit Linkages in SIHRM

Within our framework of SIHRM, the interunit linkages have been a traditional focal point for the discussion of international human resource management (Pucik & Katz, 1986; Pucik, 1988; Phatak, 1992; Bartlett & Ghoshal, 1991). These discussions have typically been around the themes such as, control of variety, in particular how to recognize the variety of several worldwide units and yet how to control and coordinate that variety (Doz & Prahalad, 1986; Edstrom & Galbraith, 1977). In some respects, these are part of the classic organizational design issues of differentiation and integration, yet they are far more complex when set in a complex global context.

In relation to SIHRM, discussions regarding interunit linkages have included: a) single SIHRM practice attention, e.g., what is the best way to prepare expatriates for foreign assignments (Black et al., 1992); b) elaborate contingency frameworks using information characteristics and forms of control along with SIHRM practices (Pucik & Katz, 1986; Galbraith, 1992); c) alternative organizational structures for global operation, their linkages and their human resource implications (Galbraith & Kazanjian, 1986); and whether or not to export people or export the HR function (Fisher, 1989).

The key objective in interunit linkages appears to be balancing the needs of variety (diversity), coordination, and control for purposes of global competitiveness, flexibility and organizational learning (Bartlett & Ghoshal, 1991). Of course, the nature of this balance is expected to vary depending on the characteristics of the MNE. As described below, this objective becomes most challenging in Bartlett and Ghoshal's transnational MNE. Here there may be several units within a global business that need to be coordinated for the success of that business. The units of separate businesses (and/or those within separate regions) need to be coordinated for the total MNE to reap advantages of the synergies of cooperation. Yet, the units need to be given the autonomy to make the best decisions for the local conditions, and they need the autonomy for motivation. Still the headquarters of the MNE may wish to utilize more global, companywide criteria (Roth, Schweiger, & Morrison, 1991). These relationships and the tensions that can arise are directly played out in HR policies and practices. The efforts by units for autonomy are often resistance to policies or, at most, acceptance of some general guidelines that allow for local discretion. This result of some general HR policies (guidelines), however, can enable the balance to be achieved (Prahalad & Doz, 1981; 1987).

Balancing the needs and demands of coordination, control and autonomy is a fundamental objective for MNEs. Following Bartlett and Ghoshal (1991, pp. 59-71) results in the following fundamental assumption in SIHRM:

> Balancing the needs of coordination, control and autonomy and maintaining the appropriate balance are critical to the success of the MNE in being globally competitive, efficient, sensitive to the local environment, flexible and capable of creating an organization in which learning and the transfer of knowledge are feasible.

This fundamental objective for MNEs and the corresponding fundamental assumption in SIHRM identifies the major objectives in interunit linkages for SIHRM:

> Balancing the needs of autonomy (thereby facilitating variety and diversity), coordination, and control for the purpose of global competitiveness, flexibility and learning through the use of the relevant SIHRM policies and practices.

This objective, along with the relevant SIHRM policies and practices directly influenced, is shown in Figure 2.

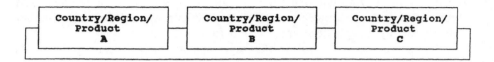

OBJECTIVE

Balancing the needs of autonomy, coordination, and control for the purpose of global competitiveness, flexibility and learning through the use of the relevant SIHRM policies and practices.

Relevant SIHRM Policies and Practices

- Maintaining an appropriate mix and flow of PCNs, TCNs, HCNs
- Systematically Developing HR Policies and Practices
- Using Management Development as Glue

Figure 2.   SIHRM Issue: Focus on Interunit Linkages

SIHRM Policies and Practices

Addressing the major objective shown in Figure 2 engages three SIHRM policies and practices rather specifically. Also impacted here are the SIHRM functions. The SIHRM policies and practices that appear to be most directly associated with interunit linkages in SIHRM include: a) determining and maintaining staffing levels that are an appropriate mix and flow of parent country nationals (PCNs), third country nationals (TCNs), and host country or local nationals (HCNs) (increasingly these three groups are being labelled "international assignees" but we use the three groups for purposes of distinguishing staffing sources); b) developing HR policies and practices that link units but also allow local adaptation; and c) using management development to create shared visions and mindsets to cohere interunit linkages.

Strategic International Human Resource Staffing: The Mix of PCNs, TCNs, and HCNs. Staffing is a major SIHR practice that MNEs have used to help coordinate and control their far-flung global operations (Pucik & Katz, 1986; Zeira & Banai, 1981; Hendry, 1992; Dowling & Schuler, 1990). Traditionally MNEs have sent parent country national or expatriates abroad to ensure that the policies and procedures of the home office were being carried out to the letter in foreign operations (Punnett & Ricks, 1992; Hailey, 1992). As costs became prohibitive and career issues made these assignments less attractive, MNEs turned to third country nationals and host country nationals to satisfy international staffing needs (Heenan & Perlmutter, 1979).

While this approach may have solved the staffing need, it raised the concern about its ability to help with the needs for coordination and control (Ouchi

& MacGuire, 1975; Hailey, 1992). As Pucik and Katz (1986) argued, firms' reactions (to the need for coordination and control) could be classified by : a) establishing rules and procedures for HCNs or TCNs to carry out; or b) socializing the HCNs or TCNs to think and behave like expatriates. Of course these pure archtypes might not be found as MNEs seek to find the most appropriate solution to fit the circumstances. For example, under conditions of rapid change, high uncertainty and the need for social information to be gathered and utilized, MNEs would more likely be found socializing employees (Van Maanen & Schein, 1979). Under conditions of stability, certainty and the need for technical information to be utilized, firms would more likely be found establishing rules and procedures for employees to carry out (Banai, 1992). But MNEs rarely ever found either one set of conditions or another. So combinations of the two approaches were common. But because socializing has a tendency to reflect the culture and norms of the parent firm, this process tends to biased (Pucik and Katz, 1986). Thus the ability of the firm to maximize the benefits of variety can be compromised. This may be diminished, however, if an MNE engages more third country nationals and host country nationals in preference to expatriates, individuals who would be expected to have been previously socialized (Cappelli & McElrath, 1992).

Resulting from this discussion is our first proposition:

> **P1(a)**. *As a means for control and coordination, MNEs will initially attempt to utilize PCNs in preference to HCNs or TCNs; however resoure considerations will give way to facilitating the utilization of HCNs and TCNs by MNEs to control and coordinate their global operations.*

> **P1(b)**. *As MNEs increase their reliance upon HCNs and TCNs to control and coordinate their global operations, they will devote more resources to socializing these employees and to developing policies and procedures that might be used to guide local decision making, while still allowing some local discretion.*

These propositions are based upon and consistent with the theoretical positions and rationale of agency theory (Jones, 1984), and resource dependence theory (Pfeffer & Salancik, 1978) as presented by Wright and McMaham (1992) in their discussions of strategic human resource management.

Systematically Linking Regions/Countries with HR Policies and Practices. While appropriate staffing mixes can be helpful in integrating and coordinating the various units of the MNE, human resource policies and practices can also assist in this objective. In doing so they must also be consistent with the needs of the business to achieve competitiveness, be flexible and facilitate the transfer of learning across units. Because of the existence of a wide variety of human resource practices this must be done consciously and systematically.

Part of the challenge in developing human resource practices to facilitate interunit linkages is simultaneously allow for some flexibility. This flexibility enables changes and its enables adaptation to local conditions. This is attained in part by ensuring that practices are not carved in stone (mentally or physically) and that the practices are formulated within a larger context. The larger context for human resource practice formulation is composed of human resource philosophy and human resource policies (Schuler, 1992).

Statements of human resource *philosophy*, while general, have the ability to proscribe limits on the actual treatment of individuals regardless of location. This is done through its top-down impact on HR policies and practices (Schuler, 1992). When the HR policies and practices are consciously and systematically linked to the strategic business needs of the MNE, they are regarded as strategic international human resource management activities. Armed with an HR philosophy, MNEs are able to further define how employees are to be treated: HR *policies* help to specify the meaning of the philosophy.

From these policies come more specific SIHRM *practices* to be implemented at the unit level. These are the human resource activities that directly have an impact on employees, e.g., types of compensation, staffing methods, appraisal methods and forms of training and development. There are many choices amongst the array of possible SIHRM practices. And because they, as the other SIHRM activities, influence the behaviors of individuals, they need to be systematically selected to be aligned with the other SIHRM activities (Begin, 1992).

Developing policies to be used as umbrellas for the practices within units, facilitates the attainment of the main objective of interunit linkage. This may be easier said than done, however, particularly if the units have dramatically different local environments and / or are pursuing different competitive strategies with different technologies. While this confounding may make the task more challenging, it does not make it impossible. Perhaps, however, it does require more resources "to get it right," i.e., to systematically develop the practices and ensure that they are linked with common human resource policies. Nonetheless, accomplishing the task enables the MNE to control the diversity of the operation while at the same time attaining the goals of competitiveness, flexibility and transfer of learning. Thus it is expected that MNEs will attempt to be systematic in developing their strategic international human resource policies and practices.

Based upon some of the rationale of behavioral theory (Jackson, Schuler & Rivero, 1989) and resource dependency theory (Pfeffer and Salancik, 1978), the following propositions are offered:

> **P1(c).**   *When the benefits from coordinating units are high, and local environments vary, MNEs will attempt to systematically develop their HR policies and practices to link with the needs of the business and accommodate to local conditions.*

> **P1(d).**   *For MNEs, linking units with systematically developed HR policies and practices will be more important and challenging to the extent the units are divergent and the benefit from coordination is high.*

Using Management Development as an Interunit Link. Although using the appropriate HR policies and practices is an important way to link regional units of the MNE, they also use management development. Evans (1992) describes management development in MNEs, as being the "glue" to bond together otherwise loose and separate entities. In MNEs that become structured to reflect the complexity of their global environments, they often decentralize operations by region, product or both. They may even become heterarchies (MNEs having multiple units with headquarters spread throughout the world). In their attempts to generate and benefit from some synergies of being a heterarchy or transnational, MNEs may try to create a pool of global managers (Bartlett & Ghoshal, 1992). This pool, through management development activities, is able to serve the MNE in any region or business. In order to operate this, the corporate or global headquarters' operation houses the management development effort. The local, regional and business HR units cooperate with the corporate HR unit in their efforts to coordinate the management development programs in order to glue the interunits together (Evans, 1992; Scullion, 1992; Vanderbroeck, 1992; Tichy, 1992; Bartlett & Ghoshal, 1991; 1992). This results in the following proposition:

P1(*e*). *MNEs will increase their utilization of management development activities as their needs to coordinate the strategic activities of separate units increase and the utility of having a global pool of managers increases.*

Internal Operations in SIHRM

While these interunit linkages just discussed tend to be the traditional focus of strategic international human resource management, the internal operations require the same degree of attention. Both have an influence on the effectiveness of an MNE (Porter, 1990; Punnett & Ricks, 1992). Each local unit remains a part of the MNE, although the degree to which it needs to be tightly integrated varies. Nevertheless, it must fit in with the local environment. It must recognize and abide by local employment law, tradition and custom of the local area. Its human resource practices must reflect those aspects of the local environment. Thus the local units need to be given some automony to adapt to the local conditions. Yet, because they need to be coordinated with the rest of the MNE, e.g., to facilitate the selection transfer, appraisal and compensation of local managers, they need to share some common human resource policies.

Beyond fitting in with the local environment and fitting with the MNE, the local unit needs to fit with its competitive strategy. That is, the local unit needs to develop human resource practices that are not only consistent with the policies of the MNE, but also fit with the competitive strategy of the unit (Schuler & Jackson, 1987). Exactly how this fit might be obtained is suggested below, but the implication here is that the local unit needs to be fitting the local human resource practices with aspects beyond the local culture in order to be effective and yet still retain some responsiveness.

More specifically, the major objective of SIHRM regarding internal operations is:

> being responsive to and effective in the local environment, yet being willing and ready to act in a coordinated fashion with the rest of the MNE units.

SIHRM Policies and Practices

This objective is executed through and reflected in three relevant SIHRM policies and practicies. The first is matching and adapting HR practices with the competitive strategy of the unit and the local culture and legal system. The second is creating a *modus operandi* whereby these HR practices can be modified to fit changing conditions. And the third is creating a set of SIHRM policies at the MNE level that can encompass and legitimate the HR practices of the local units. These are illustrated in Figure 3.

Matching and Adapting HR Practicies. In an attempt to satisfy the MNE's concerns and goals of being competitive, locally responsive and flexible, the local unit manager needs to develop human resource practices consistent with the needs of the local culture, legal system and tradition. To facilitate this the local manager (particularly an expatriate one), may staff the HR function with host country nationals. In fact, this is one of the positions that MNEs seem to insist upon filling with a host country national (Dowling & Schuler, 1990). To complement this fit, the local manager needs to inform the HR manager of the needs of the business, the competitive strategy in particular. Again, for the sake of striving for attainment of the MNE's concerns and goals, the local unit will seek to combine the knowledge of the local environment with the needs of the business (Bartlett, 1992).

As discussed above, this process of systematically aligning human resource practices, policies and philosophies with each other and with strategic needs of the business are similar for domestic corporations and MNEs. A major difference, however, appears to be in the need to balance the competitive strategy imperative (described more extensively under "Endogenous Factors") with the cultural imperative (Phatak, 1992; Punnett & Ricks, 1992; Adler, 1991).

The cultural imperative is an encompassing term that can include aspects of the local culture, economy, legal system, religious beliefs and education. The cultural imperative is important in SIHRM because of its impact upon acceptable, legitimate, and feasible practices and behaviors (Adler, 1991; Schneider, 1986; Laurant, 1986: Adler & Bartholomew, 1992). Acceptable in terms of "can we pay workers different rates, and thereby differentiate them, according to performance?" Legitimate in terms of "are there any legal statutes prohibiting us from not paying workers overtime for work on Saturday and Sunday?" Feasible in terms of "while the society is hierarchical, authoritarian and paternalistic, can we empower the workforce to make workplace decisions in order to facilitate our quality strategy?"

```
┌──────────┐
│  Local   │
│  Unit    │
└──────────┘
```

OBJECTIVE

Being responsive to and effective in the local environment yet being willing and ready to act in a coordinated fashion with the rest of the MNE units.

Relevant SIHRM Policies and Practices

- Matching and adapting HR practices with the competitive strategy of the unit and the local culture and legal system.
- Creating a modus operandi whereby these HR practices can be modified to fit changing conditions.
- Developing Global HR Policies flexible enough to be adapted for local HR practice.

Figure 3. SIHRM Issue: Focus on Internal Operations

All three components of the culture imperative are important for MNEs to consider in decisions about where to locate and about which human resource practices to use and that can be used. Because questions about which human resource practices to use are also influenced by a competitive strategy imperative (Morrison & Roth, 1992; Wickens, 1987), the potential challenge emerges: Balancing the imperatives in shaping the final set of SIHRM practices to be used on the local level.

Combining the precepts from behavioral theory (Schuler & Jackson, 1987), and requisite variety thinking (Weick, 1969), results in the three propositions below:

P2(a). *Local unit HR practices will reflect the imperative of the competitive strategy of the local unit and the cultural imperative of the local environment. Thus, local units pursuing a competitive strategy will have HR practices that reflect and support that strategy and will have HR practices that reflect the local environment.*

In attempts to attain other MNE concerns and goals, the local unit will be ready to ensure that HR practices, once developed, can also be adapted to fit with the needs of the MNE, when necessary. For example, to accommodate potential staffing and transfer needs, the local unit might adapt some staffing and development practices more consistent with those of the MNE. This may, however, be done for a limited pool of potential individuals (e.g., individuals who could be global managers). Nevertheless, this might help the MNE be more competitive. The result of this is the following proposition:

P2(b). *Units within MNEs will develop HR practices that are reflective of local conditions, and simultaneously be ready to adapt some HR practices to coordinate activities with other units particularly as the needs for coordination increase.*

Creating a Modus Operandi. As local conditions and characteristics of the MNE change, it is important for HR policies and practices to reflect these changes. Inside the local unit, the manager must establish procedures for and recognize the legitimacy of changing human resource practices to fit new conditions (Brewster & Tyson, 1991). This will help ensure the needed flexibility that is a concern and goal of MNEs today. This results in the following proposition:

> **P2(c).** *Under changing organizational and environmental conditions, MNEs will create mechanisms and policies that recognize and support the revision of HR practices in the local units.*

Developing Global HR Policies. The center has a responsibility and strategic interest in developing HR policies that are broad enough and appropriate enough for the several local units to adapt to their local environmental and competitive strategy needs.

This discussion complements the earlier discussion under "Interunit Linkages." There it was argued that policies have to be created to facilitate interunit linkage and transfer of learning, yet still recognize the needs of the local units. This discussion suggests that the local units need to systematically analyze their environmental needs and be responsible for and ensure that their needs are folded into the process whereby the global human resource policies are created. To the extent that the local units are more geographically dispersed, the more difficult it becomes to gather the necessary information. And to the extent that the local units have more dissimilar environments, the more difficult it will be to develop global HR policies that can incorporate (i.e., serve as umbrellas for) the appropriate practices within the units.

The propositions, based upon resource dependency and requisite variety precepts (Pfeffer & Salancik, 1978; Weick, 1969), that follow from our discussion include:

> **P2(d).** *As the need for integration of units increases and the respect for local conditions remains, MNEs will create HR policies that can encompass [i.e., be consistent with] the variations in HR practices within the local units.*

> **P2(e).** *As units become more geographically dispersed and more diverse, MNEs will devote more resources to developing HR policies and procedures as the need to coordinate these units increases.*

Summary of Interunit and Internal Operations

In this section the basic framework was established for describing the major impact of MNEs on SIHRM. Several propositions were suggested based upon the premise that the fundamental objective of MNEs is to establish separate units worldwide and then to identify the appropriate degrees of automony and variety, and methods of controlling and coordinating those units. The propositions suggested are those that would seem to reflect the most direct relationship between the fundamental objective of the MNE (as discussed as interunit linkages and internal operations) and the associated SIHRM issues of control and automony and local sensitivity and strategic fit as illustrated in Figure 1. While these relationships are offered for empirical examination, the results may suggest a more parsimonious way of describing the relationships of SIHRM.

Also offered for empirical examination are the following sections on Exogenous Factors and Endogenous Factors. In these sections further SIHRM propositions are offered that reflect the influence that these factors might more specifically have on the relationship between the strategic MNE components and the SIHRM Issues shown in Figure 1. While the influence of some, e.g., culture and competitive strategy, has already been alluded to, more precise expectations of the influence of all these factors are suggested.

Exogenous Factors

The Exogenous Factors are classified into two groups—*Industry Characteristics* and *Country/Regional Characteristics*. Industry Characteristics include the following factors: a) type of business or industry; b) nature of the competitors; and c) the extent of change. Country/Regional Characteristics include: a) the political environment; b) the economic environment; c) the legal environment; and d) the socio-cultural environment.

Type of Business

This factor refers to the distinction drawn by Porter (1986) between global and multidomestic business. Porter suggests that the industry (or industries if the organization is a conglomerate) in which a firm is involved is of considerable importance because patterns of international competition vary widely from one industry to another. At one end of the continuum of international competition is the *global industry*, one in which the firm's competitive position in one country is significantly influenced by its position in other countries. Examples include commercial aircraft, semiconductors, and copiers. The other end of the continuum is the *multidomestic industry*, where competition in each country is essentially independent of competition in other countries. Traditional examples include retailing, distribution, and insurance. While conceptually different from the forms of MNEs offered by Bartlett and Ghoshal (1991), Porter's description of the strategic implications for MNEs in global versus the multidomestic industries is similar to that of the multinational and transnational forms:

> The global industry is not merely a collection of domestic industries but a series of linked domestic industries in which the rivals compete against each other on a truly worldwide basis......In a multidomestic industry, then, international strategy collapses to a series of domestic strategies. The issues that are uniquely international revolve around how to do business abroad, how to select good countries in which

to compete (or assess country risk), and mechanisms to achieve the one-time transfer of know-how. These are questions that are relatively well-developed in the literature. In a global industry, however, managing international activities like a portfolio will undermine the possibility of achieving competitive advantage. In a global industry, a firm must in some way integrate its activities on a worldwide basis to capture the linkages among countries (Porter, 1986, p.12).

Commenting on the relevant human resource implications, Dowling and Schuler (1990) note that in a multidomestic industry, the role of the HR department will most likely be more domestic in structure and orientation. At times, there may be considerable demand for international services from the HR department (e.g. when a new plant or office is established in a foreign location and the need for expatriate employees arises), but these activities would not be pivotal—indeed, many of these services may be provided by consultants and/or temporary employees. The main role for the HR function would be to support the primary activities of the firm in each domestic market to achieve competitive advantage through either cost/efficiency or differentiation (value added to products or services). If, however, the firm is in a global industry, the "imperative for coordination" described by Porter would require a HR function structured to deliver the international support required by primary activities of the firm. The need to develop coordination raises complex problems for any international firm. As Laurent (1986) has noted:

> In order to build, maintain, and develop their corporate identity, multinational organizations need to strive for consistency in their ways of managing people on a worldwide basis. Yet, and in order to be effective locally, they also need to adapt those ways to the specific cultural requirements of different societies. While the global nature of the business may call for increased consistency, the nature of cultural environments may be calling for differentiation (p.97).

Thus the type of business is expected to be a major factor international HR policies and practices. This suggests the following propositions:

> **P3(a).** *In comparison to multidomestic businesses, in global businesses the need for and benefits from coordinated interunit linkages is high, thus attention and resources devoted to developing HR policies and practices to facilitate interunit linkages are also high.*

In a recent paper, however, Kobrin (1992), drawing on the work of Prahalad and Doz (1987) and Bartlett and Ghoshal (1989), suggests that characterizing businesses as being either global or multidomestic may be oversimplifying.

> Classifying businesses as either globally integrated or locally responsive can be misleading as very few fall unambiguously in either

category...although their relative intensity varies across industries, most multinationals respond to both sets of pressures *simultaneously* (p.2).

While recognizing the pitfalls of oversimplification, we offer several propositions associated with the integrative framework for strategic international human resource management:

P3(*b*). *MNEs whose dominant business is towards the global end of the industry continuum will have a HR function which is more international in orientation and will give more emphasis to the issue of international coordination and control.*

P3(*c*). *MNEs whose dominant business is towards the multidomestic end of the industry continuum will have a HR function which is less international in orientation and will give more emphasis to the issue of coordination and control at the national level.*

Theoretical and conceptual support for these propositions can be found in the early integration and differentation arguments by Lawrence and Lorsch (1967) and later expanded upon by Galbraith (1973, 1987).

Competitors

This exogenous factor refers to the major competitiors with which the MNE must contend in its various product or service markets. As Thompson and Strickland (1990) note, studying the actions and behavior of an organization's nearest competitiors is essential. Unless careful attention is paid to what competitors are doing, an MNE's intended strategy may prove to be dysfunctional. Thompson and Strickland suggest a number of factors or headings under which the objectives and strategies of competitors may be categorized. The first is *competitive scope*, which refers to whether the competitor is operating on a global, multicountry, national, or regional basis. The second is the competitor's *strategic intent*—for example, to be the dominant leader, to be among the industry leaders, or to maintain position. The third factor is the competitor's market *share objective*—for example, aggressive expansion via both acquisition and internal growth, maintaining present market share by growing at a rate equal to the industry average, or giving up market share to achieve short-term profit objectives. The fourth factor is the competitior's overall *competitive strategy*—such as low-cost leadership, niche market focus, or a differentiation strategy (Porter, 1986,1990).

Other issues relevant to competitor analysis include evaluation of potential major players in the industry and attempting to predict future strategic moves by competitors. Generally as the competition becomes more intense and aggressive, greater attention is given to competing successfully. Consequently, the enterprises devote more attention and expertise to issues of linkage and internal operations and to the management of their resources, including human

resources (Wright & McMahan, 1992). And as this competition becomes mo
intense and global, the more strategic international human resour
management issues become significant (Sundaram & Black, 1992; Kobri
1992). Propositions suggested by this discussion of competitors include:

> **P4(*a*).** *MNEs facing competitors who operate more globally will
> devote more attention to strategic international human resource
> management issues.*

> **P4(*b*).** *As competitors seek a more dominant market position
> globally, MNEs will devote more resources to strategic international
> human resource management issues. HR policies and practices to
> control and/or minimize risk will be implemented.*

> **P4(*c*).** *The strategic behavior of competitiors will impact the
> behavior of MNEs more as the competitors assume a more significant
> share of the market. HR policies and practices to gain competitive
> advantage will be implemented.*

These propositions are consistent with arguments based upon the resourc
based view of the firm (Barney, 1991), particularly those focused on usir
human resource managment as a way to gain competitive advantage (Wrigl
& McMahan, 1992).

Extent of Change

This factor refers to the extent and speed of change which the MNE face
Porter (1980) has identified a number of factors which drive the extent of chang
in various industries. These include: changes in the long-term industry growt
rate, shifts in buyer composition and the emergence of new ways to use a produ
or service, extent of product innovation, extent of technological change, exter
of marketing innovation, entry or exit of major firms, changes within nation
changes in regulatory influences, and changes in levels of uncertainty an
business risk.

As change increases in pace and intensity, more attention is directed towar
competing successfully (Porter, 1980). As such, enterprises devote resourc
ensuring that employees coordinate and cooperate their efforts. And as th
change is played out on a global basis, the more that this coordination an
cooperation occur in a global context and the more that strategic internation
human resource management issues become significant.

Rapid changes are likely to require faster and more understandabl
information exchange (Edstrom & Galbraith, 1977). The more rapid and intens
the change in the industry and the relevant external environment, the mor
exchange of information among the units that may be necessary. This exchang
typically needs to be more frequent and understandable. Time is of the essenc
Human resource practices that facilitate this timeliness, flexibility an
understandability are more likely to be found in MNEs that are in rapidl
changing environments. This may be reflected in more frequent job rotation

among expatriates and TCNs. Frequent management development programs bringing people together to facilitate familiarity and understanding are more likely (Evans, 1992; Bartlett & Ghoshal, 1991).

Based upon the extent of change the following two propositions are offered:

P5(a). *The more rapid, intensive and global the change occurring within and around the industry, the more attention and resources MNEs will devote to strategic international human resource management issues in attempts to control and minimize risk and increase certainty and predictability.*

P5(b). *The more rapid and intense the change, the greater the need for coordination and communication between units, and thus there will be a greater need for more well-developed HR policies and practices to facilitate information flow and understanding.*

These propositons are based upon a rationale offered by Edstrom and Galbraith (1977) in their arguments related to the need for control, certainty and predictability in efficiently coordinating dispersed units. They are also consistent with agency theory (Jones, 1984) and resource dependency theory (Pfeffer & Salancik, 1978; Grant, 1991).

In addition to the impact of these Exogenous Factors of Industry Characteristics, are those Exogenous Factors of Country/Regional Characteristics. Because of similar impacts, a single proposition is offered for the political and economic factors and another is offered for the legal and socio-cultural.

Political

Building on Ferris and Judge (1991), who do an excellent job in describing the importance of political influence in human resource management, this factor includes various forms of risk associated with the political environment in a particular country or region. The most important aspect of this factor is the MNE's assessment of the overall political stability of a country or region. This may be particularly important in an MNE's initial decision to enter a market (Phatak, 1992; Vernon, 1990; Root, 1987; de la Torre & Neckar, 1990).

Robock and Simmonds (1989) define political risk as "the likelihood that political forces will cause drastic changes in a country's business environment that affect the profit and other goals of a particular business enterprise" (p.378).[1] Political risk conditions create an environment of uncertainty, of political exposure (Sundaram & Black, 1992). Needing to manage this uncertainty, MNEs may act to exert more apparent control over the situation by sending more home office employees (expatriates) and imposing policies and practice prescribed by headquarters (Pucik, Tichy & Barnett, 1992).

Economic

This factor relates to the basic economic position and extent of economic development of a country or countries in a region from the perspective of investment by the MNE. Relevant economic indicators include: the economic size of a country as measured by its total gross domestic product (GDP); income level indicators, such as GDP per capita; overall growth trends; sectoral trends within a national economy; and the degree of economic integration with the global economy (ratio of exports to GDP) (Robock & Simmonds, 1989). More specific economic variables include: the ratio of foreign reserves to imports; current account balance on GDP; export growth rate; and the ratio of net foreign debt to exports (Cosset & Roy, 1991). These facets of the economy together create an overall level of economic exposure much greater than faced by domestic enterprises (Sundaram & Black, 1992; Rugman, 1980).

Consequently this represents a source of uncertainty and resource dependence that MNEs may seek to control. Engaging in complex financial transactions can be an effective response in attempting to minimize the downside risk. Another response might be to reduce the size of investment in a region by scaling back investment plans or moving operations. These moves would directly impact strategic international staffing divisions. They may also impact the political climate (and thus level of that uncertainty) in the region. Thus, based upon resource dependency and agency theory precepts, is the following proposition:

> **P6(a)**. *The higher the level of political and economic risk, the more likely the MNE is to monitor the activities of the units through SIHRM policies and practices.*

Legal

This factor refers to the basic legal code and/or legal structure of a particular country or countries which the MNE wishes to trade with and/or invest in. It is also relevant to note that some countries have dual civil and religious codes (e.g., some Muslim counties), and attitudes to the degree to which legal requirements (eg. legal contracts) are binding may vary considerably. These latter two points need to be taken into consideration in any analysis of the legal system of particular countries.

Legal issues which are of concern to MNEs include: 1) The right of establishment (the right to trade, invest, or establish and operate a business in a country); 2) Protection of intellectual property rights; 3) Taxation treaties; 4) Property protection in foreign jurisdictions: and 5) International arbitration and dispute settlement. Legal issues of importance to MNEs that impact human resource management include the varying employment and labor laws in countries throughout the world. For example, labor laws in some countries may make it mandatory for firms to provide a social plan along with their intentions to layoff employees or terminate operations. Stock option plans are not allowed as a form of compensation for employees in many countries. Of course immigration and income taxation treaties also influence staffing decisions, particularly with respect to the ability and cost of posting expatriates.

Dimensions of legal issues which may impact an MNE's strategic use of human resources include heterogeneity, complexity, relevancy, stability and predictability. While each of these dimensions has its own unique impact, generally the greater the heterogeneity, complexity and relevancy, and the less the stability and predictability, the more the need for a broader understanding of legal issues (Florkowski & Nath, 1993).[2] The more useful it is also likely to be for host country nationals to be employed in the MNE's local human resource positions.

Socio-cultural

This factor refers to the specific social and cultural norms of the host environment which the MNE must consider in assessing the business environment of a particular country. Such norms may be both pervasive and highly integrated with the other characteristics of the country or region (Hofsteade, 1993; Adler, 1991). A useful concept in discussing socio-cultural issues is the emic-etic distinction (Triandis & Berry, 1980). Emic refers to culture-specific aspects of concepts or behavior, and etic refers to culture-common aspects.

It is essential for MNEs to be aware of which business practices in any particular country or region are regarded as etic (i.e., transferable to that particular country or region) or emic (i.e., non-transferable and likely to be regarded as dysfunctional and rejected). It is equally imperative for MNEs to be aware of which specific human resource and management practices are likely to transfer abroad. This may require an analysis of cultural values deemed critical in international management. Such values as the degree of individualism, informality, materialism, change and time orientation may likely impact human resource practices such as appraisal and compensation (Phatak, 1992; Ronen, 1986; Adler, 1991).

This is not to suggest, however, that socio-cultural values are neither subject to change nor applicable to only some individuals in a society, but that MNEs must systematically consider them in managing their local units. Indeed, it appears that some human resource practices, e.g., group-oriented job design, can even work well in cultures that may be typically classified as high on individualism (Wickens, 1987; IBM/Towers Perrin, 1992). Nevertheless, emic-etic differences may influence the success of an MNE (Punnett & Ricks, 1992).

Thus, MNEs can be expected to increase their chances of success by understanding the socio-cultural systems of the regions in which they operate and share this knowledge among their units, e.g., through expatriate assignment preparation (Adler, 1991; Schneider, 1986; Laurent, 1986; Early, 1987; Tung, 1981; Adler & Bartholomew, 1992).

This success, however, may be enhanced by considering the fact that the socio-cultural factor is likely to interact with other Country/Regional Characteristics. Clearly, these factors are inter-related with culture, and it may be difficult at times, to make this differentiation when analyzing very complex events for MNEs such as the dramatic changes in Eastern Europe following the collapse of the Berlin Wall in 1989. Nevertheless, MNEs will develop policies which respond to these characteristics and enable them to operate as effectively as possible with regard to any national or regional environment. Of course adapting to local conditions is likely to produce more strains to the extent the units really need to coordinate their operations. Thus the likelihood of an MNE needing to devote more attention to SIHRM issues increases as the need for coordination increases across units that are unique. Consequently, we suggest, consistent with requisite variety precepts (Weick, 1969), the following propositions:

> **P6(*b*).** *The greater the legal differences and socio-cultural differences, the more likely MNEs will permit the development of SIHRM practices that are unique and adapted to the local interests and diversity.*

> **P6(c).** *The greater the legal differences and socio-cultural differences under conditions where MNEs benefit from coordinating their units, the greater will be the resources devoted to integrative HR policies, practices and functions.*

Endogenous Factors

Just as the Exogenous Factors are expected to have indirect and direct effects on SIHRM, so too are the Endogenous Factors. As illustrated in Figure 1, there are four Endogenous Factors that are thought to have a significant influence on SIHRM issues and the associated HR functions and policies and practices. These factors are: a) the structure of the international operations; b) the headquarter's international orientation of the MNE; c) the MNE's competitive strategy; and d) the MNE's experience in managing international operations.

Structure of International Operations

MNEs have several choices in structuring their international operations (Phatak, 1992; Bartlett & Ghoshal, 1991). Perhaps the most salient for SIHRM is captured in the distinction between the international *division* and a variation on the *global* form of organization (Phatak, 1992; Dowling & Schuler, 1990).[4]

International Divison Structure. In the international division structure (design) the MNE basically adds on a unit to deal with international business concerns. The original organization structure is left intact. The international division becomes a unit that mirrors the domestic businesses of the MNE abroad (Punnett & Ricks, 1992). As suggested by Bartlett and Ghoshal (1991), the key business decisions are made at the international headquarters (typically also the headquarters of the MNE). Knowledge is also developed at the center and dispersed where needed. Sensitivity to local conditions may be only minimally facilitated in this type of operation, but local commitments are also minimal. Consequently, international human resource decisions may be primarily associated with selecting the head of international operation and then the expatriate who may be sent abroad to operate the international location. Of course more human resource issues do arise for the expatriate in charge of this location, but they tend to be modest compared with similar issues faced by MNEs selecting a global form of organization.

Within the global *form* of organization there are several *structural* alternatives (Phatak, 1992; Bartlett & Ghoshal, 1991). These include the multinational structure, the global structure, the international structure, and the transnational structure.

Global Form. In the *multinational structure* the MNE is basically organized by geographical location and is very decentralized. This may range from several locations each serving single domestic markets to a few large regional locations each serving many markets (Roth, Schweiger, & Morrison, 1991). This structure has the ability to respond to local market needs, although perhaps at the loss of efficiency and economies of scale. It does facilitate the growth of the MNE as it does so through market place expansion. Strategic international human resource management needs thus become focused more on developing practices to local environments and staffing the local operations with local nationals (Dowling & Schuler, 1990; Bartlett & Ghoshal, 1991). The head of each operation, however, may be an expatriate but one with a considerable degree of autonomy. These local units tend to operate in a rather decentralized manner and can be relatively self-sufficient.

Two similar structures of MNEs described by Bartlett and Ghoshal (1991) are the global and the international. They differ in large part by the degree of centralization of decision making and the global scale of production. Whereas the *global structure* operates on a global scale in order to achieve economies of scale and to spread development costs over a larger area, the international MNE develops the ideas for operation and establishes local units, where needed, to implement them. In both cases, the major strategic decisions are made at the center, the corporate headquarters, and the local units carry out the directives. Whereas the *multinational structure* adapts well to sensing local market needs, the concerns of the global structure reflect a global agenda. This global agenda is driven by global economies of scale and is determined by the center. Strategic international human resource issues focus on operating the MNE as a singular global operation. Thus, the units tend to be coordinated by directives from the center. The local unit managers have modest levels of autonomy. Questions for strategic international human resource management that arise here include: How can the center ensure that the local employees will carry out the directives?; Does the center need to control the units with expatriate managers or will formalized policies and practices be sufficient?; and How can the MNE ensure that it gets (needed) sensitivity to local conditions?

The *transnational structure* basically seeks to obtain the advantages of both the multinational and global structures. It seeks economies of scale and local sensitivity. Bartlett and Ghoshal (1991) suggest that it even goes beyond this. They indicate that it seeks to facilitate global competitiveness, flexibility, and organizational learning. In doing so, the transnational MNE is actually more concerned about obtaining these goals than reflecting a particular structure. In fact, Bartlett and Ghoshal submit that the transnational MNE is more a mentality than an organizational structure. As such, a transnational may be reflected in a matrix or mixed-structure form or by a heterarchy form where the MNE has several global headquarters dispersed around the world (Hedlund, 1986).

Effectively serving the several goals and concerns listed, the transnational requires individuals who are able to be concerned with local needs and global needs. The strategic international human resource issues are consequently more complex here than in the other structures:

> In any complex organization, the main difficulty in obtaining individual commitment to an overall purpose is the limited perspectives and parochial interests of managers in key positions. Neither organization structure nor coordination systems can fully neutralize the typical hierarchy of managerial loyalties, which place local above global interests. Therefore, a fundamental prerequisite for the normative integration a transnational seeks is a sophisticated human resource management system. The transnational uses systems of recruitment, training and development, and career path management to help individuals cope with its diversity and complexity. (Bartlett & Ghoshal, 1991, pp. 70, 71)

The propositions resulting from this discussion are developed and supported by the theoretical insights of requisite variety and cybernetic systems (see Wright & Snell's, [1991] discussion of behavioral control and coordination) and uncertainty reduction (Galbraith, 1987; Sundaram & Black, 1992; Milliman, Von Glinow, & Nathan, 1991). They are based on the premises that: a) Different structures of international operation create different requirements for automony, localization and coordination, thus affecting the nature and extent of SIHRM policies and practices; and b) the structures of the international operations of the MNE will impact the need for coordination and flexibility on the part of the units, thereby impacting the need for the units to develop mechanisms to respond to local conditions and to develop a flexibility capability. The resulting propositions thus include:

P7(*a*).   *MNEs with an international division structure will be concerned with a singular SIHRM issue, that of selecting the top manager.*

P7(*b*).   *MNEs with a multinational structure will be concerned with SIHRM issues that primarily focus on the selection of managers who can operate units with sensitivity to local conditions under autonomous direction.*

P7(*c*).   *MNEs with a global structure will be concerned with SIHRM issues that primarily focus on selection of managers who are concerned about global operations operating under centralized control and direction.*

P7(*d*). *MNEs with a transnational structures will be concerned with SIHRM issues that focus on the selection and development of managers who effectively balance the local and the global perspectives.*

Headquarter's International Orientation

The attitudes and values of top management at headquarters are likely to be significant influence on strategic international human resource managment. Heenam and Perlmutter (1979) classified top management's attitudes and values into three orientations.

These three orientations can be briefly described in the following way:[5]

Ethnocentric: Few foreign subsidiaries have any autonomy, strategic decisions are made at headquarters, and key jobs at both domestic and foreign operations are held by headquarters management personnel. Subsidiaries, in other words, are managed by expatriates from the home country.

Polycentric: The MNE treats each subsidiary as a distinct national entity with some decision-making autonomy. Subsidiaries are usually managed by local nationals who are seldom promoted to positions at headquarters.

Geocentric: The organization ignores nationality in favor of ability. This approach to staffing without regard to nationality must be accompanied by a worldwide integrated business strategy to be successful. A subset of this orientation is referred to as *regiocentric*. This reflects the geographic strategy and structure of the MNE. Like the geocentric approach, it utilizes a wider pool of managers but in a limited way (personnel may move outside their countries but only within the particular geographic region). Regional managers may not be promoted to headquarters positions but enjoy a degree of regional autonomy in decision-making.

As these descriptions suggest, each orientation is likely to influence strategic international human resource management in a relatively specific way. For example, an MNE with an ethnocentric orientation would be likely, with regard to the management of local operations, to impose policies concerning staffing, compensation, performance appraisal, and management development which reflect parent country practice rather than sensitivity to the local environment (Banai, 1992; Phatak, 1992). Conversely, a polycentric orientation would lead to considerable autonomy with regard to HR decisions and activities in local operations. Thus, it would appear that headquarter's international orientation is an important factor which influences internal operations within MNE business units and the development and maintenance of HR policies and practices.

Perhaps as importantly, the headquarter's international orientation is likely to impact the nature of the relationships between the MNE center and the units. In some cases, e.g., the ethnocentric orientation, the center may construct a coordination through common HR policies. In other cases, e.g., the polycentric, it may construct separation. If not really consistent with the differentiation and integration needs of the MNE, efficiencies, responsiveness and competitiveness may decline. Consequently, MNEs are likely to be more effective if they match their orientations, and thus their human resource practices with the needs of the business.

As Evans (1986) states:

> The choice of a global geocentric or polycentric approach to human resource management is not dictated by product-market or industry logic; each approach represents a different way of coping with the different socio-cultural environments of a multinational company. ...Thus firms in worldwide industries where divisions and subsidiaries are interdependent would be advised to adopt global human resource strategies: the costs of such strategies would be outweighed by the potentially enormous returns of a successful global strategy. Firms where divisions and business elements can be discretely and independently defined would be advised to adopt cheaper polycentric human resource strategies. Some of the disadvantages of either extreme position can be counteracted by the use of subtle management processes (p.106).

Based upon the foregoing discussion and the premise that MNEs will attempt to match their orientations with the needs of the business, particularly those determined by the socio-cultural aspects of the environment, the following propositions emerge:

> **P8(a).** *An MNE's headquarter's international orientation will impact the ease of interaction among units such that interaction will be easier in MNEs with common or geocentric orientations and will be more difficult in MNEs with unique or polycentric orientations.*

> **P8(b).** *MNEs with a predominantly ethnocentric orientation will develop strategic IHR policies and practices regarding staffing, appraising, compensation and training which favor parent country employees.*

> **P8(c).** *MNEs with a predominantly polycentric orientation will develop strategic IHR policies and practices regarding staffing, appraising, compensation and training which are oriented towards host country employees.*

> **P8(d).** *MNEs with a predominantly geocentric orientation will develop strategic IHR policies and practices regarding staffing, appraising, compensation and training which do not differentiate between employees on the basis of nationality.*

MNE's Competitive Strategy

This factor, introduced earlier in this article, refers to the dominant competitive strategy which the MNE is using in each of its main product or service markets (cf. Morrison & Roth, 1992). The concept of competitive strategy is described by Porter (1985) as the essence of competitive advantage. Emerging from his discussion are three possible competitive strategies: innovation, quality enhancement, and cost reduction (Wright, 1987).

Briefly, the innovation strategy is used to develop products or services different from those of competitors; the primary focus here is on offering something new and different.[6] Enhancing product and/or service quality is the primary focus of the quality enhancement strategy. In the cost reduction strategy, firms typically attempt to gain competitive advantage by being the lowest-cost producer. Although we have described these three competitive strategies as pure types applied to single business units, some overlap can obviously occur. That is, it is possible for large business units to pursue two or more competitive strategies simultaneously, for different product lines or services.

These competitive strategies are included here because of their impact on strategic human resource issues. Execution of competitive strategies depends upon employees behaving in ways consistent with the strategic requirements. Facilitating these behaviors are human resource practices that signal and reward the needed behaviors (Jackson et al., 1989).

Models linking competitive strategy and human resource management practices have been identified elsewhere (Schuler & Jackson, 1987). These models have developed typologies of human resource practices for different competitive strategies such as innovation, quality enhancement and cost reduction. The rationale for the specific human resource practices is based upon employee role behaviors necessary because of the competitive strategy. These models, however, have basically been applied to the domestic (i.e., U.S.) environment. MNEs, however, are faced with the need to apply human resource practices in several locations of the international environment.

There is some evidence to suggest a common approach to managing human resources as a function of the competitive strategy, i.e., the "competitive strategy imperative" described earlier. Case studies from England (Scullion, 1991; Wickens, 1987); Belgium (Hiltrop, 1992); Australia (Dunphy & Stace, 1991); Switzerland (Krulis-Randa, 1991); and Japan (Pucik, 1984, 1992), point to the existence of a common set of needed employee role characteristics for quality improvement and a common set of human resource practices for those characteristics.

If competitive strategies depend upon similar behaviors regardless of location of operation, then units pursuing similar strategies are likely to benefit by exchanging information on their HR policies and practices. In this situation, having some units serve as centers of excellence, i.e. creators of knowledge, and thus becoming benchmarks for the other units for specific practices, may serve to benefit all units (Pucik et al., 1992). Regardless of the specific competitive strategy, however, MNEs can benefit by having their units exchange information, exchange learning, in order to enhance their competitive effectiveness (Bartlett & Ghoshal, 1991).

To the extent some human resource practices are more effective than others for a given competitive strategy, it may behoove MNEs to be systematic in selecting those practices. But being systematic takes time and experience. If this learning can be shared amongst dispersed units, this can facilitate local unit operating efficiency. Thus the impact of competitive strategy for strategic human resource management increases as the need for and benefit from learning and sharing across units increase.

The propositions resulting from this include:

> **P9(a).** *The nature of a unit's competitive strategy will determine, in part, the nature of its HR policies and practices. For example, a unit pursuing a quality enhancement competitive strategy will be more likely than a unit pursuing a cost reduction strategy to have participative, egalitarian and team-oriented HR policies and practices.*

> **P9(b).** *Units of MNEs that are pursuing the same competitive strategy will have HR policies and practices that are more similar than units of MNEs that are pursuing different competitive strategies.*

> **P9(c).** *Units of MNEs that are pursuing the same competitive strategy will have more mechanisms to share and transfer their learning across units than units of MNEs that are pursuing different competitive strategies.*

These propositions are based largely upon a behavioral theory rationale presented by Schuler and Jackson (1987) and Wright and McMahan (1992).

Experience in Managing International Operations

This last endogenous variable in our integrative framework is that of *Experience in Managing International Operations*. This variable is concerned with the extent to which managers in an MNE are experienced in international operations. It is expected that this experience is likely to affect the nature of their decisions related to strategic international HR issues, functions and policies and practices.

For example, a study by Dowling (1989), which surveyed international HR directors, found that the length of time which firms had been involved in international operations was positively correlated with the structure of their international HR operations. Firms with more years of overseas experience had a more diverse set of HR practices than those with fewer years experience. One interpretation of this finding is that the longer firms operate internationally, the more likely they are to change their HR practices to accommodate local or regional demands if the situation deems it appropriate. They are also more likely to have acquired the expertise to deal with more complex organizational needs, such as those found in the transnational structure (Bartlett & Ghoshal, 1991).

The results reported by Dowling (1989) also suggest that the MNE with limited international experience will assume that one set of HR practices can work everywhere, thus it will have a predominantly ethnocentric IHR orientation. Propositions suggested by this discussion include:

P10(*a*). *MNEs with limited experience in managing international operations will be less likely to change their strategic international HR policies and practices to accommodate local or regional demands.*

P10(*b*). *MNEs with more experience will be more likely to be effective in operating a more complex organizational structure than MNEs with less experience.*

Contribution of The Integrative Framework

As had been outlined earlier in this article, the integrative framework presented shows the influences and interrelationships of the factors relevant to Strategic International Human Resource Management. Much of the existing research literature on international HRM has focused on expatriate assignments and the management of expatriates. The next task for researchers is to examine the influence of exogenous and endogenous factors on strategic international HRM and to consider the consequences of these influences and interrelationships. This framework attempts to offer a conceptual map which describes a number of interrelationships and influences and which offer a number of propositions for future research.

Our framework may also enable academics and HR professionals to identify, analyze and manage the factors involved in SIHRM. In this context we define strategic international human resource management as developing a fit between exogenous and endogenous factors and balancing the competing demands of global versus local requirements, and the needs of coordination, control, and autonomy (Adler and Ghadar, 1990).

Implications for Academics and HR Professionals

For Academics

As suggested by Sundaram and Black (1992), studying the multinational enterprise goes significantly beyond studying the domestic enterprise. While it can certainly benfit from knowledge of the domestic enterprise, the MNE is unique and does warrant separate attention and focus. We argued here that this applies equally as well to the study of strategic human resource management, particularly at a time when a current theme in human resource management practice is to "link to the needs of the business." Thus we offered an integrative framework for the study and understanding of strategic international human resource management. While this builds on the work of strategic human resource management (Wright & McMahan, 1992; Schuler, 1992), it incorporates several features unique to the international (global) context (Sundaram & Black, 1992; Adler & Bartholomew, 1992).

For academics, our framework of strategic international human resource management implies a need for multidisciplinary knowledge, e.g., political science, economics, law, strategic, management, sociology, anthropology, organizational theory, psychology and human resource management. And while specific research agendas are feasible without drawing upon all of these knowledge bases (e.g., in examining many of the propositions proposed here), a cross-disciplinary research effort may be most effective for a complete understanding of strategic international human resource management just as it is for the understanding of the MNE as an organizational form (Sundaram & Black, 1992; Gregersen & Black, 1992; Naumann, 1992).

Admittedly, multidisciplinary research is difficult at best, so to facilitate the study of strategic international human resource management, we offered several propositions, testable with a more delimited research design. This research, however, would still benefit by reflecting a multidisciplinary appreciation and understanding. The integrative framework shown in Figure 1 illustrates the numerous exogenous factors that are based upon several different disciplines. This, of course, is what, in part, differentiates strategic international human resource management from the study of strategic human resource management.

The study of strategic international human resource management, however, can benefit enormously by understanding and utilizing strategic (domestic) human resource management. For example, the propositions offered here reflect the theoretical perspectives of behavioral theory (Schuler & Jackson, 1987); agency/transaction cost theory (Jensen & Meckling, 1976; Jones & Hill, 1988); a resource view of the firm (Connor, 1991); open systems theory (Katz & Kahn, 1978); and resource dependency theory and institutional theory (Meyer & Rowan, 1977), applied so adroitly to strategic human resource management by (Wright & McMahan, 1992). Having available and using these multiple theoretical perspectives, can enable the strategic international human resource management researcher to get a better understanding of the phenomenon to be examined, thereby enabling a better design to investigate testable and theoretically-based propositions. This process also facilitates the process of explaining findings and revising the propostions, instrumentation and even the design itself. One result of this may be the improved practice of strategic international human resource management (Dubin, 1976).

For Professionals

The field of human resource management is becoming more linked to the needs of the business (Walker, 1992). In so doing, the focus of human resource management has moved to the strategic arena (Schuler, 1992). As the needs of the business have become more international and strategic, the field of human resource management has become extended to the field of strategic international human resource management. Along with the challenge that this development offers for human resource professionals, is the satisfaction of knowing that the contribution of human resource management to the business can be further improved. Indeed, some would argue that the success of global businesses depends first and foremost on the quality of the MNE's human resources and how effectively the enterprise's human resources are managed and developed (Bartlett & Ghoshal, 1992).

Effectively managing an MNE's human resources is a complex task which is subject to a variety of exogenous and endogenous factors as illustrated in Figure 1. While the specific parts and propositions of the integrative framework shown in Figure 1 remain to be empirically investigated, practitioners have been operating in this reality in their attempts to manage their MNE's human resources. In many cases, guides for directions and answers to questions are elusive at best. There appear to be too many contingencies, too many uncontrollable factors and perhaps even too many unknown factors. Our attempt at an integrative framework is a partial response to this situation. By offering a framework, we hope to reduce the unknowns, narrow the relevant contingencies and make more manageable some of the uncontrollable factors. Our hope also is to convey to professionals the academic state of the field of strategic international human resource management so that this state can be revised, based in part on the experience of HR professionals.

Conclusion

The issues, challenges and propositions associated with MNEs are different from those of domestic firms (Sundaram & Black, 1992). This applies to all functional areas of managing an MNE, particularly human resource management.

MNEs confront many international human resource management issues and challenges. Those that are linked to the unique global strategic needs of these enterprises were designated in this article to be those of strategic international human resource management. Consistent with the increased recognition of the importance of strategic human resource management (Wright & McMahan, 1992), this article sought to present a framework for thinking about strategic international human resource management. Building upon some of the theoretical and conceptual arguments used by Wright and McMahan (1992) and Sundaram and Black (1992), we offered several testable propositions.

Because the field of strategic international human resource management is an emerging one, we utilized many sources of information and research, some academic and some applied, that could be fruitfully brought to bear upon our integrated framework. As suggested by Sundaram and Black (1992), approaching the study of MNEs requires a broad perspective and a set of multidisciplinary tools: e.g., business, psychology, sociology, anthropology, law and organizational theory. In approaching the area it is useful to identify and incorporate all the exogenous and endogenous factors that might be applicable to a specific issue or activity in strategic international human resource management. At this time, the propositions offered here might be best thought of as tentative, subject to revision and modification. While we have tried to incorporate as many relevant factors as possible, we may have omitted some. We may have also failed to generate all the appropriate and useful propositions relevant to academic and professional use. Hopefully we have been able to convey some information, some perspectives and some propositions that might serve the interests of those studying and practicing strategic international human resource management.

Acknowledgment: The authors wish to thank David Ricks, Steve Kobrin, Stewart Black, Moshe Banai, Cal Reynolds, Susan Jackson. Gary Florkowski, Bob Kane, Steve Barnett and three anonymous reviewers for their comments and suggestions. This article is appearing simultaneously in the *International Journal of Human Resource Management*, by special permission of the editors, Ricky Griffin and Michael Poole.

Notes

1.   For a detailed discussion of political risk for MNCs, see P.S. Ring, S.A. Lenway & M. Govekar, 1990. Management of the political imperative in international business. *Strategic Management Journal, 11*, 141-151. Also see J.D. Simon, (1984). A theoretical perspective on political risk. *Journal of International Business Studies*, (Winter), 123-143; and S.J. Kobrin, (1982), *Managing Political Risk Assessment*. Berkeley: University of California Press.

2.   A more specific description of these legal dimensions is provided by G. Florkowski and R. Nath, (1993), MNC responses to the legal environment of international human resource management. *International Journal of Human Resource Management, 4*. Briefly they are defined as follows:

Regulatory heterogeneity: The degree of similarity in the legal systems that must be accommodated. Encompasses the amount of differentiation in employment rights and legal superstructures. Varies from homogeneous to heterogenous environments.

Regulatory complexity: The level of knowledge needed to ensure compliance with the prevailing set of employment laws. Includes the diversity of issues addressed as well as the extensiveness of the substantive and procedural requirements withhin each arena. Varies from simple environments that impose limited standards in a small number of areas to complex ones with cumbersome demands in numerous facets of employment.

Regulatory relevancy: The extent to which enforcement efforts will be directed against the MNE. Economic, social, or historical factors may influence the willingness of the controlling sovereignties to challenge noncomplying firms. Varies from environments where employment laws have a low enforcement priority to those where they have a high enforcement priority.

Regulatory stability: The likelihood that significant, employment-related changes (substantive or procedural) will occur in the governing legal systems. Affected by political, economic, and cultural trends within the home and host countries, as well as the amount of turbulence (the level and speed of interconnections between elements and trends in the environment). Varies from unstable to highly stable environments.

Regulatory predictability: The extent to which the MNE can accurately forecast material changes in the applicable employment laws. Affected by political, economic, and cultural trends within the home and host countries. Varies from unpredictable to highly predictable environments.

On this legal factor, also see Chapter 8, The legal environment, in S.H. Robock & K. Simmonds (Eds.), (1989). *International Business and Multinational Enterprises*, 4th ed. Homewook, IL: Irwin. and M. Litka, (1991). *International Dimensions of the Legal Environment of Business*. Boston: PWS-Kent.

3.   There is a voluminous research literature which examines the topic of socio-cultural differences in international business. For example, see C. Geertz, (1973), *The Interpretation of Cultures*. New York: Basic Books; J.D. Child, (1981), Culture, contingency and capitalism in the cross-national study of organizations. In L.L. Cummings & B.M. Staw (Eds.). *Research in Organizational Behavior*, Vol. 3. Greenwich, CT: JAI; L. Kelly & R. Worthley, (1981), The role of culture in comparative management: A cross-cultural perspective. *Academy of Management Journal, 24*, 164-173; R.S. Bhagat & S.J. McQuaid, (1982), Role of subjective culture in organizations: A review and directions for future research. *Journal of Applied Psychology, 67*, 653-685; G. Hofstede, (1983), The cultural relativity of organizational practices and theories. *Journal of International Business, 14*(2), 75-89; and N.A. Boyacigiller & N.J. Adler, (1991), The parochial dinosaur: Organizational science in a global context. *Academy of Management Review, 16*(2), 262-290.

4.   For a detailed review of the issue of internationalization, see S. Young, J. Hamill, C. Wheeler & J.R. Davies, (1989), *International market entry and development: Strategies and management*, Hemel

Hempstead, U.K.: Harvester Wheatsheaf -Prentice Hall. Note that we are not addressing the *stages* of internationalization specifically. While these tend to incorporate some of the structural alternatives described here, they also include a discussion of such issues as sales subsidiaries and export offices (Phatak, 1992) which, while having some effect on the fundamental objective of an MNEs, have only a modest impact on SIHRM. Similarly, this discussion does not include SIHRM issues that are associated with alliances and international joint ventures (IJVs) of MNEs (see Slocum & Lei, 1991). While having an impact on SIHRM, they are beyond the preview of this article. For a review of the SIHRM issues in IJVs see R. Schuler and E. Van Sluijs, (1992), Davidson -Marley BV: Establishing and Operating an International Joint Venture. *European Management Journal*, (December), 428-437; and Y. Zeira and O. Shenkar, (1990), Interactive and specific parent characteristic: Implications for management and human resources in international joint ventures. *Management International Review, 30*, 7-22. This discussion also does not include a discussion of the possible interaction effects between MNE structure (design) and strategy. For a review of this subject, however, see Roth, Schweiger and Morrison (1991).

5.   This description is based on D.A. Ondrack (1985) International human resources management in European and North American firms, *International Studies of Management and Organization, 15*(1), 6-32. These descriptions are based upon the orientations of top management originally articulated by Perlmutter and then expanded upon Heenan and Reynolds (personal communication with Calvin Reynolds, 28 January 1993). In the subsequent expansion of these ideas, the relationship of compensation practices to these top management orientations was developed.

6.   This description is drawn from R.S. Schuler and S.E. Jackson, (1987), Linking competitive strategies with human resource management practices. *Academy of Management Executive, 1*, 207-219.

References

Adler, N.J. (1991). *International dimensions of organizational behavior*. Boston: PWS-Kent.
Adler, N.J. & Bartholomew, S. (1992). Managing globally competent people. *Academy of Management Executive, 6*, 52-64.
Adler, N.J. & Ghadar, F. (1990). Strategic human resource management: A global perspective. Pp. 235-260 in R. Pieper (Ed.), *Human Resource Management: An International Comparison*. New York: Walter de Gruyter.
Banai, M. (1992). The ethnocentric staffing policy in multinational corporations: a self-fulfilling prophecy. *The International Journal of Human Resource Management, 3*, 451-472.
Bartlett, C. (1992). Christopher Bartlett on transnationals: an interview. *European Management Journal*, (September), 271-276.
Bartlett, C. & Ghoshal, S. (1987). Managing across borders: New organizational responses. *Sloan Management Review, 29*, 43-53.
_____. (1988). Organizing for worldwide effectiveness: The transnational solution. *California Management Review, 31*, 54-74.
_____. (1989). *Managing across borders: The transnational solution*. Cambridge, MA: Harvard Business School Press.
_____. (1991). *Managing across borders: The transnational solution*. London: London Business School.
_____. (1992). What is a global manager? *Harvard Business Review*, (September/October), 124-132.
Barney, J. (1991). Firm resources and sustained competitive advantage. *Journal of Management, 17*, 99-120.
Begin, J.P. (1992). Comparative human resource management (HRM): A systems perspective. *International Journal of Human Resource Management, 3*, 379-408.
Black, J.S., Gregersen, H.B., & Mendenhall. (1992). *Global assignments*. San Francisco: Jossey-Bass.
Boam, R. & Sparrow, P. (1992). *Designing and achieving competency*. London: McGraw-Hill.
Boyacigiller, N. (1990). The role of expatriates in the management of interdependence, complexity and risk in multinational corporations. *Journal of International Business Studies, 21*(3), 357-381.
Brewster, C. (1991). *The management of expatriates*. London: Kogan Page.
Brewster, C. & Tyson, S. (1991). *International comparisons in human resource management*. London: Pittman.
Buckley, P.J. & Casson, M.C. (1976). *The future of the multinational enterprise*. London: Macmillan.
Butler, J.E., Ferris, G.R., & Napier, N.K. (1991). *Strategy and human resources management*. Cincinnati, OH: South-Western.
Cappelli, P. & McElrath, R. (1992). The transfer of employment practices through multinationals. Working paper, The Wharton School, Philadelphia.
Casson, M.C. (1982). Transaction costs and the theory of the multinational enterprise. Pp. 24-43 in A.M. Rugman (Ed.), *New theories of the multinational enterprise*. New York: St. Martin's Press.

Conner, K.R. (1991). A historical comparison of resource-based theory and five schools of thought within industrial organization economics: Do we have a new theory of the firm? *Journal of Management, 17*, 121-154.

Cosset, J-C. & Roy, J. (1991). The determinants of country risk ratings. *Journal of International Business Studies, 22*(1), 135-142.

de la Torre, J. & Neckar, D. (1990). Forecasting political risk for international operations. Pp. 194-214 in H. Vernon-Wortzel & L.H. Wortzel (Eds.), *Global strategic management: The essentials.* New York: Wiley.

Desatnick, R.L. & Bennett, M.L. (1978). *Human resource management in the multinational company.* New York: Nichols.

Dowling, P.J. (1986). Human resource issues in international business. *Syracuse Journal of International Law and Commerce, 13*(2), 255-271.

———. (1988). International human resource management. In L.D. Dyer (Ed.), *Human resource management: Evolving roles and responsibilities.* Washington, DC: BNA Books.

———. (1989). Hot issues overseas. *Personnel Administrator, 34*(1), 66-72.

Dowling, P.J. & Schuler, R.S. (1990). *International dimensions of human resource management.* Boston: PWS-Kent.

Dowling, P.J. & Welch, D.E. (1988). International human resource management: An Australian perspective. *Asia Pacific Journal of Management, 61*(1), 39-65.

Doz, Y.L. & Prahalad, C.K. (1981). Headquarters influence and strategic control in MNCs. *Sloan Management Review, 23*(1), 15-29.

Dubin, R. (1976). Theory building in applied areas. Pp. 17-40 in M. Dunnette (Ed.), *Handbook of industrial and organizational psychology,* 1st ed. Chicago, IL: Rand McNally.

Dunphy, D. & Stace, D. (1991). *Under new management: Australian organizations in transition.* Sydney: McGraw-Hill.

Earley, P. (1987). International training for managers: A comparison of documentary and interpersonal methods. *Academy of Management Journal, 30*, 685-698.

Edstrom, A. & Galbraith, J. (1977). Transfer of managers as a coordination and control strategy in multinational organizations. *Administrative Science Quarterly, 22*, 248-263.

Egelhoff, W.G. (1988). *Organizing the multinational enterprise: An information processing perspective.* Cambridge: Ballinger Publishing Company.

Evans, P. (1986). The context of strategic human resource management policy in complex firms. *Management Forum, 6*, 105-107.

———. (1992). Management development as glue technology. *Human Resource Planning, 15*(1), 85-106.

Evans, P., Doz, Y., & Laurent, A. (Eds.) (1989). *Human resource management in international firms.* London: MacMillan.

Ferris, G.R. & Judge, T.A. (1991). Personnel/human resources management: A political influence perspective. *Journal of Management, 17*(2), 447-488.

Fisher, C. (1989). Current and recurrent challenges in HRM. *Journal of Management, 15*, 157-180.

Florkowski, G.W. & Nath, R. (1993). MNC Responses to the legal environment of international human resource management. *International Journal of Human Resource Management, 4*, 305-324.

Fulkerson, J.R. & Schuler, R.S. (1992). Managing worldwide diversity at Pepsi-Cola International. In S.E. Jackson (Ed.), *Diversity in the workplace.* New York: Guilford Press.

Galbraith, J.R. (1987). Organization design. Pp. 343-357 in Lorsch, J. (Ed.), *Handbook of organization behavior.* Englewood Cliffs: Prentice-Hall.

———. (1973). *Designing complex organizations.* Reading, MA: Addison-Wesley.

———. (1992). *The value adding corporation.* Los Angeles: CEO Publication, University of Southern California.

Galbraith, J.R. & Kazanjian, R. (1986). *Strategy implementation: The role of structure in process.* St. Paul: West Publishing.

Ghoshal, S. (1987). Global strategy: An organizing framework. *Strategic Management Journal, 8*, 425-440.

Ghoshal, S. & Bartlett, C.A. (1990). The multinational corporation as an interorganizational network. *Academy of Management Review, 15*(4), 603-625.

Grant, R. (1991). The resource-based theory of competitive advantage: Implications for strategy formulation. *California Management Review,* (Summer), 114-135.

Gregersen, H.B. & Black, J.S. (1992). Antecedents to commitment to a parent company and a foreign operation. *Academy of Management Journal, 35*, 65-90.

Hailey, J. (1992). *Localization and expatriation the continuing role of expatriates in developing countries.* Presented at the 1992 EISAM workshp, Cranfield, England, September.

Hamel, G. & Prahalad, C.K. (1986). Do you really have a global strategy? *Harvard Business Review,* (July-August), 139-148.

Hambrick, D.C. & Snow, C.C. (1989). Strategic reward systems. In C.C. Snow (Ed.), *Strategy, Organization Design and Human Resource Management*. Greenwich, CT: JAI.

Hedlund, G. (1986). The hypermodern MNC—A heterarchy? *Human Resource Management, 25*(1), 9-35.

Heenan, D.A. & Perlmutter, H.V. (1979). *Multinational organization development*. Reading, MA: Addison-Wesley.

Hendry, C. (1992). *Human resource management in the international firm*. Paper presented to the VET Forum Conference on 'Multinational Companies and Human Resources: A Moveable Feast?', University of Warwick, June 22-24.

Hennart, J.F. (1982). *A theory of the multinational enterprise*. Ann Arbor: University of Michigan Press.

Hiltrop, J.M. (1992). *Human resource practices in European firms*. Unpublished working paper, IMD.

Hofstede, G. (1980). *Cultures consequences*. Beverly Hills, CA: Sage.

———. (1993). Cultural constraints in management theories. *Academy of Management Executive, 7*, 81-94.

IBM/Towers Perrin. (1992). *Priorities for gaining competitive advantage*. New York: Towers Perrin.

Jackson, S.E., Schuler, R.S., & Rivero, C. (1989). Organizational characteristics as predictors of personnel practices. *Personnel Psychology, 42*, 727-786.

Jensen, M. & Meckling, W. (1976). Theory of the firm: Managerial behavior, agency costs, and ownership structure. *Journal of Financial Economics, 3*, 305-360.

Jones, G. (1984). Task visibility, free riding, and shirking: Explaining the effect of structure and technology and employee behavior. *Journal of Financial Economics, 3*, 305-360.

Jones, G. & Hill, C. (1988). Transaction cost analysis of strategy-structure choice. *Strategic Management Journal, 9*, 159-172.

Kanter, R.M. (1991). Transcending business boundaries: 12,000 world managers view change. *Harvard Business Review*, (May/June), 151-164.

Katz, D. & Kahn, R. (1978). *The social psychology of organizations*. New York:John Wiley & Sons.

Kogut, B. (1989). A note on global strategies. *Strategic Management Journal, 10*, 383-389.

Kobrin, S.J. (1988). Expatriate reduction and strategic control in American multinational corporations. *Human Resource Management, 27*(1), 63-75.

———. (1991). An empirical analysis of the determinants of global integration. *Strategic Management Journal, 12*, 17-31.

———. (1992). *Multinational strategy and international human resource management policy*. Unpublished paper, The Wharton School, University of Pennsylvania.

Kochan, T.A., Batt, R., & Dyer, L. (1992). International human resource studies: A framework for future research. In D. Lavin, O.S. Mitchael & P.D. Sheren (Eds.), *Research frontiers in ir and nr*. Madison: IRRA.

Krulis-Randa, J. (1991). *Human resource practices in Swiss-based firms*. Working paper, University of Zurich.

Laurent, A. (1986). The cross-cultural puzzle of international human resource management. *Human Resource Management, 25*, 91-102.

Lawrence, P.R. & Lorsch, J.W. (1967). *Organization and environment*. Boston: Harvard University Press.

Lengnick-Hall, C.A. & Lengnick-Hall, M.L. (1989). Strategic Human Resources Management: A review of the literature and a proposed typology. *Academy of Management Review, 13*, 454-470.

Meyer, J.W. & Rowan, E. (1977). Institutionalized organizations: Formal structure as myth and ceremony. *American Journal of Sociology, 83*, 340-363.

Miller, E., Beechler, S., Bhatt, B, & Nath, R. (1986). The relationship between the global strategic planning process and the human resource management function. *Human Resource Management, 9*,9-23.

Milliman, J., Von Glinow, M., & Nathan, B. (1991). Organizational life cycles and strategic international human resource management in multinational companies: Implications for congruence theory. *Academy of Management Review, 16*, 318-339

Morrison, A.J. & Roth K. (1992). A taxonomy of business-level strategies in global industries. *Strategic Management Journal, 13*, 399-418.

Naumann, E. (1992). A conceptual model of expatriate turnover. *Journal of International Business Studies, 23*, 499-531.

Ondrack, D.A. (1985). International human resources management in European and North American firms, *International Studies of Management and Organization, 15*(1), 6-32.

Ouchi, W. & MacGuire, M. (1975). Organizational control: Two functions. *Administrative Science Quarterly, 20*, 559-569.

Pfeffer, J. & Salancik, G. (1978). *The external control of organizations: A resource dependence perspective*. New York: Harper & Row.

Phatak, A.V. (1992). *International dimensions of Management*, 3rd ed. Boston: PWS-Kent.

Porter, M.E. (1980). *Competitive strategy: Techniques for analyzing industries and competitors*. New York: The Free Press.

458   SCHULER, DOWLING AND DE CIERI

_____. (1985). *Competitive advantage: Creating and sustaining superior performance.* New York: The Free Press.

_____. (1986). Changing patterns of international competition. *California Management Review, 28*(2), 9-40.

_____. (1990). *Competitive advantage of nations.* New York: The Free Press.

Prahalad, C.K. & Doz, Y.L. (1981). An approach to strategic control in MNCs. *Sloan Management Review, 22,* 5-13.

Prahalad, C.K. & Doz, Y. (1987). *The multinational mission: Balancing local demands and global vision.* New York: The Free Press.

Pucik, V. (1984). White-collar human resource management in large Japanese manufacturing firms. *Human Resource Management, 23,* 257-276.

_____. (1988). Strategic alliances, organizational learning, and competitive advantage: The HRM agenda. *Human Resource Management, 27,* 77-93.

_____. (1992). *Human resource practices in large Japanese firms.* Unpublished working paper, Cornell University.

Pucik, V. & Katz, J.H. (1986). Information, control human resource management in multinational firms. *Human Resource Management, 25,* 121-132.

Pucik, V., Tichy, N.M., & Barnett, C.K. (1992). *Globalizing management.* New York: Wiley.

Punnett, B.J. & Ricks, D.A. (1992). *International business.* Boston: PWS-Kent.

Reynolds, C. (1992). Developing global strategies in compensation. *ACA Journal,* (Autumn), 74-83.

Robock, S.H. & Simmonds, K. (1989). *International business and multinational enterprises,* 4th ed. Homewood, IL: Irwin.

Ronan, S. (1986). *Comparative and multinational management.* New York: Wiley & Sons.

Root, F. (1987). *Entry strategies for international markets.* Lexington, MA: Heath.

Roth, K., Schweiger, D.M., & Morrison, A.J. (1991). Global strategy implementation at the business unit level. Operational capabilities and administrative mechanisms. *Journal of International Business Studies, 22*(3), 369-402.

Rugman, A.M. (1980). Internalization as a general theory of direct foreign investment: A reappraisal of the literature. *Weltwerschaftliches Archiv, 49,* 365-379.

Schneider, S. (1986). National vs. corporate culture: Implications for human resource management. *Human Resource Management, 27,* 133-148.

Schneider, S. & De Meyer, A. (1991). Interpreting and responding to strategic issues: The impact of national culture. *Strategic Management Journal, 12,* 307-320.

Schuler, R.S. (1992). Strategic human resource management: Linking the people with the strategic needs of the business. *Organizational Dynamics,* (Summer), 18-31.

Schuler, R.S., Fulkerson, J.R., & Dowling, P.J. (1991). Strategic performance measurement and management in multinational corporations. *Human Resource Management, 30,* 365-392.

Schuler, R.S. & Huber, V.L. (1993). *Personnel and Human Resource Management,* 5th ed. St. Paul: West Publishing Co.

Schuler, R.S. & Jackson, S.E. (1987). Linking competitive strategy and human resource management practices. *Academy of Management Executive, 3,* 207-219.

Scullion, H. (1992). Strategic recruitment and development of the international managers: Some European considerations. *Human Resource Management Journal, 3,* 57-69.

Slocum, J.W. & Lei, D. (1991). *Designing global strategic alliances: Integration of cultural and economic factors.* Working paper 91-092, Southern Methodist University.

Sundaram, A.K. & Black, J.S. (1992). The environment and internal organization of multinational enterprises. *Academy of Management Review, 17,* 729-757.

Teece, D. (1983). A transaction cost theory of the multinational enterprise. In M. Casson (Ed.), *The growth of international business.* London: Allen & Unwin.

Thompson, A.A. & Strickland, A.J. (1990). *Strategic management: concepts and cases,* 5th ed. Homewood, IL: Irwin.

Tichy, N. (1992). Global development. Pp. 206-225 in V. Pucik, N. Tichy, & Barnett (Eds.), *Globalizing Management.* New York: Wiley & Sons.

Townsend, A.M., Scott, K.D., & Markham, S.E. (1990). An examination of country and culture-based differences in compensation practices. *Journal of International Business Studies, 21*(4), 667-678.

Toyne, B. (1989). International exchange: A foundation for theory building in international business. *Journal of International Business Studies, 20,* 1-18.

Triandis, H.C. & Berry, J.W. (Eds.) (1980). *Handbook of cross-cultural psychology,* Vol. 2, *Methodology.* Boston: Allyn & Bacon.

Tung, R. (1981). Selection and training of personnel for overseas assignments. *Columbia Journal of World Business,* (Spring), 74-80.

————. (1984). Strategic management of human resources in the multinational enterprise. *Human Resource Management, 23*(2), 129-143.

Vanderbroeck, P. (1992). Long-term human resource development in multinational organizations. *Sloan Management Review*, (Fall), 95-99.

Van Maanen, E. & Schein, E. (1979). Toward a theory of organizational socialization. Pp. 209-264 in B. Staw & L.L. Cummings (Eds.), *Research in organizational behavior*, Vol. 1. Greenwich, CT: JAI.

Vernon, R. (1990). Organizational and institutional responses to international risk. In H. Vernon-Wortzel & L.H. Wortzel (Eds.), *Global strategic management: The essentials*. New York: Wiley.

Vernon, R. & Wells, L.T. (1991). *The manager in the international economy*. Englewood Cliffs: Prentice Hall.

Walker, J. (1992). *Human resources strategy*. New York: McGraw-Hill.

Weick, K.E. (1969). *Social psychology of organizing*. Reading, MA: Addison-Wesley.

Welch, L. & Luostarinen, R. (1988). Internationalization: Evolution of a concept. *Journal of General Management, 14*(2), 34-55.

Wickens, D. (1987). *The road to Nissan*. London: MacMillan.

Williamson, O.E. (1985). *The economic institutions of capitalism*. New York: Free Press.

Wright, P. (1987). A refinement of Porter's strategies. *Strategic Management Journal, 8*, 93-101.

Wright, P. & McMahan, G. (1992). Theoretical perspectives for strategic human resource management, *Journal of Management, 18*(2), 295-320.

Wright, P. & Snell, S. (1991). Toward an integrative view of strategic human resource management. *Human Resource Management Review, 1*, 203-225.

Zeira, Y. & Banai, M. (1981). Attitudes of host-country organizations towards MNC's staffing policies: A cross-country and cross-industry analysis. *Management International Review, 2*, 38-47.

[18]

Conceptualizing the global competency cube: a transnational model of human resource

Allen D. Engle Sr
Eastern Kentucky University, Richmond, Kentucky, USA
Mark E. Mendenhall
University of Tennessee, Chattanooga, Tennessee, USA
Richard L. Powers
Eastern Kentucky University, Richmond, Kentucky, USA
Yvonne Stedham
University of Nevada, Reno, Nevada, USA

Keywords
Human resource development,
Strategy, Management, Model

Abstract
Presents a conceptual framework
that attempts to bridge the lag
between strategic need and
international human resource
(IHR) support practices. Looks at
the idea of competencies being an
alternative to the traditional
construct of jobs. Presents a
model consisting of three
balanced transnational
competencies. Concludes with a
series of HR applications of the
model.

Introduction

Over the past 30 years, the conceptualization of global strategies by multinational corporations has developed dramatically (Adler, 1997; Ghoshal and Bartlett, 1997; Perlmutter, 1969), and the implication of these global strategic models for international human resource (IHR) processes and practices has been no less dramatic (Black *et al.*, 1999; Dowling *et al.*, 1999). Despite these important developments, however, major discontinuities between these global structures and the IHR processes that are required to implement them remain.

A significant and unresolved issue involves the implications of the inherent differences between multinational strategies and transnational strategies for IHR processes. Multinational strategies employ organizational design and structure as the primary control devices to implement the strategy, and advocate the use of job-based IHR practices to support structural controls. In transnational strategies, however, these roles are reversed and personal competency-based IHR processes and practices become the dominant control devices in support of a more nimble "mind matrix," while jobs and structure act in secondary support roles (Adler and Ghadar, 1992; Bartlett and Ghoshal, 1993; Engle and Stedham, 1998).

These fundamental shifts in primary form of control, unit of analysis, and the performance requirements of the firm require theorists and practitioners alike to reconceptualize all the major aspects of IHR when dealing with transnational strategies. Traditional, structurally-embedded, job-based IHR processes are inadequate to address the complexities and pace created by the need to "globally" balance an in-depth local understanding with the orchestration of global capabilities and resources (Ghoshal and Bartlett, 1997). A significant lag has resulted between the IHR requirements of a transnational strategy and their realization. This lag requires that researchers and practitioners revisit IHR activities and construct new frameworks in support of these transnational requirements. This paper is an attempt to add to, and to stimulate further development of, this important dimension in the field of international human resource management.

The purpose of this paper is to offer a conceptual framework that attempts to bridge the aforementioned lag between strategic need and IHR support practices. The paper will first present the idea of "competencies" being an alternative to the traditional construct of "jobs" in the transnational context, and will argue that it is the appropriate unit of analysis for transnational IHR processes. Next, a model consisting of three balanced transnational competencies (cultural, functional, and product competencies) will be presented; this discussion will then be followed by a delineation between the three competencies and competence in the process of acquiring these three competencies. The paper will conclude with a series of IHR applications of the model in the areas of planning, recruitment and selection, training and development, executive leadership, and strategic control.

Why competencies, or "are you experienced?"

A key to the reconceptualization of IHR activities for transnational modes of organizing relates to the necessity of moving away from the construct of "job" to that of "competency" as the ideal focus of analysis in

Allen D. Engle Sr,
Mark E. Mendenhall,
Richard L. Powers and
Yvonne Stedham
*Conceptualizing the global
competency cube: a
transnational model of human
resource*

IHR policy decisions. Before discussing this notion of "competency," first the traditional approach to IHR decision making in the multinational context will be reviewed.

In multinational firms the dominance of structure as the primary device to implement strategy on the macro level is normally reflected by the dominance of job-centered IHR processes on the micro level. The goal of the multinational strategy is to create a strategy-structure-job "fit." Human resource processes play the not-so-strategic role of ensuring that jobs happen (Stedham and Engle, 1999).

In the multinational strategic context, Mahoney (1989) noted that performance is naturally a primary dimension of work; however, in some firms the accurate and direct assessment of performance becomes too difficult or expensive to achieve. In these situations, Mahoney observes, proxies for performance are created by organizational decision makers. A job can be a proxy for performance. Jobs are paid rates and decision makers in the firm assume that, if the process of the job is being carried out, the outcome of performance will inevitably follow.

However, Mahoney (1989) also notes that a second proxy exists; namely, a person's knowledge and maturity. We term this proxy as the "competencies" that reside within a manager. In this view, an individual's qualifications, certifications and "maturity" in an occupation are the basis for pay. People are paid based on their qualifications and competencies. Decision makers in the firm assume that, if people who possess needed competencies are hired, then performance will follow. Another way of visualizing this unit of analysis is to view competencies as inputs, job characteristics as contextual process, and performance qualities as outputs. In this case, the "job/person dichotomy" is viewed as placing (inputting) persons into job contexts (processes) and expecting stable performance outputs to result from this combination (Perlman, 1980).

Most IHR processes traditionally operate at the job level of analysis, and yet this job focus is really a historical compromise between person and performance. Many IHR issues may be more effectively assessed at higher levels of analysis (occupation or job family) or lower (position or person) levels of analysis (Perlman, 1980; Wallace, 1983). Thus there is no reason to assert the universalistic superiority of job based models – especially in transnational strategic contexts.

As long as the context is stable and relatively uniform, then "job" is an acceptable proxy for performance. When contexts become unstable (as they do in global business), and must increasingly be made more variable and customized to local conditions in order to achieve performance, then "job" becomes a less acceptable proxy for performance. Success at a job (i.e. a connection between job context and performance outcomes) in one cultural context does not ensure success of the same job processes operating in a different cultural context.

For example, multinational companies normally use the criterion of technical competence as the primary selection criterion for expatriate assignments (Black *et al.*, 1999). The assumption behind this selection technique is that, if a manager performs well in New York, it stands to reason that he/she will also perform well in Tokyo. The problem with this reasoning is that it assumes that the job in Tokyo is embedded in the same social, cultural and work contexts as the job in New York. This is obviously not the case; however, corporate headquarters usually do not rework the job description (or work process) to fit the Japanese context. The expatriate winds up having to make that adjustment incrementally and informally on his/her own. Thus, the job process does change in an international assignment, but not formally, and out of view of corporate headquarters.

Additionally, corporate headquarters' staff are entirely unaware that any job process changes have been made at all, since their focus is on the job performance (output) of the expatriate's efforts. When the expatriate returns to the USA, the social memory and learning about culturally-specific job processes leave with the expatriate and his/her replacement must undergo the same self-generated job process adjustments as were made by his/her predecessor.

To avoid this inefficiency, attention should be focused on the inputs (personal competencies) and the outputs (performance experiences) of work. This competency/experience focus is robust enough to deal with the instabilities and complexities of transnational work environments. This focus is also more aligned with the macro refocus on processes as opposed to structures as the dominant form of strategic implementation (Ghoshal and Bartlett, 1997).

Past performance, from both the worker's and the firm's perspectives, equates to what we will call "experience." The accumulation of experiences may or may not create enduring and stable personal competencies. As long as we specify the cultural context of these experiences, they will make better proxies – in the transnational environment at

Allen D. Engle Sr,
Mark E. Mendenhall,
Richard L. Powers and
Yvonne Stedham
*Conceptualizing the global
competency cube: a
transnational model of human
resource*

least – for performance than would job processes. Another challenge in the transnational workplace is that experience must often be applied in contexts that did not produce it. Global activities are often characterized by their complexity as well as by the turbulence of the global business marketplace. Thus, transnational firms require IHR process cycles measured in weeks or a few months rather than in months or years. IHR processes must be operated at dramatically reduced cycle times in order to take advantage of the potential flexibility and responsiveness of the transnational strategy (Overman, 1999; Schell and Solomon, 1997; Tichy, 1993).

It may be dangerous to underestimate the practical issues related to replacing job with person as the focal unit of analysis. At the same time, the leap from one unit of analysis to another is not insurmountable. According to Sanchez and Levine (1999, p. 57), "... the primary difference between traditional job analysis and competency modeling lies in the level of analysis", so that " competencies are broader sets of human attributes than the narrowly defined knowledge, skills and abilities (KSAs) of the past". These authors go on to state that the broader unit of analysis captured by competencies may be particularly promising in task situations characterized by "continuous flux", when "group-related tasks" are critical, or when "missions", "core business values" and "organizational factors" such as location call for flexibility and change (Sanchez and Levine, 1999, p. 57).

The selection of competency dimensions

Which competencies will more accurately capture the nature of global work contingencies and forward the implementation of a transnational strategy? Bartlett and Ghoshal (1993) present the idea of a "mind matrix," the internalization of control by cadres of socialized managers, to replace the rigidity and expense of external structural control. This mind matrix control, a form of "social" as opposed to "bureaucratic" control, appears well suited to more nimbly carry out the locally responsive, yet globally directed transnational strategy (Adler and Ghadar, 1992; Engle and Stedham, 1998; Ouchi, 1981).

Looking to structure and strategy for dimensions

Our premise is not that structural solutions are inaccurate in their assessment of critical

dimensions of control, but rather that external structures are too clumsy, slow and/or expensive to implement the low cost, "mass customization" that a transnational strategy requires (Adler and Ghadar, 1992; Bartlett and Ghoshal, 1993).

Structurally, three dimensions are most commonly applied in some one-, two- or even three-part combinations. These dimensions are traditionally called "geographic," "functional," and "product" structures (Egelhoff, 1988). Multinational strategies are most often related to global product structures, which combine geographic and product line differentiation (Adler and Ghadar, 1992; Jones, 1998), while more rudimentary international strategies are associated with stand-alone global division structures. Transnational firms, however, look to external cultural, functional and product matrix structures, an expensive and cumbersome proposition, or the promises of the "mind matrix" (Bartlett and Ghoshal, 1993; Jones, 1998).

A basic contention of the proponents of the "mind matrix" is the need to balance the three dimensions, so that no single dimension dominates at the expense of the other two dimensions (Doz and Prahalad, 1986). In the language of organizational design, structures must articulate, or "differentiate" along, those areas of variation existing within the firm (Jones, 1998, Ch. 4). The "structural articulation" provided by organizational design – over variations in functions, products and cultures – must be translated into "competence articulation" provided by IHR activities – over these same three dimensions – if the mind matrix is to provide adequate levels of control.

Strategic control is not diminished by focusing on IHR competencies. Rather it is enhanced by eliminating the translation device of jobs and more directly and explicitly connecting corporate-level effectiveness (to provide a balance of global standardization, local differentiation and diffused innovation) to individual-level competencies (to develop, assess and reward a balance of functional, cultural and product based capabilities). This direct "line of sight" (Lawler, 1990), unencumbered by clumsy and time-consuming person-to-job-to-firm effectiveness translations (Lawler, 2000), between balanced individual competence and balanced organizational effectiveness criteria may be the single greatest potential contribution of the proposed model.

The greater the strategic range of response (range in functions provided, products produced or geographic markets served), the greater the need to create differentiated units

Allen D. Engle Sr,
Mark E. Mendenhall,
Richard L. Powers and
Yvonne Stedham
*Conceptualizing the global
competency cube: a
transnational model of human
resource*

to respond to these areas of variation. Subsequently there is a greater need to create more effective integrative mechanisms across these units to coordinate and share the results of these responses (Burns and Stalker, 1961; Ghoshal and Bartlett, 1997; Evans and Doz, 1993).

Domains (breadth) and ranges (depth) within the three competency dimensions

It is the contention of this paper that firms moving toward a transnational mode of strategic operation must focus on competencies related to markets (cultures), functions and products (see Figure 1).

Note in Figure 1 that the three competency dimensions (cultural, functional, and product competencies) are represented by three planes. Most competency based pay systems recognize not only a breadth (domain) of different behavioral competency indicators but also a depth (range or "level") of understanding within each indicator domain (Milkovich and Newman, 1999, Ch. 6; Zingheim *et al.*, 1996). The approach taken here is to map demonstrable interpersonal capabilities (inputs) rather than emphasize the job-specific contextual space (process).

Cultural breadth and depth
To illustrate the breadth and depth issues inherent in transnational IHR systems, consider the cross-cultural training of expatriates. The breadth (domain) dimension has been labeled in the literature "cultural toughness" (Mendenhall and Oddou, 1985) and alternatively "cultural novelty" (Black *et al.*, 1991). This refers to the degree to which the host culture differs from the expatriate's home culture in terms of numerous cultural indicators, such as values, assumptions about human life, or norms, for example. Countries can be ranked in terms of their culture novelty (Torbion, 1982) and the implication of culture novelty for expatriates is as follows:

Figure 1
Cultural, functional and product competencies – breadth and depth

degree of need for the acquisition of new cross-cultural skills rises proportionately with the degree of cultural novelty.

Thus, an expatriate transferring to Tokyo will need to work much harder at acquiring the skills necessary to succeed in their overseas assignment than the same expatriate would, if he/she was assigned to a less culturally novel country. As cultural novelty increases, so does the amount of time that is necessary for cross-cultural training before the assignment, and in-country training during the overseas assignment. Similarly, the higher the cultural novelty, the more rigorous the cross-cultural training needs to be.

Currently, most US based MNCs offer training programs that are standardized and low in rigor – no matter to what country their people are assigned. This does not enhance the potential for expatriate success (Black *et al.*, 1999). Cultural depth refers to the length and task complexity of the expatriate assignment as well as the requirement to work closely with coworkers from different cultural backgrounds. Again, the deeper the assignment, the more in-depth and detailed the cross-cultural training needs to be (Mendenhall *et al.*, 1987).

Functional breadth and depth
Functional breadth refers to the traditional arrangement of work design based on common expertise, experiences, and use of common resources; for example, organizational structure that is created around the dimensions of accounting, marketing, finance and production functions. Also, individual domestic and global careers and training often are focused and/or delimited in the universe of these functional domains.

Functional depth refers to the level of specialized expertise available within a particular functionality; for example, advanced and specialized auditing and forensic accounting capabilities within the accounting function (Jones, 1998). This dimension relates to the degree to which an individual is delimited to a specific function in terms of their competencies, and is unable to span functional boundaries.

Product breadth and depth
Global product competencies required vary dramatically. The classification of the product as an industrial good (generally needing little or no modification) or a consumer good (generally needing moderate to extensive modification), the product's position in the product life cycle, the number of product lines in the firm's product mix, and the number of product items available to the market in the firm's product line, must all be understood and

Allen D. Engle Sr,
Mark E. Mendenhall,
Richard L. Powers and
Yvonne Stedham
*Conceptualizing the global
competency cube: a
transnational model of human
resource*

taken into account (Templeton and Treece, 1994). Firms entering new consumer goods markets with new products or existing products that are new to the market have found it strategically favorable to intentionally shorten the product's life cycle. By making periodic product adaptations to the newly introduced products before competitors can bring out a product to effectively compete against the original offering, the firm is able to capture and maintain a larger market share (Rugman and Hodgetts, 1995).

Global firms must, as a matter of strategy, have a number of product items in their product line to fit local and regional preferences. Understanding these items and lines and the underlying personal preferences they meet requires greater product competency depth. The manager will be expected to make product offering (product features, branding, packaging, warranty, etc.), channel and logistical, promotional (advertising, personal selling, sales promotion) and pricing decisions for each product item in their product line marketed within their market (country or region).

Furthermore, they must continue making product modifications that will insure a competitive advantage. As the organization moves from being multinational to transnational, product competency requirements will continue to increase in both breadth and depth. The global product will be guided by the same strategic principles, use the same name (global brand), maintain a similar image and positioning, but with a marketing mix (product, price, promotion, and place) that may vary from country to country (Keegan, 1999). Here the manager needs not only skill and knowledge breadth but also skill and knowledge depth in order to maintain the continuity needed by a global product as it moves into various global markets.

Combining the three competency dimensions into a "global competency cube"

Combining the three dimensions along the domains and ranges of the various breadths and depths results in a three-dimensional "global competency cube" (see Figure 2). This cube graphically represents a three-dimensional space that captures the "location" – analogous to longitude, latitude and altitude – of all salient global competencies. The cube comprises an IHR measurement schema. This schema can be used to map, individually and in the aggregate, the mind matrix (Bartlett and Ghoshal, 1993; Ghoshal and Bartlett, 1997).

An enhanced ability by managerial groups to explicitly focus on identifying and, perhaps more importantly, balancing

Figure 2
The global competency cube

strategically linked competencies, is an absolute necessity in the transnational mode of operation. The mind matrix culture of the transnational organization requires a high degree of socialized agreement and coordination among the cadre of global managers (Bartlett and Ghoshal, 1993). This model is intended to provide a cultural frame, common vocabulary and referencing blueprint in order to mobilize and coordinate the global cadre.

The exact nature of the competencies required along cultural, functional, and product dimensions will vary from firm to firm according to strategic intent. The firm-specific "coordinates" within the domains and ranges associated with the three dimensions can be programmed or specified during strategic decision sessions. These coordinates have the potential to be utilized in a number of IHR processes, and possible implications will be discussed in the conclusion section of this paper. Before this discussion, however, it is important to distinguish further between the construct of "competencies" and the actual acquisition process involved in building the competencies necessary for the successful implementation of transnational strategies.

Acquiring transnational competencies

"Process competence" relates to how individuals acquire or update new content or outcome knowledge that is important for success in the transnational context. Process competence is that quality of mind, those "traits and characteristics" (Dowling *et al.*, 1999, p. 86), which facilitate speedy adaptation to new environments. Process competence can be conceptualized as the ability to reduce learning cycle time at the individual level. The exact nature of process competence is not currently comprehensively known; however, scholars are beginning to study this important aspect of IHR management.

Allen D. Engle Sr,
Mark E. Mendenhall,
Richard L. Powers and
Yvonne Stedham
*Conceptualizing the global
competency cube: a
transnational model of human
resource*

Some authors conceptualize process competence in terms of cultural flexibility, willingness to communicate, ability to develop social relationships, perceptual abilities, conflict resolution style and leadership style (Black *et al.*, 1999). Referring to IHR system competencies, but equally applicable to the transnational capabilities of individual employees, Claus (1999) refers to business savvy, cross-cultural awareness, communication skills, leadership skills, frame of reference and personal attributes. Kets de Vries and Mead (1993) refer to cultural adaptability. Phatak (1992) presents abilities related to cultural empathy, adaptability, diplomacy, language ability, positive attitude, emotional stability and maturity. Murray and Murray (1986) speak in terms of effectiveness and coping skills. Finally, Schell and Solomon (1997) present a list comprising of expectations, open-mindedness, respect for other beliefs, trust in people, tolerance, internal *locus* of control, flexibility, patience, social adaptability, initiative, risk taking, a sense of humor, interpersonal interest and spouse communication (for a more complete review of the notion as applied to global leadership development ... see Mendenhall (2000)).

These various traits and characteristics facilitate the speed and efficiency with which managers encounter, assess, and ultimately cope with new environments. A competence in the process of adapting to new environments results in the more permanent and enduring outcome competencies in the areas of cultural, functional and product knowledge. Exactly how these traits produce process competence, and the actual dynamics of process competence, have yet to be cogently theorized. Until this occurs, conclusive applications for IHR training and development cannot be drawn.

However, by differentiating between process competence and outcome competencies it is possible to distinguish between the means to achieve a goal quickly and efficiently – a transitory process – and more enduring ends. In the case of a manager in a transnational company, the end is a balanced, integrated and in-depth understanding of the cultures, functions and product lines required in order to implement the transnational strategy. Thus, though the goal becomes clearer from our model in terms of IHR policy focus, the "hows" of achieving IHR policy ends remain elusive.

Potential human resource applications of the global cube

This framework, which contends for the utility of balanced cultural, functional, and product competencies, has the potential to be applied to all major IHR processes. On the macro or strategic level, the assessment and planning for firm, SBU, divisional or regional activities may be analyzed by inventorying and aggregating existing competencies and experiences. Also on the macro level, decisions related to joint ventures and merger and acquisitions may be assessed using this framework (Harrigan, 1984; Lorange and Probst, 1987). Finally, this model can provide a framework to assist strategic decisions related to movement into or out of selected markets, product lines and functions.

Recall the earlier discussion of the primacy of personal competencies as a control device over job-based structural control in the transnational firm. On the micro level, unit managers can assess existing competency mixes within the firm and recruit and select individuals or teams for assignments. These individuals and teams would be determined to have the combination of cultural, functional and product line experiences that match the requirements of the assignment. Advanced databases can facilitate the assembly and access of worker assignments, performance management assessments, and any number of competency indicators and most closely match those combinations with the competency requirements of the assignment at hand (Peppard, 1999).

Training and development needs may also be more completely assessed using this model. The supervisors of employees who have adequate competencies along functional or product dimensions may be unaware of the cultural gaps in experiences and those competencies related to doing business with a certain culture. Individual "imbalances" in the three competencies may be more quickly uncovered, communicated and redressed by training or assignments that build competencies in deficient areas (Tichy, 1993). Supervisors will not have to estimate naïvely the level of candidate capabilities for global assignments – a practice with potentially devastating results for employees and firms alike (Black *et al.*, 1999).

The "Global Cube" provides both a framework and a template to assist the operating level "entrepreneurs," senior management "developers," and top level "leaders" in developing and maintaining those new and radically different management roles required by the

Allen D. Engle Sr,
Mark E. Mendenhall,
Richard L. Powers and
Yvonne Stedham
*Conceptualizing the global
competency cube: a
transnational model of human
resource*

"individualized" transnational firm (Ghoshal and Bartlett, 1997, pp. 218-41). Managerial development may be enhanced by allowing senior management "developers" to more thoroughly and accurately track the cultural, functional and product acumen of operating level "entrepreneurs". The developers would then be able to provide the line entrepreneurs with more timely assignments, mentoring interventions and orchestrate those task experiences required to build a global sensibility and develop senior level replacements for the future (Ghoshal and Bartlett, 1997).

Top level "leaders" may look to this global framework to identify and challenge unbalanced, unidimensional biases, while at the same time visualizing new cultural, functional and product goals. By publicly referencing and applying the values embedded in the framework, the visionary leaders can "build a context of cooperation and trust" and grow the "mind matrix" of social control (Ghoshal and Bartlett, 1997, p. 222).

The conceptual framework of the Global Competency Cube is not an automatic pilot that mechanically assesses and determines IHR processes. Rather it should be considered as the shared "artifact" of a transnational culture (Schein, 1985). As such, its role is to evoke, and remind members of, those shared values and assumptions – related to balancing competencies, striving to achieve "overarching purposes" and tapping more completely the human potential – so essential in order to efficiently combine local responsiveness with a global perspective (Ghoshal and Bartlett, 1997, p. 222).

References and further reading

Adler, N.J. (1997), *International Dimensions of Organizational Behavior*, 3rd ed., South-Western College Publishing, Cincinnati, OH.

Adler, N.J. and Ghadar, F. (1992), "International strategy from the perspective of people and culture: the North American context", in Lane, H.W. and DiStefano, J.J. (Eds), *International Management Behavior*, PWS-Kent, Boston, MA, pp. 217-44..

Bartlett, C.A. and Ghoshal, S. (1993), "Matrix management: not a structure, a frame of mind", in Pucik, V., Tichy, N.M. and Barnett, C.K. (Eds), *Globalizing Management*, John Wiley & Sons, New York, NY, pp. 107-18.

Black, J.S., Mendenhall, M.E. and Oddou, G.R. (1991), "Toward a comprehensive model of international adjustment: an integration of multiple theoretical perspectives", *Academy of Management Review*, Vol. 16, pp. 291-317.

Black, J.S., Gregersen, H.B., Mendenhall, M.E. and Stroh, L.K. (1999), *Globalizing People through International Assignments*, Addison-Wesley Publishing, Reading, MA.

Burns, T. and Stalker, G.M. (1961), *The Management of Innovation*, Tavistock Publications, London.

Claus, L. (1999), "Globalization and human resource professional competencies", paper presented in the Master's Series, 22nd Annual Global HR Forum, Orlando, FL.

Dowling, P.J., Welch, D.E. and Schuler, R.S. (1999), *International Human Resource Management*, 3rd ed., South-Western College Publishing, Cincinnati, OH.

Doz, Y. and Prahalad, C.K. (1986), "Controlled variety: a challenge for human resource management in the MNC", *Human Resource Management*, Vol. 25 No. 1, pp. 55-71.

Egelhoff, W.E. (1988), "Strategy and structure in multinational corporations: a revision of the Stepford and Wells model", *Strategic Management Journal*, Vol. 9, pp. 1-14.

Engle, A.D. and Stedham, Y. (1998), "Multinational and transnational strategies – implications for human resource practices", *Proceedings of the 6th Conference on International Human Resource Management*, Paderborn, CD-ROM Track III-1.

Evans, P.A.L. and Doz, Y. (1993), "Dualities: a paradigm for human resource and organizational development in complex organizations", in Pucik, V., Tichy, N.M. and Barnett, C.K. (Eds), *Globalizing Management*, John Wiley & Sons, New York, NY, pp. 85-106.

Ghoshal, S. and Bartlett, C.A. (1997), *The Individualized Corporation*, Harper Business Publishers, New York, NY.

Harrigan, K.R. (1984), "Joint ventures and global strategies", *Columbia Journal of World Business*, Vol. 19 No. 2, pp. 7-13.

Jain, S.C. (1989), "Standardization of international marketing strategy: some hypotheses", *Journal of Marketing*, Vol. 53, pp. 70-9.

Jones, G.R. (1998), *Organizational Theory*, 2nd ed., Addison-Wesley, Reading, MA.

Keegan, W.J. (1999), *Global Marketing Management*, Prentice-Hall, New York, NY.

Kets de Vries, M.F.R. and Mead, C. (1993), "The development of the global leader within the multinational corporation", in Pucik, V., Tichy, N.M. and Barnett, C.K. (Eds), *Globalizing Management*, John Wiley & Sons, New York, NY, pp. 187-205.

Lawler, E.E. III (1990), *Strategic Pay: Aligning Organizational Strategies and Pay Systems*, Jossey-Bass, San Francisco, CA.

Lawler, E.E. III (2000), *Rewarding Excellence*, Jossey-Bass, San Francisco, CA.

Lorange, P. and Probst, G.J.B. (1987), "Joint ventures as self-organizing systems: a key to successful joint venture design and implementation", *Columbia Journal of World Business*, Vol. 22 No. 2, pp. 71-8.

Mahoney, T.A. (1989), "Employment, compensation, planning and strategy", in

Allen D. Engle Sr,
Mark E. Mendenhall,
Richard L. Powers and
Yvonne Stedham
*Conceptualizing the global
competency cube: a
transnational model of human
resource*

Gomez-Mejia, L.R. (Ed.), *Compensation and Benefits*, Bureau of National Affairs, Washington, DC, pp. 1-28.

Mendenhall, M., Dunbar, E. and Oddou, G. (1987), "Expatriate selection, training, and career-pathing: a review and critique", *Human Resource Management*, Vol. 26 No. 3, pp. 331-45.

Mendenhall, M.E. (2000), "New perspectives on expatriate adjustment and its relationship to global leadership development", in Mendenhall, M.E., Kuhlman, T.M. and Stahl, G.K. (Eds), *Developing Global Leaders: Policies, Processes and Innovations*, Quorum Publishers, Westport, CT.

Mendenhall, M.E. and Oddou, G. (1985), "The dimensions of expatriate acculturation: a review", *Academy of Management Review*, Vol. 10, pp. 39-47.

Milkovich, G.T. and Newman, J.M. (1999), *Compensation*, 6th ed., Irwin/McGraw-Hill Publishers, Boston, MA.

Murray, F.T. and Murray, A.H. (1986), "Global managers for global business", *Sloan Management Review*, Vol. 27 No. 2, pp. 75-80.

Ouchi, W.G. (1981), *Theory Z*, Addison-Wesley Publishing, New York, NY.

Overman, S. (1999), "Speed of change said to leave very little room for error", *HR News*, Vol. 18 No. 12, p. 12.

Peppard, J. (1999), "Information management in the global enterprise: an organising framework", *European Journal of Information Systems*, Vol. 8, pp. 77-94.

Perlman, P. (1980), "Job families: a review and discussion of their implications for personnel selection", *Psychological Bulletin*, Vol. 87 No. 1, pp. 1-28.

Perlmutter, H. (1969), "The tortuous evolution of the multinational corporation", *Columbia Journal of World Business*, Vol. 12, pp. 9-18.

Phatak, A.V. (1992), *International Dimensions of Management*, 3rd ed., PWS-Kent, Boston, MA.

Rugman, A.M. and Hodgetts, R.M. (1995), *International Business: A Strategic Management Approach*, McGraw-Hill, New York, NY.

Sanchez, J.I. and Levine, E.L. (1999), "Is job analysis dead, misunderstood or both?", in Kraut, A.I. and Korman, A.K. (Eds), *Evolving Practices in Human Resource Management*, Jossey-Bass Publishers, San Francisco, CA, pp. 43-68.

Schein, E.H. (1985), *Organizational Culture and Leadership*, Jossey-Bass Publishers, San Francisco, CA.

Schell, M.S. and Solomon, C.M. (1997), *Capitalizing on the Global Workforce*, McGraw-Hill Publishing, New York, NY.

Sheth, J. and Eshghi, G. (1989), "Introduction", in Sheth, J. and Eshghi, G. (Eds), *Global Strategic Management Perspectives*, South-Western Publishing, Cincinnati, OH, pp. vii-xiii.

Stedham, Y. and Engle, A.D. (1999), "Multinational and transnational strategies: implications for human resource management", paper presented at the 8th Biannual Research Symposium of the Human Resource Planning Society, Ithaca, NY.

Templeton, J. and Treece, J.T. (1994), "BMW's comeback", *Business Week*, 14 February, pp. 42-4.

Tichy, N.M. (1993), "Global development", in Pucik, V., Tichy, N.M. and Barnett, C.K. (Eds), *Globalizing Management*, John Wiley & Sons, New York, NY, pp. 206-24.

Torbion, I. (1982), *Living Abroad: Personal Adjustment and Personnel Policy in the Over-seas Setting*, John Wiley & Sons, New York, NY.

Wallace, M.J. Jr (1983), "Methodology, research practice and progress in personnel and industrial relations", *Academy of Management Review*, Vol. 8, pp. 6-13.

Zingheim, P., Ledford, G.E. Jr and Schuster, J.R. (1996), "Competencies and competency models: does one size fit all?", *ACA Journal*, Vol. 5 No. 1, pp. 56-65.

Diversity Management

[19]

STRATEGIC HUMAN RESOURCE MANAGEMENT: EMPLOYEE INVOLVEMENT, DIVERSITY, AND INTERNATIONAL ISSUES

Gary C. McMahan
Myrtle P. Bell
Meghna Virick
University of Texas-Arlington

The new millennium will necessitate many changes in organizations and therefore in the issues we study. The field of strategic human resource management has certainly come to an evolutionary crossroads. It has evolved quite rapidly during the past decade, growing from early definitional and theoretical beginnings to the current state of an accumulation of empirical work exploring the fit among human resources practices, strategy, and performance. We attempt to stretch the boundaries of how we define and research strategic human resource management, by introducing three arenas for inquiry that may serve as a springboard or starting point for provocative and controversial discussion which may influence both the theoretical and empirical progress in the field. We focus on Employee Involvement, Diversity, and Strategic International Human Resource Management as presenting important challenges for current researchers and future scholars.

The field of Strategic Human Resource Management (SHRM) has evolved quite rapidly during the past decade, growing from early definitional and theoretical beginnings (Dyer 1985; Legnick-Hall & Legnick-Hall 1988; Wright & McMahan 1992) to the current state of an accumulation of a body of empirical work exploring the fit among human resources practices, strategy, and performance (Becker & Gerhart 1996; Becker & Huselid forthcoming). It could be argued that the field of strategic human resource management has certainly come to an evolutionary crossroads. This article stretches the boundaries of how we define and research strategic human resource management. We introduce three new arenas for inquiry that may serve as a springboard or

194 HUMAN RESOURCE MANAGEMENT REVIEW VOLUME 8, NUMBER 3, 1998

starting point for provocative and controversial discussion which may influence both the theoretical and empirical progress in the field. As we approach the new millennium, it is probably a healthy time to "push the envelope" forward to tackle some of the issues that are currently being verbally debated or that should be given the opportunity to be discussed and included in research concerning the strategic use of human resources (HR) in organizations. This article attempts to open the door to these discussions.

The coming decade will necessitate many changes in organizations, many of which are obvious, others more subtle, though possibly more important than the obvious ones. For the purposes of this special issue on Strategic Human Resource Management in the 21st Century, we have chosen to focus on three arenas we argue are relevant to the field: Employee Involvement, Diversity, and Strategic International Human Resource Management (SIHRM). These three issues appear to have little overlap, perhaps to be even completely distinct, however, each is important in its own right, and each is relevant to the changes in how we think about human resources strategically.

The first arena of inquiry concerns the current state of theory development in the field of strategic human resources. Although not explicitly stated, underlying many of the recent empirical advancements in strategic human resource management is the conceptual notion of employee involvement and/or the high involvement workplace (e.g., Lawler 1986; Lawler, Mohrman, & McMahan 1996). We argue that a new arena for inquiry revolves around further formalization of employee involvement (or what is currently being called High Performance Work Systems) theory and the explicit recognition of the influence of these ideas on the current empirical work being conducted in the field of strategic HR. This should lead to greater theoretical development to our field of study which has faced continued criticism as being "atheoretical" (Becker & Gerhart 1996; McMahan, Virick, & Wright forthcoming).

The second arena for inquiry concerns increased attention to workplace diversity in both the theoretical and empirical advancements in the field of strategic human resources. We argue that, though its inclusion to date has been virtually non-existent, diversity has a place in the field. We use the resource-based view of the firm to demonstrate this theoretical fit, and to provide evidence of the applicability of current theories from SHRM to the study of diversity and vice-versa.

Finally, we address the issue of strategic human resource management versus strategic international human resource management. This discussion centers around the basic issue of why these two areas have developed so separately and explores the differences between the areas with regard to definition and scope. Issues are raised that lead to the conclusion that not only do we have different conceptualizations of SHRM, but that research efforts within the U.S. are not cognizant of the efforts outside the U.S. and vice versa. Synergy in advancement of theory and research is therefore absent. What underlies the separate studies of domestic versus international strategic HR may deal directly with the question of value-added research.

STRATEGIC HUMAN RESOURCE MANAGEMENT: SECOND GENERATION EMPLOYEE INVOLVEMENT?

One new area for inquiry concerns the theoretical development of the study of strategic human resource management. Since the beginning of this relatively new approach to studying human resource management, researchers have been criticized for the lack of theory in the development of testable hypotheses (Becker & Gerhart 1996; McMahan, Virick, & Wright forthcoming; Wright & McMahan 1992). The issue here centers around the current usage of "High Performance Work Systems" (HPWS) (Huselid 1995) in the strategic human resource management literature. Huselid (1995) and others have used the term to refer to the bundling (MacDuffie 1995) of HR practices to determine their impact on firm performance measures. While this terminology is certainly not new, we argue here that the concept of HPWS may well be the next generation of an area of study that has been influencing the management of human resources for decades.

Brief Evolution of SHRM

As previously mentioned, the study of strategic human resource management is a relatively new body of research. The area of strategic HR had its beginning in the late 1970's and early 1980's when the field of HR was being influenced by the rapid emergence of the area of strategic management (Swiercz 1995). During this time HR research was centered around a silo approach to studying HR subfunctions (selection, training, compensation, performance appraisal, etc.). As the strategic management influence gained prominence, research appeared with terms such as "strategic staffing," "strategic pay," and so forth (Dyer 1983; Fomburn, Tichy, & Devanna 1984). In retrospect, it is interesting to note how each HR practice, which has an independent body of research associated with it, developed its own "strategic" jargon in order to appear current with the boom of the strategic management area. The traditional approach to the study of human resources, coupled with the same "siloed" approach to the emergence of the strategic management literature is but one factor in the evolution of the area of strategic human resource management as it is known today.

We argue that the primary contributor to the evolution of contemporary strategic human resource management thought may well come from the area of employee involvement/high involvement management (e.g., Lawler 1986). When reviewing the involvement area there seems to be two significant contributions both arguably influenced by an organizational development (OD) perspective (Swiercz 1995). First, the work of Lawler (1986, 1988) emphasizes involvement systems, which contrary to Becker and Huselid (forthcoming), affects most HRM subsystems of selection, training, appraisal and compensation. Second, the work of Dyer and Holder (1988) identified an "Involvement" type in their study of HR strategies. Empirical work by Swiercz (1995) and

Sivasubramaniam and Kroeck (1994) provides convincing evidence that an involvement orientation to human resource management strategy does exist.

As stated, the current study of SHRM seems to be at a crossroads. Most of the empirical research has focused either on the HR practices to performance relationship or the strategy-HR practice-performance fit (Delery forthcoming). Our argument is that many of the current measures of human resource practices in the strategic human resource management literature are actually the operationalizations of employee involvement concepts.

SHRM and Employee Involvement

We use Lawler's conceptualization of a high involvement/empowerment approach to organizations to make the employee involvement argument. At the core of his employee involvement model are four organizational processes or elements (i.e., Lawler 1986, 1988): power, information, knowledge and rewards. These elements are briefly described below.

Power refers to the decision making processes in the organization. There are obviously numerous types of decisions to be made in organizations, from organizational strategy decisions to the day to day operational decisions (Lawler 1986). Any form of decision-making that is made within the organization, but outside the top management team, could be argued as a form of participative decision-making.

Information refers to many types of shared communications ranging from business performance to actual employee output to almost any type of knowledge transfer. Information is a source of power in organizational coordination and cooperation (Lawler 1986).

Knowledge refers to the skills, abilities and knowledge of the employees. Central to any attempt to involve employees in an organization decision is their expertise and knowledge regarding the decision and the operation of the organization (Lawler 1988). Lawler further states that employee involvement programs vary widely in the degree to which they provide training and develop people's knowledge as part of the empowerment effort.

Rewards are a critical component of employee involvement effectiveness. In particular, sharing organizational rewards is crucial as employees obtain more power, information and knowledge; and they expect more when they feel their participation has made the organization more effective (Mohrman & Lawler 1985). Economic participation must be combined with participation in decisions for employee involvement to be most effective (Lawler 1986). All employees who are part of an involvement effort should be rewarded, at least in part, based on organizational performance.

At the root of Lawler's conceptualization is that power, information, knowledge and rewards must be pushed down to the lowest appropriate levels of the organization. Another factor is the degree of diffusion of an empowerment effort or practice inside an organization. This refers to the extent to which an organization is affected. The success of an employee involvement effort depends on how widely it is implemented into an organization (Lawler, Mohrman, & Ledford 1995). Some efforts that are limited to a few individuals or a few groups often have trouble surviving because they are foreign entities in an environment that is hostile to them (Goodman 1979). Therefore, it is important to understand that the degree of diffusion of HR practices is a critical issue in studying the relationships among firm performance, HR practices, and strategy.

Delaney and Huselid (1996) recently stated that "It has long been recognized and widely asserted that people are the preeminent organizational resource and the key to achieving outstanding performance. Until recently, this assertion was largely a statement of faith. Our results add to the growing empirical evidence suggesting that such assertions are credible" (pp. 964–965). Their study found a positive relationship between "progressive practices" and perceived measure of organizational performance. Therefore, it is not people alone, but it is the coupling of the employees and the effective HR progressive practices that affect employees' behaviors that produce this positive relationship. We further argue that these progressive practices (i.e., selective staffing, training, and incentive compensation) all fit precisely within the four elements of employee involvement/empowerment defined by Lawler (1986). Therefore, to some extent, a theory guiding the field of SHRM comes from the employee involvement/participation literature. Today, what we call strategic human resource management may well be "second generation" employee involvement with a relationship to firm strategy and performance. In essence, we might have called this area of research "Strategic Employee Involvement," however, the term "High Performance Work Systems" refers to the same thing.

Upon close inspection, almost all authors measuring strategic HR practices in the past few years have implicitly relied on the employee involvement/empowerment concepts without explicitly acknowledging this almost natural evolution of HR management thought (e.g., Arthur 1994; Huselid 1995; MacDuffie 1995; Pfeffer 1994; Youndt, Snell, Dean, & Lepak 1996). We discuss a few examples highlighting this point below.

Huselid (1995) incorporates factor structures (a) employee skills and organizational structure, and (b) employee motivation. A variety of employee involvement-oriented items create these primary factors used in this major research contribution to the field. Youndt, Snell, Dean, and Lepak (1996) define a human-capital-enhancing system as one of their primary HR systems. The items that define this system are arguably employee involvement or high involvement work practices. Delaney and Huselid (1996) attempt to differentiate HR measures from employee involvement measures; however, their process of determining what constitutes an employee involvement or high involvement practice from an HR practice is questionable. Finally, Pfeffer (1994) in his list of practices for managing people, includes information sharing, incentive pay, employee ownership, self-managed teams, etc., which certainly implies an involvement orientation.

The problem seems to be the fit of the conceptual or theoretical contributions of the employee involvement literature (Lawler 1986, 1988; Lawler, Mohrman, & Ledford 1995) with the empirical work that we have come to

198   HUMAN RESOURCE MANAGEMENT REVIEW   VOLUME 8, NUMBER 3, 1998

know as contemporary strategic human resource management. The theoretical development of the employee involvement literature has most certainly been slow to develop into formal, testable hypotheses which might explain the concept being somewhat ignored by SHRM researchers. We believe a weakness in strategic HR research might be the inability to tie together employee involvement concepts with the empirical analyses. This may well be a theoretical "missing link" and researchers should strongly consider this challenge.

This discussion attempted to provide an opportunity to link explicitly the not-yet-so developed theory of employee involvement (i.e., high involvement, empowerment, etc.) to the current study of strategic human resource management. It is hard to argue with the fact that many of the HR practices being measured today, both individually or in bundles, have evolved from the employee involvement literature which suggests pushing down responsibility and accountability for power, information, knowledge, and rewards to lower levels in the organization. It is this concept which guides many of the HR practices that researchers study but has been absent in our theoretical discussions. As mentioned earlier, the field of strategic HR continues to struggle with establishing a strong theoretical foundation, and it may well be necessary to work on establishing a more complete theory of employee involvement to help support much of the ongoing empirical work in the field. Quite possibly, we may find that employee involvement research is the earlier generation of the current study of contemporary strategic human resource management. Enhanced efforts by scholars to develop involvement concepts into testable hypotheses with the intention of building theory may well be one bright future for strategic human resource management research.

THE FIT OF DIVERSITY IN THE STUDY OF STRATEGIC HUMAN RESOURCE MANAGEMENT

In the past decade, considerable human resource management literature has discussed the increasing diversity of the United States' workforce (e.g., Cox 1994; Fernandez 1991; Jackson & Associates 1992; Jackson, May, & Whitney 1995; Milliken & Martins 1996; Tsui, Egan, & O'Reilly 1992; Wagner, Pfeffer, & O'Reilly 1984; Wiersema & Bantel 1993.) This research stream has been driven by the changing demographic picture of workers in the U. S. By the year 2000, approximately 85% of the new entrants to the workforce will be women and people of color (Johnston & Packer 1987; O'Hare 1992). Different human resources necessitate new ways of dealing with HR programs and practices that were designed to suit the needs of different kinds of workers. For example, benefit programs that were appropriate for and satisfactory to a married white male single earner family of 4 may be inappropriate for a dual-income African American family of 5, for a single-income white woman and her 2 children, and for an unmarried disabled person. As these "non-traditional" workers become an increasingly large portion of the workforce, researchers have begun to investigate potential HR ramifications.

Much of the existing literature addresses the need to value or effectively manage diversity and the potential benefits of doing so (e.g., Copeland 1988; Cox 1994; Cox & Blake 1991; Fernandez 1991). Another contingent of this research discusses some negative aspects of increasing diversity, such as turn-over and lowered attachment of whites and males (Tsui, et al. 1992), sexual harassment (Gruber & Bjorn 1982; Gutek, Cohen, & Konrad 1990; Mansfield et al. 1991) and other negative outcomes (Jackson, et al. 1991). A third contin-gent of this research recognizes the potential for both positive and negative outcomes from organizational diversity, which may change over time (e.g. Harrison, Price, & Bell 1998; Watson, Kumar & Michaelsen 1993).

While each of these three research streams has acknowledged the inev-itability of increasing diversity and sought to investigate ramifications of these changes, the majority of these investigations have been at the micro-level (individual or group). That is, most research has looked at the effects of diver-sity on individual outcomes such as turnover, group cohesiveness, or attach-ment. Limited research has addressed how those individual outcomes affect larger organizational outcomes (see Wright, Ferris, Hiller, & Kroll 1995; Wier-sema & Bantel 1993, for exceptions) or a strategic human resource manage-ment perspective.

In which context can increasing diversity be placed and what kinds of mac-ro-level theory and research on this subject may help organizations in the 21st century? Is there a competitive advantage to having a diverse workforce, as argued by some (e.g., Fernandez 1993)? We investigate these questions and make suggestions for the directions of SHRM in the year 2000 and beyond as related to diversity in organizations, applying arguments from the resource-based view of SHRM to workforce diversity. In the context of this work, diver-sity includes differences in race/ethnicity, sex, religion, age, sexual orienta-tion, physical ability, attitudes, skills, perspectives, and background (Joplin & Daus 1997; Robinson & Dechant 1997). "Valuing" diversity refers to the desire to include and utilize the assets of workers from various groups as potential employees, rather than excluding or limiting contributions of any potential employee because of any factor related to diversity (e.g., being male, Jewish, and/or aged).

SHRM, Competitive Advantage, and Diversity

The resource-based view of SHRM suggests that firms can develop and sustain competitive advantage using valuable, rare, inimitable, and non-sub-stitutable (human) resources (Barney 1991; Wright & McMahan 1992). Sim-ilarly, as discussed above, one contingent of diversity researchers argues that effectively managing and "valuing" diversity can provide organizations with a competitive advantage over organizations that do not do so. Combining SHRM with diversity research suggests that workforce diversity may provide organi-zations with a valuable, rare, inimitable, and non-substitutable competitive advantage.

The Value in Diversity. Wright and McMahan (1992) have argued that for hu-man resources to be considered a source of sustained competitive advantage, there must be a heterogeneous demand for and supply of labor. In other words,

200   HUMAN RESOURCE MANAGEMENT REVIEW   VOLUME 8, NUMBER 3, 1998

firms should have jobs that require workers to possess different types of skills and workers must also differ in their possession of those skills. Applied to the diversity literature, organizations that exclude workers as potential employees based on irrelevant factors limit their ability to hire some workers who may possess certain skills not possessed by other workers. In an often cited, clearly appropriate example, another name might have been beneficial for the Chevrolet car "Nova," which, translated from Spanish "no va" to English, means "it doesn't go" (Fernandez 1993).

In support of the argument for the value of having different types of skills, Watson et al. (1993) found that diverse groups were more effective in identifying problems and generating solutions than homogenous groups. Cox, Lobel, and McLeod (1991) found that differences in cultural norms of Asian, Hispanic, and African Americans when compared with those of Whites affected task behavior. The former, persons from collectivist cultural traditions, displayed more cooperative behavior during group tasks than did Whites, persons from individualist cultural traditions. These two studies provide support for the idea that an organization that employs a diverse workforce would have workers who possessed different types of skills, providing one aspect of the requirements for sustainable competitive advantage.

Rarity in Diversity. For a resource to be a source of sustained competitive advantage, it must be rare. Wright and colleagues (Wright, McMahan, & McWilliams 1994) argued that the ability to attract and retain applicants of the highest ability could be a source of such advantage. They reasoned that high ability applicants, due to the normal distribution of ability, are necessarily rare. Organizations that exclude potential employees based on irrelevant factors again may limit their capability to hire high ability applicants, who may also happen to be gay, Asian, and/or disabled. Further, by including all potential applicants as candidates, an organization is able to choose the cream of the entire crop (Cox & Blake 1991), rather than focusing simply on a (shrinking) subset of potential workers.

In addition, though not discussed by resource-based theorists in this context, having a truly diverse workforce is in itself "rare." Larger organizations tend to be more heterogeneous than smaller ones, however, having a fairly homogeneous workforce in any size organization is not uncommon. In addition, employees tend to be segregated *within* organizations. Job segregation by sex, in which women tend to work with women and men tend to work with men, continues to exist (Jacobs 1989; Reskin 1995). Further, women and minorities tend to be concentrated in lower level occupations across organizations (Federal Glass Ceiling Commission 1997). Having a workforce in which diverse people exist at various levels, in various occupations, working among diverse people, is rare.

Diversity as Inimitable. Researchers have argued that for an organization's human resources to be considered a sustained competitive advantage, competitors should be unable to duplicate or imitate them (Becker & Gerhart 1996; Wright & McMahan 1992). Wright and McMahan included unique historical conditions, causal ambiguity, and social complexity while Becker and Gerhart used causal ambiguity and path dependency as important to the inimitability of human resources. Though there are differences in terminology, those researchers describe similar aspects as part of inimitability.

Historical conditions refer to "historical events that have shaped a firm's practices, policies, and culture" (Wright & McMahan 1992, p. 302) and are similar to Becker and Gerhart's (1996) path dependency. Both path dependency and historical conditions refer to long-standing policies that exist in an organization that cannot be easily duplicated. Long-standing policies supportive of diversity in an organization may have been put into place as a result of past discrimination lawsuits which resulted in certain policy changes and measurement practices, or from having a company history of a leadership in hiring diverse employees.

Causal ambiguity and path dependency may result in deeply embedded HR strategies that are particularly difficult to imitate (Becker & Gerhart 1996). A "deeply embedded" strategy of workforce diversity would require the interplay of all HR functions (e.g., recruitment and selection, performance evaluation, compensation and benefits) and would interact with other organizational functions (i.e., marketing and customer support) to create inimitability. From the valuing diversity perspective, causal ambiguity and path dependency are closely related. Causal ambiguity as competitive advantage refers to the inability of competitors to identify and therefore copy the source of the competitive advantage (Gerhart & Becker 1996; Wright & McMahan 1992). Important HR strategies that could be used to create causal ambiguity are related to the standard HR functions (e.g., recruitment and selection, performance management, compensation and benefits, etc.). Recruitment practices designed to provide a competitive advantage through diversity work to ensure all potential employees see the organization as the employer of choice. That is, all potential employees should perceive that there are opportunities for people like them (e.g., over 40, female, and/or African-American) in such an organization and that those opportunities are not related to or limited by irrelevant factors, such as age, sex, race, or other diversity.

Recruitment strategies at such an organization might include actively seeking employees at universities with diverse student bodies, at historically black colleges, at women's universities, through minority or female-member organizations; or advertising in publications likely to be read by diverse populations or on Spanish-language television. Having diverse workers as recruiters might also indicate to applicants that there are people like them working in the organization. Once the organization became known as one that seeks (and values) having a diverse workforce, recruitment would be increasingly easy as persons of color, women, the aged, the disabled, and gays and lesbians made more direct applications. Once more diverse workers were employed, using employee referrals and informal networks—who can be reliable sources of employees and tend to be similar to current workers (Shelton 1987)—would continue to yield diverse workers. In that vein, some researchers have argued that a firm's ability to utilize existing resources and accumulate new ones can affect sustained competitive advantage (Lado & Wilson 1994).

Causal ambiguity is apparent if the ideas just presented are reversed. Does having diverse employees result in greater numbers of diverse applicants or does having greater numbers of diverse applicants result in having more employees who are diverse? Does having diverse recruiters result in more job acceptances when recruiting diverse workers or does receiving more job acceptances from diverse applicants result in having more diverse recruiters? Does being the employer of choice result in the direct application of more (diverse) workers?

Selection practices in organizations that value diversity might also work to create causal ambiguity. Such organizations would have systems in place to ensure their selection practices are non-discriminatory and continue their goals of increasing diversity. An analysis of such practices would include validating tests and performing job analyses to ensure potential candidates were not unnecessarily and unjustifiably excluded (e.g., irrelevant height and weight requirements, which might exclude women or Asian-Americans). Interviewers would be diverse, including members of the population to which the pool of applicants belonged. Interviewers would be aware of potential biases that might exclude diverse workers or which might alienate diverse workers during recruitment and selection processes.

Again, the causal sequence of such selection practices would be ambiguous to organizations seeking to emulate. Does having a diverse employee population result in those persons making an effort to be non-discriminatory in selection or does making an effort to be non-discriminatory in selection result in having diverse employees? Does having interviewers who are aware of potential biases result in the successful selection of diverse workers or does having diverse workers result in the selection of more workers who are diverse, perhaps through the similarity-attraction paradigm (Byrne 1971; Schneider 1987)?

Regarding path dependence, an organization that used workforce diversity to its competitive advantage would have over time developed systems to ensure that diverse workers would desire to and be chosen to enter the organization. After entering, diverse workers would see continued opportunities, rather than meet with systems to ensure they remained in entry-level positions without opportunities for advancement. Entering the organization is related to recruitment efforts and selection mechanisms (discussed above); seeing opportunities for advancement is related to performance evaluation, training and development, and the diversity of other (higher-level) employees.

Research suggests that the higher turnover of women and minorities (the largest groups of diverse workers) may result from their perceptions of a lack of opportunities and barriers to advancement after entering organizations (Federal Glass Ceiling Commission 1997). Greenhaus, Parasuraman, and Wormley (1990) found that African American managers in three organizations felt less accepted, were more likely to have plateaued in their careers, and received lower performance and promotability ratings than did comparison White managers. Thus, one system that might be in place at an organization that valued diversity might be a mentoring program for new entrants to the organization. A valuing diversity organization might focus on conducting valid, unbiased performance evaluations that included higher-level management or human resources review to ensure their validity and freedom from contamination. Such organizations might train managers to avoid biases which may result in diverse employees receiving lower performance evaluations than earned. Instruments and methods of evaluation would be evaluated for ethnocentric biases, updated accordingly, and continually re-validated. For example, a rating for "aggressive" might be naturally associated with males (Broverman, Vogel, Broverman, Clarkson, & Rosenkrantz 1972) and might perhaps be replaced with "actively seeks out new customers."

Social complexity refers to the competitive advantage that stems from social relationships in organizations, for example, in team production (Wright & McMahan 1992). Research on group performance, in general, suggests that groups may outperform persons working alone in various situations. Specific to diverse groups, as discussed earlier, some research has found complex relationships between diversity and group performance (e.g., Watson et al. 1993). The diverse teams capitalized on the strengths and knowledge of group members, which were more varied than those of the culturally homogeneous groups. Other researchers have found that diverse groups produced more and a wider variety of ideas than did homogenous groups (Jackson 1992; McLeod, Lobel, & Cox 1996).

Non-substitutability. This concept refers to the inability to find substitutes for a resource (Wright & McMahan 1992), in this case a diverse workforce. A diverse workforce is inherently comprised of people who are different and who bring to the organization different backgrounds, knowledge, skills, and abilities. An organization employing such a workforce will necessarily have employees who learned from each other and whose assets could be best utilized when circumstances warranted (such as the need for cooperation, rather than competition). Theoretically, these employees would be highly motivated, since non-job or non-performance related factors would not affect their opportunities, rewards, or future. One study indicated that females were required to be more highly qualified to be promoted, receiving fewer promotions than similarly qualified males (Olson & Becker 1983). If, as would be expected in a diverse organization, all employees (men, women, persons of color, whites, gays, lesbians, heterosexuals, etc.) believed that their qualifications and performance would be the only factors affecting their opportunities, theoretically, everyone would all have the same performance motivations and none of the de-motivating effects of having irrelevant factors affect their opportunities.

Other SHRM Theories and Diversity

We have shown that the resource-based view of SHRM may be applied to valuing diversity arguments. Though based on and well supported by diversity research, these arguments are speculative. Portions of the cybernetic view of SHRM might be applied as well as, or perhaps better than, the resource-based view has been applied. The cybernetic view of SHRM suggests that outcomes such as job satisfaction and turnover are related to human resource practices.

Diversity research argues that women and persons of color may leave organizations more frequently and be less satisfied than Whites and men as a result of the organizations' failure to value their presence and provide opportunities for advancement (Cox 1994). We could have argued, then, that valuing diversity would be related to higher job satisfaction and lower turnover of diverse workers as has been suggested by other research (e.g., Cox 1994), which would result in more positive organizational outcomes overall. These arguments would be weakened by the finding of Tsui & colleagues (Tsui et al. 1991) that heterogeneity lowered attachment for Whites and men (but not for persons of color and women). Such contradictions re-emphasize the need to see which, if any SHRM theories are appropriate to this area with such important human resource implications.

Perhaps there are better-suited SHRM approaches than the resource-based approach that could be applied to the concept of valuing diversity. Finding the SHRM theory *most* applicable to the concept of human resource diversity was not our goal, however. Instead, our goal was to stimulate thinking about this previously neglected, at least in the SHRM research arena, but important area. Given the inevitability of an increasingly diverse workforce and the growing categories of persons included under the rubric of diversity, we believe diversity as a competitive advantage is an area worthy of greater attention in SHRM research in the next millennium.

As a final note, we suggest that employee diversity itself emphasizes the potential limitations of existing SHRM theories, given organizations comprised of increasingly different types of workers. We described valuing diversity as attempts to include and utilize the assets of workers from *various* groups as potential employees. Much of SHRM research, however, argues that certain practices are best with little regard to the diversity of employees within organizations. This research makes unstated assumptions about worker similarity that may not be appropriate in the next millennium. What effects will individual incentive pay systems have upon organizations comprised of persons from individualist (typically Anglo) and collectivist (typically African, Hispanic, and Asian) cultures? How might incentive pay systems be reconfigured to address persons having different goals and motivations? That some of the fundamental assumptions of SHRM research may need to be re-assessed given increasing worker diversity would appear to be another critical challenge for SHRM researchers.

SHRM VERSUS SIHRM?: DEBATING THE ISSUES

The issue of challenging fundamental assumptions as seen above is not only reflected in the intra-national diversity arena which has emerged as a result of changing demographics in the U.S. Another significant change is the speed of global communication and its impact on business around the world. Few firms today are truly non-global and we have seen its impact on current research in what was originally the "personnel function" re-align itself as human resource management and develop a different orientation and status. Over time, the growth of multinational firms and increasing overseas operations by companies has led to the growth of a new literature on the international human resource management of such firms. Issues that emerged as a result of cross cultural interactions and movements of people around the world were those of expatriate management, staffing, compensation and matters that dealt with differences in parent and host company personnel policies. Several authors examined these issues of expatriate management with the focus on the examination and improvement of specific HR practices that aimed at specific HR outcomes such as the reduction of turnover or the maintaining of internal equity. With the advancement of strategy as a separate field of study came the realization of the importance of creating a bridge between strategy and human resources. Thus emerged the field of strategic human resource management, which adopted a new macro orientation and aimed at demonstrating a bottom-line impact of the role of people management in organizations.

The incorporation of firm-level outcomes in the study of the SHRM and the re-evaluation of the domain of study as it struggles with trying to obtain a new identity has led it to a crossroads. Research findings suggest that the use of progressive HR practices does have a financial impact on organizations and this has been very encouraging to the field. As a result there have also been investigations on the "fit" of SHRM with the overall strategy of the firm, that is, vertical integration as well as the alignment among the various practices i.e. horizontal integration (Wright & McMahan 1992). This strategic focus, which began in the United States, is now gaining ground internationally. The international stream of thought in strategic human resource management, however, has adopted a slightly different orientation from the original conception of SHRM, as formulated in the United States. This perspective has led to concerns that although researchers in the United States are making advances on both the theoretical and empirical front, they may be taking a view of strategic international human resource management that is narrow and ethnocentric, and therefore, that is leading researchers to make generalizations to the international context that are inappropriate.

In this section we inquire into the role of SIHRM, and raise issues that have relevance to the advancement of the field. We examine the contributions of current research in SHRM in the U.S. and compare it with research being done in other countries. We raise issues that lead us to conclude that not only do we have different conceptualizations of SHRM, but that research efforts within the U.S. are not cognizant of the efforts outside the U.S. Synergy in advancement of theory and research is therefore absent.

One approach that may be used in trying to understand conceptualizations of SHRM and SIHRM, is the definition offered by Schuler, Dowling, and De-Cieri (1993) who define strategic international human resource management as "human resource management issues, functions and policies and practices that result from the strategic activities of multinational enterprises and that impact on the international concerns and goals of those enterprises" (pp. 720). This definition is somewhat consistent with the definition of SHRM offered by

Wright and McMahan (1992) and has received endorsement from other re-searchers in the field as well (Taylor, Beechler, & Napier 1997). Certain basic questions however, need to be raised on the precise scope of the field because of the existence of a literature that is considered to be strategic international human resources, but that does not involve the study of multinational firms. This is the research by non-U.S. researchers on SHRM issues. Let us first examine the multinational firm issue.

Multinational Firm Issue

This issue relates to the type of companies that are encompassed in SIHRM theory. There has been a trend to create a SIHRM theory that applies strictly to multinational companies. Global, transnational, and joint ventures would fall under this category. A different variation of this would be to use the classi-fication of multinational organizations as ethnocentric, polycentric, or global (Perlmutter 1969). The focus of such studies is to explore the dynamics of the parent companies vs. the host company, or headquarters vs. subsidiaries. One important variable in studies that examine this relationship is the level of control that the parent has over the subsidiary. Firms with low control give significant autonomy to their subsidiaries and there has been considerable research debating the pros and cons of host company firms having enough autonomy to adopt local and culture specific practices. In the SHRM literature, there is evidence of the use of the resource-dependence theory to examine the dynamics between parent companies and their subsidiaries.

The growing integration of markets, and increasing homogenization, how-ever, has resulted in the growth of "transnational" (Bartlett & Ghoshal 1989) companies that aim at internal consistency as opposed to local isomorphism (Rosenweig & Nohria 1993). These are related to the second variable common-ly included in these studies: level of differentiation and integration in firms. Schuler et al. (1993) incorporate both these strategic components in their inte-grative framework of SIHRM, and refer to them as interunit linkages and internal operations (Hennart 1982; Phatak 1992). Interunit linkages are con-cerned with issues of differentiation and integration (Lawrence & Lorsch 1967), and the choices associated with selecting the different options. Internal operations are concerned with those operations that arise out of units working within the confines of local environment and conditions.

With the growth of transnational firms, and what Ferner (1994) calls "multi-centered" organizations, comes a greater diffusion of authority and control among the different parts of the organization such that organizations are becoming loosely coupled political systems, rather than controlled systems. Some organizations such a ABB, for instance are progressing to a new "federal-ism" (O'Toole & Bennis 1992), where the headquarters is extremely lean and subsidiaries are both highly homogenous and autonomous. In cases where cross cultural differences exist, and integration is neither desirable or possible, however, the situation is quite different and researchers have instead focused on issues of internal and external fit (e.g. Milliman, Von Glinow & Nathan 1991).

The above discussion presupposes that the scope of SIHRM is the study of HR issues in multinational firms. In presenting their integrative framework, Schuler and his colleagues (1993) make that quite explicit. Using the same logic, several authors have examined the relationship between parent companies and subsidiaries by developing hypotheses aimed at clarifying those relationships (e.g., Hannon, Huang, & Jaw 1995). Bird and Beechler (1995), likewise using Miles and Snow's (1984) typology of prospector, defender, and analyzer, examined issues of fit in U.S. based Japanese subsidiaries.

Research Ideology Issue

As mentioned earlier, the conceptualization of SIHRM as the study of SHRM exclusively within multinational firms, does not have extensive support. Although this has never been explicitly stated, it becomes evident in doing a review of the literature and seeing different conceptualizations of the meaning of SIHRM. Most U.S. researchers consider SIHRM as research on SHRM conducted by non-U.S. researchers, and done primarily outside the U.S. This artificial separation of the field has occurred predominantly as a result of the difficulties in transplanting U.S. based theories to other countries as well as ideological differences in the research paradigms of the U.S. based researchers as opposed to the European tradition.

A review of the literature of international authors in SHRM makes the differences in ideology with respect to research paradigms clearly evident. There have traditionally been differences in the American and European traditions with respect to research methodology, the former favoring the logical positivist approach, while the latter favoring the idiographic or inductive approach. As a result we see a lot more of empirical data and statistical analysis, using large sample sizes, in U.S. based studies (e.g., Delaney & Huselid 1996; MacDuffie 1995; Snell & Dean 1992) and many more cases studies with rich, contextual detail among non-U.S. researchers (Ropo 1993; Paauwe 1996). Brewster (forthcoming), in trying to elucidate the respective roles of the two different traditions, elaborates on the two different paradigms he calls "universalistic" and "contextual." He argues that in the SHRM literature, the aim of the universalistic paradigm is to improve organizational performance with the strategic deployment of human resources. This paradigm is predominant in the U.S. The contextual paradigm, on the other hand, delves into issues of contextual differences, and aims at gaining a better understanding of the antecedents of differences, with a relatively low emphasis on firm performance.

Both the paradigms have advantages and disadvantages. What is dangerous is that the two streams of research clearly do not work together or believe in drawing from the strengths of both traditions. Brewster (1995) calls for using the insights from one paradigm to another in the hope that learning from one another will further our understanding of SHRM. The qualitative or id-

208   HUMAN RESOURCE MANAGEMENT REVIEW   VOLUME 8, NUMBER 3, 1998

iographic tradition can, no doubt, play an important role in hypothesis development, while the logical positivist tradition can be used for measurement of constructs and analysis of data. Whether or not this happens remains to be seen.

While differences in research paradigms do play a part in causing resultant differences in conceptualizations of the scope of SHRM, it appears that these differences in ideology also impact the *content* of study in SHRM. This is of serious concern. These content areas include issues such as the inclusion/ exclusion of contextual variables (Brewster 1993), issues of fit (Boxall 1996), best practices (Guest 1997), and lack of theory building. Recognition of the fact that the theories developed in the United States cannot be generalized to all international contexts is crucial. However, being "siloed" in one's approach to the study of SHRM is also unacceptable. Yet, current research in SHRM has not addressed or even acknowledged this issue. There is some literature in "traditional" HR on international dimensions of human resource management arising out of concerns of multinational firms such as expatriate turnover and cross cultural management. However, most of these international issues deal with *individual* HR practices and how these can be optimized to achieve specific outcomes and benefits in various international settings.

In the emerging field of SHRM, the acknowledgment and inclusion of a broad range of contextual influences on management's choice of HR strategy is extremely important. That recognition is more prevalent in the idiographic tradition. Brewster, for example (forthcoming) argued that U.S. models fail to take into consideration external factors such as cultural differences, unionism, role of governments and the like. Therefore, we need to acknowledge that there may be certain types of HR practices that may be more or less appropriate in certain cultures. For example, high performance work systems, as defined by U.S. researchers may conceivably be considered *low* performance work systems in other cultural contexts if we move to the level of detail of specific HR practices. As a consequence, the recent spate of research on high performance work practices has come under criticism. Starting with Pfeffer's (1994) best practice approach, in which he outlined 16 best practices, which later were reduced to 13, and subsequently to 7 (Pfeffer 1998) researchers have been conducting studies that have a high level of statistical advancement. However, researchers differ on what constitutes a high performance work practice (Becker & Gerhart 1996). Further, there is reason to believe that if authors within the U.S. disagree on what constitutes a HPWS, there is little possibility of agreement among international researchers who encounter a wide variety of situations and cultural scenarios. Nonetheless, efforts are underway to continuously refine and improve measurement issues related to the measurement of HPWS and the various formulations of "fit," both internal and external.

Non U.S. researchers (e.g., Boxall 1996) also have some basic issues with the concept of fit, i.e. fit as strategic interaction. The concept of fit, also referred to as the "matching model" is premised on the assumption that a good fit between HR strategy and business strategy will promote organizational effectiveness. In studies that examine this fit, typologies of strategies such as those by Porter

(1980), and Miles and Snow (1984) have been used as appropriate strategic types to which HR must be aligned. Critics have argued that the strategic types may not be appropriate and that the concept of fit implies non-flexibility (Boxall 1996; Chadwick & Cappelli forthcoming; Wright & Snell forthcoming).

From a fit perspective, in an international context multiple fits may have to be considered if there are subsidiaries. However, from the point of view of application of theories to specific cultural contexts, our observation is that the contextual tradition is seeking a model of SHRM that would apply universally. The move to "internationalize" SHRM is an attempt to build a theory of SHRM that has external validity, that is applicable outside the U.S. While the goal of theory building necessitated the establishment of both internal and external validity, there is little doubt that theories from different countries, whatever their origin, tend to show some cultural specificity, and run into difficulties when transplanted into other countries (Brewster, et al. 1996).

Developing theories that are universally applicable in all contexts is a very big challenge. Some may even argue that this is fruitless to attempt because the model will be so complex so as to lessen its usefulness. Contextual factors will also vary from country to country, so mapping out each of the detailed contextual issues will be a near impossible task. However, recognizing the fundamental importance of synergy in the efforts SHRM researchers, both within and outside the U.S., is an essential challenge that requires research attention.

NEW ARENAS OF INQUIRY: CONCLUDING COMMENTS

Given our goal to be provocative, thought-provoking, and interesting, this article has provided three very important arenas for inquiry and development in the field of Strategic Human Resource Management. In our attempt to do this, we risked making some uncomfortable. If there is some agreement that the current state of strategic human resource management is at a crossroads, hopefully some of our ideas may allow us to step "out of the box" as we go about creating and developing interesting and relevant theory and research in this exciting field. The areas of employee involvement/empowerment, diversity, and the globalization of organizations are issues that are continually growing in importance and are at the forefront of issues organizations are confronting on a daily basis.

The academic study of SHRM is undeniably at a critical stage in its evolution. We suggest that there are three possible future scenarios for the field: the first, one of stagnation and retrenchment, the second of stability, slow growth, and replication, and the third would find the field of strategic human resource management moving in exciting new directions with a focus on improving our understanding and prediction of human contributions to the improvement of organizational systems. The new arenas for inquiry introduced here would support the third scenario, which is the most likely future for the field of strategic human resource management.

ACKNOWLEDGMENT

The authors wish to thank Drs. Paul Swiercz, Patrick Wright, Ken Wheeler, David Gray, and an anonymous reviewer for their helpful comments on an earlier draft of this article.

REFERENCES

Arthur, J. B. 1992. "The Link Between Business Strategy and Industrial Relations Systems in American Steel Minimills." *Industrial and Labor Relations Review* 45: 488–506.

————. 1994. "Effects of Human Resource Systems on Manufacturing Performance and Turnover." *Academy of Management Journal* 37: 670–687.

Barney, J. 1991. "Firm Resources and Sustained Competitive Advantage." *Journal of Management* 17: 99–120.

Bartlett, C. A. and G. Ghoshal 1989. *Managing Across Borders: The Transnational Solution*. London: Hutchison.

Becker, B. and B. Gerhart. 1996. "The Impact of Human Resource Management on Organizational Performance: Progress and Prospects." *Academy of Management Journal* 39: 779–801.

Bird, A. and S. Beechler. 1995. "Links Between Business Strategy and Human Resource Management Strategy in U.S. Based Japanese Subsidiaries: An Empirical Investigation." *Journal of International Business Studies* 26: 23–47.

Boxall, P. F. 1996. "The Strategic HRM Debate and the Resource-Based View of the Firm." *Human Resource Management Journal* 6: 59–75.

Brewster, C. 1993. "Developing a 'European' Model of Human Resource Management." *The International Journal of Human Resource Management* 4: 765–784.

————. 1995. "Towards a 'European' Model of Human Resource Management." *Journal of International Business Studies* 26: 1–22.

————. forthcoming. "Different Paradigms in Strategic HRM: Questions Raised by Comparative Research." In *Research in Personnel & Human Resource Management,* edited by G. Ferris. Stamford, CT: JAI Press.

Brewster, C. and H. H. Larsen. 1992. "Human Resource Management in Europe." *The International Journal of Human Resource Management* 3: 409–434.

Brewster, C., O. Tregaskis, A. Hegewisch, and L. Mayne. 1996. "Comparative Survey Research in Human Resource Management: A Review and an Example." *International Journal of Human Resource Management* 7: 585–604.

Broverman, I. K., S. R. Vogel, D. M. Broverman, F. E., Clarkson, and P. S. Rosenkrantz. 1972. "Sex Role Stereotypes: A Current Appraisal." *Journal of Social Issues* 28: 59–78.

Byrne, D. 1971. *The Attraction Paradigm*. New York: Academic Press.

Caliguiri, P. M. and L. K. Stroh. 1995. "Multinational Corporate Management Strategies and International Human Resource Practices: Bringing IHRM to the Bottom Line." *International Journal of Human Resource Management* 6: 494–507.

Chadwick, C. and P. Cappelli. forthcoming. "Alternatives to Generic Strategy Typologies in Strategic Human Resource Management." In *Research in Personnel and Human Resource Management,* edited by G. Ferris. Stamford, CT: JAI Press.

Campbell, P. R. 1996. *Population projections for states by age, sex, race, and Hispanic origin: 1995 to 2025*. U.S. Bureau of the Census Population Division, p. 1–47.

Copeland, L. 1988. "Valuing Diversity: Making the Most of Cultural Differences at the Workplace." *Personnel* 65: 52–60.

Cox, T. 1994. *Cultural Diversity in Organizations.* San Francisco: Berrett-Koehler Publishers.

Cox, T. and S. Black. 1991. "Managing Cultural Diversity: Implications for Organizational Competitiveness." *Academy of Management Executive* 5: 45–56.

Delaney, J. T. and M. A. Huselid. 1996. "The Impact of Human Resource Management Practices on Perceptions of Organizational Performance." *Academy of Management Journal* 39: 949–969.

Delery, J. E. and D. H. Doty. 1996. "Modes of Theorizing in Strategic Human Resource Management: Tests of Universalistic, Contingency, and Configurational Performance Predictions." *Academy of Management Journal* 39: 802–835.

Ferner, A. 1994. "Multinational Companies and Human Resource Management: An Overview of Research Issues." *Human Resource Management Journal* 4(3): 79–87.

Federal Glass Ceiling Commission. 1997. "The Glass Ceiling." In *Workpace / Women's Place: An Anthology,* edited by D. Dunn. Los Angeles: Roxbury. (Reprinted from *A Solid Investment: Making Full Use of the Nation's Human Capital,* by Federal Glass Ceiling Commission, 1995, Washington, DC: Government Printing Office).

Fernandez, J. P. 1991. *Managing a Diverse Work Force.* Lexington, MA: Lexington Books.

Fernandez, J. P. with M. E. Barr. 1993. *The Diversity Advantage.* Lexington, MA: Lexington Books.

Fomburn, C. Tichy, N. M., and M. A. Devanna. 1984. *Strategic Human Resource Management.* New York: John Wiley & Sons.

Goodman, P. 1979. *Assessing Organizational Change: The Rushton Quality of Work Experiment.* New York: Wiley Interscience.

Greenhaus, J. H., S. Parasuraman, and W. M. Wormley. 1990. "Effects of Race on Organizational Experiences, Job Performance Evaluations, and Career Outcomes." *Academy of Management Journal* 33: 64–86.

Gruber, J. E. and L. Bjorn. 1982. "Blue-Collar Blues: The Sexual Harassment of Women Autoworkers." *Work and Occupations* 9: 271–298.

Gutek, B. A., A. G. Cohen, and A. M. Konrad. 1990. "Predicting Social-Sexual Behavior at Work: A Contact Hypothesis." *Academy of Management Journal* 33: 560–577.

Guest, D. E. 1997. "Human Resource Management and Performance: A Review and Research Agenda." *The International Journal of Human Resource Management* 8: 263–276.

Hannon, J. M., L. C. Huang, and B. S. Jaw. 1995. "International Human Resource Strategy and Its Determinants: The Case of Subsidiaries in Taiwan." *Journal of International Business Studies* 26: 531–554.

Harrison, D. A., K. H. Price, and M. P. Bell. 1998. "Beyond Organizational Demography: Time and the Effects of Surface-Versus Deep-Level Diversity on Work Groups." *Academy of Management Journal* 41: 96–107.

Hennart, J. F. 1982. *A Theory of the Multinational Enterprise.* Ann Arbor: University of Michigan Press.

Huselid, M. A. 1995a. "The Impact of Environmental Volatility on Human Resource Planning and Strategic Human Resource Management." *Human Resource Planning* 16: 35–51.

———. 1995b. "The Impact of Human Resource Management Practices on Turnover, Productivity, and Corporate Financial Performance." *Academy of Management Journal* 38: 635–672.

Jackson, S. E. 1992. "Consequences of Group Composition for the Interpersonal Dynamics of Strategic Issue Processing." *Advances in Strategic Management* 8: 345–382.

Jackson, S. E. and Associates. Eds. 1992. *Diversity in the Workplace: Human Resource Initiatives.* New York: Guilford Press.

Jackson, S. E., J. F. Brett, V. I. Sessa, D. M. Cooper, J. A. Julin, and K. Peyronnin. 1991. "Some Differences Make a Difference: Interpersonal Dissimilarity and Group Heterogeneity as Correlates of Recruitment, Promotion, and Turnover." *Journal of Applied Psychology* 76: 675–689.

Jackson, S. E., K. E. May, and K. Whitney. 1995. "Understanding the Dynamics of Diversity in Decision Making Teams." In *Team Decision Making Effectiveness in Organizations,* edited by R. A. Guzzo and E. Salas. San Francisco: Jossey-Bass.

Jackson, S. E., V. K. Stone, and E. B. Alvarez. 1993. "Socialization Amidst Diversity: Impact of Demographics on Work Team Oldtimers and Newcomers." In *Research in Organizational Behavior* (Vol. 15), edited by L. L. Cummings and B. M. Staw. Greenwich, CT: JAI Press.

Jacobs, J. A. 1989. "Long-Term Trends in Occupational Segregation By Sex." *American Journal of Sociology* 95: 160–173.

Johnston, W. and A. Packer. 1987. *Workforce 2000: Work and Workers for the 21st Century.* Indianapolis: Hudson Institute.

Joplin, J. R. W. and C. S. Daus. 1997. "Challenges of Leading a Diverse Workforce." *Academy of Management Executive* 11: 32–47.

Lawler, E. E. III. 1986. *High-Involvement Management.* San Francisco: Jossey-Bass.

———. 1988. "Choosing an Involvement Strategy." *Academy of Management Executive* 2: 197–204.

Lawler, E. E. III, S. A. Mohrman, and G. E. Ledford. 1995. *Creating High Performance Organizations: Survey of Practices and Results of Employee Involvement and TQM in Fortune 1000 Companies.* San Francisco: Jossey Bass.

Lawler, E. E. III, S. A. Mohrman, and G. C. McMahan. 1996. *New Directions for the Human Resources Organization.* Center for Effective Organizations, University of Southern California.

Lawrence, P. and J. W. Lorsch. 1967. *Organization and Environment.* Boston, MA: Harvard Business School Press.

Lado, A. A. and M. C. Wilson. 1994. "Human Resource Systems and Sustained Competitive Advantage: A Competency-Based Perspective." *Academy of Management Review* 19: 699–727.

Legnick-Hall, C. A. and M. L. Legnick-Hall. 1998. "Strategic Human Resources Management: A Review of the Literature and a Proposed Typology." *Academy of Management Review* 13: 454–470.

MacDuffie, J. P. 1995. "Human Resource Bundles and Manufacturing Performance: Organizational Logic and Flexible Production Systems in the World Auto Industry." *Industrial and Labor Relations Review* 48: 197–221.

Mansfield, P. K., P. B. Koch, J. Henderson, J. R. Vicary, M. Cohn, and E. W. Young. 1991. "The Job Climate for Women in Traditionally Male Blue-Collar Occupations." *Sex Roles* 25: 63–79.

Miles, R. and C. Snow. 1984. "Designing Strategic Human Resource Systems." *Organizational Dynamics* (Summer): 36–52.

McLeod, P. L., S. A. Lobel, and T. H. Cox. 1996. "Ethnic Diversity and Creativity in Small Groups." *Small Group Research* 27: 246–264.

Milliken, F. J. and L. L. Martins. 1996. "Searching for Common Threads: Understanding the Multiple Effects of Diversity in Organizational Groups." *Academy of Management Review* 21: 402–433.

Milliman, J., M. A. Von Glinow, and M. Nathan. 1991. "Organizational Life Cycles and Strategic International Human Resource Management in Multinational Companies: Implications for Congruence Theory." *Academy of Management Review* 16: 318–339.

Mohrman, A. M. and E. E. Lawler. 1985. "The Diffusion of QWL As a Paradigm Shift." In *The Planning of Change,* edited by W. G. Bennis, K. D. Benne, and R. Chin. New York: Holt, Rinehart & Winston.

O'Toole, J. and W. Bennis. 1992. "Our Federalist Future." *California Management Review* (Summer): 73–90.

O'Hare, W. P. 1992. "America's Minorities—the Demographics of Diversity." *Population Bulletin* 47: Washington, DC: Population Reference Bureau.

Olson, C. A. and B. E. Becker. 1983. "Sex Discrimination in the Promotion Process." *Industrial and Labor Relations Review* 36: 624–641.

Paauwe, J. 1996. "Key Issues In Strategic Human Resource Management: Lessons From the Netherlands." *Human Resource Management Journal* 6: 76–93.

Perlmutter, H. 1969. "The Tortuous Evolution of the Multinational Corporation." *Columbia Journal of World Business* (January-February): 9–18.

Pfeffer, J. 1994. *Competitive Advantage Through People.* Boston: Harvard Business School Press.

———. 1998. *The Human Equation: Building Profits by Putting People First.* Harvard Business School Press.

Phatak, A. V. 1992. *International Dimensions of Management* (3rd ed.), Boston, MA: PWS-Kent.

Porter, M. 1980. *Competitive Strategy.* New York: The Free Press.

Reskin, B. F. 1997. "Sex Segregation In the Workplace." In D. Dunn. *Workplace / Women's* Place: An Anthology. Los Angeles: Roxbury. (Reprinted from Paula England, *Comparable Worth: Theories and Evidence,* 1992, by Walter de Gruyer, Inc.).

Robinson, G. and K. Dechant. 1997. "Building a Business Case for Diversity." *Academy of Management Executive* 11: 21–31.

Ropo, A. 1993. "Towards Strategic Human Resource Management: A Pilot Study In a Finnish Power Industry Company." *Personnel Review* 22: 35–53.

Rosenweig, P. M. and N. Nohria. 1994. "Influences On Human Resource Management Practices In Multinational Corporations." *Journal of International Business Studies* 25: 229–251.

Schuler, R. S., P. J. Dowling, and H. De Ceiri. 1993. "An Integrative Framework of Strategic Human Resource Management." *The International Journal of Human Resource Management.* 4: 173–198

Smith, S. A. and M. Tienda. 1988. "The Doubly Disadvantaged: Women of Color in the U. S. Labor Force." Pp. 61–80 in *Women Working,* edited by A. H. Stromberg and S. Harkess. Mountain View, CA: Mayfield.

Schneider, B. 1987. "The People Make the Place." *Personnel Psychology* 40: 437–454.

Shelton, B. A. 1987. "Racial Discrimination at Initial Labor Market Access." *National Journal of Sociology* 1: 100–117.

Sivasubramaniam, N. and G. K. Kroeck. 1995. *Alternative Conceptualizations of fit in Strategic Human Resource Management.* Unpublished paper presented at the 1995 Human Resource Planning Society Research Symposium.

214   HUMAN RESOURCE MANAGEMENT REVIEW   VOLUME 8, NUMBER 3, 1998

Snell, S. A. and J. W. Dean, Jr. 1992. "Integrated Manufacturing and Human Resource Management: A Human Capital Perspective." *Academy of Management Journal* 35: 467–504.

Swiercz, P. M. 1995a. Strategic HRM. *Human Resource Management* 18: 53–59.

———. 1995b. *Strategic Human Resource Management Orientation: Developing and Testing a Measure.* Unpublished paper presented at the 1995 Human Resource Planning Society Research Symposium.

Taylor, S., S. Beechler, and N. Napier. 1996. "Toward an Integrative Model of Strategic International Human Resource Management." *Academy of Management Review* 21: 959–985.

Tsui, A. S. and C. A. O'Reilly, III. 1989. "Beyond Simple Demographic Effects: The Importance of Relational Demography in Superior-Subordinate Dyads." *Academy of Management Journal* 32: 402–423.

Tsui, A. S., T. D. Egan, and C. A. O'Reilly, III. 1992. "Being Different: Relational Demography and Organizational Attachment." *Administrative Science Quarterly* 37: 549–579.

Turban, D. B. and A. P. Jones. 1988. "Supervisor-Subordinate Similarity: Types, Effects, and Mechanisms." *Journal of Applied Psychology* 73: 228–234.

Wagner, W. G., J. Pfeffer, and C. A. O'Reilly, III. 1984. "Organizational Demography and Turnover in Top-Management Groups." *Administrative Science Quarterly* 29: 74–92.

Watson, W. E., K. Kumar, and L. K. Michaelsen. 1993. "Cultural Diversity's Impact on Interaction Process and Performance: Comparing Homogeneous and Diverse Task Groups." *Academy of Management Journal* 36: 590–602.

Wiersema, M. F. and K. Bantel. 1993. "Top Management Team Demography and Corporate Strategic Change." *Academy of Management Journal* 35: 91–121.

Wright, P., S. P. Ferris, J. S. Hiller, and M. Kroll. 1995. "Competitiveness Through Management of Diversity: Effects on Stock Price Valuation." *Academy of Management Journal* 38: 272–287.

Wright, P. M. and G. C. McMahan. 1992. "Theoretical Perspectives for Strategic Human Resource Management." *Journal of Management* 18: 295–320.

Wright, P. M., G. C. McMahan, and A. McWilliams. 1994. "Human Resources and Sustained Competitive Advantage: A Resource-Based View Perspective." *International Journal of Human Resource Management* 5: 301–326.

Wright, P. M., D. L. Smart, and G. C. McMahan. 1995. "Matches Between Human Resources and Strategy Among NCAA Basketball Teams." *Academy of Management Journal* 38: 1052–1074.

Wright, P. M. and S. A. Snell. (forthcoming). "Toward a Unifying Framework for Exploring Fit and Flexibility in Strategic Human Resource Management." *Academy of Management Review.*

Youndt, M. A., S. A. Snell, J. W. Dean, Jr., and D. P. Lepak. 1996. "Human Resource Management, Manufacturing Strategy, and Firm Performance." *Academy of Management Journal* 39: 836–866.

[20]

Strategies for managing human resource diversity: From resistance to learning

Parshotam Dass and Barbara Parker

Executive Overview

Most writing on the subject suggests there is one best way to manage workforce diversity in organizations. We argue that there is no single best way, but that the organization's approach depends on the degree of pressure for diversity, the type of diversity in question, and managerial attitudes. Strategic responses for managing diversity are presented in a framework of proactive, accommodative, defensive, and reactive modes. These responses are discussed in terms of episodic, freestanding, and systemic implementation practices.

Does diversity by race, gender, ethnicity, or anything else improve organizational performance?[1] Finding reliable answers to this question is difficult because people define diversity in different, even conflicting ways. Consequently, an increasingly diverse workforce is variously viewed as opportunity, threat, problem, fad, or even nonissue. These disparate views lead people to manage workforce diversity in distinct ways, resulting in different costs and benefits. Despite the claim by some that there is one best way to manage a diverse workforce, there is little agreement on what it is.

The Framework

This article proposes a framework that links executives' perspectives and priorities to managing workforce diversity, organizational conditions, and performance.

Figure 1 presents an outline of the general framework, which shows that different steps in the process of managing diversity are related and can occur simultaneously. In practice, most U.S. organizations have assembled a more diverse workforce in response to external and/or internal pressures. For example, customers, suppliers, civil liberties groups, or others representing social, legal, economic, and other imperatives might exert external pressures to hire more people of color. At the same time, diversity champions, employee groups, or change managers might apply internal pressures for diversity in organizational hiring. The unique set of pressures

brought to bear on a single organization combine to influence managers' perspectives, priorities, and strategic responses. Other managers may assemble more diverse workforces even when there are few pressures to do so. Their choices affect strategic responses and implementation, which, in turn, alter pressures for diversity.

While some pressures have usually favored greater organizational diversity, other pressures also arise to reduce it.[2] Some firms, for example, have been lobbied to eliminate same-sex benefits policies. A fit or match among diversity pressures, perspectives, and strategic responses is likely to improve organizational performance, whereas a mismatch is likely to entail economic and noneconomic costs. Managers who acknowledge they face strong legal and social mandates for diversity may conclude that accommodating racial diversity provides a better fit with organizational circumstances than resisting it. This implies that the best approach to diversity management is particular rather than universal. Because pressures for diversity can vary and even conflict, matches made within an organ-ization may also differ, producing different initiatives on sexual orientation, gender, ethnicity, or other types of human difference.

Diversity Perspectives and Associated Strategic Responses

In the U.S., affirmative action and Equal Employment Opportunity regulations have helped to

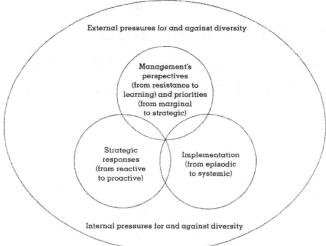

FIGURE 1
General Framework for Managing Diversity

make organizations more diverse in race, gender, and national origin. Yet, as several writers have observed, diversity can be viewed through lenses other than legal or ethical,[3] and diversity has been defined, studied, and approached in quite different ways.[4] Researchers examining how organizations manage workforce diversity have identified three different perspectives:[5] the discrimination and fairness paradigm, the access and legitimacy paradigm, and the learning and effectiveness paradigm. Since we believe that different perspectives can be effective under some circumstances,[6] we call the third paradigm learning. We also have identified a fourth perspective: resistance. (See Figure 2.)

Resistance Perspective and Reactive Strategic Response

Resistance to diversity occurred during the pre-civil rights movement in the U.S. and the post-colonial era in Europe, when there were fairly clear lines between racial and ethnic groups and few pressures for workforce diversity. As the pressures increased in the 1960s, concerns that minorities might displace the established majorities became an important reason to resist diversity. Individuals embodying some visible form of difference—nationality, color, or gender—were seen as

not like the homogeneous insiders in business organizations. Growing pressures for diversity are likely to be perceived as threats.

By some accounts, the resistance perspective is alive and well in some organizations.[7] Videotapes showed that Texaco executives used racial epithets and planned to destroy evidence of discriminatory practices. Both Mitsubishi Motor Manufacturing of America and Astra Pharmaceuticals were accused of sexual harassment,

Growing pressures for diversity are likely to be perceived as threats.

suits were filed, and managers were subsequently fired or reassigned. Many other organizations worldwide face discrimination claims from immigrants, ethnic groups, gays, lesbians, aging employees, and women.

The dominant response for the resistance perspective is reactive,[8] characterized by denial, avoidance, defiance, or manipulation.[9] Although it was traditional for male agents and their regional managers to hire male relatives, State Farm Insurance avoided change and denied any alleged effects in a nine-year gender-bias suit that the company lost.

DIVERSITY PERSPECTIVES	PROBLEM STATEMENT	INTERNAL DEFINITION	PRESCRIPTION	DESIRED OUTCOME	STRATEGIC RESPONSE
Resistance perspective	Diversity as non-issue or threat	Not "us"	Sustain homogeneity	Protect the status quo	Reactive
Discrimination and fairness perspective	Differences cause problems	Protected groups	Assimilate individuals	Level the playing field for members of protected groups	Defensive
Access and legitimacy perspective	Differences create opportunities	All differences	Celebrate differences	Access to employees and consumers	Accommodative
Learning perspective	Differences and similarities offer opportunities and bear cost	Important differences and similarities	Acculturate: pluralism	Individual and organizational learning for long term effect	Proactive

FIGURE 2
Diversity Perspectives and Associated Strategic Responses

Demands for organizational change can be deflected by defiant assertions that changes are inefficient or unacceptable to shareholders because they increase costs and reduce profits. When Shoney's then-CEO J. Mitchell Boyd organized sensitivity sessions for the 60 top managers, the board fought the sessions on the basis of their cost. An organization under court order to hire more minorities and women used manipulation tactics when it counted the same person three times in the same compliance report because one parent was black, the other Asian, and she was female. Such responses may be found in monolithic organizations[10] where bias in human resources and other systems is ubiquitous.

A reactive strategic response may be appropriate when pressure for a particular type of diversity is low. A women's sports league might make hiring of male athletes a nonissue; religious entities are likely to resist hiring priests from other religions to preserve the nature and character of their organizations; and multinational organizations that otherwise hire from a diverse workforce may be less diverse in homogeneous nations.

Discrimination and Fairness Perspective and Defensive Strategic Response

The discrimination and fairness paradigm is adopted most in U.S. organizations facing moderate pressures to incorporate diversity. This perspective assumes that prejudice has kept members of certain groups out of organizations, but that with equal access and fair treatment under the law are available remedies. This perspective is based primarily on legal decisions, particularly on affirmative action policies and Equal Employment Opportunity legislation.

The discrimination and fairness perspective perceives diversity as an organizational problem to be solved.[11] It focuses on members of historically disadvantaged groups[12] more than on individuals or on the organization as a whole. Employees may be encouraged to view people of different color, gender, or national origin as the same and thus be pressured to "make sure that differences among them do not count."[13]

This perspective gives rise to a defensive strategic response that includes such tactics as negotiating with, balancing, and pacifying different interest groups. Organizations may seek to pacify a minority group by selecting the director of affirmative action from that group. Similarly, many colleges and universities advertise their positions in minority publications, and many businesses include minority and female vendors among their suppliers. In practice, these actions may improve equity and fairness, providing economic resources as well as role models for members of historically disadvantaged groups. However, these actions can have negative effects, as well, if there is confusion about what diversity or legal compliance means. When organizational leaders allow or encourage employees to view affirmative action as a barrier to their own advancement, the result may be defensive employees who feel the leaders are unfair to them in order to be more fair to others.

When organizational leaders allow or encourage employees to view affirmative action as a barrier to their own advancement, the result may be defensive employees who feel the leaders are unfair to them in order to be more fair to others.

Similarly, enforcing quotas can create backlash if unqualified people are hired. Another challenge occurs when surface-level forms of diversity are mistaken for deep-level diversity.[14] For example, Thurgood Marshal's Supreme Court seat was filled by Clarence Thomas, an African-American, but many felt Thomas identified more with Caucasians than with other African-Americans. Such a view can generate homogeneity, assimilation, colonization, and control rather than diversity.[15]

Access and Legitimacy Perspective and Accommodative Strategic Response

Workforce 2000, a widely cited landmark study, predicted that more women, minorities, older workers, and immigrants would join the U.S. work force.[16] Such demographic changes in Europe and the U.S., as well as growing competitive pressures worldwide, created the context for the access and legitimacy perspective, which can emphasize access or legitimacy or both. For example, 44 percent of managers in 34 multinational firms believed that the most compelling reason to implement diversity programs was to tap diverse markets and customers.[17] Legitimacy may be sought by IBM managers who believe it is important for customers to look inside the company and see people like themselves,[18] but Alpine Bank sought access when it recruited bilingual employees to attract Spanish-speaking customers. Some organizations often advocate acceptance and even celebration of differences based on a perception that differences create opportunities (Figure 2).

Companies operating from the access and legitimacy perspective tend to emphasize bottom-line reasons for incorporating diversity. To leaders like

Pitney Bowes CEO Michael Critelli, diversity "is a business necessity."[19] Bottom line objectives can include cost reductions, reduced turnover, enhanced profitability resulting from improved morale or team spirit, or improved market value. Leaders may refer to studies that demonstrate links between diversity initiatives and annual returns or stock market values.[20]

This perspective typically defines diversity in broad terms that affirm differences throughout the workforce whether they are legally protected or not. Among these differences are a propensity for risk-taking, birth order, family relationships, nationality, sexual orientation, and values. Pillsbury defines diversity as "all those ways in which we differ."[21] An organization operating from this perspective often draws on concepts of inclusion to manage the many differences it endorses. While the discrimination and fairness perspective is typically adopted because of social or legal mandates, organizations following the access and legitimacy perspective usually do so by choice. This perspective not only recognizes differences but also values them. While improved performance may be one result of feeling valued, diverse communities may also feel they are being used to serve interests of a dominant class.[22] Valuing all differences equally may seem to ultimately value none. Celebrations of diversity can normalize differences and mask homogeneous values and practices.[23]

The access and legitimacy perspective is likely to be associated with an accommodative strategic response. Rather than tolerate diversity until people can be assimilated, this perspective promotes greater diversity in the workplace. Organizations with an accommodative response are likely to reflect a higher level of heterogeneity and inclusion than those with a defensive one. Their perspective is often guided by demographic pressures. Tyson Foods hired hundreds of Mexican immigrants in its poultry processing plants because of labor market shortages, presumably caused by low wage rates in the industry. Similarly, long-distance telephone companies in the U.S. often select sales representatives from immigrant groups because they may attract immigrant users. The restaurant and hospitality industries recognized that diverse consumers and employees stimulate industry growth.[24]

Learning Perspective and Proactive Strategic Response

Three characteristics distinguish the learning perspective from other perspectives on diversity: a) it sees similarities and differences as dual aspects of workforce diversity; b) it seeks multiple objectives from diversity, including efficiency, innovation, customer satisfaction, employee development, and social responsibility; c) it views diversity as having long-term as well as short-term ramifications.

The learning perspective encourages legal compliance and training, but encourages active participation in finding better, faster, or more efficient ways of compliance beyond those legally mandated. Learning motivations might also include a desire to gain access to employees and new customer groups, with the purpose of learning from employees' different perspectives. Its focus is on identifying important similarities and differences[25] and managing them in the interests of long-term learning. Its emphasis on the unity-in-diversity less evident in other perspectives could be described as multiculturalism. IBM's slogan that "none of us is as strong as all of us" expresses the synergy it seeks.

The learning perspective is primarily associated with active strategic initiatives. Organizations that take this perspective are often early adopters of diversity policies. These policies seek to nurture homogeneity and diversity, and to address core issues of race, ethnicity, and gender along with other similarities and differences important to the organization. Creativity is necessary to generate a sense of similarity among cultural, functional, and hierarchical groups accustomed to differences, and is essential for identifying options when downsizing and diversity clash. AT&T believed downsizing would reduce diversity, but a new leave policy enabled redundant employees to travel or study. As openings occurred, these employees returned to AT&T, restoring diversity and bringing enhanced skills and experience.

Organizational leaders who act strategically to manage diversity usually recognize the important role that conflict and debate can play in creating a common sense of vision and beliefs within an organization. Honest expression of differences can lead to a synthesis of conflicting perspectives,[26] but destructive conflict also can emerge to prevent synergies.

Implementing Three Useful Strategic Responses

Pressures for diversity range in intensity and can vary and even conflict. In the U.S., some pressures favor immigrant hiring, while other pressures oppose it. The implementation of diversity initiatives depends not only on these pressures, perspectives, and responses, but also on where managers place diversity on their lists of organizational priorities.

One manager might view all forms of diversity as strategic, while another sees gender diversity as marginal and ethnic diversity as strategic. In either case, these priorities and pressures combine to yield three general approaches to implementation. These are shown in the diagonal cells of Figure 3, which managers can use as a diagnostic tool to gauge the match between pressures and their own priorities for managing diversity. The options described on the diagonal suggest the best fit as measured by past and current conditions, but there are other options.

Of the three general approaches to implementation, two were suggested by DeLuca and McDowell,[27] who view diversity initiatives as either programmatic (what we call freestanding) or nonprogrammatic (what we call systemic). We believe a third episodic approach to implementation exists. These three approaches to implementation are more or less integrated with core organizational activities: the episodic approach represents the lowest level of integration, the systemic approach the highest.

These three approaches to implementation are more or less integrated with core organizational activities: the episodic approach represents the lowest level of integration, the systemic approach the highest.

The Episodic Approach

This approach is usually dominant when there are few pressures for diversity and managers view diversity as a marginal issue. The diversity initiatives of these managers tend to be isolated, disjointed, and separate from core organizational activities. They may make it difficult to identify, understand, or connect various diversity issues and pressures. Denny's Restaurant leaders dismissed racial problems in West Coast U.S. stores as isolated misunderstandings[28] rather than as signals of a widespread problem. Organizations may also use an episodic approach to experiment with new ideas. Goodyear sent upper-level managers to a week-long seminar on diversity and race relations to learn if that was a good way for them to improve managerial understanding of diversity. Except when it is used to experiment, the episodic approach usually results in few changes in organizational policies or practices.

Priorities for managing diversity

		Marginal	Significant	Strategic
Pressures for diversity	Low	**Episodic** Structure: Ad hoc, isolated Controls: Vary Rewards: Vary		
	Moderate		**Freestanding** Structure: Ongoing, stand alone Controls: Staff positions Rewards: Negative	
	High			**Systemic** Structure: Ongoing, intergrated Controls: Line positions Rewards: Positive and negative

FIGURE 3
Implementation of Strategic Responses for Managing Diversity

The Freestanding Approach

Executives who experience moderate pressures for diversity and think of it as a significant but side issue are likely to formalize diversity initiatives, but without integrating them fully with core activities. R. R. Donnelly sponsors an exchange program where counterparts in two nations swap positions for several weeks to learn about each other's countries and customs. When such programs are independent of each other and core activities, the organization can easily add or drop them as circumstances change.

This approach can create a plethora of unrelated programs, and generate more sanctions than rewards, as when ombudsman offices focus exclusively on compliance failures. If multiple freestanding programs and projects are introduced serially, diversity may be viewed as serving political expediency more than organizational plans. Some of these challenges may be avoided if it is clear that individual freestanding programs are consistent with pressures for diversity.

The Systemic Approach

Executives who experience high pressures for diversity and view diversity as a strategic issue are most likely to adopt a systemic approach to diversity. This approach involves linking diversity initiatives with existing systems and core activities of the organization. Responsibilities for monitoring and managing diversity are typically assigned to line organizational positions and are coupled with positive rewards and with sanctions. While a systemic approach is expected to be comprehensive, it also incorporates simplicity and flexibility. When an audit showed units were defining diversity in different ways, GTE responded by asking a multiunit group to create a definition of diversity broad enough to apply to the whole, but flexible enough to permit unit adaptations. S. Kirk Kinsell, Apple South's president, believes diversity management is successful only when it is "integrated fully—that is, made a part of all customer, vendor and employee programs."[29]

Although both the freestanding and systemic approaches may involve such diversity initiatives as work and family issues or veterans' affairs, only systemic approaches would integrate programs with one another and with structural mechanisms. At Motorola, diversity progress includes training programs to hire and develop from diverse groups, but retention and promotion then become part of every manager's appraisal and compensation package. Deep systemic change necessarily takes time, and may create challenges when diversity pressures call for immediate or demonstrable change.

Pulling It All Together

The twelve cells shown in Figure 4 pull together the four perspectives, the associated strategic responses toward diversity depicted in Figure 2, and the three general approaches to implementing them shown in Figure 3. The following section describes diversity initiatives typical for each of the 12 cells.

Implementing Reactive Strategic Response

Episodic Approaches—Cell 1

Episodic approaches for implementing a reactive strategic response could include denial and projection. According to employees, Denny's Chairman Raymond Danner "sometimes ordered managers to fire blacks if they were too visible to white customers,"[31] and managers rearranged work shifts to ensure that Danner did not see black employees during scheduled visits. Similarly, when CEO J. Mitchell Boyd tried to change Shoney's cul-

ture, the board resisted and ignored warnings of a pending discrimination lawsuit.[32] Projection occurred when North American managers concluded that Japanese business men would not like working with women,[33] and when a small company refused to expatriate an African-American because it believed he would not be well received in Europe.[34]

Freestanding Approaches—Cell 2

Managers can purposefully design programs and policies to ávoid diversity, such as creating a legal defense fund to fight rather than follow affirmative action mandates. One organization instructed human resource employees to use secret codes on application forms so black applicants would not be called for interviews. Freestanding resistance also can be unintentional. Robert E. Flynn, CEO of NutraSweet, reported that some executives had an unconscious yet ongoing program of filling key positions with individuals similar to themselves

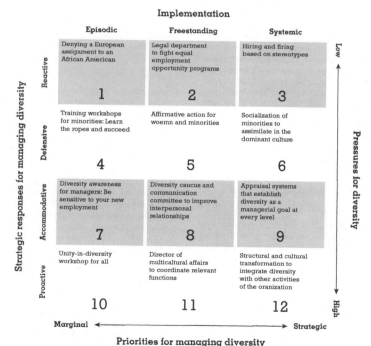

FIGURE 4
Strategic Responses for Managing Diversity and their Implementation

without posting the jobs for females, minorities, or others.[34]

Systemic Approaches—Cell 3

Organizations often resist diversity in a systemic manner. Selecting or rejecting employees based on stereotypes, for example, may be an unconscious yet systemic way of excluding diversity. Most existing systems were designed to screen out variation, which makes it difficult to incorporate greater diversity in organizations.[35] Efforts to maintain the status quo also result from malice, the degree of difficulty involved with change, or perceptions that other demands are more immediate. Shoney's culture, for example, showed systemic opposition to diversity because it neither discussed nor implemented affirmative action at any level by 1988.[37] Even while expressing a desire to incorporate greater diversity, some managers claim they cannot do so because other demands, such as global competition, are more pressing.

Another tactic to resist diversity is deflection. Claims that diversity in hiring and promotion conflict with existing merit or seniority systems may be valid, but they also deflect further diversity. For firms facing few legal or social mandates for diversity, a primary mode of organizational resistance may be as passive or evasive as keeping a low public profile. Still another systemic approach to resisting diversity may involve manipulation. Some organizations sponsor research to show why the organization or industry should or cannot accommodate diversity, and others mount public relations campaigns to discredit those who champion diversity or highlight failures of diversity programs in other settings.

Implementing Defensive Strategic Response

Episodic Approaches—Cell 4

Following a discriminatory event, organizations may assume a defensive posture by launching an investigation to disarm public concern, but little change occurs when investigations continue for months or even years. Some organizations may provide suggestion boxes, toll-free telephone lines, or counseling sessions to keep pressures from building. Organizations also may respond with explanations, apologies, or cosmetic changes, particularly when such incidents invite public scrutiny. Mitsubishi Motor Manufacturing of America claimed that sexual harassment complaints in its Illinois plant were not widespread and said subsequent changes in top management were unre-

lated. Organizations often tend to focus on symptoms without seeing the bigger picture. Although a Navy tribunal found fault with high-ranking officers in the Tailhook incident, subsequent discriminatory behavior in other branches of the U.S. armed forces suggest the hearings fostered little awareness of the overall problem.

Freestanding Approaches—Cell 5

Organizations pursuing this approach may shape diversity parameters, perhaps emphasizing dos and don'ts of affirmative action compliance or avoiding sexual harassment claims. They may also set up separate interest groups for women, African-Americans, and others. For example, Sun Microsystems initially formed five focus groups to help recruit, hire, and develop new employees from particular groups. Other organizations may emphasize concrete affirmative action programs that usually concentrate on objectively measurable goals. An advantage of this approach is to specify organizational intentions and set measurable standards. Disadvantages are that managers may be encouraged to set low goals or to adopt quotas that objectify people or prevent hiring good candidates from nonprescribed categories.

Systemic Approaches—Cell 6

Organizations may assimilate members of diverse groups via socialization. In the late 1980s, GE Silicone asked minority and women employees to meet informally to discuss why they were not assimilating effectively into the dominant culture. Organizations may institutionalize like-to-like mentoring relationships, for instance, Hispanic mentors for Hispanic mentees, to reduce gaps between affirmative action targets and results. In addition, organizations may design systems for continuous evaluation and control of their diversity efforts. American Express institutionalized a process to implement and measure the effectiveness of diversity initiatives.

Implementing Accommodative Strategic Response

Episodic Approaches—Cell 7

Many organizations offer diversity awareness sessions. At a U.S. Tyson Foods plant, managers organized diversity-training sessions for supervisors to help them understand how cultural values of Hispanics in the workplace differed from dominant U.S. culture. Likewise, when faced by pressures for diversity, organizations may review existing practices. *The Seattle Times* conducted a content audit to count the number of news stories covering different constituent activities.

Freestanding Approaches—Cell 8

According to a Conference Board survey of 131 organizations, 60 percent located diversity positions at the director or vice presidential level.[37] This is one way to place more emphasis on diversity initiatives. Other organizations may institute diversity caucuses and communication committees to improve interpersonal relationships among diverse individuals and groups. Still other organizations may establish independent diversity departments with the objectives of matching internal diversity with external diversity. These departments may organize a celebration of diversity week, as at Rockwell. Such initiatives are likely to have an impact on external constituencies, as well. Gannett's diversity goal is to assemble a workforce that reflects the communities where the company does business.[38] Hoechst Celanese set a 2001 target to hire 34 percent women and minorities to mirror the anticipated workforce.[39] Stereotyped or blanket celebration of diversity may divert attention from important historical discrimination issues and generate backlash.

> **Stereotyped or blanket celebration of diversity may divert attention from important historical discrimination issues and generate backlash.**

A Workways consultant described a bank that featured an unsuccessful Black History Month celebration featuring watermelon and collard greens as the lunch offering.

Systemic Approaches—Cell 9

Organizations may alter existing systems to accommodate diversity. Harris Bank and John Hancock Financial Services both use standard forms for employees who want flexible work hours[40] to encourage a systemic approach to flexible scheduling. This approach incorporates the kind of counting required for affirmative action reports, and results in altered evaluation systems to accommodate changing needs of new parents, caregivers for elderly parents, or disabled employees. Hoechst Celanese conducts regular salary reviews to identify and adjust pay differentials between white males and other employees. It also uses a

computerized succession review plan to show where high potential women or minority employees encounter roadblocks. General Mills has designed a mentoring system that leads to an individual development plan meant to identify actions that enhance personal growth and effectiveness. This formal aspect of mentoring is supplemented by informal ones to nurture employee networks and forums. Organizational socialization may encourage values exploration to help individuals recognize their own stereotypes and implicit assumptions. A focus on inclusion is evident in Honeywell's belief that each individual is unique and valuable. At Gannett, diversity involves recognition of all the differences among workers and the variety of perspectives and values that are part of each person.

Implementing Proactive Strategic Response

While the essential point in the systemic approach is full integration with organizational core activities, an organization does not have to fully integrate diversity in its system to learn from it. The organization can also learn from taking action on an occasional basis or in an ongoing program.

Episodic Approaches—Cell 10

Some diversity trainers suggest that organizational leaders may use the episodic approach to test the waters in their own organizations, using an introductory workshop to explore the topic's continuing relevance to the workforce. At AT&T, a 1989 workshop on "Homophobia in the Workplace" proved successful and subsequently became an offering in the regular diversity curriculum.[41] Recognizing that organizations must be dynamic, managers may occasionally organize informal discussions to monitor emerging diversity issues. Subsequent support for grass-roots organizing helps constituents learn which among many diversity issues are central to their long-term interests and can be incorporated in organizational processes. Digital Equipment Corporation's core groups have evolved over the years to include similarities as well as differences.

Freestanding Approaches—Cell 11

Motorola requires that employees enroll in 40 hours of training per year. Any employee can enroll in courses covering diversity as a competitive advantage, the spirit of diversity, or transition to diversity, but other courses target specific audiences. There are two-day courses for senior managers, special workshops on sexual harassment and diversity awareness for other managers, and diversity awareness and interviewing for managers and directors. Sears became a model for Americans with Disabilities compliance by benchmarking other firms practices and then shaping them for their workforce. Sara Lee defined diversity in terms of women because they consider them the critical constituency to represent in the organization. American Express created a new program called Diversity Learning Labs to focus on diverse market segments, such as the women's market, to improve learning about specialized groups, and to identify learning generalizable to other groups. From these groups, American Express learned that leaders of diverse client acquisition efforts also need strong project management experience. Vendors or suppliers operating from different perspectives sometimes frustrated US West's diversity goals. They and other firms therefore externalized diversity programs to encourage vendors and suppliers to learn about diversity and help them meet their diversity objectives.

Systemic Approaches—Cell 12

Systemic approaches to incorporating diversity may lead to more diverse structures and processes as well as to more diverse people in the organization. Resulting realignments often entail mutual learning and adjustment. Business units as well as top managers identify and develop the diverse skills and competencies that Hewlett-Packard will need in the next millenium. Safeco institutionalized a process to rehire promising minority candidates during university vacations to nurture long-term learning opportunities for employees and employers. Coopers & Lybrand framed child care, elder care, and work/life balance issues as relevant for the entire workforce, not just women. The firm then developed an ongoing process by which the field units could propose, experiment, evaluate, and share relevant common solutions.[42]

Organizations use different methods to incorporate a systemic approach to learning from diversity, including organization development, transition management, transformational leadership, team entrepreneurship, action research, reengineering, total quality management, and team learning. But a diverse group of top managers who embody the change desired may be the best catalyst for this transformation. Thomas and Ely suggest other preconditions they believe would apply.[43] However, systemic changes may be easier to describe than to achieve. In particular, learning is most likely to be oriented toward management's

interests and a possible result may be increased managerial control instead of employee buy-in or stakeholder interests. In other words, the learning perspective on diversity entails opportunities and costs just as does any other perspective.

Some writers suggest a normative pattern of organizational approaches to diversity.[44] However, we think that while some organizations may evolve from episodic to freestanding to systemic, others can successfully follow different patterns when they are congruent with pressures for diversity and managers' priorities for managing different types of diversity. Further, whether an organization can achieve commitment to any particular strategic response depends on external pressures (e.g., government, community, supplier, customer, societal), internal pressures (e.g., employees, stakeholders, internal consultants, change managers), and managerial perspectives, as outlined in Figure 1 and detailed in Figures 2–4.

Implementation in Complex Situations

In practice, diversity initiatives usually will not be organized in the mutually exclusive categories shown in the figures. On the contrary, diversity management in many organizations may seem more a potpourri of ideas, programs, and pet projects. Perspectives on diversity have evolved over time and thinking consistent with different time periods is likely to be embedded in diversity practices. Although top executives usually select the organization's strategy for managing workforce diversity, it is up to middle and lower-level managers to implement them and to employees to operationalize them, often according to personal perspectives and priorities. Every variety of resistance, discrimination, fairness, access, legitimacy, and learning operates today within, as much as between, organizations.

Growing pressures for diversity have led many executives to revise their perspectives and priorities for managing diversity and to introduce many diversity initiatives. But these initiatives occur in a

Every variety of resistance, discrimination, fairness, access, legitimacy, and learning operates today within, as much as between, organizations.

specific context. For example, the founder of Denny's Restaurants became a champion for diversity after decades of documented resistance to it, but implementation may be made difficult by the organization's past.

Although our proposed framework represents ideal rather than actual types, it has practical merit. Executives can use Figure 1 to examine current pressures for and against diversity and anticipate future ones. The figure also suggests that managing diversity can be approached in a step-by-step manner or as a process requiring simultaneous consideration of pressures, perspectives, and strategic responses. The categories shown in Figure 2 provide a check list to assess any organization's dominant perspective on diversity and establish a beginning point for assessing actual or intended matches with internal definitions, strategic responses, and initiatives related to managing diversity. Inconsistencies or gaps can be used to align the organization with present or future conditions, and to develop a more purposeful and cohesive approach to managing diversity.

Organizational responses to strategic issues such as diversity have an important impact on organizational performance.[45] Most theorists and practitioners believe that matching internal resources and external opportunities can yield strategic advantages, and this argument for fit should encourage leaders to carefully choose their strategic response to managing diversity with regard for the type of diversity under consideration. Organizational leaders also need to examine their internal and external environments to adopt an approach to implementation that matches their particular context[46] or with a context they believe will emerge. Consequently, research examining the relationship between diversity and performance needs to consider the perspectives and priorities adopted, as well as the organization's strategic response, its approach to implementation, and the type of diversity under consideration.

Organizations operating on the diagonal in Figure 3 where current pressures and perceptions match probably experience the fewest costs and the most benefits from their approach to managing diversity. If diversity pressures are low, then efficiency may best be served with a low involvement approach, like that practiced by domestic firms operating in homogeneous nations. Similarly, high pressures for diversity are best met with recognition that diversity is a core issue calling for a systemic approach.

This approach to thinking about diversity management suggests opportunities for achieving fit, but it also is an argument for purposefully choosing an approach to managing diversity. Random acts of kindness may be enough in some cases, whereas systemic acts of engagement may be es-

sential in others. Either choice entails opportunities and costs. Executives who become champions for organizational diversity, even when pressures for it are low, may confront stockholder alarm, internal resistance, or criticism when their efforts raise unfulfilled aspirations.

> *Executives who become champions for organizational diversity, even when pressures for it are low, may confront stockholder alarm, internal resistance, or criticism when their efforts raise unfulfilled aspirations.*

Similarly, those who resist high pressures for diversity risk public censure. Yet, there may be good reasons for operating outside the box. Becoming a champion may be appropriate for an organizational leader who foresees industry or demographic change, and resistance can be appropriate when pressures for a particular type of diversity are perceived to be transitory or to entail more costs than benefits. The important point is that the ideas presented in this article provide executives with a framework that can help them systematically consider approaches to managing diversity, choose appropriate ones, and establish priorities. A review of diversity initiatives throughout the organization should help executives organize and act on what may appear to be chaotic or disorganized behavior. Fragmented and freestanding diversity programs resulting from good intentions at different points in time represent a different challenge than fragmented programs that arose because leaders changed firm directions. Efforts and good intentions may become the glue for a revised, more cohesive set of diversity initiatives, but employees may be cynical and adept at resisting changes in the name of diversity. In either case, consistency between perspectives and action is certain to reduce employee confusion about roles they are expected to play in managing diversity.

Our examples throughout this paper have come primarily from U.S., European, and Japanese firms that operate in multiple domestic and increasingly global environments, where social, legal, cultural, and competitive pressures combine and seem to require greater diversity in personnel and organizational structures and processes. Ideal transnational firms will be those whose strategic capabilities include global competitiveness, flexibility, and worldwide learning,[47] capabilities that are enhanced by high degrees of human diversity in organizations.

Confusion, wariness, and cynicism may be produced by conflicting pressures and approaches to
managing diversity. However, executives who reflect on their own perspectives and diversity practices may become more aware of available alternatives and uncover unspoken assumptions and
biases that guide their practices and theories.
Such awareness may raise challenging new questions about managing workforce diversity.

Acknowledgment

An earlier version of this article was published
in Kossek, E.E., and Lobel, S.A., (Eds.) 1966. *Managing Diversity: Human Resource Strategies for
Transforming the Workplace*, Cambridge, MA:
Blackwell Business.

Endnotes

¹ Deadrick, D., & Kochan, T. 1997. A call for research on diversity and organizational effectiveness, a session at the Academy of Management meeting in Boston, MA; Glick, W. Miller, C.,
& Huber, G. 1993. The impact of upper echelon diversity on
organizational performance. In Huber, G. & Glick, W. (Eds.),
Organizational Change and Redesign (176–214). New York: Oxford University Press; Watson, W. E., Kumar, K., & Michaelsen,
L. K. 1993. Cultural diversity's impact on interaction process and
performance: Comparing homogeneous and diverse task
groups. *Academy of Management Journal*, 36, 590–602; Wright,
P., Ferris, S., Hiller, J., & Kroll, M. 1995. Competitiveness through
management of diversity: Effects on stock price valuation.
Academy of Management Journal, 38: 272–287.
² Ginsberg, A. 1988. Measuring and modeling changes in
strategy: Theoretical foundations and empirical directions.
Strategic Management Journal, 9: 559–575.
³ Thomas, R. R. 1991. *Beyond race and gender: Unleashing the
power of your total workforce by managing diversity*. New York:
AMACOM; Herriot, P. & Pemberton, C. 1995. *Competitive advantage through diversity*. London: Sage Publications.
⁴ For example, Nkomo and Cox identified six major bodies of
research contributing to diverse identities and social relations
in organizations. Nkomo, Stella M., & Cox, Taylor H. Jr. 1996.
Diverse identities in organizations. In Stewart Clegg, Cynthia
Hardy, & Walter Nord (Eds.), *Handbook of organization studies*
(338–356). London: Sage.
⁵ Thomas, D. , & Ely, R. J. 1996. Making differences matter. A
new paradigm for managing diversity. *Harvard Business Review*, 79–90.
⁶ Bowens, H., Merenivitch, J., Johnson, L. P., James, A. R. &
McFadden-Bryant, D. J. 1993. Managing cultural diversity toward true multiculturalism: Some knowledge from the black
perspective. In R. R. Sims & R. F. Dennehy (Eds.), *Diversity and
differences in organizations* (33–45). Westport, CN: Quorum
Books; Thomas and Ely, op. cit.
⁷ Nkomo and Cox, op. cit.
⁸ For more details on the reactive, defensive, accommodative,
and proactive strategic responses and their performance implications, see Clarkson, M. B. E. 1995. A stakeholder framework for
analyzing and evaluating corporate social performance. *Academy of Management Review*, 20: 92–117.
⁹ Oliver, C. 1991. Strategic responses to institutional processes. *Academy of Management Review*, 16: 145–79.

¹⁰ Cox, T. 1993. *Cultural diversity in organizations: theory,
research, and practice*. San Francisco: Berrett-Koehler.
¹¹ Nemetz, P. & Christensen, S. L. 1996. The challenge of cultural diversity: Harnessing a diversity of views to understand
multiculturalism. *Academy of Management Review*, 21(2): 434–
462.
¹² For a thorough review of individual and group identity
issues, see Nkomo & Cox, op. cit.
¹³ Thomas & Ely, op. cit.
¹⁴ Harrison, D. A., Price, K. H., & Bell, M. P. 1998. Beyond relational demography: Time and the effects of surface- and deep-
level diversity on Work Group Cohesion, *Academy of Management Journal*, 41: 96–107; Jackson, S. E., May, K. E., & Whitney, K.
1995. Understanding the dynamics of diversity in decision-making teams. In R. A. Guzzo & E. Salas (Eds.) *Team decision-making effectiveness in organizations* (204–261). San Francisco, Jossey-Bass; Milliken, F. J. & Martins, L. J. 1996. Searching for
common threads: Understanding the multiple effects of diversity in organizational groups, *Academy of Management Review*, 21: 402–433.
¹⁵ Humphries, M. & Grice, S. 1995. Equal employment opportunity and the management of diversity: A global discourse of
assimilation? *Journal of Organizational Change Management*,
8, 5, 17–32.
¹⁶ Johnston, William B., & Packer, Arnold E. 1987. *Workforce
2000*. Indianapolis, IN: Hudson Institute.
¹⁷ *Business Week*. 1996, Dec 9. Diversity: making the business
case. (1996). Special advertising section.
¹⁸ Ibid.
¹⁹ Cox, T. H. Jr., & Blake, S. 1991. Managing cultural diversity:
implications for organizational competitiveness. *Academy of
Management Executive*, 5: 45–56.
²⁰ Koretz, G. 1991, October 21. An acid test of job discrimination in the real world. *Business Week*, 23; Covenant Investment
Management. 1993, April 21. Equal opportunity, stock performance linked. Press Release, Chicago, IL; Wright, Ferris, Hiller,
and Kroll, op. cit.
²¹ *Business Week*, op. cit.
²² Calas, M. & Smircich, L. 1993. Dangerous liaisons: The
'feminine-in-management' meets 'globalization'. *Business Horizons*, March–April, 71–82.
²³ Humphries and Grice, op. cit.
²⁴ Hayes, J., & Prewitt, M. 1998, August 24. Operators explore
diversity at 1st multicultural conference. *Nation's Restaurant
News*, 32 (34): 3, 127.
²⁵ Ofori-Dankwa, J., & Ortega Sysak, C. L. 1994. DiverSimilarity: The re-engineering of diversity training. In *DiverSimilarity:
The paradigm for workforce 2000* (1–25). Conference Readings,
May 12–13. Saginaw Valley State University, Saginaw, Michigan.
²⁶ Ofori-Dankwa, & Ortega Sysak, op. cit.; Thomas, 1991, op.
cit.
²⁷ DeLuca, J. M. & McDowell, R. N. 1992. Managing diversity: A
strategic "grass-roots" approach. In S. E. Jackson & Associates
(Eds.), *Diversity in the workplace: Human resources initiatives*,
227–47. New York: Guilford Press.
²⁸ Rice, Faye. 1994, Aug 8. How to make diversity pay. *Fortune*,
pp. 78–86.
²⁹ Hayes, & Prewitt, op. cit.
³⁰ *The Wall Street Journal*. 1996, April 16. Eating crow: How
Shoney's, belted by a lawsuit, found the path to diversity, A1,
A11.
³¹ Gaiter, op. cit.
³² Adler, N. J. 1987. Pacific basin managers: A *Gaijin*, not a
woman. *Human Resource Management*, 26: 169–191.
³³ Gentile, M. C. 1994. The case of the unequal opportunity. In

M. C. Gentile (Ed.), *Differences that work—Organizational excellence through diversity* (223–38). Boston: Harvard Business School Press.

[34] *Business Week.* January 31, 1994. White, male, and worried, pp. 50–5.

[35] Milliken & Martins, op. *cit.*

[36] Gaiter, op. *cit.*

[37] Wheeler, Michael L. 1994. *Diversity training.* New York: Conference Board. 1083-94-RR.

[38] Jennings, op. *cit.*

[39] Rice, op. *cit.*

[40] *Wall Street Journal.* 1995. How accommodating workers' lives can be a business liability. January 4, B1.

[41] *The Wall Street Journal.* 1995, Nov. 10. AT&T class teaches an open workplace is profitably correct. B1. *Fortune.* 1996, May 13. Denny's changes its spots, pp. 133–142.

[42] Deluca & McDowell, 1992, op. *cit.*

[43] Thomas & Ely, 1996, op. *cit.*

[44] Bowens et al., op. *cit.*

[45] Ansoff, H. I. 1980. Strategic issue management. *Strategic Management Journal,* 1: 131–148; Mintzberg, H., Raisinghani, D., & Theoret, A. 1976. The structure of unstructured decision processes. *Administrative Science Quarterly,* 21: 246–75.

[46] Micklethwait, J., & Wooldridge, A. 1997. *The witch doctors: making sense of the management gurus,* Heinemann, UK.

[47] Bartlett, C. A., & Ghoshal, S. 1989. *Managing across borders: The transnational solution.* Boston: Harvard Business School Press.

Parshotam Dass teaches in the Department of Management at the Sam M. Walton College of Business Administration, University of Arkansas. His current research interests are in changes in product and in international geographic diversity. Dass coedited *Readings in strategic management* with Michael Moch, Pixel Press, 1993. Contact: *pdass@comp.uark.edu.*

Barbara Parker is an associate professor at the Albers School of Business and Economics, Seattle University. She publishes frequently on diversity and other challenges of globalization. Her book, *Globalization and business practice: Managing across boundaries,* was published by Sage in 1998. Contact: *parker@seattleu.edu.*

Global Teams

[21]

A two-year study of international teamwork at thirteen companies shows how to. . .

Use Transnational Teams to Globalize Your Company

CHARLES C. SNOW

SUE CANNEY DAVISON

SCOTT A. SNELL

DONALD C. HAMBRICK

In 1985, Fuji-Xerox sent 15 of its most experienced Tokyo engineers to a Xerox Corporation facility in Webster, New York. For the next five years, the Japanese engineers worked with a group of American engineers to develop the "world copier"—a huge success in the global marketplace. In 1991, Eastman Kodak formed a team to launch its latest consumer product, the photo CD. That group of experts, based in London, developed a strategy for the simultaneous introduction of the photo CD in several European countries. The photo CD has been Kodak's most successful multicountry product introduction in this decade. At IBM-Latin America in 1990, a group of managers and technical specialists formed their own team to market, sell, and distribute personal computers in 11 Latin American countries. It took the team leader about a year to convince his boss that the team should be formally recognized and allowed to operate as an autonomous business unit. The team now has the authority to hurdle any bureaucratic barrier that gets in its way.

What do all of those situations have in common? In each case, a transnational team is contributing to a company's efforts to globalize—to extend the firm's products and operations into international markets. Today's global competitive strategies are complex and expensive, and they are often administered best by a transnational team of managers and specialists whose talents have been carefully blended. Teams that are responsible for the conduct of those strategies are highly visible within their own firms. Their leaders and members have significant opportunities to build international business competence.

Transnational teams present challenges to the companies that use them. For example, senior line executives who form transnational teams and are responsible for their successes and failures must regularly monitor team performance and decide on which techniques could improve performance. Human resource professionals, too, must keep abreast of new management approaches, as they are frequently called upon to help select team leaders and members as well as to design team development programs. And, of course, transnational teams are challenging for their own members—an individual's personal and professional success may hinge directly on how well team members work together and achieve results.

We conducted a comprehensive, worldwide study of successful transnational teams, examining particularly how such teams are designed and managed to help their firms pursue global business strategies. Subsequently, the findings from our study served as the basis for a large demonstration project in one of the sample companies (The Wellcome Foundation, now Glaxo-Wellcome). In that project, members of the corporate human resources department developed a sound support process to help the company's international R&D and marketing teams reach maximum effectiveness. (See the box on page 53 for further details of both the research study and the demonstration project.)

We first discuss how transnational teams come into being and how they are used. Next, we present a comprehensive model of team effectiveness that includes the key characteristics differentiating a transnational team from other types of work teams. We use the model to show how transnational teams operate—how they are staffed and led, communicate across great distances, and cope with cross-cultural issues. Finally, we describe how a company's human resources department can help an "international" or "multinational" team become a "transnational" team—one that has successfully transcended the cultural, geographic, and managerial barriers to team effectiveness.

FORMATION AND USES OF TRANSNATIONAL TEAMS

Transnational teams come into existence in two ways: from the top down or from the bottom up. Most teams are formed from the top down. That is, senior managers see a competitive need, decide that a transnational team should be formed, and put together a team with a particular mandate. For example, in 1991 Heineken formed the European Production Task Force, a 13-member team representing five countries. In the preceding several years, Heineken had closed more than 10 of its brewing plants in Italy, Spain, France, and Holland, and top managers did not have a clear sense of how the company's European production facilities should be configured for the twenty-first century. The task force wrestled with the issue of how many breweries the company should operate in Europe, what size and type they should be, and where they

should be located. Essentially, the team determined how Heineken could maximize production economies of scale across Europe, an efficiency concern, while remaining responsive to the needs and preferences of its national operating companies. Eighteen months after it was formed, the task force presented its findings and recommendations to Heineken's board of directors. The board enthusiastically accepted the recommendations, the team disbanded, and the team leader accepted an assignment as general manager of one of the region's breweries.

In contrast, other transnational teams are emergent; they evolve naturally from the existing network of individuals who depend on each other to accomplish their work objectives. Such teams may cut across functions, business units, and countries and may even incorporate "outsiders" from other organizations, either temporarily or permanently. In some cases, the teams develop their own mandate and challenge higher managers to accept and support it. For example, the concept of one transnational team was hatched around a dinner table at an annual quality assurance convention held internally by a large pharmaceutical company, Glaxo-Wellcome. As quality assurance specialists, the core members of the current International Quality Assurance Coordination Team (IQACT) had met informally for several years at the company's annual conference. Over time, they had come to believe that a formal team was needed to integrate the worldwide quality assurance function within the firm. IQACT chose its own leader (a medical doctor), and she approached senior executives to obtain authorization and funding for the team.

Once formed, transnational teams can be used in a variety of ways. Adopting a framework developed by Professors Christopher Bartlett (Harvard) and Sumantra Ghoshal (London Business School) some firms use the teams primarily to help achieve *global efficiency*—to develop regional or worldwide cost advantages, standardize designs and operations, and so forth. Heineken's European Production Task Force was that kind of team.

Other teams enable their companies to be

EXHIBIT 1
A MODEL OF TRANSNATIONAL TEAM EFFECTIVENESS

Transnational Team Drivers	Design and Management Levers	Team Process Measures	Key Business Results
• Task complexity and importance	• Contribution to business strategy • Leadership roles and skills • Staffing • Alignment with company structures and systems • Communications and decision-making technologies • Group process facilitation	• Safe and trusting environment • Camaraderie • Flexibility • Dependability • Shared responsibility • Commitment	• Time to peak sales • Regulatory approvals • Study protocol • Statistical analysis plan • Data management plan • Clinical development plan
• Multicultural dynamics	• Cross-cultural management		

locally responsive. They are expected to help their companies attend to the demands of different regions' market structures, consumer preferences, and political and legal systems. Local responsiveness was the main concern of Eastman Kodak's photo CD team as it sought to tailor the marketing strategy for the new product to each major country in the European market.

A third use of transnational teams is for *organizational learning.* Teams whose main contribution is learning are expected to bring together knowledge from various parts of the company, transfer technology, and spread innovations throughout the firm. For example, IBM has a global network of experts, led by a core team of six people headquartered outside London, that consults around the world for clients in the airline industry. That team, the International Airlines Solutions Centre (IASC), is composed of both permanent and temporary members who fuse technical, consulting, and industry expertise to provide information technology to airlines and airport authorities. IASC identifies knowledge located in one part of the world and applies it to

problems that arise in another—in effect, it institutionalizes learning throughout the global air transportation industry. Within IBM, the team itself is seen as a highly flexible learning organization that may serve as a prototype for many of the company's future transnational teams.

Nearly half of the transnational teams in our study were expected to contribute to all three strategic objectives simultaneously—in other words, to help their firms become "glocal" corporations that can act both big (efficiently) and small (responsively) while learning how to adapt continuously. Such high expectations mean that the typical transnational team faces a daunting challenge at the outset: how to succeed at a very complex task with little guidance.

A MODEL OF TRANSNATIONAL TEAM EFFECTIVENESS

Broadly defined, a transnational team is *a work group composed of multinational members whose activities span multiple countries.* Two key fac-

THE RESEARCH STUDY AND DEMONSTRATION PROJECT

The transnational teams research study was funded by The International Consortium for Executive Development Research (ICEDR) in the fall of 1991. ICEDR, a consortium of 31 international companies and 22 prominent business schools, sponsors research inside its member companies on management topics of common interest.

The two-year study was conducted in three phases. In the first phase, researchers identified successful transnational teams and interviewed more than 100 team members and their leaders in 13 companies.

The second phase of the study was a questionnaire survey. Researchers designed two questionnaires, one for the team leader and the other for team members. Questionnaires were completed by 35 transnational teams selected from companies both within and outside ICEDR. The questionnaire data were used to develop profiles of each team in the areas of mission, stage of development, staffing, leadership, decision making, training, and performance.

The third phase was a demonstration project in which human resource specialists from The Wellcome Foundation (now Glaxo-Wellcome PLC) worked closely with two members of the research team to develop a practical, four-stage approach for improving team effectiveness. That approach is currently being used with the company's transnational R&D and marketing teams.

tors strongly affect a transnational team's composition, operations, and performance. (See Exhibit 1.) First, *task complexity and importance* differentiate transnational teams from other types of work teams. Transnational teams typically work on projects that are highly complex and have considerable impact on company objectives. Further, many transnational teams are geographically dispersed, with members on different continents in some cases. Geographic distance may lead to psychological distance, making it difficult for members to share information, make group decisions, and so on.

Second, transnational teams have a *multicultural dynamic*. If a transnational team is to obtain a maximum contribution from each of its members, it must be adept at handling a variety of cross-cultural issues—issues related to national culture, occupational culture, and company culture.

Task Complexity and Importance

British Petroleum's European Gas Business Development team (EGBD) provides an excellent illustration of task complexity and importance. Formed in 1991, the EGBD team was charged with developing a business plan for locating, producing, transporting, and selling natural

gas on the European continent. Because natural gas resources are located in widely dispersed areas, such as North Africa (e.g., Algeria), the North Sea (e.g., Norway), and various parts of the former Soviet Union, EGBD has a considerable challenge in bringing natural gas to the European market. One of the company's most versatile young executives, a British expatriate working in the United States, was brought in as EGBD's team leader.

The team is staffed to deal effectively with the different regions of the world involved in its business strategy. One team member, a French engineer, works regularly with various officials of the Algerian government. Two members are Norwegian engineers, and their geographic responsibility is the North Sea. Another is a German economist and lawyer who looks after matters in Eastern Europe. The remaining members are British. As most team members travel extensively, the entire team is rarely able to meet face to face.

Defining how to measure the EGBD team's performance is difficult. For example, even if British Petroleum chose to acquire some other company's natural gas assets, it would be 1997 at the earliest before any natural gas would reach the European market. Therefore, evaluating the team on so-called

EXHIBIT 2
LEADERSHIP ROLES AND TEAM DEVELOPMENT

Team Startup	**Advocacy Skills**
	• Building team legitimacy • Linking team mission and company strategy • Networking to obtain resources • "Bureaucracy busting"—eliminating old routines, facilitating • experimentation, and knowledge dissemination
Team Evolution	**Catalytic Skills**
	• Working with external constituents • Differentiating individual roles and responsibilities • Building commitment • Rewarding members for valuable contributions
Team Maturity	**Integrative Skills**
	• Emphasizing excellence and accomplishment • Coordinating and problem solving • Measuring progress and results

"hard" performance measures such as revenues generated or market share would make little sense. The team's performance can only be assessed subjectively. Team members cite factors such as progress in negotiations, the ability to add staff during an overall company downsizing, and the continued support of BP's board of directors as evidence of strong performance. In late 1993, the board of directors approved EGBD's multimillion-dollar business plan and authorized the team to begin implementing it. Shortly afterward, the team's leader was transferred to another natural gas development project that was just beginning in Alaska.

In sum, the EGBD team is an entrepreneurial business unit within its large parent firm. It has a challenging, complex mission of obvious strategic importance to the company. With such a large amount of company resources at stake, the team simply cannot afford to break down. A similar feeling of urgency permeates many transnational teams.

Contribution to Business Strategy. Careful attention to the factors shown as "management levers" in Exhibit 1 help a team deal with task complexity, importance, and urgency. Of

utmost importance is the link between the team's mission and corporate strategy. Because a transnational team's tasks are so complex, its relationships with regional and corporate headquarters, as well as its expected contribution to business strategy, are seldom straightforward and must be carefully defined. Team members must understand and commit to the team's mission if the group is to succeed.

For example, in 1990 British Airways merged two parts of its Japanese business to fulfill the mandate "grow revenues." The BA-Japan Management Team, headed by the area manager for Japan, was made responsible for British Airways' service in the Asia Pacific region. The team consisted of the top 10 managers in Japan, who were spread across five locations in and around Tokyo. After two highly successful years, a new manager was appointed with a different mandate, "route profitability." The new manager, aided by an international human resources specialist from BA headquarters, worked off site with the management team to develop the new mission and gain the team's acceptance of the new corporate goals.

In a new or reconfigured transnational

team, the team-building process must begin with a discussion of company strategy and how the team's mission will contribute to it. In mature teams, it is wise to review the mission periodically. Strategy reviews can be conducted at off-site retreats run by a facilitator, by inviting relevant line managers to team meetings, and in a variety of other ways. Some teams, especially those pushing for formal recognition as a business unit, are very aggressive in clarifying and perhaps expanding their connection to the firm's business strategies.

Leadership. To maintain the link between a transnational team's mission and the company's business strategy, the team leader must perform multiple roles, which vary over the team's life span.

New teams face challenges that are different from those of mature teams. (See Exhibit 2.) Prior to the official formation of a transnational team, the team leader commonly plays the role of *advocate*—arguing for the business necessity of a particular work group, defining a team's mission in relation to corporate strategy, and garnering the resources needed for a successful team. For example, the team leaders of Glaxo-Wellcome's IQACT (quality assurance) and British Petroleum's EGBD (natural gas development) were widely viewed as advocates within their respective companies. EGBD's leader was respected for his strategic thinking skills, and he was adept at making persuasive business presentations throughout the company hierarchy and obtaining needed resources. The individual nominated to be IQACT's leader was respected for her managerial style as well as her technical expertise. Her medical training gave her tremendous credibility among senior executives, many of whom also were doctors, when she argued for a coordinated global quality assurance function. Moreover, senior executives' confidence in her as a manager encouraged them to authorize her team formally and provide it with resources.

The lesson to be learned from the experience of these and other emergent teams is that senior line executives should listen closely to proposals emanating from the organiza-

tion. Some of the proposals may contain the core elements of a functional or business unit, complete with its own leader. Emergent teams are also full of energy and highly committed to their chosen mission.

As a transnational team evolves, the main leadership role shifts to that of *catalyst*—properly differentiating the team to match the complexity of its task, encouraging individuality, and rewarding team members for generating and implementing ideas. That role is well played by the leader of Unilever's Personal Care/Rinse Conditioners Management Team. For a group of key brands (Lux, Dove, Comfort, Ballerina, and Snuggle), Unilever created a transnational team charged with achieving efficiencies on a pan-European basis while simultaneously being responsive to the local requirements and preferences of each country.

The team leader works with five marketing managers, each based in a different country, to coordinate the marketing and sale of Unilever's personal care products across Europe. Much work is delegated to the team members who, after achieving consensus among themselves, propose their ideas and action plans to the leader for his review and guidance. This particular leader says that his overall managerial philosophy is to "get individuals to initiate and act on their own ideas."

As a transnational team matures, the primary leadership role shifts to that of *integrator*—combining the actions of individuals into an integrated whole. Integrative behaviors include maintaining a clear operational mission for the team, coordinating activities, emphasizing performance goals, and perhaps working side-by-side with team members in performing tasks similar to theirs.

The leader of Eastman Kodak's Photo CD European Launch Team, for example, proved to be a particularly skilled integrator. In Europe, where the photo CD system was viewed as having perhaps the most market potential, the launch team consisted of representatives from 14 countries. To achieve desired variety on the team, members were drawn from each of the functional areas and business units that would play an important role in the launch.

Charles C. Snow is the Mellon Bank Professor of Business Administration in The Smeal College of Business Administration at Penn State University. His most recent co-authored book is *Fit, Failure, and the Hall of Fame: How Companies Succeed or Fail* (1994). He is currently conducting a study on human resource management practices in twenty-first century organizations.

The launch team's work progressed through three major phases. The first phase, overall strategy development, was the most conceptual part of the launch and involved developing a "strategic intent" document that laid out the team's major goals and tactics. During that phase, the team tried to achieve consensus about what the overall launch agenda should encompass and how to best address the needs of each country market. The second phase, launch plan development, was an action stage in which individuals were delegated pan-European responsibility for separate tasks. Each of the assignments was negotiated (even bid for) on the basis of a particular country organization's available resources and level of expertise. At the beginning of the third phase, launch implementation, the launch team formally transferred responsibility for executing the various assignments to their respective country organizations within Kodak.

The leader of the launch team, a Belgian, had both the technical experience and diplomatic skills to work with different European country representatives. His boss, a German who was in charge of the photo CD launch worldwide, had been part of a failed global product launch in the past and had gained much useful knowledge from that experience. Together, those two individuals, plus key members of each country organization, had a good sense of what the European launch would entail, so the primary leadership role was to integrate all of the various countries' efforts. The team leader, therefore, worked closely with team members to develop a clear action plan, a division of labor based on acknowledged expertise, and a communications process that would keep each country organization updated on the progress of the launch plan.

In a fully established transnational team, no one leadership role dominates. Instead, all three roles (advocate, catalyst, integrator) may be useful, and it is a rare individual who is expert at performing all of them. Hence, in selecting a transnational team leader, senior managers must pay close attention to the critical contingencies facing the team at the time. The team's expected contribution to corporate strategy, as well as the stage of the team's development, largely determines the roles the team leader must play.

As either of those factors changes over time, it may be necessary to replace the team leader with another leader more suited to the team's new tasks and challenges. In addition, team leaders themselves need to set a personal learning agenda to develop knowledge and skills consistent with all three leadership roles. Finally, the human resources department should be prepared to provide executive development training and experiences that nurture the major leadership roles. Companies such as Unilever, Heineken, and Glaxo-Wellcome invest heavily in management development education that includes a significant team leadership component.

Staffing. Staffing transnational teams is a process fraught with tradeoffs and ambiguities, and even the most sophisticated global firms struggle with it. At least three important considerations are involved: (1) the tradeoff between local hiring and the use of expatriates, (2) consideration of group as well as technical skills among team members, and (3) size of the team.

The expectation of where the transnational team is to be based strongly influences staffing decisions. For example, team members can be based in the company's home country, enabling the team to be heavily stocked with managers and specialists from that country. A variant of that approach is to bring in team members from the various areas with which the team is interdependent. Such a team is likely to be more multicultural, and specific steps must be taken to integrate the members.

An alternative approach is to base the team outside the company's home country. Increasingly, multinational companies are hiring local workers to staff foreign-based teams—including the knowledge workers who constitute many transnational teams today. At the same time, large international companies are cutting back on their use of expatriates in order to save money. Consequently, foreign-based teams may have to focus on blending professional and corporate

Scott A. Snell is associate professor of business administration in The Smeal College of Business Administration at Penn State University. He is co-author of two books, *Managing Human Resources* (1996) and *Management: Building Competitive Advantage* (1996), as well as several articles on the strategic management of human resources.

Sue Canney Davison is a visiting research fellow at the Centre for Organisational Research at London Business School and the founder of Pipal International, a management consulting firm. She enhances productivity in international and geographically dispersed teams.

cultures as well as different nationalities.

A final staffing approach, used only sparingly to date, is to allow team members to locate themselves wherever they desire. It requires especially careful attention to leadership, communications, and decision-making issues. In short, the decision of where to locate a transnational team has major implications for the company's travel and other costs, team-building needs, and use of expatriates.

The composition of a transnational team is also driven by the need to include all of the technical skills required to pursue the team's mission. An R&D team in a large multinational pharmaceutical firm, for example, can require the cooperative efforts of many different specialists, from organic chemists to biologists, molecular geneticists, pharmacologists, toxicologists, statisticians, and data managers. At the latter stages of the research and development process, the team will work with—and may temporarily include—medical doctors, quality assurance specialists, and regulatory and marketing personnel from various regions of the world where clinical trials are being conducted and where the drug will be sold.

Even if the team succeeds in meshing the diverse technical specialists, however, there is still the question of being similarly effective interpersonally and multiculturally. Some companies have found paper-and-pencil instruments such as the Parker Team Player Survey useful for identifying individual members' inclinations toward performing certain team roles. Often, the team facilitators attempt to determine the distribution of group roles and skills after a transnational team has been staffed, as part of a team-building process. However, given the importance of establishing a strong group process prior to the pursuit of business goals, companies would do well to make earlier and heavier use of team diagnostic instruments in the staffing process.

A final staffing issue, optimal team size, came to our attention in a somewhat paradoxical way. The most energized, committed teams appeared to us to be the ones whose members complained most about being overworked and understaffed. Gradually, we began to refer to that phenomenon as "N minus one" staffing. That is, the best approach for producing a highly enthusiastic team seemed to be to deliberately understaff it—and perhaps keep it "lean and mean" in terms of other resources as well. Many years ago, Professor Chris Argyris coined the term "optimal undermanning" in reference to this group characteristic. Our interpretation of such staffing "practice" today is that transnational teams that do their own work feel better about themselves and their accomplishments than teams that offload activities to support staff, interns, outsiders, and others. Although no optimal team size can be specified, the average size of the transnational teams in our study was 12 persons, with a range of six to 21.

Alignment with Company Structures, Programs, and Systems. As a transnational team develops an effective alignment of key internal features such as its mission, leadership, and so on, it must also develop an "external" fit with the rest of the company. Achieving such a fit can be frustrating for some teams because company structures and systems can affect performance negatively as well as positively.

We studied some of the most visible and successful teams in international companies, but even those teams had plenty of stories about their struggles within their own organizations. For example, at one time The Wellcome Foundation had a research organization known within the company as the "Twin Towers" because the R&D management hierarchy in England was essentially replicated in the United States. Transnational R&D teams had to contend with both hierarchies when making decisions, obtaining approvals, and allocating resources. Glaxo-Wellcome has since abandoned the dual structure, to the substantial benefit of the company's R&D teams.

In addition to structural barriers, a company's programs and management systems may have deleterious effects on its transnational teams. For example, one well-known multinational company operates two man-

Donald C. Hambrick is the Samuel Bronfman Professor of Democratic Business Enterprise in the Graduate School of Business at Columbia University. An active researcher on chief executive and top management teams topics, Hambrick has two books in press: *Strategic Leadership: Top Executives and Their Effects on Organizations* and *Senior Leadership: CEOs, Boards, and Top Management Teams in Turbulent Times*. He is a consultant to many companies internationally, as well as a former president of the Academy of Management.

agement development programs (one at the corporate level and the other at the divisional level) for its high-potential managers. Both programs involve regular and frequent job rotation. On one occasion, three "hi-po" managers from the two programs ended up on the same transnational team, and one of them was the team leader. Everyone on the team knew that those individuals were likely to be transferred in the next 12 to 18 months, so team planning and operations had to take that possibility into account. Thus, company programs and systems can serve their own purposes while simultaneously creating problems for the company's teams, and any negative effects arising from such sources must be minimized.

Transnational teams generally are not in a position to make major changes to company structures and systems. Their efforts are best directed at figuring out how to use company processes most efficiently and effectively. One powerful vehicle for obtaining that understanding, used by companies such as Unilever and Glaxo-Wellcome, is an executive education program designed to link team activities to the company's business strategies and resources. Glaxo-Wellcome's program is aptly called "Molecule to Market." Some companies go even further and authorize their teams to break through any bureaucratic barrier that interferes with their work. For example, all Goldstar teams at LG Group (formerly The Lucky-Goldstar Group) are empowered to do that. Practically, however, it is the senior executive group that must assume major responsibility for achieving an effective alignment between a transnational team and the total company, for only members of that group have the proper vantage point to assess the quality of the fit among teams, structures, programs, and systems, as well as the power to make changes.

Communications and Decision-Making Technologies. Many transnational teams must communicate and make decisions across vast geographic distances. Geographic distance can be both an advantage and a disadvantage. For example, some companies have capitalized on differences across time zones to ac-

celerate the product development process. Texas Instruments divided a mobile telephone R&D team among locations in California, France, and Japan. The results of each day's work were transmitted electronically to the group in the next time zone so that the total team could work 24 hours a day.

Conversely, large geographic distances between members of a transnational team can aggravate the difficulties of assembling an integrated, cohesive work group. A feeling of "out of sight, out of mind" can be harmful to a team that must process a lot of information to accomplish its task.

Clearly, the first information technology needed by a transnational team is a *communications system*. Such a system must enable geographically dispersed team members to communicate with each other, with others in the company, and with outsiders. Transnational teams therefore make heavy use of telephones, voice mail, e-mail, and fax machines, and members must agree on how those communications devices should be coordinated and prioritized. Some teams use teleconferencing and videoconferencing, but those communication modes have not been adopted extensively.

Many transnational teams also use *databases* of various sorts. Some teams, such as Glaxo-Wellcome's medical R&D teams, create a database to store clinical-trial information. The efficiency with which the data are collected and analyzed significantly affects R&D costs and time, both strategically important. Other teams, such as Eastman Kodak's Photo CD Launch Team, need to be able to access databases that contain information about customers, distributors, and other parties. In general, transnational teams must analyze their data needs and then either acquire or construct appropriate databases.

Finally, transnational teams increasingly use computer-based *decision support systems*. Such "groupware" includes group scheduling, group authoring, real-time conferencing, project management, and much more. Transnational teams in the future will rely heavily on this technology as members become more comfortable with computerized

EXHIBIT 3
TRANSNATIONAL TEAM CULTURES

National Culture

An individual's orientation toward:

- universalism vs. particularism
- analyzing vs. integrating
- individualism vs. communitarianism
- inner-directedness vs. outer-directedness
- time as sequence vs. time as synchronization
- achieved status vs. ascribed status
- equality vs. hierarchy

Corporate Culture

A particular company's:

- values
- rituals
- heroes
- symbols

Occupational Culture

A given occupation's:

- analytical paradigm
- work norms and practices
- code of ethics
- jargon

---

decision-making aids and as groupware becomes more sophisticated.

Multicultural Dynamics

Besides task complexity and importance, the other defining feature of transnational teams is multicultural dynamics. A multinational team, in contrast to teams from a single culture, entails differences among members in language, interpersonal styles, and a host of other factors. Such differences can create a balance (cohesion and unity) or an imbalance (subgroup dominance, member exclusion, and other undesirable outcomes), depending on how they are handled.

Effective transnational teams directly confront the multicultural issues that inevitably arise in the group and search for ways to resolve them. Ineffective teams either ignore such issues or hope they can be re-

solved by the human resources department or through some type of outside training.

Group Process Facilitation. As indicated in the team effectiveness model (Exhibit 1), we believe strong business results follow from the establishment of an effective group process. Successful teams are characterized by leaders and members who trust each other, are committed to the team's mission, can be counted on to perform their respective tasks, and enjoy working with each other. Such process outcomes do not occur by chance, nor are they likely to develop naturally. Most often, they occur because the team has engaged in a well-conceived, facilitated process that takes multiculturalism into account.

In many transnational teams, three powerful cultures operate simultaneously. (See Exhibit 3.) The most obvious cultural characteristics (to an outsider) are those associated with a particular nationality: language, gestures, modes of dress, and so on. When a geographically dispersed transnational team holds a face-to-face meeting, the various national cultures are all on display—merging or colliding with each other depending on how much cultural synergy the team has developed.

In addition, corporate culture affects team dynamics. For example, British Petroleum hires some of the best graduates of the top British universities, and its main business involves a globally important natural resource. This creates a different corporate climate from that of, say, PepsiCo, which hires thousands of people every year, many of them semiskilled, in a variety of fast-changing consumer businesses. Both companies operate numerous transnational teams, but the teams work in very different corporate environments.

Last, some teams have a very strong occupational culture, as was evident among members of the Century Team, the joint venture between Xerox Corporation and Fuji-Xerox referred to earlier. Most team members had strong engineering backgrounds, and the similarities of this occupational culture clearly outweighed differences based on American and Japanese cultures or the two companies' corporate cultures.

Our study, including the videotaped analysis of transnational teams in European and East Asian multinational companies, suggests that the development of a healthy group process must take into account five major factors reflecting national and corporate cultures: (1) degree of similarity among the cultural norms of the individuals on the team, (2) extent to which such norms are manifested in the group, (3) level of fluency in the common language used by the team, (4) communication styles and expectations of what constitutes effective group behavior, and (5) management style of the team leader.

Cross-Cultural Management. How should transnational teams address culture-laden issues such as group norms, language, and styles of communication and leadership? In other words, how can a "multinational" team become a "transnational" team—a group of people whose effective interpersonal relationships recognize and integrate cultural differ-

ences? One way to build such a team is the approach used by MacGregor Navire, a subsidiary company of Finland's Kone Corporation.

MacGregor Navire, a small company of approximately 900 employees, is the global market leader in shipboard cargohandling equipment. It was created more than ten years ago by the merger of two companies, one Finnish and the other British. The company must enable a Norwegian shipbuilder, for example, to design cargohandling equipment in Norway, build it in Taiwan, and service it in South America. Hence, although it is a small firm, MacGregor Navire has all of the core elements of a "boundaryless" international organization.

The CEO of the newly merged company hand-picked his executive team of five managers, all of whom he knew and trusted and who shared his vision of where the company should be headed. Because he allowed each of them to choose where to live, the team is spread across Finland, Denmark, Sweden, and England. Each executive is multilingual, but team members speak in English during their weekly teleconference. Every month the team meets at one of the company's divisional headquarters and spends the next day with the managers of that division. The team leader encourages all team members to be part of every discussion, whether it is within their specific field of expertise or not. However, the roles and responsibilities for implementation are kept very clear so that interaction on a day-to-day basis across geographic distances is unnecessary. Above all else, the team emphasizes high performance goals for all members.

The MacGregor Navire Executive Team is a model of cross-cultural management. It meets all of the criteria of a healthy team. Essentially, the team was assembled by selecting people who were preprogrammed to be part of a transnational team. Team members all knew each other, spoke multiple languages, agreed on the team's mission from the outset, and shared the same business values. In most firms, however, designers of transnational teams must rely on some sort of team-building process to create interpersonal trust, shared vi-

EXHIBIT 4
A FOUR-STAGE TEAM-BUILDING PROCESS

Stage 1	**Forming the Team**
	• Company investment of HR department resources in team development
	• Senior management sponsorship
	• Use of diagnostic instruments to determine team resources
	• Understanding of business context and objectives
Stage 2	**Focusing the Team and Its Mission**
	• Team-building exercises
	• Development of team mission and norms
	• Clarification of objectives and performance measures
	• Cultural sensitivity intervention
Stage 3	**Maintaining the Team**
	• Group memory (visual record of agreements and action plans)
	• Transfer of facilitation skills to team members
	• Time spent practicing to become a better team
	• Continual update with sponsor
Stage 4	**Transfering Learning Throughout the Organization**
	• Celebrate, publicize, and reward success
	• Review group process with team and sponsor
	• Transfer learning to other teams and facilitators

sion, effective group decision making, and so on. Our demonstration project illustrates one successful team-building process.

PUTTING IT ALL TOGETHER

Our transnational teams research project coincided with a global restructuring process taking place within The Wellcome Foundation (now Glaxo-Wellcome), a large pharmaceutical company with R&D facilities in Great Britain and the United States. Before the restructuring process, both the U.K. and U.S. research facilities were often working on the same drug applications. The delays and redundancies associated with that approach resulted in lost opportunities in the global market for ethical drugs. For example, it can take 10 to 15 years and cost half a billion dollars to bring a drug to market. If the introduction of an efficacious drug is held up for any reason,

a large pharmaceutical firm can lose $5 to 10 million in sales a day. With such enormous financial sums at stake, a concerted effort to get medical R&D teams up and running smoothly can be easily justified.

Background

Turning our research results into improved practice proved to be challenging. The company first assembled a high-caliber human resources team, composed of the firm's top organization development (OD) practitioners from both the U.K. and U.S., to work with the medical R&D teams. The new team used the research findings to identify the "best practices" it wanted to convey to the R&D teams. In addition, the company invested substantial financial and human resources in the demonstration project.

Next, the HR team assessed the human resources department as a whole. They devised a matrix grid to evaluate the skills necessary to support a transnational team and found that the department had some very strong competencies, but some weak areas as well. To correct the weak areas, team members obtained needed skills from universities and consulting firms with which they had worked previously, thus putting into place an external network of OD professionals. To meet the new demand for global service delivery that arose from reorganization, the company expanded the number of transnational team facilitators from the originally planned 20 to more than 50. Staffing the HR function itself took about eight months, and the HR department explicitly committed itself to becoming one of the world's best facilitators of transnational team development.

Finally, the HR team implemented its plan and periodically evaluated results. The OD practitioners were immediately "overbooked"—many R&D teams wanted their help, but each facilitator could work in depth with only a few teams. Also, by means of a mentoring process, the new facilitators were quickly educated about the company's business strategies, structures, and systems so that each team's mission and operations could be properly integrated with the rest of the organization.

The Four-Stage Approach

The approach that ultimately emerged as "best practice" within Glaxo-Wellcome is shown in Exhibit 4. In stage 1, which precedes team launch, the members of an R&D project group meet with a skilled group-process facilitator. The team must first determine what kind of sponsorship it has. Whether the sponsor is a section head, therapeutic department head, or a division leader, that sponsor must be brought into the team process early because he or she is the primary link to company strategy. The facilitator often uses paper-and-pencil diagnostic instruments to uncover team members' knowledge of group processes and team roles. The team then determines how it is expected to contribute to corporate strategy. Throughout stage 1, the facilitator

must work closely with the team's project leader, the team's sponsor, and other members of management.

In stage 2, when team members first begin to work together, they determine what skills (technical and group) each member brings to the team and how the team's mission fits operationally into the overall business context. During this stage (and in the preceding one as well), the focus is on building an effective group process: developing team norms, articulating useful team roles, identifying success criteria, and so on. Facilitators typically meet with a team five to six times over a period of a year to help the team get through stage 2. The facilitators firmly believe that unless a sound group process develops during this stage, the team probably will not achieve superior business results in the years ahead.

One important activity in stage 2 is a cultural sensitivity intervention. It includes the introduction of key cultural concepts and discussions about the characteristics of the specific nationalities represented on the team. The overall purpose of the intervention is to legitimize cultural differences and to encourage the team to capitalize on those differences, rather than suppress or ignore them. The facilitator helps the team gain a clear conceptual understanding of national culture's impact on the group and develop a customized team language for discussing cultural issues.

In stage 3, a maintenance stage, the team has been in existence for five to nine years and is working well together. Facilitation skills are transferred from the OD practitioner to the team leader and members. Depending on the speed of the transfer, the process consultant may spend a lot of time with the team or may become less involved. One of the most important milestones of stage 3 is getting the team to take responsibility for its own outputs—not just the team's formal deliverables, but also the outcomes of team meetings. Teams are encouraged to keep a visual record of their action plans and to spend time practicing to become a better team.

The team's membership may change during the maintenance stage. When new mem-

EXHIBIT 5

MANAGERIAL LESSONS DRAWN FROM THE DEMONSTRATION PROJECT

1. **Multiple Uses of Valid Performance Measurement**

   Credible, team-specific performance measures aid managers in conducting appraisals, providing feedback, and rewarding teams.

2. **Value of Post-Project Evaluations**

   Post-project evaluations not only provide specific do's and don'ts for team effectiveness, but also create a learning orientation in the company.

3. **Importance of Group Financial Rewards**

   Teams are motivated by the prospect of receiving rewards for accomplishing their goals — if goals are realistic and performance measures are relevant.

4. **Relationship Between Team and Company Effectiveness**

   Team effectiveness begins with the development of a sound group process for communicating information, making decisions, handling conflicts, and so on. Teams can then rely on their process to produce desired business results.

5. **Role of the Human Resources Department**

   A competent, well-managed HR group can help transnational teams in a variety of ways, including team-building, leader and member selection, and manager education and development.

bers come on board, either temporarily or permanently, team dynamics change, and some teams invite back their facilitator to help the group fine-tune its process. Such efforts might take the form of total team building, or could involve aligning new members with the team's and company's business strategy, goals, and success criteria.

In stage 4, regardless of whether the drug project is canceled or the new drug receives regulatory approval, the team still has something to accomplish. In the past, the company did not transfer what was learned from team to team. In the four-stage approach, not only do HR practitioners transfer information among teams, but the teams' project leaders also get together on a regular basis to exchange advice based on their successes and failures. Successful projects are celebrated and rewarded by the company, but so too are certain types of breakdowns. Senior managers have agreed that when an R&D project is canceled, there is reason to celebrate—the team did well to abandon the project by not wasting company resources, and other teams probably can learn something useful from the experience.

Lessons Learned

The demonstration project strengthened the effectiveness of Glaxo-Wellcome's transnational R&D teams in several ways. (See Exhibit 5 for a description of the major lessons for managers.) One way involved *performance measurement*. The HR team conducted focus groups with medical researchers in the U.K. and U.S., asking, "What are the real drivers behind team performance?" From the focus group results, the HR team developed specific performance criteria and indicators as well as a 360-degree evaluation instrument to guide both the development and appraisal of team members. Valid performance measures have been created for 37 R&D projects to date (see, for example, the list of key business results in Exhibit 1).

Another outcome of the demonstration

project was recognition of the value of *post-project evaluations*. Glaxo-Wellcome now performs regular evaluations after its R&D and marketing projects—analyses of what worked well and what did not. In one case, the company launched a new drug in 18 countries within one week—an unprecedented move. The post-project evaluation revealed several success factors that were applied to other marketing projects that were underway.

A third outcome was a heightened management awareness of the importance of *group financial rewards* in motivating team performance. The annual goal-setting and performance appraisal process in the company had been based on bosses working individually with subordinates. That process aided in determining annual merit increases, but did little to promote team effectiveness. After the company adopted a compensation scheme based on group performance indicators (called key business results in Exhibit 1), team members began to share more information with each other, searched for ways to remove bottlenecks in the work process, and tried in other ways to enhance team performance.

Probably the most valuable lesson to emerge from the demonstration project was that *team effectiveness precedes company effectiveness*. Moreover, the demonstration project proved that the effectiveness of the typical transnational team can be improved considerably—particularly a team's ability to make quick and sound group decisions. One of the more experienced OD specialists who was closely associated with the demonstration project said, "Now most of our teams have a clearly defined mission and objectives. They know exactly what they're supposed to deliver, and they know what their performance measures are. They know what success will look like. This particular approach allows a project leader to form a solid team before he or she has to handle the crises of clinical development. It gives team leaders and members the tools they need to manage those crises when they come along later."

CONCLUSIONS

Transnational teams are at the heart of the globalization process. As companies spread their operations around the world, transnational teams are almost always used to both launch and manage the process. From our research and the accompanying demonstration project, we believe that international companies can systematically create high-performing transnational teams. The model of transnational team effectiveness can be used to examine the key variables that must be addressed to have a successful team, and the demonstration project offers a practical, step-by-step approach for improving team performance. Today's international companies—even large, sophisticated global leaders—probably will discover that they must dramatically improve their human resources departments to support transnational teams properly, and they will want to develop innovative and customized compensation schemes to reward teams for their accomplishments.

SELECTED BIBLIOGRAPHY

Although the literature on work teams is extensive and expanding rapidly, there are very few writings on, or empirical studies of, transnational teams. Our study is the first to identify the basic ways international companies use transnational teams to pursue global business strategies. The overall challenge of managing a transnational team has been described by Nancy J. Adler, *International Dimensions of Organizational Behavior* (Kent Publishing Company, 1991), Chapter 4. She presents a set of approaches for managing cultural diversity, particularly highlighting the goal of "cultural synergy," whereby the strengths of different cultures represented on a team are combined to achieve superior group performance.

An excellent review article on multicultural work groups is by Catherine Kirchmeyer and Aaron Cohen, "Capitalizing on Ethnic Diversity: An Approach to Managing the Diverse Workgroups of the 1990s," *Canadian Journal of Administrative Sciences*, June 1991. The authors provide a model of conditions of

security and challenge that together can lead to creative tension and thereby enhance team problem solving.

For discussions of more specific aspects of creating and managing transnational teams, see Sue Canney Davison, "Leading and Facilitating International Teams," in M. Berger (ed.), *Cross-Cultural Team Building* (New York: McGraw-Hill, in process); and Mary O'Hara-Devereaux and Robert Johansen, *GlobalWork: Bridging Distance, Culture and Time* (San Francisco: Jossey-Bass, 1994), Chapters 3-5.

For a broad understanding of the globalization process and how international companies are organizing to cope with it, see Kenichi Ohmae, *The End of the Nation State: The Rise of Regional Economies* (New York: The Free Press, 1995); Christopher A. Bartlett and Sumantra Ghoshal, *Managing Across Borders: The Transnational Solution* (Cambridge: Harvard Business School Press, 1989); and Ron Ashkenas, et al., *The Boundaryless Organization: Breaking the Chains of Organizational Structure* (San Francisco: Jossey-Bass, 1995).

[22]

Are Virtual International Assignments Feasible?

Denice E. Welch/Verner Worm/Marilyn Fenwick

Abstract

- Some international companies are using advanced communication and information technology to manage virtually, rather than sending a traditional expatriate into the foreign location.

- This article explores the feasibility of using virtual assignments as a replacement for the traditional expatriate international posting.

Key Results

- A schema is presented to illustrate elements of a virtual assignee's work relationship.
- The virtual assignment is a viable option but is unlikely to replace traditional expatriate assignments.

Authors

Denice E. Welch, Professor of International Management, Mt Eliza Business School, Melbourne, and the University of Queensland, Australia.
Verner Worm, Associate Professor of International Management, Asia Research Center, Department of International Economics and Management, Copenhagen Business School, Copenhagen, Denmark.
Marilyn Fenwick, Senior Lecturer, Department of Management, Faculty of Business and Economics, Monash University, Melbourne, Australia.

Denice E. Welch/Verner Worm/Marilyn Fenwick

Introduction

Foreign operations place particular demands on management due to the inherent economic and political risks involved in operating in multiple markets. Of course, these management demands vary across industries, firm size and geographical spread, and mode of foreign operation utilized. However, there are generic management concerns that internationalising firms face, as indicated in the burgeoning volume of scientific literature on international management. Within this work, there is general recognition that the need for effective performance monitoring and control of global activities is of critical importance. A common response has been to use staff transfers as a control mechanism (Edström/Galbraith 1977, Ondrack 1985, Fenwick/ De Cieri/Welch 1999). This approach allows the internationalising firm to fill key positions in foreign units with expatriates, whether from headquarters or from other subsidiaries. The challenge is that, as activities spread globally, the demand for internationally mobile staff becomes more acute and may become a barrier to further globalisation (Novicevic/Harvey 2001, Harris 1999, Latta 1999, Tung 1998, Welch 1994).

In this article, we explore the feasibility of using a "virtual" assignment as a replacement to the traditional expatriate international posting as a way of meeting the staffing challenge. The virtual assignment has been defined as a situation where "an employee does not relocate to a host location, but has international responsibilities for a part of the organisation in another country which they manage from the home country" (PricewaterhouseCoopers 2000, p. 31). It is an appointment to a specific, defined role in a foreign operation, for a specific period of time. The difference is that the traditional expatriate assignment requires the person to relocate to the foreign work setting. Companies therefore require persons/family units that are internationally mobile. However, demographic changes such as the increasing number of dual career couples, as more females seek equal opportunities to advance their international careers, are affecting the available pool of potential, mobile, expatriates. The traditional family unit – a male breadwinner supported by a spouse who has either no career outside the family work environment, or has a part-time attachment to the paid workforce – is declining. Compensation for the loss of income of the accompanying spouse/partner has become an issue adding to the expense of using traditional expatriate postings. Therefore, increasing staff immobility and cost constraints appear to be important drivers in the search for alternative ways of handling international staffing requirements than through the traditional form of expatriation. Recent Danish and Australian research into International Human Resource Management (IHRM) trends (conducted by two of the authors of this article) highlights this. For example, Danish line managers reported that, when potential expatriates were approached, half of them refused to accept an international assignment.

96   **mir** vol. 43 · Special Issue · 2003/1

As barriers to staff mobility increase, international companies are utilising other staffing options to reduce their reliance on traditional expatriate assignments. One alternative has been to try to localise as soon as practicable – the expatriate trains his/her replacement. For example, ABB China has made localisation a business goal. To achieve this, profit and market share targets are linked to expatriates' annual monetary bonuses, determined by the speed by which they have successfully developed a local who can take over expatriates' roles. As a result ABB has comparatively the lowest number of expatriates with a ratio of 1:100 among seven major European MNCs in China. By focusing so strongly on localisation, they were able to reduce cost considerably because an expatriate's remuneration including allowances per year is around ten times more than the typical salary of a local manager (Worm/Selmer/de Leon 2001).

Another option is to select from the many forms of what has been termed non-standard assignments – that is, other than the traditional expatriate assignment. These include: *short term assignments* (transfers abroad that range in duration from longer than a business trip, but shorter than the typical long term assignment); *commuter assignments* (special arrangements where the person concerned commutes from the home country on a weekly or bi-weekly basis to the place of work in another country); *rotational assignments* (employees commute from the home country to a place of work in another country for a short set period followed by a holiday in the home country – used on oil rigs for example); and *contractual assignments* (used in situations where employees with specific skills vital to an international project are assigned for a limited duration of six to twelve months).

The consulting firm, PricewaterhouseCoopers conducts periodic surveys of international firms operating in Europe. Its 1997/1998 survey identified a trend towards increased use of non-standard international assignments, and this trend was confirmed in its follow-up survey in 2000. The PricewaterhouseCoopers surveys also identified the emergence of the growing use of the so-called '*virtual assignment*'. The 2000 survey found that 28% of respondent firms anticipated an increasing use of virtual assignments, compared with 17% in the 1997/1998 survey. 65% of respondents who use virtual assignments reported having seen an increase in the number of virtual assignments used by their company and the same proportion indicated an expected increase in the next two years. The survey data indicates that the importance and use of virtual assignments has increased most significantly, in relative terms, compared with the other types of non-standard and the traditional expatriate assignments.

Given the above, this article now examines the virtual assignment as an alternative form of international staffing. We seek to provide a window on this alternative through the exploration of the virtual assignment concept. What are the key issues in using a virtual rather than the traditional form of expatriate assignment, considering that it involves managing discrete activities, involving foreign-based work groups, remote from the actual location? What are the impli-

Denice E. Welch/Verner Worm/Marilyn Fenwick

cations of relying on telecommunication and information technology such as telephone, e-mail and video conferencing as a *substitute for actual physical presence* in the foreign work context? Is it a long-term, viable international staffing
option that will be an effective replacement for the traditional expatriate assignment or just a variant of the traditional expatriate assignment, its use influenced
by the hype that has surrounded the Internet and E Commerce? These questions
form the starting point for our examination of the virtual assignment as a non-
standard form of staffing foreign operations and activities. While the central
focus is the nature of the virtual assignment, we also attempt to delineate aspects
that may affect the working relationship between the Virtual Assignee and the Virtual Workgroup involved in the host location. Through iteration with the relevant
extant literature, and drawing upon the limited empirical work in this area, a sche-
matic portrayal of factors (Figure 1) influencing virtual assignees and their work
groups is presented and discussed.

There is a substantial body of research into the management of expatriates in
traditional, longer-term assignments (for a review of this literature, see for
example, Dowling/Welch/Schuler 1999). However, while non-standard assignments have long been used in conjunction with, or instead of, traditional expatriate assignments, this has yet to translate into a comparable body of academic
inquiry. Consequently, there has been a dearth of research into the international
management issues, particularly human resource implications, of using other than
traditional expatriate assignments. This article seeks to assist in redressing this
imbalance by focusing on one form of non-standard assignment – the virtual assignment.

Confirming Trends

As mentioned above, the use of virtual and other forms of non-standard international assignments appear to be increasing. In this section, we draw out issues that emerged from our Australian and Danish studies that were conducted in
2000 and 2001 to identify trends in multinational staffing approaches regarding
non-standard assignments. These studies have formed the basis for on–going empirical investigations into the virtual assignment. Both studies used in-depth interviews that were tape recorded with the interviewees' permission, transcribed
verbatim, and subsequently manually content-analysed (within-case and across
case) following the pattern-matching approach outlined by Miles and Huberman
(1994).

Are Virtual International Assignments Feasible?

An Australian Perspective

Five expert informants were interviewed in order to explore staffing trends and whether or not virtual assignments featured in their lines of sight. Consistent with a Delphi-type research design, four consultants and one senior human resource practitioner were selected for interview on the basis that such professionals have been found to be reliable expert informants (Chen/Farh/MacMillan 1993). The five experts were: the Managing Director of an Australian-owned and operated international relocation consultancy; a senior consultant with a large multinational consultancy specialising in reward and recognition practices; a senior consultant in international assignment management with a large multinational management consultancy; the Human Resources Director with a multinational trading company; and, a principal in the Human Resources and Remuneration consulting division of a worldwide consulting firm.

The changing demographics of those undertaking international assignments, and an increase in project-based international assignments of shorter duration (such as those found in the PricewaterhouseCoopers surveys) were the main themes that emerged from the interviews. The following comment is illustrative:

> There's definitely a shift for younger people to go on assignment. Rather than having [international assignees who] go in as country heads at the age of 42 ... I would say that 60–70% of the people that we move around are under 37.

In the opinions of the expert informants, there were indications this shift might be more characteristic of information and high technology industries in particular. The consultants indicated that project-based international assignments of shorter duration were increasingly a feature across the banking, mining, information technology and trading organisations for example. For instance, a relocation consultant commented:

> We started the business [over a decade] ago and the average length of assignment then would have been three years ... I'd say the average length of assignment now is 18 months.

Interviewees also considered that international assignments, particularly the non-standard types, were increasingly being undertaken by all management levels, including supervisory and line management levels. The use of 'virtual teams' appears to be increasing, according to all the experts interviewed, driven by the advent of intra- and inter- net communications and advances in teleconferencing technology. For example,

Denice E. Welch/Verner Worm/Marilyn Fenwick

> *I would say we are using a lot more virtual teams and electronic communication to reduce expensive and risky expatriate postings.*

The expert informants also identified the increased frequency of the classic business trip – the frequent-flyer-type assignment – used by companies to build interpersonal relationships and for control purposes.

The reasons these expert informants attributed to increasing levels of international assignments, particularly the non-standard types, indicated that the extent to which international assignments are initiated by employers might also be changing. For instance, employees are more likely to initiate international transfer in some form or another now than they were three to five years ago. While this appears to contradict our earlier comments about the declining availability of staff willing to relocate internationally, the parameters for such self-initiated assignments are very much defined by the employees. As one Australian expert explained:

> *Employees are being a bit more selective about preserving their chosen lifestyle, rather than allowing the employer to dictate it.*

It was apparent from the interview data the five Australian expert informants considered that virtual assignments are indeed a part of an international staffing repertoire.

A Danish Perspective

Based on the PricewaterhouseCoopers (2000) report, six of the Danish companies that had been part of the PricewaterhouseCoopers 2000 survey agreed to take part in an in-depth study to examine more fully the dynamics of expatriation. This study, conducted by the second author during 2001, involved two stages. Firstly, semi-structured, in-depth interviews were conducted with 11 HR directors of the six companies, except one where the interviewee was the person within the company in charge of expatriation management. From these interviews, it emerged that non-standard international assignments tended to fall outside the jurisdiction of the HR department in the case companies. Consequently, interviews with this group concentrated on traditional expatriate management issues and concerns, such as staff availability for international assignments. In response to this somewhat surprising result, however, further discussions with the participating HR managers were conducted and these were illuminating. For example, when informed as to how one multinational used virtual assignments, two HR managers related that their companies used virtual assignments in situations where employees had regional responsibilities. In the original interviews, this arrangement was not mentioned – it was not thought about as a 'virtual assignment'.

Are Virtual International Assignments Feasible?

Concurrent interviews were conducted with 15 line managers across the six case companies about their attitude towards non-standard international assignments. In contrast to their HR counterparts, the line managers were more familiar with their employees' various experiences with non-standard assignments as they were more actively involved in selecting and deploying staff for non-standard international assignments. Thus, line managers could volunteer specific cases: for example, the use of commuter assignments (one case was an employee who worked three days in another Nordic country and two days in the Danish headquarters); and short-term international assignments.

The second part of the Danish study included a questionnaire sent to potential expatriates chosen by each case company's HR-division after consultation with relevant line managers. The main interest here was to gauge staff willingness to relocate internationally, and what types of assignment postings these potential international assignees were willing to accept. Of the 141 potential candidates surveyed, 70 percent answered that they would accept a virtual assignment, making it the most popular of the non-standard international assignments. 60 percent of the respondents would accept a short-term assignment, 41 percent a commuter assignment and 46 percent a rotational assignment. Further, while only four percent (five respondents) were prepared to state that they would *not* accept a long-term international assignment in the foreseeable future, the nature of the assignment seemed an important factor in determining staff availability.

In sum, by providing perspectives from HR and line managers and potential expatriates, the Australian and Danish studies confirmed the general trends exposed by broader surveys such as that conducted by PricewaterhouseCoopers. First, in interviews, Danish HR and line managers, and Australian expert informants, agreed that it has become more difficult to send people on foreign assignments. Second, prospective expatriates selected the virtual assignment as the most attractive option among the non-standard international assignments. This result strengthens the impression from interview data in the six Danish case companies that it is becoming more difficult to persuade young people to accept a traditional expatriate assignment. It also confirms the findings of the Pricewaterhouse Coopers surveys that virtual assignments were being considered by more companies as a solution to staff immobility.

Based on the data gained, a pilot study was conducted in early 2002 to explore issues surrounding the use of virtual assignments. This involved two interviews with Danish subsidiary staff of a large IT multinational. The firm was selected because was well known for using virtual assignments for project management and as a way of managing its regional offices. One interviewee managed the operations in the other three Nordic countries. It was therefore considered an appropriate pilot case site. Each interview took one-and-a-half hours. In the next section, data from these pilot interviews, combined with the findings of the

Denice E. Welch/Verner Worm/Marilyn Fenwick

broader studies referred to above, are used to support our exploration into the nature of the virtual assignment. For ease of reading, *italics* font is used when qualitative data, in the form of verbatim quotations from interviewees/respondents, is presented. To protect confidentiality, interviewees are identified by a country code – that is, D1 refers to Danish interviewee 1, A1 refers to Australian interviewee 1 – and company names are disguised.

Managing Virtually

By definition, the virtual assignee straddles both HQ/unit and foreign unit in a special way. For a majority of the time, the Virtual Assignee is physically located in the home unit, that may or may not be company headquarters – it could be in another subsidiary unit. In reality, the split between the country of living and the countries where the employee hold responsibilities is not that clear cut, because many people on virtual assignments also have some responsibilities in the country where they live.

It is important here to state that we are not assuming that all virtual assignments involve work in virtual teams. Even though it appears the terms are used interchangeably in the literature (see for example, Cascio 2000, Townsend/ DeMarie/Hendrickson 1998), we make a distinction between virtual teams and Virtual Workgroups. Virtual team members remain in their geographically and organisationally distant locations but work on a defined project using telecommunications and information technologies – dispersed in terms of space in geographical isolation from each other, and operate asynchronously in terms of time (Montoya-Weiss/Massey/Song 2001). In the virtual assignment, only one member (the Virtual Assignee) is geographically distant. Virtual teams often remain together for the life of the project, whereas in the virtual assignment context, the work group is real – less transient in form and substance. It functions in the traditional co-located sense, a "powerful unit of collective performance" (Katzenbach/Smith 1993, p. 10), but not necessarily bound by the levels of commitment and synergistic performance terms associated with teams. While teams might feature within the Virtual Workgroup, we suggest that the relationship between the Virtual Assignee and the Virtual Workgroup does not *necessarily* equate to virtual teamwork.

The somewhat unique work arrangement that results from a virtual assignment poses both advantages and disadvantages for the Virtual Assignee, and the work groups involved in both the home and host locations. These are now discussed, with reference to Figure 1.

Are Virtual International Assignments Feasible?

Figure 1. Factors Influencing Virtual Workgroup Relations

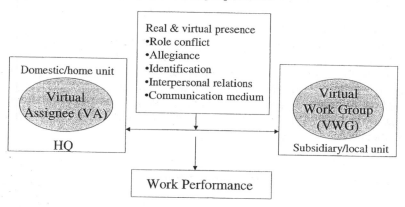

Real and Virtual Presence

The appeal of the virtual assignment, from the organisation's perspective, is that it either removes or lessens some of the barriers to the traditional assignment, particularly staff immobility and cost containment, due to savings on relocation expenses and other aspects of a traditional assignment, and accommodation of dual career concerns and other family-related barriers to staff mobility. At the same time, the organization can expect to reap at least some of the benefits usually accrued to the traditional expatriate assignment. For example, expatriates are at the boundary of the parent company and the local unit as they seek simultaneously to achieve headquarters goals while building and maintaining good relations with various stakeholders in the host location. This boundary-spanning role assists in transferring information and knowledge about the subsidiary environment to the centre, enhancing global control (Janssens 1994).

For the individual, there are many advantages to agreeing to manage virtually. The main attraction is not having to relocate to a foreign country, with the accompanying issues such as disruption to spouse/partner's career and childrens' education. In addition, the loss of visibility, often mentioned as a traditional expatriate concern as being 'out-of-sight, out-of-mind' would be lessened, as a Virtual Assignee is still visible in the home location. The dangers inherent in a lengthy period abroad, such as being passed over for promotion, and the nature of the repatriation position, are thereby lessened or negated. A similar argument could be mounted for other non-standard assignments, by nature of the shorter duration of the foreign assignment component.

Somewhat paradoxically, from a HQ perspective, one of the concerns of using expatriates on long-term assignments is that they may so identify with the foreign

Denice E. Welch/Verner Worm/Marilyn Fenwick

operation that they lose sight of headquarters' objectives, and the global perspective inherent in the expatriate role. This so-called 'going native' phenomenon is often cited as a reason for limiting the duration of the traditional expatriate assignments from three to five years (Black/Gregersen/Mendenhall 1992, Welch/Welch 1994). By remaining physically located in the home unit at least for the majority of the time, one would expect that the closer monitoring of the individual due to proximity would alert co-located workers to any signs of 'going native'. However, as Figure 1 shows, the real and virtual presence raises questions about loyalty which, in turn, may exacerbate critical aspects such as role conflict and dual allegiance.

Role Conflict, Dual Allegiance and Identification

The question of loyalty between home and host work units may contribute to intra-personal role conflict. Gregersen and Black (1990) discuss how an expatriate's role conflict can be engendered by dual allegiances to the home and host unit, with the potential of causing the expatriate to be pulled in two directions. These authors argue that having to 'choose sides' in conflict situations between headquarters and the subsidiary may provoke intra-personal role conflict, as the expatriate may be expected to show loyalty to headquarters' position. The Virtual Assignee may even be pulled in three directions – having to cater for global concerns (represented by headquarters), home work unit concerns and the concerns of the Virtual Workgroup – thus increasing the potential of intra-personal role conflict. This may be further exacerbated if, by identifying with the home unit or headquarters, the Virtual Assignee is perceived by the Virtual Workgroup concerned as an agent for headquarters rather than the work group's champion at headquarters. In the PricewaterhouseCoopers 2000 survey, 55% of responding firms that used virtual assignments reported that lack of assignee (Virtual Assignee) integration into the local workplace was a major problem. 35% of responding firms also mentioned resentment from host company employees as a further problem encountered in the use of Virtual Assignees.

Work time remains a finite resource despite recent technological developments and the placement of priorities may present often-conflicting loyalties and choices. The two Danish interviewees stressed the need to distribute one's time between work locations, and to cater for task and non-task performance when in the foreign location. For example:

> *Sometimes when I come to Stockholm I have to go out and have a beer with my people in Sweden and then go home next day* (D1).

Further, intra-personal role conflict may be heightened by a virtual assignment rather than lessened, simply because that is where the Virtual Assignee's primary responsibility and performance accountability lies. Vested self-interest may dictate placing primary allegiance with the Virtual Workgroup in the short-term, but generally one's career path is with the home unit, and ultimately with headquarters. A contributing factor to the Virtual Assignee's dilemma is that the virtual assignment requires frequent support visits to the foreign location, during which time the Virtual Assignee may foster an identify with the work unit, similar to that of a 'real' expatriate assignment. For the Virtual Assignee, identifying more with Virtual Workgroup members might well result in developing or increasing psychic, or mental, distance with those in the home office, even if it simultaneously reduces the psychic distance between the Virtual Assignee and the Virtual Workgroup. Where to place one's priorities and loyalties becomes as valid a concern as with traditional expatriate assignments.

The proportion of daily activities that is allocated to the Virtual Assignee's international responsibilities is another aspect to be considered. Conceivably, the greater the Virtual Assignee's international responsibilities, the more work time is spent interacting with the Virtual Workgroup, the less time there is available for interacting with co-located co-workers. Further, Virtual Workgroup members will expect the Virtual Assignee to champion their cause where necessary at the headquarters or home location. This may have important consequences for group dynamics and work performance, as a mutual lack of trust between group members might result (Jones/George 1998). Another danger is that Virtual Assignees may be treated as outliers – not accepted as full members of either the home unit or the host unit, by virtue not being one hundred percent present in either location, where time present physically is equated with the degree of organisational or unit commitment. In other words, at best the Virtual Assignee is regarded as a part-time worker in both locations. As one interviewee explained: "*You have to sell your self all the time in a virtual group*" (D2). It would seem that, to be effective, a virtual assignment would require deliberate investment in forums for face-to-face interaction and trust-building, particularly in the initial stages, to overcome some of the difficulties involved in a long distance working relationship.

From the perspective of the Virtual Workgroup, the real or virtual presence of the Virtual Assignee could be of relevance in determining identification to global operations. Reade's (2001a, b) work on the antecedents of identification in multinational corporations (MNCs) highlights the importance of fostering employee identification with the global level of the MNC in order to preserve overall cohesion. Her findings suggest "negative interpersonal relations with colleagues in the global network have a statistically significant negative impact on global identification" (2001b, p.1284). If this is indeed the case, then perceived negative relations with a Virtual Assignee located geographically distance will affect Virtual Workgroup members' identification with the global organization. Building the right work relationship between the Virtual Assignee and the Virtual Workgroup becomes a strategic issue. As Reade (2001a, p. 419) argues, strong local and glo-

Denice E. Welch/Verner Worm/Marilyn Fenwick

bal identification "may be an important ingredient not only for the success of the subsidiary but ultimately for the MNC as a whole".

Interpersonal Relations

Workgroup dynamics, social cohesion and positive interpersonal relations are well-recognised contributory factors to group performance. Despite members' separation, it is still possible to form group identity, as one Danish interviewee remarked:

> *A strong coherence can develop in a virtual group. It depends on the group. A good chemistry within a group is extremely important for the group's performance* (D2).

By its very nature though, the virtual assignment alters the processes by which a real group forms and operates. Firstly, geographical distance means that the normal daily interaction in the workplace that encourages social cohesion is diminished somewhat in the virtual context, as the following interviewee's comment reveals: "*One does not phone [a work colleague just] to ask how was the holiday*". The frequency and duration of supportive visits become an important group maintenance task, as the following interviewee explains:

> *When I travel, I don't get any "work" done. I mainly talk with people in my organisation. I don't go there only for the meetings. You have to know your people extremely well, otherwise you cannot deal with them* (D1).

Frequent visits are time consuming, as one of the Danish interviewees pointed out: *I have travelled 22 days in the first two months of this year* (D2). Naturally though, supportive visits to the host location provide the Virtual Assignee with more than the opportunity to forge social bonds. As Johannesen et al. (2001, p. 4) point out: "tacit knowledge is difficult to communicate to others as information, and can at best be difficult to digitalize". Such knowledge is highly person-bound. Face-to-face contact plays an important role in how information is exchanged, tacit knowledge is shared, and work is monitored (Roberts et al. 1998). In addition, the interview data suggests the necessity to build formal structures for operational and systemic procedures to support the lack of real presence of all group members when important decisions need to be made. For example:

> *If decisions are to be made during teleconferences, then all group members must know the* [underlying] *premises and know each other well* (D1).

Secondly, the virtual nature of the assignment may introduce or heighten areas for conflict. If the majority of a Virtual Assignee's time is spent in the home location, with daily interaction with Virtual Workgroup members largely work related, heavily reliant on the use of faxes, emails and telephone calls, the potential for misunderstanding and giving unintended offence increases. High-context cultures rely more heavily on one's ability to read the non-verbal cues than in low context cultures (Hall 1976). Such cues are missing from electronic media:

> *One cannot see their facial expression* [over the telephone] *although I think I am good at hearing voices* [picking up non-verbal cues]. *I can feel if there are problems* (D2).

Thirdly, being a Virtual Assignee requires more flexibility than in traditional assignments:

> *As a person you have to be incredibly flexible. If something goes wrong I must be able to take the plane to* [European city] *and phone my wife that I will not come back until 2−3 days later. When I was working* [as a traditional expatriate] *my work day was more structured* (D1).

Communication Medium

As Figure 1 illustrates, another factor that may influence the work relations between the Virtual Assignee and the Virtual Workgroup, is the communication medium used. In the virtual assignment situation, less direct communication channels become the important means of linking the two parties together so that the negative aspects of absence of daily physical presence is minimised. The PricewaterhouseCoopers survey data indicated that email, video conferencing and telephone calls are important media for communication between the Virtual Assignee and the Virtual Workgroup. This was borne out in our interview data. For example:

> *Communication is mainly conference calls and emails. Lots of decisions are made by conference calls* (D1).

Working virtually requires both the Virtual Assignee and the Virtual Workgroup to be comfortable with the various forms of electronic media, and may also place demands on work schedules and procedures. One interviewee stressed the time factor involved:

Denice E. Welch/Verner Worm/Marilyn Fenwick

> *You have to be very much aware of how you use your time. I structure my time mainly according to topics. Monday we talk about opportunities. Tuesday about HR issues and so on. We know how long [a] time each phone meeting takes. Monday half an hour, Tuesday one hour. I spend a lot of time on the phone* (D1).

Using emails to communicate presented challenges for the Danish interviewees, as revealed by the following examples:

> *I can motivate people by emails [by, for example,] saying that they get so much money if the contract is signed, or I can follow up on things but I cannot make people run in the same direction by emails . . .*
> *Many [of my Virtual Workgroup] write all too many emails. It takes time to answer them.* (D1).

> *Emails . . .can easily give a wrong impression and convey a meaning that was not intended* (D2).

Interviewees also pointed out that the greater the physical distance between the Virtual Assignee and the Virtual Workgroup, the more use of emails, because of time differences. As one interviewee added: *"one does not call a colleague in the middle of the night, because it would influence his or her work the next day"*. However, time differences can be utilized constructively – one can send an email at the end of the day so that a colleague can continue working on the matter on the other side of the globe. Of course, this assumes that emails will be answered, and there is a cultural element to be considered here. A Virtual Assignee interacting via email with Virtual Workgroup members in a situation that involves a large cultural distance may encounter difficulties[1].

Another medium of communication is via videoconferencing. 35 % of responding firms in the PricewaterhouseCoopers 2000 survey indicated they encouraged the use of videoconferencing as a way of addressing the lack of face-to-face, daily contact inherent in the virtual assignment situation.

> *Virtual leadership can be done over long distances, but it is difficult. Last year I was involved with a customer who had a subsidiary both in the USA and Australia. In such a case one has to be extremely careful with the timing of teleconferences. It would not work over a long period of time.* (D2)

Videoconferencing is also used as a substitute for visits to a foreign location. As one Australian expert informant observed:

Are Virtual International Assignments Feasible?

The advent [and] wider use of electronic communications ... [such as] videoconferencing means business [can be conducted] without hopping on an aeroplane to do it" (A1).

It is not, though, a perfect substitute for face-to-face communication and contact. As Kezsbom (2000, p. 34) points out, "even in the best of videoconferencing, facial expressions can be difficult to pick up if the transmission is poor, if someone is off camera, or when the mute button is pressed". Some people find videoconferences constraining and this may be reflected in their body language. Misunderstandings may arise if, for instance, discomfort with the medium is interpreted as discomfort with the person receiving the message. One Australian expert who had experience with this form of electronic communication, found that, along with its advantages, videoconferencing has:

[A] kind of mechanical aspect to it where you can see people but you feel like you're kind of game playing, almost role playing rather than engaging in real conversations. And you've got time limits set and you're subject to technology and that everything works properly (A2).

The Danish interviewees indicated a preference for using videoconferences to follow up earlier made decisions, but it was not considered as effective for the conduct of dialogues and discussions. Videoconferencing was useful for training purposes however. Frequent use of this medium, they both agreed, had allowed them to develop some competence in listening to the voices of their Virtual Workgroup members so that they had a 'feel' for attitudes and moods conveyed over the telephone.

Conclusions

The above exploration of the virtual assignment suggests that it may become an important component of the portfolio of non-standard options available to an internationalising firm. However, it is unlikely to completely replace the traditional expatriate assignment. There are several reasons for this conclusion. First, the limited available empirical evidence indicates an industry bias. For example, 69% of respondents in the PricewaterhouseCoopers 2000 survey who indicated using the virtual assignment were in the oil and gas industry. The Danish and Australian informants suggested that the IT industry lends itself to virtual management situations due, perhaps, to a general familiarity and ease with the communication techniques that support this work arrangement. For example, a Danish interviewee stated: *"More companies will come to work like us if they want to be international"*(D2).

Denice E. Welch/Verner Worm/Marilyn Fenwick

Second, the nature of the task or work involved is another factor in determi
ning its applicability: respondents in the PricewaterhouseCoopers survey indicate
they were using virtual assignments to manage local operations (55 %); for troubles
hooting, establishing a global company culture, for project operations and to ope.
new operations (35 % for each of these respectively); 20 % indicated they woul
use a virtual assignment to fill a skills gap, and 15 % to train staff. Two of the Da
nish case companies indicated that some research and development activities len
themselves to the use of virtual teams and that the virtual assignment could be
viable extension of this work approach. Virtual assignments in the Danish IT com
pany are used for leadership and coordination, such as managing regional offices

Third, it is somewhat difficult at this stage to comment on managing virtua
and traditional international assignments in foreign operations other than th
wholly-owned context, as empirical work on staff transfers has been mainly con
fined to intra-MNC movements. Little work has been conducted into othe
modes – such as international joint ventures, international projects, internationa
franchising, and the like – that require the use of international staff transfer
(Welch/Welch 1994). Moreover, with the proliferation of non-traditional forms o
multinational enterprise, such as strategic networks, the Virtual Assignee migh
not be so much a strategic reaction to cost containment and staff availability im
peratives, but a fundamental strategic requirement to facilitate such flexible mul
tinational forms. Some forms of foreign operation modes, such as project opera
tions, may lend themselves to virtual assignments more than others. A virtual as
signment may provide a low-risk way of assessing the feasibility of a new ven
ture or mode of foreign operation, as the following comment from a responden
in the PricewaterhouseCoopers survey suggests: "When you're not sure how the
project will go, virtual assignments can work [as a short term solution]". How
ever, often the foreign client demands the physical presence of key project staf
as a tangible signal of commitment to the project, thus reinforcing the use of tra
ditional expatriate assignments.

Last, our Danish and Australian interviewees concurred that traditional inter
national assignments will continue to be used for the global strategic purposes o
filling staffing vacancies, employee development, and creating organisational net
works, that can only be delivered through a real rather than a virtual presence
Traditional expatriate assignments provide actual international experience of wor
king and managing in foreign environments, and facilitate the development of in
ter-unit networks, and informal communication and information flows that forn
a critical part of the MNC's control processes and mechanisms (Fenwick/D
Cieri/Welch 1999), as indicated in the following interviewee comments:

> *People who can reach high positions should be sent out on normal assign*
> *ments . . . People come to know you . . . Networks are absolutely essentia*
> *for how people manage themselves in* [our company] (D2).

Are Virtual International Assignments Feasible?

Traditional international assignments are important . . . they promote your career opportunities. . . During normal assignments you can build networks that you can use later. (D1).

In this day and age, to be successful in the corporation, you should have had your first international assignment by the age of about 35. It doesn't necessarily have to have been a three-year assignment but you should have lived offshore even if it's only for six months or so (A1).

Areas for Future Research

Given its newcomer status, and the relative lack of empirical work, it is not possible to make definitive, or normative, statements regarding how virtual assignments should be managed. Rather than offer somewhat speculative managerial implications, we make some suggestions for future research. Our albeit limited data indicate there may be important differences between a traditional expatriate and a virtual assignee, in terms of elements such as frequent traveling between home and host location, and the Virtual Assignee's non-permanent presence in the foreign location. A starting point for further research into the nature of the virtual assignment would be to further explore these differences through a comparative cohort study of traditional expatriates and virtual assignees. The expatriate management literature is replete with studies looking at expatriate selection criteria. In contrast, little is known about the skills and abilities that may be required to handle a virtual assignment, though there may be commonalities with the skills required to work in virtual teams. The two Danish interviewees stressed an ability to deal with people in a social as well as the work context, and to be able to build personal networks as essential skills for Virtual Assignees. Ease of using new communication technologies would seem to be another critical component. In addition, what training would be required to assist a Virtual Assignee and the Virtual Workgroup members achieve the desired level of performance? Such studies would need to include members of the Virtual Workgroup involved, and include cases where the Virtual Assignee has come from a subsidiary unit, rather than from headquarters. This approach would reflect that reality of international staff transfers – it is "three-way" traffic, not just unidirectional (HQ to subsidiary), but from subsidiary to HQ, and between subsidiary units.

The interview data from the six Danish case companies suggest that some HR departments may be isolated from the management of virtual and other non-standard international assignments, and that the deployment and management of employees on these non-standard assignments fall into the ambit of line managers. If this is indeed the situation, then future empirical studies should begin with relevant line managers. HR directors could be involved as part of data triangula-

Denice E. Welch/Verner Worm/Marilyn Fenwick

tion, depending on the level of the involvement of the HR department, its relative strategic position and profile within the company, and the level of non-standard assignment positions involved. The Danish IT company is a case in point as virtual assignments were common throughout the company and were used frequently for higher level positions such as that of regional manager.

In their 1994 article, Welch and Welch point to the seeming preoccupation of the general IHRM literature with traditional expatriate management issues at the expense of other forms of international assignments. It has been evident from our examination of the literature for the purpose of this article that this preoccupation persists. Little work has been done into the management and HRM issues pertaining to non-standard international assignments. This is perhaps a curious anomaly given that the PricewaterhouseCoopers surveys and the Australian and Danish studies point to the increased usage of these types of international assignments. There may be commonalities across these non-standard types – such as between commuters, frequent business travelers and virtual assignees – that would assist in their effective management. Future research that examined the nature of these assignment types in more depth – along the lines suggested for investigating the virtual assignment – would assist in our understanding of the commonalities and differences across all types of international assignments, and the management implications thereof.

In conclusion, the information and communication technology revolution, generating technologies such as desktop video conferencing, collaborative software, and internet/intranet facilities, has enabled internationalizing companies to experiment with alternative staffing arrangements. Virtual assignments indeed may be feasible, and in some instances, for some companies, a necessity of international life, but they are just one of many ways in which multinationals can staff foreign operations. Despite the drawbacks for the parties concerned, the traditional expatriate assignment has been a feature of international business for centuries. Harnessing 21st century technology may alter some of its nature and substance, but it is unlikely to make the traditional expatriate assignment redundant.

Endnote

1 Almost on a weekly basis, one the authors of this paper receives phone calls from Danish companies asking why Chinese entities do not answer their emails. Basically the Chinese prefer to meet and come to know people before they begin exchanging emails.

Are Virtual International Assignments Feasible?

References

Black, J. S./Gregersen, H. B./Mendenhall, M. E. *Global Assignments: Successfully Expatriating and Repatriating International Managers*, San Francisco: Jossey-Bass 1992.

Cascio, W., Managing a Virtual Workplace, *Academy of Management Executive,* 14, 3, 2000, pp. 81–90.

Chen, M-J./Farh, J-L./MacMillan, I. C., An Exploration of the Expertness of Outside Informants, *Academy of Management Journal,* 36, 6, 1993, pp. 1614–1632.

Dowling P.J/Welch D. E., Schuler R. S., *International Human Resource Management: Managing People in a Multinational Context*, third edition, South-Western College 1998.

Edström, A./Galbraith, J. R., Transfer of Managers as a Coordination and Control Strategy in Multinational Organizations, *Administrative Science Quarterly*, 22, 2, 1977, pp. 248–263.

Fenwick, M./De Cieri, H., Welch, D., Cultural and Bureaucratic Control in MNEs: The Role of Expatriate Performance Management, *Management International Review*, 39, 1999, pp.107–124.

Gregerson, H./Black, J. S., A Multifaceted Approach to Expatriate Retention in International Assignment, *Group and Organization Studies*, 15, 4, 1990, pp. 461–485.

Hall, E., *Beyond Culture*, New York: Doubleday 1976.

Harris, H., Women in International management. Why Are They Not Selected, in Brewster, C., Harris, H. (eds.), International HRM: Contemporary Issues in Europe, London: Routledge, 1999, pp. 259–276.

Janssens, M., Evaluating International Managers' Performance: Parent Company Standards as a Control Mechanism, *The International Journal of Human Resource Management*, 5, 4, 1994, pp. 853–873.

Johannessen, J. A./Olaisen, J./Olsen, B., Mismanagement of Tacit Knowledge: The Importance of Tacit Knowledge, the Danger of Information Technology, and What to Do about It, *International Journal of Information Management*, 21, 2001, pp. 3–20.

Jones, G. R./George, J. M., The Experience and Evolution of Trust: Implications for Cooperation and Teamwork, *Academy of Management Review*, 23, 3, 1998, pp. 531–546.

Katzenbach, J. R./Smith, D. K., The Discipline of Teams, *Harvard Business Review,* 71, 2, 1993, pp. 111–120.

Kezsbom, D. S., Creating Teamwork in Virtual Teams, *Cost Engineering*, 42 10, 2000, pp 33–36.

Latta, G., Expatriate Policy and Practice: A Ten Year Comparison of Trends. *Compensation and Benefits Review,* 31, 4, 1999, pp. 35–39.

Miles, M.B./Huberman, M., *Qualitative Analysis*, second edition, Thousand Oaks, CA: Sage 1994.

Montoya-Weiss, M. M./Massey, A. P./Song, M., Getting It together: Temporal Coordination and Conflict Management in Global Virtual Teams, *Academy of Management Journal*, 44, 6 2001, pp.1251–1262.

Novicevic, M. M./Harvey, M.G., The Emergence of the Pluralism Construct and the Inpatriation Process, *International Journal of Human Resource Management*, 12, 3, 2001, pp. 333–356.

Ondrack, D., International Transfers of Managers in North American and European MNEs, *Journal of International Business Studies*, 16, 3, 1985, pp. 1–19.

Price Waterhouse, *International Assignments: European Policy and Practice,* Price Waterhouse Europe 1997.

PricewaterhouseCoopers, *Managing a Virtual World: International Non-standard Assignments, Policy and Practice*, PricewaterhouseCoopers Europe 2000.

Reade, C., Dual Identification in Multinational corporations: Local Managers and Their Psychological Attachment to the Subsidiary versus the Global Organization, *International Journal of Human Resource Management*, 12, 3, 2001a, pp. 405–425.

Reade, C. Antecedents of Organizational Identification in Multinational Corporations: Fostering Psychological Attachment to the Local Subsidiary and the Global Organization, *International Journal of Human Resource Management*, 12, 8, 2001b, pp. 1269–1291.

Roberts, K/Kossek, E. E./Ozeki, C., Managing the Global Workforce: Challenges and Strategies, *Academy of Management Executive* 12, 4, 1998, pp. 93–106.

Denice E. Welch/Verner Worm/Marilyn Fenwick

Tung, R., American Expatriates Abroad: From Neophytes to Cosmopolitans, *Journal of World Business*, 33, 2, 1998, pp. 125–144.

Townsend, A./DeMarrie, S./Hendrickson, A., Virtual Teams: Technology and the Workplace of the Future, *Academy of Management Executive,* 12, 3, 1998, pp. 17–29.

Welch, D. E., HRM Implications of Globalization, *Journal of General Management*, 19, 4, 1994, pp. 52–67.

Welch, D. E./Welch, L. S., Linking Operation Mode Diversity and IHRM, *International Journal of Human Resource Management*, 5, 4, 1994, pp. 911–926.

Worm, V./Selmer, J./de Leon, C., Human Resource Development for Localization: European Multinational Corporations in China, in Kidd, J./Li, X./Richter, F. (eds.), *Advances in Human Resource Management in Asia*, London: Palgrave 2001, pp. 188–211.

Global Integration

[23]

Converting global presence into global competitive advantage

Anıl K. Gupta and Vijay Govindarajan

Executive Overview

Global presence by itself does not confer global competitive advantage. Global presence makes available to the firm's managers five value-creation opportunities: to adapt to local market differences, to exploit economies of global scale, to exploit economies of global scope, to tap optimal locations for activities and resources, and to maximize knowledge transfer across locations. However, each of these opportunities is associated with significant obstacles and challenges that often prevent firms from exploiting them optimally. To overcome these challenges, managers need to adopt a two-step approach for analysis and action. They should first evaluate the optimality of the firm's global network for each value-chain activity along the dimensions of activity architecture, competencies at the locations, and coordination across locations. Based on this evaluation, they should then design and execute actions to mitigate or eliminate the suboptimalities.

In the early 1990s, PepsiCo, Inc. established an ambitious goal to more than triple its international soft drinks revenues—from $1.5 billion in 1990 to $5.0 billion by 1995. Charging boldly in the pursuit of these goals, Pepsi indeed built an extensive and wide-ranging global presence by the mid-1990s. Yet this global expansion did not translate into growth and profitability. In fact, by 1997, Pepsi withdrew from some major markets, such as South Africa, and had to take a nearly $1 billion loss from international beverage operations. While the global market for beverages continued to expand rapidly, Pepsi's international market share and revenues were actually shrinking, a situation that contrasted sharply with an aggressively growing Coca-Cola.[1]

As PepsiCo's experience demonstrates, securing global presence is anything but synonymous with possessing global competitive advantage. Building global presence gives you the right to play the game. However, it says little about whether and how you will actually win the game. Furthermore, winning one game does not ensure that you will win the next one. In short, transforming global presence into global competitive advantage requires systematic analysis, purposeful thinking, and careful orchestration, and is a never-ending process. Without a rigorously disciplined approach, global presence can easily degenerate into a liability that distracts management and wastes resources. The end result can even be a loss of competitive advantage in the domestic market.

Sources of Global Competitive Advantage

To convert global presence into global competitive advantage, companies must exploit five value creation opportunities: adapting to local market differences, exploiting economies of global scale, exploiting economies of global scope, tapping the optimal locations for activities and resources, and maximizing knowledge transfer across locations.

We discuss the origins of each opportunity and the specific ways in which they can yield competitive advantage. We also outline the challenges and obstacles that often prevent firms from exploiting these opportunities to the fullest extent.[2]

Adapting to local market differences

A direct implication of being present in multiple countries is that companies must respond to the inevitable heterogeneity they will encounter in these markets. Differences in language, culture, income levels, customer preferences, and distribution systems are only some of the factors to be considered. Even in the case of apparently standard products, at least some degree of local adaptation is often necessary, or at least advisable. Cellular phone manufacturers, for example, must adapt their products to different languages and the magnitude of background noise on the street. By responding to country-level heterogeneity through local adaptation of products, services, and processes, a company can reap benefits in three fundamental areas: market share, price realization, and competitive position.[3]

Increased market share. By definition, offering standard products and services across countries reduces the boundaries of the served market to only those customers whose needs are uniform across countries. Local adaptation of products and services has the opposite effect, expanding the boundaries to also include those customers within a country who value different features and attributes. One of McGraw-Hill Companies' products, *BusinessWeek*, provides a good illustration of how local adaptation of products and services can enlarge the customer base. As the magazine's editor-in-chief explained: "Each week, we produce three editions. For example, this week's North American cover story is 'The New Hucksterism.' The Asian edition cover is 'Acer, Taiwan's Global Powerhouse.' And the European-edition cover is 'Central Europe.' In addition, our writers create an additional 10 to 12 pages of stories customized for readers in Europe, Asia, and Latin America. They also turn out four pages of international-finance coverage, international editorials, and economic analysis, and a regional feature column."[4]

> Local adaptation of products and services has the opposite effect, expanding the boundaries to also include those customers within a country who value different features and attributes.

Improved price realization. Tailoring products and services to the preferences of local customers (e.g., Baskin-Robbins's introduction of green-tea flavored ice cream in Japan) enhances the value delivered to them. As a corollary, a portion of this increased value should translate into higher price realization for the firm.

Neutralizing local competitors. One of the natural advantages enjoyed by most local competitors stems from their deep understanding of and single-minded responsiveness to the needs of the local market. For example, in the Japanese soft-

drinks market, Suntory Ltd. and Asahi Soft Drinks Co. have been among the first movers in offering new concepts such as Asian teas and fermented-milk drinks. When a global player also customizes its products and services to local needs and preferences, it is mounting a frontal attack on the local competitors in their market niche. In its efforts to neutralize Suntory's and Asahi's moves and attack them on their home turf, Coca-Cola introduced several new products in Japan that are not offered by the company in other markets, including an Asian tea called Sokenbicha, an English tea called Kochakaden, and a coffee drink called Georgia.[5]

Challenges. While seeking the benefits of local adaptation, however, companies must be prepared to face a number of challenges and obstacles:

- In most cases, local adaptation of products and services will increase the company's cost structure. Given the inexorable intensity of competition in most industries, companies can ill afford any competitive disadvantage on the cost dimension. Managers have to find the right equilibrium in the trade-off between localization and cost structure. For example, cost considerations initially led Procter & Gamble to standardize diaper design across European markets, despite market research data indicating that Italian mothers, unlike those in other countries, preferred diapers covering the baby's navel. After some time, however, recognizing that this particular feature was critical to Italian mothers, the company consequently incorporated this design feature for the Italian market, despite its adverse cost implications.[6]

- In many instances, local adaptation, even when well intentioned, may prove to be misguided. When the American restaurant chain TGI Fridays entered the South Korean market, it deliberately incorporated many local dishes, such as kimchi, in its menu. This responsiveness, however, backfired. Company analysis of the tepid market performance revealed that Korean customers anticipated a visit to TGIF as a visit to America, finding local dishes on the menu was inconsistent with their expectations. Companies must take the pulse of their market continually to detect if and when local adaptation becomes misguided adaptation.

- As with many other aspects of global marketing, the necessary degree of local adaptation usually will shift over time. In many industry segments, a variety of factors, such as the influence of global media, greater international travel, and declining income disparities across countries, may pave the way toward increasing global standardization. Consistent with the earlier example of *BusinessWeek*, we foresee a diminished need over time for geography-based customization. In other industry segments, particularly where the product or service can be delivered over the Internet (such as music), the need for even greater customization and local adaptation may increase over time. Companies must recalibrate the need for local adaptation on an ongoing basis; over-adaptation extracts a price just as surely as does underadaptation.

Exploiting economies of global scale

Building global presence automatically expands a company's scale of operations, giving it larger revenues and a larger asset base. However, larger scale will create competitive advantage only if the company systematically undertakes the tough actions needed to convert scale into economies of scale. The potential benefits of economies of scale can appear in various ways: spreading fixed costs, reducing capital and operating costs, pooling purchasing power, and creating critical mass.[7]

Spreading fixed costs over larger volume. This benefit is most salient in areas such as research and development, operations, and advertising. For instance, Merck, the pharmaceutical giant, can spread R&D costs over its global sales volume thereby reducing per-unit costs of development.

Reducing capital and operating costs per unit. This benefit is often a consequence of the fact that doubling the capacity of a production facility typically increases the cost of building and operating the facility by a factor of less than two.

Pooling global purchasing power over suppliers. Concentrating global purchasing power over any specific supplier generally leads to volume discounts and lower transaction costs. For example, as Marriott has raised its stakes in the global lodging business, its purchase of such goods as furnishings, linens, and beverages has stepped up dramatically. Exercising global purchasing power over a few vendors (e.g., PepsiCo for soft drinks) is part of Marriott's efforts to convert its global presence into global competitive advantage.

Creating requisite critical mass in selected activities. A larger scale gives the global player the opportunity to build centers of excellence for the development of specific technologies and/or products. To develop a center of excellence, a company generally needs to focus a critical mass of talent in one location. In view of the potential to leverage the output of such a center on a global scale, a global player will be more willing and able to

make the necessary resource commitments required for such a center.

Challenges. Few, if any, of these potential strategic benefits of scale materialize automatically. The following challenges await firms in their efforts to secure these benefits:

- Scale economies can be realized only by concentrating scale-sensitive resources and activities in one or a few locations. Concentration is a two-edged sword, however. For example, with manufacturing activities, concentration means that firms must export centrally manufactured goods (e.g., components, subsystems, or finished products) to various markets. In making decisions about the location of any activity, firms must weigh the potential benefits from concentration against increased transportation and tariff costs.

- One unintended result of the geographic concentration of any activity is to isolate that activity from the targeted markets. Such isolation can be risky since it may cause delayed, or inadequate, response to market needs. Another management challenge is to minimize the costs of isolation.

- Concentrating an activity in a designated location also makes the rest of the company dependent on that location. This sole-source dependence implies that, unless the location has world-class competencies, a firm may create a global mess instead of global competitive advantage. A European executive of Ford Motor Company, reflecting on the company's concentration of activities during a global integration program in the mid-1990s, said: "Now if you misjudge the market, you are wrong in 15 countries rather than only one." The pursuit of global scale economies raises the added challenge of building world-class competencies at those locations in which the activities will be concentrated.

"Now if you misjudge the market, you are wrong in 15 countries rather than only one."

- In situations where global presence stems from cross-border acquisitions, as with British Petroleum's acquisition of Amoco, realizing economies of scale requires massive restructuring. Firms must scale up at those locations where activities are to be concentrated and scale down or even close shop at the other locations. This restructuring demands large financial investment, incurs huge one-time transition costs, and always results in organizational and psychological trauma. Furthermore, scaledowns or closures may damage the company's image and relations with local governments, local customers, and local communities. On top of all this, erroneous decisions in choosing locations are usually very difficult, expensive, and time consuming to reverse. Nonetheless, firms cannot realize the advantageous economies of scale without making tough decisions. Management must be willing to undertake a comprehensive and logical analysis and then have the courage of its convictions to carry out timely and decisive action.

Exploiting economies of global scope

Global scope refers to the multiplicity of regions and countries in which a company markets its products and services. Consider the case of two hypothetical advertising agencies, Alpha and Beta, whose sales revenues are roughly comparable. Assume that Alpha offers services in only five countries, whereas Beta is in 25 countries. In this instance, we would consider the global scope of Beta to be broader than that of Alpha. Global scope is rarely a strategic imperative when vendors are serving customers who operate in just one country or customers who are global but who engage in centralized sourcing. In contrast, the economic value of global scope can be enormous when vendors are serving customers who, despite being global, need the delivery of identical or similar products and services across many markets. In fulfilling the needs of such multilocation global customers, companies have two potential avenues through which to turn global scope into global competitive advantage: providing coordinated services and leveraging their market power.[8]

Providing coordinated services to global customers. Consider three scenarios: Microsoft, as it launches a new software product in more than 50 countries on the same day and needs to source advertising services in every one of the targeted markets; McDonald's, which must source virtually identical ketchup and mustard pouches for its operations in every market; and Shell Oil, which needs to source similar process-control equipment for its many refineries around the world. In all of these examples, a global customer needs to purchase a bundle of identical or similar products and services across a number of countries. The global customer could source these products and services either from a host of local suppliers or from a single global supplier that is present in all of its markets. Compared with a horde of local suppliers, a single global supplier can provide value for the global customer through greater consistency in the quality and features of products and services

across countries, faster and smoother coordination across countries, and lower transaction costs.

Market power compared with competitors. A global supplier has the opportunity to understand the unique strategic requirements and culture of its global customer. Since it takes time to build this type of customer-specific proprietary knowledge, particularly in the case of multilocation global customers, potential competitors are initially handicapped and can more easily be kept at bay. Federal Express, a major supplier of logistics and distribution services to Laura Ashley, currently enjoys this advantage. As a global logistics provider, FedEx has had the chance to deepen its understanding of its role in Laura Ashley's value chain in all of its served markets. Such understanding is customer-specific and takes time to build. As long as FedEx continues to provide effective and efficient logistics services to Laura Ashley, this knowledge will serve as a major entry barrier for other local or global logistics suppliers.

Challenges. Despite these benefits, securing economies of global scope is not without its own challenges:

- A multilocation global vendor serving the needs of a multilocation global customer is conceptually analogous to one global network serving the needs of another global network. Every global network, however effectively managed, typically has a plethora of power centers, accompanied by competing perspectives on the optimal course of action. One of the management challenges for a global vendor is to understand the ongoing tug of war that shapes the needs and buying decisions of the customer network.

> *One of the management challenges for a global vendor is to understand the ongoing tug of war that shapes the needs and buying decisions of the customer network.*

- Even for global customer accounts, the actual delivery of goods and services must be executed at the local level. Yet local country managers cannot be given total freedom in their operations with global customer accounts. They must orient their actions around their global customers' need for consistency both in product and service features and in marketing terms and conditions. Another challenge in capturing the economies of global scope lies in being responsive to the tension between two conflicting needs: the need for central coordination of most elements of the marketing mix, and the need for local autonomy in the actual delivery of products and services.

Tapping the optimal locations for activities and resources

Even though global economies have become increasingly integrated and influenced by the media so that cultures take on many of the same aspects, most countries will continue to be largely heterogeneous for years to come. Intercountry heterogeneity has an impact on the need for local adaptation in a company's products and services. But differences across countries also reveal themselves in the form of differences in cost structures and skill levels. A firm that can exploit these intercountry differences better than its competitors has the potential to create significant proprietary advantage.[9]

In performing the various activities along its value chain (e.g., R&D, procurement, component manufacturing, assembly, marketing, sales, distribution, and service), every firm has to make a number of crucial decisions, including where the activity will take place. Optimizing the location for every activity in the value chain can yield one or more of three strategic benefits: performance enhancement, cost reduction, and risk reduction.

> **Optimizing the location for every activity in the value chain can yield one or more of three strategic benefits: performance enhancement, cost reduction, and risk reduction.**

Performance enhancement. Fiat's decision to choose Brazil, rather than its native Italy, to design and launch the Palio, its "world car," and Microsoft's decision to establish a corporate research laboratory in Cambridge, U.K., are good examples of location decisions that were guided predominantly by the goal of building and sustaining world-class excellence in the selected activities. Location decisions can affect the quality with which any activity is performed in terms of availability of needed talent, speed of learning, and the quality of external and internal coordination.

Cost reduction. Two examples of location decisions founded predominantly on cost-reduction considerations are: Nike's decision to source the manufacture of athletic shoes from Asian countries such as China, Vietnam, and Indonesia; and the decision of Texas Instruments to set up a software development unit in India. Location decisions can

affect the cost structure in terms of the cost of local manpower and other resources, the cost of transportation and logistics, as well as government incentives[10] and the local tax structure.[11]

Risk reduction. Given the wild swings in exchange ratios between the U.S. dollar and the Japanese yen (in relation to each other as well as to other major currencies), a critical basis for cost competition between Ford and Toyota has been their relative ingenuity at managing currency risks. For these competitors, one of the ways to manage currency risks has been to spread the high-cost elements of their manufacturing operations across a few select and carefully chosen locations around the world. Location decisions can affect the risk profile of the firm with respect to currency, economic, and political risks.[12]

Challenges. There are challenges associated with using geographical differences to create global competitive advantage:

- The way in which activities are performed depends not only on the characteristics of the factor inputs but also on the management skills with which these inputs are converted into value-added outputs. The choice of a seemingly optimal location cannot guarantee that the quality and cost of factor inputs will be optimal. Managers must ensure that the comparative advantage of a location is captured and internalized rather than squandered because of weaknesses in productivity and the quality of internal operations. Ford Motor Company has amplified the proprietary advantage of locating some of its manufacturing operations in Mexico. People often assume that, in countries such as Mexico, lower wage rates come side-by-side with lower productivity. While this may be true statistically for the country as a whole, it does not have to be so for a specific firm. Because unemployment in Mexico is higher than in the U.S., Ford can be more selective about whom it hires in its Mexican operations. Given lower turnover of employees, the company can also invest more in training and development. Thus the net result can be not just lower wage rates but also higher productivity than in the U.S.

- The optimality of any location hinges on the cost and quality of factor inputs at this location relative to all other locations. This fact is important because countries not only evolve over time, but do so at different rates and in different directions. Thus for any particular activity, today's choice location may no longer be optimal three years down the road. A relentless pursuit of optimal locations requires the global company to remain somewhat footloose. Nike continuously assesses the relative attractiveness of various manufacturing locations and has demonstrated a willingness and ability to shift locations over time. Managers should not let today's location decisions diminish the firm's flexibility in shifting locations as needed.

- Optimal locations will generally be different for different resources and activities. Yet another challenge in fully capturing the strategic benefits of optimal locations is to excel at coordination across dispersed locations. Texas Instruments' high-speed telecommunications chip, TCM9055, was conceived in collaboration with engineers from Sweden, designed in France using software tools developed in Houston, produced in Japan and Dallas, and tested in Taiwan.[13]

Texas Instruments' high-speed telecommunications chip, TCM9055, was conceived in collaboration with engineers from Sweden, designed in France using software tools developed in Houston, produced in Japan and Dallas, and tested in Taiwan.

Maximizing knowledge transfer across locations

Foreign subsidiaries can be viewed from several perspectives. One way to view Marriott's subsidiary in the U.K. is in terms of its market position within the U.K.'s hotel industry. An alternate view of Marriott U.K. would be as a package of tangible assets, such as buildings, equipment, and capital. Yet another view would be to see Marriott U.K. as a reservoir of knowledge in areas such as real estate development, revenue management, hotel operations, and customer service. Building on this last perspective, we can view every global company not only as a portfolio of subsidiaries with tangible assets, but also as a portfolio of knowledge centers.

Given the heterogeneity of countries, every subsidiary has to create some degree of unique knowledge to exploit the resource and market opportunities of the local environment. Of course, not all locally created knowledge is relevant outside the local environment. For example, the ability to execute advertising in the Japanese language has little or no value outside Japan. However, other types of locally created knowledge may be relevant across multiple countries, and, if leveraged effectively, can yield strategic benefits to the global enterprise, rang-

ing from faster product and process innovation to lower cost of innovation and reduced risk of competitive preemption.[14]

Faster product and process innovation. All innovation requires the incorporation of new ideas, whether they are developed internally or acquired and absorbed from others. A global company's skill at transferring knowledge across subsidiaries gives these subsidiaries the added benefit of innovations created by their peers. By minimizing, if not altogether eliminating, counterproductive reinvention of the wheel, product and process innovations get accelerated across the entire global network. Procter & Gamble's highly successful launch of Liquid Tide in the U.S. market in the late 1980s occurred at least partly because the development of this product incorporated technologies pioneered in Cincinnati (a new ingredient to help suspend dirt in wash water), Japan (cleaning agents), and Brussels (ingredients that fight the mineral salts present in hard water).[15]

Lower cost of innovation. A second by-product of not reinventing the wheel is considerable savings in the costs of innovation. For example, the efficient stocklist-based distribution system developed by Richardson Vicks's Indian operations, now a part of Procter & Gamble India, found ready applicability in the company's Indonesian and Chinese operations.[16] Such cross-border replication of an innovation from one country to another eliminates or at least significantly reduces the costs associated with from-the-ground-up experimentation in that country.

Reduced risk of competitive preemption. A global company that demands constant innovations from its subsidiaries but does not leverage these innovations effectively across subsidiaries risks becoming a fount of new ideas for competitors. Procter & Gamble is keenly aware of these risks. Several of P&G's subsidiaries are dedicated to improving the fit, performance, and look of the disposable diaper. Over the last decade, P&G's ability to systematically identify the successful innovations and expedite a global rollout of these innovations has thwarted competitors from stealing its new ideas and replicating them in other markets. Effective and efficient transfer of knowledge across subsidiaries has helped P&G safeguard its innovations and enabled it to significantly reduce the risk of competitive preemption.

Challenges. Most companies tap only a fraction of the full potential in realizing the enormous economic value inherent in transferring and leveraging knowledge across borders. Some of the primary reasons are:

- Knowledge transfer from one subsidiary to another cannot occur unless the source and the target units and an intermediary, such as regional or corporate headquarters, recognize the existence of unique know-how in the source unit, and the potential value of this know-how in the target unit. Since significant geographic, linguistic, and cultural distances often separate subsidiaries, the potential for knowledge transfer can easily remain buried under a sea of ignorance. Companies face the management challenge of creating mechanisms to systematically and routinely uncover the opportunities for knowledge transfer.

Since significant geographic, linguistic, and cultural distances often separate subsidiaries, the potential for knowledge transfer can easily remain buried under a sea of ignorance.

- A subsidiary with uniquely valuable know-how is likely to enjoy a knowledge monopoly within the global enterprise. Power struggles are also both normal and ubiquitous in any organization. Thus at least some subsidiaries will view uniquely valuable know-how as the currency through which they acquire and retain power. The symptoms of this pathology are most obvious in the case of manufacturing facilities where relative superiority on an internal basis often serves as survival insurance in a footloose corporation. Management must ensure that subsidiaries are enthusiastic rather than reluctant to share what they know.

- Like the knowledge-is-power syndrome, the not-invented-here syndrome is also a chronic malady in many organizations. Two of the engines of this syndrome are ego-defense mechanisms that induce some managers to block information suggesting the greater competence of others, and power struggles that lead some managers to pretend that the knowhow of peer units is neither unique nor valuable. Global enterprises committed to knowledge transfer must also address the management challenge of making subsidiaries eager rather than reluctant to learn from peer units.

- Only a subset of an organization's knowledge exists in the form of codified knowledge, such as a chemical formula, an engineering blue-

print, or an operations manual. Such codified knowledge readily lends itself to transfer and distribution across subsidiaries through electronic or other mechanisms for document exchange. However, much valuable know-how often exists in the form of tacit knowledge that is embedded in the minds, behavior patterns, and skills of individuals or teams—for example, a vision of a particular technology's future roadmap, and competencies at managing global customer accounts. With effort and investment, it might be possible to articulate and codify some of the tacit knowledge. Nonetheless, its embedded and elusive nature often makes tacit knowledge impossible to codify and thus difficult to transfer. The global enterprise must design and erect effective and efficient bridges for the transfer of knowledge (especially, noncodifiable tacit knowledge) across subsidiaries.

Creating Global Competitive Advantage: Action Implications

Focusing on the individual business as the unit of analysis, Table 1 summarizes the key issues that must be addressed to clarify the scope of each value-creation opportunity and to uncover the underlying challenges.

Exploiting any opportunity requires action. All action occurs at the level of activities in the firm's value chain. Therefore, capturing these five sources of value requires the firm to optimize on a global basis the organization and management of each value-chain activity—such as R&D, manufacturing, selling, and customer service.

As depicted in the star framework in Figure 1, creating and managing an optimal network for each value-chain activity requires optimizing network architecture, competencies at the nodes of the network, and coordination across the nodes. In other words, for any given business, exploiting global presence requires taking actions to create optimal R&D, purchasing, and manufacturing networks.[17]

Designing an optimal architecture

For any activity, network architecture refers to the number of locations in which that activity is performed, as well as the identity and specific charter of each location. Although an infinite number of choices exist, three of the most common architectural options are: concentration in one location (e.g., management of the reservation system at Marriott); differentiated centers of excellence (e.g., dedicated vehicle program centers at Ford); and

Table 1
Issues to Consider in Exploiting Global Presence

Adapting to local market differences
- Have we accurately drawn a distinction between those attributes where the customer truly values adaptation and those other attributes where the customer is either neutral or averse to adaptation?
- For those attributes where adaptation adds value, how much is the customer willing to pay for this value?
- Do we manage our product design and manufacturing activities in such a manner that we can offer the needed intercountry variety at the lowest possible cost?
- Do we have sensing mechanisms (such as market research and experimental marketing) that would give us early warning signals about increases or decreases in customers' preferences for local adaptation?

Exploiting economies of global scale
- In designing our products, have we exhausted all possibilities to utilize concepts such as modularization and/or standardization of subsystems and components?
- Have we accurately drawn a distinction between those activities that are scale-sensitive and those that are not?
- Have we fully assessed the benefits from economies of scale against any resulting increases in other costs, such as transportation and tariffs?
- Have we established effective and efficient coordination mechanisms so that we do not squander the benefits from scale economies?
- Have we built world-class competencies in the locations where we have chosen to concentrate the scale-sensitive activities?

Exploiting economies of global scope
- Is our internal coordination of marketing activities across locations at least on par with (and preferably ahead of) the extent to which our customers have integrated their own purchasing activities?
- How well do we understand the various pulls and pushes shaping the needs and buying decisions of our customer's global network?

Tapping the optimal locations for activities and resources
- Have we ensured that our location-based advantages are neither squandered nor neutralized by competitors because of any weaknesses in the quality and productivity of our internal operations at these locations?
- Do we have the organizational and resource flexibility to shift locations over time as some other locations begin to become more optimal than our current locations?
- How frictionless is the degree of our coordination across the various locations?

Maximizing knowledge transfer across locations
- How good are we at routinely and systematically uncovering the opportunities for knowledge transfer?
- How enthusiastic are our subsidiaries to share knowledge with other units?
- How eager are our subsidiaries to learn from any and all sources including peer subsidiaries?
- How good are we at codifying the product and process innovations generated by our subsidiaries? Have we built efficient communication mechanisms for the sharing of codified know-how across locations? How good are we at keeping codified knowledge proprietary to our company?
- Have we built effective mechanisms (e.g., people transfer, face-to-face interchange) for the transfer of tacit knowledge across locations?

dispersion to regional or local units (e.g., recruitment and training at McDonald's).

While activity architecture will shape organization structure decisions, it is not the same thing as organizational structure. For example, Honda's decision to build a design center in Italy is an activity-architecture decision. In contrast, organizational structure deals with such questions as who should report to whom (e.g., who should have direct control over the Italian design center—country manager for Honda Italy, president of Honda Europe, or the corporate design chief?). Because they require commitment of investment on the ground, architectural choices are less reversible than structural ones. Therefore, getting the activity architecture right is far more important than getting the organization structure right.

The issues that must be addressed in designing an optimal global architecture are: Does the number of locations where this activity will be per-

formed ensure critical mass at each location and full exploitation of economies of scale? For each activity, does the choice of locations optimize both the quality with which this activity will be performed, and its cost competitiveness, while minimizing the political, economic, and currency risks associated with it? Is the charter of each location defined in a way that eliminates unneeded duplication across locations?

Reassessing the optimality of activity architecture on a periodic basis is essential. Some of the important factors that can render today's optimal architecture less than desirable tomorrow are: shifts in factor-cost differences across countries, changes in tariff regimes, trends in demand patterns across countries, variations in product design, and adoption of new manufacturing technologies. In 1997, Asea Brown Boveri's declaration that it would shift thousands of jobs from Western Europe to the emerging economies over the next five

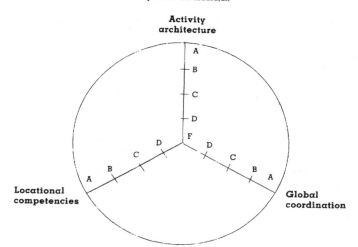

Activity architecture

A
B
C
D
F
D   D
C   C
B   B
A   A

Locational competencies

Global coordination

A- Best in industry (Ideal)
B- Above average (Good)
C- Industry average Satisfactory)
D- Below average (Poor)
F- Worst in industry (Totally unsatisfactory)

FIGURE 1
Drivers of Global Value: The Star Framework

years illustrates the need for such ongoing reassessment. The company believed that this shift in manufacturing architecture would increase efficiency, take greater advantage of lower labor costs in the emerging economies, and heighten the company's responsiveness to customers in its largest growth markets.[18]

Building World-Class Competencies

Once a firm has chosen the locations at which a particular activity will be performed, the next step is to build the requisite competencies at those locations. Otherwise, the firm could easily lose all of the gains from creating a seemingly optimal architecture. As a hypothetical example, take an American heavy machinery company that has a significant European presence and two production centers, in Germany and in France, each supplying about 50 percent of its European market needs. With labor costs a significant portion, say 21 percent, of the total cost structure, the CEO weighs the option of consolidating all European production resources into one new facility in Spain. The CEO anticipates about a 12-percent net reduction in the total cost structure: a five-percent saving due to

consolidating the two factories, and a seven-percent saving coming from the one-third reduction in labor costs that would result from lower manufacturing wages in Spain. Is this change in the architecture of the firm's European manufacturing operations the right move?

Despite the attraction of the projected reduction, the CEO should make this change only when confident that labor productivity in the Spanish plant will be greater than 67 percent of the average labor productivity in the existing German and French plants; the indirect effect of labor on other costs (e.g., raw material usage and machine utilization) will be either neutral or positive; and the quality and performance of products will remain world-class.

Many countries with relatively lower wage rates also suffer from lower levels of productivity. Nonetheless, companies should resist becoming prisoners of the aggregate statistics. It is often possible for a company to locate production in a low-labor-cost country and still achieve world-class productivity and quality levels. Both Motorola and Siemens have done this in China. This fortuitous combination of low labor costs and world-class operations is particularly feasible under the following conditions: the developing economy, despite its relative poverty, has a large pool of highly educated workers (as in India, China, and the Philippines); high unemployment levels furnish the multinational firm with a very talented and motivated pool of employees; and the company is setting up greenfield operations, where it is possible to establish world-class processes from day one, a task that often is far easier than shaking up the status quo in a well-entrenched organization.

> *It is often possible for a company to locate production in a low-labor-cost country and still achieve world-class productivity and quality levels.*

As one would expect, the greater a business's dependence on a particular location, the greater is the need to have world-class competencies in the relevant activities there. The importance of any location is likely to be very high when it is the sole location, or one of only a few locations where the activity is concentrated, as is often true in the case of upstream activities such as R&D and manufacturing. But even in the case of downstream activities, such as sales, that are often dispersed across many locations, world-class market-sensing and selling competencies are critical, especially in the major markets. For example, any weakness in Ikea's market-sensing competencies in a moderately sized market such as Spain would be far less costly for the company than in such megamarkets as the U.S. or China. Ikea's initial setbacks in the U.S. market can be attributed in part to major blindspots in its market-sensing capabilities.[19]

Ensuring frictionless coordination

The final component in creating an optimal global network is to develop and maintain smooth, seamless coordination across locations. The worldwide business team needs to foster operational coordination between units performing similar activities (e.g., two R&D labs or two production centers), as well as those performing complementary activities (e.g., manufacturing and procurement and manufacturing and marketing), and the transfer of knowledge and skills across locations. The pursuit of seamless coordination along these dimensions requires creating eagerness among those managers whose cooperation is essential, and setting up mechanisms that will put the desired cooperation into practice.

Some of the high-leverage organizational mechanisms to create eagerness for cooperation among managers working in different subsidiaries are:

- Using an incentive system that links at least part of the subsidiary managers' rewards to the firm's regional or global performance. For instance, Procter & Gamble gives explicit weight to both country and regional performance in computing annual incentive payments to country managers.[20]
- Instituting a bench-marking system that routinely compares the performance of relevant subsidiaries along key indicators and makes these comparisons visible to the subsidiaries and their corporate superiors. A system of this kind puts the spotlight and pressure on the weak performers, encouraging them to learn from peers. For example, the typical business area headquarters within Asea Brown Boveri distributes internally detailed monthly information on critical parameters such as failure rates, throughput times, inventory turns, and days receivables for each factory belonging to the business area. ABB management believes that these reports put even more intense pressure on the managers than external marketplace competition.[21]
- Giving high visibility to individuals who achieve excellent business results through collaboration with peers in other subsidiaries. For instance, Procter & Gamble regularly publicizes as success models those managers who demonstrate a zest for and ability to succeed at cross-border coordination.[22]

Some high-leverage mechanisms to make cooperation feasible are:

- Formal rules and procedures that enhance communication. Examples would be standard formats for reports, common terminology and language, and routine distribution of the reports to the relevant managers. Asea Brown Boveri's ABACUS system is an outstanding example of a formal communication system that works.[23]
- Global or regional business teams, functional councils, and similar standing committees that routinely bring key managers from various subsidiaries into face-to-face communication with each other. IBM's Global Software Team[24] and Ford's Capstone Project Team[25] are examples of effective coordination forums.
- Corporate investment in cultivating interpersonal familiarity and trust among the key managers of various subsidiaries. Managers from different subsidiaries can be brought together in executive development programs, managers

can be rotated across locations, and language skills can be developed among these managers so that these get-acquainted encounters have high leverage. Motorola's Global Organizational Leadership Development (GOLD) program brings together 30 executives at a time from various subsidiaries within the Paging Group. Similarly, Unilever has long used rotation of managers across countries, as well as its Four Acres management-training center.[26]

Table 2 summarizes the typical criteria for assessing the optimality of any global network according to activity architecture, competencies at the nodes, and coordination across the nodes.

A Two-Step Approach to Building Global Advantage

General Motors, Ford, Toyota, and DaimlerChrysler were locked in a battle for global dominance in the automobile industry in 2001. Which firm will dominate five or 10 years in the future depends largely on the ability of each to convert its global presence into global competitive advantage.

Managers should never assume that global presence by itself is the same as global competitive advantage. Having global presence implies that a firm has available to it five distinct opportunities to create global competitive advantage: local adaptation, global scale, global scope, location, and knowledge advantage. Realizing these opportunities requires firms to adopt a two-step approach for analysis and action. They should first evaluate the optimality of the global network for each activity in the value chain along three dimensions: activity architecture, locational competencies, and global coordination. Based on this evaluation, firms should then design and execute actions to eliminate, or at least reduce, the suboptimalities.

Table 2
Assessment of Global Competitive Advantage

Basis for global advantage	Typical criteria for assessment
Optimal architecture (for each value-chain activity)	• What is the size of the asset and employment base? • Have we captured economies of scale and scope in manufacturing, subcontracting, and raw material purchases? Are there any diseconomies of scale? • Do we have the needed sales and distribution strength in all key markets? Are our distribution systems too concentrated or too dispersed? • Do we have the needed critical mass in each key technology area? Is there unneeded duplication across technology centers? • Do locational choices automatically create push for excellence in the particular activity (e.g., miniaturization in Japan)? • Do we have critical talent available? • What will be the total impact on overall cost structure? • What will be the impact of government inducements and tax considerations? • What are the currency and political risks?
World-class competencies (by function; for each facility)	• Do we define quality from our customer's point of view? • Do we define quality narrowly (e.g., product durability only) or broadly (quality of products, services, and overall management)? • Do we use measurable indicators of quality or operate on gut feel? • Do we constantly compare ourselves with external benchmarks? • How do we compare with competitors on key attributes of quality- and time-based competition? • In delivering quality and speed, are we improving at a slower or faster rate than the competition?
Frictionless coordination (between similar activities; between complimentary activities)	• How direct and frictionless are the communication channels for customers' priorities and concerns to be heard, not just by marketing but also production and R&D personnel? • How direct and frictionless are the communication channels between units performing complementary activities? Between units performing similar activities? • Do reward systems encourage or discourage needed coordination? • Has the company created a frictionless internal market for ideas that rewards both the producers and the buyers of a great idea? Is the head office active or sleepy in carrying out its knowledge-broker responsibilities?

Endnotes

[1] Tomkins, R. Battered PepsiCo licks its wounds. *The Financial Times*, 30 May 1997, 26.

[2] Our ideas in this section build on and extend the work of many scholars in the area of global strategy, including Caves, R.E. 1982. *Multinational enterprise and economic analysis.* Cambridge, U.K.: Cambridge University Press; Ghoshal, S. 1987. Global strategy: An organizing framework. *Strategic Management Journal*, 8: 425–440; and Porter, M.E. 1994. Global strategy: Winning in the world-wide marketplace. In L. Fahey & R.M. Randall, (Eds.), *The portable MBA in strategy*: 108–141. New York: John Wiley.

[3] For an analysis of how local market differences affect entry strategies, see Root, F. 1994. *Entry strategies for international markets.* New York: Lexington Books.

[4] As business goes global, so does *BusinessWeek*. *BusinessWeek*, 1 July 1996.

[5] For Coca-Cola in Japan, things go better with milk. *Wall Street Journal*, 20 January 1997, B1.

[6] Remarks by John Pepper, chairman and CEO, Procter & Gamble, to MBA class at Tuck School, Dartmouth College, Hanover, NH, May 1995.

[7] See Chandler, A.D. 1990. *Scale and scope: The dynamics of industrial capitalism.* Cambridge, MA: Harvard University Press.

[8] For an interesting case study on a company's efforts at capturing the economies of global scope, see Malnight, T.W. 1994. *Citibank: Global customer management.* Case No. 9-395-142. Boston: Harvard Business School.

[9] For a recent review of the research literature dealing with choice of locations by multinational enterprises, see Dunning, J.H. 1998. Location and the multinational enterprise: A neglected factor? *Journal of International Business Studies*, 29, 1: 45–66. See also Porter, M.E. 1994. The role of location in competition. *Journal of Economics and Business*, 1(1): 35–39.

[10] See, for example, Globerman, S. & Shapiro, D.M. 1999. The impact of government policies on foreign direct investment: The Canadian experience. *Journal of International Business Studies*, 30(3): 513–532.

[11] See Dunne, K.M. & Rollins, T.P. 1992. Accounting for goodwill: A case analysis of U.S., U.K., and Japan. *Journal of International Accounting, Auditing, and Taxation*, 2: 191–207.

[12] See, for example, Miller, K.D. & Reuer, J.J. 1998. Firm strategy and economic exposure to foreign exchange rate movements. *Journal of International Business Studies*, 29(3): 493–514.

[13] Texas Instruments' global chip payoff. *BusinessWeek*, 7 August 1995.

[14] See Gupta, A.K. & Govindarajan, V. 1991. Knowledge flows and the structure of control within multinational corporations. *Academy of Management Review*, 16(4): 768–792; Gupta, A.K. & Govindarajan, V. 2000. Knowledge flows within multinational corporations. *Strategic Management Journal*, 21: 473–496; Nobel, R. & Birkinshaw, J. 1998. Innovation in multinational corporations: Control and communication patterns in international R&D operations. *Strategic Management Journal*, 19(5): 479–496; and Kogut, B. & Zander, U. 1992. Knowledge of the firm, combinative capabilities, and the replication of technology. *Organization Science*, 3(2): 383–397.

[15] Ingrassia, P. Industry is shopping abroad for good ideas to apply to products. *The Wall Street Journal*, 29 April 1985, 1.

[16] Gurcharan Das. 1993. Local memoirs of a global manager. *Harvard Business Review*, March–April: 46.

[17] Our ideas in this section build on the work of Kogut, B. 1985. Designing global strategies: Comparative and competitive value-added chains *Sloan Management Review*, 15–28; and Porter, M.E. 1986. *Competition in global industries.* Boston: Harvard Business School Press.

[18] Wagstyl, S. & Hall, W. ABB to cut jobs in Western Europe. *The Financial Times*, 9 June 1997, 1.

[19] Furnishing the world. *The Economist*, 19 November 1994, 79–80.

[20] Pepper remarks, op. cit.

[21] Taylor, W. 1991. The logic of global business: An interview with ABB's Percy Barnevik. *Harvard Business Review*, March–April.

[22] Pepper remarks, op. cit.

[23] Taylor, op. cit.

[24] Pepper remarks, op. cit.

[25] Wetlaufer, S. 1999. Driving change: An interview with Ford Motor Company's Jacques Nasser. *Harvard Business Review*, March–April: 76–88.

[26] Maljers, F. A. 1992. Inside Unilever: The evolving transnational company. *Harvard Business Review*, September–October.

Anil K. Gupta is a distinguished scholar-teacher and professor of strategy and global e-business at the Robert H. Smith School of Business, The University of Maryland at College Park. His research interests focus on managing in the digital age, managing globalization, and the quest for synergy. He is coauthor, with Vijay Govindarajan, of *The Quest for Global Dominance*, published by Jossey-Bass in 2001. Contact: *agupta@rhsmith.umd.edu*.

Vijay Govindarajan is the Earl C. Daum 1924 Professor of International Business and director of the William F. Achtmeyer Center for Global Leadership at the Tuck School of Business at Dartmouth College. He is also the faculty director for the Global Leadership 2020 Program. He is coauthor, with Anil Gupta, of *The Quest for Global Dominance*, published by Jossey-Bass in 2001. Contact: *vg@dartmouth.edu*.

Executive Commentary

....

Peter Roche
The London Perret Roche Group LLC

In a speech to the British-American Chamber of Commerce in March 1999, John Zeglis, then president of AT&T, said, "You are only going to have two kinds of companies in the future: those that go global and those that go bankrupt."[1] Zeglis's view appears to be widely shared, as there are now over 130 countries involved in global trade. Governments are lowering trade barriers with free trade agreements. Global bankers, like The World Bank and the IMF are eager to finance this internationalization of business. Further, a host of service providers and suppliers have declared themselves "global enterprises," as they step beyond their home shores to compete in the world market.

The management implications are significant for these entities. Competition is soaring. The complexity of the entity to be managed has increased exponentially because of sheer scale, business laws, business ethics, accounting procedures, and divergent cultures and habits, to name a few. The speed at which best practices are emulated is breathtaking—making that source of advantage less sustainable. Conducting business successfully in this environment requires a new business model.

The global enterprise described by Gupta and Govindarajan is a new species of organization. It is not the familiar multinational enterprise (MNE) simply expanded to a larger set of geographical locations. Rather, it is a new way of organizing designed for competitive advantage. What distinguishes a global enterprise with a competitive advantage from an MNE? According to Gupta and Govindarajan the differences are: how managers take advantage of economies of scale, rationalize production, develop a worldwide management talent pool, engage in R&D, and exchange knowledge and best practices across the globe. Many mergers designed to produce global entities have failed because they did not understand the distinctions between MNEs and global enterprises. They did not leverage the five "opportunities" outlined by Gupta and Govindarajan in their article: adapting to local market differences, exploiting economies of scale, exploiting economies of global scope, tapping the optimal locations for activities and/or resources, and maximizing knowledge transfer across locations. These opportunities are at the heart of Gupta and Govindarajan's framework. Their framework is not simplistic. Nor is it a clear-cut prescriptive set of dos and don'ts. Each of the five opportunities has multiple facets, challenges, and obstacles for each business and market. In other words, there is no single right answer, such as "always adapt the product to the local market." TGIF Fridays discovered this in South Korea, when it added local dishes to its menus. The restaurant found that local customers thought of a visit to TGIF as being a visit to America and they did not want to be served South Korean food. According to Gupta and Govindarajan, the right answer for any particular business could be adapting a little, adapting a lot, or not adapting at all. Moreover, the right answer could change over time.

> ### Many mergers designed to produce global entities have failed because they did not understand the distinctions between MNEs and global enterprises.

Gupta and Govindarajan's framework suggests that, to be successful, businesses should institute an ongoing process of discovery, along with rigorous thinking and thoughtful application across the entire firm. Their framework is not a short-cut to *the* solution. At one point in my career I was an executive with an organization that manufactured products for the construction industry around the world. Applying Gupta and Govindarajan's framework to this business, it is clear that we did abide by one of their key recommendations—we adapted to local market differences for one customer but not for another. More specifically, for construction industry customers we adapted to the local language and how the products were packaged and shipped. For the home improvement industry, which sold many of the same products, but to a different set of customers, we needed many more adaptations from one market to the next. Many of these adaptations were a result of variable retail practices and different rules about product labeling. In both cases we competed very successfully. Yet in other circumstances, the organization's thinking was essentially MNE. That is, many of our adaptations to local markets were not optimal. Clearly, we were not always systematic in exploiting the five opportunities presented in Gupta and Govindarajan's framework.

Based on Gupta and Govindarajan's model, there are many powerful questions companies should ask themselves: Are you clear about the difference between an MNE and a global enterprise with a competitive advantage? If there were a scale with MNE at one end and global enterprise with a competitive advantage at the other, where would your company fall? Finally, what are the best leverage opportunities for your business? How these questions are answered just might inspire an organization to change the way it conducts its global business.

Endnote

[1] http://www.att.com/speeches/item/0,1363,930,00.html.

Peter Roche is the managing partner and cofounder of The London Perret Roche Group LLC (LPR), an international management consulting firm dedicated to the development of extraordinary leadership and the systematic transformation of global enterprises. Prior to founding LPR 16 years ago, he was a board member and CEO of a U.K.-based multinational company. Contact: proche@lprgroup.com.

[24]

HR Issues and Activities in Mergers and Acquisitions

RANDALL SCHULER, *Rutgers University, New Jersey*
SUSAN JACKSON, *Rutgers University, New Jersey*

Mergers and acquisitions are increasingly being used by firms to strengthen and maintain their position in the market place. They are seen by many as a relatively fast and efficient way to expand into new markets and incorporate new technologies. Yet their success is by no means assured. To the contrary, a majority fall short of their stated goals and objectives. While some failure can be explained by financial and market factors, a substantial number can be traced to neglected human resource issues and activities. Numerous studies confirm the need for firms to systematically address a variety of human resource issues and activities in their merger and acquisition activities. This article proposes a three-stage model of mergers and acquisitions that systematically identifies several human resource issues and activities. Numerous examples are offered to illustrate the issues and activities in each of the three stages. The article concludes with a description of the role and importance of the HR department and leader.

Keywords: Mergers, Acquisitions, Human resource issues, Strategic alliances

Introduction

Companies today need to be fast growing, efficient, profitable, flexible, adaptable, future-ready and have a dominant market position. Without these qualities, firms believe that it is virtually impossible to be competitive in today's global economy. In some industries such as insurance or banking, firms may move into new markets. In others such as pharmaceuticals or software technology, firms may work with smaller firms that have developed or are developing new products that they can manufacture and/or distrib-

ute more efficiently, while other firms focus on their own internal growth, leadership and development. Regardless of industry, however, it appears that it has become all but impossible in our global environment for firms to compete with others without growing and expanding through deals that result in mergers or acquisitions (Lucenko, 2000; Galpin and Hemdon, 1999; Deogun and Scannell, 1998, 2001). The deals between many of the largest and most successful global firms such as Daimler–Chrysler, Chase–J.P. Morgan, McKinsey–Envision, UBS–Paine Webber, Credit Sussie–DLJ, Celltech–Medeva, SKB–Glaxo, NationsBank–Bank of America, AOL–Time Warner, Pfizer–Warner Lambert, Nestlé–Purina, Deutsche Telekom–Voice Stream and GE–Honeywell attest to this belief (Seriver, 2001; Fairlamb, 2000a; Lowry, 2000; Tierney and Green, 2000; Vlasic and Stertz, 2000a; Timmons, 2000; McLean, 2000; Ewing, 2000a,b,c; Barrett, 2000a; Silverman, 2001; Tompkins, 2001). And the future appears to be ripe for a continuation of the trend for annual increases in merger and acquisition (M&A) activity:

I personally see more consolidation: more partnerships, more strategic alliances, and more acquisitions. Jac Nasser, CEO, Ford Motor (Taylor, 2000)

And why not? The factors that have driven the M&A activity in the past decade are forecast only to intensify: need for large economies of scale, deregulation, globalization, expanding markets, risk spreading, and need for rapid response to market conditions. Even in a tough financial environment and a declining stock market in 2000, the value of global mergers and acquisition exceeded $3.5 billion for the first time (Taylor, 2001).

As a consequence of these realities, companies have become better at doing deals. Several have trained staff who can facilitate mergers and acquisitions quickly, efficiently and thoroughly such as Michael Volpi at Cisco Systems (Holson, 2000; O'Reilly and Pfeffer, 2000) However, according to Jack Procity, partner-in-charge of business integration services at KPMG, many companies still have a long way to go when it comes to effectively integrating their businesses:

This might be OK for a $1 billion business taking on a $10–$30 million acquisition. But a $1 billion company taking another $1 billion company has to make it work. The business risk is too great for failure.[1]

Some cite recent mergers and acquisitions as evidence for this, e.g., Conseco and Greentree Financial; Case and New Holland; HRS and CUC International; DaimlerChrysler; McKession and HBO; and Mattel and The Learning Company (Arndt 2000a, 2001; Sirower, 1997; Weber and Barrett, 1999). Evidence beyond these specific examples suggests that they are more the norm than the exception (Charman, 1999).

Thus many companies seem to be confronted with the need to do mergers and acquisitions successfully, yet the odds of doing so are relatively low. These odds, however, can be increased: some companies are quite successful in mergers and acquisitions. Yes, experience helps, but it is the learning from the experience that seems to be critical (Ashkenas *et al.*, 2000). In general, what their experiences appear to suggest is that firms that have a systematic approach to deal making are more likely to be successful. Underlying this successful approach is the recognition of attention to many people issues (a.k.a., human capital) that exist throughout the stages of mergers and acquisitions. The purpose of this article is to articulate a systematic, people-oriented, approach for effectively doing mergers and acquisitions from beginning to integration and post-integration. We begin by identifying the types of mergers and acquisitions, the reasons for their successes and failures, and the many people issues involved. Then a three-stage model is described. This is followed by an overview of the implication for the Human Resource (HR) Departments and HR Professionals.

Mergers and Acquisitions

Mergers and acquisitions represent the end of the continuum of options companies have in combining with each other. Representing the least intense and complex form of combination is licensing. Next come alliances and partnerships and then joint ventures. Mergers and then acquisitions conclude the combination options. It is the mergers and acquisitions that are the combinations that have the greatest implications for size of investment, control, integration requirements, pains of separation, and people management issues (Doz and Hamel, 1998; Hamel, 1991; Harbison, 1996; Sparks, 1998, 1999). With our focus

on mergers and acquisitions, it is important to distinguish them. In a merger, two companies come together and create a new entity. In an acquisition, one company buys another one and manages it consistent with the acquirer's needs.

Types

Further implications for people management issues are types of mergers and acquisitions. In general there are mergers of equals which include the merger between Citicorp and Travellers forming Citigroup; and between Ciba and Sandoz forming Novartis. There are also mergers between unequals such as between Chase and J.P. Morgan creating JPMorgan-Chase.[2] Similarly there are two major types of acquisitions: those involving acquisition and integration such as those typically made by Cicso Systems; and those involving acquisition and separation such as between Unilever and Bestfoods. Acknowledging these types of mergers and acquisitions is critical in describing and acting upon the unique people management issues each has. For example, a merger of equals often compels the two companies to share in the staffing implications; whereas a merger of unequals results in the staffing implications being shared unequally (Kay and Shelton, 2000). An acquisition that involves integration has greater staffing implications than one that involves separation. Other differences are highlighted later in this article.

Reasons

There are numerous reasons for companies to merge or acquire. Some of the most frequent include:

❖ Horizontal mergers for market dominance; economies of scale
❖ Vertical mergers for channel control
❖ Hybrid mergers for risk spreading, cost cutting, synergies, defensive drivers
❖ Growth for world-class leadership and global reach
❖ Survival; critical mass
❖ Acquisition of cash, deferred taxes, and excess debt capacity
❖ Move quickly and inexpensively
❖ Flexibility; leverage
❖ Bigger asset base to leverage borrowing
❖ Adopt potentially disruptive technologies
❖ Financial gain and personal power
❖ Gaining a core competence to do more combinations
❖ Talent, knowledge, and technology today[3]

Of these, it appears that the last one is rising in its level of importance:

There are two factors that will bring companies to the table this year (2001). First, although unemployment is rising, engineers and scientists are still in high demand, so much so that semiconductor and optical networking outfits are doing more of what bankers call HR deals (HR for Human Resource). In these acquisitions the employees are seen as more valuable than the company's product. Some banks are applying metrics like price-per-engineer to value these deals. (For example, Broadcom paid $18 million per engineer to buy chipmaker SiByte in November, a bit of a premium but far from a record.) 'HR buys are becoming more prominent. If a company can buy another firm cheap enough and pick up 50 or 100 networking engineers who have skills in technologies, it's not a bad idea,' says Mark Shafir, co-director of investment banking at Thomas Weisel Partners. These deals, though, will work only if the talent can be retained, he adds. (Creswell, 2001)

In addition, companies that are successful and inventive in combining, not only create value, but develop a core competence in combination management itself. This in turn, can give the company an edge over others who haven't been successful and/or have not learned from their past efforts.

Assumptions

Regardless of the reasons companies have for merging or combining, there are several basic assumptions being made, either explicitly or implicitly. These include:

❖ M&A's are the fastest and easiest ways to grow
❖ M&A's are likely to fall short of their initial goals
❖ M&A's are difficult to do
❖ Creating synergies is a major challenge
❖ Molding cultures is a major challenge
❖ Soft and hard due diligence are necessary but not sufficient conditions
❖ Pre-planning can help increase chances for success

It appears that companies that have gained from the experience of previous combination efforts recognize and address these assumptions more effectively than those that haven't. And the more firms have experiences, the more they appear to learn from each additional merger or acquisition, thus solidifying their core competency and competitive advantage (Ashkenas *et al.*, 2000).

Track Record

With the importance of and need for mergers and acquisitions growing, and the base of experience expanding, it may seem reasonable also to assume that success is more likely to occur than failure in these types of combinations. In fact,

Indeed, worse than this, mergers and acquisitions are more likely to fail than succeed. Statistics show that more than a staggering 75% fail. Only 15% of mergers and acquisitions in the US achieve their financial objectives, as measured by share value, return on investment, and postcombination profitability. In the European arena, a 1995 study of

large combinations — deals valued at $500 million or more — showed one-half destroyed shareholder value, 30% had minimal impact, and only 17% created shareholder returns.

In fact, more than half of the companies involved in mergers worth US $5 billion or more in 1998, underperformed in their sector. Lehman Brothers, the US investment bank, found that of 33 companies involved in mega-mergers between December 1997 and August 1998, only 14 outperformed their market in the first six months following the announcement of the combination. Of the four sectors surveyed by Lehman, financial, oil, pharmaceutical, and telecommunications, oil companies showed the weakest performance with merged entities underperforming the sector by 17.6%. Lehman's long-term analysis of 34 companies involved in high profile combinations over the last 15 years, showed more than 50% lagged behind their industry peers within 18 months of the completion of the deal.[4]

Reasons for Failure. Mergers and acquisitions fail for a variety of reasons, often several simultaneously. Typical reasons for failure include:

❖ Expectations are unrealistic
❖ Hastily constructed strategy, poor planning, unskilled execution
❖ Failure/inability to unify behind a single macro message
❖ Talent is lost or mismanaged
❖ Power and politics are the driving forces, rather than productive objectives
❖ Requires an impossible degree of synergy
❖ Culture clashes between the two entities go unchecked
❖ Transition management fails
❖ The underestimation of transition costs
❖ Financial drain
❖ Defensive motivation
❖ Focus of executives is distracted from the core business (Charman, 1999; Sparks, 1999; Doz and Hamel, 1998).

Perhaps of these, culture clashes, gaps, or incompatibility and losses of key talent are cited the most frequently, although even these become intertwined with other reasons (Bianco, 2000; Fairlamb, 2000b).

By way of an example, many outsiders believed 'from the start, the culture gap made Daimler-Chrysler's post-marriage period of adjustment more difficult than that of any other merger around' (Gibney, 1999). DaimlerChrysler believed two company cultures could simply be put in a blender and poured out as a new synergistic company. Cultural issues were all but ignored and seemed only to be addressed by executives when making broad statements to the media regarding the differences in the two companies. Either Daimler and Chrysler did not fully realize the implications of cultural differences or they chose to focus on the operational and business synergies hoping that culture would sort itself out.

Many Daimler-Benz executives initially viewed

HR ISSUES AND ACTIVITIES IN MERGERS AND ACQUISITIONS

Chrysler as a primped-up matron would regard an earnest young suitor, Chrysler marketing chief Jim Holden recalls his first meeting at the Mercedes-Benz US headquarters in Montvale, NJ. As the Germans presented their view of the brand hierarchy — Mercedes on top and everything else far, far below — the tension in the room was palpable. Says Holden: 'We felt like we were marrying up, and it was clear that they thought they were marrying down.'[5]

During the initial stages of the merger, Chrysler President Thomas Stallkamp indicated that Daimler intended to adopt Chrysler's product development methods which emphasized teamwork rather than individual-oriented work procedures. Chrysler in turn would adopt Daimler practices such as rigid adherence to timetables and their methodological approach to problem-solving. However, evidence of the lack of true sharing and cooperation was soon to emerge and could be demonstrated by Daimler executives' refusal to use Chrysler parts in Mercedes vehicles.[6]

Daimler's Chief of Passenger Cars, Juergen Hubbert, as recently as August 2000 was quoted as saying, 'We have a clear understanding: one company, one vision, one chairman, two cultures' (The Economist, 2000) While it is true that since the departure of Robert Eaton (Chrysler's former chairman) only one chairman (Juergён Schrempp) runs the company, Hubbert's other assertions are in question. Although DaimlerChrysler may be 'one' company in name, the fact remains that two separate operational headquarters were maintained; one in Michigan and one in Germany. Business operations continued to be separate as evidenced by 'Daimler's' decision to allow 'Chrysler' more leeway in the design and production of its vehicles, which more closely emulated the practices of the 'old Chrysler.' Daimler and Chrysler each had their own agenda focusing on different aspects of the automobile market, making one vision difficult to see. Finally, with the acknowledged existence of two cultures, how could DaimlerChrysler truly become one company with one vision?

By way of another example, loss of key talent is another significant reason given for a failed merger or acquisition. Consistent with NationsBank's (aka, Bank of America) strategy of acquisition, CEO Hugh McColl paid a premium price of $1.2 billion for Montgomery Securities in October 1997. Subsequently:

Most of the best investment bankers walked out after a series of rows with Montgomery's management, and culture clashes with the commercial bankers at headquarters. They are now ensconced in the thriving firm of Thomas Weisel, run by Montgomery's eponymous former boss. Though Bank of America spent a further fortune trying to revive the investment bank, Montgomery is no longer the serious force it once was in Silicon Valley. (Anon, 2000a,b)

Reasons for Success. Perhaps not surprisingly some of the major reasons for success in mergers and acquisitions include:

❖ Leadership
❖ Well-thought out goals and objectives
❖ Due diligence on hard and soft issues
❖ Well-managed M&A team
❖ Successful learning from previous experience
❖ Planning for combination and solidification steps completed early
❖ Key talent retained
❖ Extensive and timely communications to all stakeholders[7]

These reasons are corroborated by the findings of Watson Wyatt's Global M&A Survey where it is reported that the key lessons for the next M&A project suggest the need to:

❖ Develop a more realistic time scale, including allowance for the time required to prepare for effective due diligence
❖ Start the planning of integration processes sooner and get HR involved earlier
❖ Work to align expectations in the acquirer and acquired businesses
❖ Confront difficult decisions, including employee and human resource issues, earlier in the process
❖ Change managers quickly if they fail to adapt

Watson Wyatt observed a disparity between the number of respondents who felt that they had been relatively successful in their M&A experience, and the overall success rate of deals. This indicates that there is a need for companies to be more critical of their own performance in a deal to make sure that lessons are learned for the future.[8]

Thus, while there are many reasons for success and failure in mergers and acquisitions, whether in North America, Europe, or Asia, at the core of many of them are people issues.

The Human Side of M&A Activity

Plenty of attention is paid to the legal, financial, and operational elements of mergers and acquisitions. But executives who have been through the merger process now recognize that in today's economy, the management of the human side of change is the real key to maximizing the value of a deal.[9]

'Employers now recognize that human resource issues are the primary indicator of the success or failure of a deal. When we had mergers just five years ago, employers had much more leverage than they do now. The full employment economy has been a huge problem,' says Laura Carlson, a Minneapolis corporate finance lawyer at Faegre and Benson. (Armour, 2000).

The management of the human side of M&A activity, however, based upon the failure rates of M&As,

appears to be a somewhat neglected focus of the top management's attention.

'Many mergers do not create the shareholder value expected of them. The combination of cultural differences and an ill-conceived human resource integration strategy is one of the most common reasons for that failure. Given the well-publicized war for talent, I am constantly surprised by how little attention is paid to the matter of human capital during mergers,' says David Kidd, a partner at Egon Zehnder International in Chicago. (Light, 2001)

So if people issues are so critical, why are they neglected? Possible reasons include:

❖ The belief that they are too soft, and, therefore, hard to manage
❖ Lack of awareness or consensus that people issues are critical
❖ No spokesperson to articulate these issues
❖ No model or framework that can serve as a tool to systematically understand and manage the people issues; and therefore
❖ The focus of attention in M & A activity is on other activities such as finance, accounting, and manufacturing

Research, however, indicates that people issues occur at several phases or stages of M&A activity. More specifically, people issues in just the integration phase of mergers and acquisitions include: (1) retention of key talent; (2) communications; (3) retention of key managers; and (4) integration of corporate cultures.[10] From these flow numerous, more detailed people issues, e.g., evaluation and selection of duplicate managerial talent to determine who remains and who departs after the merger or acquisition. In the process of integrating corporate cultures, entire sets of human resource policies and practice from both companies may be subject to evaluation, revision, or replacement. While these human resource issues are important in M&A activity throughout the world, their importance tends to vary by the type of M&A combination. For example, if it is an acquisition that will allow for separation of the acquired company, there may be fewer evaluation, selection, and replacement decisions than in acquisitions that result in complete integration of the two companies.

In addition to these people issues in the *integration* phase of M & A activity, there are several other people issues that are evident in the phases *before* and *after* integration. Those become more evident and more manageable by detailing a model of M&A activity.

Three Stage Model of Mergers and Acquisitions

The experiences of companies in merger and acquisition activity suggest a model of M&A activity that

has three stages: (1) pre-combination; (2) combination — integration of the partners; and (3) solidification and advancement — the new entity (Charman, 1999; Habeck *et al.*, 1999). While these three stages are applicable to and encompass the larger set of business functions such as business strategy, finance, marketing, distribution, IT, and manufacturing, the issues highlighted here are those that reflect issues most closely associated with human resource management. Then to provide further focus and detail for these human resources (HR) issues in M&A activity, HR implications and actions for the several issues in each stage are identified.

Stage 1 — Pre-Combination

There are several human resource issues in this first stage of the M&A activity. While discussed together, the differences that may accompany a merger rather than an acquisition are noted. Because of the wide variation of mergers and acquisitions that are possible, however, details of all such possible differences are not fully articulated here.

In this Pre-Combination stage the most significant HR issues and their more specific implications and actions for M&A activity are illustrated in Figure 1. The HR issues are described first, followed by a discussion of the HR implications and actions.

HR Issues. As highlighted in Figure 1, an important HR issue in the Pre-Combination stage of any M&A activity is identifying the reasons to initiate the activity. As described earlier, of the many possible reasons for an M&A, a substantial number are human resource related, e.g., acquisition of key talent. At companies like Cisco and GE, retention of key talent is often the number one concern. Here the M&A is announced because a major reason for the combination is to obtain that talent in the first place (Nee, 2001).

Another important HR issue is the creation of a dedicated senior executive, such as Michael Volpi at Cisco, and a team to head the M&A process. As suggested earlier, a key reason for M&A failure is the lack of a capable leader who can focus completely on all the aspects of the M&A process, one of which is seeking out potential companies to merge with or acquire. Then after the identification of potential companies, comes the selection discussion of which one to choose. Regardless of how well the two other stages may be planned for and done, selection of the wrong partner is likely to diminish the possible success of the combination. Alternatively, selection of the right partner without a well-thought plan for managing the rest of the M&A process is also likely to diminish the possible success of the combination.[11]

A final HR issue highlighted in Figure 1 is the 'plan-

HR ISSUES AND ACTIVITIES IN MERGERS AND ACQUISITIONS

HR Issues	HR Implications and Actions
• Identifying reasons for the M & A	• Knowledge and understanding need to be
• Forming M & A team/leader	disseminated
• Searching for potential partners	• Leadership needs to be in place
• Selecting a partner	• Composition of team impacts success
• Planning for managing the process of the M and/or A	• Systematic and extensive pre-selection and selection
• Planning to learn from the process	are essential
	• Conducting thorough due diligence of all areas is vital
	• Cultural assessment
	• Planning for combination minimizes problems later
	• Creating practices for learning and knowledge
	transfer

Figure 1   Stage 1 — Pre-Combination

ning to learn from the M&A process.' According to Watson Wyatt's recent global survey:

Companies that embark on a program of M&A should build up a pool of talent, which they can redeploy to share and apply the learning gained around the organization. Similarly, they could and should be turning the knowledge and experience acquired in each deal into comprehensive, streamlined and pragmatic processes and knowledge centers, which can be applied to future deals.[12]

HR Implications and Actions. An immediate HR implication of this last HR issue is that firms that have a better understanding and knowledge base of the M&A process are likely to be more successful in their M&A activities. This understanding and this knowledge base, however, have to be shared and disseminated to have maximum impact because M&A activity is likely to affect everyone in the company, particularly if the combination results in extensive integration of the two companies. Significant HR implications result from the need to have a dedicated and skilled leader and team for M&A activities. This need is likely to be best served through the best use of a variety of HR practices working in concert, namely, recruitment, selection, development, appraisal, compensation, and labor relations.

Conducting a thorough due diligence in the M&A process also has critical HR implications: 'Many CEOs gloss over softer HR issues, including potential cultural problems, only to realize later that they've made a huge mistake,' says Mitchell Lee Marks, a San Francisco-based management consultant who has worked on more than 60 mergers over the last 15 years.[13]

Yet, the results of the extensive Watson Wyatt M&A survey concluded that the priority assigned to HR and communication in due diligence is comparatively low. Receiving more attention in due diligence are such functions as strategic business development, finance, operations, marketing, and sales.[14] While

these functions continue to be the essence of the 'hard' due diligence process, the human resource-oriented audit, the 'soft due diligence,' is gaining respect and use:

At Cooper Industries, a Houston-based manufacturer of electrical products, tools, and hardware with 28,100 employees and $3.6 billion in 1998 sales, M&A activity is a regular part of the picture. The company typically pulls the trigger on 10 to 15 deals a year, acquiring both public and private companies. George Moriarty, assistant director of pension design, typically spends several days poring over records, with the assistance of a detailed checklist. Among other things, he examines day-to-day business costs and looks for potential liability, especially related to retiree medical benefits, severance pay obligations and employment contracts for executives. When the deal involves an overseas acquisition, he often spends hours interviewing senior executives of the targeted firm.

The entire due diligence process usually takes a week to 10 days, though complex deals can require three or four weeks of analysis. Cooper Industries uses anywhere from 7 to 20 people, depending on the complexity of the due diligence. Moriarty is one of three or four HR professionals who focus on different aspects of the deal. He says, 'The idea is to understand exactly what you are buying. It's rare to spot something that kills the deal, but it isn't uncommon to uncover some information that leads to re-valuing of the deal.' Moreover, the due diligence can identify personnel who are crucial to the transaction. That allows Cooper Industries to enter long-term contracts with key executives and others, or lower the value of the deal based on the possibility that these individuals might leave for another company (Greengard, 2000, p. 69).

Consequently, cultural assessments, as an element of soft due diligence, are also becoming common (Numerof and Abrams, 1998).

Cultural assessments involve describing and evaluating the two companies' philosophies and values regarding such issues as: leadership styles; time horizons; relative value of stakeholders; risk tolerance; and the value of teamwork versus individual performance and recognition.[15] In the DaimlerChrysler combination, the importance of cultural differences, initially downplayed, became the reason for allowing the business units to function as they wished as long as they achieved their goals (Tierney, 2000; Andrews and Bradsher, 2000).

An important finding from the Watson Wyatt survey was that the above-described HR issues are best addressed through comprehensive planning and follow-through. Experience and learning from past M&A activity can help inform the planning and follow-through, but this learning process must also be well managed. Learning, knowledge sharing and transfer are acknowledged as important not only in M&A activities, but also in joint venture activity (Lei et al., 1997; Schuler, 2001). Knowledge and learning can be systematically supported by a variety of human resources practices.[16]

Stage 2 — Combination — Integrating the Companies

Although we are now at the second stage of the M&A process, it is important to acknowledge the base that has been established by the activities in the first stage. For example, for Stage 2 to be effective, it is important that planning for their integration activities be skilfully prepared in Stage 1: 'lack of integration planning is found in 80% of the M&A's that underperform' (Charman, 1999; Habeck et al., 1999).

This crucial second stage incorporates a wide variety of activities as shown in Figure 2. In general, integration is the process by which two companies combine after a merger or an acquisition is announced and pre-combination activities are completed.

Regardless of the specific area of breakdown or weakness, when poor integration occurs:

❖ Productivity drops by 50 per cent
❖ Leadership attrition soars 47 per cent within 3 years
❖ Employee satisfaction drops 14 per cent

❖ 90 per cent of high-tech mergers fail to deliver expected increases
❖ 80 per cent of employees begin to feel management cares more about financials than product quality or people[17]

Based upon the intensive J&J study of the M&A process, it was found that:

❖ A systematic, explicit integration process is at the heart of a successful acquisition
❖ All acquisitions require some degree of integration in both the area of day-to-day systems and processes and in achieving key synergies
❖ It is important to tailor what is integrated and how it is done to the specific strengths and weaknesses of the acquired company
❖ Integration efforts will differ depending on the company's characteristics
❖ Maintaining the ability to focus on the few key value drivers is a critical part of the integration process[18]

Companies the J&J study found who were particularly good at integration are listed in:

❖ *Sales and Marketing Management Best Sales Forces*: (e.g., Enron, Cisco, GE Capital, Xerox, America Online)
❖ *Fortune's* Most Admired Companies: (e.g., GE, Microsoft, Intel)
❖ *Fortune's* Best Places to Work (e.g., Deloitte and Touche, MBNA, Cisco, Microsoft)

HR Implications and Actions. Perhaps the most critical HR issue for the success of this integration stage is selection of the integration manager.[19] Combinations that were guided by the integration manager:

❖ Retained a higher % of the acquired companies' leaders
❖ Retained a higher % of the total employees
❖ Achieved business goals earlier

The results suggest several things about the integration manager:

HR Issues	HR Implications and Actions
• Selecting the integration manager	• Selecting the appropriate candidate
• Designing/implementing teams	• Creating team design and selection are critical for
• Creating the new structure/strategies/ leadership	transition and combination success
• Retaining key employees	• Communicating is essential
• Motivating the employees	• Deciding on who stays and goes
• Managing the change process	• Establishing a new culture, structure, and HR policies
• Communicating with and involving stakeholders	and practices is essential
• Deciding on the HR policies and practices	

Figure 2   Stage 2 — Combination — Integration of the Companies

HR ISSUES AND ACTIVITIES IN MERGERS AND ACQUISITIONS

❖ It is important to have an integration manager to focus exclusively on the particular acquisition or merger
❖ This person is not one of the people running the business
❖ Usually it is someone on loan to the business for a period of time to focus solely on integration issues
❖ This person helps to provide continuity between the deal team and management of the new company. Such people 'understand the company,' 'feel ownership,' and 'are passionate about making it work'
❖ The integration manager may be part of a 'steering committee' along with other top executives. This is the group responsible for setting the role, process and objectives of the integration and overseeing the progress of integration teams across various M&A projects.[20]

The roles of the integration manager are several including serving as a:

❖ Project Manager
❖ Communicator
❖ Advisor
❖ Advocate
❖ Relationship Builder
❖ Facilitator
❖ Team Leader
❖ Ombudsperson
❖ Negotiator[21]

Assisting the integration manager are integration teams (Marks and Mirvis, 2000). DaimlerChrysler created over 100 integration teams. Specific teams were assigned to various functional areas and organizational levels within the two companies.[22] J&J found that integration teams should be first focused on key priorities or value drivers:

❖ One of the first steps in the integration planning process that happens between signing and closing is to better identify those few key value drivers that will significantly impact the performance of the new acquisition
❖ Recognize that there will be a number of day-to-day systems and processes that must be integrated in order to support efforts to attain synergies. Examples are sales reporting systems, certain IT systems, access to the global e-mail network, and the distribution chain
❖ It is important to limit these activities to areas that are required to support the achievement of key synergies
❖ One J&J executive has stated: 'We only attacked things that would bring benefits to the business. We did not integrate just for the sake of integrating'
❖ Once these key areas are identified, it may help to make sure that each one of these value drivers has a team of people associated with it and those teams are tracked for their progress[23]

Another critical HR issue is the selection of a leader who will actually manage the new business combination. If an acquired business has unclear or absent leadership, the result will be crippling uncertainty, lack of direction, stalled new product development, and the postponement of important decisions. Strong leadership is essential to acquisition success — perhaps the single most important success factor. A strong leader's influence will be quickly recognized and praised.[24]

Successful leaders of the new business are described as being:

❖ Sensitive to cultural differences
❖ Open-minded
❖ Flexible
❖ Able to recognize the relative strengths and weaknesses of both companies
❖ Committed to retaining key employees
❖ Good listeners
❖ Visionary
❖ Able to filter out distractions and focus on integrating key business drivers such as R&D and customer interfaces[25]

To the extent that the acquired firm is closely integrated with the acquirer, it is critical that the leader of the acquiring company has a solid knowledge about the acquired company.

Some of the essential tasks this new business leader can perform include:

❖ Providing structure and strategy
❖ Managing the change process
❖ Retaining and motivating key employees
❖ Communicating with all stakeholders

It appears to be crucial that restructuring should be done early, fast, and once. This minimizes the uncertainty of 'waiting for the other shoe to drop.' A historical problem has been a tendency to restructure slowly and to rely heavily on people rather than structures and processes. A lesson learned by the folks at GE Capital that greatly aids successful integration is:

Decisions about management structure, key roles, reporting relationships, layoffs, restructuring, and other career-affecting aspects of the integration should be made, announced, and implemented as soon as possible after the deal is signed — within days, if possible. Creeping changes, uncertainty, and anxiety that last for months are debilitating and immediately start to drain value from an acquisition (Ashkenas *et al.*, 2000, p. 172).

The experiences at Johnson & Johnson affirm the lessons at GE Capital and suggest not to dismantle something until its use is understood and there is something to replace it with; and that restructuring should not be confused with integrating. It is one piece in a larger process. To facilitate this restructur-

HR ISSUES AND ACTIVITIES IN MERGERS AND ACQUISITIONS

ing phase, the leader can manage the process of change itself.

There is no doubting the pressure of work caused by the need to manage integration as well as 'doing the day job'. Add to that the tendency for people to resist change and the shortage of appropriately qualified management talent and you have a recipe for an over-stressed, under-performing work environment.[26]

Managing this involves preparing the staff for the change, involving them to help ensure understanding, preparing a schedule for the changes, making the changes, and then putting in place all the structures, policies and practices to support the new operation.

Integral to the integration and the activities of restructuring and change management are the activities involving staff selection, retention, and motivation; communications and cultural integration. Watson Wyatt's survey results found that:

❖ In the US, Europe, and around the world, retention of key talent, communication and cultural integration are rated most often as critical activities in the HR integration plan, as illustrated in Figure 3
❖ Cultural incompatibility is by far the most common 'bottleneck' affecting the integration process, cited by 42 per cent of European respondents
❖ Clearly, more advance planning and work done in the areas of retention, communication and cultural integration will help achieve success in M&A's[27]

The J&J study found that:

❖ Many acquired businesses lose key people after the acquisition
❖ Retention of key employees is crucial to achieving performance goals through the transition period and the long-term competitive advantage associated with specialized knowledge
❖ Uncertainty due to unclear strategy, no prior HR assessment, and insufficient communication can drive away many desirable employees

According to Kay and Shelton:

People problems are a major cause of failed mergers, and

you must ensure that most if not all of the people you want are still in place at the end of the integration period. This is best achieved by carrying out an employee selection process whose pace and substance match the kind of merger involved. (Kay and Shelton, 2000, p. 28)

This selection process needs to be closely aligned with incentives for these employees to remain. So acquiring companies today are:

❖ *Negotiating financial deals with key employees.* Senior employees may be covered by agreements that allow stock options to be exercised when there is a change in ownership. To keep these workers from taking the money and running, acquiring firms are offering new packages that vest over time.
❖ *Giving retention bonuses.* Companies are offering cash to workers who stay through a merger or until a specific project is completed.
  Florida Power, for example, has given retention bonuses to more than 200 employees to keep them on staff during this year's merger of its parent company and Carolina Power & Light. It also increased severance packages to keep employees who were worried about pending layoffs, from jumping ship prematurely.
  'It's all about helping them to stay on,' says Melanie Forbrick, a spokesperson for Florida Power in St. Petersburg. 'Overall, it's worked.'
❖ *Writing employment agreements.* Employees who get financial incentives may be asked to sign written agreements indicating they will remain with the new entity for a specific time span. The agreements are generally signed before the deal closes. 'It's really identifying your winners at all levels, in top sales, marketing, and technical leaders,' says Jeff Christian, a Cleveland-based executive recruiter.[28]

Managing the communication process is also a valuable way to retain and motivate key employees. It also plays a critical role in the process of change and the entire stage of integration. The process of communicating can take several forms:

Acquiring companies are using the Internet, internal company Intranets and e-mail to dispel rumors and keep employees updated about pending changes.

People Activity	%
Retention of key talent	76
Communication	71
Retention of key managers	67
Integration of corporate cultures	51

Source: Kay, I.T. and Shelton, M. (2000)"The People Problem in Mergers," The McKinsey Quarterly, (Number 4): 28

Figure 3   Percent of Respondents who Believe People Activity is 'Critical'

HR ISSUES AND ACTIVITIES IN MERGERS AND ACQUISITIONS

Some talk directly with the newly acquired hires they are determined to keep. When his former company, Intervu, took over Seattle-based Internet software firm Netpodium, CEO Harry Gruber met with every engineer at the newly acquired firm.

'All of our senior people went up [to the company headquarters],' Gruber says (Marks, 2000).

The J&J study found that:

❖ Communication is critically important.
❖ Where it is practised effectively, it is seen as very positive.
   Acquired companies have reported satisfaction with communication as practised by many individual J&J employees, both with the initial welcome they received from J&J, and with the communication in 'mandatory transactional' areas including benefits, options and payroll.
❖ It is important that the communication/information be proactive and correct. For example, do not say *merger* when you mean *acquisition*.[29]
❖ A lack of communication can lead to confusion, decreased productivity as acquired company employees try to learn how to function within their new corporation, high levels of uncertainty, and low morale.

A final HR issue is the need to create policies and practices for learning and knowledge sharing and transfer. As J&J found, many of the same lessons were learned repeatedly and simultaneously across business units as well as from other companies. Thus, sharing those lessons enhances integration and improves the likelihood of success. Forums for information sharing and the Intranet are tools that companies can use to facilitate the sharing knowledge.

Helping ensure that knowledge and learning are shared across units are HR policies and practices that appraise and reward employee sharing, flexibility, development and long-term orientation (McGill *et al.*, 1992).

Overall, this second stage of integration in an M&A activity is extensive and complex. Whereas Stage 1 activities set the scene for M&A activity, those in Stage 2 are the ones that make the activity come to life. Clearly there are differences here between a merger and an acquisition, differences between a merger of equals and non-equals, and differences between an acquisition with inclusion and an acquisition with separation. These differences probably impact the degree of applicability rather than the kind of activities shown in Figures 1 and 2. Nonetheless these differences must be kept in mind, particularly in the Stage 3.

Stage 3 — Solidification and Assessment of the New Entity

Particularly for a merger of equals with high levels of inclusion, there is a clear and specific new entity that is created. This new entity, the new company, e.g., DaimlerChrysler, needs to address several HR issues to ensure its viability and success. These HR issues and their implications are outlined in Figure 4.

HR Issues and HR Implications and Actions. As the new combination takes shape, it faces issues of readjusting, solidifying and fine-tuning. These issues take on varying degrees of intensity, although not importance, depending upon whether it is a merger of inclusion rather than one of separation or an acquisition of relative equals versus unequals. DaimlerChrysler, an acquisition of relative equals, provides an example. DaimlerChrysler went through this for more than two years after the formal combination was completed[30] They addressed virtually all the issues listed in Figure 4.

Shown at the top of Figure 4 is 'solidifying leadership and staffing.' During the past two years since the combination was announced Daimler has gone through several leadership changes in the Chrysler Group, as the unit is now called (Tierney, 2000; Vlasic and Stertz, 2000b).

HR Issues	HR Implications and Actions
• Solidifying leadership and staffing	• Elective leadership and staffing of the new
• Assessing the new strategies and	entity are essential
structures	• Creating and evaluating a new structure
• Assessing the new culture	• Melding two cultures needs assessment
• Assessing the new HR P & P	revision
• Assessing the concerns of stakeholders	• The concerns of all stakeholders need to be
• Revising as needed	addressed and satisfied
• Learning from the process	• The new entity must learn

Figure 4   Stage 3 — Solidification and Assessment

At the beginning of 2001, Dieter Zetsche, a veteran Daimler executive took over Chrysler's leadership, replacing a former Chrysler head James Holden. Zetsche in turn has created his own top management team composed of one Daimler veteran and five Chrysler veterans. All these changes were made because the earlier top management team of former Chrysler veterans failed in its efforts to stop the 'breathtakingly fast decline of the bottom line' (Green and Tierney, p. 48).

Similarly, the strategy and structure had to be assessed and revised. The new top management is being given more control over the Chrysler Group largely because a senior Daimler executive is running it. He and his team developed a new strategy of cost cutting by reducing supplier costs and reducing product offerings. Instead of running the Chrysler Group as a cash-rich growth business, management is managing it as a turnaround. Consequently, staff is being reduced as well. Along with this the culture changed, both to reflect the new strategy and the new leadership. Zetsche and his team are much more egalitarian: 'They are eating in the employee cafeteria rather than the executive dining room at the headquarters in Auburn Hills, Michigan' (Muller *et al.*, 2001, p. 49). This new culture, combined with the new strategy and structure, is reshaping the thrust of performance appraisal and compensation to focus more on cost cutting objectives, supplier management, flexibility and employee morale.

DaimlerChrysler CEO Jurgën Schrempp, reflecting on these changes in the post-combination stage of the acquisition, estimates that recovery will take two to four years. Initially, back in 1998 upon purchasing Chrysler, Shrempp discussed immediate global synergies and probability. Perhaps the earlier success in its acquisition of Freightliner gave him the confidence that the Chrysler acquisition would be as successful. The contrasting experiences provided DaimlerChrysler with excellent opportunities for learning.

This brief description of just one combination illustrates the HR issues and activities that can be expected to occur after the Combination Stage has been completed. Of course, change is a constant in almost any company today, as the macro factors in the global environment continue to change and present new conditions for all companies.

Role of the HR Department in M&A Activity

As illustrated in the Three-Stage Model of M&A's, there are many people issues on which the relative success or failure depends, particularly at the combination or implementation stage. Yet research indicates that only 35 per cent of senior HR executives are involved in M&A activities (Liberatore, 2000; Giles, 2000). Not surprisingly, other research reports that:

80% of combinations fail at the implementation stage as a result of the following factors; an inadequate road map, senior HR professionals brought in too little, too late; senior HR professionals lacking in either/both business/global experience; an inadequate skills base overall; and ultimately, failed organizational change. (Charman, 1999; Greengard, 2000)

Yet there are many activities that are consistent with and appropriate for the HR professional's skills and competencies. These include:

1. Developing key strategies for a company's M&A activities. 85 per cent of HR executives say they should be involved (Liberatore, 2000)
2. Managing the soft due diligence activity. This can mean:
   - ❖ Gaining knowledge of the make-up and motivation of the two workforces
   - ❖ Accessing management team of the other company
   - ❖ Conducting analysis of its organizational structure
   - ❖ Comparing benefits, compensation policies, and labor contracts of both firms
   - ❖ Assessing the cultural match between the two firms
3. Providing input into managing the process of change:
   - ❖ HR is a change champion providing the change management skills to align the right people with the appropriate knowledge and skills base to meet the shared goals of the enterprise (Charman, 1999)
4. *Advising* top management on the merged company's new organizational structure. Almost 75 per cent of HR executives think this, and only 9 per cent think that HR should have *full responsibility* (Charman, 1999)
5. Creating transition teams, especially those that will:
   - ❖ Develop infrastructure for new organization
   - ❖ Process and design systems
   - ❖ Address cultural issues
   - ❖ Provide training
   - ❖ Managing the activities associated with staffing, in particular, developing and overseeing
   - ❖ Selection processes
   - ❖ Retention strategies
   - ❖ Separation strategies
6. Overseeing the communications. Developing a communication plan aimed at realizing a vision of the new organization through:
   - ❖ Assessing issues re: audience, timing, method and message
   - ❖ Information delivery
   - ❖ Information gathering
   - ❖ Change galvanization
   - ❖ Helping employees cope with change[31]

HR ISSUES AND ACTIVITIES IN MERGERS AND ACQUISITIONS

7. Managing the learning processes, e.g.,
   ❖ Building learning into the partnership agreement
   ❖ Staffing to learn
   ❖ Setting up learning-driven career plans
   ❖ Using training to stimulate the learning process
   ❖ Responsibility for learning should be specified
   ❖ Rewarding learning activities
8. Re-casting the HR department itself:
   ❖ Develop new policies and practices consistent with vision of new organization
   ❖ Develop HR structure and staffing
   ❖ Determine service delivery model
9. Identifying and embracing *new roles* for the HR leader, namely,
   ❖ Partnership
   ❖ Change Facilitator
   ❖ Strategy Implementor
   ❖ Strategy Formulator
   ❖ Innovator
   ❖ *Collaborator*
10. Identifying and developing *new competencies*, such as those shown in Figure 5.

Conclusions

There are numerous conclusions that can be made about M&A activity, both at the company level and at the HR level.[32]

At the Company Level

❖ It is important that business and integration strategies be clear
❖ When the deal is concluded, there must be a clear vision of what the new combination will look like:
   ● How will it be structured and run?
   ● Will it be stand-alone or connected?

❖ It is important that such decisions be made as early as possible and avoid ambiguity in decision-making guidance
❖ It is critical to have a clear plan on whether to merge acquired companies or leave them alone
❖ It is important that performance expectations be reasonable and take into account market conditions, capital investment requirement, etc.
❖ The seller's picture is too often the starting point for ongoing operations (e.g., artificially inflated sales, lagging capital investment) — but is not realistic as a performance goal
❖ Inflated performance expectations can lead executives to adopt short-term focus and delay making investments in the business
❖ Financial expectations must be made clear, along with expectations with respect to other things
❖ Discovery is a broader concept than legal 'due diligence,' covering internal and external analysis, of all key functions and culture (soft and hard due diligence).
❖ Thinking through the membership of due diligence teams and the responsibilities of key participants is critical
❖ It is important to also make sure that areas such as HR, IT, Operations and R&D are represented on the teams — participation will depend upon key value drivers of the deal
❖ This has implications for capital expenditures, new product development, management retention, etc.
❖ For acquisitions or mergers in new markets, it is essential to understand market dynamics and customers

At the HR Level

❖ Companies should put their best people in charge of implementing M&A deals
❖ More emphasis needs to be placed on early planning of the integration process
❖ Difficult decisions should be dealt with quickly

Business competencies	Leadership competencies
● Industry knowledge	● Strategic analysis
● Competitor understanding	● Managing cultural diversity
● Financial understanding	● Creator of learning culture
● Global perspective/knowledge	● Planning skills
● Strategic visioning	● Adaptability
● Partner orientation	● Learning facilitator
● Multiple stakeholder sensitivity	● Value shaper
● Merger and acquisition knowledge	

Change and knowledge management competencies
   ● Consulting and communicating
   ● Group process facilitation
   ● Designing and working in flexible structure
   ● Partnering and parenting
   ● Negotiating
   ● Network building
   ● HR alignment
   ● Managing learning transfer

Figure 5   Competencies for HR Leader

HR ISSUES AND ACTIVITIES IN MERGERS AND ACQUISITIONS

❖ The time taken to complete the integration of a deal should not be underestimated

❖ Employee communications, retention of key employees and cultural integration are the most important activities in the HR area for successful M&A integration

❖ Acquired company employees often identify cultural elements (e.g., flexibility in decision-making) as integral to the company's success

❖ It is important to be sensitive to cultural differences

❖ Acquired companies often view their culture as faster moving than that of their new, larger parent

❖ It is possible that each side will perceive its culture as 'better' and does not want to give it up

❖ Unmanaged cultural differences will lead to miscommunications and misunderstandings

❖ It is also important to remember that each separate integration activity changes the acquired company in some way. It is important to recognize and preserve the important elements of the acquired company's culture

❖ HR professionals still need to prove their worth in order to get a more central role in the M&A process

❖ Companies with M&A as part of their future strategy should review how they have managed M&A deals in the past and learn from these experiences when embarking on future deals. This review should focus on:

• How to deal with inadequate information during due diligence
• Employee communication
• Identifying and dealing with integration bottlenecks

❖ M&A management can become a core competency for an HR department

Overall, with the likelihood of continued merger and acquisition activity around the world for the next several years, the future seems bright for a significant contribution to be made by the HR department and its professionals in partnership with line managers and the employees and their representatives.

Acknowledgements

The authors wish to thank Shirley Bobier, Kristin Nordfors, Sara Cooperman, Russ Biosjoly and Joanna Eriksen for assistance in the preparation of this paper.

Notes

1. Lucenko, op cit.
2. Charman; Taylor.
3. Arndt (2000b) and Charman (1999).
4. Charman (1999). A.T. Kearney study conducted in 1998 and reported in Habeck et al. (2000).
5. Ibid.
6. 'Daimler To adopt aspects of Chrysler culture, Stallkamp says,' http://detnews.com/1998/autos/9809/05/0905033.htm

7. http://www.watsonwyatt.com/homepage/eu/res/Surveys/MergersandAquisitions/0600/page 12/19/2000; Viscio et al. (1999) http://www.strategy-business.com/bestpractice/99404/page1.html (12/7/99); and Habeck et al. (2000)
8. Watson Wyatt Survey.
9. Kay and Shelton op.cit.; Gunther (2001).
10. Charman (1999); Watson Wyatt; Delta Consulting Group.
11. O'Reilly and Pfeffer, op cit; Holson, op cit.
12. Watson Wyatt.
13. Greengard (2000) and Romanchok and Arzac (2000), Holson, op cit.
14. Watson Wyatt.
15. Numerof and Abrams, op cit.
16. Watson Wyatt; Slocum and Lei (1993).
17. Survey on mergers and acquisitions conducted by the Ortho McNeil division of Johnson and Johnson under the direction of and presented by Shirley Bobier, V.P., HR, November 7, 2000. This study is referred to here as the 'J&J Study'. Also see Habeck et al. (2000).
18. J&J Study.
19. Ashkenas and Francis (2000). Delta Consulting Group Study.
20. J&J Study.
21. J&J Study.
22. Charman (1999); Vlasic, B. 'Transition teams smooth the way for big merger,' http://detnow.com/1998/autos/9809/05/09030079.htm
23. J&J Study.
24. J&J Study.
25. J&J Study.
26. Charman (1999); Bianco, op cit; Barrett (2000b) and Metha (2000)
27. Watson Wyatt; Yang (2001).
28. Armour, S. op cit.
29. J&J Study.
30. Muller et al., 2001 Gunther, op cit.
31. J&J Study.
32. Conclusions based upon the studies of J&J, Watson Wyatt, A.T. Kearney, The Delta Consulting Group, and Charman.

References

Anon (2000a). Performance Measurement During Mergers and Acquisitions Integration. The Conference Board, New York.

Anon (2000b). Employee Communication during Mergers. The Conference Board, New York.

Andrews, E. and Bradsher, K. (2000) This 1998 model is looking more like a lemon. The New York Times, November 26, section 3, pp. 1–11.

Armour, S. (2000) Merging Companies Act to keep valuable employees. USA Today, November 24, section B.

Arndt, M. (2000a) Let's talk turkeys. Business Week, December 11, pp. 44–48.

Arndt, M. (2000b) Alcoa wants one of these, and one of those.... Business Week, September 11, pp. 63–68.

Arndt, M. (2001) A merger's bitter harvest. Business Week, February 5, pp. 112–114.

Ashkenas, R.N. and Francis, S.C. (2000) Integration managers: special leaders for special times. Harvard Business Review Nov–Dec, 108–114.

Ashkenas, R.N., DeMonaco, L.J. and Francis, S.C. (2000) Making the deal real: how GE capital integrates acquisitions. Harvard Business Review Jan–Feb, 165–178.

Barrett, A. (2000a) Jack's risky last act. Business Week, November 6, pp. 40–45.

Barrett, A. (2000b) Pfitzer: how big is too big? Business Week, August 28, pp. 216–222.

Bianco, A. (2000) When a merger turns messy. Business Week, July 17, pp. 90–93.

Charman, A. (1999) Global mergers and acquisitions: the human resource challenge. International Focus (Society for Human Resource Management).

HR ISSUES AND ACTIVITIES IN MERGERS AND ACQUISITIONS

Creswell J. (2001) First cold front. *Fortune*, February 5, p. 26.

Deogun, N. and Scannell, K. (1998). *Creating and Leading Strategic Combinations*. Delta Consulting Group Inc, New York.

Deogun, N. and Scannell, K. (2001) Market swoon stifles M&A's red-hot start, but old economy supplies a surprise bounty. *The Wall Street Journal*, January 2, p. R4.

Doz, Y.L. and Hamel, G. (1998). *Alliance Advantage: The Art of Creating Value Through Partnering*. Harvard Business School Press, Boston.

Ewing, J. (2000a) Sommer's crunch. *Business Week*, December 4, pp. 144–146.

Ewing J. (2000b) Glaxo, SKB fail to inpress. http://cnnfn.com, February 16.

Ewing J. (2000c) Pfizer sees merger savings. http://cnnfn.com, December 11.

Fairlamb, D. (2000a) The continent regains its allure. *Business Week*, June 26, pp. 226–227.

Fairlamb, D. (2000b) This bank keeps growing and growing and…. *Business Week*, September 11, p. 134.

Galpin, T.J. and Hemdon, M. (2000) In *The Complete Guide to Mergers and Acquisitions*, pp. 107–108. Jossey-Bass, San Francisco.

Gibney, F. Jr. (1999) Daimler-Benz and Chrysler merge to DaimlerChrysler. *Time*, May 24, www.geocites.com/Motor City/Downs/9323/dc.htm, p. 5.

Giles, P. (2000) The importance of HR in making your merger work. *Workspan* **August**, 16–20.

Greengard, S. (2000) Due diligence: the devils in the details. *Workforce* **October**, 69.

Gunther, M. (2001) Understanding AOL's grand unified theory of the media cosmos. *Fortune*, January 8, pp. 72–82.

Habeck, M.H., Kroger, F. and Tram, M.R. (1999). *After the Merger*. Financial Times/Prentice Hall, London/New York.

Habeck, M.H., Kroger, F. and Trum, M.R. (2000). *After the Mergers: Seven Rules for Successful Post-Merger Integration*. Prentice Hall/Financial Times, New York/London.

Hamel, G. (1991) Competition for competence and inter-partner learning within international strategic alliances. *Strategic Management Journal* **12**(Special issue), 83–104.

Harbison, J.R. (1996). *Strategic Alliances: Gaining a Competitive Advantage*. The Conference Board, New York.

Holson L.M. (2000) Whiz kid: young deal maker is a force behind a company's growth. *The New York Times on the Web*, June 28.

Kay, I.T. and Shelton, M. (2000) The people problems in mergers. *The McKinsey Quarterly* **4**, 29–37.

Lei, D., Slocum, J.W. Jr. and Pitts, R.A. (1997) Building cooperative advantage: managing strategic alliances to promote organizational learning. *Journal of World Business* **32**(3), 202–223.

Liberatore, M.D. (2000) HR's relative importance in mergers and acquisitions. *Human Resource Executive*, March 2, p. 48.

Light, D.A. (2001) Who goes, who stays? *Harvard Business Review* **January**, 39.

Lowry, T. (2000) AOL Time Warner: the thrill is gone. *Business Week*, October 16, pp. 158–160.

Lucenko, K. (2000) Strategies for growth. *Across the Board* **September**, 63.

Marks, M.L. (2000) Mixed signals. *Across the Board* **May**, 21–26.

Marks, M.L. and Mirvis, P.H. (2000) Creating an effective team structure. *Organizational Dynamics* **Winter**, 35–47.

McGill, M.E., Slocum, J.W. Jr. and Lei, D. (1992) Management practices in learning organizations. *Organizational Dynamics* **Summer**, 5–17.

McLean, B. (2000) Chasing J.P. Morgan's assets and prestige. *Fortune*, October 2, p. 48.

Metha, S.N. (2000) Lucent's new spin. *Fortune*, August 14, pp. 30–31.

Muller, J., Green, J. and Tierney, C. (2001) Chrysler's rescue team. *Business Week*, January 15, pp. 48–50.

Nee E. (2001) Cisco: how it aims to keep right on growing. *Fortune*, February 5, pp. 91–96.

Numerof, R.F. and Abrams, M. M.I (1998) Integrating corporate culture from international M&A's. *HR Focus* **75**(6), 11–12.

O'Reilly, C. and Pfeffer, J. (2000). *Hidden Value: How Great Companies Achieve Extraordinary Results with Ordinary People*. Harvard Business School Press, Boston.

Romanchok, R.A. and Arzac, J.R. (2000). *Journal* **3rd quarter**, 49–56.

Schuler, R.S. (2001) HR issues in international joint ventures. *International Journal of Human Resource Management* **February**, 1–50.

Seriver A. (2001) Swiss-American bank mergers — while one works? *Fortune*, February 5, pp. 201–202.

Silverman, G. (2001) Good times ending for Bank of America. *Financial Times*, January 8, p. 19.

Sirower, M.L. (1997). *The Synergy Trap*. The Free Press, New York.

Slocum, J.W. and Lei, D. (1993) Designing global strategic alliances: integrating cultural and economic factors. In *Organizational Change and Redesign: Ideas and Insights for Improving Performance*, eds G.P. Huber and W.H. Glick, pp. 295–322. Oxford University Press, New York.

Sparks, D. (1998). *Creating and Leading Strategic Combinations*. Delta Consulting Group, New York.

Sparks, D. (1999) Partners. *Business Week*, October 25, pp. 106–112.

Taylor, A. (2000) Bumpy roads for global auto makers. *Fortune*, December 18, p. 284.

Taylor A. (2001) The great mergers wave breaks. *The Economist*, January 27, pp. 59–60.

The Economist (2000) The DaimlerChrysler emulsion, July 29–August 4 http://members.tripodasia.com.sg/batsmile/article05.html

Tierney, C. (2000) Defiant Daimler. *Business Week*, August 7, pp. 89–92.

Tierney, C. and Green, J. (2000) Daimler's Board: not exactly crisis managers. December 11, p. 47.

Timmons, H. (2000) The chase to become a financial supermarket. *Business Week*, September 25, pp. 42–44.

Tompkins, R. (2001) McKinsey moves deeper into branding. *Financial Times*, January 15, p. 19.

Viscio, A.J., Harbison, J.R., Asin, A. and Vitaro, R.D. (1999) Post-merger integration: what makes mergers work? http://www.strategy-business.com/bestpractice/99404/page1.html (12/7/99)

Vlasic, B. and Stertz, B.A. (2000a). *Taken for a Ride: How Daimler-Benz Drove off with Chrysler*. HarperCollins Publishers Inc, New York.

Vlasic, B. and Stertz, B.A. (2000b) Taken for a ride. *Business Week*, June 5, pp. 84–92.

Weber, J. and Barrett, A. (1999) Volatile combos. *Business Week*, October 25, p. 122.

Yang, C. (2001) Show true for AOL Time Warner. *Business Week*, January 15, pp. 57–64.

RANDALL S. SCHULER, *Rutgers University, Department of Human Resource Management and Labor Relations, 94 Rockafeller Road, Rm 202, Piscataway, New Jersey 08854-8054, USA. E-mail: schuler@rci-.rutgers.edu*

Randall Schuler is Professor of Human Resource Strategy and Director of the Center for Strategic HRM at Rutgers University. His interests are in global HRM, strategic HRM, the HRM function in organizations, and the interface of business strategy and human resource tasks. A prolific author, he has written or edited over 40 books, many in multiple editions and published over 100 research papers in journals.

SUSAN E. JACKSON, *Rutgers University, School of Management and Labor Relations, 94 Rockafeller Road, Piscataway, New Jersey 08854-8054, USA. E-mail: sjacksox@rci.rutgers.edu*

Susan Jackson is Professor of Human Resources Management at Rutgers University, and Graduate Director for the Doctoral Program in Industrial Relations and Human Resources. Her expertise lies primarily in strategic HRM, managing team effectiveness, workforce diversity, stress and burn-out. She has authored well over 100 research papers in journals on these subjects, and several major books.

[25]

HRD in multinationals: the global/local mix

Olga Tregaskis, De Montfort University
Noreen Heraty and Michael Morley, University of Limerick

Human Resource Management Journal, Vol 11 No 2, 2001, pages 34-56

This article is concerned with how MNCs (multinational corporations) differ from indigenous organisations in relation to their human resource development (HRD) practices, and whether this relationship changes across countries. We question whether local isomorphism is apparent in the HRD practices of MNCs, or whether MNCs share more in common with their counterparts in other countries. A series of hypotheses are put forward and tested, using survey data from 424 multinational and 259 indigenous organisations based in the UK and Ireland. The results suggest a hybrid form of localisation, where MNCs adapt their practices to accommodate national differences, but that these adaptations do not reflect convergence to domestic practice. The results also indicate that MNCs are selective in the HRD practices that are adapted. Evidence from this study indicates that country differences in career traditions and labour market skill needs are key drivers in the localisation of associated HRD practice. In contrast, MNCs, irrespective of national context, adopt comparable systematic training frameworks, ie training-need identification, evaluation and delivery.

Contact: Olga Tregaskis, Leicester Business School, De Montfort University, The Gateway, Leicester LE1 9BH. Email: otregas@dmu.ac.uk

A s multinational corporations (MNCs) and their overseas subsidiaries have become increasingly important players in the global economy, interest in and research on the strategies and management practices of these firms has also grown (Hamel and Prahalad, 1985; Rosenzweig and Singh, 1991; Taylor *et al*, 1996). Linked to this is a growing consensus that the effectiveness of human resources will provide the key to competitive differentiation between these firms. MNCs are physically dispersed in environmental settings that represent very different economic, social and cultural milieus (Fayerweather, 1978; Hofstede, 1980; Humes, 1993), and are internationally differentiated in complex ways to respond to both environmental and organisational differences across businesses, functions and geographic locations (Brewster, 1995; Maurice *et al*, 1986; Tregaskis, 1997; Bartlett and Ghoshal, 1986). Both Schuler *et al* (1993) and Rosenzweig and Nohria (1994) highlight that one of the central questions in the literature on MNCs is the extent to which their various foreign subsidiaries act and behave as local firms, or adopt practices that resemble those of the parent. Solomon (1995) argues that multinationals are paying greater attention to cross-cultural issues as they search for ways to improve human resource development (HRD) in their overseas operations. She argues that, increasingly, global companies are exporting their management development and training systems. The leitmotif of this article relates to those critical influences on HRD practices at the organisational level. HRD practice in this context refers to organisational mechanisms used to support the training and development of individuals. Our prime objective is to

Olga Tregaskis, Noreen Heraty and Michael Morley

attempt to explain the relative impact of the host-country context on domestic and MNC practices. In order to achieve this we posit two critical questions. First, does country context influence organisational HRD practice? Secondly, do MNCs localise their HRD practices to account for national demands?

To test these questions empirically we focus first on the degree to which HRD practices differ between organisations based in two European countries: the UK and Ireland. Secondly, we look at the degree to which MNCs differ from indigenous organisations across these two country contexts.

The debate on what influences HRD is a largely dichotomous one, with many contributors suggesting that the country context, and the institutionalisation that flows from it, is all important. Others contend that practices of this nature are not subject to the constraints of context and, consequently, multinationals have the ability to import practices at will. In this respect, recent research has examined how organisational and institutional arrangements shape labour market outcomes, rekindling interest in how and why labour management relations, employment and HRD practices vary across organisations (Tolbert and Zucker, 1983; Baron et al, 1986; Mezias, 1990; Berger and Dore, 1996; Westphal et al, 1997). Other research concentrates on a convergence theory which argues that only antecedents that are specific to the organisation explain the existence of HR policies (including HRD), while country-specific influences are of less importance (Weber et al, 2000; Williamson, 1996; Sparrow et al, 1994). The convergence thesis is frequently used to explain commonality in multinational practice. It is argued that MNCs reflect practices of leading-edge organisations and, as such, they act as vehicles for transferring 'best practice' across national borders (Peters and Waterman, 1982). Since such management practice transcends national borders, this tends to create common global practices. However, the term 'global' in this context is not synonymous with strategy (Prahalad and Doz, 1987), but instead is indicative of commonality in MNC practice.

The question, therefore, is whether MNCs, in developing and implementing their range of HR policies and practices (including HRD), are free to impose policies and practices in each country, or whether they must accommodate or conform to local or national norms, and so adjust their policies and practices accordingly. This is the central question underpinning this article, and one that has sparked considerable debate in recent years.

INSTITUTIONAL AND FREE AGENT PERSPECTIVES

For quite some time now, considerable efforts have been made to understand how and why organisations are created and managed in the way that they are, and what likely implications their constructions have for those who work within them (Heraty and Morley, 1998a). Recent years have seen the emergence of a cadre of researchers who have sought to describe and explain the construction of organisations from an institutional theory perspective. Institutional theory grew out of the early work of Selznick (1949), Schultz (1962) and Berger and Luckmann (1967), who all conceived of organisations as socially embedded in their external environment and affected by external forces that require them to adapt their structures and behaviour to deal with these forces.

Barley and Tolbert (1997) describe the central tenet of institutional theory as emphasising contextual and cultural influences on decision making and structural formation in organisations. Specifically they highlight the notion that organisations and the individuals who populate them are suspended in a web of values, norms, rules, beliefs and taken-for-granted assumptions. Similarly, Greenwood and Hinings (1996) note that institutional theory emphasises convergence around these institutionally embedded tenets, and is used to explain the similarity and stability of organisational arrangements in a given population.

The core idea of institutional theory is that organisations are shaped by the institutional environment that surrounds them, and that 'organisations are likely to copy what is done elsewhere, doing so to obtain legitimacy and the approval of key outside agencies, such as government' within a given society (Strauss and Hanson, 1997: 1426). Scott (1987) argues that institutional theories have focused attention on the importance of symbolic aspects of organisations and their environment.

More recently, research by, among others, Meyer and Rowan (1977), Meyer and Scott (1983), DiMaggio (1988) and DiMaggio and Powell (1983, 1991) demonstrates multiplicity and diversity of institutional sources and belief systems found in modern societies. They argue that these have a considerable influence on the way organisations are structured and managed within their cultural context. The work of DiMaggio and Powell emphasises the ways in which institutional practices are brought into organisations. Organisations in the same field develop isomorphic tendencies as they exchange employees in professional jobs, and face common exigencies such as governmental policies, regulatory constraints, education systems, changing consumer tastes and so forth. This approach to institutional theory argues that it is the nature of these nationally-bounded external actors that shape organisational life, both directly by imposing constraints and requirements, and indirectly by creating and promulgating new rational myths (Scott, 1987). For example, Maurice *et al* (1986), in comparing the economic performance of France and Germany, found evidence of the existence of powerful social *filieres* in education, along which members of the workforce travelled and were shaped before arriving in the workplace. The education system, as an institutional factor, can be seen to exert considerable influence on the HRD activities of firms, shaping the skills and knowledge of the workforce who, in turn, shape the training systems as a result of their requirements for training and their career aspirations (Hosking and Anderson, 1992).

DiMaggio and Powell (1983) argue that 'institutional isomorphism' is now the dominant reason why organisations assume the forms that they have or, as Deephouse (1996) suggests, it might explain the similarity among a set of organisations at a given point in time. DiMaggio and Powell (1983) cite three reasons for this isomorphism: first, there are coercive forces that arise from broad-based societal expectations and organisational interdependencies (coercive institutional pressures), such as government regulations and cultural and intra-organisational expectations, that can impose standardisation on organisations; secondly, organisations mimic or model each others' structures/practices in order to minimise uncertainty (mimetic institutional pressures); and, thirdly, cultural expectations concerned with the professional training of organisational members (normative pressures) emerge as the workforce, and especially management, becomes more professionalised (*cf* Jepperson, 1991; Walsh, 1995). Both professional training and the growth and elaboration of professional networks within organisational fields lead to a situation in which the managerial personnel in organisations in the same field are barely distinguishable from one another. As people participate in trade and professional associations, their ideas tend to homogenise and, once intentions and actions are formed, many are quite resistant to change (Weick, 1995). Institutional theory perceives the firm as taking actions to improve its survival chances by making

Olga Tregaskis, Noreen Heraty and Michael Morley

changes either internally or in external relations with the environment, and thus it adopts structural elements that fit better with the preferences of the surrounding institutional system.

Despite some weaknesses that are associated with institutional theory – that it lacks a definitive boundary (Tolbert and Zucker, 1996); that it provides over-socialised explanations of organisational behaviour that ignore the role of power, interest and agency (Martinez and Dazin, 1999; Oliver, 1991; Powell, 1991) – the perspective has explanatory value in the analysis of the adoption of HRM approaches and innovations (see for example Daniels *et al*, 2001; Hill *et al*, 1997; Gooderham *et al*, 1999; Gooderham and Nordhaug, 1997; Andersën, 1997; Hausner *et al*, 1995; Roche and Turner, 1994; Dobbin *et al*, 1993). As such, it provides one important set of tools for analysing continuities and discontinuities in patterns of HRD that cannot be explained solely by reference to purely economic or technological factors (Hill *et al*, 1997; Andersën, 1997; Martin *et al*, 1996; Guillen, 1994).

The corollary of institutionalism in the context of this article is represented by the universal theory of the firm, which reached prominence in the academic literature in the 1970s. It argues that there exists a set of pervasive organisational features that are independent of the country context in which that company finds itself (Pugh and Hickson, 1976; Hickson and McMillan, 1981), and that organisations can significantly deviate from the society in which they are embedded (Clark, 1987). Clark and Staunton (1989) identify what they term 'a stock of knowledge about organisations' that is free of specific contexts and of the contingency and heterogeneity of time. This perception of the organisation as 'culture-free' argues that competitive forces resulting from markets, industrialisation and/or technology obviate the influence of varying national cultures (Child, 1972; Blau and Schoenherr, 1971) or that the rationale by which managers make decisions is guided mostly by efficiency-centred considerations (Williamson, 1996). Beechler and Yang (1994), in an investigation of the transfer of Japanese-style management practices to the US, argue that three literature streams offer plausible explanations for the transfer of home-country practices overseas: the culturalist school, which concentrates on the MNC's country of origin as the major factor in determining what types of HR practices will be put in place in the subsidiary (Abegglen, 1958; Clark, 1979); the rationalistic school, which focuses on the universalistic aspects of management techniques that develop in response to industrial development, competitive pressures and production technologies, *ie* geography is not important (Aoki, 1988); and the technology-HRM-fit school, which suggests that firms with different technologies tend to adopt different HR and industrial relations (IR) practices to fit their technologies (Kujawa, 1983). It is argued that MNCs are deeply embedded in the business systems in which they originate (Hu, 1992) and that, in spite of globalisation, the role of the home situation is more significant than ever before because it is the source of the main technologies and skills that underpin competitive advantage (Porter, 1990, 1991).

In summary, these theoretical perspectives reflect the dichotomous nature of the convergence/divergence debate. There are those who suggest country context, and the institutionalisation that flows from it, is all important, while others contend that practices are not subject to the constraints of context. The former argument would suggest that HRD practices diverge across national contexts as MNCs localise their practices. Alternatively, it is argued that HRD practices are unaffected by country-context factors, and so MNCs can readily impose their particular brand of HRD practices.

GLOBAL OR LOCAL: THE EVIDENCE

The literature reviewed above, which focuses attention on the national level of explanation and prescription, increasingly emphasises institutional and cultural constraints. The question of which of the two counteracting logics of local isomorphism (localisation) or internal consistency (globalisation) characterises MNCs' HR practices has received considerable attention in recent literature. There is long-standing evidence that foreign firms behave differently from their domestic counterparts (Daniels, 1970; Little, 1978; Glickman *et al*, 1989) and, more recently, that foreign ownership may provide a platform for the diffusion of best practices (Whitley, 1992; Voss and Blackmon, 1996). Noble (1997) suggests that MNCs are potentially important to the national vocational education and training systems in which they operate. To the extent that they develop and implement efficient and effective training and development programmes, MNCs may also exert a leadership role or model of 'good practice'. At the enterprise level, comparison may point to directly transferable practices and provide a means of monitoring performance.

One might expect to witness high levels of internal consistency in HRM/HRD practices to ensure internal equity, particularly where international mobility is encouraged. On the other hand, previous empirical research has tended to point towards an overall tendency for HRM/HRD activities to closely resemble local practice. Rosenzweig and Nohria's (1994) research is illustrative here. They argue that countervailing forces have an impact on the provision of training and development in MNCs: on the one hand, training and development needs are context-specific and so vary according to local conditions, as will the requirement to provide comparable opportunities; on the other hand, many MNCs have corporate-wide policies regarding employee training, as well as management philosophies favouring certain types of training that serve to exert pressure to adhere to parent practice. Their study, from an overall perspective, concluded that HR practices, including training and development provision, were primarily shaped by local isomorphism. Similarly, Gooderham et al's (1999) research concludes that the national, institutional embeddedness of firms plays a far more important role in shaping personnel practices than does their industrial embeddedness.

In his comparative study of MNCs in the UK and Australia, Noble (1997) found that the MNCs under investigation had evolved an approach to the organisation and management of training that suited their complex structures. The MNCs in his study allowed considerable autonomy to their subsidiaries in developing and implementing training and development strategies. However, despite the high level of autonomy, there existed many areas of similarity in the organisation and management of the training and development function – a corporate role for activities such as planning, co-ordination and management development was maintained. He argued that 'it is possible that MNCs are polycentric in training but ethnocentric in their broader competitive strategies. Although subsidiaries may be operationally independent, they may be influenced by the international strategies of the parent which prescribe the role of the subsidiary.' Wickam's (1989) study of aspects of local branch management autonomy in MNCs in Ireland supports the polycentric or local isomorphic view where, he argues, the managers of these subsidiaries can form a distinct social group who develop interests and aspirations that are independent from those of corporate headquarters.

To what extent, then, do national factors shape relationships at the level of the organisation, and thus the organisation's competitive position? The remaining section

Olga Tregaskis, Noreen Heraty and Michael Morley

of this article focuses on the extent to which multinational firms' HRD efforts differ from those provided by indigenous/domestic firms and whether and how these efforts vary with the country context within which they are embedded.

THE HYPOTHESES

In this research we examine the issue of localisation of MNC practice in the context of organisations operating in Ireland and the UK. To answer our research questions, it is first necessary to establish whether the practices of organisations in these two country contexts differ and, if so, to what extent MNC practices are convergent with these country differences.

We use country of operation as a proxy for country context, defined in terms of the aspects of a country's institutional and cultural environment that have an impact on HRD practice. We separate out from country context the impact of factors associated with the heterogeneity of organisations, namely differences arising from being an MNC or non-MNC, or on the basis of sector or size. In doing this we address, to some extent, Ferner's (1997: 34) concerns that country differences are based on a composite of responses from very heterogeneous organisations.

There is also a question of what aspects of HRD practice are affected by country differences and organisational heterogeneity. This in turn helps us to appraise which aspects of MNC practice are localised or affected in some other way. We argue that country and organisational heterogeneity differences depend on whether the practices concerned are macro or micro in nature.

Micro HRD practices

In this research we use two indicators of micro-level HRD practice. One concerns the degree to which organisations adopt an internal career development system to facilitate organisational progression and personal development. A second indicator includes the degree to which organisations perceive a need for skill enhancement to equip employees with the relevant skills for future work demands. Arguably, career development is an aspect of a company's HRD system that is highly influenced by the career traditions and business system in the host country. For example, management career paths and development practices in German companies are often characterised as functionally specialised, as a result of their ability to operate a long-term skill development process. This is made possible as a result of a pay-bargaining system that sets wages, thus restricting companies applying their own wage patterns and, in turn, minimising opportunities for companies to poach skills (McCartney and Teague, 1999). Career patterns are further reinforced through the high-calibre education system and approach to apprenticeship training. It is argued that the strong impact of the *Grande Ecole* institutions in the education of managers and public control in business leads to an elitist and highly political career process for managers in France (Barsoux and Lawrence, 1994). In the UK management careers are more generalist in nature and focused to a greater degree on learning through experience than formal qualifications (Handy, 1987). Although there is some evidence that the adoption of a competence-based model for vocational education and pressure from professional organisations *eg* IM (Institute of Management), and the CIPD (Chartered Institute of Personnel and Development) has increased the focus on qualifications (*eg* Thompson *et al*, 1998). In Ireland management education is similarly generalist in nature but with a high predisposition for certified professionalisation (Garavan *et al*, 1995). We argue then that, where HRD systems are primarily concerned with career development, isomorphic pressures for convergence to host-country patterns of management/career development are likely to be stronger than competing isomorphic pressures from the MNC's home context. The same can be argued for future employee training requirements, which are defined as the skills companies identify as critical for future functioning. The close relationship between employee skills and national educational systems is one of the key motivators for government intervention in this field (Heraty and Morley, 1998a; Tregaskis, 1997). Equally, local business markets and competition define the types of skills needed in the field of continuing or lifelong learning as much as at the initial labour market entry level.

Given these arguments, we could expect country context to have a significant impact on organisational practice in the field of careers and future skill requirements. To test the impact of country context, we propose:

Hypothesis 1a There will be significant country differences between Irish-based and UK-based organisations in their micro-level (ie career development and future skill needs) HRD practice.

Furthermore, we would expect these country differences to have an impact on MNC practice. Evidence from Rosenzweig and Nohria (1994) suggests that, where HR practices in multinational organisations are focused on local employees' concerns as opposed to those of international managers, and consequently are more micro in nature, isomorphism to host country practices is more likely. We would therefore expect MNCs in Ireland and the UK to differ in the approach to career development and perceptions for skill enhancement in line with the country differences revealed from the testing of hypothesis 1a. To test if this is the case, we pose the following hypothesis:

Hypothesis 1b MNCs in Ireland and the UK will significantly differ from each other in their micro HRD practices to account for country differences.

Support for hypothesis 1b would suggest that MNCs adapt their practices to account for country differences. This raises the question of whether this adaptation reflects convergence with indigenous company practice or whether a distinct MNC approach prevails. This relationship is explored through hypotheses 2a and 2b.

Macro-HRD practices

We use three indicators of macro-HRD practice, namely, methods used to identify training need, to evaluate training effectiveness and to deliver training. In each case we would argue that these practices are macro in the sense that they are about organising systems for organisational-level HRD needs. They constitute an integral part of the generic systematic training cycle, and so are less likely to be influenced by country-specific factors. This is likely to be particularly true of country contexts where there is little cultural distance or commonality of management thinking on employee development issues, as is the case for Ireland and the UK. We hypothesise, then, that:

Hypothesis 1c There will be no significant country differences between Irish- and UK-based organisations in their macro-level HRD practice.

Support for hypothesis 1c would suggest that MNCs do not need to localise macro-HRD activities, as there are few differences in how companies operate in Ireland and the UK. Nevertheless, we would expect differences between MNC and indigenous company practice to persist, partly as a consequence of the economies of scale argument. In addition, it could be argued that macro-level HR practice concerned with guiding principles, standardising tools and procedures or use of parent resources are more likely to be affected by isomorphic pressures from international

Olga Tregaskis, Noreen Heraty and Michael Morley

business. These pressures will pull MNC practices in the direction of parent practice or 'best practice' norms, and away from the norms of indigenous company practice. In summary, we would expect country differences in the preferences of micro-HRD practices between UK- and Irish-based MNCs and contrasts between MNCs and indigenous companies in relation to both micro- and macro-HRD practice. Restated as hypotheses, this would read:

Hypothesis 2a *The micro-HRD practices of MNCs in Ireland and the UK will differ significantly from each other and from their indigenous counterparts.*

Hypothesis 2b *The macro-HRD practices of MNCs in Ireland and the UK will not significantly differ from each other but will significantly differ from those of indigenous organisations.*

Support for hypotheses 2a and 2b would suggest that multinationals operating in Ireland and the UK adopt a hybrid localisation strategy to HRD issues. We would argue that the economies of scale associated with MNCs – and existing research evidence that suggests that MNCs have greater resources to invest in HRD – are more likely to lead to a form of hybrid localisation in relation to micro HRD activities (hypothesis 2a).

Our hypotheses above specify the main relationships we are interested in for the purposes of answering our research questions. However, it is important to point out that, as part of the analysis and resulting explanation of the data, we also address issues of organisational sector and size. Many studies have indicated that training and development activity can be sector-specific. As we are primarily interested in the effects of country context and organisational status on HRD practice, we have controlled for the effect of sector in the analysis. This means that any differences in HRD practice assigned to country context or organisational status differences exist irrespective of the sector in which the company operates. Consequently, country and organisational differences do not merely reflect sector differences; organisational size is also included in the analysis as a control variable. The methods section discusses in detail the differences in the size of the organisations in the two country samples. Our analysis specifically addresses the question of whether there are country differences in the HRD practices of organisations of different sizes. Again, the aim is to establish that any country differences are not merely reflecting differences in organisational size but are in fact additional effects.

In summary, we have established hypotheses designed to assess what aspects of HRD practice differ in Ireland and the UK; whether MNC practice is localised to account for country differences; and what form this localisation takes. In addition, through our research design and analysis process, organisational factors associated with sector and size will also be accounted for.

METHOD

Data are drawn from the 1995 round of the Cranet-E survey of strategic human resource management. This is a comparative survey of organisational-led HRM practices conducted across 20 European countries on four successive occasions. A collaborative network of business schools throughout Europe, known collectively as Cranet-E, carries out the research. Data is collected from HR/personnel directors using a postal survey. For the purposes of this article, only Cranet-E survey data from Ireland and the UK have been used. A review of the research development and design for the additional countries involved in this project is presented in Brewster *et al* (1994, 1996).

TABLE 1 *Status and country characteristics of the organisations*

	UK n = 517		Ireland n = 166		Total
Company status					
Multinational	308	(60)	116	(70)	424
Indigenous	209	(40)	50	(30)	259
Sector					
Manufacturing	341	(66)	115	(69)	456
Services	176	(34)	51	(31)	166
Size					
Small	50	(10)	81	(49)	131
Medium	273	(53)	58	(35)	331
Large	194	(37)	27	(16)	221

Sample

HR/personnel specialists based in companies in Ireland and the UK completed the survey questionnaire. The sample consists of 517 UK-based private sector organisations and 166 Irish-based private sector organisations, of which 424 are multinationals and 259 indigenous organisations. Table 1 highlights full sample details.

The organisations are small (50-199 employees), medium (200-499 employees) and large (500-999), with 227 from the service sector and 456 from the manufacturing sector. We chose not to conduct the analysis solely on the basis of one industry sector, as we wanted to draw general conclusions across organisations nationally. We therefore included industry as a control variable within the statistical analysis, to allow us to take into account and assess the relative strength of industry sector in influencing HRD practice.

The proportion of MNCs in the UK and the Ireland sample are approximately matched. The same can be said for the proportions of manufacturing and service organisations in the two country samples. However, the size distributions for the samples show that, on the whole, the UK sample consists of larger organisations (Table 1). A further breakdown of the size structure of organisations (Table 2) shows that the numbers of multinational and indigenous organisations in each size band are similar

TABLE 2 *Size structure of multinational and indigenous organisations in the UK and Ireland*

	Multinational % of organisations	Indigenous % of organisations
UK		
Small	10	9
Medium	50	56
Large	39	35
Ireland		
Small	47	54
Medium	38	28
Large	15	18

Olga Tregaskis, Noreen Heraty and Michael Morley

within each country. Therefore, the sample differences in organisational size are not due to bias in company status; instead, they reflect national patterns of organisational size. We chose not to restructure the two country samples to match them in terms of company size, as this would affect our ability to extrapolate to the national level. We therefore controlled for the effects of size within the analysis.

Survey measures

Thirty-four questionnaire items were used to measure five aspects of HRD practice. Two micro-HRD measures examined the approach to career development, and perceived areas for future skill enhancement. Three macro-HRD measures examined aspects of the systemic training cycle, namely training needs analysis, training and development evaluation and training and development delivery. The items covering each of the five areas were summated and the reliability of each scale assessed using Cronbach's alpha. The alpha co-efficients for each scale were above the recommended minimum of .50.

Micro-HRD indicators Career development (alpha = 0.59) was measured through six questions relating to the use of formal career plans, assessment centres, succession plans, planned job rotation, high-flier schemes and international experience as mechanisms used to manage the employee's career. The coding for this scale ranged from 0 to 1, with the latter indicating high use of a formal organisationally-managed internal career development process. Skill enhancement requirements (alpha = 0.79) were measured on a five-point Likert scale, with 1 indicating high training need and 5 indicating low training need. The scale included nine skill areas: people management; computers and new technology; business administration; strategy formulation; marketing and sales; health and safety and the work environment; customer service skills; management of change; and quality management.

Macro-HRD indicators The training needs analysis scale (alpha = 0.83) was made up of five questions concerning the frequency of use of training audits, performance appraisals, analysis of project business/service plans, line management requests and employee requests to identify training needs. The training and development evaluation scale (alpha = 0.77) included five questions referring to the use of formal evaluation immediately after training; formal evaluation some months after training; informal feedback from line managers; informal feedback from trainees; and tests to assess the effectiveness of training and development activity. The training and development delivery scale (alpha = 0.59) included the use of internal training staff; line managers; external training providers; on-the-job training; internal seminars/training courses; external seminars/training courses; coaching; computer-based packages; open-learning programmes; and mentoring. All three scales applied a Likert-type scaling measure of use, with 1 indicating high use and 4 low use, of each aspect of the systematic training cycle.

Analysis

MANOVA (multivariate analysis of variance) is a technique that allows the researcher to test the influence of two or more independent variables on a set of dependent variables. Control variables can be included that enable the effect of the key independent variables to be assessed as additional to any effect expected by control variables. For this article, the dependent variables were represented by the micro- and macro-HRD measures, while our independent variables were the company status and country context, with the effects of industry sector and organisational size being controlled for.

MANOVA has the specific advantage of being able to test for interaction effects, where the dependent variables are changed as a result of an interaction between two or more of the independent variables. To test for localisation effects, it was important that we were able to establish if HRD practices altered for MNCs and indigenous companies based in two different country contexts. An interaction between country and organisational size was also tested; given the unequal size distributions of organisations in the two country samples, we might expect an effect.

One of the assumptions placed on data used in a MANOVA analysis is that the data is normally distributed. The responses by organisations on the HRD scales tended to be skewed either to the left or the right. This data was de-skewed using a logarithm transformation.

RESULTS

The results support the argument that country context has a differential impact on micro- and macro-level HRD practices. The findings suggest country differences in career traditions and skill needs influence organisational practice, while the commonality in the use of a systemic model of training and development affirms the closeness of the UK and Ireland contexts in relation to the management of employee skill development. On the issue of the localisation of MNC practice, the results support the hypotheses proposed, namely that MNCs operating in Ireland and the UK adapt their practices in the light of country differences. This adaptation of practice does not conform to the HRD practice of indigenous companies, thus suggesting a form of hybrid localisation. With a few exceptions, these relationships were found consistently across organisations of different sizes and in organisations operating in different sectors. Overall, the most important predictor of HRD practice was whether an organisation was an MNC or not (accounting for 6 per cent of the variation in the scores on the HRD measures – Wilks .93592, df 5/627, p .000). Country context, in comparison, was only as important in predicting HRD practice as company size and sector, each accounting for 3 per cent of variation in HRD scores (country – Wilks .97181, df 5/627, p .003; sector – Wilks .97191, df 5/627, p .003; and size – Wilks .92838, df 10/1254, p .000). This suggests that, in the case of Ireland and the UK, country differences are marginal in comparison with issues associated with the internationalisation of business. Below we examine these findings in detail.

The first set of hypotheses explored the link between country effects on micro- and macro-level HRD indicators. As proposed, the results indicate that companies operating in Ireland and the UK vary significantly in their adoption of an internal career management model and in concerns for skill enhancement (Table 3). Specifically, organisations operating in Ireland perceived that they had greater training requirements to enhance skills for the future than companies operating in the UK (Table 4). Companies in Ireland were also more likely to adopt an internal career model than UK-operating companies. However, this finding needs to be considered in the light of the significant interaction effect between country and organisational size. This finding indicates that the preference by Irish organisations for an internal career model is more true for larger organisations than for small and medium ones. In the UK, by contrast, both medium and larger organisations were significantly more likely to adopt

Olga Tregaskis, Noreen Heraty and Michael Morley

an internal career management model than smaller ones. This finding is therefore not only tied into national career models but also issues of organisational size. Larger organisations, by their nature and structure, can offer a wider range of career development opportunities and are also more likely to have the resources to invest in sustaining an internal labour market. By contrast, smaller organisations are more reliant on external labour markets to fulfil their skill needs, as they have fewer resources and promotion opportunities to support the use of an internal career model. The lack of an interaction effect between country and company status (*ie* MNC or indigenous company) suggests that these country differences on the micro-HRD issues persist in multinational companies. This would, therefore, support hypothesis 1b that MNCs adapt to account for country differences in organisational practice.

The analysis found no country differences in macro-HRD practices. Evidence of the adoption of a systemic training model, measured through the use of training evaluation, training need and delivery practices, is fairly common to both UK- and Ireland-based companies (Table 3, *overleaf*). Here, the significant interaction between company size and country indicated that large companies in the UK are less likely to evaluate the effectiveness of training than their Irish counterparts. Arguably, the fact that large companies in Ireland demonstrate such a high disposition towards training evaluation is a function of ownership as much as it is about resources. Large companies in Ireland tend to be foreign-owned, and a sizeable majority of these are US subsidiaries of MNCs. Since the 1960s, Ireland's industrial policy has focused on attracting foreign direct investment (FDI), with the result that close to one-quarter (24 per cent) of all available US manufacturing investments in Europe are now located in Ireland (*The Economist*, 1997). US-owned MNCs are characterised by their range of HRM-style policies, and they tend to place a considerable value on evaluation of HR systems, including training (*eg* Enderwick, 1986; Young *et al*, 1985). Since so many of Ireland's large companies are foreign-owned and US-owned, it is likely that the data here is reflecting the practices of these US-owned organisations. In the case of all other aspects of HRD practice, smaller organisations consistently (*ie* in both Ireland and the UK) do less than their medium and larger counterparts (Table 4, *overleaf*). These country differences are applicable to companies in both service and manufacturing sectors with one exception: training evaluation (Table 3). This difference shows that service sector companies in Ireland are more likely to carry out evaluation of the effectiveness of training undertaken than manufacturing companies (Table 4). The service sector sample is not dominated by multinational organisations but indigenous companies. As such, this finding cannot be explained primarily in terms of ownership. However, the nature of the service sector industry in Ireland, which is inextricably linked to the multinational company, may explain the findings. Ireland, like many European counterparts (including the UK), has witnessed a considerable expansion of its services sector in recent years. Much of this expansion is as a result of the establishment of a number of 'new' (to Ireland) services. A typical example in this instance is the telecommunications call centre sector in Ireland, which is one of the biggest in Europe. Payne (1997) notes that one-third of all US call centres in Europe are now located in Ireland. The call centre market was actively targeted since it was felt that it would slot in well with the explosive growth taking place in both the computer and software sectors in Ireland. Since so many of these companies are overseas-owned, there may be a combined influence of ownership and market sector. However, the data limitations mean we are unable to test the validity of this speculation. Notably, training evaluation is the one area that all organisations in both countries engage in the least. This is perhaps

TABLE 3 *MANOVA output indicating significant and non-significant effects of company status, country, organisational size and sector on responses to the HRD scales*

	Multivariate F	Univariate F	ETA²	Sig. of F
Company status	8.5861	–	.064	.000**
Training needs analysis		17.117	.026	.000**
Evaluation of training effectiveness		13.071	.020	.000**
Career development		33.902	.051	.000**
Training and development delivery methods		11.229	.017	.001*
Future training and development needs		6.175	.010	.013*
Country	3.6372	–	.028	.003*
Training needs analysis		1.467	.002	.226
Evaluation of training effectiveness		2.749	.004	.098
Career development		12.066	.018	.001*
Training and development delivery methods		2.008	.003	.157
Future training and development needs		8.001	.012	.005*
Size	4.7074	–	.036	.000**
Training needs analysis		4.402	.014	.013*
Evaluation of training effectiveness		7.599	.023	.001*
Career development		15.034	.045	.000**
Training and development delivery methods		11.041	.034	.000**
Future training and development needs		2.241	.007	.107
Sector effects	3.6248	–	.028	.003*
Training needs analysis		0.666	.001	.415
Evaluation of training effectiveness		5.666	.010	.018*
Career development		3.375	.005	.067
Training and development delivery methods		1.692	.003	.194
Future training and development needs		2.127	.003	.145
Country x status	.7592	–	.006	.579
Training needs analysis		12.8358	.003	.144
Evaluation of training effectiveness		8.6237	.000	.721
Career development		3.3318	.000	.486
Training and development delivery methods		7.9234	.000	.633
Future training and development needs		9.5350	.000	.917
Country x size	2.1965	–	.017	.016*
Training needs analysis		12.836	.007	.116
Evaluation of training effectiveness		8.6235	.001	.028*
Career development		3.3319	.011	.025*
Training and development delivery methods		7.9234	.004	.319
Future training and development needs		9.5350	.003	.415*

$*P < .01$, $**p < .001$

Olga Tregaskis, Noreen Heraty and Michael Morley

not too surprising, as it is the one area of the systematic training cycle that is often expensive and difficult to implement, and therefore dealt with less effectively by organisations (Hamblin, 1974).

The second set of hypotheses suggests that MNCs adapt their practices in line with country-isomorphic pressures, but not necessarily in line with domestic company practice. The results of the analysis support this line of argument. The MANOVA showed, first, that multinational organisations and indigenous organisations differed significantly on all five HRD measures (Table 4). Examination of the mean scores (Table 5) for multinational and indigenous organisations on each of the HRD scales

TABLE 4 *Mean scores for HRD measures by company status, country, size and sector*

	Training needs analysis		Tr'g/dvlpm't evaluation		Career development		Tr'g/dvlpm't delivery		Future tr'g/ dvlpm't need	
	Mean	SD	Mean	SD	Mean	SD	Mean	SD	Mean	SD
Status	*		*		*		*		*	
Multinational	.37	.141	.42	.119	.09	.080	.30	.116	.23	.118
Indigenous	.42	.147	.44	.114	.05	.065	.32	.118	.25	.133
Country					*				*	
UK	.39	.147	.43	.121	.07	.074	.30	.115	.25	.123
Ireland	.39	.141	.43	.114	.08	.081	.31	.118	.23	.126
Size	*		*		*		*			
Small	.42	.143	.46	.112	.05	.067	.34	.109	.26	.134
Medium	.38	.147	.42	.120	.07	.074	.30	.117	.23	.121
Large	.38	.141*	.41	.116	.09	.081	.29	.113	.24	.122
Sector			*							
Manufacturing	.39	.141	.43	.116	.07	.078	.30	.111	.24	.122
Services	.39	.154	.41	.123	.07	.072	.29	.125	.23	.127

* Significant differences between the means

Note Because of the reverse scoring used for all the HRD dimensions with the exception of career development, the lower the score, the higher the use of/importance attached to HRD practices

TABLE 5 *Mean scores for HRD measures of interaction between country and size*

	Training and development evaluation		Career development	
	Mean	SD	Mean	SD
Small	p .451		p. 408	
UK	.47	.116	.05	.067
Ireland	.45	.111	.04	.067
Medium	p .832		P .003**	
UK	.41	.123	.06	.070
Ireland	.42	.111	.10	.084
Large	p .001**		P .047*	
UK	.42	.117	.09	.080
Ireland	.34	.092	.12	.079

*P<.05, **p<.01

shows that multinational organisations are more likely to adopt a systematic training model approach through the use of training needs analyses, training evaluation and training delivery methods than indigenous organisations. MNCs are also more likely to adopt internal career development practices and to perceive a need for skill enhancement than indigenous organisations. The lack of any interaction between country and company status means that there is no alteration in the main effects reported for differences across countries and in company status. This means that, for micro-HRD issues, MNCs adapt to country differences in organisational practice by adopting a hybrid localisation strategy. For macro-HRD issues, MNCs adopt a common approach, irrespective of country context. This approach differs to that of indigenous companies; MNCs are more likely to use methods of training needs analysis, training evaluation and training delivery, supporting a systemic training-cycle approach, than are indigenous companies.

DISCUSSION AND CONCLUSIONS

In summary, there are three overarching conclusions that can be derived from this research. First, MNCs in Ireland and the UK respond to country differences by developing HRD practices that are a hybrid of local and international practice. Secondly, the localisation of HRD practice is, in part, a function of the micro nature or embeddedness of the issues within the local context; consequently, not all HRD practice will be localised to the same degree, if at all. Thirdly, commonality in HRD practice across national borders can be explained in terms of the cultural closeness of national contexts and the macro nature of the HR issues. Taking each of these points in reverse order, we will consider the implications of these findings.

As predicted, the results showed a high degree of similarity across companies in response to macro-level HRD practice. One conclusion of this finding is that organisations adopt a common managerial approach to organising training and development activity. This is likely to be promoted through the transfer of common management thinking in this field, partially facilitated by professional organisations such as the CIPD. The CIPD may be of particular significance in this context, as it accredits courses in both the UK and Ireland. However, we would also conclude that the findings are an outcome of the relative commonality between the two cultural contexts. Using Hofstede's (1980) model of cultural contexts, it is arguable that there is a relatively high level of homogeneity between the environmental contexts of the UK and Ireland, and thus one could reasonably expect to see similarity in macro-level HRD practices. An examination of the key national institutional labour market actors and systems supports the contention that, while institutions are variously constructed in each country, one can broadly observe some similarities in each country's institutional approach to training and development. (For a detailed treatise of the national training environments in the UK and Ireland, see Tregaskis and Brewster (1998) and Heraty and Morley (1998b) respectively.) The evidence may suggest that, where country contexts share many common institutional features as a consequence of being geographically or culturally close, there is a level of isomorphism that transcends national boundaries. For multinationals operating in different cultural environments, these findings suggest that the successful adoption of parent-country practices, if this is desired, will be more likely where the parent and host country are more similar in some of their institutional arrangements or traditions affecting HRD. Equally, the transference of ideas that, on HRD issues, originate in one country may be more easily applied in other settings

Olga Tregaskis, Noreen Heraty and Michael Morley

where the cultural distance is minimal. This would be applicable to MNCs adopting a global or transnational strategy that may wish to transfer practices around their subsidiary operations for standardisation, control or good practice reasons (Prahalad and Doz, 1987), or to indigenous companies that may be interested to learn from the organisational practice in other countries.

However, significant cultural bias is evident in respect of two particular micro-level HRD interventions, namely career development and perceptions of skill-enhancement needs. This finding would appear to lend some support to the institutionalist assertion that country-contextual factors tend to play a considerable role in shaping organisational practice. In particular, this finding may attest to Hosking and Anderson's (1992) assertion that the education system, as a key labour market institutional actor, exerts considerable influence on organisational-level training and development activity. These findings would clearly point to the need to consider the role of specific sources and manifestation of institutional pressure to provide a more comprehensive understanding of how organisational practice is affected. These findings also highlight that, although the UK and Irish contexts appear quite similar, differences remain that require organisations to alter their practices. From this research we might conclude that the closeness of HRD issues to the skill capability, career aspirations and motivations of employees is an indication of which areas of HRM practice need to be localised in international companies. As such, this 'closeness' identifies and defines what constitutes micro-level practice. It could also be argued in terms of resource theory that the greater the dependency of the subsidiary on local resources, such as the skills of its employees, the greater the need for localisation (Flood *et al*, 1996).

On the issue of localisation of MNC practice, the evidence suggests that, in relation to HRD issues, MNCs in Ireland and the UK did localise their practices. Wolf (1997) argues that the structure and processes of an MNC's HRM have to be aligned to the heterogeneity of the foreign environments in which they operate. Equally, subsidiary HR managers usually have different views of the role of employees in the firm and the way they should be hired, trained, compensated and so forth. This raised the question of the nature of the localisation. The differences in practices of MNCs and indigenous companies, despite the adaptation of MNC practices in line with country variation in micro-HRD practices (*ie* career development and perceived skill enhancement), suggested what we called a hybrid form of localisation. This meant that MNC practice, where country differences existed, showed some evidence of adaptation. However, MNCs were still more likely to adopt an internal approach to career development, perceive skill-enhancement needs and adopt a systemic training model in comparison with indigenous companies. It is possible that this level of commitment to HRD is indicative of MNCs championing good or 'best' practice in this area (Weber *et al*, 2000; Schuler *et al*, 1993). Studies have repeatedly shown that HRM and IR policies of US MNCs are relatively centralised and formalised (eg Hamill, 1984; Harzing, 1999; Young *et al*, 1985), but that they have also been consistent HR innovators (eg Enderwick, 1986: 115-19). MNCs tend to have considerably more resources at their disposal, both in terms of personnel and finances, and so can more readily respond to good practice demands. However, as a number of researchers have pointed out, MNC practice may not necessarily be a 'good' model for the long-term skill development and career needs of local employees. For example, Keep and Mayhew (1996) and Hendry (1994) point to the role of MNCs in promoting demand for low skills among the UK labour market in line with low-quality, mass-production business strategies. Equally, Bonache and Cervino (1997) point out how expatriate managers are used to fill senior management positions in subsidiaries in line with the company's international strategy. Consequently, many international management strategies promote investment in the careers of home-country nationals and international managers to the detriment of local managers' careers (Adler and Ghadar, 1990). The transfer of management practice in line with international business priorities in developing countries is potentially more concerning, as the power base within these countries to combat the pressures of international isomorphism may be weaker than in the developed countries.

One of the weaknesses of the research presented here is that we were only able to use a relatively crude or proxy measure of country-context influence. A limitation of the survey methodology is that it can only provide a superficial analysis (Ferner, 1997). To unravel the specific institutional factors or employee values that may underpin these country differences, and to test further the explanations posed in this article, would require more in-depth study. For example, a historical case-study approach would enable the research to track the dynamic relationship of the interplay between country factors and organisational factors (Quintanilla, 1998). This approach would also allow the researchers to assess the two-way interactions between the organisation and its environment, acknowledging the non-static relationship between the parent and subsidiary (Prahalad and Doz, 1987). In this analysis we have assumed that the national context is the proactive force, while the organisation is the passive subject of this influence. We must also consider the fact that convergence to local practice is a moving target. Multinational organisations are significant change agents at a national level. The significant internationalisation of both Ireland and the UK is likely, over time, to have had an impact on the nature of indigenous organisational practice as companies learn from each other.

We might conclude that, for the MNCs included in this study, there is some evidence of localisation of HRD practice, yet the distinctiveness between MNC and indigenous practice would support the argument for a hybrid localisation approach. Whether this form of hybrid localisation is true across all host-country contexts is beyond the limits of this article to comment on. Evidence by Gooderham *et al* (1999) found US companies in Ireland, the UK, Denmark and Norway to exhibit a common North American approach to their HRM with limited adaptation to country contexts. In Muller's (1998) study of US and UK MNCs operating in Germany, within what he defines as an institutionally strong environment, MNCs again only partially conform to local isomorphic demands.

The effects of organisational size reflect a very similar pattern of HRD activity among small firms in both Ireland and the UK. The limited provision of HRD reported here is indicative perhaps of a general 'economy-of-scale' model being applied for MNCs, but may also attest to similar difficulties in training provision being experienced by small firms across both countries. While successive national policy initiatives have attempted to target small firm training, the data here confirm the continuing lag between HRD provision in large versus small concerns. There is some evidence to indicate differences between HRD provision in medium and large organisations in Ireland and the UK that can be partially explained in terms of structural differences in the local business markets.

These findings suggest considerable variability in the degree of institutionalisation attained and support the argument that localisation of MNC HRD practice, or the implementation of generic or global HRD practices, is not an either/or option. Instead, organisations are likely to need to accommodate both, depending on a variety of organisational and contextual contingencies. The need for organisations to develop HR practices that are consistent will increase as companies move towards a greater

Olga Tregaskis, Noreen Heraty and Michael Morley

utilisation of the internal international labour market. For example, the movement of employees internationally, not just expatriate managers, creates a greater need for MNCs to promote common standards in the performance assessment of these individuals. However, in levering advantage from the local labour market and local internal resources, organisations cannot ignore employee expectations on issues such as pay and conditions, industrial relations or job security or career opportunities. As such, local and global HRD practices can each be used at the same time to lever competitive advantage from subsidiary resources and the internal international labour market. The combination of local and global HR practices should reflect and be responsive to the company's international strategy and the international markets it operates in. It could be argued that, as we enter the transnational era of competition (Harzing, 1999: 38), the need to recognise the value of both approaches becomes greater. The integrated management of local and international human capabilities can potentially offer multinationals a means of addressing the demands for local customer responsiveness; cost efficiencies enabled by global operations; and product/service innovation on a worldwide scale created through knowledge flows.

In summary, the findings suggest that the need for internal consistency can be met by organisations at the level of macro-HR activities, and pressures of local responsiveness can be met through micro HR activities. This study helps illuminate the question of when to maximise the benefits of internationalisation while simultaneously meeting demands for cultural sensitivity. We would argue that the answer lies, in part, in the extent to which the HRD system's components are concerned with micro or macro employee development concerns. However, the complexity of the convergence/divergence debate when dealing with multinational organisations should not be understated, and these findings make but a small piece of the jigsaw. Since all organisations, including MNCs, are embedded in a social, cultural and technological setting, they are inevitably subject to the myriad pressures that stem from these institutional settings, and so, as Adler and Ghadar (1990: 245) suggest:

> The central issue for MNCs is not to identify the best international HRM policy per se, but rather to find the best fit between the firm's external environment, its overall strategy and its HRM policy and implementation.

This issue of fit, be it in response to the national cultural embeddedness of the firm resulting in local isomorphism or to other demands, and the convergence/divergence debate, will continue to attract attention for at least as long as high levels of direct foreign investment remain a feature of European business.

REFERENCES

Abegglen, J. (1958). *The Japanese Factory*, New York: The Free Press.

Adler, N. and Ghadar, F. (1990). 'Strategic human resource management: a global perspective' in *Human Resource Management: An International Comparison*, R. Pieper (ed), Berlin: De Gruyter.

Andersën, T. (1997). 'Do institutions matter? Convergence and national diversity in the restructuring of employment in British and Danish banking'. *European Journal of Industrial Relations*, 3: 1, 107-124.

Aoki, M. (1988). *Information, Incentives and Bargaining in the Japanese Economy*, New York: Cambridge University Press.

Barley, S. and Tolbert, P. (1997). 'Institutionalization and structuration: studying the links between action and institution'. *Organization Studies*, 18: 1, 93-117.

Baron, J., Dobbin, F. and Jennings, P. (1986). 'War and peace: the evolution of modern personnel administration in US industry'. *American Journal of Sociology*, 92: 2, 350-383.

Barsoux, J.-L. and Lawrence, P. (1994). *Management in France*, London: Cassell.

Bartlett, C. and Ghoshal, S. (1986). 'Tap your subsidiaries for global reach'. *Harvard Business Review*, 4: 6, 87-94.

Beechler, S. and Yang, J. (1994). 'The transfer of Japanese-style management to American subsidiaries: contingencies, constraints and competence'. *Journal of International Business Studies*, 25: 3, 467-492.

Berger, S. and Dore, R. (eds). (1996). *National Diversity and Global Capitalism*, London: Cornell UP.

Berger, P. and Luckmann, T. (1967). *The Social Construction of Reality*, New York: Doubleday.

Blau, P. and Schoenherr, R. (1971). *The Structure of Organisations*, New York: Basic Books.

Bonache, J. and Cervino, J. (1997). 'Global integration without expatriates'. *Human Resource Management Journal*, 7: 3, 89-100.

Brewster, C. (1995). 'Towards a European model of human resource management practice'. *Journal of International Business Studies*, 26: 1, 5-21.

Brewster, C., Hegewisch, A., Mayne, L. and Tregaskis, O. (1994). 'Methodology of the Price Waterhouse Cranfield project' in *Policy and Practice in European Human Resource Management*. C. Brewster and A. Hegewisch (eds), London: Routledge.

Brewster, C., Tregaskis, O., Hegewisch, A. and Mayne, L. (1996). 'Comparative research in human resource management: a review and an example'. *International Journal of Human Resource Management*, 7: 3, 585-604.

Child, J. (1972). 'Organisational structure, environment and performance: the role of strategic choice'. *Sociology*, 6: 1, 1-22.

Clark, P. (1987). *Anglo-American Innovation*, Berlin: De Gruyter.

Clark, P. and Staunton, N. (1989). *Innovation in Technology and Organisation*, London: Routledge.

Clark, R. (1979). *The Japanese Company*, Newhaven, Conn: Yale University Press.

Daniels, J. (1970). 'Recent foreign direct manufacturing investment in the United States'. *Journal of International Business Studies*, 1: 1, 125-132.

Daniels, K., Lammond, D. and Standen, P. (2001). 'Teleworking: frameworks for organisational research'. *Journal of Management Studies*, forthcoming.

Deephouse, D. (1996). 'Does isomorphism legitimate?'. *Academy of Management Journal*, 39: 4, 1024-1039.

DiMaggio, P. (1988). 'Interest and agency in institutional theory' in *Institutional Patterns and Organisations: Culture and Environment*. L. Zucker (ed), Cambridge, MA: Ballinger.

DiMaggio, P. and Powell, W. (1983). 'The iron cage revisited: institutional isomorphism and collective rationality in organisational fields'. *American Sociological Review*, 48: 2, 147-160.

DiMaggio, P. and Powell, W. (1991). 'The iron cage revisited: institutional isomorphism and collective rationality in organisational fields' in *The New Institutionalism in Organisational Analysis*. W. Powell and P. DiMaggio (eds), London, University of Chicago Press.

Dobbin, F., Sutton, J., Meyer, J. and Scott, W. (1993). 'Equal opportunity law and the construction of internal labour markets'. *American Journal of Sociology*, 99: 2, 396-427.

Economist, The (1997). 'Green is good – advantages of Ireland as a host For FDI'. 17 May, 343: 8017, 21-24.

Olga Tregaskis, Noreen Heraty and Michael Morley

Enderwick, P. (1986). 'Multinationals and labour relations: the case of Ireland'. *Journal of Irish Business and Administrative Research*, 8: 1, 1-11.

Fayerweather, J. (1978). *International Business Strategy and Administration*, Cambridge: MA, Ballinger.

Ferner, A. (1997). 'Country of origin effects and HRM in multinational companies'. *Human Resource Management Journal*, 7: 1, 19-37.

Flood, P. C., Gannon, M. J. and Paauwe, J. (1996). 'Competitive advantage through strategic innovation in human resource management' in *Managing Without Traditional Methods*. P. Flood, M. Gannon and J. Paauwe (eds), Wokingham: Addison-Wesley.

Garavan, T. N., Costine, P. and Heraty, N. (1995). *Training and Development in Ireland: Context, Policy and Practice*, Dublin: Oak Tree Press.

Glickman, N., Glasmeier, A., Bannister, G. and Luker, W. (1989). 'Foreign investment, industrial linkages and regional development'. *Working Paper No. 55*, Austin: University of Texas.

Gooderham, P. and Nordhaug, O. (1997). 'Flexibility in Norwegian and UK firms: competitive pressure and institutional embeddedness. *Employee Relations*, 19: 6, 568-580.

Gooderham, P, Nordhaug, O. and Ringdal, K. (1999). 'Institutional and rational determinants of organisational practice: human resource management in European firms'. *Administrative Science Quarterly*, 44: 3, 507-531.

Greenwood, R. and Hinings, C. (1996). 'Understanding radical organisational changes: bringing together the old and the new institutionalism'. *Academy of Management Review*, 21: 4, 1022-1054.

Guillen, M. (1994). *Models of Management: Work, Authority, and Organisation in a Comparative Perspective*, Chicago: University of Chicago Press.

Hamel, G. and Prahalad, C. (1985). 'Do you really have a global strategy?'. *Harvard Business Review*, 63: 4, 139-148.

Hamblin, A. C. (1974). *Evaluation and Control of Training*, Maidenhead: McGraw-Hill.

Hamill, J. (1984). 'Labour relations decision making in multinational corporations'. *Industrial Relations Journal*, 15: 2, 30-34.

Handy, C. (1987). *The Making of Managers: A Report on Management Education, Training and Development in the United States, West Germany, France, Japan and the UK*, London: NEDO.

Harzing, A. W. (1999). *Managing the Multinationals, an International Study of Control Mechanisms*, Cheltenham: Edward Elgar.

Hausner, J., Jessop, B. and Nielsen, K. (1995). *Strategic Choice and Path Dependency in Post Socialism: Institutional Dynamics in the Transformation Process*, Aldershot: Elgar.

Hendry, C. (1994). *Human Resource Strategies for International Growth*, London: Routledge.

Heraty, N. and Morley, M. (1998a). 'Of paradigms, policies and practices: the changing contours of training and development in five European economies'. *Journal of European Industrial Training*, 22: 4/5, 154-228.

Heraty, N. and Morley, M. (1998b). 'Training and development in the Irish context: responding to the competitiveness agenda?'. *Journal of European Industrial Training*, 22: 4/5, 190-205.

Hickson, D. and McMillan, C. (eds) (1981). *Organisation and Nation: The Aston Programme IV*, Farnborough: Gower.

Hill, S., Martin, R. and Vidinova, A. (1997). 'Institutional theory and economic transformation: enterprise employment relations in Bulgaria'. *European Journal of Industrial Relations*, 3: 2, 229-251.

Hofstede, G. (1980). *Culture's Consequences: International Differences in Work Related Values*, Beverly Hills, CA: Sage.

Hosking, D. and Anderson, N. (1992). *Organisational Change and Innovation: Psychological Perspectives and Practices in Europe*, London: Routledge.

Hu, Y.-S. (1992). 'Global or stateless corporations are national firms with international operations'. *California Management Review*, 32: 2, 107-26.

Humes, S. (1993). *Managing the Multinational: Confronting the Global-Local Issue*, New York: Prentice Hall.

Jepperson, R. (1991). 'Institutions, institutional effects and institutionalism in *The New Institutionalism in Organisational Analysis*. W. Powell and P. DiMaggio (eds). Chicago: Chicago University Press.

Keep, E. and Mayhew, K. (1996). 'Evaluating the assumptions that underlie training policy' in *Acquiring Skills*. A. Booth and D. Snower (eds). Cambridge: Centre for Economic Policy Research.

Kujawa, D. (1983). 'Technology strategy and industrial relation: case studies of Japanese multinationals in the United States'. *Journal of International Business Studies*, 14: 3, 9-22.

Little, J. (1978). 'Location decisions of foreign direct investors in the United States'. *New England Economic Review*, July/August, 43-63.

Martin, R., Vidinova, A. and Hill, S. (1996). 'Industrial relations in transitional economies: emergent industrial relations institutions in Bulgaria'. *British Journal of Industrial Relations*, 34: 1, 3-24.

Martinez, R. and Dazin, M. (1999). 'Efficiency structures and normative forces: combining transaction costs and institutional logic'. *Journal of Management*, 25: 1, 75-96.

Maurice, M., Sellier, F. and Silvertre, J. (1986). *The Social Foundations of Industrial Power: A Comparison of France and Germany*, Cambridge, MA: MIT Press.

McCartney, J. and Teague, P. (1999). 'Private sector training and the organisation of the labour market: evidence from the Republic of Ireland'. Paper presented at the Irish Academy of Management Conference, University of Limerick.

Meyer, J. and Rowan, B. (1977). 'Institutional organisations: formal structures as myth and ceremony'. *American Journal of Sociology*, 83: 2, 340-363.

Meyer, J. and Scott, W. (1983). *Organisational Environments: Ritual and Reality*, Beverly Hills, CA: Sage.

Mezias, S. (1990). 'An institutional model of organisational practice: financial reporting at the Fortune 200'. *Administrative Science Quarterly*, 35: 3, 431-457.

Muller, M. (1998). 'Human resource and industrial relations practices of UK and US multinationals in Germany'. *International Journal of Human Resource Management*, 9: 4, 732-749.

Noble, C. (1997). 'The management of training in multinational corporations: comparative case studies'. *Journal of European Industrial Training*, 21: Feb/March102-110.

Oliver, C. (1991). 'Strategic responses to organisational processes'. *Academy of Management Review*, 11: 1, 145-179.

Payne, D. (1997). 'Irish answer to world's calls'. *The European*, 25 September, 29.

Peters, T. and Waterman, R. (1982). *In Search of Excellence: Lessons from America's Best Run Companies*, New York: Harper and Row.

Porter, M. (1990). *The Competitive Advantage of Nations*, New York: Free Press.

Porter, M. (1991). 'Towards a dynamic theory of strategy'. *Strategic Management Journal*, 12, 95-117.

Powell, N. (1991). 'Expanding the scope of institutional analysis' in *The New Institutionalism in Organisational Analysis*. W. Powell and P. DiMaggio (eds). Chicago:

Olga Tregaskis, Noreen Heraty and Michael Morley

University of Chicago Press.

Powell, W. and DiMaggio, P. (1991). *The New Institutionalism in Organisational Analysis*, Chicago: University of Chicago Press.

Prahalad, C. K. and Doz, Y. (1987). *The Multinational Mission: Balancing Local Demands and Global Vision*, New York: The Free Press.

Pugh, D. and Hickson, D. (1976). *Aston Programme: Volume 1*, London: Saxon House Press.

Quintanilla, J. (1998). 'The configuration of human resources management policies and practices in multinational subsidiaries: the case of European retail banks in Spain'. PhD thesis: University of Warwick, UK.

Roche, W. and Turner, T. (1994). 'Testing alternative models of human resource policy effects on trade union recognition in the Republic of Ireland'. *The International Journal of Human Resource Management*, 5: 3, 721-753.

Rosenzweig, P. and Singh, J. (1991). 'Organisational environments and the multinational enterprise'. *Academy of Management Review*, 16, 340-361.

Rosenzweig, P. M. and Nohria, N. (1994). 'Influences on human resource development practices in multinational corporations'. *Journal of International Business Studies*, 25: 2, 229-251.

Schuler, R. Dowling P. and De Cieri, H. (1993). 'An integrative framework of strategic international human resource management'. *Journal of Management*, 19: 2, 419-459.

Shultz, A. (1962). 'Common-sense scientific interpretation of human action; and concept and theory formulation in the social services' in *Collected Papers 1: The Problem of Social Reality*. M. Natanson (ed). The Hague: M. Nijhoff.

Scott, W. (1987). 'The adolescence of institutional theory'. *Administrative Science Quarterly*, 32 4, 493-511.

Selznick, P. (1949). *TVA and the Grass Roots*, Berkeley: University of California Press.

Solomon, C. (1995). 'Learning to manage host-country nationals'. *Personnel Journal*, 74: 3, 60-66.

Sparrow, P, Schuler, R. and Jackson, S. (1994). 'Convergence or divergence: human resource practices and policies for competitive advantage worldwide'. *International Journal of Human Resource Management*, 5: 2, 267-299.

Strauss, G. and Hanson, M. (1997). 'Review article: American anti-management theories of organisation: a critique of paradigm proliferation'. *Human Relations*, 50: 9, 1426-1429.

Taylor, S., Beechler, S. and Napier, N. (1996). 'Towards an integrative model of strategic international human resource management'. *Academy of Management Review*, 21: 4, 959-985.

Thompson, A., Mabey, C. and Storey, J. (1998). 'The determinants of management development: choice or circumstance?' *International Studies of Management and Organisation*, 28: 1, 91-113.

Tolbert, P. and Zucker, L. (1983). 'Institutional sources of change in the formal structure of organisations: the diffusion of civil service reform, 1880-1935'. *Administrative Science Quarterly*, 28: 1, 22-39.

Tolbert, P and Zucker, L. (1996). 'The institutionalization of institutional theory' in *Handbook of Organisational Studies*. S. Clegg, C. Hardy and W. Nord (eds). London: Sage.

Tregaskis, O. (1997). 'The role of national context and HR strategy in shaping training and development practice in French and UK organisations.' *Organisation Studies*, 18: 5.

Tregaskis, O. and Brewster, C. (1998). 'Training and development in the UK: an emerging polarisation?'. *Journal of European Industrial Training*, 22: 4/5, 180-190.

Voss, C. and Blackmon, K. (1996). 'The impact of national and parent company origin on world class manufacturing: findings from Britain and Germany'. *International Journal of Operations and Production Management*, 16: 11, 98-116.

Walsh, J. (1995). 'Managerial and organisational cognition: notes from a trip down memory lane'. *Organisation Science*, 6: 3, 280-320.

Weber, W., Kabst, R. and Gramley, C. (2000). 'Human resource policy in European organisations – an analysis of country and company specific antecedents' in *New Challenges to European Human Resource Management*. W. Myrhofer, C. Brewster and M. Morley (eds), London: Routledge.

Weick, K (1995). *Sensemaking in Organisations*, Thousand Oaks: Chicago.

Westphal, J., Gulati, R. and Shortell, S. (1997). 'Customisation or conformity? An institutional and network perspective on the content and consequences of TQM adoption'. *Administrative Science Quarterly*, 42: June, 366-394.

Whitley, R. (1992). 'The comparative study of business systems in Europe' in *European Business Systems*. R. Whitley (ed), London: Sage Publications.

Wickam, J. (1989). 'The relative autonomy of branch plant management'. Paper presented to the Annual Conference on Organisation and Control of the Labour Process, University of Manchester Institute of Science and Technology.

Williamson, O. (1996). 'Economic organization: the case for candor'. *Academy of Management Review*, 21: 1, 48-57.

Wolf, J. (1997). 'From starworks to networks and heterarchies? Theoretical rationale and empirical evidence of HRM organisation in large multinational corporations'. *Management International Review* (special edition), 37: 2, 145-169.

Young, S., Hood, N. and Hamill, J. (1985). 'Decision-making in foreign-owned multinational subsidiaries in the United Kingdom'. *ILO Working Paper No. 35*, Geneva: ILO.

Zucker, L. (1987). 'Institutional theories of organisation'. *Annual Review of Sociology*, 13, 443-464.

[26]

Toward the boundaryless career: a closer look at the expatriate career concept and the perceived implications of an international assignment

Günter K. Stahl[a], Edwin L. Miller[b,*], Rosalie L. Tung[c]

[a]INSEAD, Asian Business Area, Singapore, Singapore
[b]Department of Management, University of Michigan Business School, Ann Arbor, MI, USA
[c]Faculty of Business, Simon Fraser University, Burnaby, BC, Canada V5A 1S6

Abstract

Based on survey questionnaire data of 494 German expatriate managers on assignment to 59 countries, this study explored the nature of the expatriate career concept, the perceived impact of an international assignment on career advancement and personal development, and the effectiveness of corporate expatriate career management systems. The findings revealed that the majority of expatriates view their international assignment as an opportunity for personal and professional development and career advancement, despite perceived deficits in corporate career management systems and a widespread skepticism that the assignment will help them advance within their companies. The findings thus support the emerging notion of "boundaryless" careers. The implications for theory and practice of International Human Resource Management are discussed.

Expatriate assignments play an increasingly critical role in the execution of international business strategies and the development of global managers (Mendenhall, 2001; Stroh & Caligiuri, 1998). However, despite their strategic importance, the successful completion of international assignments do not always enhance managers' careers. In a study of management succession in U.S. companies with annual revenues in excess of U.S.$1 billion, over 93% of responding executives did not consider international experience one of the top three criteria for promotion into the ranks of senior management (Tung & Miller, 1990). As a consequence, managers are often reluctant to accept the offer of an international assignment for fear that it may result in a negative career move (Selmer, 1998; Tung, 1988).

Although relatively little is known about the long-term impact of international assignments on managers' careers, empirical research corroborates such fears. In a survey of U.S. companies, while 65% of HR executives thought an international assignment had a positive career impact, 77% of expatriates felt it had a negative effect on their careers

* Corresponding author. Tel: +1-734-764-1408.
E-mail addresses: guenter.stahl@insead.edu (G.K. Stahl), elmiller@umich.edu (E.L. Miller), tung@sfu.ca (R.L. Tung).

(Black, Gregersen, Mendenhall, & Stroh, 1999: 193). These findings are not confined to U.S. multinationals. A study of German expatriate managers found that respondents perceived career-related problems, such as anticipated difficulties finding a suitable reentry position, lack of long-term career planning, and inadequate advancement opportunities after reentry, as the most troublesome problems in their international assignments (Stahl, 2000). In fact, research has shown that the majority of returning expatriates feel their overseas assignment had a neutral, and sometimes negative, impact on their careers (Adler, 2001; Hammer, Hart, & Rogan, 1998). Not surprisingly, a substantial percentage of expatriates resign upon return and seek employment elsewhere; others become professionally unproductive and personally dissatisfied because their companies fail to capitalize upon their overseas experiences (Black et al., 1999; Caligiuri & Lazarova, 2001). Thus, from the individual manager's point of view, an expatriate career may appear as an increasingly unattractive and risky alternative (Selmer, 1998).

Then, why do managers continue to accept offers of international assignments? While few systematic attempts have been made to examine the nature of the expatriate career concept, the findings of a study conducted by Tung (1998) indicate that managers increasingly view an international

G.K. Stahl et al. / Journal of World Business 37 (2002) 216–227   217

assignment as enhancing their internal, rather than external, careers. The emerging notions of "internal" or "boundary-less" careers (Arthur & Rousseau, 1996; Parker & Inkson, 1999) suggest that managers value an international assign-ment for the opportunity it brings for skill acquisition, personal development, and career enhancement, even though it may not help them advance within their company.

The purpose of this study is to explore the nature of the expatriate career concept and to examine how it affects International Human Resource Management (IHRM) theory and practice. Much of the existing body of knowledge on expatriate career orientations has been derived from study of U.S. expatriate managers and professionals employed by American firms. A review of the literature on expatriation provides little information about how careers are interpreted by expatriates who are members of other countries.

Building on previous research on U.S. expatriates (e.g., Feldman & Thomas, 1992; Tung, 1998; Tung & Arthur Andersen, 1997) this study is one of the few to examine the career development implications of international assign-ments in a non-U.S. sample of expatriates. Consequently, career orientations will be examined from a different national perspective. Expatriates of German companies were selected for this study because Germany is a leading eco-nomic player in the world and, after the United States and Great Britain, is the world's third-largest investor abroad. In the recent past, German companies have been heavily involved in cross-border alliances and mergers and acquisi-tions, and there are large numbers of German managers and professionals working abroad (Kühlmann, 2001). Tradition-ally, German employees, particularly those at the manage-ment level, are very loyal to their companies as exhibited by low turnover rates. By studying expatriate career issues in a non-U.S. sample, it is possible to assess potential cross-cultural differences in the expatriate career concept when the findings are compared against those from U.S. expatriates, where relevant. These findings can yield some insight into whether the emerging concept of "boundaryless careers" is beginning to take hold in countries other than the U.S.

1. Expatriate career transitions and the management of international assignments

While a substantial body of research exists with regard to the selection, training, career-pathing, and repatriation of expatriates (see Black et al., 1999; Brewster, 1991; Dowling, Welch, & Schuler, 1999 for reviews), relatively little is known about whether expatriates perceive an international assignment as having a positive or negative impact on their long-term career advancement and what motivates expatri-ates to accept an international assignment.

In one of the first studies that examined the decision to accept an overseas position, Miller and Cheng (1978) found that advancement in the organization hierarchy was the primary motive influencing managers to accept an interna-

tional assignment. Other important motives were the appeal of increased pay, the opportunity to obtain greater job responsibility, and the possibility of improving one's man-agement skills and to gain international experience. The results also suggested that there are certain risks associated with an overseas assignment, including missed opportunities for advancement in the home office and difficulties finding a suitable position upon return. Yurkiewicz and Rosen (1995) also found that managers consider the opportunity to go abroad to be a mixed blessing.

International assignments provide expatriates with an opportunity to improve their general management skills and intercultural competencies, assets important at higher organization levels (Gregersen, Morrison, & Black, 1998; Mendenhall, 2001). Some scholars and senior executives even believe that international assignments are the "most powerful experience in shaping the perspective and capabil-ities of effective global leaders" (Black et al., 1999: 2). Given that the development of global leaders is key to success in today's highly competitive and rapidly changing global business world, one would expect that companies should reward managers for pursuing an overseas assign-ment and developing an international perspective. Yet, empirical research indicates that the majority of repatriates feel their international assignment had a negative impact on their careers, and that the company does not value their overseas experience and their newly acquired skills (Adler, 2001; Hammer et al., 1998).

Thus, there seems to be a discrepancy between the stated strategies of most companies to internationalize their busi-nesses and their actual IHRM policies and practices.

2. Toward the boundaryless career: a closer look at the expatriate career concept

If companies usually fail to reward managers for acquir-ing international expertise and to integrate expatriate assign-ments into long-term career paths, as the preceding literature review indicates, why do managers accept an international assignment? To explain this apparent contradiction, Tung (1998) suggested that for many expatriates, the internal career has taken precedence over the external career. According to Schein (1996), the "internal" career involves a subjective sense of where one is going in one's work life, whereas the "external" career essentially refers to advance-ment within the organizational hierarchy. For individuals pursuing internal careers, one's work life may no longer be perceived as a progression of jobs within a single organiza-tion. Rather, individuals will move from one company to another to pursue the best opportunities for their professional development. Thus, career progress comes not from intra-company hierarchical advancement, but rather from inter-company self-development (Parker & Inkson, 1999). Under this perspective, careers can be viewed as "boundaryless" (Arthur & Rousseau, 1996).

218 *G.K. Stahl et al. / Journal of World Business 37 (2002) 216–227*

Tung (1998), in a survey of U.S. expatriate managers in more than 50 countries, found that managers increasingly view international assignments as enhancing their internal, rather than external, careers. Most expatriates surveyed were seriously concerned about repatriation, yet an overwhelming majority of them perceived an international assignment as essential to their subsequent career advancement either in their current organization or elsewhere. Further, most of the expatriates in the sample viewed their overseas position as an opportunity to acquire skills and expertise usually not available at home. These findings suggest that expatriates value an overseas assignment primarily for the experience and the opportunities it brings for personal development and career enhancement, even though it may not be with their current company. The positive attitude that many expatriates have toward their international assignments, despite problems with repatriation, support the emerging notion of boundaryless careers.

Other authors (Caligiuri & Lazarova, 2001; Inkson, Pringle, Arthur, & Barry, 1997) have also suggested that "boundaryless" careers are becoming the pattern for international assignees—as with other high demand professionals, such as management consultants or information technology engineers. Since international experience is a competitive asset that makes managers more valuable for the external labor market, companies that do not provide adequate opportunities for professional growth and career advancement upon repatriation may lose a valuable human capital investment to a competitor (Caligiuri & Lazarova, 2001). Research done by Black et al. (1999: 237) has shown that the retention of internationally experienced professionals is in fact a major challenge for companies. They found that some European and U.S. companies have lost between 40% and 55% of their repatriates within 3 years after repatriation through voluntary turnover. The emerging notion of boundaryless careers suggests that many of these repatriates have deliberately chosen to leave for a better job offer elsewhere, and that they did not perceive the organizational exit as a negative career move.

3. Research questions

Because of the exploratory character of this study, no hypotheses were generated. Instead, several research questions were formulated to guide the empirical research process.

Previous research suggests that professional motives such as increased prospects of future promotion and monetary considerations are the primary reasons influencing managers to accept an international assignment (Miller & Cheng, 1978; Yurkiewicz & Rosen, 1995). Although this research has increased our understanding of the expatriate job choice process, it has offered relatively little insight into the personal and professional tradeoffs associated with the decision to accept an international assignment, and the potential negative consequences of refusing such an offer. Moreover, in

light of recent findings that the expatriate career concept is undergoing significant change (Inkson et al., 1997; Tung, 1998), previous research dealing with the motives for accepting an international assignment may be outdated. Therefore, the following research question was addressed:

Research Question 1: What motivates managers to accept an international assignment and what factors influence them in their decision to go abroad?

Prior research has shown that there is a discrepancy between the stated strategies of most companies to internationalize their businesses and their actual IHRM policies and practices. Corporate expatriate management systems have been characterized as insufficient (Feldman & Thomas, 1992), haphazard (Mendenhall, Dunbar, & Oddou, 1987), and irrelevant (Selmer, 1998). As a consequence, expatriates may perceive a disconnection between their international assignments and their long-term career plans. Therefore, a question can be raised as to whether expatriates perceive corporate IHRM policies and practices, in particular those related to the development and career-pathing of international managers, as enhancing their career advancement.

Research Question 2: Do expatriates perceive corporate IHRM policies and practices as enhancing their career advancement? Are they satisfied with how their companies approach the expatriation and repatriation process?

In explaining why managers continue to accept offers of international assignments, despite the lack of systematic career planning in most companies, it has been argued that managers increasingly view international assignments as a chance to enhance their internal, rather than their external, careers (Tung, 1998). Accordingly, expatriate managers may value an international assignment for the opportunities it brings for skill development and career advancement, even though it may not be with the same company. Up to this point, however, few attempts have been made to empirically examine the nature of the expatriate career concept and the significance that the notion of boundaryless careers has in motivating managers to accept an international assignment. Therefore, the following research question was addressed:

Research Question 3: What is the nature of the expatriate career concept? Specifically, are boundaryless careers becoming the pattern for international assignees?

4. Method

4.1. Organizational context and sample characteristics

In attempting to better understand what motivates expatriates to accept an international assignment, whether they perceive corporate IHRM policies and practices as enhancing

G.K. Stahl et al. / Journal of World Business 37 (2002) 216–227   219

their careers, and what the nature of their career concept is, we surveyed expatriate managers of 30 German companies in 59 countries. Among the companies were 7 of the 20 largest German firms. They represented a variety of industries, including electronics, cars, pharmaceuticals, consumer products, and financial services. We selected expatriates of German companies for this study because we were interested in exploring expatriate career issues in a non-U.S. sample, and comparing the findings against those obtained from U.S. subjects (e.g., Tung, 1998; Tung & Arthur Andersen, 1997). Given the slightly different focus of this and Tung's study, comparative data are not available for all items.

A survey questionnaire, along with self-addressed envelopes for return, were sent to HR executives working in the corporate head offices in Germany. The HR executives then forwarded the questionnaires to the expatriates abroad. The completed questionnaires were returned directly to the first author to ensure confidentiality of responses. Of the 1058 survey questionnaires mailed, 549 were returned; 494 were usable, for a response rate of 47%.

As Table 1 indicates, the "typical" respondent in this study was a college-educated male, between 30 and 40 years old, married, occupying a middle management position, had

been posted to a North-American, Western-European, or Southeast-Asian country, and had been on the expatriate assignment between 6 and 18 months. Since some of the research questions focused on aspects of the expatriate job choice process prior to the international assignment (e.g., motives for going abroad), the sample for this study was drawn from expatriates who had been posted to their overseas locations no longer than 2 years. It was hoped that this group of expatriates would be able to provide more reliable retrospective accounts of the job choice process prior to their international assignments than expatriates who had been living abroad for many years.

Interestingly, the demographic profile of respondents suggests that there is a slow but steady increase in the use of women in international assignments. In the early 1990s, less than 3% of German expatriates were women; this figure increased to 5% in the mid-1990s, to 7% in the late 1990s (Stahl, 2000), and to 10% in the present study. A similar trend has been observed for U.S. expatriates (Adler, 2001; Tung, 1998).

4.2. Instruments and measures

Based on an extensive review of the expatriate career literature and previous research conducted by the authors, a survey questionnaire was developed to examine expatriates' attitudes toward their international assignments and their experience abroad, including the perceived career implications of an international assignment.

The survey questionnaire comprised five sections. The first section contained demographic questions, including those related to spouse and family characteristics. The second section contained questions related to the expatriate job choice process. A sample item in this section presented expatriates with a list of motives for going abroad and asked them to rank order the five most important considerations in their decision to accept an overseas assignment. The third section contained questions regarding career expectations, including the perceived impact of an overseas assignment on the career. A sample item in this section measured opportunities for career advancement within the company. The fourth section contained questions related to satisfaction with corporate expatriation policies and practices, including perceived discrepancies between the company's stated strategy to internationalize its business and its actual policies and practices. A sample item in this section measured satisfaction with the compensation and benefits package. The final section contained questions regarding repatriation. A sample item in this section measured concern about reduced responsibility and autonomy upon repatriation.

In addition, expatriates were asked to respond to several open-ended questions. A sample item asked expatriates if and why they believed that their international assignment had a positive impact on their overall career. Responses to the open-ended questions were extracted from the questionnaires and analyzed by using content analytical techniques.

Table 1
Demographic profile of expatriate sample

Demographic variables	Frequency	Percentage
Gender		
Male	440	90
Female	47	10
Age (years)		
<30	49	10
30–40	302	62
>40	136	28
Marital status		
Married	317	65
Not married	170	35
Position level		
Senior management	109	23
Middle/lower management	266	55
Professional/technical	98	20
Other	10	2
Region of assignment		
North-America	163	34
South- and Latin-America	38	8
Western-Europe	119	25
Eastern-Europe	43	9
South-East Asia	105	22
Africa and Middle East	17	3
Length of stay in host country		
<6 Months	33	7
6–12 Months	182	37
12–18 Months	196	40
18–24 Months	75	16

220 G.K. Stahl et al. / Journal of World Business 37 (2002) 216–227

Table 2
Motives for accepting an international assignment

Motives	Among five most important (%)	Most important[a] (%)
Personal challenge	83	39
Professional development	78	17
Importance of the job itself	68	22
Future opportunities for advancement	61	7
Geographic location of the assignment	54	4
Monetary considerations	50	5
Anticipated job success	39	2
Normal career advancement pattern	21	1
Family considerations	18	2
Encouragement from spouse or partner	15	1
Encouragement from colleagues and superiors	6	0
Fear of restricted career opportunities within the home office	3	1

[a] Respondents were asked to rank order the five most important considerations in their decision to accept an international assignment ($n = 435$).

5. Results

In this section, the findings of descriptive statistical analyses are presented to address the main research questions under investigation.[1]

5.1. Expatriate job choice

The first research question sought to examine what motivates managers to accept an international assignment and what factors influence expatriates' career decisions. Table 2 presents the various motives for accepting an international assignment, rank ordered according to their perceived importance. The findings indicate that motives such as personal challenge and professional development are more important than opportunities for career advancement in influencing managers to accept an international assignment. Thus, aside from viewing the overseas assignment as a prerequisite for subsequent career advancement, the findings suggest that expatriates place a high intrinsic value on the personal challenge posed by living and working overseas and the concomitant professional development that comes from overcoming such challenges.

"Intrinsic" motivation refers to the notion that something is worth doing it for its own sake, e.g., because it is interesting and creates a learning opportunity, and not because it is rewarded with money or praise (Deci, 1975). The expatriates in this study ranked "personal challenge"— a clearly intrinsic motive—as the most important reason why they had accepted the assignment. In contrast, monetary reasons were considered only moderately important in the decision to go abroad. Interestingly, compared to U.S. managers who consistently rank financial rewards as one

of the top reasons for accepting an international assignment (Tung & Arthur Andersen, 1997; Yurkiewicz & Rosen, 1995), German expatriates seemed to put a higher emphasis on intrinsic motives. This finding may in part be explained by the fact that most German companies have reduced the sizes of compensation packages for expatriates in recent years.

Torbiörn (1982: 82) distinguishes between negative motives or "push factors" that drive employees toward an international assignment (e.g., dissatisfaction with the situation in the home country) and positive motives or "pull factors" (e.g., the expectation that an overseas assignment could provide great satisfaction). In order to find out more about the "push factors," expatriates were asked whether they anticipated any negative consequences if they had refused the overseas assignment. The findings revealed that 69% of respondents believed that a manager can never or at most decline an international assignment only once without it negatively affecting his/her subsequent career advancement; 61% believed that rejection of the job offer would have limited their subsequent career opportunities within the company. Thus, although the expatriates in the sample were positively and intrinsically motivated to go abroad, they also anticipated serious negative consequences if they had refused the international assignment.

5.2. Satisfaction with IHRM policies and practices

Prior research has found that corporate IHRM policies and practices are often non-strategic and *ad hoc* (Mendenhall et al., 1987; Selmer, 1998). Asked whether they see a discrepancy between their company's stated strategy to internationalize its business and its actual IHRM policies and practices, 65% of the expatriates in this study felt there was such a discrepancy, while 35% said there was no such discrepancy. Table 3 summarizes the reasons given by those expatriates who saw a discrepancy. Note that the percentage

---

[1] The results of additional data analyses (e.g., significance tests on the basis of region of assignment, position level, and gender) can be obtained from the first author.

G.K. Stahl et al. / Journal of World Business 37 (2002) 216–227   221

Table 3
Reasons why expatriates perceive a discrepancy between their company's stated internationalization strategy and actual IHRM policies and practices

Perceived discrepancy between strategy and IHRM policies and practices[a]	Percentage of expatriates[b]
Lack of career planning and support during the international assignment	
Lack of long-term career planning and/or reentry planning	53
No systematic development of managers for international careers	
Lack of company support during the international assignment	
IHRM policies reflect low degree or early stage of internationalization	
Ethnocentric staffing and/or compensation policy	30
Top management is parochial and/or has no international experience	
International experience is not valued/rewarded at corporate headquarters	
Deficits in implementing a global strategy	
There is no visible/clear strategy to internationalize the business	17
There is a gap between statements of top management and actual practice	
Speed of implementation of global strategy is too slow	

[a] Responses to an open-ended question were content-analyzed.
[b] Percentage data refer to sub-sample of expatriates who perceived a discrepancy and responded to the question ($n = 242$).

data likely provide conservative estimates of the actual figures, because few expatriates provided more than one explanation. The results indicate that a lack of long-term career planning and company support during the overseas assignment are the most important reasons why expatriates perceive a discrepancy.

To investigate further about the perceived career implications of an international assignment, respondents were asked to indicate the extent to which their company rewards its employees for acquiring international expertise. Table 4 shows that respondents were rather skeptical that their company will reward them for pursuing an international

Table 4
Expatriates' perception of corporate IHRM policies and practices

Perception of IHRM policies and practices	Percentage of expatriates[a]		
	Very little/little extent	Neutral	Very great/great extent
Rewards for international assignment			
Rewards for pursuing an international assignment	30	33	37
Rewards for developing an international perspective	33	31	37
Rewards for developing a worldwide network of associates	39	31	30
Rewards for acquiring fluency in a foreign language	40	36	25
	Dissatisfied/highly dissatisfied	Neutral	Satisfied/highly satisfied
Satisfaction with expatriation policies and practices			
Pre-departure preparation for requirements of the new job	41	33	26
Pre-departure cross-cultural training	42	34	24
Compensation and benefits package	39	26	35
Ongoing support during the international assignment	44	32	24
Long-range planning of the repatriation	64	22	14
	Concerned/highly concerned	Neutral	Not/not at all concerned
Concerns about repatriation			
Career advancement upon repatriation	20	23	58
Reduced responsibility and autonomy on the job	42	22	36
Reduced size of compensation package upon repatriation	33	21	47
Limited opportunities for using new knowledge and skills	37	22	41
Spouse's/partner's job and career upon repatriation	30	18	52

[a] Sample sizes vary between $n = 441$ and 465 for perceived rewards; $n = 451$–483 for aspects of satisfaction; and $n = 318$–474 for aspects of repatriation.

G.K. Stahl et al. / Journal of World Business 37 (2002) 216–227

assignment, for developing an international perspective, for developing a worldwide network of associates, and for acquiring fluency in a foreign language. Expatriates who perceived a discrepancy between their company's stated strategy to internationalize its business and its actual IHRM policies and practices were particularly pessimistic that their company will reward them for pursuing an international assignment, for developing an international perspective, for developing a worldwide network of associates and for acquiring fluency in a foreign language than were respondents who saw no such discrepancy. Apparently, expatriates who perceive corporate IHRM policies and practices as nonstrategic do so because they see a disconnection between their overseas assignment and their subsequent career advancement within the company.

Given the prevailing doubts among expatriates that they will be rewarded for acquiring international expertise, how satisfied are respondents with the way their company approaches the expatriation and repatriation process? Table 4 indicates that the majority of expatriates in this study were not very satisfied with how the HR department handled their overseas assignment, especially the long-range planning of their repatriation. This finding is consistent with prior research indicating that repatriation may be the most problematic stage in the expatriation cycle (Adler, 2001; Stahl, 2000; Tung, 1998). In Tung (1998), while American expatriates expressed overall satisfaction with an international assignment, when asked to assess separately their satisfaction with expatriation and repatriation, there was a marked discrepancy between the two.

In order to find out more about the anticipated reentry difficulties of expatriates, several items addressed concerns about different aspects of the repatriation process. Table 4 indicates that relatively few respondents were concerned about different aspects of their repatriation, such as career advancement, degree of autonomy and responsibility, size of the compensation package, and opportunities for using the newly gained international expertise upon return. Thus, although the majority of expatriates were dissatisfied with how their company approached the repatriation process, many of them were relatively nonchalant regarding the outcomes of their repatriation.

There are several possible interpretations of this finding. First, the expatriates in the sample had been on their overseas assignments for less than 2 years. Despite their dissatisfaction with how the company planned for their reentry and future careers, it is plausible that they were not overly concerned about repatriation at such an early stage of their overseas assignment. Second, 83% of expatriates were guaranteed a reentry position upon completion of the overseas assignment. This figure is much higher than the 40% found in a study of U.S. expatriates conducted by Tung (1998) where most expatriates expressed a serious concern about repatriation. Having a guaranteed position upon return may have resulted in a higher degree of job security and hence less worry about repatriation. Finally, the changing nature of the expatriate career concept may explain respondents' nonchalance regarding their repatriation. Issues related to the career orientation of expatriates will be addressed in the following section.

5.3. Expatriate career concept and career aspirations

In order to find out whether boundaryless careers are indeed becoming the pattern for international assignees, expatriates were asked to indicate the likelihood that successful performance in their current overseas assignment will advance their career within or outside the company. Table 5 indicates that an overwhelming majority of respondents believed that their international assignment will have a positive impact on future career opportunities among other possible employers, while considerably fewer expatriates were confident that it will help them advance within their current company. Also, expatriates were very optimistic that their overseas assignment will help them improve their professional and management skills, and they firmly believed that it will enhance their intercultural skills as well. The finding that the vast majority of expatriates viewed their international assignment as an opportunity for skill development and future career advancement, even though it may not be with their current company, clearly supports the notion of boundaryless careers.

Additional evidence comes from the finding that a considerable number of expatriates were willing to resign upon return and seek employment elsewhere. Asked whether they would leave their company for a better job in another firm, 51% of respondents said they were willing to do so, whereas only 25% indicated that they were unwilling to leave their company. Given the traditionally high loyalty of German

Table 5
Perceived impact of the international assignment on career advancement and development

Perceived career impact	Percentage of expatriates[a]		
	Highly unlikely/unlikely	Neutral	Highly likely/likely
Advancement within the company	15	26	59
Career opportunities among other possible employers	4	7	89
Demonstration of professional or managerial skills	6	9	85
Development of professional and managerial skills	5	11	84
Development of intercultural skills	1	4	95

[a] Sample sizes vary between $n = 466$ and 483 for different aspects of career development.

G.K. Stahl et al. / Journal of World Business 37 (2002) 216–227   223

Table 6
Reasons why expatriates believe that their international assignment will have a positive impact on their overall career

Perceived positive impact of international assignment on career[a]	Percentage of expatriates[b]
Enhances personality development and enriches personal life	
Leads to a more mature personality and broadens the horizon	71
Reduces ethnocentrism, narrow-mindedness, and intolerance	
Enables one to develop a global mindset	
Forces one to take initiative and assume responsibility	
Enriches one's life in general	
Improves managerial, interpersonal, and communication skills	
Enhances professional or managerial skills	34
Enhances interpersonal and communication competence	
Enhances intercultural skills	
Allows one to acquire fluency in a foreign language	
Enables one to create a network of international contacts	
Directly affects subsequent career advancement	
Leads to job offers from possible employers in the home country	15
Creates career opportunities in the host country or other foreign subsidiaries	
Increases visibility for "headhunters"	
Is an essential part of the Curriculum Vitae of any manager	

[a] Responses to an open-ended question were content-analyzed.
[b] Percentage data refer to sub-sample of expatriates who agreed with the statement, "Even if the overseas assignment will not enhance my career prospects within my company, it will have a positive impact on my overall career," and who responded to the question ($n = 295$).

professionals toward their employers, this finding provides strong support for the notion of boundaryless careers. It may also explain why the expatriates were only moderately concerned about career advancement upon return. Apparently, respondents were confident that the demand for their international expertise on the labor market was high and, therefore, they should be able to find better jobs elsewhere.

Further insight into the expatriate career concept comes from responses to an open-ended question. Respondents were asked to indicate the extent to which they agreed with the statement that their international assignment will have a positive impact on their overall career, even if it does not enhance their advancement within their company, and to explain their answer in detail. The findings revealed that 89% of respondents agreed with this statement, while only 11% disagreed. Table 6 indicates that expatriates who were confident that their international assignment had a positive impact on their overall careers believed so because they felt it enhanced their personality development, enabled them to develop a global mindset, and enriched their personal lives. In addition, many expatriates believed that an overseas assignment will help them improve their managerial, interpersonal, and communication skills, and enable them to create a valuable network of personal relationships. However, only few expatriates believed that their overseas assignment will have a direct effect on their subsequent career advancement.

These findings suggest that expatriates perceive an international assignment as having an impact on their internal career, to use Schein's (1996) terminology, through the acquisition of knowledge, skills, and experiences that are usually not available in the home country. As such, expatriates

seem to place a high intrinsic value on the overseas assignment *per se*, rather than merely viewing it as a prerequisite for hierarchical career advancement.

6. Discussion

This study extended the current research on expatriation and repatriation in several ways. First, while empirical research on the antecedents of expatriate and repatriate adjustment abounds, few systematic attempts have been made to examine the career development aspects of international assignments. This study focused on the nature of the expatriate career concept, in particular, the significance of "boundaryless" careers in motivating managers to accept an overseas assignment, and explored how this notion of careers affects the attitudes of expatriate managers toward their international assignments.

Building on prior research on U.S. expatriates (e.g., Feldman & Thomas, 1992; Tung, 1998), this study is one of the few to examine the career implications of international assignments in a non-U.S. sample of expatriates to determine the extent to which the concept of "boundaryless careers" has extended beyond a U.S. context. The findings clearly support Tung's (1998) conclusion that boundaryless careers are indeed becoming the pattern for international assignees. Although the majority of expatriates in this sample were dissatisfied with how their company rewarded its employees for pursuing an international assignment and were critical of their company's repatriation practice, they firmly believed that their overseas assignment will help improve their professional and

G.K. Stahl et al. / Journal of World Business 37 (2002) 216–227

management skills and enhance their careers, though not necessarily within their current company. However, rather than merely viewing international mobility as a prerequisite for subsequent career advancement, the expatriates placed a high intrinsic value on the overseas experience *per se*, especially on the opportunities it brings for personality development and enrichment of their personal lives.

Perhaps it is not surprising that the concept of "boundaryless careers" has indeed extended beyond the U.S. After all, the executives who accept international assignments are typically more adventurous and less risk averse (Tung, 1999). Furthermore, given the extensive socialization of expatriates abroad, particularly among those from industrialized countries and from an Anglo-Saxon background (Tung, 1998), different career aspects (including challenges and opportunities) become frequent topics of discussion.

6.1. Implications for practice

One of the most striking findings of this study was the positive attitude that expatriates had toward their international assignment, despite a widespread dissatisfaction with how their company rewarded international experience and approached the repatriation process. While there is a growing recognition that managers who work for companies that are less sympathetic to career development concerns will be more reluctant to accept offers of international assignments (Selmer, 1998), the fact that expatriates place a high intrinsic value on the overseas experience suggests that companies will continue be able to *recruit* capable managers for international assignments in the future. However, this does not imply that companies will also be able to *retain* these managers upon repatriation. This study found that the majority of expatriates were confident that the demand for their international expertise on the external labor market was high, and they were prepared to leave their company for a better job elsewhere.

These findings have important implications for IHRM practice. In terms of organizational career development programs, the notion of integrating international assignments into logical career paths seems to be the most critical variable in facilitating expatriation and repatriation success (Feldman & Thomas, 1992; Oddou & Mendenhall, 1991). Organizational career development programs and repatriation practices, such as managing expatriates' career expectations, providing career-path information, organizing participation in networking activities that allow expatriates to stay in touch with key people in the organization, providing ongoing coaching or mentoring, continuously reviewing performance during the international assignment, and improving expatriates' career self-management skills can facilitate the career-pathing and repatriation of international managers (Caligiuri & Lazarova, 2001; Selmer, 1999). While well meaning organizational career development programs and repatriation practices are necessary for managing expatriates' career expectations, there are preparatory activities and commitments the organization must under-

take. If the organization fails to meet these requirements, there is little chance that its career development and repatriation programs will be able to successfully respond to the growing boundaryless career orientation of expatriates and the increasing turnover rates among repatriates.

If the organization expects to develop a well-meaning career development program and implement effective repatriation practices several preliminary steps must be undertaken. It will be critical for the IHRM function and management to seek a thorough understanding and explanation to the following questions: (1) "Who is leaving or recently left, and who is staying?" (2) "Are there professional and personal characteristics of those repatriates who are preparing to leave or have left the organization after repatriation which differentiate them from their repatriate peers who have chosen to remain with the organization over the same time period?" With a better understanding of the dimensions of repatriate turnover, the IHRM function will be able to propose steps to rectify the problem. Typically turnover data are reported in the aggregate and little attention has been directed toward a more refined and detailed analysis of repatriate turnover. Clearly, some turnover upon repatriation is functional and beneficial to the firm because the repatriate's skills and experiences are no longer needed by the organization as it competes in the global marketplace. Consequently, there may be no available job for the repatriate, and termination is the best personnel decision for the repatriate and for the organization.

In other cases repatriate turnover may be dysfunctional to the organization because it inflicts a costly expense (time-, money-, and human resource-wise) in terms of lost investment in human resources, particularly if the repatriates had been members of the firm's managerial and professional elite or if they had joined companies which are considered to be the firm's competitors in the global marketplace. These lost investments are costly time-wise because there is downtime required to select a candidate for an international assignment and to allow the expatriate to relocate and settle in his/her new position abroad. These lost investments are expensive money-wise because of the relocation expense and the premiums paid for international assignments, particularly to high-cost cities. The amount paid to an expatriate averages two to three times base salary. Furthermore, the lost investment is costly human resource-wise because many international assignments now are used for career development purposes as opposed to the past practice of merely filling a position abroad. When these managers with high potentials are lost to one's competitors in a global economy where an international mindset is pivotal to success, the damages to the company in the long-term can be immeasurably high.

Thus, it is imperative that a company gain a better appreciation of who is leaving and who is staying because it will provide the basis for designing career development programs and repatriation practices that will address the needs of repatriates who are motivated by a boundaryless

G.K. Stahl et al. / Journal of World Business 37 (2002) 216–227   225

career orientation and whose skills and talents the organization seeks to retain.

As Caligiuri and Lazarova (2001) asserted, "honesty is the best recommendation for building a repatriation system." Organizational honesty in terms of the positive contribution of international experience, requires the firm to be forthright in terms of its personnel decisions, positive expressions and actions of senior management and continuous support, commitment and communication with its expatriates during and upon completion of their global assignments. In a recent study of the antecedents of turnover intentions among repatriates, Lazarova and Caligiuri (2000) found that rather than choosing any specific type of repatriation assistance, repatriates rated visible signs that the company values overseas experience and that international expertise is beneficial to one's career as the most important elements in the IHRM system. Specifically the company's leadership must aggressively demonstrate that it values international expertise, and such experience will enhance one's career advancement and prestige within the organization. Unfortunately, only one third of the expatriates surveyed in this study felt that their international experience was appreciated by their companies.

While well-designed career development programs can assist in the effective repatriation and retention of managers after an international assignment, companies will not be able to capitalize on the overseas experience of their workforce unless they have developed a truly global corporate culture. As more and more companies move away from multinational organizations toward more global ways to organize and manage, the development of global leaders is becoming increasingly important for companies in order to succeed in the business world (Adler, 2001; Mendenhall, Kühlmann, & Stahl, 2001; Stroh & Caligiuri, 1998). An effective way to develop this new breed of managers is to send them on international assignments where they can assume a broader range of duties and improve their general management skills and intercultural competencies (Gregersen et al., 1998; Mendenhall, 2001; Tung, 1998).

From a slightly different perspective, as firms develop global strategies to guide their participation in the global marketplace, there will be implications for the management of their human resource system. The career orientation of host country managers, expatriates and "third country nationals" will become much more important in the management process. Personnel decisions including staffing, retention and repatriation of expatriates and third country nationals may prove to be incorrect if those decisions are solely based on American career concepts. Consequently, in-depth knowledge about career orientations based on country specific data will improve the likelihood of improved decisions appropriate for the staffing decisions and management of a firm's human resource system.

As the findings about the changing nature of expatriate career concept indicate, companies need to do a much better job at leveraging and rewarding the global skills of the managers in whom they have invested a lot of money during

their international assignments if they want to retain them upon repatriation. To thrive in a global economy, companies must excel in both recruitment and retention of such scarce executive talent.

6.2. Future research

This study provided some new and useful insights into the career development aspects of international assignments by suggesting that the concept of "boundaryless careers" is indeed becoming more prevalent and widespread across countries. However, its inherent limitations have to be considered, as well as avenues for future research. First, the results have to be replicated using different samples and research methodologies to establish their generalizability. While the results corroborate those of a large-scale study of U.S. expatriates (Tung, 1998), and, therefore, suggest that findings on expatriate careers are to some degree generalizable across different national samples, future studies should replicate and elaborate these findings by collecting data from nationally more diverse samples.

Second, quantitative studies that focus on hypothesis testing have to be combined with more qualitative methodologies to better understand the changing nature of the expatriate career concept. Because of the exploratory character of this study, no hypotheses were generated. However, from the findings of this and other studies (e.g., Feldman & Thomas, 1992; Tung, 1998), as well as from theoretical research dealing with the changing nature of the expatriate career concept (e.g., Inkson et al., 1997), it is now possible to derive hypotheses and empirically test them. In addition, qualitative methodologies such as in-depth interviews and case studies should be employed to find out more about the career implications of expatriate assignments.

Third, an interesting question concerns the career orientation of those managers who have dismissed an overseas assignment because they believe it is not instrumental for the development of their careers. Are those managers any less internally oriented in terms of their career development than their expatriate counterparts? These questions can provide the source for future investigations aimed at exploring other dimensions and complexities of the boundaryless career orientation.

Fourth, from a broader perspective, non-work related issues such as family situation, dual-careers, support of the spouse, etc., are important, yet understudied aspects of expatriate careers. For example, the trailing spouse's career orientation and job opportunities overseas may play an important role in the decision to accept or reject an international assignment, and may also influence the level of work performance and satisfaction overseas (Harvey, 1996). Future research—and IHRM practice as well—would probably benefit from a closer examination of non-work related variables that enhance or constrain expatriate careers.

Fifth, greater attention has to be devoted to the analysis of expatriate turnover. Disaggregating turnover into its functional versus dysfunctional aspects based on the goals of the assignment, the firm's intention for assigning an individual to a global job and repatriate's career expectations will help to improve our understanding of the determinants of turnover and possible organizational responses for coping with it. In-depth study and knowledge will contribute to the construction of expatriate turnover models as well as insights and practical recommendations to global corporations and their management cadres about how to manage the career expectations of repatriates.

7. Conclusion

This study represents an incremental advance in terms of the perceived dynamics of expatriate career development, and contributes to a better understanding of the internal or boundaryless career notion. For the academic researcher interested in IHRM, the results of this study make two contributions. First, rather than replicating what is known about how firms go about selecting individuals for overseas assignments, this study examined expatriate perceptions concerning the reasons why they accepted an overseas assignment. Given the results of this study, one can conclude that at least with respect to this sample of German expatriates their career orientation becomes an important factor in their motivation to accept an overseas assignment. Traditionally, loyalty to the firm and blind acceptance of the firm's decision had been the basis for acceptance of the overseas assignment: the firm decided where and when an employee was to be assigned abroad. This study indicates that for many of the expatriates, the assignment was evaluated in terms of what it would contribute to their personal and professional development and their subsequent career advancement. Second, the notion of the boundaryless career concept of expatriates provides new insights into the emerging body of knowledge on career orientations.

The basis for early and excessive turnover among repatriates has been expanded to include the career orientation of the repatriate as another factor that contributes to repatriation failure. Fortunately, the firm can work on this problem, and it can seek to take corrective action to deal with dysfunctional IHRM policies and practices. Some of the organizational actions have been discussed earlier in the paper. For the firm it is important to know that there is something that it can do, and that is to clearly demonstrate that it appreciates and values the expatriate's experience and that it will capitalize on that experience upon return.

Acknowledgments

We would like to thank the editor and two anonymous reviewers of the *Journal of World Business* for their helpful comments on an earlier version of this paper.

References

Adler, N. J. (2001). *International dimensions of organizational behavior* (4th ed.). Cincinnati: South-Western College Publishing.

Arthur, M. B., & Rousseau, D. M. (Eds.) (1996). *The boundaryless career: A new employment principle for a new organizational era*. New York: Oxford University Press.

Black, J. S., Gregersen, H. B., Mendenhall, M. E., & Stroh, L. K. (1999). *Globalizing people through international assignments*. New York: Addison-Wesley, Longman.

Brewster, C. (1991). *The management of expatriates*. London: Kogan.

Caligiuri, P. M., & Lazarova, M. (2001). Strategic repatriation policies to enhance global leadership development. In M. E. Mendenhall, T. M. Kühlmann, & G. K. Stahl (Eds.), *Developing global business leaders* (pp. 243–256). Westport: Quorum.

Deci, E. L. (1975). *Intrinsic motivation*. New York: Plenum Press.

Dowling, P. J., Welch, D. E., & Schuler, R. S. (1999). *International Human Resource Management: Managing people in a multinational context* (3rd ed.). Cincinnati: South-Western College Publishing.

Feldman, D. C., & Thomas, D. C. (1992). Career management issues facing expatriates. *Journal of International Business Studies, 23*: 271–294.

Gregersen, H. B., Morrison, A. J., & Black, J. S. (1998). Developing leaders for the global frontier. *Sloan Management Review, 40*: 21–32.

Hammer, M. R., Hart, W., & Rogan, R. (1998). Can you go home again? An analysis of the repatriation of corporate managers and spouses. *Management International Review, 38*: 67–86.

Harvey, M. (1996). Addressing the dual-career expatriation dilemma. *Human Resource Planning, 19*: 18–39.

Inkson, K., Pringle, J., Arthur, M. B., & Barry, S. (1997). Expatriate assignment versus overseas experience: Contrasting models of international human resource development. *Journal of World Business, 32*: 351–368.

Kühlmann, T. M. (2001). The German approach to developing global leaders via expatriation. In M. E. Mendenhall, T. M. Kühlmann, & G. K. Stahl (Eds.), *Developing global business leaders: Policies, processes, and innovations* (pp. 57–71). Westport: Quorum.

Lazarova, M., & Caligiuri, P. (2000). Retaining repatriates: The role of organizational support practices. *Paper presented at the 2000 Academy of Management Meeting*, Toronto, Canada.

Mendenhall, M. E. (2001). New perspectives on expatriate adjustment and its relationship to global leadership development. In M. E. Mendenhall, T. M. Kühlmann, & G. K. Stahl (Eds.), *Developing global business leaders* (pp. 1–16). Westport: Quorum.

Mendenhall, M. E., Dunbar, E., & Oddou, G. R. (1987). Expatriate selection, training, and career-pathing: A review and critique. *Human Resource Management, 26*: 331–345.

Mendenhall, M. E., Kühlmann, T. M., & Stahl, G. K. (Eds.) (2001). *Developing global business leaders: Policies, processes, and innovations*. Westport: Quorum.

Miller, E. L., & Cheng, J. L. (1978). A closer look at the decision to accept an overseas position. *Management International Review, 3*: 25–33.

Oddou, G. R., & Mendenhall, M. E. (1991). Succession planning for the 21st century: How well are we grooming our future business leaders? *Business Horizons, 34*: 26–34.

G.K. Stahl et al. / Journal of World Business 37 (2002) 216–227   227

Parker, P., & Inkson, K. (1999). New forms of career: The challenge to human resource management. *Asia Pacific Journal of Human Resources, 37*: 76–85.

Schein, E. H. (1996). Career anchors revisited: Implications for career development in the 21st century. *Academy of Management Executive, 10*: 80–88.

Selmer, J. (1998). Expatriation: Corporate policy, personal intentions and international adjustment. *International Journal of Human Resource Management, 9*: 996–1007.

Selmer, J. (1999). Corporate expatriate career development. *Journal of International Management, 5*: 55–71.

Stahl, G. K. (2000). Between ethnocentrism and assimilation: An exploratory study of the challenges and coping strategies of expatriate managers. *Academy of Management Proceedings,* IM: E1–E6.

Stroh, L. K., & Caligiuri, P. M. (1998). Strategic human resources: A new source for competitive advantage. *International Journal of Human Resource Management, 9*: 1–17.

Torbiörn, I. (1982). *Living abroad: Personal adjustment and personnel policy in the overseas setting.* New York: Wiley.

Tung, R. L. (1988). Career issues in international assignments. *Academy of Management Executive, 2*: 241–244.

Tung, R. L. (1998). American expatriates abroad: From neophytes to cosmopolitans. *Journal of World Business, 33*: 125–144.

Tung, R. L. (1999). International Human Resource Management. In R. L. Tung (Ed.), *The IEBM Handbook of International Business* (pp. 215–231). London: Thomson Learning.

Tung, R. L., & Miller, E. L. (1990). Managing in the twenty-first century: The need for global orientation. *Management International Review, 30*: 5–18.

Tung, R. L., & Arthur Andersen (1997). *Exploring international assignees' viewpoints: A study of the expatriation/repatriation process.* Chicago IL: Arthur Anderson.

Yurkiewicz, J., & Rosen, B. (1995). Increasing receptivity to expatriate assignments. In J. Selmer (Ed.), *Expatriate management* (pp. 37–56). Westport: Quorum.

[27]

Creating and Sustaining Ethical Capability in the Multi-National Corporation

Paul F. Buller   **Glenn M. McEvoy**

Multinational corporations are continually seeking sources of competitive advantage. In addition to strategic, technological, financial, and organizational capabilities as sources of competitive advantage, this paper argues that ethical capability also can be an important source of sustainable advantage. The paper presents the challenges of ethics in an international context, discusses the resource-based view of competitive advantage, and describes how a multinational company can develop and sustain ethical capability through the related processes of transformational leadership, organizational learning, and human resource management.

Multi-national corporations (MNCs) face a variety of questions regarding the appropriate business practices to use in the different countries in which they compete. MNCs face challenges in determining the right product, market, finance, and human resource management strategies across different national cultures. Increasingly, among the many questions facing MNCs are those concerning business ethics, that is, the rightness or wrongness of certain business actions across cultures. Recent writings on international business ethics suggest that the decisions regarding ap-

propriate ethical actions are complex and multifaceted (Buller, Kohls, & Anderson, 1997; DeGeorge, 1993; Donaldson, 1989, 1996; Jackson, 1997). Further, there is little guidance in the literature about how an MNC can enhance its capability in dealing with international business ethics. This paper briefly reviews current approaches to addressing questions of ethics in a cross-cultural context. It then builds on Litz's (1996) contention that sound ethical practice is an overlooked potential source of competitive advantage to the MNC. A discussion of the resource-based perspective of competitive advantage serves as the foundation of our proposition that ethical capability is a sustainable source of competitive advantage. The paper concludes with a

Paul F. Buller, School of Business Administration, Gonzaga University, Spokane, WA 99258, USA. Glenn M. McEvoy, Department of Management & Human Resources, College of Business, Utah State University, Logan, UT 84322, USA.

description of how transformational leadership, organizational learning, and human resource management (HRM) are integral to building MNC capabilities in global ethics.

Ethical Capability

The central premise of this article is that an MNC's ethical capability may be an overlooked source of competitive advantage. Ethical capability is defined here as an organization's ability to identify and respond effectively to ethical issues in a global context. Ethical capability involves firm-specific: 1) knowledge and skills to understand ethical frameworks and respond effectively to cross-cultural ethical situations; 2) leadership, team work, and organizational culture that facilitate ongoing dialogue and learning about global ethics; and 3) human resource systems and other organizational practices that acquire, develop, and sustain these capabilities. The proposed positive relation of ethical capability to competitive advantage is built on a resource-based perspective of the firm. This perspective argues that firm-specific resources and capabilities, that are valuable, rare, and inimitable, are sustainable sources of competitive advantage. Before developing this argument further, it is important to understand the nature and challenges of global ethics.

Frameworks for Examining Cross-Cultural Ethics

Several frameworks and algorithms have been proposed to address business ethics in a global context (Buller et al., 1997; DeGeorge, 1993; Desai & Ritten-burg, 1997; Donaldson, 1989, 1996; Jackson, 1997). These frameworks suggest that there is no simple answer to the question of what is right and wrong ethical behavior across different national cultures. Donaldson (1996), for example, observed that U.S. businesses have tended to adopt one of two extreme positions when faced with ethical questions across cultures: relativism or absolutism. The relativist perspective takes the familiar stance— "when in Rome, do as the Romans do." At the other extreme, the absolutist perspective argues that the home country cultural (and ethical) values must be applied everywhere as they are at home. According to Donaldson (1996):

> "Companies must help managers distinguish between practices that are merely different and those that are wrong. For relativists, nothing is sacred and nothing is wrong. For absolutists, many things that are different are wrong. Neither extreme illuminates the real world of business decision making. The answer lies somewhere in between." (1996, 52).

Donaldson (1996) proposed several core values that broadly define the moral imperatives for MNCs and provide a moral compass for global business practices: respect for human dignity, respect for basic rights, and good citizenship. He then provided a set of algorithms that guide decision making in situations where ethics collide across cultures. He proposed the concept of "moral pluralism" to show how the outcomes of these algorithms can range from the MNC insisting on its own (home country) ethical principles to the MNC accommodating the ethical values of the host country. Thus, although Donaldson concludes that there is a set of core values that can serve as a basic threshold for all MNCs, there also should be "moral free space" that allows for judgment based upon the unique circumstances involved in a given situation.

DeGeorge (1993) also has proposed several international moral norms that can be applied to MNCs. In contrast to Donaldson, he argued that the complexity of multinational situations makes the use of simple algorithms inadequate. Rather, he suggested that each situation requires judgment and moral imagination. He offered a number of guidelines, particularly for MNCs operating in less developed countries, and for dealing with issues of hazardous products or processes and corruption. In addition, DeGeorge identified three types of ethical conflicts: 1) pressures on individuals to violate personal norms, 2) inconsistent cultural norms, and 3) host country versus home country interests and values. He argued that each of these types of conflicts ultimately needs to be resolved at a higher level of influence, a concept he termed *ethical displacement*. Ethical displacement involves the development of sufficient policies, procedures, structures, rewards, and background institutions to reinforce ethical practices.

Jackson (1997) also observed that MNCs:

"face an intricate multilayered array of cultural, ethical, and legal norms. The norms subsist at local, national, regional, international, and global levels. The presence of such normative complexity and depth signals the need for ethics programs

that assimilate such characteristics." (p. 1128).

He suggested a number of pragmatic steps toward building a "cosmopolitan" culture of ethical awareness in the MNC. This cosmopolitan culture is one that is neither relativistic or absolutist, but that is sensitive to cross-cultural differences regarding ethics. Such a culture goes beyond simple rule formulations or ethical algorithms, and is characterized by a higher level of moral sensitivity based on ongoing education and collaboration among decision makers across-cultures. This notion of a cosmopolitan culture is similar to Vega's (1997) concept of "common norming" in which conflicting parties attempt to find the common moral ground through ongoing dialogue.

Buller et al. (1997) have proposed a pragmatic framework to guide managerial decision making in situations involving cross-cultural ethical conflict. Their model, based on conflict management theory, suggests that there is a continuum of at least six possible alternative strategies for responding to cross-cultural ethical conflict ranging from adaptation to the host country's ethical standards to complete insistence on the application of home country standards. They provide a decision tree to guide managers through the decision process in situations where ethics collide across cultures. The decision tree is intended to encourage contingency thinking and identify plausible courses of ethical action.

In summary, these emerging frameworks are consistent in their view that making appropriate ethical decisions in the MNC is a complex process. Although there may be situations in which the MNC can rightfully insist on universal moral principles, there may be other instances in which the MNC should adopt the local ethical norms. There are also situations in which the MNC is compelled, through collaboration and/or imagination, to develop a unique response to a cross-cultural ethical dilemma, one that attempts to find the common ground among disparate moral views. For the purposes of this paper, we propose three possible general responses of the MNC when faced with a cross-cultural ethical conflict: *relativism* (i.e., adopting the local norms), *cosmopolitanism* (i.e., identifying the common moral ground), and *universalism* (i.e., enforcing universal moral principles).

ETHICAL CAPABILITY AS A SUSTAINABLE SOURCE OF COMPETITIVE ADVANTAGE

An organization's capability to be ethically and socially responsible across cultures may be an overlooked source of competitive advantage (Litz, 1996). This section of the paper builds on the resource-based theory of competitive advantage by proposing that ethical capability is a potential source of sustainable competitive advantage. It then describes how a firm's leadership, learning processes, and human resource management activities can be primary means through which ethical capability is created and sustained in the MNC.

Resource-Based Perspective of Competitive Advantage

A prominent emerging perspective in the strategic management literature is the resource-based view of the firm (Wenerfelt, 1984; Barney, 1991). Resource-based theory proposes that a firm is defined by the resources that it controls. Further, it assumes that all competitors are not homogeneous but, rather, they differ based on the resources that they possess. These resource-based differences explain differences in performance across firms. If a firm possesses resources that are valuable, rare, inimitable, and the firm has the organizational capability to exploit these resources, it possesses a sustainable competitive advantage (Barney, 1991). Three general types of resources can be sources of competitive advantage: physical capitol (e.g., plant, equipment, finances), organizational capitol (e.g., structure, planning, systems), and human capitol (e.g., skills, judgment, adaptability). Note that sources of advantage include both tangible and intangible resources. Barney (1991) and others (Senge, 1990; Brenneman, Keys, & Fulmer, 1998) have argued that certain firm-specific, intangible sources of advantage (such as organizational history, culture, and learning) can be particularly important to sustaining competitive advantage precisely because these resources are extremely difficult to imitate.

Litz (1996) has pointed out that the strategic management literature has overlooked social responsibility and ethical response capabilities as potential sources of competitive advantage. He argued that:

> "to the extent that the firm is able to recognize its interdependence, reflect on the ethical standards appropriate to the situation, and react in a timely and responsive manner, it possesses valuable, rare, inimitable, and non-substitutable assets, that is, it possesses strategic resources." (1996, 1360).

Litz (1996) identified three crucial resources for competitive advantage based on ethical capability: perceiving interdependence, thinking ethically, and responding effectively. Perceiving interdependence specifically acknowledges the stakeholder perspective of the firm. With respect to the MNC, important stakeholders include host country institutions as well as the MNCs foreign suppliers, customers, and employees. According to stakeholder theory, a firm that recognizes and effectively satisfies the diverse needs of its various stakeholders will be able to sustain its institutional legitimacy (Freeman, 1984). There is increasing evidence that effective management of stakeholders can improve the financial performance of the firm (Waddock & Graves, 1997). For example, effectively balancing the needs of various stakeholders can lead to enhanced corporate reputation (Royal Society for the Encouragement of the Arts, Manufacture and Society, 1996), increased solidarity, commitment, loyalty, and productivity of employees, and lower costs in maintaining complex networks of suppliers, customers, agents and geographically dispersed employees, particularly in globalization strategies (Zadek, 1998). In addition, an or-

ganization's ability to engage in ongoing, constructive dialogue with its various stakeholders can be an important source of competitive advantage (Fulmer, Gibbs, & Keys, 1998; Wheeler & Sillanpaa, 1997). As Sharma and Vredenburg (1998) found, such dialogue can lead to the development of greater capabilities for stakeholder integration, higher order learning, and continuous innovation, that in turn can contribute to competitive advantage.

Thinking ethically involves the resource of ethical awareness. In the context of the MNC, ethical awareness includes an understanding of the various ethical frameworks (e.g., utilitarianism, rights-based, justice) as well as sensitivity to the differences among ethical perspectives across cultures. As noted above, effective dialogue among stakeholders can be an important source of organizational learning. Dialogue is a process of collective thinking and exploration of underlying assumptions, beliefs and values. According to Fulmer et al. (1998):

> When organizations must "unlearn" previously unsuccessful patterns, dialogue offers a path to follow. As companies move to global operations, dialogue becomes even more important. . . . (p. 15)

The organizational learning that emerges from the dialogue among diverse stakeholders in the MNC allows for greater awareness of and sensitivity to the ethical values, beliefs and practices across cultures. This organizational learning can be a highly sustainable source of advantage (Fulmer et al.; 1998; Senge, 1990).

Responding effectively involves the resource contribution of effective issues management, that is, taking the appropriate ethical action in a timely manner. As discussed earlier, discerning the appropriate ethical response in an international context is complex and the ability to apply relevant cross-cultural ethics models is critical to the decision-making process. This capability assumes that the first two capabilities—perceiving interdependence and thinking ethically—are in place. In addition, it involves the requisite structures, processes, procedures and other means of creating and sustaining ethical behavior and decision-making.

In summary, we argue that MNCs, to the extent that they can develop the capability to perceive, deliberate about, and respond effectively to ethical issues across cultures, can enhance their competitive advantage. These capabilities can be developed through effective dialogue with international stakeholders and through organizational practices designed to facilitate organizational learning and appropriate action regarding global ethics. In the next section, we argue that the MNCs human resource management systems can be a primary means for developing ethical capability.

Human Resources Management as a Key Source of Advantage

Assuming that ethical capability can be a source of sustainable competitive advantage, how can such capability be developed? There is a growing consensus that the key to developing competitive advantage in MNCs is the effec-tiveness of the human organization (Bartlett & Ghoshal, 1995; Pfeffer, 1994; Pucik, Tichy, & Barnett, 1992). More specifically, MNCs can enhance their competitiveness by integrating their human resource management activities with their strategic goals (Schuler, Dowling, & De Cieri, 1993; Taylor, Beechler, & Napier, 1996). These so-called strategic international human resource management (SIHRM) systems are optimally designed in accordance with the MNCs strategic challenge—achieving the appropriate balance between global integration and local responsiveness (Taylor et al., 1996). Strategic choices for the MNC include focusing primarily on multidomestic strategy (i.e., emphasis on meeting local needs), global strategy (i.e., emphasis on global efficiency), or transnational strategy (i.e., simultaneous emphasis on local responsiveness, global efficiency, and worldwide organizational learning) (Bartlett & Ghoshal, 1995). The appropriate international strategy is a largely a function of industry characteristics and firm resources.

The challenge of effective strategic human resource management in MNCs is to design human resource systems and practices that are consistent with strategy. In this regard, Taylor et al. (1996) suggested three possible MNC orientations regarding human resource management practices: adaptive (i.e., adapting to practices in the host country), exportive (i.e., imposing home country practices), or integrative (i.e., using some combination of best practices regardless of origin). In addition to strategy, an MNCs approach to SIHRM may also be determined by the relative

Table 1
Possible Configurations in the MNC

	Local Responsiveness --Global Consistency		
STRATEGY	multidomestic	transnational	global
HRM	adaptive	integrative	exportive
ETHICS	relativist	cosmopolitan	universal

influence of home country and host country culture, values and practices.

Table 1 summarizes possible configurations of strategy, human resource management, and ethical responses for the MNC. Although the separate literatures on international strategy, human resource management, and ethics suggest that approaches should differ based on the relative importance of local versus global demands, it is not clear how strategy, human resources, and ethics are (or should be) best integrated in the MNC. For example, a company following a multidomestic strategy may well employ an adaptive approach to human resource management. It does not necessarily follow, however, that this company would also follow a relativistic approach to ethics. There may be some ethical issues (e.g., employment of child labor) that might require the MNC to follow a universal policy (e.g., a code legislating against child labor) under any circumstances, even if local customs and values allow the employment of young children. Alternatively, a global strategy may require some consistency across cultures regarding human resource and ethics practices. However, there may be instances (e.g., gift giving or nepotism) in which one could argue from an ethical perspective that local values and norms should be honored. Although beyond the scope of

this paper, a fruitful avenue for future research would be to develop and test various configurations of strategic, human resource management, and ethics practices of MNCs.

Taylor et al. (1996) argued that an effective SIHRM system "should be constructed around specific organizational competencies that are critical for securing competitive advantage (p. 960)." Barney and Wright (1998) have shown how resource-based theory applies specifically to human resource management as a source of competitive advantage. They proposed that human resource practices contribute to competitive advantage only if they provide value (i.e., enhance cost leadership or differentiation), are rare, are difficult to imitate, and the organization has the systems and practices in place to derive the potential of its human resources. In particular, they contend that, to the extent that a firm can develop firm-specific skills, effective teamwork and culture among diverse employees, and human resource systems that are synergistic across the disparate organizational units, the firm can harness valuable, rare, and inimitable resources.

Extending this notion, ethical capability would include firm-specific: 1) knowledge and skills to understand ethical frameworks and respond effectively to diverse ethical perspectives across

Figure 1. Creating and Sustaining Ethical Capability

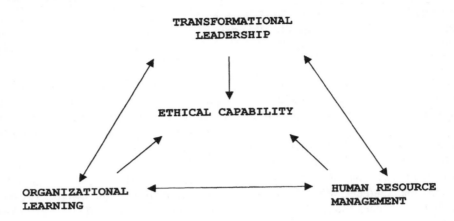

cultures; 2) leadership, team work, and organizational culture that facilitates effective ongoing dialogue on ethical differences; and 3) human resource management and other organizational practices that create and sustain these capabilities. Thus, we would argue that ethical capability in a global context is certainly one source of competitive advantage that an SIHRM system could build.

CREATING AND SUSTAINING ETHICAL CAPABILITY

Specific ways in which the MNCs human resource (HR) function can help to build and maintain ethical capability include three primary interrelated aspects that are shown in Figure 1: **transformational leadership, enhancing organizational learning** and **implementing specific HR practices**. Each of these elements is described next. It is important to acknowledge, however, that

while we are focusing primarily on the role of the HR function, ethical capability is developed in partnership with line managers, HR professionals, ethics officers, and other employees. However, as Ulrich and Lake (1990) have shown, the HR function can play a key role as a catalyst for developing and maintaining ethical capability. We build on their work in the following discussion.

Transformational Leadership

The process for creating and sustaining ethical capability is best initiated and facilitated through transformational leadership on the part of the CEO and other key leaders, including those responsible for human resources. Transformational leaders articulate a vision that includes ethical principles, communicate the vision in a compelling way, and demonstrate consistent commitment to the vision over time (Tichy & Devanna, 1986). Tichy (1993) described transformational leadership as a complex drama played out over three stages: *Awakening*, when the need for changes is recognized; *Envisioning*, when a vision is created and employees become committed to it; and *Re-architecting*, that entails the creation of an organization to support the vision. In the awakening stage, leaders must carefully articulate why the move to ethical capability is necessary and generate broad support for change among other key leaders in the organization. Part of working through this initial stage is recognizing and addressing points of resistance to change. There are a number of reasons why managers and employees might resist adopting new skills and organizational practices necessary for creating ethical capability. The transformational leader must be sensitive to these sources of resistance while instilling a compelling motivation to change. The envisioning stage helps overcome resistance by engaging employees in a definition of what ethical capability will look like for the MNC. Collaboration among the MNCs various stakeholders is essential in developing this vision or mind set. Re-architecting involves building the requisite structures, systems, policies, and practices to support the vision of ethical capability. The reputation for strong ethical cultures in companies like Johnson & Johnson, Motorola, Royal Dutch/Shell, Texas Instruments, and others can be traced directly to transformational leaders who consistently, by their words and deeds, signaled the importance of and commitment to high moral standards (Brenneman et al., 1998; Moorthy et al., 1998).

Enhancing Organizational Learning

Ulrich and Lake (1990) state that at the heart of building organizational capability (and by extension, ethical capability) is creating "shared mindsets" among the internal and external stakeholders of the company regarding its strategic goals and the processes to reach those goals. In developing a shared mindset, it is critical that the senior HR managers, in partnership with other senior managers in the MNC and from the overseas affiliates, develop consensus on the appropriate HR agenda, including a specific attention to the challenge of cross-cultural ethics (Eisenstat, 1996). Successful MNCs have learned that they cannot simply export practices that are effective domestically to overseas operations. As Table 1 suggests, although exporting human resource management or ethics practices might be appropriate under certain conditions, other possible configurations might be required. Developing the capability to deal with this complexity demands that the organization learn from its international stakeholders.

Several conditions facilitate organizational learning. First, it is critical that top managers of the MNC provide leadership in recognizing the value of human resources and developing a broader cross-cultural understanding and sensitivity (Barney & Wright, 1998; Brenneman et al., 1998). Second, the MNC must engage its various international stakeholders, including employees from home and host countries, in a collaborative effort to find the common ground with respect to human resources and ethical practices (Donaldson, 1996). As noted earlier, cross-cultural dialogue is an important tool for developing new mindsets and creating shared meanings (Fulmer et al., 1998). For example, Snow, Davidson, Snell, and Hambrick (1996) have described how MNCs can use transnational teams to develop values, policies, and practices to achieve global efficiency, local responsiveness, and organizational learning. Through ongoing research, dialogue, and action learning, these transnational teams can create a set of human resource management practices and ethical principles that could be applied in various contexts in which the MNC operates (Fulmer et al., 1998; Luthans, Marsnick, & Luthans, 1997). The outcome of this collaborative effort would be a set of human resource practices that are adaptive, integrative, and/or exportive, and a set of moral principles that are locally responsive, cosmopolitan, and/or universal in their application across different situations (See Table 1).

The ultimate goals of this initial organizational learning process are: 1) to establish a *corporate code of ethics* that is globally integrative yet locally responsive, consistent with the models of global ethics described above; 2) to create mechanisms for an *ongoing process of organizational learning and responsiveness*; and 3) to create an *ethical culture* across all MNC operations. Based on a clear corporate code of ethics and a continuous learning process, the MNC can develop specific management practices to shape and reinforce an ethical corporate culture. These practices are described more fully below.

Implementing Specific HRM Practices

As noted, an international code of ethics is a necessary, but not sufficient, step in building ethical capability. Codes of ethics are essential in providing clear direction about ethical behavior in various situations. However, employees must have the ability and motivation, and the organizational support, to understand and implement the code of ethics. Moreover, formal codes, rules, and legal guidelines cannot cover all possible situations and do not obviate the need for moral judgment and imagination (DeGeorge, 1993; Donaldson, 1996). So, ethical capability must be further enhanced through developing specific human-resource management practices linked to cross-cultural ethical competencies. Below we focus on the major human resource activities of selection, training and development, appraisal, compensation, and organization design and change, although other organizational activities are certainly relevant in building ethical capability. It is also important to recognize that there is not one prescribed set of human resource management practices for MNCs to follow. Rather, specific practices should vary (e.g., adaptive, integrative, exportive) depending upon the strategy of the MNC and the unique cultural characteristics of countries in which it operates (Luthans et al., 1997; Taylor et al., 1996).

Although "shared mindsets" (i.e., assumptions, values, and beliefs) are at the heart of ethical capability, these core values and beliefs must be created and reinforced by the various management practices that govern employees' behaviors in the organization. Human resource management practices that are central to shaping ethical values, beliefs, and behaviors can be organized into three general areas: generating competencies, reinforcing competencies, and sustaining competencies.

Generating Competencies

Generating competencies involves acquiring the necessary ethical values and behaviors through *selection* processes and/or developing values and behaviors through *training and development*.

Selection

Top executives agree that one of the most important things they can do to influence firm performance is to hire and promote the right people. Staffing decisions in the MNC are particularly complex. For example, in many MNCs, lower level employees tend to be host country nationals, while higher level managers tend to be parent country expatriates, often without much intercultural experience (Bell & Harrison, 1996). One reason for the traditionally high failure rate among U.S. expatriates is that selection criteria for these managers historically have emphasized technical, rather than relational or cultural, skills (Mendenhall, Dunbar, & Oddou, 1987). It is now widely recognized that relational and intercultural skills also are critical to expatriate effectiveness (Tung, 1993). Intercultural competence may allow expatriate employees to be more effective, in part, because it better equips them to "cope

with the stress of acculturation" (Bell & Harrison, 1996, p. 50).

Due to the challenges of global ethics, selection criteria for managers and other employees working across cultures should certainly include ethical competence (e.g., moral development), sensitivity to differences in ethics across cultures, and ability to make sound decisions in situations when home and host country ethics collide. Previous cross-cultural experience would certainly be valuable. Other useful selection criteria would include, adaptability, flexibility, and the capacity to learn in the face of changing conditions. Of course, staffing decisions should be made based on: 1) a thorough needs analysis to identify the specific jobs to be filled as well as the knowledge, skills and abilities needed for effective performance; 2) careful screening of candidates based on multiple structured interviews and other valid selection procedures; and 3) realistic job previews that communicate the kinds of situations that the new employee is likely to face. The screening of candidates should also include an assessment of ethical awareness, sensitivity, and responsiveness perhaps through the use of ethical dilemmas that are likely to confront employees in the company.

In addition, MNCs should expand their search for job candidates beyond the domestic labor pool to attract the best global talent. Leading companies such as Unilever and IBM have developed sophisticated databases that enable managers and human resource professionals to identify qualified job candidates from across their international operations (Snell, Snow, Davison, & Hambrick, 1998). Ideally, these databases would include information about employees' experience, competencies, and preferences. Such systems would be valuable in staffing management, human resources, and other relevant job positions (e.g., ethics advisors/ committees) with individuals who are sensitive and responsive to the diverse moral values and issues across the MNC's operations.

Training and Development

Training and development activities also are important in building ethical capability. Resource-based theory suggests that training in firm-specific rather than general skills creates greater potential for competitive advantage because firm-specific skills are more rare, valuable, and difficult to imitate (Barney & Wright, 1998). So, to the extent possible, ethics-related training should emphasize firm-specific rather than general moral issues, principles and practices. As discussed earlier, firm-specific skills can be identified and developed through dialogue among international stakeholders across the MNCs geographical units.

Training and development activities can enhance several types of competencies. First, all employees must be trained to understand and apply the MNC's code of ethics, as well as the multitude of international laws and codes of conduct. Training in various ethical frameworks and models is also warranted. Beyond that, cross-cultural training can be effective in developing greater cultural awareness and ability to interact across cultures (Black & Mendenhall, 1990). Presumably, this kind of training also would be effective with respect to cross-cultural differences in ethics. Bell and Harrison (1996) suggested that cross-cultural training should emphasize both content (e.g., knowledge of other cultures) and process (e.g., how culture influences cognition and behavior). However, as Husted, Dozier, McMahon, and Kattan (1996) have observed, cross-cultural training may be more effective in transmitting attitudes than in transmitting moral reasoning across cultures. For this reason, some have suggested that selection of individuals with diverse cultural experience may be preferred to cross-cultural training in generating ethical competencies in the MNC (Bell & Harrison, 1996; Jackson, 1997).

An alternative approach that addresses some of the shortcomings of cross-cultural training is cross-cultural team building for transnational teams, used by such companies as Motorola, Shell, Ford, and Glaxo–Wellcome (Snell et al., 1998). This approach goes one step further than traditional cross-cultural training programs by

"developing coherent work processes that take advantage of differences on the team by establishing ground rules and protocols that integrate members. When coupled with training in conflict resolution and negotiation skills, cross-cultural team building can substantially improve integration and efficiency." (Snell et al., 1998, 153)

Motorola's *Ethics Renewal Process* provides one example of how organizations can implement this approach (Moorthy, DeGeorge, Donaldson, Ellos,

Solomon, & Textor, 1998). With a trained core of senior executives, Motorola's Director of Global Leadership and Organizational Development facilitates ethical awareness, skill development, and team building in diverse teams of managers in the company's foreign operations. The teams identify ethical issues and collaborate on possible solutions. Particular attention is paid to dialogue on local ethical perspectives that may differ from the Motorola corporate code of ethics. Local ethics committees are formed, trained in various ethical frameworks, and authorized to develop policies and guidelines to address local ethical issues. For example, Motorola has developed specific guidelines for gift giving in Japan that differ from the company's guidelines on gift giving in other countries. The products of these local ethics committees are then shared with other similar committees around the world. To date, Motorola has formed fourteen ongoing ethics committees across its global operations. Clearly, this kind of comprehensive approach to cross-cultural ethics training and development can enhance the organizational learning process and create the firm-specific knowledge and skills that contribute to sustainable competitive advantage.

Reinforcing Competencies

Once they have been acquired or developed, cross-cultural ethical competencies must be reinforced through *performance appraisal* and *compensation/ rewards* systems.

Performance Appraisal

Appraisal processes should signal clearly the MNC's standards and expectations regarding ethical behaviors. To be effective, ethical standards should include both behavioral and outcome measures. In addition, employees should receive timely and regular feedback regarding their performance. Effective performance feedback reinforces behaviors that are consistent with expectations and helps the employee make any necessary improvements. Finally, the performance appraisal process itself (i.e., appraisal interviews, goal setting, feedback, coaching) can be an effective tool for enhancing trust and communication between managers and employees. Increased trust and communication can in turn reinforce the shared mindset regarding ethics in the MNC (Barney & Wright, 1998).

Performance expectations regarding ethics should also be developed between the MNC and its suppliers and customers (Donaldson, 1996). It is incongruent when the MNC has high internal ethical standards whereas its own suppliers and customers engage in unethical behaviors. Ideally, acceptable ethical standards should be jointly developed with suppliers and customers. This process will help to clarify for managers the kinds of suppliers and customers with which the MNC can do business. And, as with internal appraisal processes, effective processes designed and implemented with suppliers and customers also can enhance trust and communication reinforcing a shared mind set regarding ethics.

Rewards and Recognition

One purpose of performance appraisal is to provide a systematic basis for allocating rewards. To be effective, compensation and recognition systems should be: 1) linked directly to ethical behaviors and outcomes; 2) timely; 3) visible; 4) durable (i.e., produce long-term motivation); and 5) contribute to a shared mindset regarding ethical values and behaviors (Ulrich & Lake, 1990). In addition, thoughtfully designed reward systems include both monetary and non-monetary rewards linked to ethical performance. Effective leaders, such as Jack Welch at General Electric, are renowned for their prompt, hand-written notes acknowledging exemplary employee performance (Byrne, 1998). This type of informal recognition can provide strong reinforcement for company values. An example provided by Donaldson (1996) emphasizes the power of recognizing and rewarding ethical behavior:

"Around 1950, a senior (Motorola) executive was negotiating with officials of a South American government on a $10 million sale that would have increased the company's annual net profits by nearly 25%. As the negotiations neared completion, however, the executive walked away from the deal because the officials were asking for $1 million for 'fees.' CEO Robert Galvin not only supported the executive but also made it clear that Motorola would neither accept the sale on any terms nor do business with those government officials again. Retold over the decades, this story demonstrating Galvin's resolve has helped cement a culture of ethics for thousands of employees at Motorola". (p. 60).

This example also demonstrates the particular challenge of linking rewards with appropriate behaviors in instances where ethical and other outcomes (e.g., financial) may be in conflict. The MNC must be clear about its priorities and reinforce them accordingly to reduce employees' ambiguity under these circumstances.

Sustaining Competencies

Organizational mechanisms for sustaining ethical competencies over time include *organization design* (e.g., structure and reporting relationships), *communication*, and *ongoing capacity for change*.

Organization Design

The central purpose of organization design is to allocate and coordinate the key tasks that must be completed to create and sustain competitive advantage. Consequently, emphasis should be placed on organizing those tasks and resources that add value, are rare and inimitable (Barney & Wright, 1998). In building ethical capability, the HR department adds value through its selection, training, appraisal, and compensation activities that are linked to ethical behavior (Schuler et al., 1993; Taylor et al., 1996). Ideally, these activities are internally consistent and continually aligned with the organization's needs as it evolves in a changing global environment. In this respect, organization design is best viewed as a process for continually identifying key tasks and modifying the reporting relationships, responsibilities, and coordinating mechanisms to accomplish those tasks. Further, in a dynamic, global environment, organic forms such as networks, team-based organizations, and temporary structures, can enhance organizational learning, stimulate moral imagination, and allow for greater flexibility and re-sponsiveness to changing conditions (Fulmer et al., 1998; Nonaka & Takeu-chi, 1995; Snell et al., 1998).

Another aspect of organization design is creating partnerships with suppliers, customers, and other organizations that can enhance the organization's competi-tiveness. Effective strategic alliances can produce resources that are valuable, rare and difficult to imitate (Barney, 1991). International partners are sources of learn-ing regarding different ethical values and practices. Through exploring different perspectives, partners may discover com-mon ethical ground or forge a cosmopol-itan ethical culture that achieves a higher level of moral development (Donaldson, 1996; Jackson, 1997).

Additionally, MNCs have a moral obligation to support their organiza-tional units and employees by develop-ing appropriate structures, systems, pol-icies, procedures, and other background institutions to reinforce ethical practices (DeGeorge, 1993). In this regard, an increasing number of MNCs are estab-lishing ethics officers, advisors, om-budsmen, and/or committees to focus more attention on ethical issues and practices (Center for Business Ethics, 1992; Ethics Officer Association, 1997). The HR function can be instru-mental in facilitating the staffing of these positions with individuals of di-verse cultural perspectives. Many com-panies have found that it is important for the ethics function to be highly vis-ible and accessible, as well as some-what independent, within the organiza-tion. This type of structure may provide quicker access and greater confidential-ity for employees who have concerns about ethics.

Communication

Clear and consistent organizational communication is central to creating and sustaining a shared mindset of eth-ics in the MNC. As noted earlier, there is no question that the CEO and other top managers are critical in establishing ethical capability in the MNC. Top managers signal expectations by their words and, more importantly, by their example. Moreover, effective global companies like Royal Dutch/Shell (The Shell Report, 1998) and Motorola (Moorthy et al., 1998) have developed explicit statements of their global ethics principles and values and made them available to their employees throughout the world. The worldwide web, email, and other communication technologies have made it possible for these and other companies to solicit real time feedback and facilitate ongoing dis-cussion regarding their ethical values and principles. In addition, many com-panies have established ethics hotlines via telephone or computer to provide immediate and confidential support for employees facing ethical dilemmas. In countries where the telecommunica-tions infrastructure is less developed, "hot boxes" (manual systems) provide a means for communication. These vari-ous approaches provide an essential in-frastructure for ongoing dialogue on ethical practices throughout the MNC.

Ongoing Capacity for Change

Paradoxically, a key task for transformational leaders is to instill in the organization an ongoing capacity for change (Tichy, 1993). Several activities are central in creating a capacity for continuous improvement in ethical capability: 1) conducting periodic audits of the ethical and cultural climate; 2) developing a vision and a plan for continually improving ethical capability; 3) understanding and overcoming possible points of resistance to change; and 4) identifying and implementing the right tasks, structures, processes, systems, and other resources necessary to develop and sustain ethical capability. The HR function, in partnership with key managers and ethics professionals, can be instrumental in facilitating this process of ongoing organizational change and improvement.

Summary

MNCs operate in a context of diverse, sometimes conflicting, moral values and norms. The emerging consensus is that companies must become more sensitive to cross-cultural ethical differences and more sophisticated in applying the appropriate ethics in any given situation. This global ethical capability can be a sustainable source of advantage for the multinational corporation because it involves developing resources that are valuable, rare, and inimitable. The organization can enhance its ability to exploit and sustain its ethical capability through transformational leadership, ongoing organizational learning, and the design and implementation of its human resource management practices.

Acknowledgment: The authors would like to thank two anonymous reviewers for their helpful suggestions in the preparation of this manuscript.

References

Barney, J. (1991). Firm resources and sustained competitive advantage. *Journal of Management, 17*: 99–120.

Barney, J., & Wright, P. (1998). On becoming a strategic partner: The role of human resources in gaining a competitive advantage. *Human Resource Management, 37*(1): 31–46.

Bartlett, C., & Ghoshal, S. (1989). *Managing across boarders: The transnational solution.* Boston: Harvard Business School Press.

Bartlett, C., & Ghoshal, S. (1995). Changing the role of top management: Beyond structure to purpose. *Harvard Business Review, 73*(1): 86–96.

Bell, M., & Harrison, D. (1996). Using intranational diversity for international assignments: A model of bicultural competence and expatriate adjustment. *Human Resource Management Review, 6*(1): 47–74.

Black, S., & Mendenhall, M. (1990). Cross-cultural training effectiveness: A review and a theoretical framework for future research. *Academy of Management Review, 15*: 113–136.

Brenneman, W. B., Keys, J. B., & Fulmer, R. M. (1998). Learning across a living company: The Shell companies' experience. *Organizational Dynamics,* (Autumn): 61–70.

Buller, P., Kohls, J., & Anderson, K. (1997). A model for addressing cross-cultural ethical conflicts. *Business and Society, 36*(2): 169–193.

Byrne, J. (1998). Jack: A close-up look at how America's #1 manager runs GE. *Business Week,* June, 8: 90–106.

Center for Business Ethics (1992). Instituting ethical values in large corporations. *Journal of Business Ethics, 11*: 863–867.

DeGeorge, R. (1993). *Competing with integrity in international business.* New York: Oxford University Press.

Desai, A., & Rittenburg, T. (1997). Global ethics: An integrative framework for MNEs. *Journal of Business Ethics, 16*: 791–800.

Donaldson, T. (1989). *The ethics of international business.* New York: Oxford University Press.

Donaldson, T. (1996). Values in tension: Ethics away from home. *Harvard Business Review.* (Sept-Oct): 47–62.

Eisenstat, R. (1996). What corporate human resources brings to the picnic: Four models for functional management. *Organizational Dynamics,* (Autumn): 7–22.

Freeman, R. (1984). *Strategic management: A stakeholder approach.* Boston: Pitman Publishing, Inc.

Fulmer, R. M., Gibbs, P, & Keys, J. B. (1998). The second generation learning organizations: New tools for sustaining competitive advantage. *Organizational Dynamics,* (Autumn): 7–20.

Husted, B., Dozier, J., McMahon, J. T., & Kattan, M. (1996). The impact of cross-national carriers of business ethics on attitudes about questionable practices and form of moral reasoning. *Journal of International Business Studies (Vol 2),* : 391–411.

Jackson, K. (1997). Globalizing corporate ethics programs: Perils and prospects. *Journal of Business Ethics, 16*: 1227–1235.

Litz, R. (1996). A resource-based view of the socially responsible firm: Stakeholder interdependence, ethical awareness, and issue responsiveness as strategic assets. *Journal of Business Ethics, 15*: 1355–1363.

Luthans, F., Marsnik, P, & Luthans, K. (1997). A contingency matrix approach to IHRM. *Human Resource Management, 36*(2): 183–200.

Mendenhall, M., Dunbar, E., & Oddou, G. (1987). Expatriate selection, training, and career pathing: A review and critique. *Human Resource Management, 26*: 331–345.

Moorthy R., Donaldson, T., Ellos, W., So-lomon, R., & Textor, R. (1998). *Uncompromising integrity: Motorola's global challenge: 24 global case studies with commentaries.* Shaumberg, IL: Motorola University Press.

Nonaka, I., & Takeuchi, H. (1995). *The knowledge-creating company: How Japanese companies create the dynamics of innovation.* New York: Oxford University Press.

Pfeffer, G. (1994). *Competitive advantage through people.* Boston: Harvard Business School Press.

Pucik, V., Tichy, N., & Barnett, C. (1992). *Globalizing management: Creating and leading the competitive organization.* New York: John Wiley & Sons.

Royal Society for the Arts, Manufacture & Commerce (1996). *Tomorrow's company: The role of business in a changing world.* London: RSA.

Schuler, R., Dowling, P., & De Cieri, H. (1993). An integrative framework of international human resource management. *International Journal of Human Resource Management, 1*: 717–764.

Senge, P. M. (1990). *The fifth discipline.* New York: Doubleday.

Sharma, S. & Vredenburg, H. (1998). Proactive corporate environmental strategy and the development of competitively valuable organizational capabilities. *Strategic Management Journal, 19*: 729–753.

Snell S., Snow, C., Davison, S., & Hambrick, D. (1998). Designing and supporting transnational teams: The human resource agenda. *Human Resource Management, 37*(2): 147–158.

Snow, C., Davison, S., Snell, S., & Hambrick, D. (1996). Use transnational teams to globalize your company. *Organizational Dynamics,* (Spring):50–66.

Taylor, S., Beechler, S., & Napier, N. (1996). Toward an integrative model of strategic human resource management. *Academy of Management Review, 21*: 959–985.

The Shell Report (1998). *Statement of General Business Principles.* London: Shell International, Group External Affairs.

Tichy, N., & Devanna, M. (1986). *The transformational leader*. New York: John Wiley & Sons.

Tung R. (1988). Career issues in international assignments. *Academy of Management Executive, 11*: 241–244.

Tung R. (1993). Managing cross-national and intra-national diversity. *Human Resource Management, 32*: 461–477.

Ulrich, D. & Lake, D. (1990). *Organizational capability: Competing from the inside out*. New York: John Wiley & Sons.

Vega, G. (1997). *Caveat emptor*: Ethical chauvinism in the global economy. *Journal of Business Ethics, 16*: 1353–1362.

Waddock, S. & Graves, S. (1997). The corporate social performance-financial performance link. *Strategic Management Journal, 303*–319.

Wernerfelt, B. (1984). A resource-based view of the firm. *Strategic Management Journal, 5*: 171–180.

Wheeler, D. & Sillanpaa, M. (1997). *The stakeholder corporation: A blueprint for maximizing stakeholder value*. London: Pitman Publishing.

Zadek, S. (1998). Balancing performance, ethics, and accountability. *Journal of Business Ethics, 7*: 1421–1441.

[28]

Think Global, Act Local: From Naïve Comparison to Critical Participation in the Teaching of Strategic International Human Resource Management

Helen De Cieri, Julie Wolfman Cox, & Marilyn S. Fenwick. **Tamara : Journal of Critical Postmodern Organization Science**. Las Cruces: 2001. Vol. 1, Iss. 1; pg. 68, 11 pgs

Abstract (Article Summary)

In this paper, we examine the implications of ethnocentrism and paternalism in teaching approaches for the field of strategic international human resource management (SIHRM), as an example of management studies. We argue that the teaching of SIHRM has been approached in a colonizing fashion, joining and extending the territories of human resource management and organizational strategy through the definition and teaching of a new language and conceptual vocabulary. We explore philosophical approaches and processes involved in teaching SIHRM, and consider implications of pedagogical developments in this field of management education.

A major aspect of international management is based in the field of strategic international human resource management (SIHRM) (Schuler, Dowling & De Cieri, 1993; Taylor, Beechler & Napier, 1996), which is essentially focused on strategic human resource management in multinational enterprises (MNEs). In this paper, we argue that issues identified in critiques of the development and teaching of international management, and, in particular, SIHRM, raise issues and questions that are also important in the more general context of managing teaching internationally. Are we walking our theoretical talk? How might we guard against the oversimplifications of naïvete, the narrow exclusiveness of ethnocentrism or even the patronization of paternalism in teaching internationally? Rather than attempt to judge or to provide standards for evaluation, our purpose is to introduce questions and terminologies that may assist in encouraging reflexive discussion and debate. The aim of this paper is, therefore, two fold; first, to introduce the subject area of SIHRM and to articulate some of the theoretical and pedagogical critiques that are relevant to that subject area, and second, to draw on this analysis to reflect on our own teaching and to raise questions that may also be of interest to others.

The Development of SIHRM

The field of SIHRM (Milliman, Von Glinow & Nathan, 1991; Schuler et al., 1993; Taylor et al., 1996) emerged from the study of human resource management. An early extension of HRM was the inclusion of attention to cross-cultural issues (see, for example, Laurent, 1986). Since then, the broader consideration of HRM in multinational enterprises has been defined as international HRM (IHRM; Dowling, Welch & Schuler,

1999; Edwards, Ferner & Sisson, 1996; Teagarden & Von Glinow, 1997). While HRM is relevant within a single country, IHRM addresses added complexity due to diversity of national contexts of operation, the inclusion of different national categories of workers (Tung, 1993), and co-ordination across national borders via the cross-national transfer of management and management practices (e.g., Gregersen, Hite & Black, 1996). A related area of research has developed in comparative HRM research (Brewster, Tregaskis, Hegewisch & Mayne, 1996). In parallel with (and not unrelated to) the internationalization of HRM has been the increasing recognition of the importance of linking HRM policies and practices with organizational strategy in a domestic (single-country) context (Becker & Gerhart, 1996; Wright & McMahan, 1992).

As researchers and practitioners have paid increasing attention to the strategic nature of IHRM and the implications for organizational performance (Caligiuri & Stroh, 1995), we have witnessed the emergence of SIHRM, which has been defined as "human resource management issues, functions, and policies and practices that result from the strategic activities of multinational enterprises and that impact the international concerns and goals of those enterprises" (Schuler et al., 1993, p. 422).

Schuler et al. (1993) presented an integrative framework of SIHRM, in which they acknowledged that a fundamental issue is the tension between the needs for global co-ordination (integration) and local responsiveness (differentiation) (Doz & Prahalad, 1991; Nohria & Ghoshal, 1994). In addition to the strategic MNE components, the framework showed factors exogenous and endogenous to an MNE that influence SIHRM issues, functions, policies and practices, thereby influencing the realization of MNE concerns and goals. Schuler et al. (1993) presented their framework as a conceptual model of exploratory analysis, and the framework has been noted in recent literature as a useful tool that brings together the strategic and international dimensions of HRM (Kamoche, 1996; Taylor et al., 1996).

We suggest that developments in theory and research since the publication of Schuler et al.'s framework in 1993, have brought the need for revision of both the content of this framework and its integrative assumptions. For example, Taylor et al. (1996) draw upon this framework, but present a simplified version of SIHRM constituents, reducing Schuler et al.'s (1993) rather cumbersome `SIHRM issues, functions, policies and practices' to `SIHRM orientation' (analogous to HR function strategy) and `SIHRM functional focus' (comprising all HR practices). While this development and simplification appear to be of value, we should consider the implications of such reductionism. If we simplify when we teach, do we dilute the quality and quantity of knowledge shared with students?

SIHRM and Colonization Considerations

With regard to the development of SIHRM, we suggest that revisiting and refining of theory, definitions and research should occur in the context of theoretical developments in related fields. As Willmott has stated, while HRM seems at first somewhat remote from organization theory, the design and operation of HRM activities is dependent on notions of "organizing and organization" (1995, p. 33). Thus the operation of such activities "has consequences for the maintenance and transformation of how work and employment are organized" (Willmott, 1995, p. 33). Therefore, we examine the teaching of SIHRM in the context of recent developments in critical organizational theory.

For example, if we consider the way(s) in which the field of management strategy is taught in business schools we can see that this field has been the subject of critical re-interpretation (Alvesson & Willmott, 1996; Knights & Morgan, 1991; Whipp, 1996). In particular, we note Alvesson and Willmott's (1996) reference to the work of Habermas in describing management as a colonizing power. Alvesson and Willmott defined colonization as "the way that one set of practices and understandings, which are strongly associated with the instrumental reason that is dominant in the organization and management of complex systems, comes to dominate and exclude other practices and discourses" (1996, p. 105; see also Power & Laughlin, 1992). Kerfoot and Knights (1993) have commented on the masculinist nature of management strategy discourse, and Alvesson and Willmott suggested that strategic management is a senior management activity that occurs "as a condition and consequence of wider, institutionalized forms of domination" (1996, p. 132). Indeed, access to strategic territory has become a contested source of power, "a number of occupational or functional groupings... competing to establish supremacy over the area of strategic discourse" (Knights & Morgan, 1991, p. 265). If they succeed, they engage in strategy talk, where:

> The term `strategic' is bandied around to add rhetorical weight, misleadingly one might say, to managerial activity and academic research projects....Like other discourses that have a colonizing impact, by weakening alternative ways of framing issues and assessing values, its effect is to close rather than open debate (Alvesson & Willmott, 1996, p. 133).

Further, we argue that the development of the field of SIHRM is itself a colonizing force, not only joining the intellectual territories of HRM and organizational strategy, but also extending those territories into international geographic domains and perhaps, in doing so, further privileging a senior strategic perspective to the exclusion of those more marginal to internationalization decisions.

Internationalization Strategies and the Teaching of SIHRM

Let us consider the particular case of the university, in which SIHRM is both taught within the management curriculum and practised in the internationalization of operations, for consideration of the internationalization of management education raises important issues about how and what and where we teach (and, indeed, who `we' are).

The globalization of business has included the education industry, particularly tertiary education. Business schools and management educators have entered global markets following much the same `foreign market entry' strategies as the multinational corporations (Barkema, Bell & Pennings, 1996; Benito & Welch, 1994). Monash

University, Australia's largest university, provides an excellent example of an institution engaged in many documented forms of internationalization in the education industry. These include:

1. establishment of wholly-owned foreign subsidiaries (foreign campuses and research centres). This essentially provides 'exporting' education to students outside the parent country. Malaysia, in addition to Singapore and Hong Kong, has provided strong markets for such developments (Celestino, 1999). For some universities, this is explicitly intended to provide 'American-style' university education abroad (Celestino, 1999). They attract international students seeking a 'Western' education approach without travelling outside their own home country;

2. formation of strategic alliances, partnerships and joint ventures with local firms and educational institutions, to offer cross-institutional credit for subjects and even joint degrees;

3. recruiting foreign students for the home campus (i.e., developing a global customer base, by recruiting in the host country student/customer market for 'in'patriation to the parent headquarters (home campus);

4. flexible learning, utilizing multi-media technology to enable students to complete programs at a distance. Wilson & Meadows (1998) examined the implications of information technology in education, particularly with respect to Australian education providers and their strategies in the emerging Asian markets;

5. expatriation via student and faculty exchange programs; and

6. short-term international assignments, such as study tours, international internships and intensive study experience. One example of this is the Asian Intensive School in Advanced Management conducted in Penang, Malaysia in July each year by the Australian National Business School.

The last two strategies are perhaps those most explicitly aimed to provide parent-country students (and faculty) with some exposure to other cultures in order to better understand and manage international business.

Issues in (and from) the Pedagogy of SIHRM

Is each approach to the internationalization of management, and, in this case, management education, both sustainable and ethically defensible? In considering the relative merits of these various strategies, we suggest that two issues important in the development of pedagogy in SIHRM warrant particular consideration. First, we recognise the tendency for ethnocentrism in teaching SIHRM. Second, we suggest that it is important to avoid paternalism in SIHRM pedagogy.

Ethnocentrism and SIHRM teaching. A major challenge for development of SIHRM theory development and research is to overcome the ethnocentrism of one's own perspective and experience (Perlmutter, 1969). Theories, research methods, and practices may be applicable and effective in one cultural setting, but changes to suit local requirements are inevitable for transfer across cultural and national boundaries. This, of course, is particularly the case for teaching.

Ethnocentrism, or the assumption of the superiority of one's cultural approach, is perhaps most evident in the use of the `parent country' language in teaching and curricula. One dominant feature of the forms of internationalization listed above is that English is most often the language of instruction. This is generally applicable for US, UK and Australian universities, although cannot be assumed. Exceptions include the University of Technology Sydney, Australia, which conducts MBA courses (including Strategic HRM) in Mandarin (S. Teo, personal communication, 1999). Also, numerous programs have utilized knowledge transfer from expatriates to locals, with translation of materials and eventual handover of all teaching to locals (e.g., Yan Jiao China-Australia Management Centre, Beijing, China). Some business schools also encourage students to study in another language, and award specific certificates to acknowledge proficiency in the language.

As with many training and development strategies, we have seen a rush to develop new training programs, yet we suggest that more time could be spent in evaluation of such programs. For example, Hong (1999) reported that a survey of students in a U.S. university found that, after 3 semesters of Chinese business language learning, the students still lacked cultural knowledge in Chinese business contexts. Hong (1999) concluded that improvements remain necessary, such as integrating cultural knowledge into such teaching programs.

In addition, it is not only in the spoken/written language of instruction that ethnocentrism may be evident. For example, the content of SIHRM may limit its pedagogical possibilities. Due to colonization by senior, Western perspectives, the SIHRM classroom may well be foreign territory where the experiences discussed are those of the guest speaker who plays the role of the experienced traveler or adventurer, telling stories of the journey, of adventure and misadventure as a means of appeal to the (supposedly) naïve audience (cf. Jeffcutt, 1994). Or, maybe not. Perhaps we should allow for new possibilities, not only in the topics we cover but also in the way we cover them and in our forms of assessment (e.g., writing `letters home', choosing gifts for those who have assisted our passage). We should not leave it to the guest speaker to present and represent something a little too presumptuous, too provocative, and too risky for the mainstream curriculum or class co-ordinator to cover.

One important mechanism for the colonization of SIHRM is provided by the definition and teaching of a new, and potentially exclusive, language and conceptual vocabulary (cf. Abrahamson, 1996; Czarniawska & Sevón, 1996). Like all others, the language of SIHRM has its own vocabulary. In this respect, the field of SIHRM has followed the example set by international business research in developing and utilizing jargon that ranges from aphorisms to abbreviations. For example, `think global, act local' has been widely adopted as an aphorism reflecting a `transnational mindset' (Bartlett & Ghoshal, 1998). This is sometimes supported by the hybrid `glocal', or `glocalization' (Parker, 1996). While the terms `global' and `globalization' have been central to the development of SIHRM research and practice, there remains debate about definition and implications. For example, we note that many US-based researchers and practitioners (mis-)use `global' when referring to `transnational' issues (e.g., Pucik, 1997). While there is a need for `knowledge transfer', or content-based delivery of SIHRM constructs, we raise concerns about the oversimplification of SIHRM subject matter in efforts to `assist' students' and practitioners' comprehension.

Paternalism in the teaching of SIHRM. Some of these examples of ethnocentrism might also be interpreted as examples of paternalism, a concept most commonly defined as "a system of management under which the employer creates a workforce dependent for more than just the wages exchanged for work" (Wray, 1996, p. 702). Padavic and Earnest (1994, p. 340) suggest, counter to Weber, that paternalism is one of many forms of managerial control. They differentiate two forms of paternalism: "(1) an exploitative power asymmetry, suffused at the social-psychological level with deference and loyalty grounded in a familial sentiment; (and) (2) the institutional forms within which this asymmetry is exercised, such as company-subsidized community projects or housing."

In a similar but more extensive classification, Wray (1996) discussed three forms. Traditional paternalism "transferred family or domestic `authority' into the workplace as a basis for industrial organization" and is "authoritarianism tempered with generosity" (Wray, 1996, p. 702, with reference to Martin & Fryer, 1973). Welfare paternalism took the form of routinized benefits such as long-term employment contracts, pension schemes, company-owned housing, and provision of medical benefits, education, parks and sports. Finally, sophisticated paternalism is where "(t)he personal indulgency patterns established by traditional paternalist employers are maintained through the institutionalisation of largesse through profit share systems and social and welfare benefits financed by the organisation" (Wray, 1996, p. 703).

If we apply this to teaching internationally, we can perhaps become sensitized to the politics of our actions. For example, do we make superficial alterations to curriculum and content in order to indulge local interests, perhaps still teaching American perspectives on international management? Students may `feel free' to disagree, particularly with each other, but that freedom is always within the constraints of the standard, imported theory and assessment base. We suggest that such an approach is not dissimilar to a paternalistic employer allowing an employee some minor indulgence. What may be a well-intentioned technique that is successful in an `Anglo-culture' classroom setting may violate local norms concerning discussion and debate when used in other cultural contexts.

From naïve comparison… In addition to teaching in the host country's language, oversimplifying terminology, and making only modest changes to host country curriculum and content, one of the most obvious forms of ethnocentrism (if not paternalism) in teaching internationally is probably adopting a naïve comparative approach. This approach "regards culture as the basic explanatory variable" (Cray & Mallory, 1998, p. 23). According to Cray and Mallory (1998), 'naïve' in this context involves the absence of theory to inform the comparative analysis. In particular, while culture is viewed as the motivating determinant for any differences noted, the way in which culture and behavior are linked is seldom explained or analyzed (Cavusgil & Das, 1997). More often, the comparison employs the teacher's own culture as the baseline for comparison, with the underlying assumption that, once similarities and differences have been identified, only an adjustment to management style, in this case SIHRM, is required for success. Thus, cultural 'differences' may become cultural 'realities' resulting in culture-bound, explanation-poor representations. For example, the end result is often little more than a set of cultural stereotypes with minimal or no theoretical foundation for behavioral predictability. Yet, these stereotypes, which predispose 'us' to see collective 'others' as similar to or different from 'us' and to behave in certain 'culturally sensitive ways' towards 'them', may solidify 'our' views of 'them' (cf. Fine. 1994).

Alternatives have been dominated by culture-free and culture-bound approaches (Cray & Mallory, 1998). According to Cray & Mallory, (1998, p. 24) a culture-free, or 'etic' approach seeks "underlying regularities across national boundaries". For example, a culture-free approach to research attempts to use variables which are generalizable across cultures to study social phenomena in relatively culture-free (culture-common), universal terms (Bhagat & McQuaid, 1982). Supporters of this approach argue that the basic tasks in any organizations, but particularly in industrialized organizations, are the same worldwide. This argument reflects a convergence perspective (Hickson, Hinings, McMillan & Schwitter, 1974). In contrast, a culture-bound, or 'emic' approach emphasizes differences among cultures (Cray & Mallory, 1998), and has been aligned with a divergence perspective (McGaughey & De Cieri, 1999). An emic approach to research attempts to describe a particular culture by investigating culture-specific aspects of concepts or behaviors, based on historical and social developments that have influenced people. The stream of research influenced by Hofstede (1984) has been an influential example of the culture-bound approach.

Both etic and emic approaches may be legitimate in the research and teaching of SIHRM, but difficulties may be encountered if the distinction between the two approaches is ignored. Hence, a major issue for SIHRM researchers and teachers is to ensure that an etic approach is not inappropriately assumed and imposed (De Cieri & Dowling, 1995; Dowling et al., 1999). This is an important point because a true etic is "one that emerges from the given phenomena" (Ronen, 1986, p. 48). The emic-etic issue has been one of the most frequently examined in cross-cultural research and various suggestions for overcoming the difficulties inherent in this area of research have been offered (Bhagat & McQuaid, 1982; Morey & Luthans, 1984; Teagarden & Von Glinow, 1997; Triandis & Martin, 1983).

Recognition of the differences among the naïve comparative/ culture-free/ culture-bound perspectives is important, not only in terms of raising awareness of the content of what is taught, but in providing a terminology to assist in raising awareness of process and epistemological issues. This recognition is necessary, as the naïve comparative/ culture-free/ culture-bound distinctions, which assume culture to be a measurable entity, apply just as much to teacher-student dynamics as to syllabus and task decisions. To move beyond these traditional approaches to the teaching of SIHRM, we might consider developing more participative, student-teacher critique.

...Towards critical participation. In this analysis, our intent is not only to criticize but also to raise awareness of possibilities for teaching of SIHRM. Can we go further than raising awareness of the differences among naïve comparative/ culture-free/ culture-bound approaches in international education? This question is in line with the suggestion that while the use of critical theory in the classroom is often met with `institutional resistance', "critical theory has much to offer the management classroom and therefore may well be worth the effort. More than anything else, it encourages students and practicing managers not to take organizational "realities" at face value" (Prasad & Caproni, 1997, p. 289).

One means of doing this is suggested by Grey, Knights and Willmott (1996) in their discussion of an approach in which both teachers and students reflect critically on management knowledge. In this way, teaching "becomes an activity that points to continuities and discontinuities between students' experience and bodies of literature" (Grey et al., 1996, p. 101). However, we suggest that such reflection may be difficult where the subject matter is that of SIHRM and where the student group is not a group of experienced senior managers. In any other group, and including classes comprising students of differing nationalities, it may be difficult to move beyond the level of discussing cross-cultural stereotypes, communication norms, and the importance of `managing diversity' (Hostager, Al-Khatib & Dwyer, 1995; Ramsey & Calvert, 1994). However, in the teaching of SIHRM, issues of distance not only relate to physical geography but also to the elevation of the content matter to international and strategic, and hence hierarchically remote matters.

`Western' knowledge and thinking about teaching and learning approaches has changed significantly in recent decades, with increasing emphasis on notions of `deep' or `active learning' and `independent learning' (McLean, Reid & Scharf, 1998/99). This refers to students who search for deep conceptual understanding, take responsibility for their own learning, are concerned with skill development as well as knowledge, and seek to apply their learning to the broader context of career and social experience. This active learning approach has been extended to students' involvement in the assessment process, through self and/or peer assessment system. Stefani (1994, cited in McLean et al., 1998/99) claimed that self and peer assessment increases student motivation and critical processing. While there is some empirical evidence of success with this approach with `Western' students, the cross-cultural applicability remains to be investigated. If we, as Western writers, cannot escape the centrism and colonization of Western teaching styles, perhaps we can at least open up some discussion of the dilemmas involved.

Cross-cultural training as inoculation: A re-presentation. As one example, let us consider an unconventional approach, or re-presentation, of cross-cultural training (CCT). Indeed, the major focus of training related to SIHRM has been CCT programs that are designed to educate employees, usually in the pre-expatriate phase, in the key cultural values and behaviors of the host country (Harrison, 1994).

As usually presented, CCT has been advocated as important in developing 'effective interactions' with host country nationals (HCNs) as strange people from strange lands. CCT is positively correlated with expatriate adjustment and performance: effective use of CCT, and the effectiveness of pre-departure preparations in all areas of staffing and maintenance, has implications for the success of the expatriation and repatriation process (Deshpande & Vishwesvaran, 1992). One example of the cross-cultural issues in training programs is provided by Farhang (1999). A study of Swedish firms in China was used to show that training success depends not only on the knowledge and teaching ability of those providing the teaching as well as the willingness to learn and knowledge of the students. The need for adequate identification and analysis of training needs is viewed as crucial.

With respect to cross-cultural learning experiences, it is important to recognise that the roles of teacher and student may apply both to expatriates and locals. Hence, the knowledge and willingness to teach and to learn are relevant to both groups. Porter and Tansky (1999) argued that a learning orientation is a determining factor of expatriate success; expatriates with stronger learning orientation are more likely to adapt to the new environment and continue in their expatriate assignment.

Models for CCT (e.g., Mendenhall & Oddou, 1986; Harrison, 1994), including methods of immersion versus passive learning, provide examples of the teaching technology of SIHRM. Empirical testing and evaluation of such CCT models is scarce in the literature (cf. Deshpande & Vishwesvaran, 1992), but the apparent reasoning behind CCT is that it raises sensitivity to and tolerance of 'others', avoiding or reducing the chances of unpleasant encounters. In this sense, CCT can be viewed as a means of prophylaxis and, in particular, inoculation against 'host country nationals', invoking images of biological colonization in addition to the geographical and discursive senses of colonization discussed above.

Rather than train for or teach about CCT as (implied) inoculation, we can consider other models. If we move beyond the 'safari mode' of taking the uninitiated out of the classroom on a 'Cook's Tour' into SIHRM territory, we might shift attention from the expatriate to the HCN. For example, we could take heed of Linstead's (1996) comments that social anthropology proceeds by a methodology of 'ethnographic immersion', and of his suggestions for a pedagogy that seeks to develop the manager as anthropologist that includes "becoming receptive to others and otherness" (Linstead, 1996, p. 22). He gives the example of an exercise that involved briefing and discussion sessions to allow 'actors' to take on or feel 'inside the skin' of a particular employee role. Leaving biology aside, we suggest that it is also important to examine pedagogical implications of such suggestions for the teaching of SIHRM due to the predominance of Western educational techniques such as experiential learning and participative classes; techniques which may be much less effective for non-Western learners (Vance & Ring, 1994). Perhaps we can learn from Calas and Smircich (1996), who identify post (colonial) feminist deconstructions of colonial stories and testimonial writings from the points of view of those such as HCNs, non-managerial employees and/or expatriate partners and families whose voices are not otherwise heard.

Summary and Conclusion

In presenting these arguments in several academic fora, we have been struck by the polarisation of our reception. Our presentations have been met by a combination of positive and outraged reactions, the latter including concerns with our critical perspective, our feminism, and our tone of writing. Others again have suggested we increase the strength of our argument, though this is not our intention as we realise that internationalised management education is in the early stages. However, our critique introduces the relevant and important concepts of ethnocentrism and paternalism and we raise these concepts so that we may open up further discussion and consideration.

The issues raised in this paper highlight the importance of reflexive contemplation, discussion, and strategy formulation and implementation in order to develop sustainable approaches to internationalised management education. This requires examination not only of what we teach or how we teach others, but how we act ourselves. We must question our actions as researchers and educators in the field of SIHRM, and develop awareness of our role as definers and disseminators of information. We hope that, by exploring the implications of SIHRM for research, practice and teaching, we may raise awareness of current deficiencies and unasked questions.

References

[Reference]
Abrahamson, E. (1996). Technical and aesthetic fashion. In B. Czarniawska, & G. Sevón (Eds.), Translating organizational change (pp. 117-137). Berlin: Walter de Gruyter.

[Reference]
Alvesson, M., & Willmott, H. (1996). Making sense of management: A critical introduction. London: Sage.

[Reference]
Barkema, H.G., Bell, J.H.J., & Pennings, J.M. (1996). Foreign entry, cultural barriers, and learning. Strategic Management Journal, 17, 151-166.

[Reference]
Bartlett, C., & Ghoshal, S. (1998). Managing across borders: the transnational solution. (2nd ed.). Boston, MA: Harvard Business School.

[Reference]
Becker, B., & Gerhart, B. (1996). The impact of human resource management on organizational performance: Progress and prospects. Academy of Management Journal, 39, 779-801.

[Reference]
Benito, G.R.G., & Welch, L.S. (1994). Foreign market servicing: beyond choice of entry mode. Journal of International Marketing, 2 (2), 7-27. Bhagat, R.S., & McQuaid, S.J. (1982). Role of subjective culture in organizations: A review and directions for future research. Journal of Applied Psychology, 67, 653-685.

[Reference]
Brewster, C., Tregaskis, O., Hegewisch, A., & Mayne, L. (1996). Comparative survey research in human resource management: a review and an example. International Journal of Human Resource Management, 7, 585-604.

[Reference]
Calas, M.B., & Smircich, L. (1996). From `the woman's' point of view: Feminist approaches to organization studies. In S. R. Clegg, C. Hardy, & W. R. Nord (Eds.), Handbook of organization studies. London: Sage.

[Reference]
Caligiuri, P.M., & Stroh, L.K. (1995). Multinational corporate management strategies and international human resource practices: bringing IHRM to the bottom line. International Journal of Human Resource Management, 6, 494-507.

[Reference]
Cavusgil, S.T., & Das, A. (1997). Methodological issues in empirical cross-cultural research: A survey of the management literature and a framework. Management International Review, 37 (1), 71-96.

[Reference]
Celestino, M.L. (1999). Graduate education programs with international vision: How graduate business schools are transcending borders. World Trade, 12 (7), 86-91.

[Reference]
Cray, D., & Mallory, G. (1998). Making sense of managing culture. London: International Thomson.

[Reference]
Czarniawska, B., & Sevón, G. (1996). Introduction. In B. Czarniawska, & G. Sevón (Eds.), Translating organizational change (pp. 1-12). Berlin & New York: de Gruyter.

[Reference]
De Cieri, H., & Dowling, P.J. (1995). Cross-cultural issues in organizational behavior. In C.L. Cooper, & D.M. Rousseau (Eds.), Trends in Organizational Behavior, 2, (pp. 127-145). Chicester, U.K.: John Wiley & Sons.

[Reference]
Deshpande, S.P., & Viswesvaran, C. (1992). Is cross-cultural training of expatriate managers effective: A meta analysis. International Journal of Intercultural Relations, 16, 295-310.

[Reference]
Dowling, P.J., Welch, D.E., & Schuler, R.S. (1999). International HRM: Managing People in a Multinational Context (3rd ed.). Cincinnati, OH: South-Western.

[Reference]
Doz, Y., & Prahalad, C.K. (1991). Managing DMNCs: A search for a new paradigm. Strategic Management Journal, 12, 145-64.

[Reference]
Edwards, P., Ferner, A., & Sisson, K. (1996). The conditions for international human resource management: two case studies. The International Journal of Human Resource Management, 7, 20-40.

[Reference]
Farhang, M. (1999). The human resource dimension of international technology transfer: Identification and analysis of training needs. Journal of Euro-Marketing, 7 (3), 79-93.

[Reference]
Fine, M. (1994). Working the hyphens: reinventing self and other in qualitative research. In N. Denzin, & Y. Lincoln (Eds.), Handbook of Qualitative Research (pp.70-82). Thousand Oaks, CA: Sage.

[Reference]
Gregersen, H.B., Hite, J.M., & Black, J. S. (1996). Expatriate performance appraisal in U.S. multinational firms. Journal of International Business Studies, 27, 711-738.

[Reference]
Grey, C., Knights, D., & Willmott, H. (1996). Is a critical pedagogy of management possible? In R. French, & C. Grey (Eds.), Rethinking management education (pp. 94-110). London: Sage.

[Reference]
Harrison, J. Kline (1994). Developing successful expatriate managers: A framework for the structural design and strategic alignment of cross-cultural training programs. Human Resource Planning, 17 (3), 17-35.

[Reference]
Hickson, D.J., Hinings, C.R., McMillan, C.J., & Schwitter, J.P. (1974). Comparative and Multinational Management. New York: Wiley and Sons.

[Reference]

Hofstede, G. (1984). Culture's consequences: International differences in work related values. Beverly Hills: Sage Publications.

[Reference]
Hong, W. (1999). Explorations in the teaching of Chinese business culture. The Journal of language for International Business, 10 (1), 72-85.

[Reference]
Hostager, T.J., Al-Khatib, J., & Dwyer, M.D. (1995). National, social and organizational identity: The effective managerial exploration of diversity. International Journal of Management, 12, 297-304. Jeffcutt, P. (1994). From interpretation to representation in organizational analysis: Postmodernism, ethnography and organizational symbolism. Organization Studies, 15, 241-274.

[Reference]
Kamoche, K. (1996). The integration-differentiation puzzle: a resource-capability perspective in international human resource management. The International Journal of Human Resource Management, 7, 230- 244.

[Reference]
Kerfoot, D., & Knights, D. (1993). Management, masculinity and manipulation: From paternalism to corporate strategy in financial services in Britain. Journal of Management Studies, 30, 659-677.

[Reference]
Kilduff, M., & Mehra, A (1997). Postmodernism and organizational research. Academy of Management Review, 22, 453-481.

[Reference]
Knights, D., & Morgan, G. (1991). Corporate strategy, organizations, and subjectivity: A critique. Organization Studies, 12, 251-273.

[Reference]
Laurent, A. (1986). The cross-cultural puzzle of international human resource management. Human Resource Management, 25, 91-102.

[Reference]
Linstead, S. (1996). Understanding management: Culture, critique and change. In S. Linstead, R. Grafton Small, & P. Jeffcutt, (Eds.), Understanding management (pp. 1-33). London: Sage.

[Reference]
Martin, R., & Fryer, R. H. (1973). Redundancy and paternalist capitalism. London: George Allen & Unwin.

[Reference]
McLean, C., Reid, C., & Scharf, F. (1998/99). The development of transferable skills in business studies in degrees. Irish Business and Administrative Research, 19/20 (1), 47-

64.

[Reference]
McGaughey, S.L., & De Cieri, H. (1999). Reassessment of convergence and divergence dynamics: Implications for international HRM. International Journal of Human Resource Management, 10 (2), 235-250.

[Reference]
Mendenhall, M.E., & Oddou, G.R. (1986). Acculturation profiles of expatriate managers: Implications for cross-cultural training programs. Columbia Journal of World Business, 21, 73-79.

[Reference]
Milliman, J., Von Glinow, M.A., & Nathan, M. (1991). Organizational life cycles and strate gic international human resource management in multinational companies: Implications for congruence theory. Academy of Management Review, 16, 318-339.

[Reference]
Morey, N., & Luthans, F. (1984). An emic perspective and ethnoscience methods for organizational research. Academy of Management Review, 9 (1), 27-36.

[Reference]
Nohria, N., & Ghoshal, S. (1994). Differentiated fit and shared values: Alternatives for managing headquarters-subsidiary relations. Strategic Management Journal, 15, 491-502.

[Reference]
Padavic, I., & Earnest, W. R. (1994). Paternalism as a component of managerial strategy. The Social Science Journal, 31, 389-405.

[Reference]
Parker, B. (1996). Evolution and revolution: from international business to globalization. In S.R. Clegg, C. Hardy, & W.R. Nord (Eds.), Handbook of organization studies (pp. 484-506). London: Sage.

[Reference]
Perlmutter, H.V. (1969). The tortuous evolution of the multinational corporation. Columbia Journal of World Business, 4 (1), 9-18.

[Reference]
Porter, G., & Tansky, J.W. (1999). Expatriate success may depend on a "learning orientation": Considerations for selection and training. Human Resource Management, 38 (1), 47-60.

[Reference]
Power, M., & Laughlin, R. (1992). Critical theory and accounting. In M. Alvesson & H. Willmott (Eds.), Critical management studies (pp. 113-135). London: Sage.

[Reference]

Prasad, P., & Caproni, P.J. (1997). Critical theory in the management classroom: Engaging power, ideology, and praxis. Journal of Management Education, 21, 284-291.

[Reference]
Pucik, V. (1997). Human resources in the future: An obstacle or a champion of globalization? Human Resource Management, 36, 163-167.

[Reference]
Ramsey, V. J., & Calvert, L. McGee. (1994). A feminist critique of organizational humanism. Journal of Applied Behavioral Science, 30, 83-97.

[Reference]
Schuler, R.S., Dowling, P.J., & De Cieri, H. (1993). An integrative framework of strategic international human resource management. Journal of Management, 19, 419-459.

[Reference]
Taylor, S., Beechler, S., & Napier, N. (1996). Towards an integrative model of strategic international human resource management. Academy of Management Review, 21, 959-985.

[Reference]
Teagarden, M., & Von Glinow, M.A. (1997). Human resource management in cross-cultural contexts. Management International Review, 37 (1), 7-20.

[Reference]
Triandis, H.C., & Martin, G. (1983). Etic plus emic versus pseudo etic. Journal of Cross-Cultural Psychology, 14 (4), 489-500.

[Reference]
Tung, R.L. (1993). Managing cross-national and intra-national diversity. Human Resource Management, 32, 461-477.

[Reference]
Vance, C.M., & Ring, P.S. (1994). Preparing the host country workforce for expatriate managers: The neglected other side of the coin. Human Resource Development Quarterly, 5, 337-352.

[Reference]
Whipp, R. (1996). Creative deconstruction: Strategy and organizations. In S.R. Clegg, C. Hardy, & W. R. Nord (Eds.), Handbook of organization studies (pp. 261-275). London: Sage.

[Reference]
Willmott, H. (1995). What has been happening in organization theory and does it matter? Personnel Review, 24 (8), 33-53.

[Reference]

Wilson, R.E., & Meadows, C.J. (1998). Tele-teaching: Australia's competitive question. Journal of Global Information Management, 6 (1), 15-26.

[Reference]

Wray, D. (1996). Paternalism and its discontents: A case study. Work, Employment & Society, 10, 701-715.

[Reference]

Wright, P.M. & McMahan, G.C. (1992). Theoretical perspectives for strategic human resource management. Journal of Management, 18, 295-320.

[Author(s) Affiliation]

Helen De Cieri is an associate professor in the Department of Management, Monash University Australia. She has a PhD in management and her current research interests are related to strategic human resource management in multinational enterprises and international alliances. Helen is the Editor of the Asia Pacific Journal of Human Resources.

Marilyn Fenwick has a qualitative PhD in strategic international human resource management and expatriate performance management from the University of Melbourne, Australia. As a senior lecturer with the Department of Management, Monash University, Australia, she is interested in critical theory and pedagogy in international management and human resource management. Marilyn's research interests are forms of multinational organization; the dyadic relationship between organizational control and individual performance; individual-level identities and commitments in multinational organizations.

Julie Wolfram Cox is a Senior Lecturer in the Department of Management at Monash University,Australia, where she teaches in the areas of management theory, organisational behaviour and organisational change. She received B.A.(Honours) and M.A. (Research) degrees from the University of Melbourne and holds a PhD in organisational behaviour from Case Western Reserve University in Cleveland, USA. Her research interests include critical perspectives on emerging and established topics in management theory and research, craft, and healthcare, and she has published in Organization Studies and Journal of Management Studies.

Name Index